Contents

P9-DNZ-576

OPPOSITE GOKYO LAKES AND EVEREST **PREVIOUS PAGE** YOUNG MONKS AND PRAYER WHEELS

Introduction to
Nepal

Nepal is the very watershed of Asia. Squeezed between India and Tibet, it stretches from rich subtropical forest to soaring Himalayan peaks: from jungly tiger habitat to the precipitous hunting grounds of the snow leopard. Climbing the hillside of one valley alone, you can be sweltering in the shade of a banana palm in the morning, and sheltering from a snowstorm in the afternoon.

Nepal's **cultural landscape** is every bit as diverse as its physical one. Its peoples belong to a range of distinctive ethnic groups, and speak a host of languages. They live in everything from dense, ancient cities erupting with pagoda-roofed Hindu temples to villages perched on dizzying sweeps of rice-farming terraces and dusty highland settlements clustered around tiny monasteries. **Religious practices** range from Indian-style Hinduism to Tibetan Buddhism and from nature-worship to shamanism – the indigenous Newars, meanwhile, blend all these traditions with their own, intense tantric practices.

The cultural richness owes something to the shaping force of the **landscape** itself, and something else to the fact that Nepal was never colonized. This is a country with profound national or ethnic pride, an astounding flair for festivals and pageantry and a powerful attachment to traditional ways. Its people famously display a charismatic blend of independent-mindedness and friendliness, toughness and courtesy – qualities that, through the reputations of Gurkha soldiers and Sherpa climbers in particular, have made them internationally renowned as people it's a rare pleasure to work with or travel among.

But it would be misleading to portray Nepal as a fabled Shangri-la. Long politically and economically backward, it has developed at uncomfortable speed in some areas while stagnating in others. Heavily reliant on its superpower neighbours, Nepal was, until 1990, the world's last remaining absolute Hindu monarchy, run by a regime that combined China's repressiveness and India's bureaucracy. Following a soul-scouring Maoist insurgency, which ended in 2006, it has ended up as a federal republic, led, for the time at least, by the Nepali Congress party. Nepal seems always to be racing to catch up with history, and the sense of **political excitement** in the country is thrillingly palpable.

ABOVE CHANGU NARAYAN TEMPLE; THE HIMALAYAS; A TREKKING PORTER

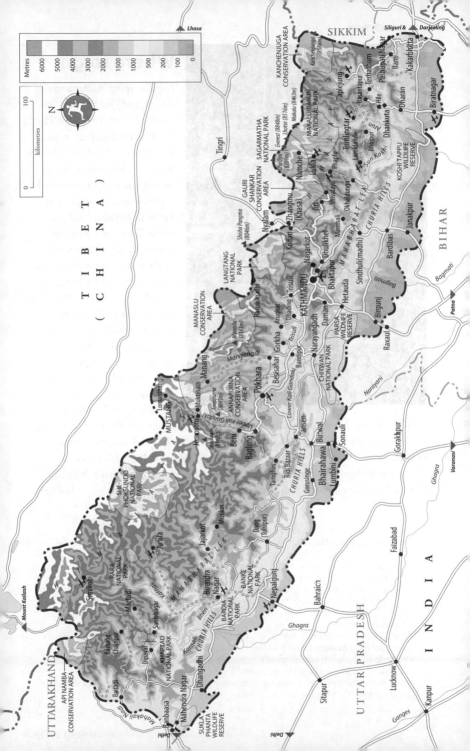

Where to go

Nepal's capital, **Kathmandu**, is electrifyingly exotic, with its medieval warren of alleys, Hindu temples and Buddhist stupas, and its uniquely relaxed nightlife. The city is increasingly hectic, however, so many visitors make day-trips into the semi-rural **Kathmandu Valley**, and the astoundingly well-preserved medieval cities of **Patan** and **Bhaktapur**, or overnight at one of the mountain viewpoints on the valley rim, such as **Nagarkot**, in the **Central Hills**. A few explore the valley's wealth of temples, towns and forested hilltops in more depth, or make road trips to the Tibet border or down the tortuous Tribhuwan Rajpath towards India. Most people will take the tourist bus six hours west of Kathmandu to **Pokhara**, an engagingly easy-going resort town in the **Western Hills**, set beside a lake and under a towering wall of white peaks. While many visitors are happy just to gaze at Pokhara's views, or hangout in its bars, it also makes a great base for day hikes and mountain-bike rides, yoga and meditation courses, and even paragliding and microlight flights. Other towns

On April 25, 2015, as this book went to press, Nepal was devastated by a massive **7.8-magnitude earthquake** – the country's worst in over eighty years – and several powerful aftershocks, killing thousands and creating a humanitarian disaster. The epicentre was in Gorkha district, in the Western Hills, but the densely populated Kathmandu Valley was badly hit too. There were also avalanches on Everest, killing climbers and Sherpas and leaving many others stranded; it was the deadliest ever incident on the mountain. Along with the horrifying loss of life, the earthquake destroyed significant parts of the country's cultural heritage, including much of the historic durbar squares in Kathmandu, Patan and Bhaktapur.

It was Nepal's third tragedy in just over twelve months: on April 18, 2014, sixteen Sherpas were killed in an **avalanche** on Everest's Khumbu Icefall; some six months later at least 41 people died when **freak blizzards** and avalanches swept across the Annapurna region (see box, p.306). The impact of these disasters will be felt in Nepal, one of Asia's poorest countries, for many years to come: tourism, one of the biggest sectors of the economy, has a vital role in helping the country recover.

ABOVE PUPPETS, BHAKTAPUR **OPPOSITE** DAAL BHAAT

in the Western Hills – notably **Gorkha** with its impressive fortress, **Manakamana** with its wish-fulfilling temple, and **Bandipur** with its old-world bazaar – offer history and culture as well as scenery.

Few travellers head into the flat **Terai**, along the border with India, unless it's to enter the deservedly popular **Chitwan National Park**, with its endangered Asian one-horned rhinos. **Bardia National Park** and two other rarely visited wildlife reserves are out there for the more adventurous. In the Western Terai, **Lumbini**, Buddha's birthplace, is a world-class pilgrimage site, as is **Janakpur**, a Hindu holy city in the east.

Nepal is most renowned, however, for **trekking** – hiking from village to village, through massive hills and lush rhododendron forests and up to the peaks and glaciers of the high Himalayas. The thrillingly beautiful and culturally rich **Annapurna** and **Everest** regions are the most oriented to trekkers, but other, once-remote areas are opening up, notably **Mustang** and **Manaslu**. Meanwhile, **rafting** down Nepal's rivers, and **mountain biking** through its scenic back roads, offer not only adventure but also a different perspective on the countryside and wildlife.

When to go

Nepal is broadly temperate, with four main **seasons** centred around the summer monsoon. The majority of visitors, prioritizing mountain visibility, come in the **autumn** peak season (late Sept to late Nov), when the weather is clear and dry, and neither too cold in the high country nor too hot in the Terai. With the pollution and dust (and many bugs) washed away by the monsoon rains, the mountains are at their

FACT FILE

- With a land **area** of 147,000 square kilometres, Nepal is about the size of England and Wales combined. Useable land, however, is in short supply due to the precipitous terrain and a growing population of 27 million or more, over a third of whom are less than 15 years old.

- Eight of the world's ten highest **mountains** are found in Nepal, including Everest, the tallest of them all.

- Prior to 1951, only a handful of Westerners had ever been allowed into Nepal. Today, the country receives as many as 800,000 **tourists** annually; increasingly they are coming from neighbouring India and China.

- Despite the fame of its Tibetan and Sherpa Buddhist communities, Nepal was long the world's only Hindu kingdom, and **Hindus** still officially make up some eighty percent of the population. In truth, many Nepalis combine worship of Hindu gods with shamanic and animist practices.

- The decade-long **Maoist insurgency** ended in 2006, along with the career of the notorious King Gyanendra. Nepal's politics are now noisily turbulent but largely peaceful.

- With an average per capita annual **Income** of US$730, Nepal was ranked 145th out of 187 countries in the UN's 2014 Human Development Index.

most visible, making this an excellent time for trekking. Two major festivals, Dasain and Tihaar, also fall during this period. The downside is that the tourist quarters and trekking trails are heaving, prices are higher and it may be hard to find a decent room.

Winter (Dec & Jan) is mostly clear and stable. It never snows in Kathmandu, but mornings can be dank and chilly there – and in trekking areas, the fierce cold can make lodge owners shut up shop altogether. This is an excellent time to visit the Terai, and if you can face the cold, a rare time to be in the mountains too.

Spring (Feb to mid-April) is the second tourist season, with its warmer weather and longer days. Rhododendrons are in bloom in the hills towards the end of this period, and as the Terai's long grasses have been cut, spring is the best time for viewing wildlife – despite the increasing heat. The downsides are that haze can obscure the mountains from lower elevations (though it's usually possible to trek above it) and stomach bugs are more common.

The **pre-monsoon** (mid-April to early June) brings ever more stifling heat, afternoon clouds, rain showers – and more stomach upsets. It also brings edginess: this is the classic time for popular unrest and illness. Trek high, where the temperatures are more tolerable.

Nepalis welcome the **monsoon**, the timing of which may vary by a few weeks every year, but typically begins in mid-June and peters out in the last weeks of September. The fields come alive with rushing water and green shoots, and this can be a fascinating time to visit, when Nepal is at its most Nepali: the air is clean, flowers are in bloom, butterflies are everywhere and fresh fruit and vegetables are particularly abundant. But there are also drawbacks: mountain views are rare, leeches come out in force along the mid-elevation trekking routes, roads and paths may be blocked by landslides, and flights may be cancelled.

OPPOSITE NEPALI WOMEN COOKING; TIGER, BARDIA NATIONAL PARK

Author picks

Our authors have bussed and walked and rafted and biked the length and breadth of Nepal to research this book. Here are some of their own favourite travel experiences and places.

Nepali people It's the Nepali people themselves who make the country so special. Learning some Nepali (p.45), volunteering (p.45) or simply accepting that invitation for tea are all great ways to get to know them.

Festivals Catch one of Nepal's many religious festivals (p.34). It's an experience you'll never forget, and will show you an important part of Nepali culture.

Bardia National Park Skip the commercialism of Chitwan and head east to explore the less-visited, unspoiled Bardia (see p.271). It's the best place in Nepal to spot tigers, too.

Treks The Everest Base Camp (p.341) and Annapurna (p.322) treks justify their fame, but going off-piste brings rich rewards. That might mean a tough walk-in through the eastern hills to Everest (p.346); a thrilling side trip, such as Muktinath's Lupra route (p.330); or even a glorious day hike, like Tansen to Rani Ghat (p.235).

Newar cities Bhaktapur (p.154), Patan (p.86) and even central Kathmandu (p.62) are arguably the best-preserved medieval cities in all of Asia.

Food Astounding pickles enliven the national dish of *daal bhaat* (p.30), while spicy Newari food is an adventure in meat-eating: try it in restaurants such as Kathmandu's *Thamel House* (p.107), Pokhara's *Newari Kitchen* (p.220), Tansen's *Nanglo West* (p.234) and, most authentically, Kirtipur's superb *Newa Lahana* (p.143).

Janakpur Little-visited by Western travellers, the fascinating Terai city of Janakpur (p.286) is an important stop on the Hindu pilgrimage circuit, with an ornate temple and a bustling old town.

Our author recommendations don't end here. We've flagged up our favourite places – a perfectly sited hotel, an atmospheric café, a special restaurant – throughout the guide, highlighted with the ★ symbol.

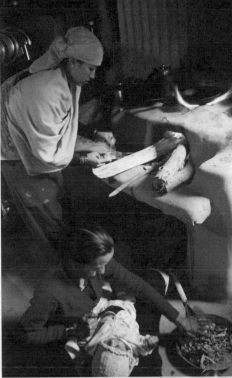

17

things not to miss

It's not possible to see everything that Nepal has to offer in one trip – and we don't suggest you try. What follows, in no particular order, is a selective taste of the country's highlights, including beautiful mountains, outstanding national parks, ancient cities and unforgettable experiences. All highlights have a page reference to take you straight into the Guide, where you can find out more. Coloured numbers refer to chapters in the Guide section.

1

2

1 TREKKING
Page 302

Nepal's ultimate activity: an unequalled scenic and cultural experience.

2 BHAKTAPUR
Page 154

The exquisitely preserved Kathmandu Valley town of Bhaktapur is built in dark carved wood and glowing pink brick, and adorned with fine stone sculptures.

3 BOUDHA
Page 130

Clustered round the great white stupa, with its all-knowing Buddha eyes, is a thriving Tibetan Buddhist community and pilgrimage centre.

3

4

4 MOUNTAIN BIKING
Page 368

From precipitous descents (and, if you're fit enough, ascents) to relaxed countryside ambles, Nepal is an epic place to explore on two wheels.

5 MOMO
Page 31

These steamed meat or vegetable dumplings, resembling plump ravioli, are an addictive snack. They're served with a chilli sauce, and you can find them everywhere from street stalls to fancy restaurants.

6 DASAIN
Page 35

Dasain is the high point of the busy Nepali festival calendar. Masked dancers perform elaborate rituals in Bhaktapur and Kathmandu, people travel for days to be at home with their families, and children celebrate by playing on bamboo swings.

7 THE HIMALAYAS
Pages 176 & 225

Even if you don't trek, don't miss a hilltop view of the world's greatest mountain range. Nagarkot is the classic viewpoint outside Kathmandu. Sarangkot, near Pokhara, is a good alternative.

5

गकाली एभरेष्ट म

होम प्याकिङ्गको पनि सुबिधा छ

8

9

8 SHIVA RAATRI
Page 34
This winter festival brings tens of thousands of Shiva devotees to Pashupatinath, the holiest of river gorges.

9 JANAKI MANDIR
Page 288
Worshippers flock to Janakpur's Mughal-style Janaki Mandir to pay homage to legendary lovers Ram and Sita.

10 JUNGLE WILDLIFE
Pages 249 & 271
You'll get closer to a wild rhino than might seem advisable at Chitwan and Bardia national parks.

11 OLD KATHMANDU
Page 62
An intensely urban quarter of narrow alleys, noisy markets, fabulously carved temples and rowdy political rallies.

12 BUS JOURNEYS
Page 24
Chickens under the seats, sunbathers on the roof and spectacular hairpin bends: rides on a public bus may be uncomfortable, but they get you close to everyday life.

16

17

Itineraries

The best way to explore Nepal, of course, is to use this guide to create your own itinerary, but below we offer three recommended routes. "The Best of Nepal" covers the highlights – deservedly popular destinations, but you'll never be far off the beaten track. "Kathmandu and Everest" adds a few Kathmandu Valley sights onto the Everest Base Camp trek, while "Exploring the West" gives you a memorable trip well away from most tourist itineraries.

THE BEST OF NEPAL

You could do a whistle-stop tour of the classic sights in eight to ten days. If you trek into the Annapurna region, you'll need another week or two – depending how far and how fast you walk.

❶ Kathmandu The capital has boomed in recent years, becoming a busy, polluted, modern city, but it still preserves a stunning medieval heart and an easy-going restaurant and nightlife scene. **See p.54**

❷ Pashupatinath and Boudha At the holy riverbank of Pashupatinath, the Hindu dead are cremated in the open; just down the road lies the dizzyingly exotic Tibetan Buddhist community of Boudha. **See p.125 & p.130**

❸ Bhaktapur The stunningly preserved micro-city of Bhaktapur offers a taste of what Kathmandu was like before the modern world arrived. **See p.154**

❹ Bandipur Poised on a precipitous ridge, the old-world bazaar town of Bandipur has become an easy-going haven, packed with gorgeous boutique hotels and friendly homestay lodges. **See p.202**

❺ Pokhara Set under the white peaks of the Annapurna range, lakeside Pokhara is Nepal's biggest tourist centre. You can paraglide, meditate or just relax on a boat or in a bar. **See p.206**

❻ Annapurna trekking The Annapurna range rises above some of Nepal's lushest, steepest and loveliest foothills – perfect for a shorter trek to the viewpoint of Poon Hill, or, with a few more days in hand, on to the uplifting Annapurna Sanctuary and then back to Pokhara. **See p.322**

❼ Chitwan From Pokhara, head off next to the jungle, grassland and rivers of Chitwan National Park. You're almost guaranteed sightings of rhinos, deer, monkeys, crocodiles and countless species of birds. You might not spot the elusive tigers, though. **See p.249**

KATHMANDU AND EVEREST

Altitude enforces a minimum 14- to 16-day schedule for the Everest Base Camp trek, but three weeks would allow some exploration of Kathmandu and its valley as well.

❶ Shivapuri and Budhanilkantha Start acclimatizing with a day hike from Kathmandu up to the valley rim at Shivapuri, taking in the Sleeping Vishnu at Budhanilkantha. **See p.137 & p.139**

❷ Lukla Fly from Kathmandu to the world's most insane airstrip, and in minutes you're at the gates of Khumbu, the profoundly Buddhist Everest region, ready to start walking up to Namche. **See p.341**

ABOVE ANNAPURNA TREK; BHAKTAPUR; RAFTING

❸ Thame A "rest" day at Namche Bazaar, the Sherpa capital, might involve a six-hour round-trip hike to Thame. **See p.341**

❹ Buddhist monasteries The slow ascent necessary for acclimatization above Namche allows time for monastery visits. On the trail between Namche and Base Camp, the serene *gompa* at Tengboche, Pangboche and Deboche are rich with gilded statues and *thangka* paintings. **See p.341 & p.342**

❺ Chhukhung Another "rest day" takes you exploring off the main Base Camp trail up to the Imja Glacier or the peak of Chhukhung Ri, overnighting at the tiny settlement of Chhukung. **See p.342**

❻ Kala Pattar The high point of the Everest trek isn't the relatively disappointing Base Camp itself (5300m) but the breathtaking (literally) viewpoint hillock of Kala Pattar (5545m). **See p.344**

❼ Cho La In good conditions, experienced walkers can cross the Cho La into the Gokyo valley, for more views and a descent to Lukla by the western trail. **See p.345**

❽ Kathmandu A post-trek day or two in Kathmandu could be happily wasted browsing for handicrafts, eating and drinking – or seeing the sights. **See p.54**

EXPLORING THE WEST

Few travellers head any further west than Pokhara, but as soon as you get off the well-travelled track you start tasting a rougher, richer side of Nepal. This itinerary is for those with weeks to spare – though you could reduce it to a fortnight by settling for just the Karnali, Bardia and Pokhara.

❶ The Karnali from Dungeshwar This remote rafting-and-camping trip begins with a flight to Nepalgunj, a bus or jeep ride via Birendra Nagar to the put-in point at Dungeshwar, then a raft descent through remote, far western hills for about eight days towards Bardia. What a way to begin. **See p.364**

❷ Bardia National Park The rafting trip can end at Bardia, which has all the spectacular wildlife of Chitwan, but a fraction of the visitors – and preserves its laidback mud-and-thatch lodges. **See p.271**

❸ Lumbini The birthplace of the Buddha sits in the burning hot plains, amid astounding monasteries and ancient archeological sites. **See p.261**

❹ Tansen A friendly town on the edge of the hills offering appealing homestays, a fine restaurant, a palace, Himalayan views and a great day hike to Rani Ghat. **See p.231**

❺ Biking the Tamghas Highway You'll see no other tourists on this rough, multi-day mountain-biking (or, if you must, bus and hitchhiking) route between Tansen and Pokhara. If it's too much, the sinuous Siddhartha Highway is (relatively) fast and fabulous. **See p.379**

❻ Pokhara If you arrive in Pokhara from the west, you'll deserve all that basking by the lake, and all those relaxed bars and restaurants. **See p.206**

❼ Gorkha An impressive royal palace looms on the ridge above the hill town of Gorkha. **See p.198**

❽ Manaslu Circuit You could make a two- to three-week detour from Gorkha around Nepal's "teahouseable" trekking route – no camping required. **See p.333**

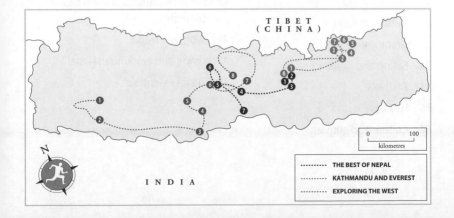

NEWAR MEN EATING SACRED MITHAI SWEETS

Basics

Getting there

In the autumn and spring tourist high seasons (late Sept to mid-Nov and late Feb to late March), flights to Kathmandu – Nepal's only international airport – often fill up months ahead. Most people book tickets through to Kathmandu, but you can also make your own way to a major regional air hub such as Delhi, and arrange transport from there. Airfares depend on the time of year, but timings of the high, low and shoulder seasons are calculated differently by each airline, and may not always coincide with tourist seasons.

You can sometimes cut costs by going through a specialist flight agent such as STA Travel (ⓦstatravel.com) or Trailfinders (ⓦtrailfinders.com), but the best deals tend to be found online (compare prices on an aggregator like ⓦmomondo.com or ⓦkayak.com). **Round-the-World** tickets are worth considering, but cheaper off-the-peg tickets don't generally allow you to fly both into and out of Kathmandu. Figure on around at least £1500/ US$2250 for a ticket that includes Nepal.

Flights from the UK and Ireland

There are no direct **flights** from London, Ireland or indeed Europe as a whole to Kathmandu, so you'll have to make at least one stop en route. Fares are seasonal, and airlines generally charge full whack (around £650–900) from late September to mid-November, late February to late March, and during the Christmas period. It's often possible, however, to find discounted fares (around £550–700), especially on less convenient routes, and prices drop outside of these periods, when you may be able to get a flight for as little as £500.

From London, Emirates (ⓦemirates.com) and Qatar Airways (ⓦqatarairways.com) offer the most direct routings via the Middle East. Another good option is to fly on Jet Airways (ⓦjetairways.com) or Air India (ⓦairindia.com) via Delhi/Mumbai. Travelling by other routes takes longer (sometimes with long stopovers), but relatively inexpensive deals can often be found on carriers such as Etihad Airways (ⓦetihad .com), Oman Air (ⓦomanair.com) or a Virgin Atlantic/ Jet Airways combo (through an online agent). Flights on Malaysian Airlines (ⓦmalaysiaairlines.com) and Singapore Airlines (ⓦsingaporeair.com) aren't really worth considering because you'll have to double back from Kuala Lumpur or Singapore.

> **MOUNTAIN VIEWS**
>
> If you're flying into or out of Kathmandu via Delhi or the Gulf, it's worth trying to book a daytime flight, as the **views** on clear days are astounding. Flying west from Kathmandu, many flights now take a particularly astonishing route, during which the western Himalayas scroll right past your window. Check in early to ensure a window seat on the best side: on the left on the way in (seats lettered A), and on the right on the way out.

Travellers **from Ireland** will generally have to journey via London or another European city.

Flights from the US and Canada

If you live on the **east coast** it's quicker to fly to Nepal via Europe and then – typically – the Middle East or India (see p.22). From the **west coast** it's easier to go via the Far East on a carrier like Singapore Airlines (ⓦsingaporeair.com), Thai Airways (ⓦthaiairways.com), Malaysian Airlines (ⓦmalaysiaairlines.com) or Cathay Pacific (ⓦcathay pacific.com). Expect to spend 20–24 hours on planes if you travel via these routes.

Seasonal considerations may help determine which route you fly; note that these airline seasons don't necessarily coincide with Nepal's autumn and spring tourist seasons. Most airlines consider high season to be summer and the period around Christmas; low season is winter (excluding Christmas), while spring and autumn may be considered low or shoulder season, depending on your route. High-season prices from both the east and west coasts are around US$1350–2000.

From **Canada**, the cheapest flights tend to be from Toronto, flying eastwards, and cost around Can$1750–2400 in the high season.

Flights from Australia, New Zealand and South Africa

The cheapest flights by far **from Australia** (and more or less everywhere else in Asia) are with Air Asia (ⓦairasia.com). These can cost as little as Aus$850 return, and are often quicker than travelling with other airlines. Air Asia don't fly from New Zealand however.

Flying from Australia or **New Zealand** with a **mainstream carrier** invariably means travelling with Malaysian Airlines (ⓦmalaysiaairlines.com) via Kuala Lumpur, Air India (Ⓦairindia.com) via Delhi, or combo-flights with Singapore Airlines (Ⓦsingaporeair.com) via Singapore, with a stopover en route. Some airlines such as Virgin Australia (Ⓦvirginaustralia.com) via Abu Dhabi, are well-priced but go via very circuitous routes.

Fares with the mainstream carriers depend on the time of year. Generally, low season runs from mid-January to late February, and from early October to the end of November; high season is from around mid-May to August, and early December to mid-January; shoulder season takes up the rest of the year. Low-season prices to Kathmandu via Singapore or Bangkok start at roughly Aus$1100–1600 from Australia, and NZ$2000–2500 from New Zealand, and can be several hundred dollars (in either currency) higher in peak season.

Fares **to Delhi** are about the same as to Kathmandu, so another possibility – although not the most economical – is to fly into India and fly or travel overland from there (see below).

From **South Africa**, the cheapest flights are with Emirates (Ⓦemirates.com) via Oman, or Jet Airways (Ⓦjetairways.com) via India, though both these flights can have long stopovers; Qatar Airways (Ⓦqatarairways.com) via Doha is a bit more expensive but tends to be shorter. Try different combinations of flights/carriers online for the best price and shortest durations. Expect to pay around ZAR9500–13000.

Getting there from neighbouring countries

Many travellers combine Nepal with a trip to India, even if they're just making the connection with a flight to or from Delhi. There are numerous **border crossings** between the two countries, and overland routes can easily be planned to take in many of northern India's most renowned sights. Travel agencies in India and Nepal offer bus package deals between the two countries, but these are generally overpriced and it is far better to organize things yourself.

Three border crossings see the vast majority of travellers: **Sonauli/Belahiya**, reachable from Delhi, Varanasi and most of North India (via Gorakhpur); **Raxaul/Birgunj**, accessible from Bodhgaya and Kolkata via Patna; and **Kakarbhitta**, serving Darjeeling and Kolkata via Siliguri. A fourth, **Banbaasa/Mahendra Nagar**, in the little-visited west of Nepal, is handy for the Uttar Pradesh hill stations and (relatively speaking) Delhi too. All these border crossings are described in the relevant

sections of the Guide. Two other border points (near Nepalgunj and Dhangadhi) are also open to tourists, but they're rarely used. Other crossings near Janakpur, Biratnagar and Ilam rarely admit foreigners.

Flying between Delhi and Kathmandu rewards you with Himalayan views (see box, p.21) and opens up a wider choice of international flights. Air India (Ⓦairindia.in), IndiGo (Ⓦgoindigo.in), Jet Airways (Ⓦjetairways.com), SpiceJet (Ⓦspicejet.com), and Nepal Airlines (Ⓦnepalairlines.com.np) all serve this route for around US$100–150 one-way, or half that on one of the low-cost carriers if you're lucky.

Travel from **Tibet** is possible as long as you have the correct permit; entering Tibet from Nepal, however, is limited to group tours (see p.96). It is also possible to fly to Kathmandu from **Bhutan**, though again it needs to be as part of an organized tour.

The classic **Asia overland** trip is just about alive and kicking, and several operators, including Dragoman (see p.23) run trips to Nepal.

Specialist agents and tour operators

The following operators are good options for special interest, sightseeing, wildlife and trekking **tours** in Nepal. It's worth bearing in mind that, while booking a package through an operator in your own country might be much easier, and perhaps more secure, the more agencies you put between you and the product the more expensive it gets – there are very few things that can't be organized more cheaply (and with more benefit to the local economy) by a Nepali agency, or by using this book to organize yourself.

A BETTER KIND OF TRAVEL

At Rough Guides we are passionately committed to travel. We feel that travelling is the best way to understand the world we live in and the people we share it with – plus tourism has brought a great deal of benefit to developing economies around the world over the last few decades. But the growth in tourism has also damaged some places irreparably, and climate change is exacerbated by most forms of transport, especially flying. All Rough Guides' trips are carbon-offset, and every year we donate money to a variety of charities devoted to combating the effects of climate change.

IN THE UK

Audley Travel ☎ 01993 838300, Ⓦ audleytravel.com. Quality tailor-made and small-group tours in Nepal.

Classic Journeys ☎ 01773 873497, Ⓦ classicjourneys.co.uk. Nepal specialist offering the usual range of treks, plus several tours run by professional photographers.

Dragoman ☎ 01728 885644, Ⓦ dragoman.com. Extended overland journeys taking in Nepal and India.

Exodus ☎ 0845 863 9600, Ⓦ exodus.co.uk. Established company with trekking, cycling and sightseeing trips to Nepal, India, Tibet and Bhutan.

Explore Worldwide ☎ 01252 884223, Ⓦ explore.co.uk. Recommended operator offering Nepal and Tibet trips, featuring trekking and cultural activities. Good for single travellers.

Footprint Adventures ☎ 07546 872801, Ⓦ footprint-adventures .co.uk. Specializes in wildlife and birdwatching tours, plus trekking.

High Places ☎ 0114 279 2790, Ⓦ highplaces.co.uk. For the more serious trekker, focusing on high-altitude trekking and scaling peaks.

Jagged Globe ☎ 0114 276 3322, Ⓦ jagged-globe.co.uk. Climbing, mountaineering and serious trekking expeditions.

Mongoose Travel ☎ 01271 850224, Ⓦ mongoosetravel.co.uk. Small company offering cultural tours and treks, with good ethical and environmental credentials.

Mountain Kingdoms ☎ 01453 844400, Ⓦ mountainkingdoms .com. Smallish specialist company with particular expertise on Nepal.

Naturetrek ☎ 01962 733051, Ⓦ naturetrek.co.uk. Leading specialist in birdwatching and wildlife tours.

On The Go Tours ☎ 020 7371 1113, Ⓦ onthegotours.com. Established operator offering tours throughout Nepal, as well as trips to India, Tibet and Bhutan, and a pan-Himalayan tour travelling between them.

Traidcraft ☎ 0191 265 1110, Ⓦ meetthepeople.skedaddle.co.uk. Sustainable "meet the people" tours involving stays with small-scale farmers who produce fair trade products.

Wildlife Worldwide ☎ 01962 302086, Ⓦ wildlifeworldwide .com. Trips for wildlife enthusiasts.

IN THE US AND CANADA

Above the Clouds Trekking ☎ 1 800 233 4499, Ⓦ aboveclouds .com. Family-run operator offering some unusual treks, including "heli-trekking"; good for family treks.

Adventure.com Ⓦ adventure.com. Traveller community that specializes in finding the right tour operator for those who want to get off the beaten path.

Canadian Himalayan Expeditions ☎ 1 800 563 8735, Ⓦ himalayanexpeditions.com. Wide range of small-group treks and climbing expeditions.

Friends in High Places ☎ 1 781 354 9851, Ⓦ fihp.com. US-Nepali company offering mostly customized itineraries, especially treks.

Journeys International ☎ 1 800 255 8735, Ⓦ journeys.travel. Worldwide trekking agency covering the standard routes, plus a few off-the-beaten-track options.

Mountain Travel Sobek ☎ 1 888 831 7526, Ⓦ mtsobek.com. High-end trekking and rafting company, with easy to strenuous routes, plus wildlife and customized trips.

IN AUSTRALIA AND NEW ZEALAND

Abercrombie and Kent Australia ☎ 1300 851924, New Zealand ☎ 0800 441638, Ⓦ abercrombiekent.com. Upmarket tours of Nepal and India.

Intrepid Travel Australia ☎ 1300 797010, New Zealand ☎ 0800 600610, Ⓦ intrepidtravel.com. Small-group tours, mostly treks on standard routes, but also wildlife, rafting and India trips, with an ethical emphasis.

Peregrine Adventures Australia ☎ 1300 854445, Ⓦ peregrine adventures.com. Tours across Nepal, some combining visits to India, Bhutan or Tibet.

Ultimate Descents International Australia ☎ 03 543 2301, Ⓦ ultimatedescents.com. Pioneering rafting operator with an extensive range of trips.

Getting around

Getting around is one of the biggest challenges of travelling in Nepal. Distances aren't great, but the roads are poor and extremely slow, and public buses are crowded and uncomfortable. Tourist buses are available on the main routes, however, and you can always hire a motorcycle, or charter a taxi, car or 4WD vehicle, or catch a flight.

Nepal's **highways** are irregularly maintained, and each monsoon takes a toll on surfaces. Wherever you travel, the route will probably be new in parts, disintegrated in places, and under construction in others. The country has a truly appalling road safety record, and accidents are common. And, in

> ## NEPALI PLACE NAMES
>
> Even though Devanaagari (the script of Nepali and Hindi) spellings are phonetic, **transliterating** them into the Roman alphabet is a disputed science. Some places will never shake off the erroneous spellings bestowed on them by early British colonialists – Kathmandu, for instance, looks more like Kaathmaadau when properly transliterated. Where place names are Sanskrit-based, the Nepali pronunciation sometimes differs from the accepted spelling – the names Vishnu (a Hindu god) and Vajra (a tantric symbol), for instance, sound like Bishnu and Bajra in Nepali. We have followed local pronunciations as consistently as possible in this guide, except in cases where to do so would be out of step with every map in print.

addition, blockades or general strikes (*bandh*) can at times make travel virtually impossible, though it's got a lot better in recent years.

By bus

Allowing for bad roads, overloaded buses, tea stops, meal stops, the constant picking up and letting off of passengers, and the occasional flat tyre or worse, the average bus speed in the hills is barely 25–30km per hour, and on remote, unpaved roads it can be half that. Along the Terai's Mahendra Highway, it's more like 50km per hour in an express bus.

Bus **frequencies** and approximate journey times are given throughout this guide. Inevitably, these figures should be taken with a pinch of salt: the bus network seems to grow every year, but political troubles or festivals can dramatically reduce the number of buses, and some gravel or dirt roads are closed altogether during the monsoon.

Open-air **bus stations** (also known as *bas parks* or *bas islands*) are typically located in the dustiest parts of town. Tickets are generally sold from a small booth. Destinations may not be written in English, but people are almost always happy to help you out if you ask.

In Kathmandu and Pokhara you may find it easier to make arrangements through a travel agent (though make sure it's one you've been recommended), while in cities you can ask your hotel to buy a ticket for you.

Even the longest journeys on public buses should **cost** no more than Rs500.

Tourist buses

Regular **tourist buses** connect Kathmandu with Pokhara, Sauraha (for Chitwan National Park) and Sonauli, as well as Pokhara with Sauraha and Sonauli. The vehicles are usually in good condition, making for a safer ride than in a regular bus. They aren't supposed to take more passengers than there are seats, so the journey should also be more comfortable and quicker too. Some companies use minibuses, which are somewhat quicker – occasionally dangerously so. Book seats at least one or two days in advance. Note that ticket agents often add an undisclosed commission onto the price.

Express buses

Long-distance public bus services generally operate on an **express** basis – meaning they stop at scheduled points only. They're faster and more comfortable than local buses.

Express buses fall into two categories: **day buses**, which usually set off in the morning, and night buses, which usually depart in the afternoon or early evening. **Night buses** are generally more comfortable, though legroom is always in short supply, and between all the lurching, honking, tea stops and blaring music you won't get much sleep (bring earplugs and an eye mask). Night journeys are also significantly more dangerous, and it's not uncommon for drivers to fall asleep at the wheel or drink alcohol.

Like tourist buses, and unlike local buses, express buses allow you to **reserve seats** in advance. Do this, or you could end up in one of the ejector seats along the back. Numbering begins from the front of the bus: the prized seats #1A and #2A, on the left by the front door, often have the most legroom. You can usually get away with buying a ticket just a few hours beforehand, except during the big festivals, when you should book as far in advance as possible.

Most express buses give you the choice of stowing your **baggage** on the roof or in a locked hold in the back. Having all your things with you is of course the best insurance policy against theft. Putting bags in the hold is usually the next-safest option, especially on night buses. Baggage stowed on the roof is probably all right during the day, but you can never be completely sure – if possible, lock your bag to the roofrack, and keep an eye out during stops.

Local buses

Serving mainly shorter routes or remote roads, **local buses** are ancient, cramped and battered contraptions. A bus isn't making money until it's nearly full to bursting, and it can get suffocating inside. Once on the road, the bus will stop any time it's flagged down.

Local buses often depart from a separate bus park or just a widening in the road, and tickets are bought on board. The only way to be sure of getting a seat is to board the bus early and wait. If you're just picking up a bus along the way you're likely to join the crush standing in the aisle.

Unless your **bag** is small, it will have to go on the roof; during daylight hours it should be safe there as long as it's locked, but keep all valuables on your person. **Riding on the roof** can be quite appealing, but it's dangerous and illegal. Even if you've got a seat, safety is a concern: these buses are often overworked, overloaded and poorly maintained.

By 4WD and truck

Almost every roadhead in Nepal is being extended, often on local initiative, by way of a dirt track making its painful way deeper into the countryside. And where the bus comes to the end of the road, you can rely on finding a **gaadi** (the all-purpose word for a vehicle) to take you further. This will often be a Tata Sumo or similarly extended 4WD; on the roughest routes you'll even find tractor transport.

Another option is to travel by **truck**, many of which do a sideline in hauling passengers. Trucks aren't licensed as passenger vehicles, and take little interest in passenger **safety**; you should also watch your luggage. Women travelling by truck will probably prefer to join up with a companion.

If you're really stuck, you could try **hitching**, though this carries obvious risks.

By plane and helicopter

Aircraft play a vital role in Nepal's transport network, and there will be times when US$150–200 spent on an **internal flight** seems a small price to pay to avoid 24 hours on a bus. Most flights begin or end in Kathmandu, but two other airports in the Terai – Nepalgunj and Biratnagar – serve as secondary hubs. The less profitable destinations tend to be served exclusively by the state-owned Nepal Airlines Corporation (NAC; Ⓦnepalairlines.com.np), which has a justifiably poor reputation.

Numerous **private airlines** operate fairly efficiently on the main domestic inter-city and tourist trekking routes. They include Air Viva (Ⓦair-viva.com); Buddha Air (Ⓦbuddhaair.com); Gorkha Airlines (Ⓦgorkhaairlines.com); Tara Air (Ⓦtaraair.com); and Yeti Airlines, (Ⓦyetiairlines.com).

An hour-long scenic loop out of Kathmandu, the so-called "**mountain flight**", is popular among tourists who want to get an armchair view of Everest (see box, p.97).

Tickets

Almost all domestic airlines now allow booking **online** using a credit card, though you can also book through a **travel agent** for a small fee. Tickets bought through travel agents must be paid for in hard currency only, usually US dollars. At off-peak times you shouldn't have any trouble getting a **seat**, but during the trekking season flights to airstrips along the popular trails may be booked up months in advance. Agencies frequently overbook, though, releasing their unused tickets on the day of departure, so you may be able to buy a returned ticket from the airline on the morning you want to travel. Make sure to **check in early** for popular flights, as they are often overbooked. There is a Rs200 **departure tax** for all internal flights flying into Kathmandu (it's included in outbound ticket prices).

Safety and delays

Government scrutiny of the airline industry is minimal, and there have been 42 major **crashes** in Nepal since 1992, when two international flights went down, though most crashes occur at remote airstrips. The mountainous terrain is the main problem, particularly during the monsoon – "In Nepal, clouds have rocks in them", as the saying goes – although baggage overloading and lack of maintenance checks are contributing factors. Radar was installed at Kathmandu airport after the crashes of 1992, and mountain airstrips now have limited warning systems in place, but for the most part you are relying on pilot skill and experience. It's a close

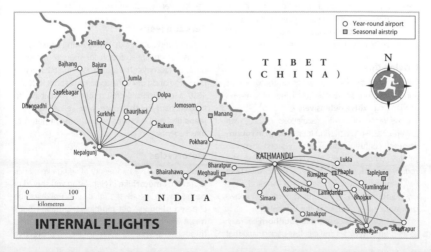

INTERNAL FLIGHTS

call as to whether flying is more, or less, dangerous than travelling by bus, especially during the perilous monsoon period.

Another problem with flying in Nepal is the frequency of **delays and cancellations**, usually due to weather. Few airstrips have even the simplest landing beacons, and many of them are surrounded by hills, so there must be good visibility to land – if there's fog or the cloud ceiling is too low, the plane won't fly. Since clouds usually increase as the day wears on, delays often turn into cancellations. If your flight is cancelled, you may be placed at the bottom of a waiting list, rather than being given space on the next available flight.

Helicopters

Several companies – including Mountain Helicopters Nepal (W mountainhelicoptersnepal.com) and Fishtail Air (W fishtailair.com) – offer charter **helicopter services**, which are mainly used by trekking parties with more money than time, who charter a chopper for upwards of US$1000 to save them several days' backtracking. Companies are supposed to charter only entire aircraft, but in practice if a helicopter is returning empty from a trekking landing strip, the pilot will take on individual passengers for about the same price as a seat on a plane. Helicopter tours are also available.

Driving and cycling

In addition to being faster and more comfortable than a bus, travelling by **car**, **4WD** or **motorbike** will enable you to get to places you'd never go otherwise, and to stop whenever you like. **Rental cars** always come with a driver in Nepal. If you bring your own vehicle you'll need a carnet de passage and an international driving licence; you'll just need the latter if you rent a motorcycle.

Driving tips

Driving your own car or riding a motorbike is sometimes fun, sometimes terrifying, and always challenging – **drive defensively**.

Observance of traffic regulations is lax, with drivers constantly jockeying for position. On **roundabouts**, confusion arises (for visitors) because priority officially goes to vehicles *entering* the roundabout. Most vehicles you want to **overtake** will want you to wait for their signal – a hand wave or, confusingly, a right-turning indicator (slow-moving vehicles often leave the latter on).

Follow local practice and **use your horn** liberally: to alert other vehicles and careless pedestrians that

you're there, when rounding sharp corners, and when overtaking – so more or less all the time. Driving without using your horn will almost certainly result in an accident.

Watch your **speed** on the highways, which are rarely free of unmarked hazards. Try to keep speeds to a maximum of 50–60kmph, and slow down when passing through towns and villages, keeping an eye out for vehicles, cyclists and people or animals who often wander into the road without looking. And watch out for those **cows**: the penalty for killing one is up to twelve years in prison, the same as for killing a human being.

If you do have an **accident**, the first locals on the scene will always help, and for minor accidents a lively discussion will ensue (with passers-by taking sides) as to where to apportion blame. If it's a straightforward case with no injuries, you can negotiate and pay/receive damages there and then. If one side is not happy about this, or there are injuries, the police will get involved, fill out a report and help with arbitration.

Never drive **at night** if you can help it: there are no dipped headlights, and all the dangers above are magnified. Aim to arrive at your destination at least an hour or two before sunset.

Petrol stations can be found in towns and cities, as well as along major routes, though you should fill up when you have the opportunity (start looking when you've got half a tank) as they often run out of fuel – it's always wise to carry an extra container of petrol just in case. Off the beaten path, most villages will have at least one shop which sells bottles of petrol, though it's usually watered down or contaminated – this is sometimes the case at the pumps too. Petrol currently costs around Rs150 a litre.

Cars and jeeps

In Kathmandu and Pokhara, chartering a **taxi** by the day is the cheapest option for short or medium-distance journeys. The going rate for trips within the Kathmandu or Pokhara valleys is about Rs3000–4000 a day (plus petrol), though you'll have to bargain hard for that price. More expensive cars, **jeeps** and 4WDs can be rented through hotels or travel agents.

Motorcycles

You'll want to have had plenty of riding experience to travel by **motorbike** in Nepal, and you should of course have a licence, though it's very unlikely to be checked (though your red/blue registration book might well be) – police usually just wave foreigners through checkpoints. Wear as much **protective**

clothing as possible (especially a helmet, which is the law).

You will almost certainly break down at some point, in which case you will need a **mechanic** (*mistri*), who can be found in larger villages, towns and cities. If you're in the middle of nowhere, stop any passing vehicle and ask them to call a mechanic out to you; you'll be expected to pay Rs100–150 extra for a call-out. Figure on paying about Rs10 for something that's very quick to fix (under 5min), or for bigger problems around Rs100/hour, plus parts. It's a good idea to watch the work being done, as unscrupulous mechanics have been known to take new parts from within the engine and replace them with old ones.

When **renting**, you may have to leave an air ticket, passport or sum of money as a deposit. Check brakes, oil and fuel level, horn, lights and indicators before setting off, and note that rented bikes carry no insurance – if you break anything, you pay for it. Street bikes can be rented from about Rs500–650 a day, excluding petrol. Most visitors tend to plump for the larger Enfield, which cost more like Rs1500 (and up) a day; these have a lot more heft for long-distance cruising, but are also heavy and hard to handle off-road, and more expensive to run and maintain.

If you **buy a bike**, note that Enfields are considerably more expensive in Nepal than in India (some people buy them in India, and drive them to Nepal to sell for a profit) – a newish secondhand Enfield will set you back over Rs300,000 in Kathmandu. Secondhand, smaller 100–150cc bikes can be bought easily from as little as Rs15,000. Added to these costs are an extra Rs4700 for the ownership registration transfer (which should be arranged by the seller). It's possible to get to most places on a 100cc bike (this edition was partly researched on one), though for the mountains something over 150cc is far preferable – the Bajaj Pulsar 200cc or 220cc is the most popular bike for locals in more remote mountainous regions.

Finally, bear in mind that biking around Nepal is a great experience, but roads are atrocious and drivers can be reckless. If you don't have experience driving in similar conditions, it would be advisable to start out by taking an **organized motorcycle tour**, which are not only much safer as you're in a group, but easy to organize in Kathmandu (see p.97).

Bicycles

A rented **bicycle** (*saikal*) is the logical choice for most day-to-day getting around. One-speeders are good enough for most around-town cycling, and cost Rs150–300 per day. **Mountain bikes** will get you there in greater comfort, and are essential for longer distances or anything steep – a few shops in Kathmandu and Pokhara rent top-quality models for Rs1000–2500.

Bike rental shops are rare beyond Kathmandu, Pokhara and Sauraha, but you can often strike a deal with a lodge owner. Check the brakes, spokes, tyres and chain carefully before setting off; a bell is essential. Repair shops are everywhere, but don't have mountain-bike parts. Theft is a concern with flashier bikes.

City transport

Taxis are confined mainly to Kathmandu and Pokhara. Although they have meters, you'll almost always have to negotiate the fare. Fixed-route **tempos**, three-wheeled vehicles, set off when they're full and stop at designated points; they're noisy and most of them – except Kathmandu's white electric Saafa ("clean") tempos – put out noxious fumes. Cycle **rikshaws** – rare now outside the Terai and Thamel – are slow and bumpy, but handy for short distances; establish a fare before setting off. **City buses**, **minibuses** (shorter ordinary buses) and **microbuses** (white Toyota people-carriers) are usually too crowded, slow or infrequent to be worthwhile, but can be useful in the Kathmandu Valley.

Accommodation

Finding a place to sleep is hardly ever a problem in Nepal, although only the established tourist centres offer much of a choice. Prices vary considerably, depending on where you stay and when. You can pay anything from a couple of dollars per night in a trekking lodge to more than US$350 in a wildlife resort, but guesthouses, where most travellers stay, typically charge between US$5 and US$35.

Outside the **high seasons** (late September to mid-November and late February to late March), or if things are unusually quiet, **prices** can drop by up to fifty percent: the simple question "*discount paunchha?*" ("any discount?") will often do the trick. Note that official tariffs don't generally include the government and service **taxes** (13 percent and 10 percent respectively); rates are usually quoted as "plus plus", meaning that both need to be applied. Offers made on the spot at ordinary guesthouses, however, are generally all-in – make sure you check.

Most places have a range of rooms, from budget, shared-bathroom boxes to en suites with a/c and

ACCOMMODATION PRICES

The accommodation **prices** quoted in this guide are based on the cost of the least expensive double room in the **high season** (late Sept to mid-Nov and late Feb to late March), and include the government (13 percent) and service taxes (10 percent) that are not generally included in the official tariff quoted by the hotel.

Room prices are given in the currency quoted by the hotel, generally either **Nepali rupees** or **US dollars**, though some places quote in euros. Note that prices quoted in foreign currency don't tend to change much, but those given in Nepali rupees are likely to be considerably higher than quoted due to annual inflation of 8–10 percent.

TVs. **Single rooms** are usually doubles offered at between half and two-thirds of the full price. Hotels and guesthouses take **bookings**, and reservations are often necessary in the busy seasons, during local festivals or if you're arriving late at night.

Lodges

Off-the-beaten-track **lodges** are aimed at Nepali travellers, and are usually known as "hotel and lodge" (confusingly, the "hotel" bit means there's somewhere to eat). Some are reasonably comfortable, but more often than not you'll have to settle for something fairly insalubrious. Stark concrete floors, cold-water showers and smelly squat toilets are the rule, though you'll rarely **pay** more than Rs350–500. It's a good idea to bring your own sleeping-bag liner to protect against bedbugs and lice, and earplugs to block out the inevitable noise. In the Terai, try to get a room with a mosquito net and a working fan (or a/c).

This is not to say that Nepali lodges are to be avoided. Often the most primitive places – where you sit by a smoky fire and eat with your hosts – are the most rewarding. **Trekking lodges** on less-travelled routes (see p.314) can take this form, though there are some remarkably comfortable ones out there too.

Guesthouses

Many tourist-oriented places to stay in Nepal call themselves **guesthouses**. This category covers everything from primitive dosshouses to well-appointed small hotels. Most places offer a spread of rooms at different prices, and sometimes dorm beds too. By and large, those that cater to foreigners do so efficiently; most innkeepers speak excellent English, and can arrange anything for you from laundry to trekking/porter hire.

Despite assurances to the contrary, you can't necessarily count on constant **hot water** (many places rely on solar panels) nor uninterrupted electricity (power cuts are a daily occurrence, though some establishments have generators). If constant hot water is important to you, ask what kind of water-heating system the guesthouse has – best of all is "*geyser*" (pronounced "geezer"), which means an electric immersion heater or backup.

All but the really cheap guesthouses will have a safe, and the smarter places sometimes have security boxes in each room.

Budget guesthouses

Kathmandu and Pokhara have their own tourist quarters where fierce competition among **budget guesthouses** ensures great value. In these enclaves, all but the very cheapest places provide hot running water (though perhaps only sporadically), flush toilets, foam mattresses and clean sheets and blankets. Elsewhere in Nepal, expect rooms to be plainer and scruffier. Most guesthouses also offer some sort of roof-terrace or garden, a phone and TV. They're rarely heated, however, making them rather cold in winter. Rooms in most budget places **cost** Rs350–1000, and standards vary considerably; the cheapest options often have **shared bathrooms**.

Mid-range guesthouses

Mid-range guesthouses (for lack of a better term) are increasingly popular. Rooms tend to be bigger and come with a fan (or even a/c), and often a phone and TV. Toilet paper is provided in the bathrooms, and the hot water is more reliable. The better ones will provide a portable electric heater in winter. Expect to **pay** Rs1000–3500 for a double room of this sort. Most mid-range guesthouses quote their prices in dollars, though you can pay in rupees and sometimes even with credit cards.

Hotels and resorts

It's hard to generalize about the more expensive **hotels and resorts**. Some charge a hefty premium to insulate you from the Nepal you came to see, while others offer unique experiences. Prices for international-type features begin at around the US$50 mark, but you should expect to pay in the region of US$100 a night or more for a genuinely classy place. This guide also recommends several smaller resort hotels that offer something unique, such as a breathtaking view or historic building. **Jungle lodges** near the Terai wildlife parks are typically the most expensive options of all, charging US$250 plus a night.

Village stays and homestays

A growing number of programmes enable visitors to stay overnight in private homes in traditional villages far from the tourist trails. **Village stays** (also called village tourism or homestays) offer a unique opportunity for comfortable cultural immersion, and could become a good way to disperse visitors and spread the economic benefits of tourism into rural areas. The idea is that a tour operator contracts with a whole village to accommodate and entertain guests; rooms in local houses are fitted with bathrooms and a few tourist-style comforts, host families are trained to prepare meals that won't disturb delicate Western constitutions, and a guide accompanies the guests to interpret, if necessary.

There are numerous **village tourism programmes**, including one in **Chisapani**, southeast of Pokhara near Rup Tal, run by the reputable Pokhara-based Child Welfare Scheme (Ⓦcwsn.org), another at the Gurung village of **Sirubari** (see box, p.230), and others that can be organized in and around **Tansen** (see p.234) and **Bandipur** (see p.204).

SUSTAINABLE TOURISM

While tourism is a key part of Nepal's economy, it doesn't always have a positive impact on the country. The **Responsible Travel Nepal** initiative provides Nepali tourism companies – hotels and resorts, trekking and adventure companies, travel agencies and so on – with training and support to encourage them to ensure their activities and management practices follow sustainable tourism principles. Crucially, it emphasizes the business benefits of adopting these principles, helping the companies to build links with operators and travellers, improve their marketing work and expand their businesses. Responsible Travel Nepal's website (Ⓦrt-responsibletravel.com) provides information about the companies participating, and is a useful first port of call when planning activities in Nepal.

A few language institutes and other organizations in Kathmandu and Patan also organize homestays with families in and around the valley; try Nepal Face to Face (☏980 883 8447, Ⓦnepalfacetoface.com). A quick internet search will put you in direct contact with dozens of other options.

Eating and drinking

Nepal – and specifically Kathmandu – is renowned as the budget eating capital of Asia. Sadly, its reputation is based not on Nepali but on pseudo-Western food: pizza, chips (fries), "sizzling" steaks and apple pie are the staples of tourist restaurants. Outside the popular areas, the chief complaint from travellers is about the lack of variety, though with a little willingness to experiment, a range of dishes can be found.

Indeed, a vast range of flavours can be found just in **daal bhaat**, the national dish of rice, lentils, lightly curried vegetables and pickles; though it can also, sometimes, be disappointingly bland. In the Kathmandu Valley, the indigenous **Newars** have their own unique cuisine of spicy meat and vegetable dishes, while a vast range of Indian curries, breads, snacks and sweets comes into play in the **Terai**; in the high **mountains**, the traditional diet consists of noodle soups, potatoes and toasted flour. "*Chow-chow*" packet noodles, cooked up as a spicy soup snack, are ubiquitous. **Vegetarians** will feel at home in Nepal, since meat is considered a luxury. Tourist menus invariably include veggie items.

Outside the tourist areas food is very **inexpensive**, and a simple meal and drink may well set you back less than Rs100. In places like Kathmandu and Pokhara, however, costs can quickly add up: you might pay around Rs300–800 for a main meal at a tourist-oriented restaurant, and even more at a posher place. Note that few restaurants in tourist areas include government **taxes** (13 percent) and service charges (10 percent) in their menu prices, though we have added these to the sample prices quoted in our listings.

Where to eat

Tourist restaurants in Kathmandu, Pokhara and a few other well-visited places show an amazing knack for sensing what travellers want and simulating it with basic ingredients. Some specialize in particular cuisines, but the majority attempt to cover most bases. Outside these tourist hubs, options are more limited, though Terai cities always have a fancy (by Nepali standards) restaurant or two, generally serving a mix of Nepali, Indian and Chinese food.

Local **Nepali diners** (known as *bhojanalayas*, roadside *dhabas* in the Terai, or, confusingly enough, *"hotels"*) are traditionally humble affairs, offering a limited choice of dishes or just *daal bhaat*. Menus don't exist, but the food will normally be on display or cooking in full view, so all you have to do is point. Utensils are usually available on request, but if not, try doing as Nepalis do and eat with your right hand – and bear in mind the various social taboos relating to eating (see p.41). In towns and cities, places to eat tend to be dark, almost conspiratorial places, unmarked and hidden behind curtains. On the highways they're bustlingly public and spill outdoors in an effort to win business.

Teahouses (*chiyapasal*) really only sell tea and basic snacks, while the simple **taverns** (*bhatti*) of the Kathmandu Valley and the Western hills put the emphasis on alcoholic drinks and meaty snacks, but may serve Nepali meals too. **Trailside**, both *chiyapasal* and *bhatti* are typically modest operations run out of family kitchens. **Sweet shops** (*mithaipasal or misthan bhandar*) are intended to fill the gap between the traditional mid-morning and early evening meals; besides sweets and tea, they also do South Indian and Nepali savoury snacks.

Street vendors sell fruit, nuts, roasted corn, and various fried specialities. As often as not, food will come to you when you're travelling – at every bus stop, vendors will clamber aboard or hawk their wares through the window.

Nepali food

The most popular meal in Nepal is *daal bhaat tarkaari*, a simple dish of lentils, rice and vegetables, usually just known as **daal bhaat** (see box below). Most Nepalis begin the day with a cup of tea and little else, eating *daal bhaat* some time in the **mid-morning** (often around 9am or 10am) and again in the **evening**, with just a snack of potatoes, *makkai* (popcorn) or noodles in between. *Daal bhaat* times in Kathmandu are pushing nearer to lunchtime but, outside the city, it's worth remembering that if you turn up for *khaanaa* (food) at noon it'll either be cold or take hours to cook from scratch.

You'll usually be able to supplement a plate of *daal bhaat* with small side dishes of *maasu* (meat) – chicken, goat or fish. In Indian-influenced Terai towns you can often get *roti* instead of rice. **Sukuti** (dried, spiced meat fried in oil) is popular everywhere. You could make a meal out of rice or *chiura* (beaten, dried rice) and **sekuwa** (spicy kebabs) or **taareko maachhaa** (fried fish), common in the Terai. If you're invited into a peasant home in the high hills you might be served **dhedo** (a toasted corn, millet or wheat flour dough) instead of rice. Some say *dhedo* with *gundruk*, not *daal bhaat*, is the real national food of Nepal, though it's only just started to appear on the menu of Thakali restaurants.

DAAL BHAAT

For many Nepalis **daal bhaat** – or *daal bhaat tarkaari* (*daal* means lentil, *bhaat* rice and *tarkaari* vegetable) – is the only meal they ever eat, twice a day every day of their lives, and they don't feel they've eaten properly without it. Indeed, in much of Nepal, *bhaat* is a synonym for food and *khaanaa* (food) is a synonym for rice.

The *daal bhaat* served in restaurants ranges from excellent to derisory – it's a meal that's really meant to be eaten at home – so if you spend much time trekking or travelling off the beaten track you'll probably quickly tire of it. It's worth looking out for establishments sporting the name **Thakali** – Nepalis believe this ethnic group (originating in the hills around Annapurna) produces a particularly good *daal bhaat*, and they are usually right.

That said, a good **achhaar** (a relish or pickle made with tomato, radish or whatever's in season) can liven up a *daal bhaat* tremendously. There are endless subtle variations in the flavours and grades of rice and in the idea of what constitutes a good *daal*, from the buttery, yellow gunge of *raharkodaal* to the king of winter lentils, *maaskodaal*, cooked in an iron pot until it turns from green to black.

Daal bhaat is often served on a gleaming steel platter divided into compartments similar to an Indian *thali*; add the *daal* and other condiments to the rice, knead the resulting mixture into mouth-sized balls with the right hand, then push it off the fingers into your mouth with the thumb. One price covers unlimited refills, except in tourist-savvy establishments.

Nepali **desserts** include *khir* (rice pudding), *sikarni* (thick, creamy yoghurt with cinnamon, raisins and nuts) and various versions of Indian sweets.

Newari food

Like many aspects of Newari culture (see p.153), **Newari food** is all too often regarded as exotic but too weird for outsiders. It's complex, subtle, delicious and devilishly hard to make. Most specialities are quite spicy, and based around four mainstays: buffalo, rice, pulses and vegetables (especially radish).

The Newars use every part of the buffalo, or "buff": **momocha** (meat-filled steamed dumplings – differentiated from Tibetan *momos* by their purse-like rather than half-moon shape), **choyila** (buff cubes fried with spices and greens), **palula** (spicy buff with ginger sauce) and **kachila** (a paté of minced raw buff, mixed with ginger and mustard oil) are some of the more accessible dishes; others are made from tongue, stomach, lung, blood, bone marrow and so on. Because of caste restrictions, Newars rarely eat boiled rice outside the home. Newari restaurants therefore serve it in the form of **baji** (*chiura* in Nepali) – rice that's been partially cooked and then rolled flat and dried, looking something like rolled oats – or **chataamari** (a sort of pizza made with rice flour, usually topped with minced buff).

Pulses and beans play a role in several other preparations, notably **woh** (fried lentil-flour patties, also known as *buuru*), **kwati** (a soup made with sprouted beans), **musyapalu** (roasted soya beans and ginger) and **bhuti** (boiled soya beans with spices and herbs). Various vegetable mixtures are available seasonally, including **pancha kol** (a curry made with five vegetables) and **alu achhaar** (boiled potato in a spicy sauce). The best veggie option is *alutama*, a sour soup made with bamboo shoots and potatoes. Radish turns up in myriad forms of *achhaar*.

International food

The tourist restaurants of Kathmandu and Pokhara offer tastes of virtually every cuisine under the sun. There's no denying that this **international food** is tasty, but the sheer range of choice available to visitors has the unfortunate side effect of isolating many visitors from Nepali cooking. Many restaurants try to offer a bit of everything, but some are moving upmarket into dedicated cuisines, notably Chinese, French, Italian, Japanese, Korean, Mexican and Thai. Outside of Kathmandu and Pokhara, international food is almost always a crashing disappointment and best avoided.

Indian food

Indian food is widely available. The dishes you're most likely to encounter are from **North India**: thick, rich **curries**, *tandoori* **dishes**, and breads like *rotis, chapatis, naans, parathas* and *puris*.

In the Terai you'll also run across **South Indian canteens**, which serve a predominantly vegetarian cuisine. The staple dish here is the *masala dosa*, a rice-flour pancake rolled around curried potatoes, served with *sambhar* (a savoury *daal* flavoured with tamarind) and coconut chutney. There is also an incredible array of **sweets**, including *laddu*, yellow-and-orange speckled semolina balls; *jalebi*, orange pretzel-shaped tubes of deep-fried, syrup-soaked treacle; *gulab jamun*, spongy balls in super-sweet syrup; and *ras malai*, cream cheese balls in a milky, perfumed syrup.

Tibetan food

Strictly speaking, "Tibetan" refers to nationals of Tibet, but the people of several other highland ethnic groups eat what could be called Tibetan food.

Momo, arguably the most famous and popular of Tibetan dishes, are available throughout upland Nepal. Similar to dim sum, the half-moon-shapes are filled with meat, vegetables and ginger, steamed, and served with hot tomato salsa and a bowl of broth. Fried *momo* are called *kothe*. *Shyaphagle*, made from the same ingredients, are Tibetan-style pasties. Tibetan cuisine is also full of hearty soups called **thukpa** or *thenthuk*, consisting of noodles, meat and vegetables in broth. For a group feast, try the huge **gyakok** (chicken, pork, prawns, fish, tofu, eggs and vegetables), which gets its name from the brass container it's served in. In trekking lodges you'll encounter pitta-like Tibetan or "Gurung" **bread**.

The average peasant seldom eats any of the above. **Potatoes** are common in the high country, and Sherpa potatoes – usually eaten boiled in their skins with a dab of salt and chilli paste – are justly famous for their nutty sweetness. **Tsampa** (toasted barley flour) is another staple, and often, especially for trekkers, mixed with milk or tea to make a porridge paste.

Road food

Common food on the road includes **pakora** (vegetables dipped in chickpea-flour batter, deep fried), and **bean curry** served with *puris* or *roti*. Another possibility is **dahi chiura**, a mixture of yoghurt and beaten rice. If you're in a hurry, you can grab a handful of **samosas** (curried vegetables in fried pastry triangles), *baara* (fried lentil patties), or other titbits on a leaf plate. In the hill towns and around Kathmandu, huge aluminium steamers placed by the restaurant door advertise **momo**. If nothing else, there will always be packet **noodles** ("*chow-chow*").

Other snacks

Imported **chocolates** are sold in tourist areas, and waxy Indian substitutes can be found in most towns. **Biscuits** and cheap boiled **sweets** (confusingly enough, called *chocolet* in Nepali) are sold everywhere. **Cheese**, produced from cow, buffalo and occasionally yak milk (nak milk in fact – the yak is the male and the nak the female), comes in several varieties and is sold in tourist areas along trekking routes. Watch out for *churpi*, a native cheese made from dried buttermilk – it's so hard as to be inedible.

Fruit

Which fruits are available depends on the season, but there's usually a good choice imported from India. Lovely **mandarin oranges**, which ripen throughout the late autumn and winter, grow from the Terai up to around 1200m and are sweetest near the upper end of their range. Autumn and winter also bring **papaya** in the Terai and lower hills, **Asian pears**, **apples** and **sugar cane**. **Mangoes** from the Terai start ripening in May and are available throughout most of the summer, as are **lychees**, **watermelons**, **pineapples** and **guavas**. **Bananas**, harvested year-round at the lower elevations, are sold everywhere.

Drinks

Water (*paani*) is automatically served with food in Nepali restaurants – but it may not be safe, so it's best to pass. Bottled water is widely available and usually safe; check that the seal is intact. You can also purify your own water (see p.38), which is cheaper and doesn't create plastic waste (plastic bottles are not recycled in Nepal). **Soft drinks** (*chiso*) are sold everywhere; lemon soda, made with soda water and lime juice, makes a good sugar-free alternative.

Tea (*chiya*) is traditionally brewed by boiling tea dust with milk (*dudh*) and water, with heaps of sugar (*chini*) and a bit of ginger, cardamom or pepper. In tourist restaurants you'll be offered "black" or "milk" tea with a teabag – you have to specify "Nepali" or "*masala*" tea if you want it made the traditional way. You can also ask for lemon tea or "hot lemon". Tibetans take their tea with salt and

---

TOBACCO AND PAAN

Nepalis love their **cigarettes** (*churot*). The cheaper brands like Yak and Khukuri are harsh and strong for most Western tastes. Marlboro is widely available, while the most similar luxury domestic brand is Surya. After the evening meal, old men may be seen smoking tobacco in a hookah (hubble-bubble), or occasionally passing around a chilam (clay pipe).

Many Nepali men make quite a production of preparing **chewing tobacco** (*surti*), slapping and rubbing it in the palm of the hand before placing behind the lower lip. *Surti* comes in little foil packets hung outside most general stores.

At least as popular, particularly near India, is the digestive and mild stimulant **paan**. A *paan* seller starts with a betel leaf, upon which he spreads various ingredients, the most common being *jharda* (tobacco) or *mitha* (sweet). *Paan*-wallahs also sell foil packets of *paan parag*, a simple, ready-made mix.

---

yak butter, which is definitely an acquired taste. Locally produced (often organic) **coffee** and fancy espresso machines are increasingly seen in Nepal, though non-touristy restaurants just do a very milky instant.

Roadside stalls serve freshly squeezed **fruit juices** and **lassis**, but the practice of adding water and sugar is widespread – and if the water comes from the tap, as is usually the case, your chances of catching something are high. Fruit juice is sold widely, and in trekking areas you will find the rosehip- or cherry-like sea buckthorn juice, which is high in Vitamin C.

Alcohol

Beer (*biyar*) makes a fine accompaniment to Nepali and Indian food. It isn't cheap, though: you could spend more on a bottle than on a full meal. Domestic beers include Everest (locally considered to be sweet, and therefore feminine) and Gorkha (stronger), while the "foreign" brands available, including San Miguel, Carlsberg and Tuborg, are all brewed in Nepal. Most are sold in 650ml bottles, though 330ml cans are increasingly available.

An amazing selection of **spirits** is distilled in Nepal, ranging from the classic Khukuri rum (dark and raisiny) to a myriad of cheap whiskies and vodkas. They're mostly rough, but tolerable when mixed – "Mustang coffee", made with Khukuri and instant coffee, is a classic. Lookout for regional specialities like the apricot and apple brandies of Marpha, north of Pokhara. Imported spirits and **wine** are available at inflated prices; many tourist restaurants and bars serve wine by the glass, and make cocktails.

Home-brewed *jaar*, or beer often made from rice or millet, is commonly referred to by the Tibetan or hill word, **chhang**. **Raksi**, which is ubiquitous in hill Nepal, is a distilled version of the same and bears a heady resemblance to tequila or grappa. It's made in a series of *pani*, or distillations: *ek pani*, or the first distillation of the liquor, is the strongest. Harder to find, but perhaps the most pleasant drink of all, is a highland home-brew called **tongba**. The ingredients are a jug or tankard of fermented millet, a straw and a flask of hot water: you pour the water in, let it steep, and suck the mildly alcoholic brew through the straw until you reach the bottom.

Festivals

Stumbling onto a local festival may prove to be the highlight of your travels in Nepal – and given the sheer number of them, you'd be unlucky not to. Though most are religious in nature, merry-making, not solemnity, is the order of the day, and onlookers are always welcome. Festivals may be Hindu, Buddhist, animist or a hybrid of all three.

Hindu events can take the form of huge pilgrimages and fairs (*mela*), or more introspective gatherings such as ritual bathings at sacred confluences (*tribeni*) or special acts of worship (*puja*) at temples. Many see animal sacrifices followed by family feasts, with priests and musicians usually on hand. Parades and processions (*jaatra*) are common, especially in the Kathmandu Valley.

Buddhist festivals are no less colourful, typically bringing together maroon-robed clergy and lay pilgrims to walk and prostrate themselves around stupas (dome-shaped monuments, usually repainted specially for the occasion).

Many of Nepal's **animist** peoples follow the Hindu calendar, but local nature-worshipping rites take place across the hills throughout the year. **Shamanic rites** usually take place at home, at the request of a particular family, although shamans themselves have their own calendar of fairs (*mela*) at which they converge on a particular holy spot. You'll have to travel widely and sensitively to have the chance to witness a shaman in action.

Jubilant Nepali **weddings** are always scheduled on astrologically auspicious days, which fall in the greatest numbers during the months of Magh, Phaagun and Baisaakh. The approach of a wedding party is often heralded by a hired *band baajaa* or brass band and open-air feasts go on until the early hours. The bride usually wears red, and for the rest of her married life she will colour the parting of her hair with red *sindur*.

Funeral processions should be left in peace. The body is normally carried to the cremation site within hours of death by white-shrouded friends and relatives; white is the colour of mourning for Hindus, and the eldest son is expected to shave his head and wear white for a year following the death of a parent. Many of the hill tribes conduct special shamanic rites to guide the deceased's soul to the land of the dead.

THE NEPALI YEAR

Nepal's calendar has three major differences from the Western one: it is 57 (or, for three months of the year, 56) years ahead of the Western calendar; its months start and finish approximately two weeks out of kilter with their international equivalents; and the New Year officially begins with the month of Baisaakh, in mid-April. This **"Bikram Sambat"** calendar was established by the legendary Indian emperor Vikramaditya; India long since went over to the European model but Nepal, which resisted colonization, has maintained tradition. Inevitably, there are calls for change. Some want to return to use the "Nepal Sambat" of the Kathmandu Valley's indigenous Newari people; others prefer to modernize.

The decisions of astrologers, on whom festival dates (see p.34) depend, are notoriously unpredictable, as they are based around the phases of the moon. The common names of the **Nepali months** are listed below; alternative spellings, sometimes based on classical Sanskrit, are often seen.

Baisaakh (April–May)	**Bhadau (Aug–Sept)**	**Poush (Dec–Jan)**
Jeth (May–June)	**Asoj (Sept–Oct)**	**Magh (Jan–Feb)**
Asaar (June–July)	**Kaattik (Oct–Nov)**	**Phaagun (Feb–March)**
Saaun (July–Aug)	**Mangsir (Nov–Dec)**	**Chait (March–April)**

A festival calendar

Knowing when and where festivals are held will not only enliven your time in Nepal, but should also help you avoid annoyances such as closed offices and booked-up buses. Unfortunately, as most are governed by the lunar calendar, **festival dates** vary annually, and determining them more than a year in advance is a highly complicated business best left to astrologers. Each lunar cycle is divided into "bright" (waning) and "dark" (waxing) halves, which are in turn divided into fourteen lunar "days". Each of these days has a name – *purnima* is the full moon, *astami* the eighth day, *aunshi* the new moon, and so on. Thus lunar festivals are always observed on a given day of either the bright or dark half of a given Nepali month. The following list details Nepal's most widely observed festivals, plus a few notable smaller events. For upcoming festival dates, check one of the **online** Nepali calendars (try Ⓦ visitnepal .com or Ⓦ www.nepalhomepage.com).

MAGH (JAN–FEB)

Magh (or **Makar**) **Sankranti** Marking a rare solar (rather than lunar) event in the Nepali calendar – the day the sun is farthest from the earth – the first day of Magh (Jan 14 or 15) is an occasion for ritual bathing at sacred river confluences, especially at Devghat and Sankhu. The day also begins a month-long period during which families do daily readings of the Swasthani, a compilation of Hindu myths, and many women emulate Parvati's fast for Shiva, one of the Swasthani stories. See p.258.

Basanta Panchami This one-day spring festival is celebrated on the fifth day after the new moon in most Hindu hill areas. The day is also known as Saraswati Puja, after the goddess of learning, and Shri Panchami, after the Buddhist saint Manjushri. School playgrounds are decorated with streamers and children have their books and pens blessed; high-caste boys may undergo a special rite of passage.

PHAAGUN (FEB–MARCH)

Losar Tibetan New Year falls on the new moon of either Magh or Phaagun, and is preceded by three days of drinking, dancing and feasting. The day itself is celebrated most avidly at Boudha, where morning rituals culminate with horn blasts and the hurling of *tsampa*. Losar is a time for families, and is the highlight of the calendar in Buddhist highland areas, as well as in Tibetan settlements near Kathmandu and Pokhara.

Shivaraatri Falling on the new moon of Phaagun, "Shiva's Night" is marked by bonfires and evening vigils in all Hindu areas, but most spectacularly at Pashupatinath (see p.125), where tens of thousands of pilgrims and sadhus from all over the subcontinent gather for Nepal's best-known *mela*. Fervent worship and bizarre yogic demonstrations can be seen throughout the Pashupatinath complex. Children collect firewood money by holding pieces of string across the road to block passers-by. Nepalis say the festival is usually followed by a final few days of winter weather, which is Shiva's way of encouraging the Indian sadhus to go home.

Holi Nepal's version of the springtime water festival, common to many Asian countries, lasts about a week, and commemorates a myth in which the god Krishna, when still a boy, outsmarted the demoness Holika. During this period, anyone is a fair target for water balloons and coloured powder. It culminates in a general free-for-all on Phaagun Purnima, the full-moon day of Phaagun.

CHAIT (MARCH–APRIL)

Chait Dasain Like its autumn namesake, the "little Dasain", observed on the eighth day after the new moon, involves lots of animal sacrifices. The goriest action takes place at goddess temples, such as the one at Gorkha, and in the Kot courtyard near Kathmandu's Durbar Square, where the army's top brass come to witness the beheading of numerous buffalo and goats.

MUSIC

Folk music (*git lok*) is an important aspect of life in Nepal, particularly during festivals and holidays. The **maadal** double-ended drum plays a focal role, often accompanied by the harmonium, *murali* (bamboo piccolo) or *bansuri* (flute). A group member will strike up a familiar verse, and everyone joins in on the chorus.

Folk music traditions vary among the country's many ethnic groups, but the true sound of Nepal can be said to be the soft, melodic and complex music of the hills. **Jhyaure**, the *maadal*-based music of the Western hills, is the most popular. **Selo**, the music of the Tamangs, has also been adopted by many other communities. Meanwhile, the music of the **Jyapu** (Newari farmers) has a lively rhythm, though the singing has a nasal quality.

The improvised, flirtatiously duelling duets known as **dohori**, traditionally performed by young men and women of the hill tribes, have become the soundtrack of modern Nepal. You'll hear them on personal radios, mobile ringtones and bus music systems, as well as in the dedicated *rodi ghars* (nightlife restaurants), and will soon come to recognize the repetitive back-and-forth, him-then-her structure, with wailing flutes and unison choruses punctuating each verse.

While folk music is by definition an amateur pursuit, there are two traditional castes of **professional musicians**: wandering minstrels (*gaaine* or *gandarbha*) who play the *sarangi* (a four-stringed fiddle), and *damai*, members of the tailor caste who serve as wedding musicians.

Ram Nawami The birthday of Lord Ram is observed on the ninth day after the full moon at all temples dedicated to Vishnu in his incarnation as the hero of the Ramayana, one of the great Hindu epics. By far the biggest and most colourful celebrations take place in Janakpur, where thousands of pilgrims flock to the Ram temple.

Seto Machhendranath Jaatra Kathmandu's answer to Patan's Machhendranath Rath Jaatra (see below), this sees a lumbering wooden chariot containing the white mask of the god Machhendranath pulled through the narrow lanes of the old city for four days, starting on Chait Dasain.

BAISAAKH (APRIL–MAY)

Nawa Barsa Nepali New Year, which always falls on the first day of Baisaakh (April 13 or 14), is observed with localized parades. Culminating on Nawa Barsa, Bhaktapur's five-day celebration, known as Bisket or Biska, is the most colourful, combining religious processions with a rowdy tug-of-war (see p.159); the nearby settlements of Thimi and Bode host similarly wild scenes.

Machhendranath Rath Jaatra Nepal's most spectacular festival: thousands gather to watch as the image of Machhendranath, the Kathmandu Valley's rain-bringing deity, is pulled around the streets of Patan in a swaying, 18m-high chariot. It moves only on astrologically auspicious days, taking four weeks or more to complete its journey. See p.93.

Buddha Jayanti The anniversary of the Buddha's birth. Enlightenment and death is celebrated on the full-moon day of Baisaakh at all Buddhist temples, but most visibly at Swayambhu, where the stupa is decorated with thousands of lights, and ritual dances are performed by priests dressed as the five aspects of Buddhahood. Processions are also held at the Boudha stupa and in Patan. Curiously, observances at the Buddha's birthplace, Lumbini, are rather sparse.

SAAUN (JULY–AUG)

Janai Purnima The annual changing of the sacred thread (*janai*) worn by high-caste Hindu men takes place at holy bathing sites throughout the country on the full-moon day of Saaun. Men and women of any caste may also receive a yellow-and-orange "protective band" (*raksha bandhan*) around one wrist, which is then worn until Tihaar, when it's supposed to be tied onto the tail of a cow. Mass observances are held at Gosainkund, a holy lake high in the mountains north of Kathmandu; Pashupatinath; and most prominently at Patan's Kumbeshwar temple, where priests tie strings and bestow *tikas*, and *jhankri* (hill shamans) perform sacred dances.

Gaai Jaatra Newari tradition has it that Yamraj, the god of death, opens the gates of judgement on the day of the full moon, allowing departed souls to enter. Falling on the day after the full moon, Gaai Jaatra honours cows (*gaai*), who are supposed to lead departed souls to Yamraj's abode. Processions in Kathmandu, Bhaktapur and other Newari towns are both solemn and whimsical: an occasion for families to honour loved ones who have died in the past year, but also for young boys to dress up in fanciful cow costumes or masquerade as sadhus. In Bhaktapur, where the festival is known as Gunhi Punhi and starts a day earlier (coinciding with Janai Purnima), men parade around town in humorous costumes. Satirical street performances are less common nowadays than they once were, but newspapers and magazines publish caustic Gaai Jaatra specials.

Nag Panchami On the fifth day after the new moon, Kathmandu Valley residents quietly propitiate the *nag* (snake spirits), who are traditionally held to control the monsoon rains and earthquakes, by pasting pictures of *nag* over their doorways with cow dung and offering milk, rice and other favourite *nag* foods to the images. Wells are cleaned only on this day, when the *nag* are believed to be away worshipping their ancestral deities.

Ghanta Karna On the fourteenth day after the full moon, residents of Kathmandu Valley towns celebrate the victory of the gods over the demon Ghanta Karna ("Bell Ears") by erecting effigies and then burning or tearing them down.

BHADAU (AUG–SEPT)

Krishna Astami (also called **Krishna Jayanti** or **Krishna Janmastahmi**). Krishna temples such as Patan's Krishna Mandir throng with thousands of worshippers celebrating the god's birth on the seventh day after the full moon. Vigils are also held the night before.

Tij The three-day "Women's Festival", which starts on the third day after the new moon, sees groups of women clad in red singing and dancing through the streets. Letting their families fend for themselves for once, they start with a girls' night out, feasting until midnight when they begin a day-long fast. On the second day they queue up to worship Shiva at the Pashupatinath temple outside of Kathmandu, and break the fast and ritually bathe to remove their sins on the final day.

Indra Jaatra A wild week of chariot processions and masked-dance performances in Kathmandu, held around the full moon of Bhadau. On the last day, which is also known as Kumari Jaatra, beer flows from the mouth of an idol in Durbar Square. See p.65.

Yartung A swashbuckling fair held at Muktinath, in the Annapurna trekking region, centred around the full-moon day and featuring horse racing, dancing, drinking and gambling.

ASOJ (SEPT–OCT)

Dasain (or **Dashera**). Although Hindu in origin, Nepal's longest and greatest festival is enthusiastically embraced by members of almost all religious and ethnic groups. It stretches over fifteen days, from the new moon to the full moon of Asoj, with the liveliest action taking place on the seventh, ninth and tenth days. Normally falling just after the summer rice harvest is in, Dasain is a time for families to gather (buses get extremely crowded with homeward-bound passengers), children to be indulged (with kites, makeshift swings and miniature ferris wheels), and animals to be sacrificed (roads and markets all over the country are filled with doomed goats). On the first day, known as Ghatasthapana, people plant *jamura* (barley) in a *kalash* (sanctified vessel), representing Durga, Dasain's honoured goddess; the seedlings will be picked and worn in the hair on the tenth day. Devotees congregate at local goddess temples throughout the next nine nights. A separate festival, Panchali Bhairab Jaatra, features late-night processions between the Bhairab's shrine and the Kumari Ghar in Kathmandu, and coincides with the fourth and fifth days of Dasain. On the seventh day, Fulpati, a bouquet of sacred flowers (*fulpati*) is carried in a procession from Rani Pokhari to the Hanuman Dhoka Palace in Kathmandu. The ninth day, Navami, begins at midnight with tantric buffalo sacrifices inside the forbidden Taleju (a form of Durga) temples of the Kathmandu Valley; throughout the day, animals are ritually beheaded publicly in the Kot Courtyard near Kathmandu's Durbar Square and in every village and

---

DANCE AND CULTURE SHOWS

Nepali music is inseparable from **dance**, especially at festivals. Nepali dance is an unaffected folk art – neither wildly athletic nor subtle, it depicts everyday activities such as work and courtship. Each region and ethnic group has its own traditions, and during your travels you should get a chance to join a local hoedown or two, if not a full-blown festival extravaganza. Lookout, too, for the stick dance of the lowland Tharus, performed regularly at lodges around Chitwan National Park. Staged **culture shows** in Kathmandu and Pokhara are a long way from the real thing, but they do provide a taste of folk and religious dances. Most troupes perform such standards as the dance of the *jhankri* (shaman-exorcists still consulted by many hill-dwelling Nepalis); the sleeve-twirling dance of the Sherpas; the flirting dance of the hill-dwelling Tamangs; perhaps a formal priestly dance, to the accompaniment of a classical *raga* (musical piece); and at least one of the dances of the Kathmandu Valley's Newars.

---

city of Nepal; their blood is sprinkled on tools, vehicles and even aircraft to impart Durga's *shakti* (power). These rituals commemorate Durga's slaying of the demon Mahisasur, and more generally, the triumph of good over evil. Bijaya Dasami, the "Victorious Tenth Day", celebrates Ram's victory over the demon Ravana – with Durga's help. Various processions and masked dance troupes ply the streets and families visit their elders to receive blessings and *tika*.

KAATTIK (OCT–NOV)

Tihaar (Diwali near India). Lasting for five days, starting two days before the new moon, the "Festival of Lights" is associated with Yamraj, the god of death, and Lakshmi, the goddess of wealth and good fortune. On the first day, Nepalis set out food on leaf plates for crows, regarded as Yamraj's messengers; on the second, they honour dogs as Yamraj's gatekeepers, giving them *tika*, flower garlands and special foods; and on the third they garland cows both as the symbol of Lakshmi and as the soul's guide to Yamaraj's underworld. The festival's most picturesque event, Lakshmi Puja, comes on the evening of the third day, when families throughout Nepal ring their homes with oil lamps, candles or electric lights to guide Lakshmi to their homes so she can bless them with prosperity for the year. Trusting in her, many Nepalis gamble on street corners, and student groups make the rounds singing "Diusire", a form of musical fundraising. Firecrackers have also become a big part of the fun for kids. To Newars, the fourth day is known as *Mha Puja* ("Self-Worship"), an occasion for private rituals, and also their New Year's Day, marked by banners, well-wishing and motorcycle parades in the Kathmandu Valley's three main cities. On the fifth day, Bhaai Tika, sisters recall the myth of Jamuna, who tricked Yamraj into postponing her brother's death indefinitely, by blessing their younger brothers and giving them flower garlands, *tika* and sweetmeats.

Chhath Coinciding with the third day of Tihaar, this festival honours Surya, the sun god, and is one of the most important for the Maithili-speaking people of the eastern Terai. Chhath is celebrated most ardently in Janakpur, where women gather by ponds and rivers to greet the sun's first rays with prayers, offerings and ritual baths.

Mani Rimdu Held at Tengboche and Chiwong monasteries in the Everest region around the full moon of the ninth Tibetan month (usually Oct/Nov), this colourful Sherpa masked dance dramatizes Buddhism's victory over the ancient Bon religion in eighth-century Tibet. A similar event is held in May or June at Thami.

MANGSIR (NOV–DEC)

Ram-Sita Biwaha Panchami As many as 100,000 pilgrims converge on Janakpur for this five-day gathering, beginning on the new moon of Mangsir. The highlight is the re-enactment of the wedding of Ram and Sita, the divine, star-crossed lovers of the Ramayana, one of the great Hindu epics. Janakpur's stature as a holy city rests on its having been the location of the original wedding.

Health

Hygiene is not one of Nepal's strong points. Sanitation is poor, and lots of bugs make the rounds, especially during spring and the monsoon. But by coming prepared and looking after yourself, you're unlikely to come down with anything worse than a cold or the local version of "Delhi belly".

This section deals with health matters mainly in the context of Western-style medicine; you could of course also turn to traditional **ayurvedic** or **Tibetan** practices (see p.44). For more detailed advice, refer to our recommended health **books** (see p.424) and **websites** (see p.53).

Before you go

No **inoculations** are required for Nepal, but hepatitis A, typhoid and meningitis jabs are recommended, and it's worth being up to date with tetanus, polio, mumps and measles boosters. Malaria tablets, injections for Japanese B encephalitis and rabies are also worth considering. All of these can be obtained in Kathmandu, but it's better to get injections done beforehand. If you have any medical conditions or concerns about your health, don't set off without seeing a **doctor** first. Medicines are sold over the counter everywhere, but it's best to bring your prescribed medications. Consider having a dental check-up before you go.

If you're planning on **trekking**, bear in mind the possibility of altitude sickness and other trekking hazards (see p.315).

Recommended inoculations

Most travellers decide to inoculate themselves against the following diseases, which are, on the whole, fairly ghastly but not fatal. Deciding which to protect yourself against is a matter of risk management. Consult your doctor well before you plan to travel for the latest inoculation advice.

Hepatitis A is an infection or inflammation of the liver that causes mild fever, nausea/vomiting, loss of appetite and jaundice. It's fairly common in Nepal, and while it won't kill you, it'll put a swift end to your travels and lay you up for several months. It's transmitted through contaminated food and water, so sensible hygiene will reduce the risk of catching it, but you can't count on fastidiousness alone.

Typhoid and paratyphoid are common in Nepal, and are also spread through contaminated food and water. These nearly identical diseases produce a persistent high fever, headaches, abdominal pains and diarrhoea, but are treatable with antibiotics and are rarely fatal. Paratyphoid usually occurs in epidemics and is less severe.

Immunizations against **mumps** and **measles** are recommended for anyone who wasn't vaccinated as a child and hasn't already had these diseases. You should also ensure you are fully vaccinated against **polio**.

Flu is no more prevalent in Nepal than elsewhere, but you might consider getting a flu jab before you leave just to reduce the risk of spending several days sick during your holiday.

Optional inoculations

The following diseases are all rare, but potentially fatal. Again, consult your doctor for the latest inoculation advice.

Meningicoccal meningitis, spread by airborne bacteria, is a very serious disease that attacks the lining of the brain, and can cause death in as little as a day. While localized cases are occasionally reported in Nepal, the chances of catching meningitis are remote. That said, the injection is very effective and causes few side effects.

Rabies is a problem in Nepal, and the best advice is to give dogs and monkeys a wide berth. It can be cured by five post-exposure injections (available in Kathmandu), administered over a month; these are 100 percent effective if given in reasonable time. The **pre-exposure vaccine** involves three injections over four weeks, which gives some protection for three years; if you get bitten, you'll still have to get two more boosters. It's probably not worth it except for long-stays and children.

Japanese B encephalitis, though potentially fatal, is mostly confined to the more jungly portions of the Terai around monsoon time. Visitors to Kathmandu and the Terai who are staying for a long period between April and October should certainly consider vaccinating against it. Rural areas where pigs are kept are most risky.

Hepatitis B is a more serious version of hepatitis A, but is passed on through blood and sexual contact. The vaccine is recommended for those working in a medical environment. Long-term travellers are sometimes vaccinated as they might have an accident and need to receive blood.

Don't bother with the **cholera** inoculation – the risk in Nepal is minimal.

Malaria prophylaxis

Most visitors won't need to take **malaria** tablets. The disease hasn't been eradicated in Nepal, but it is unknown above 1000m, and rare outside the monsoon months. The risk to short-term travellers is very low, but it's well worth taking **anti-mosquito** measures anyhow, especially during the rainy season.

Prophylaxis (regular doses of tablets) *is* worth considering if you plan to visit the **Terai** (which includes Chitwan and Bardia national parks) between June and September. Longer-term visitors and anyone visiting India should seek expert advice, and rafters should remember that valleys in the hills can be lower than 1000m. Consult your doctor before you travel for the latest information and drugs available.

Precautions

The lack of **sanitation** in Nepal is sometimes overhyped – it's not worth getting too uptight about it or you'll never enjoy anything, and you'll run the risk of rebuffing Nepali hospitality. The best advice is to follow the guidelines below when you can.

Most travellers are careful about drinking dirty water, but **food** is now thought to be the worst culprit, and it's usually tourist restaurants and "Western" dishes that bring the most grief: more people get sick in Kathmandu than anywhere else in Nepal. Be particularly wary of anything reheated, and food that's been sitting where flies can land on it. Nepali food is usually fine and you can probably trust anything that's been boiled or fried in your presence, although meat has additional risks. Raw, unpeeled fruit and vegetables – including pickles – should always be viewed with **suspicion** in local places, though all but the cheapest tourist restaurants usually have acceptable salads, fruit juices and *lassis* these days.

Kathmandu's **polluted air** gives many people respiratory infections within a few days of arrival; asthmatics and others with breathing problems are particularly affected. Minimize your exposure by staying off the main streets, and seriously consider bringing a filtering face mask if you're spending much time in the Kathmandu Valley. You can also help your immune system by keeping warm, dry and well rested. Most importantly, get out of the valley to where the air is fresh as quickly as possible.

You need to be particularly vigilant about **personal hygiene** while travelling in Nepal. That means, above all, washing your hands often – waterless antibacterial soap comes in handy. Keep any cuts clean and disinfected. If you're staying in cheap guesthouses, bring a **sleeping sheet** to keep fleas and lice at bay. Scabies and hookworm can be picked up through bare feet, so it's best to always wear **shoes**; flip-flops provide reasonable protection in bathrooms.

When travelling in the Terai, don't give **mosquitoes** the opportunity to bite you. They're hungriest from dusk to dawn, when you need to wear repellent and/or long-sleeved clothes, sleep under netting and use plug-in mosquito killing/deterring devices or smoke coils. Very few mosquitoes carry malaria, so you don't need to worry over every bite. Try not to scratch bites as infection may result.

Travellers in rural areas of the eastern Terai should protect against **sandflies** in the same way, as they transmit the disease **visceral leishmaniasis**, also called **kala-azar**, which causes fever and potentially fatal enlargement of the spleen.

Take the usual precautions to avoid **sunburn** and **dehydration**. You'll probably want at least medium suncream protection, and high protection will be essential while trekking.

Water

Untreated **water** should be **avoided** when possible and you may not always notice the risk. Plates and glasses are customarily rinsed just before use: if you're handed wet utensils it's a good idea to give them a discreet wipe. Use treated or bottled water when brushing your teeth, and keep your mouth closed in the shower. Thamel restaurants generally use clean water for **ice**, but it's probably still worth steering clear. Similarly, many guesthouses provide filtered water, but you can't guarantee it was boiled first, or that the filters are clean. **Tea** and **bottled drinks** are generally safe.

Mineral water is available everywhere but **purifying** your own – either by boiling and filtering,

or by using purification tablets – is cheaper and avoids plastic waste. Iodine tablets are more effective than chlorine (and it's possible to buy tablets to neutralize the medicinal taste) – be careful to follow the instructions, especially when it comes to giving the tablets enough time to work. Aqueous iodine solution, aka Lugol's solution, is available in pharmacies across Nepal, together with plastic pipettes; it's far cheaper than tablets brought from home, and works faster. There are high-tech alternatives; the pocket sized Steropen, which uses UV light, is portable and popular, but requires a battery, and there are various water filters that can filter most harmful bacteria. Note that iodine and chlorine do not kill cyclospora (see p.39), so drink boiled or bottled water if you can during the peak months of June and July.

HIV/AIDS

Almost **ninety percent** of transmissions in Nepal are thought to be through heterosexual contact, especially in the context of migrant workers and prostitution. Brothels are full of HIV-positive sex workers. Trekking guides can also be considered a relatively high-risk group. Carry **condoms** with you (locally available but it's best to bring some) and **insist** on using them. Condoms also protect you from other sexually transmitted diseases such as hepatitis B.

Male travellers who get a shave from a barber should make sure that the blade used is clean, and nobody should go for ear-piercing, acupuncture or tattooing unless fully satisfied the equipment is sterile. Should you need an injection, make sure new, **sterile equipment** is used. And if you need a blood transfusion, bear in mind that the Nepali blood supply isn't adequately screened.

Common ailments

Chances are that at some point during your travels in Nepal you'll feel ill. In most cases, it won't be something you need a doctor for but it may well happen somewhere remote and inconvenient. The following information should help with **self-diagnosis**, although it is *not* a substitute for professional medical advice. If you're unable to get to a clinic – a strong possibility when trekking – you might choose to **self-medicate**, and medicine and dosage information for the most common complaints are given below. It's not a bad idea to travel with a course of the drugs mentioned here (especially as fake, badly stored and out-of-date drugs are not rare in Nepal), but make sure you have the correct dosages explained to you beforehand.

Some of the illnesses and parasites you can pick up in Nepal may not show themselves immediately. If you become ill within a year of **returning home**, tell the doctor where you've been.

Intestinal troubles

Diarrhoea is the most common bane of travellers. If it's mild and not accompanied by other major symptoms, it should pass of its own accord within a few days without treatment. However, it's essential to replace the fluids and salts you're losing – cheap and effective oral **rehydration** formulas are widely available. Bananas and fizzy drinks are also good for replacing electrolytes. "Starving the bug to death" is an old wives' tale, though you're unlikely to be hungry. Tablets containing loperamide, such as **Imodium**, will plug you up if you have to travel, but won't cure anything.

If the diarrhoea comes on suddenly and is accompanied by cramps and vomiting, there's a good chance it's **food poisoning**, brought on by toxins secreted by foreign bacteria. There's nothing you can do other than keep replacing fluids, but it should run its course within around 24 to 48 hours.

If you're feverish, have severe diarrhoea that lasts more than three days or if you see blood or mucus in your stools, seek treatment. In the eventuality of serious or persistent intestinal problems, you're strongly advised to have a stool test done at a **clinic** (see p.40), where a doctor can make a diagnosis and prescription.

Bacterial diarrhoea, which causes 85 percent of identifiable cases, is recognizable by its sudden onset, accompanied by nausea and vomiting, stomach cramps and sometimes fever. The choice of treatments is Norfloxacin 400mg twice a day for three days; Ciprofloxacin 500mg twice a day for three days; or Ofloxacin 400mg twice a day for

three days. All three are available inside Nepal, though as with all drugs, it's safest to bring your own (see p.40).

About five percent of diarrhoea cases in Nepal are giardiasis (**giardia**), which produces three or four loose stools a day, and is often recognizable by copious, foul-smelling belches and farts. The cure is a 2g dose of Tinidazole at night (four 500mg tablets of locally available "tiniba"), for a maximum of two nights. This can make you tired and nauseous for 24 hours; it absolutely shouldn't be mixed with alcohol, and you should abstain from alcohol for several days afterwards as well.

Amoebic dysentery is relatively rare. Setting in gradually, it manifests itself in frequent, small, watery bowel movements, often accompanied by fever.

If the diarrhoea is associated with fatigue and appetite loss over many days, and occurs between April and November, it may be the result of **cyclospora** (sometimes called blue-green algae), another water-borne condition.

Finally, bear in mind that oral drugs, such as malaria pills or the contraceptive pill, are rendered **less effective** or completely **ineffective** if taken while suffering from diarrhoea. In all cases, remember that you must keep hydrated.

Flu and fever

Flu-like symptoms – fever, headache, runny nose, fatigue, aching muscles – may mean nothing more than the latest virus. Rest and aspirin/paracetamol should do the trick. However, strep throat, bronchial or sinus infections will require an antibiotic course such as Erythromycin or Amoxycillin. Flu symptoms and jaundice point to hepatitis, which is best treated with rest and a plane ticket home.

A **serious fever** or delirium is cause for real concern. Diagnosis is tricky; the sufferer needs to be taken to a doctor as quickly as possible. To begin with, try bringing the fever down with aspirin/paracetamol. If the fever rises and falls dramatically every few hours, it may be **malaria** (see p.37). If the fever is consistently high for four or more days, it may be **typhoid**.

Minor symptoms

Minor **muscle cramps**, experienced after exercise or sweating, may indicate you're low on sodium – a teaspoon of salt will bring rapid relief. Likewise, a simple **headache** may just mean you're dehydrated. (However, a severe headache, accompanied by eye pain, neck stiffness and a temperature, could mean meningitis – in which case get to a doctor pronto.)

Itchy skin is often traced to mosquito bites, but can also be fleas, lice or scabies. The last of these,

ANTIBIOTICS

Tourists in Nepal tend to rush for **antibiotics**, but they shouldn't be taken lightly: most tummy bugs cure themselves in around 48–72 hours, and antibiotics can increase susceptibility to other problems by killing off all organisms in the digestive system (yoghurt can replenish them to some extent, as can acidophilus tablets – also good for thrush and fungal infections). Some antibiotics may cause allergic reactions or unpleasant side effects, and the more a particular antibiotic is used, the sooner organisms become resistant to it.

caused by a burrowing mite, generally affects the spaces between fingers and toes. Shampoos and lotions are available in Nepal. Air out your bedding and wash your clothes thoroughly.

Worms may enter your body through the skin (especially the soles of the feet), or through food. An itchy anus is a common symptom, and you may even see them in your stools. They are easy to treat with worming tablets, available locally.

Animal bites and leeches

For **animal bites** or scratches, *immediately* wash the wound with soap and water for at least five minutes then rinse with Providone iodine (found in Nepal); if this isn't available, use 40–70 percent alcohol – local *raksi* may do the trick. This should kill any rabies virus on the spot but anyone bitten by an animal should immediately get themselves to a Kathmandu clinic for expensive post-exposure rabies shots (see p.117). The disease's incubation period is ten to ninety days – ideally, you're supposed to capture the animal alive for observation!

Thickly vegetated country, such as the Terai national parks or low-lying trekking areas, can come alive with **leeches** during the monsoon. Protect yourself by wearing **insect repellent**, long clothing and perhaps gaiters. There is a small risk of **infection**, particularly if you pick them off and the mouth parts get left behind in the wound. It's best to leave them – they won't take so much blood that they'll harm you. Otherwise, the advised way to remove a leech is to break its suction by gently sliding a fingernail around first the thinner, then the thicker end of the animal. Locals tend to use a rapid finger flick and take their risks – and this may be the only practicable solution in thickly infested areas. Using salt, iodine or, worst of all, heat from a lighter or match will make a leech drop-off but not before it effectively vomits into the wound.

Getting medical help

In a non-emergency, make for one of the traveller-oriented **clinics** in Kathmandu. Run to Western standards, these can diagnose most common ailments, write prescriptions and give inoculations. In other cities and towns, local clinics (often attached to pharmacies) can usually provide adequate care. An array of Indian-manufactured medicines are available without prescription in the **pharmacies** of all major towns, though be sure to check the sell-by date, and be aware that fake medicines are widespread so it's best to bring any medicines you might need from home (see below).

In the event of serious injury or illness, contact your **embassy** (see p.117) for a list of recommended **doctors**. The majority are in Kathmandu and speak English. It's a good idea to register with your embassy or consulate on arrival, especially if you go trekking or rafting.

Hospitals are listed in the Kathmandu and Pokhara sections of the guide; others are located in Dhulikhel, Tansen, Kolhalpur and the bigger Terai cities. Most are poorly equipped, and are not too hygienic – doctors routinely prescribe a course of antibiotics to all patients for this reason. Also note that you have to pay on the spot for all services, medicines and items used by the doctor, so it's important to have cash with you.

MEDICAL RESOURCES

W **cdc.gov/travel** The official US government travel health site.

W **ciwec-clinic.com** This Kathmandu clinic is an authoritative source of information.

W **iamat.org** The International Association for Medical Assistance to Travellers provides a list of English-speaking doctors in Nepal plus guidance on diseases and inoculations.

W **istm.org** Website of the International Society for Travel Medicine.

W **masta-travel-health.com** MASTA (Medical Advisory Service for Travellers Abroad) has a list of UK travel health clinics.

W **www.thehtd.org** The Hospital for Tropical Diseases Travel Clinic is the only UK medical facility dedicated to tropical diseases.

W **tripprep.com** Travel Health Online has a comprehensive database of necessary vaccinations for most destinations.

Culture and etiquette

Many different ethnic groups coexist in Nepal, each with their own complex customs. In the Kathmandu Valley, where they mix the most, there's a high degree of tolerance of different clothes and lifestyles – a fact that travellers sense, and often abuse. Away from the tourist areas, however, ethnic groups are quite parochial, and foreign ways may cause offence. That said, many taboos relax the further and higher you head into the mountains, as Hindu behavioural norms are only partially shared by Buddhist and animist ethnic groups.

The **do's and don'ts** listed here are more flexible than they sound. You'll make gaffes all the time and Nepalis will rarely say anything. When in doubt, do as you see Nepalis doing.

Common courtesies

As a foreigner, you're likely to be an **object of curiosity**, and you may be joined in the street or on the trail by someone who just wants to chat. Nepalis will constantly be befriending you, wanting to exchange addresses, take photos and extract solemn promises that you will write to them.

Giving the Nepali **greeting**, *namaste* ("I salute the god within you"), your palms held together as if praying, is one of the most attractive and addictive of Nepali customs. It isn't used freely or casually: think of it as "how do you do?" rather than "hello!" If you want to show great respect, *namaskar* is a more formal or subservient variant.

Another delightful aspect of Nepali culture is the familiar ways Nepalis address each other: it's well worth learning *didi* ("older sister"), *bahini* ("younger sister"), *daai* ("older brother"), *bhaai* ("younger brother"), *buwa* ("father") and *aamaa* ("mother") for the warm reaction they'll usually provoke. To be more formal or respectful, just add *ji* to the end of someone's name, as in "*namaste*, John-*ji*".

The word *dhanyabaad* is usually translated as "thank you" but is normally reserved for an act beyond the call of duty – so if you feel you have to say something, "thank you" in English is widely understood.

The gestures for "**yes**" and "**no**" are also confusing to foreigners. To indicate agreement, tilt your head slightly to one side and then back the other way. To tell a tout or a seller "no", hold one hand up in front of you, palm forwards, and swivel your wrist subtly, as if you were adjusting a bracelet; shaking the head in the Western fashion looks too much like "yes". To point use the chin, rather than the finger.

Caste and status

Hill Nepal is less rigid than much of India, but **caste** *is* deeply ingrained in the national psyche. Nepal "abolished" the caste system in 1963, but millennia-old habits take time to change. Though professions are changing and "love marriage" is more popular, caste and status still determine whom most Nepalis may (or must) marry, where they can live and who they can associate with. Foreigners are technically casteless, but in the remote far western hills they can be considered **polluting** to orthodox, high-caste Hindus. Wherever you travel you should be sensitive to minor caste restrictions: for example, you may not be allowed into the kitchen of a high-caste Hindu home.

Status (*ijat*) is equally important. Meeting for the first time, Nepalis observe a ritual of asking each other's name, home town and profession, which helps determine relative status and therefore the correct level of deference. As a Westerner you have a lot of status, and relatively speaking you're fabulously wealthy.

Eating

Probably the greatest number of Nepali taboos are to do with **food**. One underlying principle is that once you've touched something to your lips, it's polluted (*jutho*) for everyone else. If you take a sip from someone else's water bottle, try not to let it touch your lips (and the same applies if it's your own). Don't eat off someone else's plate or offer anyone food you've taken a bite of, and don't touch cooked food until you've bought it.

If eating with your **hands**, use the right one only. The left hand is reserved for washing after defecating; you can use it to hold a glass or utensil while you eat, but don't wipe your mouth, or pass food with it. It's considered good manners to give and receive everything with the right hand. In order to convey respect, offer money, food or gifts with both hands, or with the right hand while the left touches the wrist.

Clothing and the body

Nepalis are innately conservative in their attitudes to **clothing**, and it's worth knowing how you may come across. The following hints apply especially in temples and monasteries.

Men should always wear a shirt in public, and long trousers if possible (shorts are fine on well-used trekking trails). For **women** in villages, a sari or skirt that hangs to mid-calf level is traditional, though trousers are acceptable these days. Shoulders are usually covered, and vest-tops are considered risqué. Girls in Kathmandu and Pokhara do wear shorts or short skirts, but this is relatively new and you run the risk of being seen as sexually available. Generally, looking **clean** shows respect – and earns it. Ungroomed travellers may find themselves treated with significantly less courtesy.

Only women with babies or small children bare their breasts. When Nepali men bathe in public, they do it in their underwear, and women bathe underneath a *lungi* (sarong). Foreigners are expected to do likewise. In Nepal, the forehead is regarded as the most sacred part of the body and it's impolite to touch an adult Nepali's head. The **feet** are the most unclean part, so don't put yours on chairs or tables, and when sitting, try not to point the soles of your feet at anyone. It's also bad manners to step over the legs of someone seated.

Male friends will often hold hands in public, but not lovers of the opposite sex. **Couples** who cuddle or kiss in public will at best draw unwelcome attention. Handshaking has increased, but not all Nepali women will feel comfortable about shaking a man's hand.

Temples and homes

Major **Hindu temples** or their innermost sanctums are usually off limits to nonbelievers, who are a possible cause of ritual pollution. Where you are allowed in, be respectful: take your shoes off before entering, don't take photos unless you've asked permission, and leave a few rupees in the donation box. Try not to touch offerings or shrines. Leather is usually not allowed in temple precincts.

Similar sensitivity is due at **Buddhist temples** and monasteries. If you're granted an audience with a lama, it's traditional to present him with a *kata* (a ceremonial white scarf, usually sold nearby). Walk around Buddhist stupas and monuments clockwise.

If invited for a meal in a **private home**, you can bring fruit or sweets, but don't expect thanks as gifts tend to be received without any fuss. Take your shoes off when entering, or follow the example of your host. When the food is served you may be expected to eat first, so you won't be able to follow your host's lead. Take less than you can eat – asking for seconds is the best compliment you can give. The meal is typically served at the end of a gathering; when the eating is done, everyone leaves.

Sherpas and some other highland groups regard the **family hearth** as sacred, so don't throw rubbish or scraps into it.

Hustle and hassle

Indian-style **hustle** is on the rise in Nepal. You'll get a dose of it at the airport or any major bus station, where hotel touts lie in wait to accost arriving tourists. They also cruise the tourist strips of Kathmandu, offering drugs, treks, and, increasingly, sex. For the most part, though, Nepali touts are less aggressive than their Indian brethren, and if you're entering Nepal from North India, where aggressive touts have to be dealt with firmly, you should prepare to adjust your attitude. Ignore them entirely and they're likely to ignore you. If that doesn't work, most touts will leave you alone if asked nicely, whereas they'll take a rude brush-off personally.

The tourist zones are full of other lone entrepreneurs and middlemen – **touts** by any other name. Ticket agents, rikshaw-wallahs, guides and guest-house owners are ever-anxious to broker services and information. They usually get their commission from the seller; your price is bumped up correspondingly. In general, cutting out the middleman gives you more control over the transaction. You should find, however, that a few rupees (and smiles) given to people whose services you may require again will smooth the way and make your stay more pleasant.

Beggars

Dealing with **beggars** is part and parcel of travelling in Nepal. The pathos might initially get to you, as it should, but you will probably adjust to it fairly quickly. A current favourite is the woman with a baby who asks you to buy them milk, and then will take you to a shop where the only available milk comes in a large, expensive container – the shopkeeper and woman then split the money.

A small number of bona fide beggars make an honest living from *bakshish* (alms). Hindus and Buddhists have a long and honourable tradition of giving to lepers, the disabled, sadhus and monks. It's terrifyingly easy for a **Nepali woman** to find herself destitute and on the street, either widowed or divorced – perhaps for failing to bear a son or from a dowry dispute. There are no **unemployment benefits** in Nepal, and many who can't work and have no family turn to begging (or prostitution).

In the hills, ailing locals will occasionally approach foreigners for **medicine**: it's unwise to make any prescriptions unless you're qualified to diagnose the

---

HIRING A GUIDE

Even if you're not going on a trek, hiring a **guide** is a great way to get under the skin of Nepal. Most people only think of hiring a guide for a **trek** (see p.311), but they're even more essential when tracking **wildlife** in the Terai parks. If you find a good guide, stick with him (guides are usually male); a day guide in Chitwan, for instance, might well be willing to accompany you to Bardia National Park. In **town**, would-be guides, often masquerading as friendly students, position themselves strategically at temples and palaces, but you'll probably do better to find one through a hotel or travel agent. An inexperienced guide hired informally will usually charge about Rs800–1000 a day (plus expenses); paying around double that for an experienced and knowledgeable guide would be fair. Generally, you get what you pay for.

illness. However, before leaving the country you can donate unused medicines to the destitute through the dispensary at Kathmandu's Bir Hospital, or to the Himalayan Buddhist Meditation Centre in Kathmandu, which gives them to monks.

Children

Throughout Nepal – principally along the tourist trails – **children** will hound you. Repeatedly shouting *"namaste"* or "hello" at the weird-looking stranger is universal and often kids will ask you for "one dollar", "chocolate" or "pen". They're not orphans or beggars, just ordinary schoolkids who've seen too many well-meaning but thoughtless tourists handing out little gifts wherever they go. A firm-but-gentle *hoina holaa!* ("I don't think so!") is usually enough. Few children would ever ask a Nepali for money, so reacting like a local will quickly embarrass them. Sometimes, however, they will tag along for hours; the best defences are a sense of humour and/or a strategic lack of engagement.

Street children are a different case. Don't give (or not directly – donations to a children's charity will do more good – see box, p.72), and watch your wallet.

Spiritual pursuits and alternative therapies

Nepal has a multitude of traditional and progressive disciplines, and though the country can seem something of a spiritual supermarket, its tolerant atmosphere makes it a great place to challenge your assumptions and study other systems of thought.

The past thirty years have seen an explosion of outfits teaching yoga and meditation to both foreigners and locals. The allied health fields of ayurvedic and Tibetan medicine are also an attraction for many travellers to Nepal. Many programmes don't require a lengthy commitment, although any **residential courses** are worth booking well in advance. For more detailed background on Hinduism and Buddhism, the spiritual bases for many practices, see "Religion" (p.396).

Yoga

Yoga is more than just exercises – it's a system of spiritual, mental and physical self-discipline, designed to unify the individual's consciousness with the universe. Techniques include **Karma yoga** (basically altruism), **Bhakti yoga** (devotion, recognizable by the chanting) and **Jnana yoga** (deep meditation, best practised only after mastering one of the other kinds).

What most Westerners would recognize as yoga springs from **Raja yoga**, probably formulated around 600 BC. It has eight *astanga*, or limbs (not to be confused with the yoga style with the same name, Ashtanga), each a step to realization. Three of these have a physical emphasis, and it is from this root that yoga's reputation for pretzel poses and headstands comes. Whatever the name of a particular variation, be it Bikram, Kundalini, or Ashtanga, all types of yoga that use *asanas* (or positions) as an aid to developing the self are generally referred to as **hatha yoga**.

Most practices also include **Pranayam** – breathing exercises. You'll find several kinds in Nepal, including the **Sivanand** school (a slow style with *asanas* and lots of spiritual guidance), **Iyengar** (a very exacting school that uses some props and focuses on alignment) and practices that follow particular gurus from India, usually including elements of Raja, Bhakti and Karma yoga.

There are reviews of **yoga centres** around Kathmandu (see p.100) and Pokhara (see p.216) in the relevant sections of the guide.

Buddhist meditation and study

Meditation is closely related to yoga, and the two often overlap: much of yoga involves meditation, and Buddhist meditation draws on many Hindu yogic practices. However, meditation centres in Nepal generally follow the Tibetan Buddhist tradition.

Buddhist meditation is a science of mind. To Buddhists, mind is the cause of confusion and ego, and the aim of meditation is to transcend these. *Vipassana* ("insight") is the kernel of all forms of Buddhist meditation; related to hatha yoga, it emphasizes the minute observation of physical sensations and mental processes to achieve a clear understanding of mind. Another basic practice common to most schools of Buddhism, *shamatha* ("calm abiding") attunes and sharpens the mind by means of coming back again and again to a meditative discipline. Several centres in the Kathmandu Valley run rigorous residential courses in this practice.

Tibetan Buddhist centres start students out with *vipassana* and *shamatha* as the foundation for a large armoury of meditation practices.

An "adept" (novice) will cultivate Buddha-like qualities through visualization techniques – meditating on the deity that manifests a particular quality, while chanting the mantra and performing the *mudra* (hand gesture) associated with that deity. The Tibetan Buddhist path also involves numerous rituals, such as prayer, offerings, circumambulation and other meritorious acts; committed followers will take vows, too. Kathmandu has several centres offering introductory courses (see p.100).

A big part of Tibetan Buddhism is the **teacher-disciple relationship**. More advanced students of the *dharma* will want to study under one of the lamas at Boudha (see p.130), some of whom give discourses in English.

Ayurveda

Ayurveda (often spelled "ayurved") is the oldest school of medicine still practised. It is a holistic system that assumes the fundamental sameness of self and nature. Unlike the allopathic medicine of the West, which identifies what ails you and then kills it, ayurveda looks at the whole patient: disease is regarded as a symptom of imbalance, so it's the imbalance that's treated, not the disease.

To diagnose an imbalance, the ayurvedic doctor investigates the physical complaint but also family background, daily habits and emotional traits. Treatment is typically with inexpensive herbal remedies designed to alter whichever of the three forces is out of whack. In addition, the doctor may prescribe some yogic cleansing to rid the body of waste substances.

You'll find ayurvedic **doctors and clinics** throughout the Hindu parts of Nepal, but those who are able to deal with foreigners are confined mainly to Kathmandu (see p.101).

Tibetan medicine

Medicine is one of the traditional branches of study for Tibetan Buddhist monks. Like ayurveda, from which it derives, **Tibetan medicine** promotes health by maintaining the correct balance of three humours: *beken*, phlegm, which when out of balance is responsible for disorders of the upper body; *tiba*, heat or bile, associated with intestinal diseases; and *lung*, meaning wind, which may produce nervousness or depression.

Recommended **clinics** specializing in Tibetan medicine are listed in the Kathmandu (p.101) and Boudha (p.134) sections.

Massage

Nepali massage is a deep treatment that works mainly on the joints. It's not all that relaxing, but it can be just the job after a trek. Nepalis themselves rarely receive massages after the age of about three, but numerous masseurs ply their services to foreigners. Many practitioners also offer shiatsu, Swedish or Thai massage, reflexology and so on. Others, especially in Thamel, are actually (or additionally) offering sexual services; the best advice is that if it looks or feels dodgy, it probably is.

Women's Nepal

In most parts of the country, women will be of interest mainly as foreigners rather than for their gender, but a few specific tips are given below.

For women travellers, most parts of Nepal are relatively easy: the atmosphere is tolerant and inquisitive rather than threatening or dangerous. Nepali society is on the whole chaste, almost prudish; men are mostly respectful to foreign women. **Sexual harassment** is unlikely to upset your travels: you may encounter staring and catcalling or rarely, an attempt at groping, but it's not as bad as in India, or indeed most of the rest of the world, and seldom goes any further than words. The chief danger comes from the rare predatory trekking guide (see p.311).

Wearing **revealing clothing** will up the chances of receiving unwelcome advances. That doesn't mean you have to wear Nepali clothes (though it may help); just keep legs, breasts and shoulders covered and avoid skin-tight garments.

A woman **travelling or trekking alone** won't be hassled so much as pitied. Going alone (*eklai*) is most un-Nepali behaviour. Locals (of both sexes) will ask if you haven't got a husband – usually out of genuine concern, not as a come-on. Teaming up with another female stops the comments as effectively as being with a man. If you find yourself on a public bus, you can make your way to the front compartment, where preference is usually given to women and children.

Terai cities and **border towns** are another matter, unfortunately. As in North India, misconceptions about Western women mean men may try for a surreptitious grope or even expose themselves. Travelling with a man generally shields you from this sort of behaviour. Don't be afraid to make a public scene in the event of an untoward advance – that's what a Nepali woman would do.

Of course, you may want to strike up a relationship with a **Nepali man**. There's a long tradition of women travellers falling for trekking or rafting guides and Kathmandu has a small but growing community of women who have married and settled. However, Nepali men are not without their own agendas: exotic romance, conquest, perhaps even a ticket out of Nepal. Be aware also that many Nepali men use the services of sex workers and that HIV/AIDS is a growing and largely concealed problem.

Meeting Nepali women

A frustrating aspect of travelling in Nepal is the difficulty of making contact with **Nepali women**. Tourism is still controlled by men; women are expected to spend their time in the home, get fewer educational opportunities than men and speak much less English. If you're lucky enough to be invited to a Nepali home for a meal, chances are the women of the house will remain in the kitchen while you eat. Upper-class women, who may even work with foreigners, are often well educated and free of these restrictions, but they have few encounters with travellers.

Sexual politics are different among **highland ethnic groups**. Along trekking routes, many women run teahouses single-handedly while their husbands are off guiding or portering. Proud, enterprising and flamboyant, these "didis" are some of the most wonderful people you're likely to meet anywhere. There are a few female trekking guides now, too (see p.214).

Living and working in Nepal

Working or studying in Nepal can add a satisfying focus to your trip, and deepen your understanding of another way of life. It's certainly the best way to meet and get to know Nepalis.

Unfortunately, you can't stay longer than 150 days in any calendar year on a **tourist visa** without special permission (though that means you can stay almost a year if your trip straddles two calendar years). To stay longer, you have to get a **longer-term visa** (such as the business, residential or study visas), but they require an application from an accredited organization to the relevant Nepali government ministry.

Working

If you feel you've received a lot from Nepal, **volunteering** is a good way to give something back. The old people's hospices in Pashupatinath and Chabahil run by Mother Teresa's Sisters of Charity welcome walk-in help on a day-to-day basis. The Kathmandu Environmental Education Project (KEEP; Ⓦ keepnepal.org.org) and Himalayan Rescue Association (Ⓦ himalayanrescue.org) offices in Kathmandu always use workers, and can put you in touch with other organizations.

Orphanages have boomed in Kathmandu and Pokhara, but be cautious if signing up to volunteer with these places; a depressing number exploit both the children in their care and the volunteers who fund them, siphoning off money and gifts and, in some notorious cases, subjecting the orphans to all kinds of abuses.

For **longer-term** volunteer work, postings with the Peace Corps, VSO and other voluntary agencies abound, providing you've got the relevant skills. People with experience in education, health, nutrition, agriculture and forestry are preferred. Many other aid agencies (such as Action Aid, Save the Children, CARE and Oxfam) operate in Nepal and occasionally take on specialists.

If you just want an open-ended arrangement for a few weeks or so, **teaching English** is a good option. Language schools in Kathmandu and Pokhara occasionally take people on, although the pay is negligible. Numerous organizations run longer, more formal teaching programmes (see p.46), but you'll pay for the privilege, once you've factored in training and support fees.

Paid work is almost impossible to find locally, and it's against the law to work on a tourist visa. Some people find jobs as guides, but you may want to question the ethics of taking a job that could be done by a Nepali. Qualified masseurs and yoga/meditation instructors may be able to find work in Kathmandu or Pokhara.

If you can persuade the Department of Industry that you've got a good idea, you may qualify for a business visa.

Studying

A few **language schools** in Kathmandu offer intensive courses in Nepali, Newari or Tibetan (see p.117), and there are opportunities to study Tibetan Buddhism (see p.100). Several American universities run study programmes in Nepal; see p.133. For anything longer term or more formal you'll need to apply in writing to Tribhuvan University (Campus of International Languages, PO Box 4339, Exhibition Rd, Kathmandu ☎01 422 8916, ⓦbishwobhasa.edu .np), which runs courses in Nepali, Tibetan, Sanskrit and Newari.

STUDY AND WORK PROGRAMMES

Campus of International Languages Tribhuvan University ☎01 422 8916, ⓦbishwobhasa.edu.np. Kathmandu's most highly regarded university.

Himalayan Rescue Association ⓦhimalayanrescue.org. Accepts doctors to staff its high-altitude aid posts.

Naropa Institute ⓦnaropa.edu/studyabroad. Colorado institution that runs a pricey course on Tibetan Buddhism each autumn at Boudha.

Partnership for Sustainable Development ⓦpsdnepal.org. Small, friendly organization, running four-week to five-month programmes for international volunteers – digging wells, building classrooms, hospital internships – often incorporating tourist activities.

Peace Corps ⓦpeacecorps.gov. Places US citizens with specialist qualifications or skills in two-year postings.

Restless Development ⓦrestlessdevelopment.org/Nepal. Teaching placements and environmental education programmes for young people aged 18–25.

School for International Training ⓦsit.edu. Based in Vermont, with its own campus in Kathmandu.

School of South Asian Studies ⓦwisc.edu. Full-year study programmes with the University of Wisconsin–Madison.

Study Abroad.com ⓦstudyabroad.com. Good list of study and volunteer programmes in Nepal.

VSO (Voluntary Service Overseas) ⓦvso.org.uk. Highly respected charity that sends qualified professionals from the UK, US and EU to work for local wages on projects beneficial to developing countries. There are special programmes for young people and the over-60s too.

Travel essentials

Children

Kids always help break the ice with strangers, and Nepal can be a magical place for a child to visit. Arranging **childcare** is easy, and Nepalis generally love kids. Some children (especially those with fair skin and blond hair) may be uncomfortable with the endless attention, however.

Parents will of course have to take extra **precautions** in the light of Nepal's poor sanitation, dogs, crowds, traffic, pollution, bright sun, rooftops and steep slopes. It may be hard to keep hands clean and yucky stuff out of mouths, and you'll have to keep a firm grip on small children while out and about. If your child comes down with diarrhoea, keep them hydrated and topped up on salts – have oral rehydration formula on hand.

Naturally, you'll want to plan a more modest itinerary and travel in greater comfort with children than you might on your own. In tourist areas it should be no problem finding food that kids will eat, though in other places it might be more challenging. Baby food and disposable nappies/diapers are available in Kathmandu and Pokhara, but are hard to come by elsewhere. Some toys and books can be bought in Nepal, but bring a supply of your own. Carry small tots in a backpack or papoose – a stroller or pushchair will be virtually useless.

Trekking with children is generally a wonderful experience (see p.320), though it can be logistically awkward if they're too old to ride in a backpack and too young to hike on their own (though mules or horses can often be arranged).

Climate

Nepal's climate varies significantly through the year, with seasons showing themselves very differently at different altitudes. The **pre-monsoon** period, generally very hot and humid at lower elevations, lasts from mid-April to early June, while the **monsoon** itself, when travel is difficult but not impossible, dominates the period between mid-June and mid-September. **Autumn** sees pleasant temperatures and dry weather, while **winter** is generally cool and clear. There's a fuller rundown of Nepal's various seasons and weather changes in the introduction to this guide (see p.7).

Costs

Your money goes a long way in Nepal. Off the tourist routes, it can actually be hard to spend US$30–40 a day, including food, transport and accommodation. On the other hand, Kathmandu and some of the other tourist traps can burn a hole in your pocket faster than you might expect. Even so, it's still possible for a frugal traveller to keep to **US$20 a day** in the capital, although the figure can effortlessly balloon to US$50 or more simply by choosing slightly nicer hotels and restaurants. However, if you travel in less-touristed areas, use local buses and live as the locals, it's perfectly possible to live on as little as US$10 a day. If you like to travel in greater luxury and do a few activities, you should reckon on spending **US$60–80 or more per day**, depending mainly on standard of accommodation.

You'll inevitably **pay over the odds** for things at first, and it may even feel as if people are charging you as much as they think they can get away with, but that's hardly a market principle exclusive to Nepal. Bargain where appropriate, but don't begrudge a few rupees to someone who has worked hard for them.

Many hotels (and most tourist restaurants) quote their prices exclusive of the 13 percent "government" **tax** (essentially a value-added tax) and charge another 10 percent service charge. Hotel prices quoted in this guide (see box, p.28) include all surcharges and taxes, as do the sample prices listed in restaurant reviews.

No matter how tight your budget, it would be foolish not to splurge now and then on some of the things that make Nepal unique: organized treks, rafting, biking and wildlife trips are relatively expensive, but well worth it.

Crime and safety

Nepal is one of the world's more crime-free countries, but it would be unwise not to take a few simple precautions, especially as crime is on the rise in urban areas.

The main concern is **petty theft**. Store valuables in your hotel safe, close windows or grilles at night in cities to deter "fishing", and use a money belt or pouch around your neck. Some public bus routes have reputations for baggage theft. **Pickpockets**

(often street children) operate in crowded urban areas, especially during festivals; be vigilant.

If you're robbed, report it as soon as possible to the **police** headquarters of the district in which the robbery occurred. Policemen are apt to be friendly, if not much help. For **insurance** purposes, go to the Interpol Section of the police headquarters in Durbar Square, Kathmandu or to the Tourist Police in the Kathmandu tourist offices, to fill in a report; you'll need a copy of it to claim from your insurer once back home. Bring a photocopy of your passport and your Nepali visa, together with two passport photos.

Violent crime is rare. An occasional concern is a certain amount of hooliganism or sexual aggression in the Kathmandu tourist bars, and late-night muggings do sometimes occur. In addition, there have been a couple of well-publicized armed robberies and sexually motivated murders in the national parks on the edge of the Kathmandu Valley. A few Western women have been raped, but most problems come about within relationships with Nepali men – trekking or rafting guides, for instance (see p.311) – not due to attack by strangers. The countryside, generally, is very safe, though there is a small risk of attack by bandits on remote trekking trails. In the Terai, there are a number of armed Madhesi groups, but tourists are not targets and you are unlikely to be affected

AVERAGE TEMPERATURES AND RAINFALL	Feb	Apr	Jun	Aug	Oct	Dec
JANAKPUR (70M), TERAI PLAINS						
Max/min (°C)	26/11	35/16	35/20	33/26	31/22	25/11
Max/min (°F)	79/52	95/15	96/68	91/79	88/72	77/52
Rain (mm)	20	40	40	310	70	10
JOMOSOM (2713M), HIMALAYAN RAIN SHADOW						
Max/min (°C)	10/-2	19/4	23/12	23/13	18/6	12/-2
Max/min (°F)	50/28	66/39	73/53	73/55	64/43	54/28
Rain (mm)	10	20	20	30	30	10
KATHMANDU (1300M), CENTRAL HILLS						
Max/min (°C)	20/4	27/11	29/19	28/20	26/13	20/3
Max/min (°F)	68/39	81/52	84/66	82/68	79/55	68/37
Rain (mm)	20	60	260	320	60	150
NAMCHE (3450M), HIGH HIMALAYAS						
Max/min (°C)	6/-6	12/1	15/6	16/8	12/2	7/-6
Max/min (°F)	43/21	54/34	59/43	61/46	54/36	45/21
Rain (mm)	20	30	140	240	80	40
POKHARA (800M), WESTERN HILLS						
Max/min (°C)	22/9	30/15	30/21	30/22	27/17	20/8
Max/min (°F)	71/48	86/59	86/70	86/72	81/62	68/46
Rain (mm)	30	120	700	850	170	20

much beyond the odd delayed bus, roadblock or *bandh* (see below).

There are several ways to get on the wrong side of the law. **Smuggling** is the usual cause of serious trouble – if you get caught with commercial quantities of either drugs or gold you'll be looking at a more or less automatic five to twenty years in prison.

In Nepal, where government servants are poorly paid, a little **bakshish** sometimes greases the wheels. Nepali police don't bust tourists simply in order to get bribes, but if you're accused of something it might not hurt to make an offer, in an extremely careful, euphemistic and deniable way. This shouldn't be necessary if you're the victim of a crime, although you may feel like offering a "reward".

The worst trouble you're likely to run into is one of Nepal's **civil disturbances**, which are thankfully less common than they used to be. Political parties, student organizations and anyone else with a gripe may call a *chakka jam* (traffic halt) or **bandh** (general strike). In either case, most shops pull down their shutters as well, and vehicles stay off the roads to avoid having their windows smashed. Demonstrations sometimes involve rock-throwing, tear gas and *lathis* (Asian-style police batons), but you'd have to go out of your way to get mixed up in this.

Drugs

Drugs are illegal in Nepal, but it is impossible to walk through Thamel or any of the other tourist hot spots without being approached by a dealer offering **hash**. It would be incredibly stupid to go through customs with illegal drugs, but discreet possession inside the country carries relatively little risk. While the drug dealers are often shady characters, they are not generally informants.

Electricity

Power comes at 220 volts/50 cycles per second, when you can get it: lengthy power cuts ("load shedding") are a daily occurrence – these are sometimes random, but often planned, so ask for timings at your hotel. Smarter hotels and restaurants have backup generators; ask for a room away from them as they can be noisy. Tourist guesthouses usually offer sockets that accept almost any kind of pin, but the European standard two-pin is the most common.

Emergencies

Dial ☎ 100 for the **police**. Hospitals and other organizations have their own telephone numbers for an ambulance, but get a Nepali-speaker to do the talking. Registering with your embassy can speed things up in the event of an emergency.

Entry regulations

All foreign nationals except Indians need a **visa** to enter Nepal. These are free (for 30 days) for nationals of other South Asian Area Regional Cooperation (SAARC) countries: Pakistan, Bhutan and Bangladesh. All other nationals have to pay for them. Tourist visas are issued **on arrival** at Kathmandu airport and official overland entry points. At the former, queues can be long, so you may prefer to get one in advance from a Nepali embassy or consulate in your own country. Otherwise, have a passport-size photo at the ready; you can also save time by filling in an online application in advance, on which you can attach a digital photo (Ⓦ online.nepalimmigration .gov.np/tourist-visa). At the airport, you can pay the visa fee in US dollars, euros, pounds sterling or other major foreign currencies. At overland entry points, officials tend to demand US dollars or Nepali rupees.

The **fee** structure at the time of writing was US$25 for 15 days, US$40 for 30 days and US$100 for 90 days; all are multiple-entry visas. Fees may change without warning, however, so double-check at Ⓦ nepalimmigration.gov.np before setting out.

Tourist visas can be **extended** up to a maximum of 150 days in a calendar year: an extension of 30 days or less costs US$30. You'll need to apply online (at Ⓦ nepalimmigration.gov.np), then take the email response with you to the Kathmandu or Pokhara Department of Immigration offices. You should be able to collect your passport with the visa extension added later the same day. Submit your passport and one digital photo with your application – if you haven't submitted your photo online you can put it on a USB stick. A non-extendable **transit visa**, valid for 24 hours, can be issued at airport immigration and costs US$5; you can save time by applying online first.

Don't overstay more than a couple of days as you'll have to pay the visa extension fee plus fines, and *don't* tamper with your visa – tourists have been fined and even jailed for these seemingly minor infractions.

It is no longer necessary to have a **trekking permit** to visit the most popular trekking regions, but you will need the TIMS card, which amounts to much the same thing. You'll have to pay **national park entry fees** for the Annapurna, Everest and Langtang areas. A handful of remote regions are still restricted, and require permits to enter (see box, p.314).

EARTHQUAKE DANGER IN NEPAL

The earthquakes that periodically trouble Nepal are all too tangible proof that the Himalayas are still rising, forced ever upward by the movement of the Indian subcontinent plate as it drives into the greater Asian plate at a rate of 2cm per year. Tremors of magnitude 4 and 5 occur a dozen or so times a year, while the country was terrified by a 6.8-magnitude shake in September 2011 (fortunately, it occurred on the sparsely occupied eastern border, and killed very few).

The most recent major earthquake, in 1988, registered a terrifying 8.3 on the Richter scale and killed seven hundred people in the eastern part of the country. When a similar quake hit Kathmandu in 1934, it destroyed a quarter of the capital's buildings and killed some seventeen thousand people inside a single minute, its power amplified by the valley's soupy soil, which liquefied in places, due to the shaking.

Since then, the population has swelled dramatically, and thousands of concrete houses are built every year – the majority officially considered "highly unsafe". Unnervingly, tourist guesthouses, built ever upwards in unceasing competition for rooftop airspace, are among the main contenders for collapse – along with schools and hospitals. The best guess is that an 8-magnitude quake in the Kathmandu Valley would kill some 100,000 people and leave at least a million homeless. Survivors would be stranded, without succour: all the hospitals would collapse, and the roads into and out of the capital would be blocked by landslides.

Recent seismic studies, moreover, predict that a major earthquake, one that hits 8 or more on the Richter scale, is due to hit Nepal "soon" – which is to say probably within the next fifty years. Local experts contend that the less populated (and much less visited) western region is a more likely target than Kathmandu, but it's small comfort if you're in Pokhara. Here's what to do if there is an earthquake:

- If indoors, stay indoors. For most people, this is counterintuitive. Get under a table or stand against an interior wall. Stay clear of heavy furniture, and stand back from exterior walls and windows.
- If outdoors, find open space if you can. Stay clear of walls, buildings and power lines – if you can.
- If trekking, walk up from riverbanks and away from landslide areas.
- Expect aftershocks. Stay in a safe place and gather things you might need in an emergency: first-aid kit, blanket, emergency lights, water purification tablets, food.

It's worth noting, too, that a few sites in the **Kathmandu Valley**, including the entire city of Bhaktapur, charge entry fees.

Customs officers are fairly lax on entry, but checks are more thorough on departure, and it is illegal to export objects over 100 years old (see box, p.114).

Gay and lesbian Nepal

While the **gay scene** in Kathmandu is growing slowly, and the government is taking a more progressive line than in the past, homosexuality is still very much frowned upon. (Lesbianism is barely even considered a possibility.) In a society where men routinely hold hands and often share beds, gay **couples** may feel a certain freedom in being able to be close in public, but otherwise the same advice on sexual behaviour in public applies as for heterosexual couples (see p.40). The only approach a gay traveller is likely to get is from touts who, at the end of a long inventory of drugs and "nice Nepali girls", might also offer "boys". But it's nothing like the scene in, say, Thailand. For

more information, contact the Blue Diamond Society (W bds.org.np), a Kathmandu-based gay rights pressure group.

Insurance

It's worth taking out **insurance** before travelling, to cover against theft, loss and illness or injury. Before paying for a new policy, however, check whether you're already covered: some all-risks home insurance policies may cover your possessions when overseas, and many medical schemes include cover when abroad.

A typical policy usually provides cover for the loss of baggage, tickets and – up to a certain limit – cash, as well as cancellation or curtailment of your journey. Most of them exclude so-called **dangerous sports** unless an extra premium is paid: in Nepal this can mean whitewater rafting, trekking (especially above 4000m) and climbing. Many policies can be tailored – for example, sickness and accident benefits can often be excluded or included at will. If you do take medical coverage, ascertain whether benefits will be paid as treatment proceeds or only after return home, and whether there is a 24-hour medical emergency number. When securing baggage cover, make sure that the per-article limit will cover your most valuable possession. If you need to make a claim, you should keep **receipts** for medicines and medical treatment, and in the event you have anything stolen, you must obtain an official statement from the police.

Internet

Cyber **cafés** are abundant in Nepal. Beyond Kathmandu and Pokhara, however, connections can be painfully slow. Expect to pay around Rs50–100/hr. Find out whether a power cut is due before going online, as only a few cyber cafés have backup generators. Most hotels and restaurants in touristy areas offer wi-fi access.

Laundry

Most hotels and guesthouses provide **laundry** services, generally charging around Rs50–100/kg. In Thamel and other tourist areas, numerous laundries offer a same-day service. If you're doing your own, you'll find detergent sold in inexpensive packets in cities, or you can buy a cheap cube of local laundry soap almost anywhere.

Mail

Post generally takes at least ten days to get to or from Nepal – if it arrives at all. Postcards (Rs25–30 to anywhere in the world) go through fine, but envelopes or parcels that look like they might contain anything of value sometimes go astray. Letters can be sent to a hotel or a friend's home, or care of **poste restante** in Kathmandu (see p.117). Mail should be addressed: Name, Poste Restante, GPO, Kathmandu (or Pokhara), Nepal. Mail is held for about two months, and can be redirected on

request. In Kathmandu, American Express handles mail for cardholders and those carrying Amex cheques, and US citizens can receive mail c/o the Consular Section of the American Embassy.

When **sending mail** in Nepal, there's rarely a need to deal directly with the postal system; most hotels will take it to the post office for you. Book and postcard shops in tourist areas sell **stamps**, and many also have their own, largely reliable, mail drop-off boxes. Where no such services exist, take your letters or cards to the post office yourself, or wait to send them from Kathmandu. Never use a public letterbox: the stamps will be removed and resold.

Parcels can be sent by air or sea. Sea mail is cheaper but takes a lot longer (three months or more) and there are more opportunities for it to go missing. Again, the private sector is much easier to deal with than the official postal service. **Shipping agents** and **air freight services** will shield you from much of the frustration and red tape, but for this they charge almost twice as much as the post office. Be sure you're dealing with a reputable company.

The media

The media is fast developing in Nepal and even remote places now have access to newspapers, TV and, increasingly, the internet.

Despite a literacy rate of less than fifty percent, Nepal boasts more than a thousand **newspapers** – an outgrowth of two noble Brahmanic traditions: punditry and gossip. Several are published in English, the most readable and incisive being the weekly *Nepali Times*. Of the dailies, the *Kathmandu Post* remains the frontrunner, overshadowing *The Himalayan Times* and *República*. All are hard to find outside big cities, but are available online.

A number of **magazines** are published in English, the most interesting being *Himal* (ⓦ himalmag .com) and ECS Nepal (ⓦ ecs.com.np). Foreign publications such as the *International Herald Tribune*,

Time and *Newsweek* are available from bookshops in Kathmandu and Pokhara.

As well as several terrestrial Nepali channels, cable and satellite **TV** – broadcasting programmes from India and the West – is widespread, and more and more hotel rooms have TVs. The influential government-run **Radio Nepal** (Ⓦ radionepal.gov .np) on 103 FM has English-language news bulletins daily at 8pm. Local **FM stations** are sprouting like mushrooms and increasingly using ethnic languages and local dialects. There are a couple of English-language ones in the Kathmandu Valley; the trendiest is Kantipur (Ⓦ radiokantipur.com) on 96.1 FM. If you have a short-wave radio, you can pick up the BBC World Service: Ⓦ bbc.co.uk/world service lists the frequencies.

Money and banks

Nepal's unit of currency is the Nepali **rupee** (*ruplya*), which is divided into 100 *paisa* (which you will never see). At the time of writing, the **exchange rate** was around Rs100 to US$1, Rs150 to £1 and Rs115 to €1. Most Nepali money is paper: **notes** come in denominations of Rs1, 2, 5, 10, 20, 25, 50, 100, 250, 500 and 1000.

More upmarket tourist businesses quote prices in **US dollars**, and may even expect payment in that currency. A fistful of rupees will very rarely be refused, but if you're planning to stay in classy hotels, or book flights or rafting trips, it's worth bringing some US currency. A selection of denominations is useful; make sure the bills are relatively new. Euros and pounds sterling are accepted too, converted on the basis of the bank's tourist rate, or the one printed in that day's newspaper. The Indian rupee, also widely accepted, is known as IC for Indian Currency.

One minor annoyance of travelling in Nepal is **getting change**. Outside tourist areas, business people will hum and haw about breaking a large note. It gets to be a game of bluff between buyer and seller, both hoarding a wad of small notes for occasions when exact change is vital. It pays to carry a range of smaller bills.

Credit and debit cards

Top-end hotels and some travel agents, shops and mid-range guesthouses accept **credit cards** (charging a processing fee for doing so), but most others places don't. Most towns covered in this guide have at least one **ATM**, and places like Kathmandu have hundreds. Almost all ATMs have instructions in English and many are open 24

hours; most accept foreign debit and credit cards (although not, at the time of writing, Cirrus or American Express cards) – check with your bank before leaving home. Annoyingly, most ATMs have an Rs10,000–15,000 withdrawal limit for each transaction, the exception being Nabil Bank ATMs, which will often give you up to Rs35,000 (though not in tourist areas like Thamel). Let your bank know you intend to use your card in Nepal before leaving home, as they sometimes stop cards used abroad for fear that they have been cloned or stolen.

Some banks also issue credit card cash advances, and American Express cardholders can draw money inside branches of Himalayan Bank. A good alternative to debit or credit cards are the pre-paid "cash passport" cards (Ⓦ cashpassport.com) issued by companies such as Travelex.

Travellers' cheques

Travellers' cheques are more secure than cash, but are used less and less these days. **US dollar** cheques are widely accepted in tourist areas, and cheques denominated in other major currencies are usually accepted as well. If you're travelling off the beaten track, however, it's wiser to stick to cash.

Banks and moneychangers

Using **banks** in Nepal is, by south Asian standards, hassle free. Numerous banks vie for tourist business, as do a horde of government-registered **moneychangers**. The former tend to give slightly better rates, though the latter are often more convenient.

Moneychangers can be found wherever there are significant numbers of tourists, while banks are more widespread. **Hours** for foreign exchange vary: at least one Kathmandu airport moneychanger operates around the clock, Nepal Bank's central Kathmandu (New Road) branch stays open seven days a week, and some private banks keep extended hours, but lesser branches generally change money only from 9am to 3pm Monday to Friday, often closing early on Fridays. Moneychangers keep generous hours (usually daily 9am–8pm).

Hold on to all exchange receipts in case you want to **change money back** when you leave. Some banks (including those at Tribhuwan airport and official border crossings) will buy rupees back, though they may only give US dollars in return. If you're entering India, changing Nepali currency into Indian currency is no problem.

Opening hours and public holidays

In the Kathmandu Valley, **government offices** and **post offices** are open Monday to Friday from 9am to 5pm (sometimes closing at 4pm between mid-Nov and mid-Feb); outside the valley, they often open on Sunday as well.

Museums are usually closed at least one day a week; opening times are fairly similar to office hours. **Shops** keep long hours (usually 9–10am to 7–8pm), and in tourist areas generally open daily. Some **banks** in tourist areas and Kathmandu are also generous with their hours, but elsewhere you'll generally have to do your transactions between 9am and 3pm from Monday to Friday. Money-changers keep longer hours. **Travel agents** tend to work from around 9am to the early evening; **airline offices** are open roughly the same hours as government offices, and often close for lunch between 1pm and 2pm.

Nepal's hectic calendar of **national holidays** can shut down offices for up to a week at a time. Dates vary from year to year – Nepal has its own calendar, the Vikram Sambat, which began in 57 BC. The year starts in mid-April and consists of twelve months that are a fortnight or so out of step with the Western ones. Complicating matters further are religious **festivals**, which are calculated according to the lunar calendar, while Tibetan and Newari festivals follow calendars of their own.

Phones

All tourist areas and major towns have **telephone/internet shops** that offer a variety of

---

CALLING HOME FROM ABROAD

To make an **international call**, dial the international access code (in Nepal it's +977), then the destination's country code, before the rest of the number. Note that the initial zero is omitted from the area code when dialling the UK, Ireland, Australia and New Zealand from abroad.

Australia + 61
New Zealand + 64
UK + 44
US and Canada + 1
Republic of Ireland + 353
South Africa + 27

---

ways to make cheap international calls, including on Skype. Most have backup generators for power outages. Simpler telephone-only outfits, which advertise themselves with the acronyms ISD/STD/IDD, can be found almost everywhere there's a phone line.

Mobile phone coverage is now found across the country, even in some trekking areas. You can generally use foreign SIM cards in Nepal, but it is far cheaper to buy a local one: Ncell is currently the most popular network, though it is not the best choice when in the mountains. When you buy a SIM (from Rs99) you'll need to take photocopies of your passport and visa and a passport photo; it can take up to half an hour to process.

Nepali numbers are always eight digits long: in the Kathmandu Valley the ☏01 area code is followed by a seven-digit number; elsewhere, a three-digit area code is followed by a six-digit number; mobile phone numbers are ten digits long. You don't need to dial the area code when you're calling landlines from within that area. Numbers in the Kathmandu chapter of this guide are listed with codes, but note that you'll need to remove ☏01 when dialling from within the Kathmandu Valley. The **international dialling code** for Nepal is +977. For **directory enquiries** call ☏197; for Kathmandu numbers you can look online at ⓦnepalhomepage.com/whitepages.

Time zones

Nepal is 5 hours 45 minutes ahead of GMT. That makes it 5 hours 45 minutes ahead of London, 10 hours 45 minutes ahead of New York, 13 hours 45 minutes ahead of Los Angeles, and 4 hours 15 minutes behind Sydney. Nepal doesn't observe **daylight saving time**, so daylight saving time

---

NATIONAL HOLIDAYS

Prithvi Narayan Shah's Birthday Jan 10 or 11
Basanta Panchami Late Jan or early Feb
Shiva Raatri Late Feb or early March
Democracy Day Feb 18 or 19
Nawa Barsa (Nepali New Year) April 13 or 14
Chait Dasain Late March or early April
Ram Nawami Late March or early April
Buddha Jayanti Late April or early May
Janai Purnima Late July or early Aug
Krishna Asthami Late July or early Aug
Dasain Late Sept or early Oct (6 days)
Tihaar Late Oct or early Nov (3 days)
Constitution Day Nov 9

elsewhere reduces/increases the time difference by one hour.

Tipping

Most restaurants automatically include a ten percent **service charge** in the bill and this will almost always go straight to the staff – it's one of the few bits of useful legislation the Maoist introduced while in government. Trekking porters and guides have their own expectations (see p.312).

Toilets

Toilets range from "Western" (sit-down) flush options to a shed over a hole. In basic lodges the norm is a squat toilet. When travelling by bus you'll almost always find a bathroom available at stops – but sometimes there is nothing but a designated field. If in doubt, ask *Toilet kahaachha?* ("Where is the toilet?"). Don't flush toilet paper: put it in the basket provided. Note that paper is not provided in more basic places; Nepalis use a jug of water and the left hand.

As many villages have no covered **toilets**, it's deemed okay to defecate in the open – but out of sight of others, in the early morning or after dark. Men may urinate in public away from buildings – discreetly – but women have to find a sheltered spot.

Tourist information

The handful of **Nepal Tourism Board** offices inside the country are generally friendly, if not necessarily full of information. You'll get the most useful information from guesthouse staff and other travellers. Check the **notice boards** in restaurants and guest-houses around the tourist quarters for news of upcoming events or to find travelling or trekking companions. In the capital, the **Kathmandu Environmental Education Project** (KEEP; W keepnepal.org) and the **Himalayan Rescue Association** (W himalayanrescue.org) can provide trekking information. Nepal's English-language newspapers and magazines are also good sources of information, and there are several useful websites.

USEFUL WEBSITES

W **catmando.com** Comprehensive (if rarely updated) lists of Nepal-based businesses, including hotels, restaurants, travel and travel agencies.

W **digitalhimalaya.com** Hosted by Cambridge University in the UK, this site offers the last word in research, news and resources for Nepal and other Himalayan countries.

W **ekantipur.com** Online edition of the *Kathmandu Post*, one of the country's best dailies.

W **fco.gov.uk/travel** This UK Foreign and Commonwealth Office site is usually the most detailed government advisory service on travel to Nepal.

W **himalayanrescue.org** Useful trekking resource run by the Himalayan Rescue Association.

W **keepnepal.org** KEEP's website is good for environmental, cultural and trekking information.

W **nepalhomepage.com** Helpful Nepal gateway, with FAQs on travel in Nepal, local yellow pages, directories, and photos, though information is not always up to date.

W **nepalnews.com** Good news aggregator with links to many Nepali media outlets, including the fortnightly *Spotlight* magazine.

W **pilgrimsbooks.com** Online branch of Nepal's best bookshop.

W **travel.state.gov** The US Department of State's website details the dangers of travelling to most countries in the world.

Travellers with disabilities

Nepal is a poor country without the means to cater for **disabled travellers**. If you walk with difficulty, you'll find the steep slopes, stairs and uneven pavements hard going. Open sewers, potholes, crowds and a lack of proper street crossings will all make it hard for a blind traveller to get around. That said, guides and porters are readily available and should be prepared to provide whatever assistance you need.

With a companion, there's no reason why you can't enjoy many of Nepal's activities, including mountain flights and sightseeing by private car. If you rent a taxi, the driver is certain to help you in and out, and perhaps around the sites you visit. A safari should be feasible, and even a trek, catered to your needs by an agency, might not be out of the question – mules or horses can be used on a number of trekking routes, for example.

Basic **wheelchairs** are available in Kathmandu's airport, and smaller airports, including Pokhara, are mostly at ground level. Generally, however, facilities for the disabled are nonexistent, so you should bring your own wheelchair or other necessary equipment. Hotels aren't geared up for disabled guests, though the most expensive ones have lifts and (sometimes) ramps.

Kathmandu and Patan

DURBAR SQUARE, PATAN

1

Kathmandu and Patan

How to describe Kathmandu? A medieval time capsule? An environmental disaster? A holy city? A tourist trap? The answer is, of course, all of the above. There are a thousand Kathmandus, all layered together in an extravagant morass of chaos and sophistication. With a fast-growing metropolitan population of just over one million, Nepal's capital is easily the country's biggest and most cosmopolitan city: a melting pot of a dozen ethnic groups, and home town of the Newars – master craftsmen and traders extraordinaire. Trade, indeed, created Kathmandu – for at least a thousand years the city controlled the most important caravan route between Tibet and India – and trade has always funded its Newari artisans. Little wonder, perhaps, that the city has so deftly embraced the tourist business.

Though squeezed by traffic, the **old city** – with **Durbar Square** at its centre – is still studded with temples and splendid architecture. Its narrow lanes seethe with an incredible crush of humanity, echoing with the din of bicycle bells, motorbike engines, religious music, construction and car horns, and reeking of incense, spices, sewage and exhaust fumes. Sacred cows, holy men, beggars and street urchins roam the streets. The Kathmandu most travellers experience is **Thamel**, a thumping, developing-world theme park in the old city, north of Durbar Square, filled with hotels, restaurants, bars, souvenir shops, bookshop, imitation trekking gear, pirated DVDs, and touts flogging tiger balm and hashish.

To the south is the separate municipality of **Patan**, is once the capital of an independent kingdom; though now subsumed into the greater Kathmandu conurbation, it has its own quieter and better-preserved historic district, marked by numerous Buddhist *bahal* (monastery compounds, some still active), proud artistry and a conspicuous community of foreign residents, predominantly the staff of international NGOs and charities.

These quarters represent only part of a complex and eccentric city, which also encompasses shantytowns, decrepit ministry buildings, swanky shopping streets, sequestered suburbs and heaving bazaars. Perhaps the predominant images of contemporary Kathmandu are those that pass for progress: hellish **traffic jams** and **pollution**; suburban sprawl and rubbish heaps; crippling daily power cuts (at times up to eighteen hours a day) and backup generators; chauffeured SUVs and families on

THE BAGMATI GHATS

Highlights

❶ Kathmandu Durbar Square An old royal palace, a living goddess, temples, statues, vegetable sellers and curio hawkers come together in this touristy yet vibrant hub. **See p.62**

❷ The Bagmati ghats Little-visited relics and cremation platforms dot these neglected riverside embankments. **See p.76**

❸ Swayambhu This eye-catching hilltop temple complex is a profound microcosm of Nepali culture. **See p.78**

❹ The Patan Museum A fascinating selection of religious woodcarvings, stone sculptures, bronzes and other exhibits can be found at this excellent museum, located in Patan's refined Durbar Square. **See p.88**

❺ Meditation and yoga courses Kathmandu's spiritual supermarket caters to dabblers and serious seekers alike. For excellent classes, try the Pranamaya Yoga Centre in Patan. **See p.100**

❻ Kathmandu dining The city's restaurants serve a bewildering array of cuisines, from fine French dining to Tibetan street food – try the romantic *Kaiser Café* for a special experience. **See p.105**

HIGHLIGHTS ARE MARKED ON THE MAP ON PP.58–59

KATHMANDU AND PATAN

■ ACCOMMODATION
Dwarika's	3
Gokarna Forest Resort	2
Hyatt Regency Kathmandu	1

● SHOPPING
Dhankuta Sisters	1
Dhukuti	3
Mahaguthi	4
Jawalakhel Handicraft Center	2
Patan Industrial Estate	5

● EATING
Krishnarpan	1
Mako's	2

Sankhu & Sundarijal

Boudha stupa

SEE 'BOUDHA' MAP (CHAPTER 2)

Royal Nepal Golf Club

CHABAHIL

SEE 'PASHUPATINATH' MAP (CHAPTER 2)

Pashupati Mandir

GAUSHALA

Bagmati River

Dhobi Khola

BANSBARI

Budhanilkantha

Australian Embassy

RING ROAD

Dhum Barahi

US Embassy

Mountain Ecology Treks

MAHARAJGANJ

Teaching Hospital

Prime Minister's Residence

HADIGAUN

BALUWATAR

BHATBATENI

Police HQ

NAFA

NAKSAL

BATTISPUTALI

PURANO BANESWAR

Dhobi Khola

DILLI BAZAAR

Shital Niwas (Foreign Ministry)

LAZIMPATH

Kamal Pokhari

Royal Palace

Rani Pokhari

K A T H M A N D U

SAMAKHUSI

Ratna Park

Tudikhel

Minibuses to Trisuli Bazaar

GONGABU

Naya (New) Bus Park

THAMEL

ASAN

Kathmandu Durbar Square

Bhimsen Tower

NAYA BAZAAR

CHHETRAPATI

Bishnumati River

KALDHARA

BALAJU

Macha Pokhari Bus Station (Bypass Bus Station)

Nagarjun Ban (Raniban)

TAHACHAL

KATHMANDU AND PATAN

Bishnumati River

Kakani, Trisuli & Osho Tapoban Forest Retreat Centre

SEE SWAYAMBHU MAP

Swayambhu

CHHAUNI

Buddha Dharma Centre

National Museum

Ichangu Narayan

N

Bhaktapur & Nagarkot

Bhaktapur & Tibet border

Tribhuwan International Airport

ARNIKO RAJMARG

Hanumante Khola

Mandhara Khola

RING ROAD

KOTESWAR

Bagmati River

Mandara Khola

RING ROAD

Luhhu

Birendra International Convention Centre

NAYA BANESWAR

B&B Hospital

Haisiddhi & Godavari

Sankhamul Ghat

Golden Temple

Sports Complex

Thecho

Patan Museum 4

SEE 'PATAN' MAP

THAPATHALI

KUPONDOL

Patan Dhoka

Patan Durbar Square

P A T A N

LAGANKHEL

Bus Park

SATDO BATO

TRIPURESWAR

Bagmati River

PULCHOWK

JAWALAKHEL

Kushunti Pancheswar Mahadev Mandir

Bungmati

Ghats 2

SEE 'CENTRAL KATHMANDU' MAP

SANEPA

Zoo

5

EKANTAKUNA

NAKHU

Nakhu Khola

TEKU

RING ROAD

Hariisiddhi & Godavari

Patanjali Yoga Centre

BALKHU

Jeeps to Hetauda

Bagmati River

Chobar Gorge

Dakshinkali

Asheesh Osho Meditation Centre

KALIMATI

Used motorbike shops

PRITHVI HIGHWAY

KALANKI

RING ROAD

Tribhuwan University

CHOBAR

Thankot & Pokhara

Kirtipur

0   500
metres

1

Kathmandu was badly hit by the devastating **earthquake of April 25, 2015** (see box, p.6), which occurred as this book went to press. In addition to the tragic loss of life, infrastructure damage and destruction of property, many of the capital's architectural treasures also suffered losses. Durbar and Patan squares were both severely damaged with several building entirely destroyed at each, Dharahara tower was reduced to a stump and there was also damage to the Swayambhunath temple complex. While there is no doubt that there will be a massive rebuilding and renovation of these historic places, it is as yet unclear how long this will take, especially given the more primary needs of the city's inhabitants.

motorbikes. The city hasn't abandoned its traditional identity, but the rapid pace of change has produced an intense, often overwhelming, urban environment.

Brief history

People must have occupied what is now Kathmandu for thousands of years, but chroniclers attribute the city's founding to Gunakamadev, who reigned in the late ninth century – by which time sophisticated urban centres had already been established by the **Lichhavi** kings at Pashupatinath and other sites in the surrounding valley. Kathmandu, originally known as Kantipur, took its present name from the Kasthamandap (Pavilion of Wood) that was constructed as a rest-house along the main Tibet–India trade route in the late twelfth century, and which still stands in the city centre.

The city rose to prominence under the **Malla** kings, who took control of the valley in the thirteenth century, ushering in a golden age of art and architecture that lasted more than five hundred years. Kathmandu's finest buildings and monuments, including in Durbar Square, date from this period. At the start of the Malla era, Kathmandu ranked as a sovereign state alongside the valley's other two major cities, Bhaktapur and Patan, but soon fell under the rule of the former. The cities were again divided in the fifteenth century, and a long period of intrigue and rivalry followed.

Malla rule ended abruptly in 1769, when Prithvi Narayan Shah of Gorkha, a previously undistinguished hill state to the west, captured the valley as the first conquest in his historic unification of Nepal. Kathmandu fared well in defeat, being made capital of the new nation and seat of the new **Shah** dynasty.

Although politically outmanoeuvred from 1846 to 1951 by the powerful **Rana** family, who ruled as hereditary prime ministers and left Kathmandu with a legacy of enormous whitewashed Neoclassical palaces, the Shahs were essentially in power until April 2006, with the final decade consumed by a debilitating conflict with Maoist forces. A peace deal was struck later that year and in early 2007 the Maoists joined an interim government. A general election in April 2008 left the Maoists as the biggest party in parliament, and a month later Nepal's monarchy was abolished.

WHERE ARE THE MOUNTAINS?

They're there – behind the smog. In the 1990s, peaks such as Ganesh I, Langtang Lirung and Dorje Lakpa could be seen most mornings from Kathmandu. Now they're rarely visible from the metropolitan area except on clear mornings after a soaking rain, or on *bandh* (general strike) days when all traffic is banned.

Kathmandu is among the world's most polluted cities, and the **traffic and fumes** are appalling. The ever-increasing number of cars, motorbikes, buses and lorries, fuel adulteration, lax emissions tests, poorly surfaced roads, rapid urbanization, rubbish dumping and high levels of general pollution, mean that **air quality** frequently reaches "unhealthy" levels, according to official measurements. This toxic brew irritates lungs and eyes, weakens immune systems and increases the long-term risk of various health problems. If you can help it, don't stay more than a couple of days in Kathmandu at the start of your trip. If you do, you're likely to come down with a chest or sinus infection that will dog you for days and may be hard to shake if you go trekking.

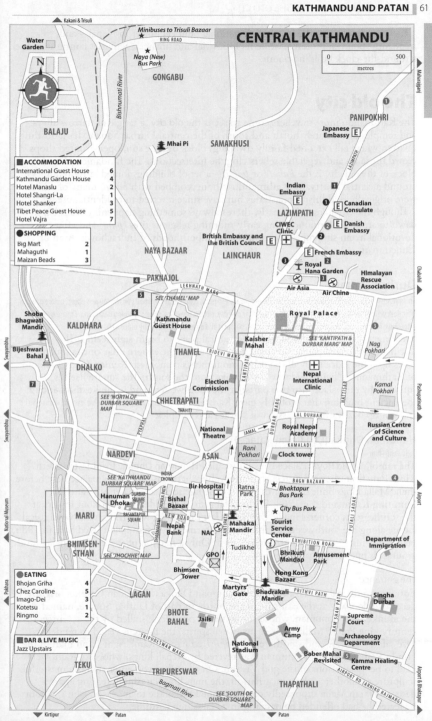

CENTRAL KATHMANDU

0 — 500 metres

Kakani & Trisuli

Water Garden

Minibuses to Trisuli Bazaar
RING ROAD
Naya (New) Bus Park

GONGABU

Bishumati River

PANIPOKHRI

Japanese Embassy E

BALAJU

Mhai Pi

SAMAKHUSI

Indian Embassy E

Canadian Consulate E

LAZIMPATH

CIWEC Clinic

Danish Embassy E

ACCOMMODATION
International Guest House — 6
Kathmandu Garden House — 4
Hotel Manaslu — 2
Hotel Shangri-La — 1
Hotel Shanker — 3
Tibet Peace Guest House — 5
Hotel Vajra — 7

British Embassy and the British Council E

French Embassy E

LAINCHAUR

NAYA BAZAAR

Royal Hana Garden

Himalayan Rescue Association

Air Asia

Air China

SHOPPING
Big Mart — 2
Mahaguthi — 1
Maizan Beads — 3

PAKNAJOL

LEKHNATH MARG

Shoba Bhagwati Mandir

KALDHARA

SEE 'THAMEL' MAP

Kathmandu Guest House

Royal Palace

SEE 'KANTIPATH & DURBAR MARG' MAP

Nag Pokhari

Bijeshwari Bahal

DHALKO

THAMEL

Kaisher Mahal

TRIDEVI MARG

KANTIPATH

Kamal Pokhari

SEE 'NORTH OF DURBAR SQUARE' MAP

Election Commission

Nepal International Clinic

CHHETRAPATI

THAHITI

PYKHALI

National Theatre

LAL DURBAR

DURBAR MARG

Royal Nepal Academy

Russian Centre of Science and Culture

NARDEVI

SEE 'KATHMANDU DURBAR SQUARE' MAP

Rani Pokhari

Clock tower

JAMAL

KAMALADI

ASAN

INDRA-CHOWK

Bir Hospital

Ratna Park

BAGH BAZAAR

Bhaktapur Bus Park

City Bus Park

MATTISAR

PUTALI SADAK

Hanuman Dhoka

DURBAR SQUARE

Bishal Bazaar

MARU

BASANTAPUR SQUARE

SHUKRA PATH

NEW ROAD

Nepal Bank

NAC

Mahakal Mandir

Tourist Service Center

EXHIBITION ROAD

Department of Immigration

BHIMSEN-STHAN

SEE 'JHOCHHE' MAP

DHARMAPATH

KANTIPATH

Tudikhe

Brikuti Mandap

Amusement Park

GPO

Bhimsen Tower

Hong Kong Bazaar

Singha Durbar

EATING
Bhojan Griha — 4
Chez Caroline — 5
Imago-Dei — 3
Kotetsu — 1
Ringmo — 2

LAGAN

Martyrs' Gate

Bhadrakali Mandir

PRITHVI PATH

Supreme Court

BHOTE BAHAL

Jails

Army Camp

RAM SHAH PATH

Archaeology Department

BAR & LIVE MUSIC
Jazz Upstairs — 1

National Stadium

Baber Mahal Revisited

Kamma Healing Centre

TEKU

Ghats

TRIPURESWAR

TRIPURESWAR MARG

Bagmati River

THAPATHALI

AIRPORT RD (ARNIKO RAJMARG)

SEE 'SOUTH OF DURBAR SQUARE' MAP

Kirtipur

Patan

Patan

Maharajganj

Chabahil

Pashupatinath

Airport

Airport & Bhaktapur

Swayambhu

Pokhara

National Museum

1

Kathmandu remains the focus of all national political power in Nepal – and, frequently, political protest – while its industrial and financial activities continue to fuel a round-the-clock building boom.

The old city

The Kathmandu most travellers come to see is the **old city**, a tangle of narrow alleys and temples immediately north and south of the central Durbar Square. It's a bustling quarter, where tall extended-family dwellings block out the sun, open-fronted shops crowd the lanes and vegetable sellers clog the intersections. The fundamental building block of the old city is the *bahal* (or *baha*) – a set of buildings joined at right angles around a central courtyard. Kathmandu is honeycombed with *bahal*, many of which were originally Buddhist monasteries but have since reverted to residential use.

Though the city goes to bed early, there's always something happening from before dawn to around 10pm, including early-morning religious rites (*puja*) and after-dinner devotional **hymn-singing** (*bhajan*) in the neighbourhoods of Indrachowk, Asan or Chhetrapati.

Durbar Square

An entrance fee (Rs750, which includes the museum and palace entries) is collected at checkpoints on the square's edges; before dawn or after dusk you can usually enter for free. Tickets are valid for one day, but the site office on neighbouring Basantapur Square gives free extensions; for three-day-plus extensions, take your ticket, passport and a passport photo • Site office ☎ 01 426 8969

Teeming, touristy **Durbar Square** is the natural place to begin sightseeing. The fascinating old royal palace (*durbar*), running along the eastern edge of the square, takes up more space than all the other monuments combined. Kumari Chowk, home of Kathmandu's "living goddess", overlooks from the south. The square itself is squeezed by the palace into two parts: at the southwestern end is the **Kasthamandap**, the ancient building that probably gave Kathmandu its name, while the northern part is taken up by a varied procession of statues and temples.

Hanuman Dhoka (Old Royal Palace)
Daily 9am–4pm

The rambling **Old Royal Palace** is usually called **Hanuman Dhoka**. Its oldest, eastern wings date from the mid-sixteenth century, but there was probably a palace here before then. Malla kings built most of the rest by the late seventeenth century, and after capturing Kathmandu in 1768, Prithvi Narayan Shah added four lookout towers at the southeastern corner. Finally, the Ranas left their mark with the garish Neoclassical facade along the southwestern flank. Nepal's former royal family last lived here in 1886, before moving to the northern end of town. Only a fraction of the five-acre palace and grounds is open to the public.

The entrance

Entrance to the palace is through the Hanuman Dhoka (Hanuman Gate), a brightly decorated doorway at the east side of the northern part of Durbar Square, named after the monkey god **Hanuman**, whose statue stands outside. Installed by the seventeenth-century king Pratap Malla to drive away evil spirits, the figure is veiled to render its gaze safe to mortals, and smothered in *abhir* (red paste). Ram's right-hand man in the Hindu Ramayana epic, Hanuman was revered by Nepali kings, who, like Ram, were held to be incarnations of the god Vishnu. On the left as you enter stands a masterful sculpture of another Vishnu incarnation, the man-lion **Narasingh**, tearing apart a demon. Pratap Malla supposedly commissioned the statue to appease Vishnu, whom he feared he had offended by dancing in a Narasingh costume.

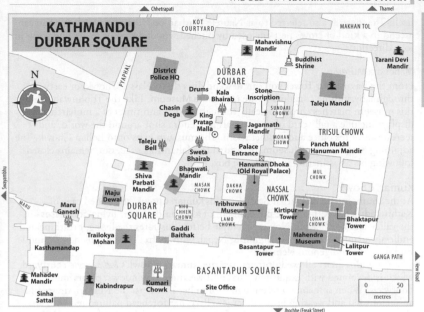

▲ Chhetrapati   ▲ Thamel

KATHMANDU
DURBAR SQUARE

KOT COURTYARD

MAKHAN TOL

Mahavishnu Mandir

Buddhist Shrine

Tarani Devi Mandir

District Police HQ

DURBAR SQUARE

PYAPHAL

N

Drums

Kala Bhairab

Stone Inscription

SUNDARI CHOWK

Taleju Mandir

Chasin Dega

King Pratap Malla

Jagannath Mandir

MOHAN CHOWK

TRISUL CHOWK

Taleju Bell

Sweta Bhairab

Palace Entrance

Panch Mukhi Hanuman Mandir

Swayambhu

Shiva Parbati Mandir

Bhagwati Mandir

Hanuman Dhoka (Old Royal Palace)

MUL CHOWK

Maju Dewal

MASAN CHOWK

DAKHA CHOWK

NASSAL CHOWK

MARU

Maru Ganesh

DURBAR SQUARE

NHU CHHEN CHOWK

Tribhuwan Museum

LAMO CHOWK

Kirtipur Tower

LOHAN CHOWK

Bhaktapur Tower

Trailokya Mohan

Gaddi Baithak

Mahendra Museum

Lalitpur Tower

Kasthamandap

Basantapur Tower

GANGA PATH

New Road

Mahadev Mandir

Kabindrapur

Kumari Chowk

BASANTAPUR SQUARE

Site Office

Sinha Sattal

0   50
metres

▼ Jhochhe (Freak Street)

Interior courtyards

The entrance opens to **Nassal Chowk**, a large central courtyard which provided the setting for King Birendra's coronation in 1975. The brick wings that form its southern and eastern flanks date from the sixteenth century and boast painstakingly carved wooden doorways, windows and struts. At the northeastern corner of the square, the five-tiered pagoda-like turret, notable for its round roofs, is the **Panch Mukhi Hanuman Mandir**: "Five-Faced Hanuman" is supposed to have the faces of an ass, man-bird, man-lion, boar and monkey. Along the northern side of the courtyard is the Malla kings' audience hall.

Although the palace has ten courtyards, visitors are allowed to enter only Nassal Chowk and **Lohan Chowk**. **Mul Chowk**, which can be glimpsed through a doorway off Nassal Chowk, contains a temple to Taleju Bhawani, the ancestral deity of the Malla kings, and sacrifices are made to her in the courtyard during the Dasain festival. To the north, but not visible, **Mohan Chowk** is alleged to have a sunken royal bath with a golden waterspout.

The Tribhuwan Museum

Housed in the west and south wings overlooking Nassal Chowk, the **Tribhuwan Museum** features a collection of memorabilia from the reign of Tribhuwan, though there's little in the way of English-language explanation. Often referred to as *rashtrapita* ("father of the nation"), Tribhuwan is fondly remembered for his pivotal role in restoring the monarchy in 1951 and opening up Nepal to the outside world. Looking at the displayed photos and newspaper clippings, you get a sense of the high drama of 1950–51, when the king sought asylum in India and then, having served as the figurehead for resistance efforts against the crumbling Rana regime, returned triumphantly to power. Also on display are thrones, jewel-studded coronation ornaments, royal furniture, guns, trophies and even a casket.

Basantapur Tower

The Tribhuwan Museum leads to the massive nine-storey **Basantapur Tower**, the biggest of the four raised by Prithvi Narayan Shah in honour of the four main cities of the Kathmandu Valley. (Basantapur means "place of spring" and refers to Kathmandu

1

itself. The tower is also referred to as Nautele Durbar, or Nine-Storey Palace.) You can ascend to a kind of crow's nest enclosed by pitched wooden screens to get fine views in four directions.

Mahendra Museum

From the Basantapur Tower you can descend directly to Nassal Chowk, or carry on through labyrinthine corridors to the **Mahendra Museum**. Like the Tribhuwan exhibit, this museum marches chronologically through the life and times of a monarch. The displays include a tally card of the animals Mahendra shot around the world, and recreations of his office and cabinet room. The museum exits onto Lohan Chowk. The adjoining **King Birendra Museum**, dedicated to Mahendra's successor, remains closed following his assassination in 2001 (see box, p.387).

Kumari Chowk

At the southern end of Durbar Square stands **Kumari Chowk**, the gilded cage of Kathmandu's Raj Kumari, the pre-eminent of a dozen or more "**living goddesses**" in the valley (see box below). No other temple better illustrates the living, breathing and endlessly adaptable nature of religion in Nepal, with its freewheeling blend of Hindu, Buddhist and indigenous elements.

Non-Hindus aren't allowed upstairs past the Kumari Chowk's *bahal*-style **courtyard**, which is decorated with exquisitely carved (if weathered) windows, pillars and doorways. When someone slips enough cash to her handlers, the Kumari, dressed in auspicious red and wearing heavy silver jewellery, her forehead painted red with an elaborate "third eye" in the middle, shows herself at one of the first-floor windows. (Your chances of a sighting are higher in the morning or late afternoon.) She's believed to answer her visitors' unspoken questions with the look on her face. Cameras are allowed inside the courtyard, but photographing the Kumari is strictly forbidden.

The chariot that carries the Kumari around during the **Indra Jaatra** festival (see box opposite) is garaged next door to the Kumari Chowk. The big wooden chariot-yokes from past processions, which according to tradition may not be destroyed, are laid out

---

LIVING GODDESSES: THE CULT OF THE KUMARI

The cult of the **Kumari** – a prepubescent girl worshipped as a living incarnation of the goddess Taleju – probably goes back to the early Middle Ages. Jaya Prakash, the last Malla king of Kathmandu, institutionalized the practice when he built the Kumari Chowk in 1757. According to legend, Jaya Prakash, a particularly paranoid and weak king, offended Taleju by lusting after her, and to atone for his sin she ordered him to select a virgin girl in whom the goddess could dwell. He also established the tradition – which ended in 2008 – that each year during the Indra Jaatra festival, the Kumari should bestow a *tika* (auspicious mark) on the forehead of the king who was to reign for the coming year.

Although the Kumari is considered a **Hindu goddess**, she is chosen from the **Buddhist Shakya** clan of goldsmiths, and the traditional selection process is reminiscent of the Tibetan Buddhist method of finding reincarnated lamas. Elders interview Shakya girls aged between three and five, ideally shortlisting those who exhibit 32 auspicious signs: a neck like a conch shell, body like a banyan tree, eyelashes like a cow's and so on. In fact, the physical exam is a standard health check, and far greater emphasis is placed on the girl's **horoscope** (see p.404).

The young goddess lives a cloistered life inside the Kumari Chowk and is only carried outside on her throne during Indra Jaatra (see box opposite) and a handful of other festivals; her feet are never allowed to touch the ground – it took the previous Kumari several weeks to regain her ability to walk after retiring. The goddess's spirit leaves her when she menstruates or otherwise bleeds, whereupon she's **retired** with a modest pension. The transition to life as an ordinary mortal can be hard, and she may have difficulty finding a husband, since legend has it that the man who marries an ex-Kumari will die young. The present Kumari, seven-year-old Unikia Bajracharya, was installed in March 2014.

1

INDRA JAATRA: EIGHT DAYS OF POMP AND PARTYING

According to Kathmandu Valley legend, **Indra**, the Vedic King of Heaven, wanted to buy flowers for his mother. Unable to find any in heaven, he descended to the valley and stole some, but was caught and imprisoned. When Indra's mother came looking for him, the people realized their mistake and to appease him, started an annual festival in his honour.

Usually held in late August or early September (see p.33), **Indra Jaatra** is an occasion to give thanks to the god for bringing the monsoon rains that make the vital summer rice crop possible. Yet Indra's humiliation is a parallel theme, as straw effigies of the god are placed in jails. Another local legend claims that an invading king, calling himself Indra, was defeated by the valley's indigenous people, and some anthropologists believe such an event may have provided the historical impetus for the festival.

Indra Jaatra features eight days of almost nonstop spectacle. It begins with the ceremonial raising of a 15m-tall **pole** in front of the Kala Bhairab statue by members of the Manandhar (oil-presser) caste. In Indrachowk, the famous blue mask of **Akash Bhairab**, a god sometimes identified with Indra, is displayed, as are lesser Bhairab images in other neighbourhoods. Locals do *puja* (an act of worship) to them by day, and light lamps by night in memory of deceased relatives. Masked dancers perform around the old city, and one group stages a tableau of the *das avatar* (the ten incarnations of Vishnu) at the base of the Trailokya Mohan.

Indra Jaatra is the fusion of two festivals, and the second, **Kumari Jaatra**, begins on the afternoon of the third day. From noon, Durbar Square steadily fills up with spectators and, in the balcony of the Gaddi Baithak, with politicians and foreign dignitaries dressed in formal attire. (Tourists are herded into an area around the Shiva Parbati Mandir, where it's hard to get a decent view unless you're right behind the police cordon; however, women can sit on the elevated steps of the Maju Dewal.) Masked dancers entertain the crowd: the one in the red mask and shaggy hair is the popular **Lakhe**, a demon said to keep other spirits at bay if properly appeased. The procession used to begin when the king and queen arrived, but now senior politicians have taken over their roles. The Kumari and two attendants, representing Ganesh and Bhairab, are pulled in wooden **chariots** around the square past the Gaddi Baithak. They then make a circuit of the southern old city, as far as Jaisi Dewal and Lagan, before returning to the square after dark.

When the procession departs, the formal ceremony gives way to all-out partying. **Dance troupes** from around the valley perform near the entrance to the old royal palace, and a pantomime **elephant** – Indra's mount – careers through the streets. Young men gravitate toward **Sweta Bhairab** where, after lengthy ritual preliminaries, rice beer flows from a pipe sticking out of the idol's mouth.

Without the VIPs and ceremonial pomp, the chariots are again pulled the next afternoon, past Nardevi and Asan. On the final day, after a few days of relative calm, the chariots are pulled for a third time to Kilagal. According to legend, this last procession was added by King Jaya Prakash Malla to allow his concubine, who lived in Kilagal, to see the Kumari. In the days of the monarchy, when the chariots returned to Durbar Square later that evening, the king would come before the Kumari to receive the **royal tika** that assured his right to rule for another year. Finally, the ceremonial pole is pulled down, and people take pieces of it as amulets against ghosts and spirits.

nearby. The broad, bricked area to the east is **Basantapur Square**, once the site of royal elephant stables, where souvenir sellers now spread their wares.

The Kasthamandap

According to legend, the **Kasthamandap**, standing at the southwestern end of the square, is Kathmandu's oldest building, and one of the oldest wooden buildings in the world. It's said to have been constructed from the wood of a single tree in the late twelfth century (**Sinha Sattal**, the smaller version to the south, was made from the leftovers), but what you see today is mostly the result of several renovations since 1630. An open, pagoda-roofed pavilion (*mandap*), it served for several centuries as a rest-house (*sattal*) along the Tibet trade route, and probably formed the nucleus of early

1

Kathmandu. This corner of the square, called Maru Tol, still has the look of a crossroads, with vendors hawking fruit, vegetables and flowers. Many of the city's homeless sleep in the Kasthamandap at night.

The Shah kings converted the Kasthamandap into a temple to their lineage deity (see box above), **Gorakhnath**, whose statue stands in the middle of the pavilion. A Brahman priest usually sets up shop here to dispense instruction and conduct rituals. In four niches set around are shrines to Ganesh, the god of good fortune, which are said to represent the celebrated Ganesh temples of the Kathmandu Valley (at Chabahil, Bhaktapur, Chobar and Bungmati), thus enabling Kathmandu residents to pay tribute to all four at once.

Kabindrapur

The building to the southeast of the Kasthamandap is **Kabindrapur**, a temple built in the seventeenth century for the staging of dance performances. Also known as **Dhansa**, it's dedicated to Shiva in his role as Nasa-dyo ("Lord of the Dance" in Newari), and is mostly patronized by musicians and dancers. Opposite Kabindrapur, occupying its own side square, is a brick *shikra* (Indian-style, corncob-shaped temple) to Mahadev (Shiva).

Maru Ganesh

Immediately north of the Kasthamandap stands yet another Ganesh shrine, **Maru Ganesh**. A ring on his bell is usually the preliminary act of any *puja*, and this shrine is the first stop for people intending to worship at the other temples on Durbar Square. Ganesh's trusty "vehicle", a rat, is perched on a plinth of the Kasthamandap, across the way. The lane heading west from here used to be called Pie Alley – in its 1970s hippy heyday it boasted many pie shops, but most have now gone.

Trailokya Mohan

The three-roofed pagoda between the Kasthamandap and the Kumari Chowk is the seventeenth-century **Trailokya Mohan**, dedicated to Narayan (a Nepali name for Vishnu). A much-photographed statue of the angelic Garud, Vishnu's man-bird vehicle, kneels in his customary palms-together *namaste* position in front of the temple.

Gaddi Baithak

The part of the Royal Palace facing the Trailokya Mohan is the **Gaddi Baithak**, a ponderous early twentieth-century addition that pretty much sums up Rana-era architecture. Some purists bemoan the Neoclassical building's distorting effect on Durbar Square's proportions, but it adds a bit of spice to the mix. The west-facing balcony serves as the VIP viewing stand during Indra Jaatra (see box, p.65).

The antiquity of the Durbar Square area was confirmed during the construction of the Gaddi Baithak, when workers uncovered what is believed to be remnants of a Lichhavi-era temple. The find spot is enclosed by a small grate in the middle of the road near the southwest corner of the Gaddi Baithak.

1

Maju Dewal

A few steps north of the Trailokya Mohan, the massive seventeenth-century **Maju Dewal** sits high atop a pyramid of nine stepped levels. If you climb up to the top you will be rewarded with an amazing view of the square.

Shiva Parbati Mandir

Only open 6–8am for *puja*

From the top of the Maju Dewal you can look straight across at the rectangular **Shiva Parbati Mandir**, erected in the eighteenth century by one of the early Shah kings. Painted figures of Shiva and his consort Parbati lean out of the first-floor window, looking like they're about to toss the bouquet and dash off to the honeymoon suite. Despite the temple's popular name, the actual objects of worship inside are nine images of the mother goddesses associated with the nine planets.

Around the Taleju Bell

North of the Shiva Parbati temple, the square narrows and then opens out to another temple-clogged area. Ranged along the left (western) side are the eighteenth-century **Taleju Bell**; the octagonal, seventeenth-century **Chasin Dega**, dedicated to Krishna the flute player; and a pair of ceremonial **drums** from the eighteenth century. The bell and drums were historically sounded as an alarm or call to congregate, but are now used only during the festival of Dasain.

Next to the palace opposite the bell, a small bas-relief depicts **Jambhuwan**, the legendary teacher of Hanuman. Just to the north of this, look up to see the **Kun Jhyal**, a gold-plated window frame flanked by two ivory ones, once used by Malla kings to watch processions in the square below.

Sweta Bhairab

Just beyond the Taleju Bell, set against the palace wall but not very visible behind a wooden screen, is the snarling 3m-high gilded head of **Sweta Bhairab** (White Bhairab), a terrifying, blood-swilling aspect of Shiva. The screen comes down during Indra Jaatra (see box, p.65). The column nearby supports a gilded statue of **King Pratap Malla** and family, a self-congratulatory art form that was all the rage among the Malla kings of the late seventeenth century.

Kala Bhairab

North of the Pratap Malla statue, on the other side of the small Degu Taleju Mandir, the massive, roly-poly image of **Kala Bhairab** (Black Bhairab) dances on the corpse of a demon. Carved from a single 3.5m slab of stone, it was found in a field north of Kathmandu during the reign of Pratap Malla, but probably dates to Lichhavi times. It used to be said that anyone who told a lie in front of it would vomit blood and die. One story has it that when the chief justice's office stood across the way, so many witnesses died while testifying that a temple had to be erected to shield the court from Kala Bhairab's wide-eyed stare.

Jagannath Mandir

Only open 6–8am for *puja*

East of Pratap Malla's column stands the sixteenth-century pagoda-style **Jagannath Mandir**, dedicated to the god whose runaway-chariot festival in India gave us the word "juggernaut". The struts supporting the lower roof of this temple contain Kathmandu's most tittered-about **erotic carvings**, although such images are actually quite common in Nepali temples.

Scholars disagree over the significance of these little vignettes, which often feature outrageous athletics, threesomes and bestiality. Some suggest that sex in this context is being offered as a tantric path to enlightenment, but a more popular belief is that the goddess of lightning is a chaste virgin who wouldn't dare strike a temple so decorated.

1

Nearby, along the palace outer wall, is a **stone inscription** in fifteen languages, carved in 1664 by King Pratap Malla, the prime architect of Durbar Square's temples, and something of a linguist. The inscription is a poem to the goddess Kali, and the story goes that if anyone can read the whole thing, milk will gush from the tap. There are two words in French and one in English.

Taleju Mandir

Set atop a twelve-tiered plinth and rising 40m above the northeast end of the square, the magnificent **Taleju Mandir** looks down on you with haughty grandeur. Kathmandu's biggest temple, it was erected in the mid-sixteenth century by King Mahendra Malla, who decreed that no building should exceed it in height – a ban that remained in force until the middle of the twentieth century. It's open only on the ninth day of Dasain, and then only to Nepalis.

Taleju Bhawani, a South Indian goddess imported in the fourteenth century by the Mallas, is considered by Hindus to be a form of the mother goddess Durga, while Buddhist Newars count her as one of the Taras, tantric female deities. Behind the Taleju Mandir, reached by a doorway from Makhan Tol, sits the brick god-house of **Tarani Devi**, Taleju's "older sister".

North of Durbar Square

Kathmandu's oldest, liveliest streets lie northeast and **north of Durbar Square**. You could make a more or less circular swing through the area, but you'll almost certainly be diverted somewhere along the way. Any "official" sights are simply a backdrop for the old city's fascinating street life.

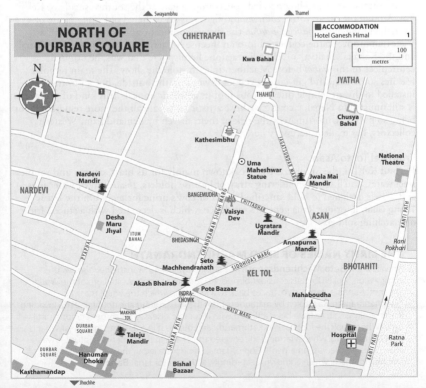

1

Indrachowk

The old trade route to Tibet passes through Durbar Square and becomes a narrow lane after it rounds the Taleju Mandir. Passing through **Makhan Tol** – the name harks back to a time when butter (*makhan*) was sold here – it runs a gauntlet of *thangka* (Buddhist scroll painting) stalls and then takes a northeasterly bearing towards Kathmandu's traditional goldsmiths' neighbourhood.

The first big intersection you reach is **Indrachowk**, named in honour of the Vedic (early Hindu) king of the gods. A sort of Asian Zeus, complete with thunderbolt, Indra fell from grace in India centuries ago, but in the Kathmandu Valley he still warrants his own festival (see box, p.65). The house-like temple on the west side of the crossroads is that of **Akash Bhairab** (Sky, or Blue, Bhairab), considered the equivalent of Indra and represented by a large snarling blue head. Newars also call this deity Aju-dyo, claiming that the idol is what's left of a native king who was beheaded in the Mahabharata epic. The upstairs temple is out of bounds to non-Hindus, while the downstairs is rented out to shopkeepers to fund the temple's upkeep.

Seto Machhendranath

From Indrachowk, the tumultuous **Chandraman Singh Marg** heads north towards Thamel, while the old Tibet road (**Siddhidas Marg**) to its right strikes off northeast towards the junction of Kel Tol. Just before the junction is the seventeenth-century temple of **Seto Machhendranath** (or Sweta Machhendranath), one of two main shrines to the protector god of the Kathmandu Valley. Like his "Red" cousin in Patan (see p.93), "White" Machhendranath (see box below) is feted in a great chariot festival during the month of Chait (March–April).

The entrance to the well-concealed courtyard is a gate at the southwest side of Kel Tol. Among the many votive *chaityas* and figures is a weathered old stone figure of Amitabha (one of the *panchabuddha*, the five personifications of Buddhahood), a Victorian bronze statue converted into an incense holder, three Tara figures on pillars, and the Kanaka Chaitya, a Lichhavi-era stone hemisphere that was the original centrepiece of this *bahal* before Machhendranath stole the show. The main temple features some beautiful gilt-copper repoussé work on the outside, but an iron grille, installed to thwart temple thieves, robs it of its aesthetic appeal. This kind of precaution is still unusual in Nepal, a country whose artistic riches are all the more remarkable for being so public. Unfortunately, the risk of theft, driven by demand from Western collectors, has made it necessary here.

From Kel Tol to Asan

Beyond Kel Tol, the Siddhidas Marg is known mainly for its brass, copper and stainless steel wares: you'll see a bewildering array of incense holders, *thaal* (trays), water jugs and vessels designed to hold sanctified water or cow's urine for *puja*. On the left is **Tilang Ghar**, a former Rana general's residence, which is decorated with a stucco frieze of marching soldiers.

THE MANY NAMES OF SETO MACHHENDRANATH

Newars know **Seto Machhendranath** as Karunamaya Lokeshwar, the *bodhisattva* of compassion, while Tibetans consider him Jowo Dzamling Karmo, White Lord of the World. Yet another name, **Jama-dyo**, traces back to a legend in which the white mask of Machhendranath was stolen by marauders from the west during ancient times. The invading king's family is said to have been afflicted with incurable diseases for six generations, until one of them took the idol back to Kathmandu and buried it in a field in Jamal, near what is now Durbar Marg. When a farmer rediscovered the image in the fifteenth century, it was immediately hailed as Jama-dyo – God of Jamal – and installed in the temple of Seto Machhendranath, which is known, accordingly, as **Jamal** (or Jana) **Bahal**.

Asan

The exuberant intersection of **Asan** is the ancestral home of many of the wealthiest Newari families in the old trading economy. Asan used to be the main fruit and vegetable market north of Durbar Square, and produce is still sold in the streets leading east and north from here, while the trade in spices, home-made balls of soap, candles, oil, incense and other household wares has shifted to Kel Tol and Indrachowk.

The gilt-roofed pagoda at the south side of the square is the **Annapurna Mandir**, dedicated to the goddess of grain and abundance, a manifestation of Lakshmi, the popular goddess of wealth. A lavish affair, the pagoda bristles with icons and imagery, and in festival seasons its roof is strung with electric bulbs like a Christmas tree.

Mahaboudha

From Asan, the trade route angles up to Kantipath and the modern city, while an alley heading south leads to **Mahaboudha**. Stuck in a rather unattractive square and said to date back to the sixth-century king Basantdev, this plain white **stupa** takes its name from the big statue of the Buddha in an adjacent brick shelter.

Bangemudha

Walk westwards from Asan and you'll first pass the small three-tiered pagoda of **Ugratara**, a goddess believed to cure eyesight problems, before returning to the main Indrachowk–Thamel lane at **Bangemudha**. Just south of this square is a somewhat odd shrine to **Vaisya Dev**, the Newari toothache god. Commonly billed as the "Toothache Tree", it's actually the butt end of a log, embedded in the side of a building; it used to be common practice to seek the god's help with dental problems by banging a nail into the log. (Bangemudha – "Crooked Stick" – refers to the legendary tree from which the log was cut.) Nowadays, many dentists advertise their services with grinning signs nearby.

At the north end of Bangemudha, a priceless fifth-century **Buddha figure** stands neglected in a tacky, tiled niche. Continuing north another 100m, you will pass a lattice doorway on the right that opens to a small recess housing a ninth-century **Uma Maheshwar statue**, a standard motif depicting Shiva and Parbati as a cosy couple atop Mount Kailash.

Kathesimbhu

Central Kathmandu's biggest stupa, **Kathesimbhu**, stands in a square off to the left about 200m north of Bangemudha. The temple is only a modest replica of the more impressive Swayambhu stupa (its name is a contraction of "Kathmandu Swayambhu"), but for those too old or infirm to climb to Swayambhu (see p.78), rites performed here earn the same merit. According to legend, it was built with earth left over after Swayambhu's construction; Lichhavi-era sculptures hereabouts attest to the antiquity of the site, but the stupa itself probably dates from the late seventeenth century. Like its namesake, Kathesimbhu has an associated shrine to the smallpox goddess Harati, located in the northwestern corner of the square.

Thahiti and around

Traffic circulates around the stupa at **Thahiti**, the square north of Kathesimbhu on the way to Thamel. Because they're continually replastered, stupas never look very old and are hard to date, but this one probably goes back to the fifteenth century. One of Kathmandu's finest old *bahal*, the seventeenth-century **Chusya Bahal**, stands about two blocks east of Thahiti. It's recognizable by the two stone lions out in front and a meticulously carved wooden *torana* (decorative shield) above the doorway.

Chhetrapati

Just west of Thahiti lies boisterous **Chhetrapati**, a six-way intersection of almost perpetual motion. Though the neighbourhood lacks any ancient monuments, it

1

KATHMANDU'S STREET CHILDREN

Ground down by rural poverty and domestic violence, many Nepalese children run away to the capital in search of a better life. Some are lured by often false promises of high-paying jobs in tourism. The children are frequently referred to as **khate**, a derogatory term referring to scrap plastic collectors. There are estimated to be around 1500 street children in Kathmandu, predominantly boys, and the problem seems to be getting worse.

The conditions street children endure are arguably more debilitating than rural poverty. Homeless, they sleep in doorways, *pati* (open shelters) or unfinished buildings. Weakened and malnourished by a poor diet and contaminated water, few are without disease. Many sniff glue or become addicted to harder drugs. They're regularly beaten by the police, and vulnerable to sexual violence and abuse (including from tourists).

Although it can be hard to say no when street children ask for money or food, in the long term your alms will do far better going to a **charity** than the beggars themselves. For more information, contact Child Workers in Nepal (☎01 428 2255, ⓦcwin.org.np), Just-One (ⓦjust-one.org) or Voice of Children (☎01 554 8018, ⓦvoiceofchildren.org.np).

---

supports a central *pati* (open shelter) resembling an Edwardian bandstand, around which religious processions and impromptu musical jamborees frequently take place. During Shiva Raatri in February, sadhus build fires on the platform and light up their chilams, and during Tihaar the iron railings are decorated with oil lamps.

Pyaphal and the Nardevi Mandir

From Chhetrapati it's a straight run south along **Pyaphal** to the Kasthamandap; this street is favoured as an assembly point for protest marches, since the police can't easily secure it. Midway along is the **Nardevi Mandir**, believed to have been established by the ninth-century founder of Kathmandu, Gunakamadev, though the present structure is merely medieval. The temple's deity, known as Sweta (White) Kali or Neta Ajima, is said to have received human sacrifice in ancient times; visible inside the temple are three silver images of Kali. The area to the west of the temple has a reputation as an important centre of **ayurvedic medicine**, with a college, hospital and many doctors' practices and pharmacies.

Thamel

Old buildings are scarce in the **Thamel** tourist zone, though **Kwa Bahal**, a traditional courtyard tucked away just off the touristy main drag north of Thahiti, is one of several *bahal* in Kathmandu and Patan that have their own Kumaris. **Bhagwan Bahal**, which lends its name to an area north of Thamel Chowk, is home to a little-used pagoda whose most notable feature is a collection of kitchen pans and utensils nailed to the front wall as offerings to the deity. ("Bikrama Sila Mahabihar", the name on the sign in front, refers to a moribund monastery contained within the complex.) During the spring festival of Holi, a portrait of the *bahal's* eleventh-century founder is displayed to celebrate his slaying of demons on his return from a trade delegation to Lhasa.

South of Durbar Square

The old city **south of Durbar Square** is home mainly to working-class castes and, increasingly, immigrant squatters from other parts of Nepal. With fewer traders, it's less touristy than the quarters north of the square, although **New Road**, which bristles and throbs with consumerism, is as lively a street as any in Kathmandu.

Bhimsensthan

A small square southwest of the Kasthamandap, down a lane leading to the Bishnumati River, **Bhimsensthan** is named after one of Nepal's favourite gods. Bhimsen, the

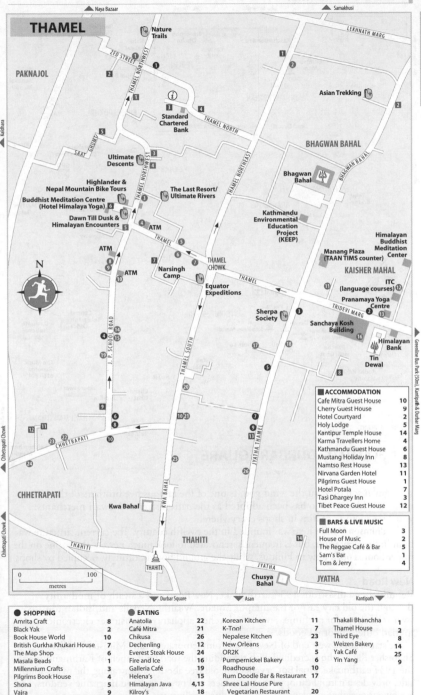

THAMEL

Naya Bazaar

Samakhusi

LEKHNATH MARG

Nature Trails

ZED STREET

THAMEL NORTHWEST

PAKNAJOL

Asian Trekking

THAMEL NORTH

Standard Chartered Bank

BHAGWAN BAHAL

SAAT GHUMTI

THAMEL NORTHWEST

Ultimate Descents

THAMEL NORTHEAST

Bhagwan Bahal

Highlander & Nepal Mountain Bike Tours

The Last Resort/ Ultimate Rivers

Buddhist Meditation Centre (Hotel Himalaya Yoga)

Kathmandu Environmental Education Project (KEEP)

Dawn Till Dusk & Himalayan Encounters

ATM

THAMEL

Himalayan Buddhist Meditation Center

ATM

Manang Plaza (TAAN TIMS counter)

THAMEL CHOWK

KAISHER MAHAL

N

ATM

Narsingh Camp

THAMEL

ITC (language courses)

J. P. SCHOOL ROAD

Equator Expeditions

Pranamaya Yoga Centre

TRIDEVI MARG

Sherpa Society

Sanchaya Kosh Building

THAMEL SOUTH

Himalayan Bank

Tin Dewal

Greenline Bus Park (50m), Kantipath & Durbar Marg

CHHETRAPATI

Kaldhara

Chhetrapati Chowk

Chhetrapati Chowk

CHHETRAPATI

Kwa Bahal

KWA BAHAL

THAHITI

THAHITI

JYATHA THAMEL

THAHITI

Chusya Bahal

JYATHA

0   100
metres

Durbar Square   Asan   Kantipath

ACCOMMODATION
Cafe Mitra Guest House	10
Cherry Guest House	9
Hotel Courtyard	2
Holy Lodge	5
Kantipur Temple House	14
Karma Travellers Home	4
Kathmandu Guest House	6
Mustang Holiday Inn	8
Namtso Rest House	13
Nirvana Garden Hotel	11
Pilgrims Guest House	1
Hotel Potala	7
Tasi Dhargey Inn	3
Tibet Peace Guest House	12

BARS & LIVE MUSIC
Full Moon	3
House of Music	2
The Reggae Café & Bar	5
Sam's Bar	1
Tom & Jerry	4

● SHOPPING
Amrita Craft	8
Black Yak	2
Book House World	10
British Gurkha Khukari House	7
The Map Shop	6
Masala Beads	3
Millennium Crafts	3
Pilgrims Book House	4
Shona	5
Vajra	9

● EATING
Anatolia	22	Korean Kitchen	11	Thakali Bhanchha	1
Café Mitra	21	K-Too!	7	Thamel House	2
Chikusa	26	Nepalese Kitchen	23	Third Eye	8
Dechenling	12	New Orleans	3	Weizen Bakery	14
Everest Steak House	24	OR2K	5	Yak Café	25
Fire and Ice	16	Pumpernickel Bakery	6	Yin Yang	9
Galleria Café	19	Roadhouse	10		
Helena's	15	Rum Doodle Bar & Restaurant	17		
Himalayan Java	4,13	Shree Lal House Pure			
Kilroy's	18	Vegetarian Restaurant	20		

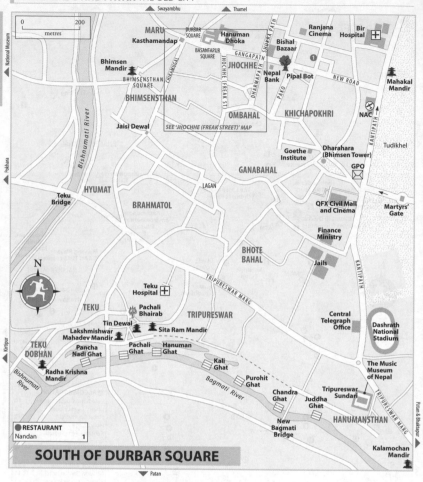

SOUTH OF DURBAR SQUARE

strongman son of Vayu the wind god, is one of the famous five brothers of the Hindu epic Mahabharata who has been adopted as the patron saint of Newari merchants: you'll see pictures of him in shops everywhere.

The **Bhimsen Mandir** here was founded in the twelfth century. The current structure was built in the eighteenth, but is frequently renovated to look much newer. The shrine on the upper floor is open only to Hindus, while the ground floor is, fittingly, occupied by shops.

New Road
Rebuilt after a disastrous 1934 earthquake, **New Road** cuts a swath of modernity through the old city east of Basantapur Square. Wealthy Nepalis and Indian tourists swarm its shops for perfume, jewellery, kitchen appliances, consumer electronics and myriad other imported goods.

The statue at the west end of New Road commemorates Prime Minister Juddha Shamsher Rana, who is credited with rebuilding the road (and much of Kathmandu) after the 1934 earthquake. **Pipal Bot**, a venerable old tree about midway along the road's south side, provides a natural canopy for shoeshiners and newspaper and magazine vendors, and is a favourite gathering place for Kathmandu's intelligentsia and gossipmongers.

Jhochhe (Freak Street)

Immediately south of Basantapur Square, **Jhochhe (Freak Street)** isn't prime sightseeing territory, but it does have unique historical associations. For a few foggy years in the late 1960s and early 1970s, this was an important stop on the hippy trail through Asia. In those days, before the invention of Thamel, Jhochhe was the place to hangout. Grass and hash were legal, and "freaks" had the freedom of the city. It all ended suddenly in 1974, with a series of stricter immigration and drug laws. To catch a whiff of those halcyon days, head to the *Snowman* (see p.108); it was a pie shop just like this that Cat Stevens eulogized in his classic – though now, much like Freak Street itself, neglected – song, *Katmandu*.

Bhimsen Tower and around

A lane heading east from Jhochhe leads to Kathmandu's main fish market and on to **Dharahara**, the tall minaret-like tower overlooking the GPO. Commonly known as **Bhimsen Tower**, it was built in 1832 by the prime minister, Bhimsen Thapa, possibly in imitation of Kolkata's Ochterlony Monument, erected four years earlier. The nearby **Sun Dhara** (Golden Water Tap), a *mandala*-shaped sunken bathing area, was created by Thapa in 1821.

Pachali Bhairab

The most interesting part of south Kathmandu begins with **Pachali Bhairab**, an open-air shrine marooned among the city's maintenance facilities. To find it, head west on Tripureswar Marg and then south on the back road to Patan; finally, bear left at a fork marked by a small park.

Compared to the uninspiring area you've just walked through it feels very peaceful here. The tiny gilded idol of Bhairab stands in a sunken sanctuary, dwarfed by a huge

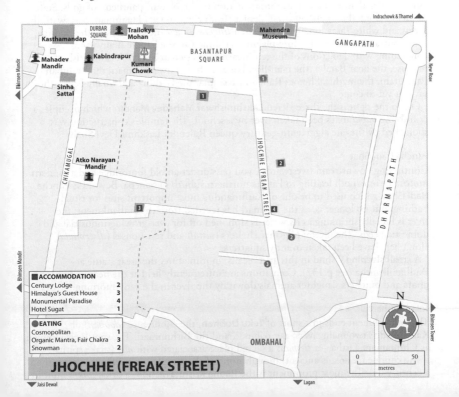

1

pipal tree and a life-sized human figure laid out like a pharaoh's casket. The repoussé figure is a **betal**, Bhairab's vehicle and a likeness of death which, in Nepali Hinduism, is believed to protect against death (the old principle of fighting fire with fire). *Betal* normally take the form of miniature skulls or skeletons at temple entrances, so this one is unusual for being so large.

According to legend this shrine was established by Kathmandu's founder, the ninth-century King Gunakamadev, to protect the city's southern gate. For many centuries, all treaties were signed with Pachali Bhairab as witness, in the belief that the god would strike dead anyone who broke the agreement. A procession starts here on the fourth and fifth nights of Dasain before moving on to Durbar Square.

The Bagmati ghats

A path from Pachali Bhairab leads to the Bagmati River **ghats**, stretching as far as the eye can see in either direction. Statues, temples and all manner of artefacts are jumbled along these stone-paved embankments – especially to the west, where the Bishnumati joins the Bagmati – and you could easily spend several hours here. The area has been the subject of a proposed restoration project for many years – several link roads that aim to reduce the city's chronic congestions are also being built – so perhaps it will some day enjoy a much-deserved renaissance. For the time being, though, it's in a pretty sorry state of neglect.

Pachali Ghat

The path forks before reaching the river, but both ways lead to **Pachali Ghat** and its remarkable collection of Hindu and Buddhist statuary. If you take the right fork, you'll enter an area that serves as a neat introduction to the Newari pantheon of gods. Statues in niches along the right-hand wall depict (from right to left) Hanuman, Saraswati, the green and white Taras, Bhairab, Ganesh, a *linga/yoni*, a standing Vishnu, the Buddha, Ram, Shiva as sadhu, and a flute-playing Krishna. On the left are many more, concluding with depictions of the ten incarnations (*das avatar*) of Vishnu: fish, tortoise, the boar Baraha, the man-lion Narasingh, the dwarf Vaman, the Brahman Parasuram, the mythical heroes Ram and Krishna, the Buddha and finally Kalki, the saviour yet to come.

Off to the right is the three-tiered **Lakshmishwar Mahadev Mandir**, which occupies a crumbling *bahal* that's been taken over by a school. The temple's construction was sponsored by the late eighteenth-century queen Rajendra Laskhmi Devi Shah.

Pancha Nadi Ghat

Continuing downstream (westwards), you pass under an old footbridge and a modern motorable one, both leading to Patan's northern suburb of Sanepa. Beyond is **Pancha Nadi Ghat**, which used to be one of Kathmandu's most important sites for ritual bathing, but no longer is, as the Bagmati has receded from the embankment: the river is literally shrinking as its water is siphoned off for ever-growing industrial and domestic needs. The several pilgrims' shelters (*sattal*) and rest-houses (*dharmsala*) along here have been taken over by squatters.

A small **sleeping Vishnu** in this area recalls, in miniature, the great statue at Budhanilkantha (see p.137). Cremations are infrequently held at the nearby **burning ghats** and butchers slaughter animals down by the river in the early morning.

Teku Dobhan

The embankment ends just short of **Teku Dobhan**, the confluence (*dobhan*) of Kathmandu's two main rivers, the Bagmati and the Bishnumati. The spot is also known as Chintamani Tirtha – a *tirtha* is a sacred place associated with *nag* (snake spirits).

The confluence area is ancient, though none of the temples or buildings is more than a century old. The most prominent is the **Radha Krishna Mandir**, a brick *shikra* built in the 1930s; flute-playing Krishna is the middle of three figures inside. The rest-house behind the temple, **Manandhar Sattal**, is named after a wealthy nineteenth-century trader who was forced to retire here after his property was confiscated by the prime minister. The next-door building is an unused electric crematorium built in the 1970s. The riverbank from here downstream to the Ring Road has been used as a landfill: this dumping site, like an earlier one further upstream near the Pashupatinath temple complex, will leak toxins into the river for decades to come.

Tin Dewal

Heading upstream (eastwards) from Pachali Ghat, you reach the atmospheric **Tin Dewal** ("Three Temples") by an entrance from the riverside. The temple's popular name refers to its three brick *shikra* sharing a common base and ground floor – an unusual combination of Indian and Nepali styles, with some fine brick detailing.

A sign identifies the site by its official name, which is transliterated into English as Bomveer Vikalashora Shibalaya. The complex was erected in 1850 by Bom Bahadur Kunwar, brother of Jang Bahadur Rana, who'd seized power in a bloody coup four years earlier. A *shivalaya* (a shrine containing a *linga*) can be seen behind each of the temple's three lattice doors.

Further east there's a 300m break in the embankment, as a path makes its way through a semi-permanent **shantytown**. Its residents – landless rubbish-pickers, day labourers and street vendors – have moved in as the river has receded, and take their chances each monsoon.

Tripureswar Sundari

From the area known as **Hanumansthan**, east of Tin Dewal, a path leads away from the river to Tripureswar Marg via the **Tripureswar Sundari**. The square's central **temple**, a massive three-tiered pagoda dedicated to Mahadev (Shiva), was erected in the early nineteenth century by Queen Lalit Tripura Sundari in memory of her husband Rana Bahadur Shah, who was assassinated in one of the period's many episodes of court intrigue. The square is currently being spruced-up as a tourist site, and the collective of low-caste families who are squatting there will be evicted to make way for craft shops.

The Music Museum of Nepal

Tripureswar Sundari • Sun–Fri 11am–4pm • Rs200 • ☎ 01 424 2741, ⓦ nepalmusicmuseum.org

On the north side of Tripureswar Sundari, the tiny **Music Museum of Nepal** holds the country's largest collection of musical instruments – over 650 in total. At any one time around two hundred instruments are exhibited, arranged by ethnic group in the museum's dusty first-floor gallery. Many of the instruments are available for you to try out, or you can listen to them using the museum's extensive sound archive, or in the hall where music students regularly come to practise on traditional instruments.

Kalamochan Mandir

Southeast of Tripureswar Marg, with its buzzing, sputtering cross-town traffic, lies the marvellously hideous **Kalamochan Mandir**, a study in Rana excess, resembling a grotesque white wedding cake, with gargoyles snarling at its four corners.

West of the Bishnumati

Most of Kathmandu **west of the Bishnumati River** was settled relatively recently, with much of the development focused on the ugly Kalimati–Kalanki corridor and the suburbs either side. The only real antiquities are the famous **Swayambhu** stupa and a few shrines and temples that can be visited en route, plus the exhibits preserved in the **National Museum**. All of these sights are within fairly easy walking distance of central

1

Kathmandu or Thamel, but to make a circuit of all of them it's more pleasant to hire a bike or taxi for the day (taxis wait at Swayambhu, but are hard to find near the museum). A visit to Swayambhu can be turned into a longer hike or bike trip by continuing on to Ichangu Narayan (see p.141).

Swayambhu

Daily 7am–7pm • Rs200, paid at booths at the main entrances • Buses run irregularly between the City Bus Park (see p.96) and Swayambhu's eastern entrance; a taxi will cost Rs200 from Thamel. On foot, from Thamel the easiest way is via Chhetrapati, from where a small road heads straight towards Swayambhu, passing Hotel Vajra en route; from Jhochhe or Durbar Square, take the lane running northwest from the Maru Ganesh shrine; either way, it should take about 20min

Swayambhu (or Swayambhunath), magnificently set atop a conical hill 2km west of Thamel, is a great place to get your bearings, geographically and culturally, in your first few days in Nepal: the hill commands a sweeping view of the Kathmandu Valley, and the temple complex is overrun with pilgrims and monkeys.

The ancient **stupa** – which has benefited from a recent renovation – is the most profound expression of Buddhist symbolism in Nepal (many *bahal* in the valley contain a replica of it), and the source of the valley's creation myth. Inscriptions date the stupa to the fifth century, and there's reason to believe the hill was used for animist rites even before Buddhism arrived in the valley two thousand years ago. Tantric Buddhists consider it the chief "power point" of the Kathmandu Valley; one chronicle states that an act of worship here carries thirteen billion times more merit than anywhere else. To call it the "Monkey Temple" (its tourist nickname) is to trivialize it.

Since the Chinese invasion of Tibet in 1959, the surrounding area has become home to many exiled Tibetans. You'll see them and many other Buddhist pilgrims making a full circumambulation (*kora*) of the hill, queuing up to spin the gigantic fixed prayer wheels and the six thousand smaller ones that encircle the perimeter, and frequently twirling their own hand-held ones. The place is so steeped in lore and pregnant with detail that you'll never absorb it all in a single visit. Try going early in the morning at *puja* time, or at night when the red-robed monks pad softly around the dome, murmuring mantras.

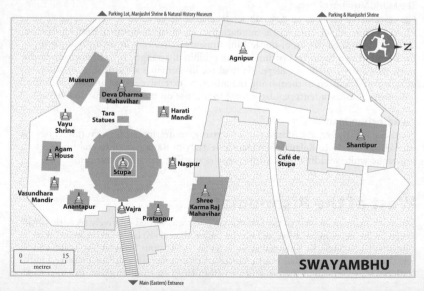

SWAYAMBHU

THE LEGEND OF MANJUSHRI

According to Buddhist scriptures, the Kathmandu Valley was once a snake-infested lake – and geologists agree about the lake (see p.381). Ninety-one aeons ago, a perfect, radiant lotus flower appeared on the surface of the lake, which the gods proclaimed to be Swayambhu ("self-created"), the abstract essence of Buddhahood. **Manjushri**, the *bodhisattva* of knowledge, drew his sword and cut a gorge at Chobar, south of Kathmandu, to drain the lake and allow humans to worship Swayambhu. As the water receded, the lotus settled on top of a hill and Manjushri established a shrine to it, before turning his attention to ridding the valley of snakes (see p.405) and establishing its first civilization. Another legend tells how, when Manjushri cut his hair at Swayambhu, the strands that fell on the ground grew into trees, and the lice turned into monkeys.

A paved road circles the base of the hill. Although there are several other ways up, the steep main path from the **eastern entrance**, with its three-hundred-odd centuries-smoothed steps, is the most dramatic. The **Buddha statues** near the bottom are from the seventeenth century, while a second group further up was donated in the early part of the twentieth century. The chiselled slates sold by entrepreneurs along the path are *mani* stones, inscribed, in Tibetan script, with the ubiquitous Buddhist mantra *Om mani padme hum* – "Hail to the jewel in the lotus" (see box, p.397).

You can get **food** at a few snack places near the eastern entrance, at the far (northwestern) side of the stupa precinct (*Café de Stupa* is overpriced but has good views) and at the southern base of the hill. Beware of the monkeys: they'll snatch at anything that even looks like food.

Swayambhu's main **festivals** are Buddha Jayanti (April or May) and Losar (Feb or March), when pilgrims throng around the stupa and monks splash arcs of saffron paint over it in a lotus-flower pattern. Many also flock here each morning during the month-long Gunla festivities (Aug or Sept) to mark the "rain's retreat" with music and offerings to the monks.

Swayambhu stupa

The apparently simple structure of **Swayambhu stupa** belies an immensely complex physical representation of Buddhist cosmology, and the purpose of walking round it is to meditate on this. The solid, whitewashed dome (*garbha*) symbolizes the womb or creation. Set in niches at the cardinal points, statues of **dhyani** (meditating) **Buddhas** correspond to the four elements (earth, air, fire and water) and a fifth, placed at an angle, to the sky or space. Each represents a different aspect of Buddhahood: the hand positions, colours and "vehicles" (the animal statues below) of each are significant. The *dhyani* Buddhas are the same characters who appear on virtually every *chaitya* around the Kathmandu Valley. At each of the sub-cardinal points sit **female counterparts**, who in tantric Buddhism represent the wisdom aspect that must be united – figuratively speaking – with the compassionate male force to achieve enlightenment.

The gilded **cube** (*harmika*) surmounting the stupa surrounds a thick wooden pillar, which may be considered the phallic complement to the female dome. The **eyes** painted on it are those of the all-seeing Adi-Buddha (primordial Buddha), staring in all four directions. Between the eyes is a curl of hair (*urna*), one of the identifying features of a Buddha; the thing that looks like a nose is a miraculous light emanating from the *urna* (it can also be interpreted as the Nepali figure "one", conveying the unity of all things). A **spire** of gold disks stacked above the pillar represents the thirteen steps to enlightenment, while the *torana*, or gold plaques above the painted eyes, also show the five *dhyani* Buddhas, known collectively as the *panchabuddha*. Finally, the umbrella at the top symbolizes the attainment of enlightenment: some say it contains a bowl filled with precious gems.

1

Around Swayambhu stupa

Swayambhu stupa is surrounded by an incredible array of **shrines** and votive items, most of which have been donated over the past four centuries by merit-seeking kings and nobles.

Vajra

The bronze sceptre-like object at the top of the steps is a vastly oversized **vajra**, a tantric symbol of power and indestructibility; its pedestal is carved with the twelve animals of the Tibetan zodiac. Until recently twin bullet-shaped *shikra* stood on either side of this, known as **Pratappur** and **Anantapur**, which were installed by King Pratap Malla during a seventeenth-century dispute with Tibet, on the advice of an Indian guru. Unfortunately, the former collapsed in 2011 after being struck by lightning; a restoration effort is planned.

Vasundhara Mandir

Moving around clockwise, as is the custom at all stupas, you will come to the brick hut to the south of Anantapur, **Vasundhara Mandir**, dedicated to the earth goddess Vasundhara, who's more or less synonymous with Annapurna and Lakshmi, the goddesses of grain and wealth respectively. Further on – beyond the priests' quarters and a number of *chaitya* – is a small marble-faced shrine to **Vayu**, the Vedic god of wind and storms.

Around the Deva Dharma Mahavihar

A little **museum** behind the Vayu shrine contains bas-relief statues of gods, Buddhist and Hindu, which are beautiful to look at, but only tersely identified. Next door and up a flight of steps is the **Deva Dharma Mahavihar**, a small, uneventful monastery, open to the public. In front of this, close to the stupa behind protective caging, stand two acclaimed bronze statues of the **White and Green Taras**, deified princess wives of an eighth-century Tibetan king.

Harati Mandir

A few paces beyond the Deva Dharma Mahavivar squats **Harati Mandir**, a gilt-roofed temple built to appease **Harati** (also known as **Ajima**), traditionally the goddess of smallpox but now regarded as governing all childhood diseases. Like many Newari deities, Harati/Ajima is both feared (as a bringer of disease) and revered (as a protectress, if properly appeased). Harati/Ajima's shrine is extremely popular, and you'll see queues of mothers with kids in tow, waiting to make offerings. The nineteenth-century idol was carved to replace an earlier one smashed by King Rana Bahadur Shah after his wife died of smallpox.

Agnipur

Agnipur, an insignificant-looking lump on the pavement in the extreme northwest corner of the complex, marked by two tiny lions in front, is a seldom-visited shrine to the Vedic fire god Agni, the relayer of burnt offerings to heaven.

Around Shree Karma Raj Mahavihar

Nagpur, a bathtub-sized tank at the north point of the stupa, propitiates the valley's snake spirits, and when it's not filled with water you can see the idol at the bottom. Nearby, the **Shree Karma Raj Mahavihar**, an active monastery at the northeast corner of the compound, contains a big Buddha and numerous butter candles, which Tibetan Buddhists light for much the same reasons as Catholics do. You can catch the sonorous chanting of the monks at around 3pm or 4pm every day.

RIGHT DURBAR SQUARE, PATAN (P.88)>

1

Shantipur

A 1500-year-old mystery surrounds **Shantipur**, the otherwise plain, box-like building northwest of Swayambhu stupa. Shanti Shri, a fifth-century holy man, is supposed to have sealed himself in a vault beneath the temple to meditate, vowing not to emerge until the valley needed him. Commentators write that he subsequently attained a mystic state of immortality, and according to devout believers he's still in there.

King Pratap Malla, who entered the chamber in 1658 to seek magical help in ending a drought, experienced adventures worthy of Indiana Jones. According to scholar Keith Dowman, the king recounted how he entered alone and descended to the second subterranean level. In the first room "bats as large as kites or hawks came to kill the light", while in the second room "ghosts, flesh-eating spirits and hungry ghosts came to beg", clutching at anyone who failed to pacify them. Of the third room he said, "If you cannot pacify the snakes by pouring out milk, they chase and bind you. Having pacified them you can walk on their bodies". Finally, Pratap Malla found the saint in an almost skeletal form, and was rewarded with a *nag* rain-making emblem.

Faded **frescoes** on the walls of the outer sanctum show scenes from the Swayambhu Purana, a seventeenth-century scripture recounting the story of Manjushri's sword act and other creation myths. Shantipur, also known as Akashpur ("Sky-place"), completes a cycle of shrines to the five elemental spirits: earth, air, fire, water (snakes) and sky.

The Manjushri Shrine

The **Manjushri Shrine**, located on a prayer-flag-capped spur of the hilltop 50m to the west of Swayambhu, comes second only to the main stupa in antiquity – the canopied *chaitya* is reckoned to be 1500 years old. Manjushri, the Buddhist god of wisdom and founder of civilization in the valley, is traditionally depicted by an empty niche in the *chaitya*, but an image of Saraswati, the Hindu goddess of learning, was placed in the niche three hundred years ago, and so the shrine is now on the pilgrimage circuit for Hindus as well. Schoolchildren make a special trip here on Saraswati Puja, in late January or early February, to have their books and pencils blessed.

The Natural History Museum

Sun–Fri 10am–4pm • Rs50; camera Rs50 • ☎ 01 427 1899

The morbidly amusing **Natural History Museum** is on your right as you follow the road from the car park down the south side of Swayambhu hill. Its jumbled collection of stuffed birds and shrivelled animals in old-fashioned display cases looks like it was cobbled together from the trophy rooms of hoary old Rana hunters; exhibits include an eight-legged lamb, an Atlas moth (the world's largest) and various pickled embryos. The weirdness is fun for its own sake though, and the specimens might give you an idea of what to look for when you get to Nepal's mountains or jungles.

Bijeshwari and around

Bijeshwari, along the west bank of the Bishnumati on the way to Swayambhu, used to be Kathmandu's execution ground. While Tibetans and other immigrants broke the taboo against settling near the cursed ground a generation ago, a fear of ghosts still endures, as do two important but little-visited temples.

Bijeshwari Mandir

Bijeshwari Bahal, perched at the top of a flight of steps above the river, is the centre of worship of an esoteric Buddhist goddess, Bijeshwari (Lord of Victory), who is also known as Akash (Sky) Yogini and sometimes counted as the fifth of the valley's Bajra Yoginis, the wrathful aspects of the tantric Tara goddesses.

1

Shoba Bhagwati Mandir

Just upstream of Bijeshwari Bahal stands a cremation pavilion, and beyond that, the Hindu **Shobha Bhagwati Mandir**. Bhagwati is a common Nepali name for the mother goddess, and this idol of her is considered to be among the most powerful manifestations in the valley: early in the morning you might see political candidates, students preparing for exams, or anyone requiring quiet strength coming here to perform *puja* for her. According to legend, the sculptor of the Shobha Bhagwati image here carved it with his feet, his hands having been cut off by a jealous king to prevent him from reproducing an earlier masterwork in the king's collection.

The National Museum

Mon 10.30am–2.30pm, Tues, Wed & Fri–Sun 10.30am–4.30pm • Rs150; camera Rs100 • ☎ 01 427 1478, ⓦ nationalmuseum.gov.np

The **National Museum**, based in an old Rana armoury 1km south of Swayambhu, is no curatorial coup, but you'll come away from it with a better appreciation of the intertwining of religion, art, myth and history in Nepal.

The art building

Count on spending most of your time in the **art building**. The collection of **stone sculptures** showcases an amazing artistic consistency spanning almost two thousand years, from the Lichhavi period (second to ninth centuries) through to the tantric-influenced Malla dynasties (thirteenth to eighteenth centuries). The oldest is a life-size statue of King Jaya Varma from 184 AD. The **metalwork** exhibit pays tribute to a later art form which blossomed under patronage from Tibet. A trio of stunning fourteenth-century bronzes of tantric deities form the centrepieces.

Other exhibits include exceptional images, window frames and *torana* (ornate shields mounted over the doors of temples) carved from **wood**. On the ground floor are a couple of dozen rare **poubha** (Nepali scroll paintings) from the sixteenth century and later.

The Buddhist Art Gallery

The red-brick building at the back of the compound houses the **Buddhist Art Gallery**, which gives a patchy overview of artistic traditions from three distinct parts of the country. The **Terai** section represents the most ancient and archeologically important area in Nepal: the environs of Lumbini, the Buddha's birthplace. The **Kathmandu Valley** section surveys the valley's considerable artistic contributions in brass, stone and painting from a Buddhist perspective. Finally, the small **Northern Himalayan** section contains *thangka*, bronzes and ritual objects.

The history building

A Rana-style mansion on the right as you enter the compound, the **history building** is aimed mainly at school groups, with a hotchpotch of animal carcasses, bones, dolls, a moon rock, and weaponry. The top floor houses the **National Numismatic Museum**, displaying coins representing the reign of every Nepali king from the Malla and Shah dynasties.

East of Kantipath

Old photographs of Kathmandu show the area **east of Kantipath** dominated by the palaces and residences of the ruling Rana family, with villages – Hadigaun, Dilli Bazaar, Baneswar – surrounded by farmland beyond. Today, the palaces have mostly been taken over by government ministries, while the boulevards around the old Royal Palace are lined with airline offices and high-end hotels; the old villages have become congested bazaars, and the farmland subdivided into walled suburban compounds.

KANTIPATH & DURBAR MARG

EATING

1905	2
Bhanchha Ghar	8
Chimney	4
Dudh Sagar	7
Kaiser Café	1
Korea Pyongyang Arirang Restaurant	6
Koto	5
Moti Mahal Delux	3

ACCOMMODATION

Hotel Yak & Yeti	1

LIVE MUSIC

Madhushala	1
Raj Gharana	2

The sacred Hindu pilgrimage site of **Pashupatinath**, which lies just east of the Ring Road, 4km from central Kathmandu, is covered in the "Kathmandu Valley" chapter (see p.118).

Kaisher Mahal

On the corner of Tridevi Marg and Kantipath • **Kaisher Library** Mon–Thurs, Sat & Sun 10am–4/5pm, Fri 10am–3pm • Free • ☎ 01 441 1318, ⊛ klib.gov.np • **Garden of Dreams** Daily 9am–10pm • Rs200 • ☎ 01 442 5340, ⊛ gardenofdreams.org.np

Kaisher Mahal, former residence of Field Marshal Kaisher Shamsher Rana (1891–1964), now serves as a government building. Inside, the **Kaisher Library** has long shelves of European books, cabinets of Sanskrit manuscripts, a suit of armour, a stuffed tiger and portraits of famous acquaintances.

Kaisher Shamsher Rana is said to have laid out the grounds of his mansion as a "**Garden of Dreams**", with areas devoted to each of the six seasons and trees planted to ensure that different fruits ripened year-round. Today this idyllic spot provides a wonderful respite from the nearby Thamel chaos, with an excellent restaurant (see p.109), photo gallery and regular cultural events. Keep an eye out for the giant fruit bats in the trees.

The Royal Palace (Narayanhiti Palace Museum)

Thurs–Mon 11am–3pm • Rs500 • ☎ 01 01 552 1492

An architectural travesty from the 1960s, the **Royal Palace** is a looming, pink-hued construction. Built in front of an earlier palace dating from around 1900, it was inaugurated in 1970 for then Crown Prince Birendra's wedding. Its Nepali name refers to a water tap (*hiti*) east of the main entrance.

Many Nepalis avert their eyes when they walk past the palace, or avoid passing it altogether, for it evokes painful memories as the scene of the inexplicable **royal massacre** of June 1, 2001, when Crown Prince Dipendra killed his entire immediate family and five other relatives before apparently turning the gun on himself (see box, p.387).

In early 2009, the government opened up part of the Royal Palace as a **museum**. It offers a fascinating snapshot of the former monarchy, with kitsch and opulent 1960s interiors, a well-stocked library, photos of past visitors and over-the-top features like tiger and crocodile skins. The building where the massacre happened was razed to the ground shortly after the event, but the museum has helpfully (and some might say gruesomely) put signs on the remaining foundations to indicate where each victim fell.

Around Rani Pokhari

Rani Pokhari (Queen's Pool), the large square tank east of Asan, was built in the seventeenth century by King Pratap Malla to console his queen after the death of their favourite son; the shrine in the middle, opened one day a year during the Tihaar festival, is more recent. The pavements around the pool and nearby **Ratna Park** (officially renamed Shankhadhar Park) are active centres for small-time trade, including prostitution.

East of Rani Pokhari rises the c.1900 **Ghanta Ghar** (clock tower) – like Bhimsen Tower, a landmark only in the functional sense – and Kathmandu's two **mosques**. Muslims first settled in Kathmandu as traders five centuries ago, and now represent only a tiny fraction of Nepal's half-million "Musalmans".

Around the Tudikhel

Kathmandu's **Tudikhel** is the biggest military parade ground in Nepal. Percival Landon, an early twentieth-century traveller, proclaimed it "level as Lord's", as in London's famous cricket ground. An institution rooted in Nepal's warring past, the *tudikhel* is a feature of every town of consequence throughout the hills. Unfortunately, although Kathmandu's Tudikhel provides a sizeable chunk of open space in the middle of the city, it's no green lung: it has few trees and actually adds to the city's pollution problem by forcing traffic to bottleneck around it.

On the Kantipath side of the Tudikhel stands the **Mahakal Mandir**, whose modern surroundings have in no way diminished the reverence of its worshippers: pedestrians and motorists commonly touch a hand to the forehead as they pass. East of the Tudikhel, **Bhrikuti Mandap** serves as an amusement park and part-time exhibition ground. The nearby **Martyrs' Gate** commemorates the four ringleaders of a failed 1940 attempt to overthrow the Rana regime.

Singha Durbar

Undoubtedly the most impressive structure ever raised by the Ranas, **Singha Durbar** dominates the governmental quarter in the southeastern part of the city. Once the biggest building in Asia, the prime ministers' palace of a thousand rooms was built in 1901 by Chandra Shamsher Rana, who employed workers round the clock for two years to complete it and fill it with European extravagances, all for the then unconscionable sum of Rs2.5 million. It's said that the entire population of Kathmandu abstained from *daal*, an ingredient in traditional mortar, during the construction.

1

The palace was mostly destroyed by fire in 1973, and only the main wing was restored for use as parliamentary offices. Numerous governmental ministries, departments and the Gallery Baithak (home of Nepal's parliament) now occupy new buildings and original outbuildings elsewhere in the vast complex. You can peek at the main wing's colonnaded facade through the sweeping front (western) gate.

Baber Mahal Revisited

Off Airport Rd • Daily 9am–11pm • Free • ⓦ babermahal-revisited.com

Baber Mahal Revisited lies off a tree-lined street south of Singha Durbar. A restored Rana palace with shops, restaurants and peaceful courtyards, it's a heavenly retreat. Many taxi drivers are unfamiliar with the complex, and will assume you mean Baber Mahal, a ministry building off the Airport Road, just to the south. Fortunately, it's only a short walk away.

Eastern neighbourhoods

While Kathmandu's eastern and northeastern neighbourhoods have little of scenic interest, they do provide insights into contemporary life in the capital.

Crowded **Bagh Bazaar** and **Dilli Bazaar** pretty much sum up one end of the spectrum, with their computer institutes, lawyers' cubbyholes, and shops selling office furniture and "suitings and shirtings". Dilli Bazaar is also the home of Nepal's stock exchange. The other extreme is found further north in the shady lanes of **Bhatbateni**, **Baluwatar** and **Maharajganj**, where old, new and foreign money hides in walled compounds, along with embassies, aid organizations and corporate mansions.

Between the two lie the hopeful settlements of a burgeoning middle class, who build their houses one floor at a time, and send their children off in uniforms to "English boarding schools" with names such as "Bright Future" and "Radiant Readers".

Hadigaun

Like most ancient cities, Kathmandu was formed by the gradual merging of once-separate villages. Excavations suggest **Hadigaun**, now a northeastern suburb, is one of the oldest of Kathmandu's original settlements. Evidence of Hadigaun's age comes from the overgrown fifth-century Vishnu shrine, **Dhum Barahi**, in a schoolyard a further 1km northeast; here, inside the small brick shelter, a whimsical fifth-century image illustrates the tale of Barahi (Vishnu in his incarnation as a boar) rescuing the earth goddess Prithvi from the bottom of the sea. To get here, head north out of Hadigaun and when in doubt always take the right fork.

Patan (Lalitpur)

Now largely absorbed by greater Kathmandu, and easy to reach from the centre of town (see p.98), **PATAN** was once the capital of a powerful independent kingdom, and still maintains a defiantly distinct identity. Compared to Kathmandu it's quieter, less frenetic and more Buddhist. Patan is sophisticated and, in a Nepali sort of way, bohemian: while Kathmanduites are busy amassing power and wealth, Patan's residents appreciate the finer things of life, which perhaps explains the area's alternate name, **Lalitpur** ("City of Beauty"). Above all, it remains a proud city of **artisans**. Patan produces much of Nepal's fine metalwork, and its craftspeople have created some of the most extraordinarily lavish temples, *hiti* and *bahal* in the country. *Bahal* – their doorways here always guarded by cuddly stone lions with overbites – are a particular feature of Patan, and a few still function as active monasteries. In the past two decades, Patan has also emerged as the de facto

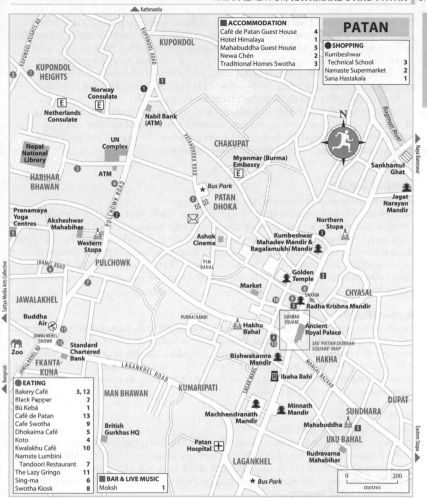

PATAN

foreign aid capital of Nepal: the offices of the UN and innumerable NGOs are scattered around the western suburbs, as are many expat residences.

Brief history

In legend and in fact, Patan is the oldest city in the Kathmandu Valley. **Manjushri**, the great lake-drainer, is supposed to have founded Manjupatan, the forerunner of Patan, right after he enshrined Swayambhu, while the so-called Ashokan stupas, earthen mounds standing at four cardinal points around Patan, seem to support the legend that the Indian emperor **Ashoka** visited the valley in the third century BC (historians are sceptical). More reliable legend ascribes Patan's founding to **Yalambar**, second-century king of the Kirats, an ancient tribe that provided the original stock for the valley's Newari population (which explains the traditional Newari name for Patan, **Yala**), or to the Lichhavi King **Arideva** at the end of the third century.

Under the long-running Lichhavi dynasty, Patan emerged as the cultural and artistic capital of Nepal, if not the entire Himalayan region. It maintained strong links with

1

the **Buddhist** centres of learning in Bengal and Bihar – thereby playing a role in the transmission of Buddhism to Tibet – and when these fell to the Muslims in the twelfth century, many scholars and artists fled to Patan, setting the stage for a renaissance under the later **Malla** kings. Patan existed as part of a unified valley kingdom until the late fifteenth century, then enjoyed equal status with Kathmandu and Bhaktapur as a sovereign state until 1769, when Prithvi Narayan Shah and his Gorkhali band conquered the valley and chose Kathmandu for their capital.

One of Patan's charms is that its historic core is frozen much as it was at the time of defeat. However, see it while you can: although a number of temples and public monuments have been skilfully restored in recent years, the city has lost many of its older private buildings in the name of modernization.

Durbar Square

Open 24hr • Tourists must pay a Rs500 admission fee 7am–7pm

Smaller and less monumental than its equivalent in Kathmandu, Patan's **Durbar Square** comes across as more refined and less touristy. Maybe it's because the city of artisans has a better eye for architectural harmony; or because Patan, which hasn't been a capital since the eighteenth century, has escaped the continuous meddling of monument-building kings. The formula is, however, similar to that in Kathmandu, with a solemn **royal palace** looming along one side and assorted **temples** grouped in the remaining public areas.

Ancient Royal Palace

Patan's richly decorated **Ancient Royal Palace** was largely constructed during the second half of the seventeenth century, but substantially rebuilt after both the Gorkhali invasion of 1769 and the 1934 earthquake. The palace consists of three main wings, each enclosing a central courtyard and reached by a separate entrance. There have been plans to open up more of the interior of the palace for some time, but they are yet to come to fruition at the time of writing.

Patan Museum

Daily 10.30am–5.30pm • Rs250 • ☎ 01 552 1492

The Royal Palace's northernmost wing, Mani Keshab Narayan Chowk, once served as the palace of another noted seventeenth-century king, Yoganarendra Malla. It was badly damaged in the 1934 earthquake, and at the time was only clumsily rebuilt. With assistance from the Austrian government, however, it has been restored to house the splendid **Patan Museum**.

The museum displays a well-curated **permanent collection** of important bronzes, stone sculptures and woodcarvings, a gilded Malla throne and archival photographs. The exhibits are arranged thematically to lead you through Hindu, Buddhist and tantric iconography, temple construction, ritual objects and metallurgical processes, all supported by excellent explanatory text.

Moreover, the building itself, with its newly stuccoed walls and artful lighting, suggests the royal palace Yoganarendra Malla might have built had he reigned at the beginning of the twenty-first century. From the interior balconies you can lookout onto the courtyard below and its central Lakshmi shrine, and watch the *kinkinimali*, leaf-shaped tin cut-outs hanging from the eaves, fluttering in the breeze. A stunning gold window above the exterior main entrance depicts Vishnu and a heavenly host.

There's a sedate **café**, run by the *Summit Hotel*, in the courtyard behind the museum (you don't need an entry ticket to eat here), and a **gift shop**. The courtyard also hosts regular **concerts**.

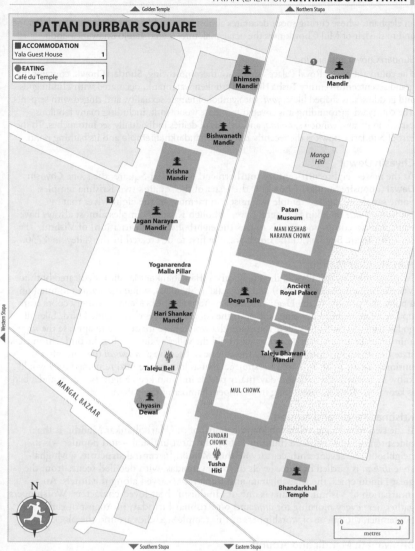

PATAN DURBAR SQUARE

ACCOMMODATION
Yala Guest House — 1

EATING
Café du Temple — 1

Golden Temple

Northern Stupa

Bhimsen Mandir

Ganesh Mandir

Bishwanath Mandir

Manga Hiti

Krishna Mandir

Patan Museum

MANI KESHAB NARAYAN CHOWK

Jagan Narayan Mandir

Yoganarendra Malla Pillar

Ancient Royal Palace

Degu Talle

Hari Shankar Mandir

Taleju Bhawani Mandir

Western Stupa

Taleju Bell

MANGAL BAZAAR

MUL CHOWK

Chyasin Dewal

SUNDARI CHOWK

Tusha Hiti

Bhandarkhal Temple

N

0 — 20
metres

Southern Stupa

Eastern Stupa

Degu Talle

The monolithic **Degu Talle**, a Taleju temple, towers just south of the museum. Seven storeys high and the tallest building on the block, it was erected in 1640 by Siddhi Narsingh Malla, during whose reign much of the palace and square were built, but had to be completely rebuilt after being razed in the 1934 earthquake.

Mul Chowk and around

Mul Chowk, the Royal Palace wing to the south of Degu Talle, served as the royal family residence until Patan's fall in 1769. A deteriorated gilt door in the right-hand wall of the courtyard, leading to the Taleju Mandir, is flanked by statues of the Indian river goddesses **Ganga** and **Jamuna**, the latter riding a *makana* – a mythical cross between a crocodile and

1

an elephant, whose curling snout decorates almost every public waterspout in Nepal. Behind and to the left of Mul Chowk rises the octagonal, three-tiered **Taleju Bhawani Mandir**.

Sundari Chowk and around

The courtyard of the Royal Palace's small, southernmost wing, **Sundari Chowk**, contains the grand seventeenth-century **Tusha Hiti**. This sunken water tank, decorated with Hindu gods and goddesses, is shaped like a *yoni*, the symbol of female sexuality, and ringed with serpents. The courtyard surrounding it is covered in ornate woodwork, including many fabulous carved doorways, windows, *torana*, and images of deities individually set into niches. To the east of Sundari Chowk is the recently restored **Bhandarkhal Temple** and its bathing pond.

Chyasin Dewal

At the newer, eighteenth-century southern end of Durbar Square, the stone **Chyasin Dewal** (opposite Sundari Chowk) is the lesser of the square's two Krishna temples. Some say the octagonal temple was raised in memory of the eight wives that committed *sati* on a king's funeral pyre, although Krishna temples almost always have eight sides to commemorate his role as the eighth *avatar* (incarnation) of Vishnu. The cast-iron **Taleju Bell** just to the north was the first to be erected in the valley, in 1736.

Hari Shankar Mandir

North of the Chyasin Dewal, the finely carved **Hari Shankar Mandir** is dedicated both to Vishnu (sometimes called Hari) and Shiva (alias Shankar), while the statue mounted on a pillar and praying to the Degu Talle depicts **Yoganarendra Malla**. An angry cobra rears up like a halo behind the king, and atop the cobra's head perches a gilded bird. Like all god-fearing rulers of the valley, Yoganarendra would have made sure to appease the *nag*, animist snake spirits who deliver or withhold the valley's rains. As for the bird, chroniclers state that the king, upon abdicating the throne to become a *sunyasan* (hermit) after the untimely death of his son, told his subjects that as long as the bird remained they would know he was still alive. To this day, many people in Patan keep a light burning, and a bed is kept ready for the absent king in an upper chamber of the palace.

Krishna Mandir and around

If the two-tiered **Jagan Narayan Mandir**, north of the Hari Shankar Mandir, is the oldest temple in the square (built in 1565), the most unusual – and popular – is its neighbour, the seventeenth-century **Krishna Mandir**. Its central structure, a Mughal-style *shikra*, is girdled by three levels of stone verandas, with detailed scenes from the great Hindu epics, the Mahabharata and Ramayana, carved along the lintels. An incarnation of Vishnu, Krishna is one of Hinduism's best-loved characters. Worshippers gather here every morning for *puja* and on Krishna's birthday, in August or early September, the queue of worshippers at this temple stretches around the block.

Bishwanath Mandir and around

The **Bishwanath Mandir** contains a copy of the Shiva *linga* of the same name in Varanasi, India. The temple collapsed in 1990, but has been seamlessly restored. On the northwest corner of the square, the seventeenth-century **Bhimsen Mandir** is dedicated to the ever-popular god of Newari traders. Non-Hindus aren't allowed inside, but you can often see and hear *puja* being performed in the open upstairs sanctuary. Across the way, one of the valley's largest sunken public bathing tanks, **Manga Hiti**, has been operational since the sixth century.

North of Durbar Square

Some of Patan's most interesting sights – the lavish **Golden Temple**, the five-tiered **Kumbeshwar Mahadev Mandir** (the oldest temple in Patan) and the **ghats** – lie north of Durbar Square.

Hiranyavarna Mahavihara (The Golden Temple)
Daily 6am–6pm • Rs50

The **Hiranyavarna Mahavihara** – Sanskrit for "Golden Monastery", although all the tour guides call it the **Golden Temple** – is the most opulent little temple in Nepal. The three-tiered pagoda occupies one side of the cramped courtyard of Kwa Bahal, a still-active twelfth-century Buddhist Newari monastery and the spiritual hub of old Patan. During early-morning *puja*, the *bahal* is a fascinating theatre of Nepali religion in all its perplexing glory. Note that nothing leather is allowed inside.

The temple's gilt facade, embossed with images of Buddhas and Taras, is regarded as the pre-eminent example of large-scale repoussé **metalwork** in Nepal, while in the middle of the courtyard, a small, lavishly ornamented shrine contains a priceless silver and gold Swayambhu *chaitya*. Both the shrine and the main temple are further decorated with what look like long metallic neckties: these *pataka* are supposed to provide a slide for the gods when they descend to answer worshippers' prayers. The *bahal* is so crammed with images, ornaments and fine details that a full account of all its wonders would fill a book.

Sakyamuni Buddha is the temple's *kwapadya* (main image). According to **legend**, it was made homeless in the twelfth century when the temple it formerly resided in collapsed. When King Bhaskardev built it a new temple, the image informed him in a dream that it wished to move to a new place where mice chased cats. One day the king saw a golden mouse chasing a cat here at Kwa Bahal, and so he set about building a new, golden temple on the spot. Rats are thus allowed to run free here, as are tortoises, for in legend the universe rests on the back of a tortoise.

Though no longer a residential monastery, the Mahavihara is an important centre of lay worship, following well-established Buddhist rituals and iconography that draw from both the Newari and the Tibetan traditions. Its principal priest, a boy no older than twelve, tends the main shrine. A Tibetan-style *gompa* upstairs on the northeastern side of the courtyard, which you can visit, is evidence of the spiritual ties forged between Patan and Tibet through centuries of trade.

Swatha Tol
Swatha Tol, an attractive intersection one block east of the Golden Temple, lies poised between Durbar Square and the more traditional neighbourhoods to the north, and seems to combine the best of both worlds. The square's centrepiece, the three-tiered **Radha Krishna Mandir**, has been restored, and the lovers Krishna and **Radha**, to whom this temple is dedicated, are a favourite subject for Indian sandalwood carvers.

The Kumbeshwar Mahadev Mandir
Patan's oldest temple, and one of only two freestanding five-tiered pagodas in Nepal (the other is in Bhaktapur), the **Kumbeshwar Mahadev Mandir** was built as a two-roofed structure in 1392, and despite the addition of three more levels in the seventeenth century, it remains well proportioned. Shiva is the honoured deity here: inside you can see a stone *linga* and a brass one with four faces; Nandi, Shiva's patient mount, waits outside. The temple owes its name to an episode in which a pilgrim at Gosainkund, the sacred lake high in the mountains north of Kathmandu, dropped a pot (*kumbha*) into the water there. Much later, the same pot appeared in the water tank here, giving rise to the belief that the tank is fed by an underground channel from Gosainkund, and adding to Shiva's roll of titles that of Kumbeshwar – Lord of the Pots.

Thanks to this connection, Kumbeshwar's water tank is regarded as an alternative venue during Gosainkund's great annual **festival**, **Janai Purnima**, which takes place on the day of the late July or early August full moon, and sees Brahmans and Chhetris formally changing the sacred thread (*janai*) that distinguishes them as members of the "twice-born" castes. Thousands come to have their threads renewed and pay respect to a *linga* erected in the middle of the tank, while Tamang *jhankri* (shamans) perform ritual dances and young boys dive and splash in the water.

1

Bagalamukhi Mandir
Though smaller and less to look at than the Kumbeshwar Mahadev, the **Bagalamukhi Mandir**, occupying the southern end of the same compound, inspires far more day-to-day devotion. Considered a powerful wish-fulfilling manifestation of the goddess Kali, Bagalamukhi traditionally appeals to women seeking domestic harmony and anyone requiring strength to overcome adversity.

The Northern Stupa
Just northeast of the Kumbeshwar Mahadev, the **Northern Stupa** stands at the edge of Patan. It's the smallest and most central of the Ashokan mounds, and the only one that's been sealed over with plaster. Although it doesn't look wildly interesting for a supposedly 2200-year-old monument, you can let your imagination dwell on what treasures or relics Ashoka might have buried here – the contents are unlikely ever to see the light of day, since archeological digs are prohibited in the valley.

Sankhamul Ghat and around
North of the Northern Stupa, the road wends through receding farmland towards Patan's **Sankhamul Ghat**, a half-kilometre-long embankment near the junction of the Manohara and Bagmati rivers and Patan's main cremation site.

East of the footbridge, flanked by sagging pilgrims' shelters and statues of Hanuman and Ganesh, a path leads under an arch and up to the exotic **Jagat Narayan Mandir** complex, named after its builder, nineteenth-century prime minister Jagat Shamsher.

West of Durbar Square
There's plenty of serendipitous exploring to be done among the back alleys **west of Durbar Square**. For more detail on this area, pick up a copy of *Patan Walkabout*, an informative booklet available from the bookshop at **Patan Dhoka**, a small bazaar area and bus park surrounding an unremarkable city gate.

From **Mangal Bazaar** at the southern end of Durbar Square, central Patan's main drag heads out towards the Western Stupa. One of Patan's less-touristed former monasteries, **Hakhu Bahal** (also known as Ratnakar Mahabihar), rises on the left after 300m and is the seat of Patan's Kumari. The **Western Stupa** comes alive one day a year when the great chariot procession of Raato Machhendranath (see box opposite) gets started just to the south.

The northwestern quarter of old Patan is a jumble of *bahal* – the lane leading from the Golden Temple west takes you past quite a few.

South of Durbar Square
South of Durbar Square, you essentially have two choices. The southbound street passes the **Machhendranath temple** and other sights en route to the Lagankhel bus park. Alternatively, head east along Mangal Bazaar – which gets quieter and more appealing as you go – to reach **Sundhara**, a sunken bathing area with four golden (*sun*) spouts (*dhara*), **Dupat**, whose close, dark alleys are brimming with atmosphere, and **Uku Bahal**, Patan's main metalsmithing area and home of the famed **Mahabuddha** temple.

Bishwakarma Mandir and around
One of Patan's most charming streets runs parallel to Mangal Bazaar, a block to the south. This is an area of metalworkers and sellers of household wares – appropriately enough, the **Bishwakarma Mandir**'s facade features hammered gilt-copper and froggy copper lions standing guard. Unfortunately you can no longer photograph the facade after a railing was installed to deter thieves. The name Bishwakarma refers both to the god of artisans and members of the blacksmiths caste. Patan's second-oldest monastery,

Ibaha Bahi, stands one block further to the south. Founded in 1427, the *bahal* was restored with assistance from the Nippon Institute of Technology.

Machhendranath Mandir

Outwardly, Patan's **Machhendranath Mandir** resembles many other such temples: a huge seventeenth-century brick pagoda adorned with beautifully carved, gaudily painted struts and *torana*. What makes this one extraordinary, however, is its idol, **Raato Machhendranath** ("Red Machhendranath"), a painted shingle of sandalwood which, for several weeks beginning in late April, is the object of one of Nepal's most extraordinary **festivals** (see box below).

Older than his white counterpart in Kathmandu, Raato Machhendranath is a god of many guises. To Newars he is Bunga Dyo, the androgynous god of agricultural prosperity and a manifestation of the great cult figure Karunamaya. To Buddhists of other ethnic groups he is Avalokiteshwara or Lokeshwar, the *bodhisattva* of compassion. As Machhendranath, the progenitor of the *nath* (lord) cult, he's the spirit of a seventh-century Hindu guru who once taught the Shah kings' beloved saint, Gorakhnath. Legend has it that Gorakhnath once visited the valley and, offended that he wasn't accorded a full reception, caused a drought by rounding up all the rain-bringing snakes. The locals sent a posse to Assam to fetch Machhendranath, who came to their rescue in the form of a bee. Wishing to pay tribute to his guru, Gorakhnath had to release the snakes, whereupon the rains returned and Machhendranath came to be revered as a rain-maker.

Minnath Mandir and around

Set behind a *hiti* (sunken bathing tank) across the street from the Machhendranath Mandir entrance, the smaller sixteenth-century **Minnath Mandir** is dedicated to another mythologized Indian saint. South of here, the main road widens to include a busy

---

RAATO MACHHENDRANATH'S BIG RIDE

The Kathmandu Valley's oldest, longest and most exciting festival, the **Machhendranath Rath Jaatra**, begins the day after the full moon of Baisaakh (April/May), when priests ritually bathe Raato Machhendranath's sandalwood idol in Patan's Lagankhel Square. Moved back to its temple, the Machhendranath Mandir, the idol spends the next ten days undergoing the life-cycle rituals of Buddhist Newars. Meanwhile, just south of the Western Stupa at Pulchowk, Machhendranath's chariot (*raath*) – more like a mobile temple – is assembled and its 18m-high tower of poles and vegetation constructed. A smaller chariot to carry Minnath is also built.

The idols are eventually installed in their chariots and the great **procession** begins. Scores of men heave at the ropes; Machhendranath's unwieldy vehicle rocks, teeters and suddenly lurches forward, its spire swaying and grazing buildings as it passes. The crowd roars, people leap out of the way, and the chariot comes to a stubborn stop until the pullers regroup and try to budge it again. Separately, local children pull Minnath's chariot. It goes on like this, in stages, for four or more weeks, until the chariots reach Jawalakhel Chowk, a journey of about 4km.

At Jawalakhel, the stage is set for the dramatic **Bhoto Jaatra**. A huge crowd begins assembling before noon on a day ordained by the astrologers – usually the fourth day after the chariots' arrival at the chowk. At around 4pm or 5pm, Patan's Kumari (see box, p.64) is carried in by palanquin. Local VIPs climb aboard Machhendranath's chariot and take turns holding aloft the god's magical jewelled vest. Since the procession culminates during the showery pre-monsoon, Machhendranath usually obliges with rain: bring an umbrella.

Machhendranath's idol is then carried to Bungmati, 6km to the south (see p.148), where it is welcomed home with great fanfare; the cult of Raato Machhendranath is believed to have originated in Bungmati, accounting for the god's Newari name, Bunga Dyo ("God of Bunga"). The idol spends the summer months in Bungmati before being transported back to the Machhendranath Mandir, but once every twelve years (last in 2015) it's kept in Bungmati all winter and the chariot procession begins and ends there.

1

open-air bazaar and the chaotic **Lagankhel** minibus park. It's not really worth travelling another kilometre south to visit the grassy **Southern Stupa**, though if you're going to the Patan Industrial Estate (see p.115), you'll pass by it.

Mahabuddha

Nicknamed "Temple of a Thousand Buddhas", **Mahabuddha** is constructed entirely of terracotta tiles – each one bearing the Buddha's image. This remarkable Rococo structure mimics the famous Mahabodhi Temple of Bodhgaya, India, where its builder, an enthusiastic seventeenth-century Patan architect, had previously meditated for several years. Although the likeness is only approximate, the temple introduced the Indian *shikra* form to Nepal, which to this day remains prevalent around Patan. Reduced to rubble during the 1934 earthquake, it was put back together again and the smaller temple beside it was built from the spare parts. The structure is so tightly hemmed in by residences you'll need to go up into one of the surrounding metal handicrafts sellers' buildings to get a decent view.

Rudravarna Mahabihar

The name of the Uku (or Oku) Bahal neighbourhood comes from the now-defunct Buddhist monastery at the intersection to the south of Mahabuddha, which also goes by the handle **Rudravarna Mahabihar** ("Red Monastery"). Though it has undergone a renovation, it's believed to be Patan's oldest – the wooden struts on the north side of the courtyard date from the thirteenth century.

Jawalakhel and around

The name **Jawalakhel** (pronounced *Jowl*-akel) applies to a wide area around the Jawalakhel Chowk roundabout and south from there down to the Ring Road. The southern part – often referred to as **Ekantakuna** ("Lonely Corner") – is Patan's **Tibetan** ghetto.

Tibetans started pouring into the Kathmandu Valley immediately after the Chinese annexation of Tibet and the flight of the Dalai Lama in 1959. By 1960 their plight prompted the International Red Cross to set up a transit camp at Jawalakhel, later assigned to the Swiss Red Cross, which in turn formed the Swiss Association for Technical Assistance (SATA) to help Tibetans on a long-term basis. SATA encouraged carpet-making and other cottage industries, and by 1964 the Jawalakhel "transit camp" was a registered company. A generation and a half on, Jawalakhel's Tibetans are prospering from the booming **carpet industry**, and many have left the centre to establish businesses and live closer to Buddhist holy places.

Ekantakuna

The former Tibetan refugee camp at **Ekantakuna** is arguably the best place in the valley to watch **carpets** being made (see box opposite). There's no big temple here, just one small monastery, and – except for the Jawalakhel Handicraft Center (see p.115) and nearby carpet shops – not a lot of commercial vitality.

The zoo

Southwest of Jawalakhel Chowk • Daily 10am–5pm • Rs500, elephant rides Rs100 • ☎ 01 521 467

Nepal's only **zoo** – often rendered "jew" by Nepali-speakers – occupies a former Rana estate just southwest of Jawalakhel Chowk. It's probably the best attraction for young children in the Kathmandu Valley: besides looking at the animals, they can see, touch and even ride on the zoo's free-roaming elephant (see our box on elephant rides on p.252), and there are also pedalo rides and a few other attractions around the lake. **Food** is available and there are picnic spots. Most of the species kept here are indigenous to Nepal (rhinos, elephants, deer, monkeys); the conditions aren't great, but not appalling.

TIBETAN CARPET-MAKING

To make a **Tibetan carpet**, typically **Tibetan wool** – from sheep bred for their unusually long, high-tensile wool – is blended with foreign processed wool. Once it is spun into yarn, much of the spinning is still done by hand, producing a distinctive, slightly irregular look. It is then dyed and rolled into balls. Tibetan-style carpets are produced by the **cut-loop** method, which bears little relation to the process employed by Middle Eastern and Chinese artisans. Rather than tying thousands of individual knots, the weaver loops the yarn in and out of the vertical warp threads and around a horizontally placed rod; when the row is finished, the weaver draws a knife across the loops, freeing the rod. Once the weaving is finished, the carpets are trimmed to give an even finish, in some cases embossed and then washed (an industrial process which **pollutes local streams** with chemicals linked with birth defects).

Most carpets are made-to-order for the export market, with distribution controlled by a small collection of traders. Many Nepali producers also produce Afghan, Middle Eastern and Kashmiri-style carpets, though these are rarely as fine as the originals.

ARRIVAL AND DEPARTURE · KATHMANDU AND PATAN

BY PLANE

The Tribhuwan International Airport (⊚ tiairport.com.np) lies 5km east of the centre. Tourist visas (see p.48) are issued on arrival, and there's an exchange counter, ATM, tourist information desk (open for incoming flights) and a booking service for the pricier hotels. Note that the baggage handling here isn't great; keep fragile or expensive items in your hand luggage.

Getting into town If you've booked in advance, many hotels offer a free pick-up from the airport, which is worth accepting (making sure you've got a number to call in case of problems). There's also a pre-paid taxi booth with fixed prices (around Rs800–1000 to most destinations in Kathmandu). Unofficial taxis charge a bit less (around Rs500–600), but are not really worth the hassle (even after apparently agreeing to take you to your stated destination, a driver may try to deliver you to a hotel offering a commission). Touts offer "free" rides to their lodges, but their commission will just be added to your room charge. Local buses are cheaper (Rs10), but inconvenient: they depart from the main intersection at the end of the airport drive – a 200m walk – and terminate at the City Bus Park.

Booking flights in Nepal Most domestic and international airlines have their offices in the Kantipath and Durbar Marg area. You can either book tickets directly, via an agent or online (most domestic airlines now allow this). International flights should be reconfirmed at least 72 hours prior to departure.

Domestic airline offices Air Viva, no office (⊚ air-viva .com); Buddha Air, Pulchowk, Patan (☎ 01 554 2494, ⊚ buddhaair.com); Gorkha Airlines, Hattisar (☎ 01 621 2096, ⊚ gorkhaairlines.com); Nepal Airlines (NAC – though still often referred to as RNAC, for Royal Nepal Airlines Corporation), corner of New Rd and Kantipath (☎ 01 422 0757, ⊚ nepalairlines.com.np); Tara Air (subsidiary of Yeti Airlines; ☎ 01 421 3012, ⊚ taraair.com); Yeti Airlines, Thamel Chowk (☎ 01 446 4878, ⊚ yetiairlines.com).

International airline offices Air Asia, c/o Incentive Tours & Travels, North Gate, Royal Palace (☎ 01 441 4739, ⊚ airasia.com); Air China, Sundar Bhawan, north side of Royal Palace (☎ 01 444 0650, ⊚ airchina.com.cn); Air India/Indian Airlines, Hattisar Kamal Pokhri (☎ 01 442 9468, ⊚ airindia.com); Gulf Air, Hattisar (☎ 01 422 0245, ⊚ gulfair.com); Jet Airways, Sundar Bhawan House, Hattisar (☎ 01 411 3005, ⊚ jetairways.com); Korean Air, Heritage Plaza, north of Kamaladi (☎ 01 416 9191, ⊚ koreanair.com); Malaysia Airlines, Kamaladi (☎ 01 424 7215, ⊚ malaysiaairlines.com); Qatar Airways, Hattisar Sadak (☎ 01 444 0849, ⊚ qatarairways.com); Thai Airways, Durbar Marg (☎ 01 422 0905, ⊚ thaiairways.com).

Destinations Bhadrapur (several daily; 45min); Bhairahawa (4 daily; 30min); Bharatpur (2 daily; 20min); Biratnagar (4 daily; 40min); Janakpur (2 daily; 25min); Nepalgunj (4–5 daily; 55min); Pokhara (14–17 daily; 40min); Siddharthanagar (2 daily; 30min); Simara for Birgunj (6 daily; 15min).

BY BUS

Gongabu (New or Naya) Bus Park Most long-distance bus services depart from the Gongabu Bus Park (also confusingly referred to as the New or Naya Bus Park) in Gongabu, 3km north of Thamel on the Ring Road; a taxi from Thamel costs around Rs300.

Destinations Bhairahawa Butwal Sonauli (every 10–30min; 8–9hr); Biratnagar (10–15 daily; around 12hr); Birgunj (every 15min; around 9hr); Dhankuta (3 night buses; 17–18hr); Dharan (9 daily; 15hr); Ghatgain (1 daily; 7hr); Gorkha (every 30min; 4–6hr); Hetauda (every 2hr; around 6hr); Hile (3 daily; 17–18hr); Ilam (1 night bus; 27–28hr); Janakpur (hourly; 10hr); Kakarbhitta (10–15 daily; around 14–15hr); Lumbini (3 daily; 9–11hr); Mahendra Nagar (6 daily; 16–17hr); Narayangadh (every 30min; 4–5hr); Nepalgunj (around 20 daily, mostly leaving around 6pm; around 13hr); Pokhara (day buses every

1

20min; night buses 6 daily; 6–7hr); Tansen/Palpa (5 daily; 11hr).

City Bus Park Buses serving destinations along the Arniko Highway leave from the City Bus Park (also known as the *purano* or "old" bus park), just east of the Tudikhel. Make things easy on yourself and get an agent to book your ticket for you. Local buses (including to destinations within the Kathmandu Valley, the Tibet border and Jiri) also start here, and generally leave when full, so get there early if you want a seat.

Destinations Banepa/Panauti (every 10min; 45min/1hr); Dhulikhel (every 5–10min; 1hr 10min); Kodari (hourly; 4hr); Nagarkot (2 daily; 2hr).

Macha Pokhari Bus Station (Bypass Bus Station) Around 3km north of Thamel (and 200m northwest of the Gongabu Bus Park) in Gongabu, this tiny, dusty bus station serves all destinations along the Trisuli Highway.

Destinations Nuwakot (3 every morning; 2hr 20min); Trisuli Bazaar (every 30min; 2hr).

Tourist buses Tourist buses (and minibuses) to Pokhara, Sauraha (for Chitwan) and Sonauli depart from Kantipath or Tridevi Marg, Thamel, around 7am or 8am. Tickets, available through travel agencies, cost roughly double the public bus fare, but services are more comfortable and generally quicker. Greenline Tours (☎01 425 7544, ⊛greenline.com.np), with its own bus park on Tridevi Marg, operates the most comfortable services (and, at US$20–23 including lunch, the priciest).

Destinations Pokhara (every 15min till late afternoon; 7–8hr); Sauraha (for Chitwan; 12 daily; 6–7hr); Sonauli (hourly; 7–8hr).

Jeeps Jeeps travel to Hetauda (3–4hr) in the Terai via a direct – though rough – scenic route through the hills south of Kathmandu (see p.284). They depart when full from the Balkhu junction, on the Ring Road where it crosses the Bagmati River.

TO INDIA

By plane The easiest way to reach India is on one of the numerous daily flights from Tribhuvan International Airport.

By bus There is a direct bus from Kathmandu to Delhi, but this is a truly horrendous journey (at least 36hr). It is far better to buy a bus ticket to the border and then make onward arrangements from there; India Railways tickets can be booked online (⊛cleartrip.com is far easier to use than the official site, ⊛irctc.co.in). Six border crossings between Nepal and India are open to foreigners; the most popular are Sonauli (see p.261), Kakarbhitta (see p.294) and Birgunj (see p.285).

Package tours Travel agents sell package deals to India, but these are notoriously unreliable and are best avoided.

Visas The Indian Embassy (☎01 441 0900, ⊛indianembassy.org.np), just off Lazimpath, has

outsourced its visa operation to Nepal SBI Bank, whose office is next door (Mon–Fri: applications 9.30am–noon, collections 3–5pm; ☎01 400 1516, ⊛nepalsbi.com.np /indian_passport); queues can be very long, so arrive early. In theory the visa process takes 7–10 working days, but in practice it's often around 5–7. A tourist visa valid up to six months costs Rs4350 (UK citizens Rs13,600), while a transit visa lasting up to fifteen days is Rs2300 (UK citizens Rs9350) – prices are in Nepalese rupees. There's also an additional Rs250 "handling fee". Note that recently the embassy has been reluctant to issue more than a three-month visa, especially if you've had other recent Indian visas, and that there must be a two-month gap between visas. Visa forms can be downloaded from the Indian Embassy website; you should also bring two colour passport photos with a light background. Visas are valid from the date of issue, not the date you enter India. If you are flying into one of the major airports, certain nationalities are eligible for an Electronic Travel Authorization-enabled thirty-day visa on arrival, which you can apply for online; check the Indian Embassy website (⊛indianembassy.org.np) as the scheme is expanding.

TO TIBET

Tours China's official policy is that foreigners wanting to enter Tibet from Nepal must join a tour – a policy strictly enforced. The standard eight-day, seven-night tour in which you travel up by road and fly back costs at least US$1320 (or around US$900 plus the flight). On this kind of package, you'll stay in basic guesthouses on the way to Lhasa, and travel in a bus rather than a more comfortable Land Cruiser. Stops usually include various viewpoints and monasteries, including Shigatse, Gyantse and Yamdruk Tso (Turquoise Lake). Longer, more adventurous (and expensive) itineraries could include trekking around Mount Kailash, cycling from Lhasa to Nepal or whitewater rafting. Visiting the north Base Camp of Everest usually adds two days to a tour, but is done in a Land Cruiser so the cost is more like US$2000, including a return flight to Lhasa. You have to stay with the group for the duration of the tour, but can – in theory – head off on your own afterwards for as long as your visa allows, and then head back to Nepal or into China; an outgoing ticket from Lhasa is a prerequisite. (That said, cyclists are known to get into Tibet if they're attached to a group at the border, after which they can peel off – though you may have to pay a US$100–200 fine if you leave Tibet ahead of your group.) The Tibet high season is April to September; monsoon landslides make the overland route more difficult in the latter part of this period, but there's almost always a way to get through. Tours don't generally run between the middle of December and early March because of the risk of snowstorms.

Tour operators Wayfarers (☎01 426 6010, ⊛wayfarers .com.np), on J.P. School Rd in Thamel, can organize trips to

Tibet, as can several of the trekking, rafting and mountain-biking operators (see p.98).

Visas The Chinese Embassy only issues group visas through travel agents; visas cost US$42 (US$132 for US nationals), and last 15–20 days. Officially visas are non-extendable, though it may be possible in Lhasa. If you already have a Chinese visa in your passport, it will be deleted when you are given a Tibetan one. Regulations are notoriously prone to change, and the Tibet border has occasionally been closed in the past, so ask around about the current situation.

GETTING AROUND

Kathmandu's roads are pretty horrendous in terms of traffic congestion and pollution, so you'll probably find you do most of your exploration of the old city **on foot**, but here's a rundown of transport options for sights further afield.

By taxi Taxis are a fairly inexpensive way to travel longer distances in Kathmandu – a trip from Patan to Thamel, for example, costs around Rs300 – though they don't work well in the crowded old city. Figure on around Rs50 per kilometre, fifty percent more at night. A couple of companies operate fleet taxis (☎01 422 4374 or ☎01 426 6642); have your guesthouse make the call. Freelance cabs tend to wait in designated areas such as Tridevi Marg, the main Thamel intersection, along Dharma Path, at the Jamal end of Durbar Marg, at the Mangal Bazaar side of Patan Durbar Square, and Jawalakhel Chowk. Drivers are supposed to use their meters, but it is standard practice to negotiate a flat rate. Try surprising them with a bit of Nepali (*Meter-maa januhunchha?* – "Will you go by the meter?").

By fixed-route tempo Tempos – including the eco-friendly electric Safaa tempos – ply routes throughout the city and cost around Rs20 a journey. Many originate from two locations along Kantipath: one, just north of Rani Pokhari; and the other outside the Nepal Airlines office (NAC or RNAC), just north of the GPO and south of the junction with New Road. You can get on at any of their frequent stopping points, but they're often full unless you pick them up at the point of origin.

By local bus Local buses cover some of the same city routes as fixed-route tempos, but they're really meant for longer journeys. They're cheap (prices fluctuate, but expect to pay around Rs30), but slow and crowded, particularly at rush hour; they're easiest to cope with if you get on at the starting point.

By microbus Microbuses tend to have the same points of origin and routes as tempos.

By cycle rikshaw Cycle rikshaws are only really found around Thamel in the centre, but are worthwhile for short distances down the backstreets. Agree a price before setting off; they should cost around Rs25 per kilometre but they'll start off quoting around four or five times that so you'll need to haggle.

By bike Cycling is a good way to get to many sights in the surrounding valley, but traffic and pollution make it miserable work in central Kathmandu. You will probably want to wear a mask or at the least a dampened handkerchief to block out fumes and dust. There are a couple of inexpensive rental places just south of Chhetrapati Chowk, but for better-quality cycles, head to one of the Thamel mountain-bike operators (see p.99). Basic, one-speed bikes rent for around Rs250 per day, mountain bikes with helmets (and sometimes handy repair kits) from Rs500–1000 and upwards. The lane south of the National Theatre, just west of Kantipath, is the place to buy a new bike.

By motorbike Riding a motorbike is a great way to explore the Kathmandu Valley and beyond (though not much fun inside the Ring Road). Several Thamel operators rent motorbikes, costing from around Rs500 a day for a moped up to Rs1500–4000 a day for an Enfield, excluding petrol, which costs almost as much as it does in Europe. You generally need to leave a plane ticket or passport as

HIMALAYAN MOUNTAIN FLIGHTS

The harder you work to see the mountains in Nepal, the greater the reward, but there's no denying the drama of the hour-long "**mountain flight**". These scenic tours depart every morning (6.30–9am), weather permitting, from Kathmandu's Tribhuwan Airport – go as early as you can bear for the best chance of clear weather. Any agent can sell you a next-day ticket, and prices are standard, at US$197 (not including the taxi fare from your hotel and the Rs200 airport departure tax). There's little to choose between the airlines, though Buddha and Yeti have good reputations. Routes are standard too: you fly close to the ranges northeast of Kathmandu, and get a slightly more distant view of Everest. Don't imagine that you'll actually be flying right in among the peaks, however, or you'll be disappointed. And bear in mind that the standard flights to the mountain airstrips of, say, Jomosom and Lukla, are arguably even more exciting, given the landing (see box, p.310). All that said, the mountain flight planes themselves are small, noisy and hugely atmospheric – and you're allowed into the cockpit too. And the views, of course, are stunning.

1

security, and you're supposed to show a driving licence. Himalayan Enfielders (☎01 444 0462, ⓦ himalayan enfielders.com), next to the Israeli embassy in Lazimpath, is a good place to start; it offers rentals, repairs, spares, tours and instruction. Singh Motorbike Centre (☎ 985 104 0595, ⓔ singh.motorbike@gmail.com), near *Thamel House* restaurant, and Bikemandu (☎ 980 352 2833, ⓦ bike mandu.com) in Patan also do rentals. If you want to buy a bike secondhand, you'll find innumerable motorbike shops on the Prithvi Highway between Kalimati and Kalanki. Before setting off on a ride, you may want to read our driving tips (see p.26).

By car Foreigners are not (officially) allowed to drive themselves in Nepal, but it is easy to hire a car and driver through a travel agent (see p.115) or your hotel; expect to pay around Rs3000–4000 per day (excluding petrol), depending on your haggling skills. It's generally cheaper to negotiate a deal with a taxi driver.

GETTING TO PATAN

By taxi A taxi from Thamel or central Kathmandu to Patan costs around Rs300.

By tempo and microbus Fixed-route tempo and microbus services run from Durbar Marg and near the Nepal Airlines office in Kantipath.

By bike Don't cycle to Patan via the main Bagmati bridge and Kupondol – you'll expire from the fumes. A better alternative is to cross the river from the Teku area of Kathmandu, south of Durbar Square, entering Patan through its northwestern suburbs.

INFORMATION

Tourist information The Tourist Service Center (Mon–Fri 10am–5pm; ☎01 425 6909, ⓦ welcomenepal.com) has free maps and leaflets, but is of limited use otherwise, and is inconveniently located in Bhrikuti Mandap, east of the Tudikhel. There's a much smaller, little-visited tourist office in Thamel (Mon–Fri 10am–5pm; ☎01 470 0750) opposite and slightly down the small lane from the Standard Chartered Bank. Both offices have tourist police booths. The notice boards in Thamel's guesthouses and restaurants are also worth checking out.

Kathmandu Environmental Education Project (KEEP) Located just off Tridevi Marg in Thamel, the KEEP office (Mon–Fri & Sun 10am–5pm; ☎01 441 0952, ⓦ keepnepal.org) offers advice, mainly on trekking, homestays and volunteering, and has a notice board, an eco-shop and a café, which is a good place to meet other trekkers.

Himalayan Rescue Association A helpful nonprofit organization just north of the Royal Palace (Mon–Fri & Sun 10am–5pm; ☎01 444 0292, ⓦ himalayanrescue.org). Like KEEP, it has a useful trekking-related notice board.

Publications Local English-language newspapers and magazines such as the *Kathmandu Post*, *Himalayan Times* and the more youth-orientated and funky *Living Magazine* (ⓦ living.com.np) are readily available at bookshops, supermarkets and vendors around town.

Maps The advertiser-supported city maps given away by the tourist offices are less detailed than the ones in this book. Bookshops sell better versions, including quality Mapple/Karto Atelier maps; Nepa's pocket map of Kathmandu and Patan is decent value.

Trekking permits You can get trekking permits and Trekkers' Information Management System (TIMS) cards at the Tourist Service Center (see box opposite).

TREKKING, RAFTING AND OTHER ACTIVITIES

Most people book organized outdoor activities such as **trekking**, **rafting** and **mountain biking** in Kathmandu because that's where most of the operators and agents are based. Pokhara (see p.206) has a similar plethora of agencies, even if most (but not all) are simply offshoots of the Kathmandu branch. Almost all agencies can organize **multi-activity adventures** in partnership with other specialists. Be aware that agencies change hands and management fairly frequently, and consolidation and/or splitting occur all the time. Increasingly, a few bigger companies – such as Adventure Centre Asia (which includes Ultimate Descents Nepal), Equator Expeditions, Himalayan Encounters and Ultimate Rivers – offer one-stop shopping for a variety of outdoor experiences.

TREKKING COMPANIES

A full discussion of the pros and cons of trekking with a group versus doing it independently is outlined in our "Trekking" chapter (see p.302). As explained there, budget trekking companies can't really be recommended because the quality of their service can vary so much from trip to trip. This is especially important given the tragic Annapurna snowstorm disaster in November 2014, where poor guiding and trekkers travelling without guides were two factors that contributed to the deaths of over forty

people. The following operators all have reputations for high standards.

Asian Trekking Bhagwan Bahal ☎01 442 4249, ⓦ asian-trekking.com; map p.73. Established company offering treks on both standard and more remote routes, as well as climbing expeditions.

Highlander Thamel Northwest ☎01 470 0563, ⓦ highlandernepal.com; map p.73. A well-respected operator, Highlander offers off-the-beaten-track treks in Nepal, India, Tibet and Bhutan.

ORGANIZING A TREK FROM KATHMANDU

Trekking **permits** are required for a few sensitive areas (see box, p.314), and are obtainable only through a trekking agency. If your trek passes through any of Nepal's national parks or conservation areas, you'll need an **entrance ticket**, which it is advisable to buy before departure. These can be picked up from the Tourist Service Center building in Bhrikuti Mandap, where the **National Trust for Nature Conservation** (daily 9am–5pm, tickets to be collected before 4pm; ⓦntnc.org.np) sells entrance tickets for the Annapurna, Manaslu and Gauri Shankar conservation areas, and the **Department of National Parks and Wildlife** (Mon–Fri & Sun 9am–2pm; ⓦdnpwc.gov.np) sells entrance tickets for essentially everywhere else.

An office in the same building (Mon–Fri 7am–7pm) sells Trekkers' Information Management System **(TIMS) cards**; these are also available at the **TAAN TIMS Counter** (Mon–Fri 7am–6am, Sat & Sun 10am–1pm) in Manang Plaza in Thamel.

Himalayan Encounters Thamel Northwest, in the forecourt of the Kathmandu Guest House ⓣ01 470 0426, ⓦhimalayanencounters.com; map p.73. Established, highly professional agency with an extensive range of treks, rafting trips and tours.

Karnali Excursions Next to Yak & Yeti in Durbar Marg ⓣ01 423 3192, ⓦtrekkinginnepal.com; map p.84. This long-standing, reliable trekking and tour agency specializes in Tibet tours, especially to the "wild west" and Mount Kailash, but also offers a wide range of treks and excursions in Nepal, and has some fantastic guides.

Nature Trail Chaksibari Marg, Thamel Northwest ⓣ01 470 1925, ⓦnaturetrailnepal.com. Experienced agency, used by VSO staff, organizing treks throughout Nepal.

RIVER OPERATORS

Because of the extra safety considerations, it's even riskier to recommend budget river operators than trekking companies. The ones listed here are reputable and more expensive. All raft the most popular rivers (scheduled departures in season) and can organize trips on other rivers on demand. Several companies are based in Pokhara (see p.214), and run kayak schools on the Seti River. All can rent out equipment. For more on whitewater rafting and kayaking in Nepal, see also our "Rafting and kayaking" chapter (see p.354).

Equator Expeditions Thamel Northwest ⓣ01 435 6644, ⓦequatorexpeditionsnepal.com; map p.73. Covers all the major rivers, provides courses for rafting and kayak guides, and offers treks and peak climbing. Affiliated with *Sukute Beach Adventure Resort* (see box, p.186).

The Last Resort/Ultimate Rivers Mandala St, Thamel Northwest ⓣ01 470 1247, ⓦthelastresort.com.np; map p.73. Very professional operation with a wide range of rafting, kayaking and canyoning trips, plus, at 160m-high, one of the world's highest bungee jumps (which have very good safety procedures). Runs *The Last Resort* camp on the Bhote Koshe (see box, p.186).

Ultimate Descents Thamel Northwest ⓣ01 470 1295, ⓦudnepal.com; map p.73. One of Nepal's biggest river operators, with good equipment, safety record and guides. Affiliated with *Borderland Resort* (see box, p.186) and Himalayan Mountain Bikes.

MOUNTAIN-BIKE TOURS

The following companies operate mountain-bike tours. For more on biking in Nepal, see also our "Mountain biking" chapter (see p.364).

Dawn Till Dusk Thamel Northwest, in the forecourt of the Kathmandu Guest House ⓣ01 470 0286, ⓦnepalbiking.com; map p.73. A seasoned operator offering short and long trips, including customized off-road itineraries and daily rental. Good bikes and repair facilities.

Nepal Mountain Bike Tours Thamel Northwest ⓣ01 470 1701, ⓦbikehimalayas.com; map p.73. Popular company that organizes the annual Nepal Mountain Bike Race (Oct or Nov) and runs tours, including the classic Nagarkot–Dhulikhel–Namobuddha circuit, starting from US$50 a day.

WILDLIFE PACKAGE TOURS

Although most of the budget lodges near Chitwan and Bardia national parks are represented by agents in Kathmandu, their packages are not recommended: Nepal's major wildlife parks are easily accessible by public transport, and arranging your own trip is a straightforward process that's much cheaper and much less rushed than a pre-arranged package. See the Chitwan (p.241) and Bardia (p.271) sections for details on doing it yourself.

Mountain Ecology Treks Chandol-4, Maharagunj ⓣ01 442 1821, ⓦmountainecologytreks.com; map p.58. This new agency is run by a highly respected, professional and experienced guide, who is also an expert birdwatcher. A wide range of treks are on offer, as well as wildlife- and birdwatching-focused tours.

1

SPORTS AND RECREATION

Golf Royal Nepal Golf Club (☎01 449 4247; temporary memberships available; around US$20–25/person, per round) has a nine-hole course near the airport, where monkeys are among the hazards. For an international-standard eighteen-hole course, head to *Gokarna Forest Resort* (p.105).

Hot-air balloon flights Balloon Sunrise Nepal (☎01 443 1078, ⓦcatmando.com/balloon) offers one-hour morning flights over the Kathmandu Valley; the price (US$195) includes hotel transfers, breakfast after the flight, and a certificate.

Hot-spring baths The *Royal Hana Garden* (☎01 441 6200), a Japanese restaurant just south of the French embassy in Lazimpath, has hot-spring baths in a green secluded grotto (daily 3–9pm; Rs340). The food's not bad either.

Swimming Many of the smarter hotels such as *Dwarika's* (see p.105), *Yak & Yeti* (see p.104) or *Hotel Shangri-La* (see p.104) will let you use their pools if you're a customer of their spas (US$10–20).

Tennis The *Yak & Yeti* (see p.105) has tennis courts open to nonresidents for a fee.

MEDITATION, YOGA AND ASTROLOGY

Not surprisingly, Kathmandu is an important centre for **spiritual pursuits**. This section concentrates on established outfits that cater specifically for Westerners; a scan through the posters in the popular lodges and restaurants will turn up many others. See also the organizations listed in the section on alternative therapies (see opposite), as there's a lot of overlap between the disciplines.

MEDITATION

Asheesh Osho Meditation Centre Tahachal ☎01 427 1385; map p.84; second branch in Kamaladi ☎01 427 1385; map p.59. Kathmandu supports a thriving Osho industry. The Asheesh centre, the first in Nepal, conducts one-hour dynamic meditation sessions every morning; these are open to all (donation expected).

Buddha Dharma Center On a high point south of Swayambhu ☎01 428 2744, ⓦsangling.org; map pp.58–59. For anyone interested in residential study of Tibetan Buddhism, this centre offers instruction under the direction of Lopon Tsechu Rinpoche. Many more opportunities exist in Boudha (see p.133).

Himalayan Buddhist Meditation Centre Hotel Himalaya Yoga, Thamel ☎980 325 4704; map p.73. Guided meditation sessions (Sat 10–11.30am), plus Tibetan Buddhism and yoga classes. HBMC is affiliated with Kopan Monastery, north of Boudha (p.133), and another monastery in Pokhara (p.216). More information is available on their Facebook page.

Nepal Vipassana Centre ☎01 425 0581, ⓦshringa .dhamma.org; map p.84. Ten-day residential courses in Budhanilkantha. These aren't for the frivolous: daily meditation begins at 4.30am, and silence is kept for the duration. To register or find out more, visit the centre's Kathmandu office (Mon–Fri & Sun 10am–5pm) in the courtyard of Jyoti Bhawan, behind Nabil Bank on Kantipath. All courses are funded by donations.

Osho Tapoban Forest Retreat Centre North of Nagarjun Ban ☎01 511 2012, ⓦtapoban.com; map pp.58–59. Meditation retreats in a beautiful setting, with full-board prices from Rs2200/person/day.

YOGA

Kamma Healing Centre Baber Mahal Revisited, off Airport Rd ☎01 425 6618; map p.61. A good choice for yoga (Rs400) and t'ai chi classes (Rs 4000/month), or join the free meditation class at 4pm on Sat (call first).

Patanjali Yoga Centre Tahachal, next to Shrestha Guest House ☎01 427 8437, ⓦyogakathmandu.com; map p.61. Daily drop-in classes, private tuition and five-day intensive courses in pure Ashtanga yoga. Contact the centre for information on residential study and its teacher training programme in Pokhara.

★**Pranamaya Yoga Centres** Above Himalaya Java and opposite Fire and Ice in Thamel; map p.73; and near Moksh bar in Patan; map p.87; ⓦpranamaya -yoga.com. This well-run outfit offers a variety of excellent daily classes (Rs700) including iyengar, power, flow and pregnancy yoga, as well as Pilates. It also runs three-day yoga retreats (US$295) in Pharping (see p.146).

ASTROLOGY

It's best not to single out individual astrologers in the Kathmandu area, partly because few of them speak English, but mostly because they all have their own flocks to look after and it wouldn't be fair to rain hordes of foreign horoscope-seekers down on them. Try offering staff at your hotel or a guide a commission to take you to their astrologer and translate for you – you'll get a fascinating glimpse into an extremely important but behind-the-scenes aspect of Newari life (see p.153). To have a horoscope prepared you'll need to provide the exact time and place of birth (if you don't know the time, the astrologer may be able to improvise by reading your palm). It'll then take up to a week to produce an annual chart, longer for a full span-of-life chart. In a separate session, the astrologer will interpret it for you. The fee for the entire service may run to Rs1500 or more. If nothing else, you'll come away with a beautiful and unique work of art, hand-calligraphed and painted on a parchment scroll.

ALTERNATIVE THERAPIES

Many of what the West calls **alternative therapies** are, of course, established practice in Nepal (see p.43). The full range of remedies is quite a bit greater than what you see in this section, which focuses on what's accessible to the average visitor.

AYURVEDIC MEDICINE

Ayurveda Health Home Tilingatar, near Hotel Shahanshah ☎01 435 8761, ⓦayurveda.com.np. Private consultations at a group practice. Daily 8am–7pm.
Dr Madhu Bajracharya Behind the Bir Hospital in central Kathmandu ☎01 422 3960. The son of Nepal's most famous practitioner offers private consultations.
Gorkha Ayurved Company East of the Royal Palace on Nagpokhari Sadak ☎01 428 6873 ⓦgorkhaayurved .com. Come here to fill ayurvedic prescriptions, or if your Nepali is up to it, go to any of the ayurvedic *pharmas* lining Yogbir Singh Marg, the lane running west from the Nardevi Mandir just north of Durbar Square.

TIBETAN MEDICINE

Kailash Medical and Astro Institute Dhobichaur (the road leading northwest from Chhetrapati Chowk) ☎01 424 8889, ⓦmen-tsee-khang.org/branch/nepal; plus other outlets elsewhere, including in Boudha ☎01 448 4869. Offers a comparable range of treatments to Kunphen Tibetan Medical Clinic, and keeps similar hours.
Kunphen Tibetan Medical Clinic Kunphen Marg, north of Chhetrapati Chowk ☎01 425 1920, ⓦkunphen .tripod.com. This is basically a front office for a Tibetan medicine company, whose products it sells, but its diagnostic services are recommended. Mon–Fri 10am–5pm.

MASSAGE

Most of the "Yoga and Massage" signs around Thamel have been put there by charlatans. Some, especially those offering "special" massages, are fronts for prostitution; studies suggest there are as many as five thousand sex workers in Kathmandu. That said, a few legitimate masseurs do exist in Thamel and other tourist/expat areas, though they come and go – check the notice boards and ask to see credentials. A Nepali massage should cost around Rs500–1000/hr; other types of massage cost more. Most of the high-end hotels will allow non-guests to use their spas for a day rate (US$10–20).
Healing Hands Center Near the Russian embassy, Maharajganj ☎985 103 8447, ⓦancientmassage.com. Thai massage, as well as t'ai chi, yoga and meditation sessions.
★ **Himalayan Healers** Tridevi Marg, Thamel ☎01 443 7183, ⓦhimalayanhealers.org; also in several other hotels across Nepal. A highly recommended organization that trains members of "untouchable" castes in massage and spa techniques. Discounts available before 2pm. Daily 9am–8pm.
Tranquility Spa Various locations in Kathmandu and Patan ☎01 441 1818, ⓦtranquilityspa.com.np. A recommended spa offering various therapies – ayurvedic, aroma, deep tissue, hot stone and spinal.

ACCOMMODATION

Kathmandu and Patan have myriad accommodation options, with something for every budget. The most popular hotels fill up early in the high season (especially in Oct), so **book ahead** if you can. During the **winter**, when the city can be chilly – if not as cold as most tourists expect – inexpensive guesthouses will provide cotton quilts, but few have portable heaters and only the more expensive hotels have central heating. Try to get a room that doesn't overlook the street: Kathmandu's barking dogs, banging pots and traffic **noise** could wake the dead. Most hotels provide internet and/or wi-fi access, and many offer free airport pick-ups. If you don't want to stay in Kathmandu or Patan you don't have to – Boudha (p.130), Bhaktapur (p.154) and numerous other places in the Kathmandu Valley are easily accessible.

THAMEL

Tourist ghettos like Thamel follow a circular logic: most people stay there because, well, most people stay there. And the more people stay there, the more Thamel turns itself into what it thinks foreigners want it to be, which increases its popularity. Especially in the high season, there's so much hype, and so little that has anything to do with Nepal, that you may wonder why it remains as popular as it does. "Thamel" nowadays refers to a large area containing a ridiculous number of hotels. The listings below are split into three geographical groupings. Central Thamel comprises the strips immediately north, south and east of the *Kathmandu Guest House*, where tourist

development began and has now reached its unholy zenith. North Thamel includes Paknajol, Bhagwan Bahal and Kaisher Mahal – neighbourhoods that are no longer distinct from Thamel proper, but are at least a bit less like a

> ### TOP 5 PLACES TO STAY ON A BUDGET
> **Cherry Guest House** (see p.102)
> **Himalaya's Guest House** (see p.104)
> **Mahabuddha Guest House** (see p.105)
> **Mustang Holiday Inn** (see p.104)
> **Tibet Peace Guest House** (see p.102)

1

circus. South Thamel spans the areas of Chhetrapati, Thahiti and Jyatha, which, while similarly in thrall to tourism, manage to preserve more of the architecture and culture of the old city.

CENTRAL THAMEL

Kathmandu Guest House Thamel Northwest ☎ 01 470 0632, ⓦ ktmgh.com; map p.73. Thamel's original and best-known guesthouse is set well back from the noisy street, with a pleasant garden and a buzzing atmosphere. There are nine classes of rooms, from a couple of "ultra-basic" backpacker boxes to modern a/c suites ($180); the cheapest standard room is US$20. In addition, there are innumerable services including a barber, beauty salon, coffee shop, restaurant, bar, souvenir shops, and a travel agency, plus a useful notice board. US$12

Hotel Potala Narsingh Camp ☎ 01 470 0680, ⓦ potalahotel.com; map p.73. Run by an incredibly friendly Tibetan family, this central place has rooms that are good value but also cramped and a little dark; some have private bathrooms, and there's also a roof terrace. Includes breakfast. US$13

NORTH THAMEL

Hotel Courtyard Zed St ☎ 01 470 0476, ⓦ hotelcourtyard.com; map p.73. Cross the bridges over the water feature to reach this charming, sheltered hotel, which has large, swish en suites, Newari architectural touches, a funky bar with cosy sofas, and a range of massage options. US$55

Holy Lodge Saat Ghumti ☎ 01 470 1763, ⓦ holylodge .com; map p.73. The carpets are a little grubby, but otherwise the rooms – set around a central courtyard – are decent enough for travellers on a budget; those with private bathrooms, a/c and TVs cost roughly triple the price of the cheapest options. US$10

International Guest House Paknajol ☎ 01 425 2299, ⓦ ighouse.com; map p.73. This hotel, featuring elegant Newari carved wood, feels far away from the Thamel bustle. While the stuffed animal heads and horns on the walls are a bit incongruous, the garden is immaculate, and the rooms and four-bed dorm are neat and tidy, though a little overpriced. Rates include breakfast. Dorms US$10, doubles US$25

Karma Travellers Home Thamel North ☎ 01 441 7897, ⓦ hotelkarma.com; map p.73. Also known as *Hotel Karma*, this economical hotel does the basics well: all of the rooms are clean and well tended and come with private bathrooms and TVs, while the staff are both welcoming and helpful. A/c rooms cost just US$10 extra. US$15

Kathmandu Garden House Paknajol ☎ 01 438 1239, ⓦ hotel-in-nepal.com; map p.73. One of a string of good-value hotels along a quiet (for Kathmandu) back lane, this lodge has a flower-filled garden, a big book exchange, welcoming staff and clean, reliable en-suite rooms with TVs. Rs1000

Pilgrims Guest House Bhagwan Bahal ☎ 01 444 0565, ⓦ pilgrimsguesthouse.com; map p.73. Although service is not always reliable, this is a reasonable choice, with a range of very clean rooms with comfy beds; top-floor suites with a/c cost twice the price. There's a restaurant-bar, small book exchange, and even a water feature in the courtyard. US$20

Tasi Dhargey Inn Thamel North ☎ 01 470 0030, ⓦ hoteltashidhargey.com; map p.73. This bustling, efficient hotel is right in the heart of things. The top-floor rooms (which have a/c, private bathrooms, TVs and phones) are the pick of the bunch and very good value at US$20, but all are fine. There's a fifteen percent discount for online bookings. US$15

★ **Tibet Peace Guest House** Paknajol ☎ 01 438 1026, ⓦ tibetpeace.com; map p.73. Something of a haven, this popular lodge offers twee but serviceable rooms with private bathrooms and TVs, and added bonuses such as security boxes, a garden, hot water and a decent Tibetan restaurant . Rs800

SOUTH THAMEL

★ **Café Mitra Guest House** Thamel South ☎ 01 425 9015, ⓦ cafemitra.com; map p.73. Attached to the restaurant of the same name, this excellent boutique hotel has just eight rooms, four looking out onto a garden courtyard. The exemplary en suites have been decorated with flair and attention – features include wood-effect floors and stylish sinks. Rates include breakfast. US$85

Cherry Guest House J.P. School Rd ☎ 01 421 5697, ⓔ cherryguesthouse@hotmail.com; map p.73. With a pink interior, small book exchange, warm welcome and loyal Japanese and Korean following, *Cherry Guest House* also has clean but decidedly spartan rooms with shared or private bathrooms at rock-bottom prices. Rs450

Hotel Ganesh Himal South of Chhetrapati ☎ 01 426 3598, ⓦ ganeshhimal.com; map p.69. Away from the tourist scrum of central Thamel, and with its own garden, *Ganesh Himal* is a very popular – if occasionally a little chaotic – hotel with a range of neat and tidy en suites with TVs, phones and fans or a/c, as well as nice touches like free filtered water. US$25

Kantipur Temple House Jyatha ☎ 01 425 0131, ⓦ kantipurtemplehouse.com; map p.73. Atmospheric Newari-style architecture, an environmentally friendly ethos (there is a "no plastic" policy for example), welcoming staff, a peaceful garden, a fine restaurant serving predominantly organic food and attractive en suites make this hotel a great choice. US$98

TOP 5 HOTELS TO SPLASH OUT ON

Dwarika's (see opposite)
Hyatt Regency (see opposite)
Hotel Shangri-La (see below)
Traditional Homes Swotha (see opposite)
Hotel Vajra (see opposite)

Mustang Holiday Inn Off Jyatha Thamel ☏ 01 424 9041, ⊛ mustangholidayinn.com; map p.73. Owned by the Mustang royal family, this hotel has worn but okay rooms with private bathrooms and TV (some also have snooker-table-green carpets). There's little difference between standard and deluxe options apart from a/c and US$30 extra. US$15

Namtso Rest House Jyatha Thamel ☏ 01 425 1238, ⊜ namtsorh@wlink.com.np; map p.73. Follow a marble staircase up to this keenly priced hotel, which has plain, forensically clean rooms with modern attached bathrooms, phones and TVs. Try to get one that catches the afternoon sun. Rs1500

Nirvana Garden Hotel Chhetrapati ☏ 01 425 6200, ⊛ nirvanagarden.com; map p.73. The carefully tended garden gives the hotel a serene air, despite the central position, though it may be a little low-key for some. The reasonably priced en suites have marble bathrooms and little seating areas; a/c costs US$31 extra. US$62

Tibet Guest House Chhetrapati ☏ 01 426 0383, ⊛ tibetguesthouse.com; map p.73. Big, professional hotel straddling the budget and mid-range brackets. All rooms come with TV and private baths, though the deluxe rooms (US$60) in the new wing are more comfortable and have a/c; if you're paying less, however, there are better cheapies nearby. Book online for a twenty percent discount. US$25

JHOCHHE (FREAK STREET)

Quieter and less touristy than Thamel, Jhochhe (aka Freak Street) is much more authentically Nepali, closer to the old city sights and noticeably cheaper. However, comprised mainly of older traditional buildings and somewhat poky family-run businesses, it also has considerably fewer of the restaurants and other facilities that make Thamel so convenient. But, of course, that's precisely what makes it an interesting place to stay.

Century Lodge Jhochhe ☏ 01 424 7641, ⊛ centurylodge.4t.com; map p.75. Despite the dull brick exterior and gloomy entrance, this lodge is not without charm. Its rooms are clean and cheerful, and those with shared facilities often have small balconies. The low ceilings in the cheaper rooms, however, rule it out for any six-footers, though you can pay Rs450 more for the much bigger deluxe room. Rs750

★**Himalaya's Guest House** Between Jhochhe and Chikamugal ☏ 01 425 8444, ⊜ himalgst@hotmail.com; map p.75. Hidden at the end of a narrow alley (follow the signs from the square), this welcoming family home has a sizeable library, roof garden and spick and span rooms, which get better the higher up the building you go (some even have TVs). Rs800

Monumental Paradise Jhochhe ☏ 01 424 6555, ⊜ mparadise52@hotmail.com; map p.75. This hotel is a touch more comfortable than most of the others in the area, though it's somewhat lacking in atmosphere. Rooms come with tiny private bathrooms (hot water during the day only), and there's also a roof terrace and bar. US$12

Hotel Sugat Basantapur ☏ 01 424 5824, ⊜ maryman @mos.com.np; map p.75. Dusty old place with a faintly hippyish air, relying on its prime Basantapur Square location. The threadbare rooms are generally clean enough, and some of those with shared bathrooms have great views (as has the roof garden terrace). Rs900

DURBAR MARG AND LAZIMPATH

Accommodation elsewhere in the city beyond Freak Street and Thamel is more spread out. Running south from the Royal Palace, Durbar Marg holds a handful of Kathmandu's poshest hotels, as well as many upscale restaurants and shops. Running north from the Royal Palace, Lazimpath boasts a selection of mid- and top-end hotels, and some interesting restaurants and bars.

Hotel Manaslu Lazimpath ☏ 01 441 0071, ⊛ hotelmanaslu.com; map p.84. In the shadow of the looming *Radisson*, this hotel has well-appointed terracotta-tiled rooms (some overlooking the garden, no extra price), with traditional carved windows, a pseudo-American bar and a pool complete with waterspouting statues. US$80

★**Hotel Shangri-La** Lazimpath ☏ 01 441 2999, ⊛ hotelshangrila.com; map p.61. One of the city's top hotels, this five-star is tucked away in embassyland and offers stylish en suites with dark wood furnishings and king-sized beds, as well as peaceful flower gardens, pool, gym, casino and restaurant-bar. US$271

Hotel Shanker Lazimpath ☏ 01 441 0151, ⊛ shankerhotel.com.np; map p.61. A refurbished palace with a sprinkling of French architectural touches and elegant en suites, some with bath tubs. There's also a great pool, manicured gardens and a couple of good eating options. US$187

Hotel Yak & Yeti Durbar Marg ☏ 01 248 8999, ⊛ yakandyeti.com; map p.84. Kathmandu's most famous hotel is in a 100-year-old former Rana palace and counts Edmund Hillary among its past guests. It offers opulent rooms, excellent restaurants, manicured grounds, two pools, tennis courts, a health club and a 24hr casino. Save fifty percent by booking online. US$298

WEST OF THE BISHNUMATI AND EASTERN NEIGHBOURHOODS

There's only one real reason to stay west of the Bishnumati, and that's to be near the popular Swayambhu stupa. There aren't many hotels and guesthouses here, though. The city's best hotel, *Dwarika's*, is close to the Pashupatinath temple complex in Battisputali.

★ **Dwarika's** Battisputali ☎ 01 447 9488, ⓦ dwarikas .com; map pp.58–59. If money is no object, this is the place to stay. *Dwarika's* is a five-star heritage hotel that makes use of woodwork and other artefacts salvaged from temple and house restorations. The Newari-style en suites are sumptuous, service is on point, there's a wonderful pool and tranquil grounds, plus several outstanding restaurants. US$362

Gokarna Forest Resort Gokarna forest, 14km from city centre ☎ 01 445 1212, ⓦ gokarna.com; map pp.58–59. Luxurious "country club" resort, with traditional Nepali-style architecture and a wonderfully peaceful location within the pristine (apart from the eighteen-hole golf course) Gokarna forest. There's also a pool, forest trails and a spa. US$160

Hyatt Regency Kathmandu Taragaon ☎ 01 491 1234, ⓦ hyatt.com; map pp.58–59. Nepal's biggest five-star hotel, which dominates the skyline 1km west of the Boudha stupa, has a bit more character than many other *Hyatts*, featuring plentiful "heritage" detailing, swish en suites, several places to eat and drink, tennis courts, fitness centre and two outdoor pools. US$165

★ **Hotel Vajra** Bijeshwari, about 1km east of Swayambhu ☎ 01 427 1545, ⓦ hotelvajra.com; map p.61. Resembling a pagoda, *Vajra* has an elaborate Tibetan fresco in the hall, a library, beautiful carvings and a theatre, as well as a restaurant and bar. The majority of rooms are en suite (US$47–75), some with their own balconies, but there are a few cheaper rooms with shared facilities. The views of Swayambhu from the roof terrace are the icing on the cake. US$20

PATAN

South of Kathmandu, Patan offers a pleasant alternative to the Kathmandu scene. Its culture is more intact, yet it has sufficient restaurants and facilities, and easy enough access to Kathmandu. However, there's a distinct lack of accommodation in the old part of Patan and what there is fills up early, so book ahead.

Café de Patan Guest House Mangal Bazaar ☎ 01 553 7599, ⓦ cafedepatan.com; map p.87. Small, very popular lodge attached to the eponymous restaurant (see p.110), with simple, bright and clean rooms (with shared or private bathrooms). Service, and the location on the edge of the square, are both excellent. Rs900

Hotel Himalaya Kupondol ☎ 01 552 3900, ⓦ himalayahotel.com.np; map p.87. Top-end hotel offering contemporary en suites with white and beige colour schemes; the more expensive options have good mountain views. It also has an appealing pool, health club, sauna, and a popular, though pricey, restaurant. There's a thirty percent discount for online bookings. US$224

★ **Mahabuddha Guest House** Uku Bahal ☎ 01 554 0575, ⓔ nfosterm@wlink.com.np; map p.87. Great budget lodge, located close to the Mahabuddha temple, with clean, homely rooms; some lack natural light, though all have private bathrooms. There's an apartment for longer stays and fabulous views from the rooftop terrace. Rs700

Traditional Homes Swotha By the Narayan temple, just north of Patan Museum ☎ 01 555 1184, ⓦ traditionalhomes.com.np; map p.87. This boutique B&B is housed in a restored Newari building just northeast of Durbar Square and the rooms are comfortable and characterful, with exposed brick walls, but modern fittings. The staff are friendly and helpful and it has a very fine international restaurant (see p.110). US$90

★ **Newa Chén** Near Durbar Square ☎ 01 553 3532, ⓦ newachen.com; map p.87. This traditional Newari house has been transformed into an outstanding, intimate and great-value hotel, with just eight rooms (five of which have private bathrooms). Carved wood, exposed brickwork, low ceilings and excellent service ensure a memorable stay. Rates include breakfast, which is taken in the beautiful courtyard. US$33

Yala Guest House Durbar Square ☎ 01 552 2187, ⓦ yalaguesthouse.com; map p.89. This backpacker favourite boasts the best location in Patan, with rooms looking out directly onto Durbar Square. Standards are a bit slack, however, and the rooms could do with a freshen-up. The restaurant has sensational views (but so-so food). Rs1500

EATING

Scores of **restaurants** and **cafés** line Kathmandu's tourist quarters, and more spring up each year. While some carry on in a funky 1970s style, a growing number have gone upmarket. If you can't be bothered to go out, many restaurants (including quite a few from our listings) will **deliver** though the ⓦ foodmandu.com website.

ESSENTIALS

Cuisine Fine Nepali/Newari food is increasingly available in both tourist and local restaurants. Tibetan, Chinese and Indian restaurants have long been widespread, but there are also numerous places serving Japanese, Thai and Korean food. You can also find good French and Italian restaurants, and even some offering more unusual choices like Bhutanese, Cajun, Turkish and Irish cuisine.

1

Innumerable restaurants cater to travellers with all-purpose "continental" menus; they're all pretty samey, featuring "buff" (buffalo) steaks, variable pastas and pizzas, and a few pseudo-Mexican and Greek dishes. Bakeries producing pastries and cakes are similarly ubiquitous. Almost every restaurant has at least a few vegetarian options.

Health Food can also be the biggest peril of staying in Kathmandu. More travellers get sick here than anywhere else, often as a result of placing too much trust in the hygiene of tourist restaurants. Indeed, local restaurants are arguably safer, as chefs know what they're doing when they prepare Nepali food. The places listed here are generally reliable, but heed the words of caution in our "Basics" chapter (see p.39).

Opening times Note that although we've given opening times for the cafés, restaurants and bars below, these should only be taken as a general guide – most places don't keep set hours.

Picnic food For picnic ingredients and other provisions, stores in Thamel sell just about everything you could want; Big Mart in Lazimpath and Namaste Supermarket in Patan have an even greater selection (see p.116).

THAMEL

As with lodgings, Thamel generally has the newest, trendiest and most professional budget restaurants. That said, many have become so stylish that they've priced themselves out of the budget category, and sampling them is one of the great pleasures of staying in the district.

CENTRAL THAMEL

Fire and Ice Tridevi Marg ☎01 425 0210, ⓦfireandicepizzeria.com; map p.73. With a name inspired by a Robert Frost poem, the ever-popular *Fire and Ice* serves thin-crust, though slightly oily pizzas (Rs590–900), plus paninis, pastas, risottos and ice cream. Service is quick, but the music can be cheesy. Generally open daily 8am–10.30pm.

K-Too! Near Thamel Chowk ☎01 250 441, ⓦkilroygroup.com; map p.73. An offshoot of *Kilroy's* (see opposite), with a pub atmosphere. It's especially known for its steaks (house steak Rs360, massive Chateaubriand Rs1175), sandwiches and burgers (around Rs250), but also serves up tacos and burritos. There's live sport on TV, board games and good beers, cocktails and wines. Daily 7.30am–11pm.

★**New Orleans** Thamel Northwest ☎01 470 0736; map p.73. One of the few Thamel restaurants expats still visit, *New Orleans* is set in the courtyard of a Newari house and has a tasty menu (with everything from Indian to Cajun food – most mains around Rs250–650) and live jazz on Wednesdays and Saturdays. The gourmet burgers are good, as is the excellent hummus. There's another branch in

Patan, which hosts a Sunday farmer's market (9am–noon). Daily 9am–9.30pm.

OR2K Thamel ☎01 442 2097, ⓦor2k.net; map p.73. Perch on cushions, enjoy the chilled, candlelit atmosphere, swap stories with the next table and tuck into generous portions of falafel (Rs335), hummus (Rs250) and other Middle Eastern treats; the "combo platter" (Rs645) is ideal for sharing. If you're in a hurry, grab a snack from the takeaway counter upstairs. Daily 9am–11pm.

Pumpernickel Bakery Thamel ☎01 425 9185, ⓦpumpernickelbakery.com; map p.73. Long-running café with a garden out back and quality baked goods – including sourdough, banana bread and cinnamon whirls – which are probably worth the slightly higher prices compared with other Thamel bakeries. Cakes Rs55–150 per slice. Generally open daily 7am–8pm.

Roadhouse J.P. School Rd ☎01 426 2768; map p.73. Drawing an older crowd than many other Thamel restaurants, *Roadhouse* has well-prepared dishes like wood-oven pizzas (Rs430–840), tiramisu and various other Western dishes such as pastas and steaks, plus Illy coffee (which you can also take away). Daily 11am–10pm.

Third Eye J. P. School Rd ☎01 426 0289, ⓦthirdeye .com.np; map p.73. Mainly high-end North Indian *tandoor*-based cuisine, with a few Western dishes thrown in, served either in a sleek interior or out on the terrace. The tandoori chicken (Rs975) is particularly good, as are the pastas (Rs400–500); other mains cost around Rs500-1000. Only serves Halal meat and no pork. Daily 10am–10pm.

Yin Yang J.P. School Rd ☎01 470 1510; map p.73. Managed by the same team as its neighbour, *Third Eye* (see above), this restaurant specializes in Thai food, with most mains in the Rs500–1000 range. The seafood, such as the sweet and sour prawns, is a highlight. Daily 10am–10pm.

NORTH THAMEL

Dechenling North of Trivedi Marg ☎01 441 158; map p.73. Although it styles itself as a beer garden, *Dechenling* is a tranquil place with wicker chairs and flower-filled grounds. The menu features unusual dishes (Rs300–1000) like *erma dhatsi* (a fiery Bhutanese cheese and mushroom curry) and *shabrel* (Tibetan meatballs), plus draught beer (Rs350). Generally open daily 9am–10pm.

Himalayan Java Tridevi Marg ☎01 442 2519, ⓦhimalayanjava.com; map p.73; another branch near the Kathmandu Guest House; map p.73. Aping the style of international coffee-house chains, *Himalayan Java* serves excellent lattes, cappuccinos, Americanos, espressos and iced and frozen coffees (Rs65–190), as well as reasonable pastries, croissants and brownies. Service can be sloppy. Daily 7am–10pm.

★**Korean Kitchen** North of Tridevi Marg; map p.73. Also known as *Picnic*, this tiny restaurant has a handful of

FIVE-STAR DINING

If you can't afford to stay in one of Kathmandu's five-star hotels, the next best thing is to have dinner in one: for not much more than the cost of a meal at a good Thamel restaurant, you'll have an experience unavailable back home at almost any price. The best **hotel restaurants** offer sumptuous food, unusual specialities, opulent decor, over-the-top service and music and/or dance performances. It's worth booking ahead and dressing up a bit if you plan to visit these restaurants, though neither is essential. Whichever one you choose, expect to pay at least around Rs2000 for a meal.

Chimney See p.109

Krishnarpan See p.109

Mako's See p.109

low tables and fiercely authentic Korean food at economical prices. Try one of the good-value vegetable, chicken, pork, fish or beef "lunchboxes" (Rs300–350). Daily 11am–8.30pm; closed on the 25th of each month.

Thakali Bhanchha Corner of Thamel Northwest and Zed St ☏01 470 1910; map p.73. A mainly local crowd comes to this unpretentious Nepali-Tibetan restaurant, which serves the food of the Thakali people of the Annapurna region, with bargain set meals (less than Rs160) and excellent *momos* – try the potato *alu dameto* ones (Rs170). Generally open daily 10am–10pm.

Thamel House Thamel Northeast ☏01 441 0388, ⊛thamelhouse.com; map p.73. Exemplary Nepali and Newari food – including unusual items like wild boar (Rs510) – served in the covered patio garden of an evocative old townhouse. Other mains start at Rs200. If you're hungry, opt for one of the generous set dinners (Rs1120–1230). Daily 11am–10pm.

SOUTH THAMEL

Anatolia Chhetrapati ☏01 425 8757; map p.73. Drawing a Muslim crowd from across Kathmandu, this halal restaurant specializes in sizzling kebabs from India, Turkey and Tibet; the *adana* kebab (Rs410) is particularly good. Just try to block out the sickly pink walls. Mains Rs95–445. Daily 10am–10pm.

Café Mitra Thamel South ☏01 425 6336, ⊛cafemitra .com; map p.73. Seductive restaurant in a quaint old house, with exposed beams, smartly laid tables and inventive – if steeply priced – dishes (Rs500–1300) such as roast quail with Asian pesto. They also do good steaks and tempting desserts. Generally open daily 10am–10pm.

Chikusa Jyatha Thamel ☏01 423 2990, ⊛chikusacafe .com; map p.73. Tiny café, popular with French-speakers, both from Nepal and abroad, serving proper coffee, *lassis* (including a strawberry-flavoured variety), economical breakfasts with thick wedges of toast (Rs230–290), sandwiches and crepes. Mon–Sat 7am–7pm, Sun 7am–2pm.

★ **Everest Steak House** Chhetrapati ☏01 426 0471; map p.73. This long-time Nepali institution, with another

branch in Pokhara (see p.220), serves tasty, cooked-to-order steaks and burgers (the beef imported from Kolkata), in comfortable surroundings. The standard steaks are 300g (Rs700–1200), though you can also opt for a 150g half-steak (Rs400–600), which are pretty filling. It gets very busy around mealtimes, so arrive early. Daily 10am–10pm.

Galleria Café J.P. School Rd; map p.73. This suave café has a stripped-back feel, Illy coffee (Rs100–250), sandwiches, salads and cakes, as well as, sadly, a cloying playlist of 80s ballads. The outdoor seats offer a good vantage point from which to survey the Thamel maelstrom. Daily 7am–10pm.

Helena's J.P. School Rd ☏01 426 6979, ⊛helenasrestaurant.com; map p.73. One of Thamel's oldest establishments, *Helena's* is located in a towering building. The highlight is the roof terrace, which has great views, especially at sunset. Although the menu holds no surprises – pasta, *momos* etc (mains Rs250–650) – the food is decent, and the steaks are reasonable value. Daily 7.30am–11pm.

Kilroy's Jyatha Thamel ☏01 425 0440, ⊛kilroygroup .com; map p.73. French-owned, and run by a highly credentialled Irish chef, *Kilroy's* has a smart dining area, a kitsch garden, slightly overbearing staff and a predominantly European and Indian menu specializing in fish (most mains Rs600–1150). Fish aside, the breast of chicken stuffed with mushrooms (Rs750) is excellent, as are the desserts, notably the light-as-air bread-and-butter pudding (Rs350). Daily 10am–10pm.

Nepalese Kitchen Chhetrapati; map p.73. A shaded, plant-filled courtyard restaurant with a good line in *thali*-style Nepali food and breakfast options – including muesli, rosti, sausages and cornflakes – from all over the world. Set breakfasts Rs115–280. Generally open daily 8am–9.30pm.

Rum Doodle Bar and Restaurant Jyatha Thamel ☏01 424 8692, ⊛therumdoodle.com; map p.73. Signed paper "footprints" of Everest summiteers are tacked up on the wall of this famous, long-running restaurant-bar, which is named after the mountaineering spoof by

1

W.E. Bowman. Pizzas, steaks and chicken in a basket are among the dishes on offer. Mains Rs360–1000. Mon–Thurs & Sun 10am–10pm, Fri & Sat 10am–midnight.

★**Shree Lal House Pure Vegetarian Restaurant** Thamel South ☎01 425 0417; map p.73. Follow a narrow passage down to this tiny subterranean restaurant, which serves excellent meat-free Indian food at very competitive prices (mains Rs160–200, *thali* Rs275). The *paneer* dishes are particularly good, and the South Indian *dosas* are a fine breakfast or lunchtime choice. Daily 8am–10pm.

Weizen Bakery J.P. School Rd; map p.73. Cheaper than, but not quite as good as *Pumpernickel* (see p.106), *Weizen* has pineapple pastries, bagels, brown rolls, brownies and much more, with cakes and pastries in the Rs65–100 range. There's a seating area at the back where good breakfasts (Rs295) and snacks are on offer, as well as highly addictive pizzas. Daily 7am–10pm.

Yak Café Kwa Bahal ☎01 425 9318; map p.73. Join the Buddhist monks who come to this dimly lit restaurant for traditional Tibetan food (Rs90–185), such as *guma* (sausages) and the *gyakok* (a brass container of meat, vegetables, tofu and vermicelli; Rs2125), which serves four and is washed down nicely with hot *tongba* beer (Rs155). It's not the very best Tibetan food, but the prices are excellent. Generally open daily 7/8am–10pm.

JHOCHHE (FREAK STREET) AND NEW ROAD

It may be noticeably cheaper than Thamel but, in the main,

Jhochhe also has a smaller and less interesting selection of restaurants. Nearby, just off New Road, there's a good Indian establishment.

Cosmopolitan Jhochhe; map p.75. Score a window seat and gaze out over the square from this cramped, smoky joint, haunted by the ghosts of travellers past. Low-cost breakfasts (Rs300–355), *momos* and international mains (Rs215–460) such as pasta are on offer. Daily 8am–10pm.

Nandan Off New Rd ☎01 424 1498, ⓦnandan.com .np; map p.74. You may have to queue for a table at lunchtime, but this vegetarian restaurant, patronized by Kathmandu's Indian residents, is worth the wait. Go for a *thali* (Rs348) and finish with a to-die-for *ras malai*. Daily 8am–9pm.

Organic Mantra, Fair Chakra Jhochhe ⓦorganic mantra.org; map p.75. Grab a stool or straw cushion and watch the world go by at this Freak Street place, which has unusual offerings such as goat's cheese sandwiches, lemongrass tea, sea buckthorn squash (available Nov–March) and various "prebiotic" concoctions. Drinks Rs35–195. Daily 8am–8pm.

★**Snowman** Jhochhe ☎01 424 6606; map p.75. Operating continuously since 1965, and still owned by the same family, this is the only original Freak Street pie shop still going, and it's got a kind of cool that doesn't go out of fashion. The apple crumble and chocolate cakes (around Rs100 a slice) are great, as are the juices and *lassis* (Rs60–80), but the atmosphere's the real attraction here. Daily 7am–9.30pm.

NEPALI, NEWARI AND TIBETAN RESTAURANTS

Kathmandu has some wonderful places at which to eat the ethnic cuisines of Nepal. Several of the **Nepali/Newari restaurants** recommended here are on the expensive side, but they're worth it. At the other extreme are the many dirt-cheap menu-less *bhojanalaya* (diners) and *bhatti* (taverns), which advertise themselves with a curtain hung over the entrance and are impossible to recommend by name. Most are Newari equivalents of a greasy spoon, but the best are fantastic. Ask around for suggestions, or try your luck in the areas north of Asan or north and west of Patan's Durbar Square. There are loads of inexpensive *sekuwa* joints on Putali Sadak Road, north of Singha Durbar, frequented by a predominantly male crowd from late afternoon onwards. They're great with a beer. You can find a rundown of Nepali and Newari dishes in our "Basics" chapter (see p.30).

    Tibetan restaurants, meanwhile offer some of the cheapest food in Kathmandu, and you pay even less at the many *momo* kitchens in the old city. Again, for descriptions of popular Tibetan dishes, turn to "Basics" (see p.31).

NEPALI AND NEWARI RESTAURANTS

Bhanchha Ghar Kamaladi. See opposite
Bhojan Griha Dilli Bazaar. See opposite
Krishnarpan Battisputali. See opposite
Nepalese Kitchen Chhetrapati, South
   Thamel. See p.107

Thakali Bhanchha North Thamel. See p.107
Thamel House North Thamel. See p.107

TIBETAN RESTAURANTS

Dechenling North Thamel. See p.106
Thakali Bhanchha North Thamel. See p.107
Yak Café South Thamel. See above

KANTIPATH, DURBAR MARG, LAZIMPATH AND BEYOND

There is a good selection of places to eat Nepali and Indian food on Durbar Marg, which is famous for its fine restaurants, while Lazimpath has a growing selection of better-value places, popular with foreign residents and Kathmandu's middle classes. Kantipath has less choice, but there are still a couple of places worth checking out.

1905 Kantipath ☎ 01 422 5272, ⊛ 1905restaurant .com; map p.84. Cross a bridge over a sunken lily pond to reach this beautiful colonial-style building (the menu tells you about its interesting history). Dishes are predominantly Asian and fusion cuisine and expensive, though you can also get a top Philly cheesesteak (Rs900). Dinner mains range from Rs620 to Rs2400, though lunch is considerably less. They also host a weekly farmer's market (Sat 9am–noon). Daily 8.30am–10pm.

Bhanchha Ghar Kamaladi ☎ 01 422 5172, ⊛ nepalibhanchha.com; map p.84. This smart restaurant serves up Nepali nouvelle cuisine – such as wild mushroom curry and buckwheat chapatis – in a beautifully converted Newari house. There are also nightly culture shows at 6.30pm and 7.30pm. Mains are Rs310 upwards, but most people plump for the extravagant set meal for Rs1370. Daily 10am–10pm.

Bhojan Griha Just off Dilli Bazaar ☎ 01 441 1603, ⊛ bhojangriha.com; map p.61. The "house of food", a fabulous 150-year-old restored Rana priest's mansion, provides a culture show with dinner (US$25, excluding drinks): much of the Nepali food is organic, and the dancing and music, from across the country, is entertaining. Daily lunch & dinner.

Chez Caroline Baber Mahal Revisited, off Airport Rd ☎ 01 426 3070, ⊛ chezcarolinenepal.com; map p.61. Classy French restaurant with outdoor courtyard seating and a patisserie. The food is of high quality, and suitably pricey (a meal isn't likely to come in under Rs2000), though there are some less expensive lunch options. Notable dishes include mango salad with duck (Rs1100), and crepes (Rs800). Daily 9am–11pm.

Chimney Hotel Yak & Yeti, Durbar Marg ☎ 01 424 8999, ⊛ yakandyeti.com; map p.84. Founded by Boris Lissanevitch, the legendary Russian adventurer who opened Kathmandu's first hotel in the 1950s, this superlative restaurant preserves his memory with dishes like borscht, Chicken Kiev and Baked Alaska. Reckon on spending around Rs1500–2000 for a full meal. Daily 6.30–9.30pm.

Dudh Sagar Kantipath ☎ 01 423 2263; map p.84. Good *misthan bhandars* – bustling canteens serving vegetarian South Indian food like dosas and toothsome sweets – are common in the Terai, but relatively rare in Kathmandu, so don't miss *Dudh Sagar*. Meals cost less than Rs150. Generally daily 9am–10pm.

Imago-Dei East of the Royal Palace on Nagpokhari Sadak ☎ 01 444 2464; map p.61. An airy, modern café, with leather sofas, attached art gallery and appealing sandwiches (including a meatball sub), wraps and other continental dishes (Rs520–1060). The desserts – chocolate brownies and cheesecake among them – are equally inviting. Daily 8am–9pm.

★ **Kaiser Café** Garden of Dreams ☎ 01 442 5341; map p.84. Run by *Dwarika's* hotel (see p.105), this tranquil place scatters its seating around stunning water gardens, full of nooks and crannies, and there's a romantic Classical pavilion, all white pillars and arches. The menu ranges from coffee and sandwiches to delicious main meals (from Rs1200) such as prawn kebabs or steaks. Check out the film nights, when you can watch movies on a big screen. Daily 9am–10pm.

Korea Pyongyang Arirang Restaurant Opposite Hotel Yak & Yeti, Durbar Marg ☎ 01 423 3288; map p.84. This is a pretty authentic North Korean restaurant, serving favourites such as *kimchi chiggae* (kimchi stew), *samgyeopsal* (BBQ pork) and very nice *pajan* (savoury pancake), with most dishes in the Rs250–400 range. The large dining area is a stage for weekend live music, and they also have *norebang* (karaoke rooms). Daily 10am–midnight.

Kotetsu Lazimpath ☎ 01 621 8513; map p.61. Widely considered to be the best Japanese restaurant in the city; if you manage to get a seat at the counter of this little place, you could find yourself eating next to the Japanese ambassador, who is a regular visitor. Mains cost around Rs600–800, but they also do very good weekday bento boxes for around Rs500. Mon–Fri noon–2.30pm & 6–9.30pm, Sat & Sun 6–10pm.

Koto Durbar Marg ☎ 01 422 0346; map p.84. This lauded first-floor Japanese restaurant, with plain tiled floors and wooden tables, has its focus firmly on the food: the teriyaki, *onigiri* (rice balls cooked in seaweed; Rs150), tempura and sushi all hit the spot, and there are some fine trout and mackerel dishes too. There's a new, tiny branch in Pulchowk too. Most dishes Rs300–800. Daily 11.30am–3pm & 6–9.30pm.

Krishnarpan Dwarika's, Battisputali ☎ 01 447 9488, ⊛ dwarikas.com; map pp.58–59. A wonderfully opulent restaurant in one of Kathmandu's finest hotels, *Dwarika's* (see p.105): the tables are made of antique latticework, and the excellent Nepali food is served on traditional tableware. Set meals run from 6 to 22 courses (US$57–80). Reservations required. Daily 6–10pm.

Mako's Dwarika's, Battisputali ☎ 01 447 9488, ⊛ dwarikas.com; map pp.58–59. Authentic, delicious and beautifully presented Japanese food in this splendid restaurant in *Dwarika's* (see p.105), one of the city's best hotels. The fish is fresh and flown in daily for the sushi and sashimi, and the Kobe beef is excellent. The two-person

1

shabu-shabu (hotpot) is popular at Rs2800, or it's around Rs2000–3000 for a meal. Reservations required. Daily 11.30am–2.30pm & 6–10pm.

Moti Mahal Delux Durbar Marg; map p.84. This superior pure veg Indian restaurant has a modern a/c interior with large glass windows, and a menu that focuses on north India, with the *paneer butter masala* (Rs615) and tandoori stuffed mushrooms (Rs555) particularly good. Other mains cost Rs350–615. Daily 11.30am–10pm.

★**Ringmo** Lazimpath ☎01 441 5327; map p.61. Still going strong after almost forty years, this hidden (and somewhat dingy) gem is an excellent place for a budget breakfast, or for superlative, thick US-style buckwheat pancake (Rs165–185; try the apple, banana or buttermilk varieties). They also do excellent *momos* for Rs120–140. The joint next door does great samosas and *chaat*. Generally daily 8am–9pm.

PATAN

Several restaurants and cafés cluster around Patan Durbar Square, targeting day-trippers. They're often packed at lunchtime, but are far more peaceful at night. The restaurants in the west side of Patan are patronized mainly by expats, NGO staff and well-heeled locals. Most are concentrated in an area dubbed Jhamel, a short way northwest of Jawalakhel Chowk.

Bakery Café Jawalakhel Chowk ☎01 552 2949, ⟨w⟩thebakerycafe.com.np; map p.87; there's another branch near the UN HQ, plus many other branches in and around Kathmandu. These branches of the *Bakery Café* chain, which provides employment opportunities for Nepalis with hearing impairments, are handy places for a drink or a quick bite. The menu features coffees, juices, smoothies and milkshakes (all Rs60–140), plus burgers and pizzas. Daily 7am–9.30pm.

Black Pepper Kupondol Heights ☎01 552 1897; map p.87. This multi-cuisine restaurant is housed in a Newari-style building with pleasant outdoor seating. Tasty food includes sirloin steak (Rs1250) and charcoal Jalkapur fish (Rs620), as well as some pretty good North Indian dishes (mains around Rs400). Generally daily noon–10pm.

Bú Kebá Kupondol Heights ☎01 552 4368; map p.87. *Bú Kebá* ("field" and "garden" in Newari) has an eco-friendly focus, and seventy percent of the menu is organic. Dishes include wraps, hummus and pita bread, pastas and – the standouts – buckwheat pancakes with mushrooms (Rs350) and trout fillet (Rs1050). Eat outside in the garden or inside reclining on cushions. Daily 11am–10pm.

Café de Patan Just off Durbar Square ☎01 553 7599, ⟨w⟩cafedepatan.com; map p.87. A travellers' favourite for more than 25 years, *Café de Patan* is still going strong. There's seating in the courtyard at the back and on the roof terrace – both good places to enjoy the well-prepared Nepali *thalis* (Rs750–800) and refreshing *lassis*. Daily 8am–10pm.

Café Swotha By the Narayan temple, just north of Patan Museum ☎01 555 1184; map p.87. Tiny and atmospheric restaurant, with just five tables, housed in the old stables of a traditional Newari house – now the *Traditional Homes Swotha* boutique B&B (see p.105). Food is an ecclectic mix of intenational foods such as a tasty lasagne (Rs600) and gourmet burgers (Rs580–680), though they also do a good Nepali *daal bhaat* (Rs500). Especially recommended are the fresh continental breakfasts and coffee. Daily 7.30am–10pm.

Café du Temple North side of Durbar Square ☎01 552 7127; map p.89. The sunny roof terrace has great views, the piped Nepali classical music is relaxing, and the Indian food (mains around Rs250–400) is pretty good too, as is the Nepali vegetarian set meal (Rs500). It's very popular with tour groups, however, so you may struggle to get a seat. Daily 9am–9pm.

★**Dhokaima Café** Patan Dhoka ☎01 552 2113, ⟨w⟩dhokaimacafe.com; map p.87. Beyond its less-than-promising entrance close to the bus stand, *Dhokaima* proves to be a sophisticated place: sit at a glass table and have a cocktail or glass of organic wine and something from the inviting menu – dishes include shiitake mushrooms on garlic toast (Rs360) and blackened Norwegian salmon (Rs1000). There are regular art and cultural events in the adjoining building. Generally daily 7am–9.30pm.

Kwalakhu Café Near the Golden Temple ☎01 621 2154; map p.87. Atmospheric café housed in a traditional Newari house, with a peaceful garden at the back – the perfect spot for a fresh lemon soda (Rs80) on a hot day, or a serving of *daal bhaat* (veg Rs700; non-veg Rs900). Daily 10am–8.30pm.

The Lazy Gringo Jawalakhel Chowk ☎01 221 0527; map p.87. Entered through an arch and up some stairs, this vaguely Mexican-looking restaurant serves excellent burritos (the "Stuffed Gringo" is highly recommended; Rs375–450), as well as tacos (Rs105–315) and quesadillas (Rs180–250). Tues–Sun 11am–9pm.

★**Namste Lumbini Tandoori Restaurant** Sign in Nepali, next to the Green Café on Jawalakhel Chowk ☎01 552 9197; map p.87. The kind of good-quality budget Indian place you could find yourself eating in every day if you're staying in the area, the *Namste Lumbini* serves great *roti* and *naan* from the *tandoor* outside, with a mean *dal* fried (Rs30) and a not so special but good-value *daal bhaat* (Rs90). Other Indian standards cost around Rs50–150. The dining area is nothing exciting, and the toilets best avoided. Daily 7am–9pm.

Sing-ma North of Jawalakhel Chowk ☎01 500 9092, ⟨w⟩singmafoodcourt.com; map p.87. This cheerful restaurant offers authentic Chinese, Singaporean and Malaysian hawker favourites at reasonable prices, with mains around Rs300–500. Dishes include crispy won tons, Hainanese chicken and a delicious beef *rendang*, as well as scrumptious blueberry cheesecake (Rs250). Mon–Fri & Sun 8.30am–9pm.

Swotha Kiosk Just off Durbar Square; map p.87. A tiny place – there are just two tables and four seats

– specializing in domestically produced and organic coffee and tea (both around Rs150), the latter produced in the Ilam region, which borders Darjeeling. Daily 9am–6pm.

NIGHTLIFE AND ENTERTAINMENT

The capital's nightlife scene has in the past been pretty subdued, with few places staying open later than midnight. However, in early 2014 the government announced that in order to encourage tourism, businesses in both Thamel and Durbar Marg would be able to stay open 24 hours; it's unclear at the time of writing what effect this will have, but bear in mind that the closing times listed below may change. Even if you're not able to have a really late night, there's plenty to keep you entertained: what follows is an overview of permanent attractions, from **bars** and **clubs** to **cultural shows** and **cinemas** – check the notice boards to find out about special events.

BARS AND NIGHTCLUBS

As with the tourist restaurants, Kathmandu's bars and nightclubs are more like a Nepali's idea of what they must be like than the real thing, but on the whole they're good for meeting, mixing and prolonging an otherwise short evening. The Thamel bars attract mainly backpackers, and a few young Nepali men hoping to hook up with Western women – some can be pretty seedy. A handful of fancier nightclubs elsewhere in the city attract a more diverse clientele; they're often cheesy and typically have a cover charge (Rs500 plus). Keep an eye out when you're heading home at night as muggings do sometimes occur.

THAMEL

★ **House of Music** Thamel Northeast ☎01 441 8209; map p.73. Slightly away from the main tourist drag, this bar – with a rooftop restaurant – is decorated with cool black-and-white photos, and owned by long-standing Nepali musicians, so a lot of the best live jazz, reggae and funk acts in the country play here (Fri & Sat 8pm–midnight). Daily 3pm–midnight.

Full Moon Thamel Northwest ☎980 102 3151, ⊛fullmooncafe.yolasite.com; map p.73. This tiny bar, on the first floor of a building in the heart of Thamel, features bamboo walls, low tables to sit crossed-legged at or chic armchairs on the terrace overlooking the street, friendly staff and an eclectic range of music. Generally daily 6am–2am.

The Reggae Café and Bar Chaksibari Marg, Thamel; map p.73. More frequented by locals than foreigners, this laidback upstairs place has a grungy feel (and decor), and a outdoor terrace for *sheesha* smoking. There's live music nightly (8–11.30pm), usually popular Nepali and English covers (to varying degrees of success), or very occasionally reggae. Daily 5pm–midnight.

Sam's Bar Thamel Northwest ☎984 949 4779; map p.73. A mix of travellers and locals hangout at this welcoming place, which has a mix of bar and terrace seating, as well as a reggae night (Sat) with a more diverse playlist than the standard Bob Marley classics. Daily 4pm–midnight.

Tom & Jerry Thamel Northwest; map p.73. Long-standing pub, popular with travellers, guides and younger NGO staff, *Tom & Jerry* has a welcoming atmosphere, a large TV screen for all the big sporting events and cold beer (around Rs400). Cocktails happy hour 5–8pm. Generally daily 4pm–midnight.

CENTRAL KATHMANDU

★ **Jazz Upstairs** Lazimpath ☎01 241 0436; map p.61. On the fourth floor (look for the guitar sign on the left) of a building just north of the Royal Palace, this welcoming bar is not to be missed: it has a great vibe, live jazz (Wed & Sat 8pm), top Darjeeling *momos* and a mixed crowd, which has on occasion included Sting. Mon 5–10pm, Tues–Thurs 9am–10pm, Fri 1pm–midnight, Sat noon–1pm & 5pm–midnight, Sun 11am–noon & 4–9pm.

PATAN

★ **Moksh** North of Jawalakhel Chowk, Patan ☎01 552 8362; map p.87. Patan's best bar draws a healthy sprinkling of local expats. Its garden and roof terrace play host to live bands (Tues, Fri & Sat), which are worth checking out, and it also serves a decent pizza (from Rs370). Generally Tues–Sun 10am–11pm.

CULTURE SHOWS

Music and dance are essential parts of Nepali life, and perhaps nowhere more so than in Kathmandu, where neighbourhood festivals, parades and weddings are an almost daily occurrence. Several Thamel restaurants host free folk music performances, and most of the top-end hotels do pricey dinner shows. Infrequent cultural evenings are held at the Royal Nepal Academy, off Kamaladi, and other venues such as the Patan Museum.

Bhojan Griha Just off Dilli Bazaar ☎01 441 1603, ⊛bhojangriha.com; map p.61. This place puts on nightly Nepali cultural performances from across the country in its atmospheric dining area, accompanied by excellent food (see p.109).

Hotel Vajra Bijeshwari ☎01 427 1695, ⊛hotelvajra.com. The *Vajra*'s resident ensemble has a superb classical

1

KATHMANDU'S FESTIVALS

The festivals listed here are just the main events; there are many others centred around local temples and neighbourhoods.

MAGH (JAN–FEB)

Basanta Panchami The spring festival is marked by a VIP ceremony in Durbar Square on the fifth day after the full moon. Children celebrate Saraswati Puja on the same day at Swayambhu.

PHAAGUN (FEB–MARCH)

Losar Tibetan New Year, observed at Swayambhu on the full moon of February, but more significantly at Boudha (see p.130).

Shiva Raatri "Shiva's Night" is celebrated with bonfires in Kathmandu on the new moon of Phaagun, but the most interesting observances are at Pashupatinath (see p.125).

Phaagun Purnima (Holi) Youths bombard each other and passers-by with coloured powder and water. The festival lasts a week, but peaks on the day of the full moon.

CHAIT (MARCH–APRIL)

Chait Dasain On the morning of the eighth day after the new moon, the army's top-ranking officers gather at the Kot compound, at the northwestern end of Durbar Square, for the beheading of dozens of buffalo and goats and to troop their regimental colours.

Seto Machhendranath Jaatra A flamboyant chariot procession in which the white idol of Machhendranath is placed in a towering chariot and pulled from Jamal to an area south of Jhochhe in at least three daily stages. The festival starts on Chait Dasain.

BAISAAKH (APRIL–MAY)

Nawa Barsa On Nepali New Year (April 13 or 14), there are parades in Kathmandu, but Bhaktapur's festivities are more exciting (see p.159).

Machhendranath Rath Jaatra An amazing, uniquely Newari extravaganza in which an immense chariot is pulled through old Patan over a period of several weeks (see p.93).

Buddha Jayanti The anniversary of the Buddha's birth, enlightenment and death, celebrated on the morning of the full moon at Swayambhu: thousands come to do *puja*, and priests dressed as the *panchabuddha* perform ritual dances.

SAAUN (JULY–AUG)

Janai Purnima The annual changing of the sacred thread worn by high-caste Hindu men (and of temporary wrist bands that may be worn by men and women of any caste), on the day of the full moon, at Patan's Kumbeshwar Mandir and other temples.

Ghanta Karna Demon effigies are burned throughout the city on the fourteenth day after the full moon of Saaun.

Gaai Jaatra Held the day after the full moon, the Cow Festival is marked by processions through the old city, led by garlanded boys dressed as cows. A good place to watch is in front of the former Royal Palace's entrance in Durbar Square.

BHADAU (AUG–SEPT)

Krishna Astami (Krishna Jayanti) Krishna's birthday, on which thousands of women queue for *puja* at Patan's Krishna Mandir.

Tij A three-day Women's Festival, starting on the third day after the full moon: women may be seen singing and dancing anywhere, but especially at Pashupatinath (see p.125).

Indra Jaatra A wild week of chariot processions and masked-dance performances held around the full moon of Bhadau (see p.65).

ASOJ (SEPT–OCT)

Dasain A mammoth ten-day festival celebrated in most parts of Nepal, concluding on the full moon of Asoj. In Kathmandu, mass sacrifices are held at the Kot courtyard near Durbar Square on the ninth day, Durga Puja, with *tikas* bestowed on all and sundry on the last day.

KAATTIK (OCT–NOV)

Tihaar The Festival of Lights, celebrated with masses of oil lamps throughout the city and five days of special observances. Lakshmi Puja, falling on the full moon of Kaattik, is the highlight.

Nepali dance, music and drama programme. Private dance, vocal and instrumental instruction is also available.

THEATRE, CINEMA AND OTHER PERFORMANCES

Beyond those put on for tourists, scheduled arts performances are relatively rare. Several cinemas show the latest Bollywood blockbusters (and the odd Hollywood hit), and some restaurants and bars show films; try *Lazimpat Gallery Café*, near *Ringmo*. In the high season, the *Kathmandu Guest House* hosts screenings and talks. The annual Kathmandu International Mountain Film Festival (W kimff.org), held in mid-December, is also worth looking out for. For live music you're limited to small bars such as *Jazz Upstairs* (see p.111) or *House of Music* (see p.111); some of these serve as venues for the annual Jazzmandu festival (W jazzmandu.org), held in October.

British Council Lainchaur ☎ 01 441 0789, W british council.org/nepal.htm. Occasional screenings and events.

QFX 317 Narayanhiti Marg, near the GPO ☎ 01 444 2220, W qfxcinemas.com; map p.74. Modern cinema screening Hollywood, Bollywood and Nepali films (Mon–Thurs Rs210–250, Fri–Sun Rs270–310).

Russian Centre of Science and Culture Kamal Pokhari ☎ 01 441 5453, W russiancultureinnepal.org; map p.61. Hosts the annual Kathmandu International Mountain Film Festival, as well as the Miss Nepal contest.

Sattya Media Arts Collective Behind the zoo in Jawalakhel, Patan ☎ 01 552 3486, W sattya.org. An interesting venue hosting everything from poetry slams to art workshops.

GHAZAL

As with so many other cultural imports from south of the border, Kathmandu has been quick to embrace *ghazal* (an Indian style of popular music). Troupes tend to work the better Indian restaurants, where they provide dinnertime accompaniment from a platform over to the side somewhere. A typical ensemble consists of an amplified tabla, guitar, harmonium and/or synthesizer. The singer, who gets top billing, croons in a plaintive voice. Love is the theme, and the sentimental lyrics – typically in Urdu or Hindi, but often in Nepali – draw on a long tradition going back to the great Persian poets.

Madhushala Durbar Marg, 200m east of Thamel ☎ 01 422 3613, W madhushalaghazal.com; map p.84. Just a five-minute walk from Thamel, this bar-restaurant hosts *ghazal* acts daily from 7.30pm to 11pm. Cuisine is Indian, but mostly just finger food, though they do have *sheesha*.

Raj Gharana Kathmandu Plaza Building, corner of Lal Durbar and Kamaladi ☎ 01 416 8760; map p.84. This restaurant, at the top of the Kathmandu Plaza Building, is a good option for *ghazal* nights.

CASINOS

A night at one of Kathmandu's casinos (W casinosnepal .com) is a weirdly memorable experience. They're frequented mainly by Indians and Westerners staying at the affiliated deluxe hotels. *Yak & Yeti* and *Hotel Shangri-La* – among numerous others – have casinos.

"DANCE BARS"

One curious trend in Kathmandu is the popularity of so-called dance bars, which involve (generally) fully clothed women dancing under lights on a makeshift stage to loud Nepali pop music. The dancing is more traditional than suggestive, but the customers are almost always men and some arrange for private services after hours.

SHOPPING

The sheer volume of stuff on sale in Kathmandu, and the fierce competition among sellers, makes it possible to get some very good deals, especially if you're adept at bargaining. **Bargain** everywhere, even when prices are supposedly "fixed"; the initial price could be anything from ten to one thousand percent over the going rate. That said, haggling in Nepal is generally a well-mannered business, and the aggressive styles used in some countries in the world will be counterproductive.

SHOPPING AREAS

Kathmandu Thamel offers Nepal's largest gathering of shops selling handicrafts and souvenirs, while Durbar Marg specializes in high-end products. Handicrafts are sold around Jhochhe and at the Durbar Square night market. Lazimpath has several boutiques and nonprofit outlets, while just south of the Singha Durbar is Baber Mahal Revisited (see p.86), a top-end shopping complex housed in a restored Rana palace. Locals shop in the old city around Asan and Indrachowk, the New Road area, and the Hong Kong Bazaar flea market encircling the Bhrikuti Mandap exhibition ground.

Patan Many items sold in Kathmandu are actually made in Patan, so shopping there will enable you to watch pieces being made and (maybe) get a lower price. The main shopping areas are the streets just north of Patan Durbar Square, Mangal Bazaar and the street running south to Lagankhel, the Tibetan-influenced Ekantakuna (Jawalakhel) district, and the busy boulevards of Kupondol.

METAL AND JEWELLERY

Patan has always been renowned for its metalsmiths, who produce religious (mainly Buddhist) statues. There are dozens of retail outlets-cum-workshops in the Uku Bahal

ANTIQUES

The Nepali government is hyper-vigilant about the **export of antiques** more than one hundred years old. Not being experts, customs officials tend to err on the side of caution and reject any item that looks like it might be old. To avoid difficulties, take any suspect items to the **Department of Archeology** next to the Supreme Court on Ram Shah Path (℡ 01 425 0688, ⓦ doa.gov.np) and for a small fee have them tag it as okay.

neighbourhood; pieces run from crude little statuettes to magnificent large-scale works of art. Simple statuettes, bells, singing bowls, bracelets and other metal items are sold throughout the city. Large, curved *khukuri* knives (as made famous by the Gurkhas) make uniquely Nepali gifts and are widely sold wherever there are tourists, though you may have problems taking them into your home country; prices start at around Rs1500–2000. Brass sets of Bagh Chal, Nepal's "tigers and goats" game, are also common. Gold and silversmiths in the old city (mainly north and west of Indrachowk) produce fine traditional jewellery; tourist shops sell cheaper ornaments. Gem sellers are grouped mainly at the east end of New Road, but watch out for scams.

British Gurkha Khukari House Jyatha, Thamel ℡ 01 422 3119. A good choice for *khukuris*, this place sells a range of both ornamental and practical blades. Daily 10am–6pm.

Masala Beads Thamel North ℡ 01 425 0450, ⓦ masalabeads.com; map p.73. Less expensive than *similar shops*, with an array of necklaces, bangles and bracelets. Generally daily 10am–8pm.

Millennium Crafts Tridevi Marg, Thamel ℡ 01 425 8999, ⓦ silvernp.com; map p.73. Specialists in quality silver jewellery and crafts. Generally daily 10am–6pm.

WOOD AND PAPER

Many Nepali carved-wood crafts – picture frames based on Newari window designs, statues of deities and animals – are best bought in Bhaktapur (see p.166), although several shops around Patan Durbar Square also deal in these items. Numerous shops in Thamel sell beautiful paper products, many made from *lokta*, handmade paper produced from the bark of an indigenous shrub. You can buy colourful papier-mâché masks and puppets all over the place, but these are produced – and better represented – in Bhaktapur (see p.166) and Thimi (see p.170).

Woodcarving Industries Patan Industrial Estate ℡ 01 552 1147, ⓦ woodcarving.com.np; map p.87. Exquisite (and expensive) traditional and non-traditional Nepali-style furniture, mirror frames and windows. Sun–Fri 10am–5pm.

THANGKA, POUBHA AND OTHER FINE ART

It's hard to say where to bargain-hunt for *thangka* (see box below) – or *poubha*, a similar ritual scroll painting in the Newari, rather than Tibetan, style – as there are so many standard depictions and levels of quality. There are numerous *thangka* shops at the north end of Kathmandu Durbar Square, around Thamel and north of Patan Durbar Square. Some also sell paintings based on traditional Tibetan medical texts, and a few in Patan display *thangka*-influenced naive landscape paintings – they're mass-produced for the tourist market, but still make nice souvenirs. Some Kathmandu artists are starting to produce more individualistic works, usually watercolours.

THE PRODUCTION AND MEANINGS OF THANGKA

A good **thangka** is the product of hundreds – or even thousands – of hours of painstaking work. A cotton canvas is first stretched across a frame and burnished to a smooth surface that will take the finest detail. The design is next drawn or traced in pencil, there is little room for deviation from accepted styles, for a *thangka* is an expression of religious truths, not an opportunity for artistic licence. Large areas of colour are then blocked in, often by an apprentice, and finally the master painter will take over, breathing life into the figure with lining, stippling, facial features, shading and, finally, the eyes of the main figure. *Thangka* can be grouped into four main genres. The **Wheel of Life**, perhaps the most common, places life and all its delusions inside a circle held firmly in the clutches of red-faced Yama, god of death. A second standard image is the **Buddha's life story**. Many *thangka* feature tantric **deities**, either benign or menacing; such images serve as meditation tools in visualization techniques. Mandala (mystical diagrams) are also used in meditation. That's just the tip of the iceberg. A full exposition of *thangka* iconography would fill volumes – ask a dealer or artist to lead you through a few images step by step, or visit somewhere like the Tsering Art School in Boudha (see p.136) to find out more.

CARPETS

The Tibetan-style handwoven carpet industry, once a modest income-generator for Tibetan refugees, has evolved into one of Nepal's biggest export earners. The carpet industry in Nepal – and throughout Asia – remains plagued by a serious child-labour problem, however. International NGO GoodWeave (⊚ goodweave.org) operates a certification scheme for responsible carpet producers and outlets. Prices vary widely: at the bottom end expect to pay around US$50 per square metre; top-of-the-range carpets can be three times this, or even more.

Jawalakhel Handicraft Center ☎ 01 552 5237, ⊚ jhcnepal.com; map pp.58–59. The easiest place to see carpets being made (see box, p.95) is in the former Tibetan refugee camp in the Ekantakuna section of Patan, Nepal's oldest and most famous carpet-weaving centre. The complex includes a fixed-price sales showroom, where profits benefit elderly and poor Tibetans, and a couple of souvenir shops. Prices are generally cheaper at many other private shops on the road leading back to Patan. Sun–Fri 9am–5pm.

SOUVENIRS AND CURIOS

Vendors in Basantapur Square and Thamel flog a vast array of Tibetan-style curios, while a few Thamel and Durbar Marg boutiques sell genuine antique Tibetan chests and dressers. Countless shops in the tourist areas carry identical ranges of Kashmiri, Rajasthani and Afghan handicrafts; others stock Nepali tea, coffee, incense, essential oils and spices, and numerous places sell Buddhist singing bowls. Small shops in Thamel, Chhetrapati and Khichapokhari (south of New Rd) stock Nepali musical instruments, while hack minstrels doggedly peddle *sarangi* (traditional fiddles). Nepali artisans turn out an ever-expanding range of contemporary crafts. The impetus for many of these innovations has come from a few income-generation projects supported by aid organizations, which operate their own sales outlets (see box, p.116), although many products are now widely imitated.

Amrita Craft First floor, J.P. School Rd, opposite the school, Thamel ☎ 01 424 0757, ⊚ amritacraft.com; map p.73. A wide range of crafts, gifts and clothes; it wholesales to a number of other shops in Thamel, so prices are keen. Generally daily 9am–7pm.

Patan Industrial Estate Just beyond the Southern Stupa ☎ 01 552 1367; map pp.58–59. The estate comprises dozens of handicraft factories and showrooms; you can learn about Nepali handicrafts and the processes used to make them, as well as buy at reasonable prices – though you'll still have to haggle hard. Generally Mon–Sat 10am–6pm.

CLOTHING

Thamel and Jhochhe are full of shops selling wool sweaters, jackets, mittens and socks, which are among Nepal's best

bargains. Cotton garments are particularly cheap, in both senses of the word, but might be just the ticket for short-term travel needs. Tailors, usually found inside the T-shirt shops, are skilled at machine-embroidering designs on clothing. Pashminas and much cheaper yak wool equivalents are sold everywhere (try the Kwa Bahal end of Thamel), and there are some very good deals to be had. *Topi*, the caps Nepali men wear, are sold around Asan. You'll find sari material in New Road and around Indrachowk, and you can have items made to order from shops east of Asan. Other textiles are sold in the nonprofit shops (see box, p.116). A number of boutiques on Durbar Marg, Lazimpath, Patan and in Baber Mahal Revisited sell designer fashions with a Nepali flavour. Tailors can also make men's suits to order.

BOOKS AND MAPS

Kathmandu has one of Asia's greatest concentrations of English-language bookshops. Almost all will buy back books for half the price you originally paid, or part-exchange them. Note that many of the books on sale are fakes, produced by pirate publishers, and quality levels vary.

Book House World Chhetrapati ☎ 01 425 2683; map p.73. Good selection of fiction, both new and used, and friendly staff. Generally daily 9.30am–8pm.

The Map Shop J.P. School Rd ⊚ himalayan-maphouse .com; map p.73. The best outlet for Nepa/Himalayan Map House, with an extensive selection of their products. There are several other lesser outlets in Thamel. Generally daily 10am–8pm.

★**Pilgrims Book House** J.P. School Rd, Thamel ☎ 01 422 1546; map p.73. The best bookshop in Nepal, with extensive sections on all things Nepali, Indian and Tibetan, from coffee-table mountaineering books to serious studies of Tibetan religion, and from Nepali English-language fiction to field guides to local butterflies. Generally daily 9.30am–9pm.

Vajra Jyatha Thamel; map p.73. A wide range of non-fiction on Nepal and Asia, plus books on religion, philosophy and travel, specializing in Tibet and Buddhism. Daily 10am–7pm.

OUTDOOR EQUIPMENT

You can buy or rent almost any sort of outdoor equipment in Kathmandu. Most of the new gear is locally produced or imported from China, and tends to be of poor quality, but you can usually specify the quality you want, and thus the price, from the cheapest fake to authentic, imported brands. Go to the tailors in Jyatha if you want something made or copied in nylon. Decent walking boots are much harder to find than other gear, and attract serious premiums for rental. A few shops specialize in quality secondhand stuff – generally expedition cast-offs and stuff sold by other trekkers: climbing hardware, gas stoves, water bottles, glacier glasses, plastic boots, authentic name-brand

1

ETHICAL SHOPPING

In many of Kathmandu's shops, only a fraction (often less than five percent) of a shopkeeper's profit on any given item actually finds its way back to the person who produced it in the first place. Meanwhile, a growing number of outlets in tourist areas spuriously claim to be fair trade or to support, for example, women's skills development programmes. The following shops, however, genuinely exist to fund **charitable causes** or sell crafts made by **income-generation** projects.

Dhankuta Sisters Kupondol ☎01 552 9161; map pp.58–59. Predominantly representing village women in the eastern hills, this place sells mainly *dhaka* clothes. Generally Sun–Fri 10.30am–7pm.

Dhukuti Kupondol, north of Hotel Himalaya ☎01 553 5107; map pp.58–59. One of Nepal's biggest nonprofit shops, run by a village and low-income project marketing association, and stocking a wide variety of cotton, leather and felt items, as well as dolls, copper vessels, pashmina, cashmere and basketry. Generally Sun–Fri 9am–7pm.

Kumbeshwar Technical School North of Kumbeshwar Mandir, Patan ☎01 553 7484; map p.87. This nonprofit school provides vocational and literacy training for destitute women, orphans and other disadvantaged people, supported in part by sales from its shop. This is one of the few places where you can buy one-hundred-percent Tibetan-wool carpets, plus other woollen garments and wooden products made by the students. Generally daily 9am–5pm.

Mahaguthi Branches in Kupondol (map pp.58–59) and Lazimpath (map p.61) ⊛mahaguthi.org. A good selection of textiles, crafts, jewellery, ceramics and home furnishings produced by artisans in Janakpur, Dang and Thimi; the money raised supports a home for destitute women. Generally Mon–Fri & Sun 10am–6.30pm, Sat 10am–5pm.

Sana Hastakala Kupundole, Lalitpur ☎01 552 2628, ⊛sanahastakala.com; map p.87. A good selection and display of woollens, *dhaka*, pashmina, dresses, ceramics, paper, Maithili paintings, toys and general gift items. Supports projects mainly run by and for women producers. Generally Sun–Fri 10am–6pm.

clothing, packs and so on. Except for the climbing hardware, it will cost at least as much as in your home country.

Black Yak Tridevi Marg ☎01 441 6483; map p.73. Official store of the outdoor equipment giants, with several other outdoor outlets nearby. Generally daily 9.30am–7pm.

Shona Jyatha Thamel ☎01 426 5120; map p.73. Good range of trekking and climbing gear to buy or rent. Generally daily 9am–7pm.

SUPERMARKETS

Big Mart Lazimpath ☎01 400 5200, ⊛bigmart.com .np; map p.61. One of the city's largest supermarkets. Daily 10am–8pm.

Namaste Supermarket Pulchowk ☎01 552 0026; map p.87. This supermarket is especially popular with NGO staff and expats for its range of imported food and drinks. Generally daily 8am–8pm.

OTHER BARGAINS

With close trading links to the Far East, Kathmandu has relatively cheap prices on consumer gadgets. Cameras, MP3 players and other electronic devices can be found at the many shopping malls on New Road near the GPO, though the selection is patchy. Sunglasses and glasses frames are also a good deal here. Charges are very reasonable for prescription lenses, too, but leave plenty of time for your order to be filled in case of mistakes.

DIRECTORY

Banks and money There are moneychangers all over Thamel, and scattered about Jhochhe, Durbar Marg and Patan Durbar Square; they typically open daily 9am–8pm. Nepal Bank on New Road, south of Durbar Square, has longer opening hours than most other banks (daily 7am–7pm) and offers good exchange rates. Standard Chartered Bank has a convenient branch on Thamel North. There are innumerable ATMs in Thamel – all accept foreign cards and several operate 24hr – and many more throughout the city. Note that most banks' ATMs give a maximum Rs10,000–15,000 per withdrawal, except those belonging to Nabil Bank, which give up to Rs35,000 (with the exception of the branch in Thamel) – there's a handy Nabil Bank on the main road as you enter Patan. Currently, American Express cards can only be used at Himalayan Bank.

Communications Most hotels provide internet and/or wi-fi access for guests. Cyber cafés are easy to find in Thamel and Jhochhe, and virtually every commercial street has one; most charge around Rs50–75/hr. If you are not using a mobile phone, head to one of the many ISD/STD/IDD centres or internet cafés; local calls cost only a few rupees, while international calls start at around Rs50 per minute.

1

Embassies and consulates Australia, Bansbari ☎01 437 1678; Belgium, Thamal Amrit Marg, off Thamel Northeast ☎01 441 8922; Canada, Lazimpath ☎01 441 5193; Denmark, Lazimpath ☎01 441 3010; Finland, Lazimpath ☎01 441 6636; France, Lazimpath ☎01 441 2332; Germany, Gyaneswar ☎01 441 2786; Israel, Lazimpath ☎01 441 1811; Italy, Baluwatar ☎01 425 2801; Japan, Panipokhari ☎01 442 6680; Netherlands, Kupondol Heights, Patan ☎01 552 3444; New Zealand, Ramalaya, Panipokhari ☎01 441 2436 (only open Mon–Fri 10am–noon); Norway, Pulchowk, Lalitpur ☎01 554 5307; South Korea, Ravi Bhawan, Kalimati ☎01 427 0172; Spain, Battisputali ☎01 447 0770; Sweden, Khichapokhari ☎01 422 0939; Switzerland, Jawalakhel, Patan ☎01 559 2759; Thailand, Bansbari ☎01 437 1410; UK, Lainchaur ☎01 441 0583; US, Maharajgunj ☎01 400 7200. For India, see the section on travelling to India (see p.96).

Emergencies Several organizations provide ambulances, including the Red Cross (☎01 422 8094), Nepal Chamber of Commerce (☎01 423 0213) and Norvic International Hospital (☎01 425 8554), but taking a taxi is generally quicker.

Hospitals, clinics and pharmacies The best Western-standard clinic is CIWEC, opposite the British Embassy in Lainchaur (daily 24hr for emergencies; clinic hours Mon–Fri 9am–5pm; ☎01 442 4111, ⓦciwec-clinic.com), which has very proficient Western and Nepali staff, and is a great source of information. The Nepal International Clinic (NIC), a block east of the Royal Palace entrance on Lal Durbar Marg (daily 9am–1pm & 2–5pm; ☎01 443 5357, ⓦnepalinternationalclinic.com), is also good, and a bit cheaper; it specializes in mountaineering-related medical treatments and vaccinations. Several clinics in Thamel offer more hit-or-miss care, and can't be recommended. Medicines can be purchased at *pharma* (pharmacies) everywhere. A number of small private hospitals operate in the valley; two with good reputations among expats and NGO staff are B&B Hospital (☎01 553 1933, ⓦbbhospital.com.np) in Patan, and Norvic International Hospital (☎01 425 8554, ⓦnorvichospital.com) in Thapathali. Of the public facilities, Patan Hospital (☎01 552 2295, ⓦpatanhospital.org.np) is reasonably modern, while Bir Hospital (☎01 422 1119, ⓦbirhospital.awardspace.info) is central but very basic and best avoided. If you're in really bad shape, you'll be sent abroad.

Language courses Kathmandu Institute of Nepali

Language, Bhagwan Bahal, Thamel (☎01 443 7454, ⓦktmnepalilanguage.com).

Police If you're the victim of a crime, first contact the Tourist Police (☎01 422 0818), in the Tourist Service Center in Bhrikuti Mandap, which is supposed to have an English-speaking officer on duty (Mon–Fri 10am–5pm). They also have officers at the Thamel tourist office (☎01 442 9750) and at booths in Durbar Square and other tourist areas. Outside regular hours, have a Nepali-speaker call ☎01 100. Report thefts to a tourist police officer or the district police headquarters, which in Kathmandu is on the west side of Durbar Square and in Patan at Jawalakhel Chowk. Ask for the Interpol section. The national police HQ and Interpol office is in Naksal.

Post and shipping The GPO (General Post Office) in Kantipath (Mon–Fri 9am–5pm) has a poste restante section. Bookshops and other stores sell stamps, and will generally (for a small charge) take mail for franking; many hotels will also do this. Shipping agents can take the headache out of sending parcels home: try Atlas de Cargo, Hattisar (☎01 444 5666, ⓦatlasdecargo.com) or Sharmasons Movers, Kantipath (☎01 554 7791). Air-freight services include DHL, Naya Baneswore (☎01 448 1303, ⓦdhl.com.np); United Parcel Service, care of Shangri La Tours, Kantipath (☎01 423 2219, ⓦups.com); and Federal Express, care of Everest De Cargo, Kantipath (☎01 426 9248, ⓦfedex.com/np). Parcels can also be sent from the Foreign Post Office (Mon–Fri 9am–5pm) next to the GPO, but although cheaper, the experience is completely exasperating – set aside the whole morning.

Travel agents Ample Travels, Thamel, in front of *Hotel Vaishali* (☎01 442 3148, ⓦampletravels.com); President Travel and Tours, Durbar Marg (☎01 422 0245, ⓦpttnepal.com); Sherpa Society, Jyatha Thamel (☎01 424 9233, ⓦsherpasocietytrekking.com); Wayfarers, J.P. School Rd (☎01 426 6010, ⓦwayfarers.com.np).

Visa extensions If you need to extend your visa (see p.48), you can now apply online first (at ⓦnepalimmigration.gov.np) and then take the email response with you to the Department of Immigration in Kalikasthan, just north of Singha Durbar (Mon–Thurs & Sat 10am–5pm, Fri 10am–1pm; ☎01 442 9659, ⓦnepalimmigration.gov.np) – this is much quicker than queuing for the sole computer entry station as the process is now paperless. You should be able to collect your passport with the visa extension added later the same day.

The Kathmandu Valley

GIRLS ON BAMBOO SWING, CHANGU NARAYAN

The Kathmandu Valley

Within the relentlessly steep terrain of midland Nepal, the Kathmandu Valley is something of a geographical freak: a bowl of gently undulating, richly fertile land, lifted up towards the sky like some kind of sacrifice. It may only be some 25km across, but it is densely packed with sacred sites. So much so, in fact, that well into modern times it was referred to as "Nepal mandala", implying that the entire valley acted as a gigantic spiritual diagram, or circle. "The valley consists of as many temples as there are houses", enthused William Kirkpatrick, the first Englishman to reach Kathmandu, "and as many idols as there are men."

2

Although the valley's sacred geography remains largely unchanged, the number of houses – and people – has soared since Kirkpatrick's day. In the 1980s, two-thirds of the valley was farmland: today it covers barely a third. The region is the country's economic engine, and pulls young Nepalis in from the hills with an irresistible force. Thanks also to refugees fleeing the Maoist insurrection of the early 2000s, the valley's **population** has doubled in the last fifteen years or so to more around 2.5 million. What was once a rural paradise is fast becoming a giant conurbation, with the concrete spreading almost to the valley rim on the north and western sides, and **smog** obscuring the view of distant mountains on all but the clearest of days.

Despite rampant development, the valley's underlying **traditions** have proved remarkably resilient. Like the other, smaller Newari towns of the valley – **Kirtipur**, **Thimi**, **Sankhu**, **Bungmati** – **Bhaktapur** preserves a distinctly medieval air, its wood- and brick-built houses tightly clustered together around alleyways and temple plazas, and the lives of its residents still bound up with the paddy fields outside the city walls. On the southern and eastern sides of the valley, meanwhile, and in the lush side valleys and on the steep slopes of the rim, the countryside continues to shimmer in an undulating patchwork of paddy fields.

> The Kathmandu Valley suffered serious damage in the **earthquake** of April 25, 2015 (see p.6), which occurred as this book went to press. Alongside the loss of hundreds of lives, many of the historic sites in this chapter were damaged or even destroyed. Bhaktapur's old town and Durbar Square and Bungmati's Machhendranath temple were particularly badly hit; the Boudha stupa was also reportedly damaged. It was unclear at the time of writing whether the damaged sites could or would be restored.

Highlights

❶ Pashupatinath The most sacred of Nepal's Hindu temple complexes is veiled by the smoke of funeral pyres. **See p.125**

❷ Boudha At dawn and dusk, Buddhist monks, nuns and pilgrims flock to the vast white dome of the stupa. **See p.130**

❸ Bajra Yogini As befits a tantric goddess demanding blood sacrifices, Bajra Yogini's forest-enfolded shrine is palpably sinister. See p.137

❹ Shivapuri Hike or bike through rich forest to the second highest (but most accessible) of the valley's summits, at 2732m. **See p.139**

❺ Newa Lahana, Kirtipur The best traditional Newari food in Nepal is found in a community-run restaurant in one of the most atmospheric Newari towns. **See p.143**

❻ Bishanku Narayan This peaceful Hindu shrine is modestly hidden in one of the valley's most delightfully rustic folds. **See p.154**

❼ Bhaktapur The most immaculately preserved of the valley's ancient cities is no museum: Newari life continues here as it has for centuries. **See p.154**

❽ Changu Narayan Exquisitely carved ancient sculptures and a rural, ridgetop setting make this the finest of the valley's temples. **See p.167**

HIGHLIGHTS ARE MARKED ON THE MAP ON PP.122–123

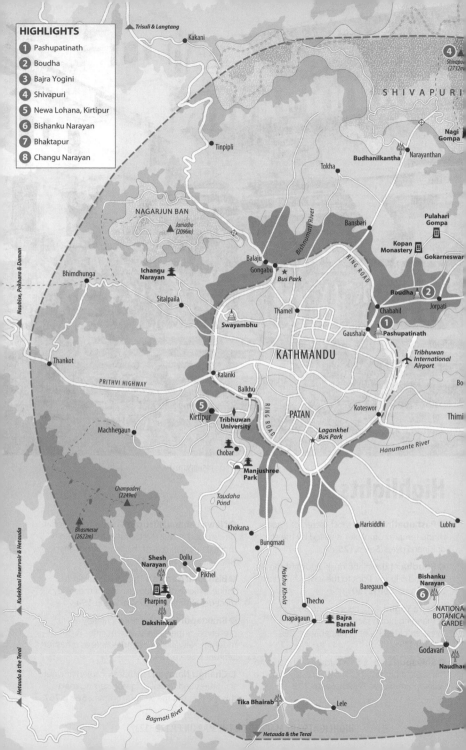

HIGHLIGHTS

1. Pashupatinath
2. Boudha
3. Bajra Yogini
4. Shivapuri
5. Newa Lohana, Kirtipur
6. Bishanku Narayan
7. Bhaktapur
8. Changu Narayan

Trisuli & Langtang

Kakani

4

Shivapuri (2732m)

SHIVAPURI

Nagi Gompa

Tinpipli

Budhanilkantha   Narayanthan

Tokha

Pulahari Gompa

NAGARJUN BAN

Jamacho (2096m)

Bansbari

Kopan Monastery   Gokarneswar

Balaju
Gongabu   *Bus Park*

RING ROAD

Naubise, Pokhara & Daman

Bhimdhunga

Ichangu Narayan

Sitalpaila

Thamel

Boudha   **2**   Jorpati

Chabahil

Swayambhu

1   **Pashupatinath**

Gaushala

Bishnumati River

KATHMANDU

Thankot

Tribhuwan International Airport

PRITHVI HIGHWAY

Kalanki

Balkhu

RING ROAD

PATAN

Koteswor

Thimi

Bo

5
Kirtipur

Tribhuwan University

Lagankhel Bus Park

Hanumante River

Machhegaun

Chobar

Manjushree Park

Champadevi (2249m)

Taudaha Pond

Khokana

Harisiddhi

Lubhu

Bhasmesur (2622m)

Bungmati

Kulekhani Reservoir & Hetauda

Shesh Narayan   Dollu

Pikhel

Bishanku Narayan

6

Nakhu Khola

Baregaun

Pharping

Dakshinkali

Thecho

Chapagaun   **Bajra Barahi Mandir**

NATIONAL BOTANICAL GARDEN

Godavari

Naudhar

Hetauda & the Terai

Tika Bhairab   Lele

Bagmati River

Hetauda & the Terai

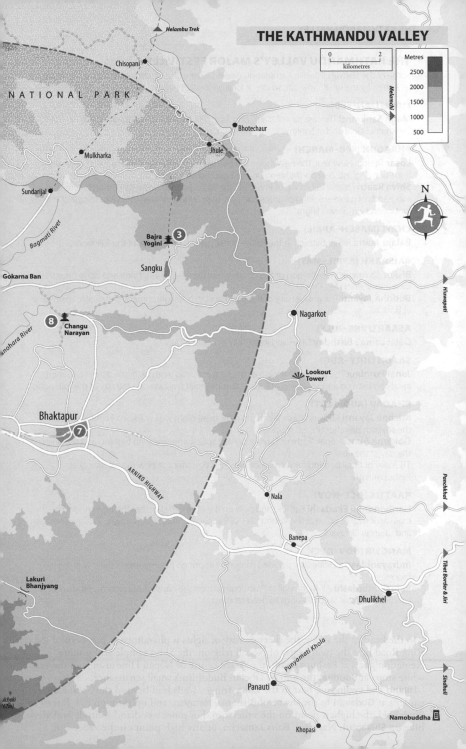

THE KATHMANDU VALLEY

Metres
2500
2000
1500
1000
500

0   2
kilometres

N

Helambu Trek

Chisopani

NATIONAL PARK

Melamchi

Bhotechaur

Mulkharka

Jhule

Sundarijal

Bagmati River

Bajra Yogini ③

Sangku

Gokarna Ban

Nagarkot

Hiuwapati

Changu ⑧
Narayan

Lookout
Tower

Manohara River

Bhaktapur ⑦

Panchkhal

ARNIKO HIGHWAY

Nala

Banepa

Tibet Border & Jiri

Lakuri
Bhanjyang

Dhulikhel

Punyamati Khola

Sindhuli

Panauti

ulchoki
(62m)

Khopasi

Namobuddha

2

THE KATHMANDU VALLEY'S MAJOR FESTIVALS

Some of the festivals listed in Kathmandu (see p.112) are also celebrated in the valley. Most are reckoned by the lunar calendar, so check locally for exact dates.

MAGH (JAN–FEB)

Magh Sankranti The first day of Magh (Jan 14 or 15), marked by ritual bathing at Patan's Sankhamul Ghat and at Sankhu.

PHAAGUN (FEB–MARCH)

Losar Tibetan New Year, the new moon of February, celebrated at Boudha with processions, horn-blowing and *tsampa*-throwing on the big third day.

Shiva Raatri On the full moon of Phaagun, the Pashupatinath *mela* (fair) attracts tens of thousands of ganja-smoking pilgrims and holy men, while children everywhere collect money for bonfires on "Shiva's Night".

CHAIT (MARCH–APRIL)

Balaju Jaatra Ritual bathing at the Balaju Water Garden on the day of the full moon.

BAISAAKH (APRIL–MAY)

Bisket Bhaktapur's celebration of Nepali New Year (April 13 or 14). Thimi and Bode have their own idiosyncratic festivities.

Buddha Jayanti The anniversary of the Buddha's birth, enlightenment and death, celebrated at Boudha.

ASAAR (JUNE–JULY)

Dalai Lama's Birthday Observed informally at Boudha (July 6).

SAAUN (JULY–AUG)

Janai Purnima The annual changing of the sacred thread worn by high-caste Hindu men, involving bathing and splashing at Patan's Kumbeshwar Mahadev on the day of the full moon.

BHADAU (AUG–SEPT)

Krishna Jayanti Krishna's birthday, marked by an all-night vigil at Patan's Krishna Mandir on the seventh day after the full moon.

Gokarna Aunsi Nepali "Father's Day", observed at Gokarneswar with bathing and offerings on the day of the new moon.

Tij A day of ritual bathing for women on the third day after the new moon, mainly at Pashupatinath.

KAATTIK (OCT–NOV)

Haribondhini Ekadashi Bathing and *puja* on the eleventh day after the new moon. The main action takes place at the Vishnu sites of Budhanilkantha, Sesh Narayan, Bishanku Narayan and Changu Narayan.

MANGSIR (NOV–DEC)

Indrayani Jaatra Deities are paraded through Kirtipur on palanquins on the day of the new moon.

Bala Chaturdashi All-night vigil at Pashupatinath on the night of the new moon, involving candles and ritual seed offerings to dead relatives.

In the heart of the valley, the sheer density of sights is phenomenal. Just beyond the Ring Road beat the twin hearts of Nepali religion: the Shiva temple and sombre cremation ghats at **Pashupatinath**, the sacred centre of Nepali Hinduism; and the vast, white stupa at **Boudha**, the hub of Tibetan Buddhism's small renaissance.

Hiking and **cycling** are best in the valley fringe. Trails lead beyond the botanical gardens at **Godavari** to the shrine of **Bishanku Narayan**, and up through rich forests to **Phulchoki**, the highest point on the valley rim. For more woodland solitude and views, hike up **Shivapuri**, Nagarjun Ban's **Jamacho**, or any high point on the valley rim.

All of the places described in this chapter are within day-tripping range of Kathmandu, although in several cases it's best to stay overnight, perhaps before continuing on to the destinations covered in the "Central Hills" chapter (see p.172).

GETTING AROUND	THE KATHMANDU VALLEY

By taxi Taxis are the quickest way to travel, though of course traffic jams affect them as much as buses. On shorter journeys, you can try to insist on going by the meter, but may find it hard to get a driver to agree and it may be fixed anyway. On longer journeys, forget the meter: you can negotiate surprisingly reasonable rates for a return trip – just make sure you specify ample waiting time.

By bus Buses and microbuses bring you into (very) close contact with the real Nepal – local fellow travellers will often enter into conversation, if you take the lead. Most destinations in the valley are served by buses running at 15min intervals or less, so you'll rarely wait long. Around the Ring Road, you can jump on and off buses pretty much at will.

By bike If you're touring around the rural parts of the valley, a bike or motorcycle is by far the most flexible option. However, getting out of the fug and crush of Kathmandu can be dangerous and unpleasant, so if you're cycling, consider loading the bike on top of a bus at least to get beyond the Ring Road.

Maps The Kathmandu city/valley maps sold in tourist areas are good enough for general sightseeing. Nepa Maps 1:60,000 *Around Kathmandu Valley* (and their 1:50,000 *Biking Around the Kathmandu Valley*, which highlights mountain-biking routes) is largely accurate, though not all the trails or even the new roads on the edge of the valley are marked.

Pashupatinath

PASHUPATINATH (pronounced Pash-*patty*-nat) is known to most people simply as the place where they burn the bodies in the open. But it is, of course, much more besides. Crammed up against the mouth of a ravine, 4km east of central Kathmandu and just beyond the Ring Road, it also straddles a *tirtha*, or sacred crossroads and is Nepal's holiest Hindu pilgrimage site, a smoky and stirring melee of temples, statues, pilgrims and half-naked holy men.

The entire complex overflows with pilgrims from all over the subcontinent during the wild **festival** of Shiva Raatri (held on the full moon of Feb–March), which commemorates Shiva's *tandava* dance of destruction, according to some, or his drinking of blue poison to save the gods (see p.138), according to others. Devout locals also come for special services on full-moon days and on the eleventh lunar day (*ekadashi*) after each full and new moon.

Pashupati Mandir

The **Pashupati Mandir** is the holy of holies for Nepali Shaivas, followers of Shiva, and has become the pre-eminent national sacred spot for Hindus. As in many temples in Nepal, admission is for Hindus only (which in practice means anyone who looks South

---

PRIESTS AND PILGRIMS AT PASHUPATI MANDIR

Pashupati Mandir emerged as a hotbed of tantric practices in the eleventh century and remained so for four hundred years, until King Yaksha Malla imported conventional Brahman **priests** from South India, although the *bhandaris* (temple assistants) are always Newars born in the immediate area. Wearing the ceremonial orange robes of the Pashupata sect, the priests array the *linga* in brocade silk and bathe it with curd, ghee, honey, sugar and milk. (They also allegedly cream off vast profits from the donations of worshippers – which was one factor in the 2009 row, when the Maoist government tried to expel the Indians from the temple; popular outrage prevented them from succeeding.) Hindu **pilgrims** are expected to distribute offerings and then make a circuit of the temple and the 365 *shivalinga* and other secondary shrines scattered about the precinct. Most also distribute alms to beggars lined along some of the nearby lanes. If you choose to give, arm yourself with a sufficient stockpile of small change (*saano paisa*), available from nearby vendors.

2

Asian). From the outside, though, you can glimpse the two familiar symbols of Shiva, found here in gargantuan scale: a two-storey-*trisul* (trident), and the enormous golden backside of Nandi, Shiva's faithful bull.

The gold-clad pagoda dates from the late seventeenth century, but the origin of the site as a sacred place may date back to the third century BC, and probably to a pre-Hindu animistic cult. Certainly, the benign **Pashupati, Lord of the Animals,** is not Shiva in his ordinary guise. Nepali schoolchildren are taught that Shiva, to escape his heavenly obligations, assumed the guise of a one-horned stag and fled to the forest here. The other gods pursued him and, laying hold of him, broke off his horn, which was transformed into the powerful Pashupati *linga*. The *linga* was later lost, only to be rediscovered by a cow who magically began sprinkling the spot with her milk. According to nation-building legend, she was seen doing this by a cowherd named Ne, a legendary ur-ancestor, who dug up the *linga* and established the shrine.

Hidden inside, the famed, fourteenth-century **Pashupati linga** displays four carved faces of Shiva, plus a fifth, invisible one on the top (Buddhists claim one of the faces is that of the Buddha). Hindus associate this *linga* with the story of how Shiva transformed his phallus into an infinite pillar of light and challenged Brahma and Vishnu to find its ends. Brahma flew heavenward, while Vishnu plumbed the depths of hell. Both were forced to abandon the search, but Brahma falsely boasted of success, only to be caught out by Shiva. Shaivas say that's why Brahma is seldom worshipped, Vishnu gets his fair share, and Shiva is revered above all.

The riverbank ghats

Tourist entrance opposite the Pashupati Mandir's south entrance • Daily 6am–8pm • Rs1000, payable at the main gate

From the **main gate** to the **riverbank ghats** complex it's just a step to the twin footbridges that cross the Bagmati River between the ghats – or cremation and bathing places – on the stone embankments. To die and be cremated here is the pinnacle of religious achievement, virtually guaranteeing release from the cycle of rebirths.

Notwithstanding the ritual and actual pollution, or the lack of water during the winter and spring (when most tourists visit), **bathing** is considered second only to cremation. It's still widely believed that husbands and wives who bathe here together will be remarried in the next life. Most days, you won't see many willing to brave what water there is, except perhaps children, or during the meritorious full-moon days, on Magh Sankranti (usually Jan 14) and Bala Chaturdashi (late Nov or early Dec), and, for women, during the festival of Tij (late Aug or early Sept).

Arya Ghat

Arya Ghat, on the upstream side of the footbridges, is reserved for the higher castes. The cremation platform furthest upstream (so placed for obvious reasons) was once exclusively dedicated to the royal family; next down, just above the bridge, is the ghat for "VVIPs", including prominent politicians and anyone else who can afford it. After the palace massacre in June 2001 (see box, p.387), the army had to build a temporary ghat between the two to accommodate all the royal bodies.

Even if there's no cremation in progress, you may see people lying prone on stretchers with their feet in the Bagmati River. Many of the buildings around the main temple are *dharmsala* (pilgrims' rest-houses), set aside here for devout Hindus approaching death. In their final hour, they are laid by the river and given a last drink of the holy water – which probably hastens the end.

The Virupaksha statue

Housed in a small stone reliquary beside Arya Ghat (which unfortunately means you can't get up close to it) is a famed seventh-century statue of **Virupaksha**, the "Three-Eyed Shiva", whose Mongoloid features are said to betray the figure's pre-Hindu origins. The image is also associated with Kalki, the tenth and final incarnation of Vishnu, a sort of messiah figure who will bring the present Kali Yuga (Age of Kali) to a close and usher in a new, virtuous cycle of history. The statue is half-submerged in the Bagmati River: some claim that the idol is gradually sinking, and its final disappearance will mark the end of the age; others say that Virupaksha will be released from the waters when he has earned enough merit from visiting pilgrims.

Vatsala Mandir

The small, two-storey pagoda between the bridges is the **Vatsala Mandir**, dedicated to Shiva's consort Parbati in one of her wilder mother-goddess roles; she is said to have demanded human sacrifice in the past, but is nowadays satisfied with an annual washing-down with beer.

RESPECTING THE DEAD

Perhaps more than anywhere else in Nepal, Pashupatinath is a place to modestly cover legs and arms – for women especially. It's also important to **respect** the privacy of bathers, worshippers and, indeed, the dead. You may see other people poking their long lenses into the cremation pyres, but you have to question whether this is appropriate, particularly when grieving families are present.

2

Ram Ghat and around

Cremations are held almost continuously at the next embankment downstream from the Vatsala Mandir, **Ram Ghat**, which is used by all castes. You're usually allowed access to the terrace immediately behind. Photography is discouraged.

Towards the southern end of Ram Ghat, a small eleventh-century (some say fifth-century) **Buddha statue** sticks out of the paving. Just beyond is a bumper-sized, tipped-over *linga* ensconced in a round brick battlement; it's believed to date from the fifth century. The southernmost building shelters two temples in its open courtyard. The oval **Raj Rajeshwari** is named after a powerful, nineteenth-century queen who was forced to commit *sati* after her husband's death, while the gilded pagoda of **Nawa Durga** is devoted to the nine fierce manifestations of the goddess Durga.

Pancha Dewal

Behind Ram Ghat stands the **Pancha Dewal**, which is a centre for the old, sick and infirm, partly run by Mother Teresa's Missionaries of Charity. You can enter to see the five Mughal-style cupolas in the courtyard, which give it its name. Better still, arrive early in the morning to volunteer for a week's humble nursing work such as washing residents, cleaning pots and sheets and so on; look for the sisters (who speak English) in their trademark white saris with blue trim.

SADHUS

Sadhus, the dreadlocked holy men usually seen lurking around Hindu temples, are essentially an Indian phenomenon. However, Nepal, the setting for many of the amorous and ascetic exploits of **Shiva** – the sadhus' favourite deity – is also one of their favourite stomping grounds. Sadhus are especially common at **Pashupatinath**, which is rated as one of the subcontinent's four most important Shaiva pilgrimage sites. During the festival of Shiva Raatri, Pashupatinath hosts a full-scale sadhu convention, with the government laying on free firewood for the festival.

Shaiva sadhus follow Shiva in one of his best-loved and most enigmatic guises: the wild, dishevelled **yogin**, the master of yoga, who sits motionless atop a Himalayan peak for aeons at a time and whose hair is the source of the mighty Ganga (Ganges) river. Traditionally, sadhus live solitary lives, always on the move, subsisting on alms and owning nothing but what they carry. They bear Shiva's emblems: the *trisul* (trident), *damaru* (two-sided drum), a necklace of furrowed *rudraksha* seeds, and perhaps a conch shell for blowing haunting calls across the cosmic ocean. Some smear themselves with ashes, symbolizing Shiva's role as the destroyer, who reduces all things to ash so that creation can begin anew. The trident-shaped *tika* of Shiva is often painted on the sadhus' foreheads, although they may employ scores of other *tika* patterns, each with its own cult affiliation and symbolism.

Sadhus have a curious role model in Shiva, who is both a mountaintop ascetic and the omnipotent god of the phallus. Some, such as the members of the Gorakhnath cult (which has a strong presence at Pashupatinath), follow the tantric **"left-hand" path**, employing deliberately transgressive practices to free themselves of sensual passions and transcend the illusory physical world. The most notorious of these spiritual exercises is the tying of a heavy stone to the penis, thus destroying the erectile tissues and helping to tame the distractions of sexual desire. **Aghoris**, the most extreme of the left-hand practitioners, are famed for their cult of death, embracing the forbidden in order to destroy it. Cremation grounds like Pashupatinath are effectively their temples, and they are even rumoured to ingest human flesh – all in pursuit of the liberation of the soul.

Like Shiva, sadhus also make liberal use of **intoxicants** as a path to spiritual insight. It was Shiva, in fact, who supposedly discovered the transcendental powers of ganja (cannabis), which grows wild throughout the hills of Nepal. Sadhus usually consume the weed in the form of *bhang* (a liquid preparation) or *charas* (hashish, smoked in a vertical clay pipe known as a chilam). With each toke, the holy man intones *"Bam Shankar"*: "I am Shiva".

The east bank

The east bank of the river has a palpably restful atmosphere thanks to **Mrigasthali Ban**, the woods in which Shiva is supposed to have cavorted as a stag. Deer are still kept here, safe behind a protective fence, ready for the god's enjoyment. Upstream of the twin bridges, the stone terraces are studded with fifteen great **shivalaya** (boxy *linga* shelters). Erected in the mid-nineteenth century by the Ranas and the royal family, they honour women who committed *sati* on their husband's pyres opposite; the practice was outlawed early in the twentieth century. Nowadays, photo-me sadhus stake out lucrative perches around them.

Above the terraces, it's possible to pick your way northwards along the top of the cliff heading towards the **Kirateshwar Mahadev Mandir** (see p.130). The path teeters somewhat between the forest fence and the gorge below, but offers good views of the river. You can peer down to **Surya Ghat**, the site of several meditation caves hewn out of the cliffs, and still used by sadhus today.

The Vishnu temples

To the south of the chief stone staircase ascending the hill stands a wide, paved enclosure, which during Shiva Raatri is chock-a-block with sadhus and other spiritual exhibitionists. The three rather undistinguished, Indian-donated temples are dedicated to **Ram**, Vishnu's incarnation as a mortal; **Lakshmi Narayan**, Vishnu's alter ego, and his wealth-bringing wife Lakshmi; and **Ram Janaki**, referring to the family of Ram's beloved wife Sita. They seem out of place in this Shaivite power place. The fenced-off forested area to the right belongs to a more indigenous tradition: it is a **cemetery** set aside for Nepal's few "burying" groups, which include Rais and Limbus of the eastern hills.

Gorakhnath Mandir

The main stairway up the east bank of the Bagmati River heads up past troupes of occasionally aggressive monkeys towards the mellow **Gorakhnath Mandir**, a modest *shikra* structure dedicated to the patron deity of the Shah kings. The adjoining rest-houses are home to resident and passing sadhus. All around, scores of **shivalaya** lie in crumbling rows in the forest, mottled by shade and shafts of sunlight. It feels like a romantically overgrown cemetery, but the *shivalaya* are not tombs, but Shiva shrines, as their iconography proclaims: most have the *trisul*, statues of Nandi and Shiva (always with an erection), and the *linga* atop the *yoni*.

The onion dome rising above the trees to the southeast of Gorakhnath is the **Bishwarup Mandir** (entrance only to Hindus), dedicated to Vishnu in his many-limbed "universal form". Dominating the sanctum is a 6m-tall statue of Shiva and Parbati in the state of *yab-yum* (sexual union).

Ghujeshwari Mandir

The **Ghujeshwari Mandir** (or Ghuyeshwari) sits at the bottom of the path that continues downhill from Gorakhnath, overlooking a giant sacred fig tree. Here, too, non-Hindus can only peek in from outside. The story goes that Shiva's first wife, Sati, offended by some insult, threw herself onto a fire (giving rise to the term *sati*, or *suttee*). Shiva retrieved her corpse and, blinded by grief, flew to and fro across the subcontinent, scattering parts of the body in 51 sacred places. Ghujeshwari is where Sati's vagina fell. As a consequence, the temple here represents the female counterpart to the Pashupati *linga* and is held to be every bit as sacred, its chief focus being a *kalash* (vessel) kept in a sunken pit and containing an "odiferous liquid". Buddhists consider Ghujeshwari to be one of the valley's four mystic Bajra Yoginis – powerful tantric goddesses – and the site to be the seed from which the Swayambhu lotus grew.

Across the river you can see a **sewage treatment centre** whose construction sparked a curious row between the secular authorities, who wanted to clean up the effluents upstream, and the temple priests, who objected to the treated water being reintroduced

2

above the complex on the grounds that it wasn't holy. In any case, it can't cope with the volume, so untreated water bypasses it anyway.

Kirateshwar Mahadev Mandir

From Ghujeshwari a lane follows the river downstream past the **Kirateshwar Mahadev Mandir**, which serves the Kirati ethnic groups of the hills – chiefly Rais and Limbus. You can often hear worshippers singing *bhajan* (devotional song) here, especially on full-moon evenings. Below lies **Gauri Ghat**, a peaceful spot where the river enters the Pashupatinath ravine. You can cross the river here and circle back around over the grassy knoll of **Kailash Hill**; or exit the complex and walk on to Boudha (see box, p.136). From the eastern edge of Kailash, a steep staircase leads down to Surya Ghat (see p.129), or you can continue on to the Pashupati Mandir's main gate.

ARRIVAL AND DEPARTURE PASHUPATINATH

By bus In Kathmandu, tempos and microbuses (every 10–15min; 20–30min) originate next to the Nepal Airlines office (NAC, also often referred to as RNAC) on Kantipath; all are numbered #2, and will drop you at the Gaushala crossroads on the Ring Road before continuing on towards Boudha. From the crossroads, walk down the eastward, downward-sloping road, then turn almost immediately left down a lane that leads through a scrubby park and past flower and trinket stalls for 500m to the complex.
By taxi A taxi costs about Rs500 from Thamel.
By bike You could cycle from Kathmandu to Pashupatinath, past the Royal Palace, then via Kamal Pokhari and Gaushala, on the Ring Road, but the traffic is horrendous.

INFORMATION

Guides Visitors are usually approached by guides, who sometimes ease the introduction by presenting themselves as "students". Some are knowledgeable and friendly, others out for what they can get; most ask to be paid what you think the tour was worth.
Food There are few concessions to Western visitors beyond a small snack stall beside the Gorakhnath temple.

SHOPPING

Pilgrim stalls There are no shops as such, but many pilgrim stalls along the road up to the Gaushala crossroads. If you're looking for an authentic Pashupatinath souvenir, check out the things Nepalis buy there: cheap votive icons, *linga* replicas, conch shells, *shaligram* (fossil-bearing stones), *motimala* (pearl necklaces, supposed to be good for the health of the mind) and the *rudraksha* or "tears of Shiva" necklaces, made from the seeds of the Utrasum bead tree.

Boudha

The great white stupa at **BOUDHA** (or **BOUDHANATH**), about 5km northeast of central Kathmandu, is the swollen sacred heart of a thriving Tibetan Buddhist community. One of the world's largest stupas – Tibetans call it simply Chorten Chempo, "Great Stupa" – it is also the most important Tibetan Buddhist monument outside Tibet. Since 1959, Boudha has been the focus for **Tibetan exiles** in Nepal, but it has been a sacred site on the Kathmandu–Tibet trade route for centuries. The 10km corridor from Pashupatinath to Sankhu was known as the auspicious zone of *siddhi* (supernatural beings), and Boudha was – and still is – its biggest, most auspicious landmark.

VOLUNTEERING IN BOUDHA

One of the simplest ways to spend some time in Boudha without committing to full-time study (see p.133) is to volunteer with one of the many **charities** sponsored by the Tibetan monasteries. One of the biggest is **Karuna Shechen** (🔘 karuna-shechen.org), run by French author and monk Mathieu Ricard and based at Shechen monastery, which operates clinics and schools in Nepal, Tibet and India. Another, **Rokpa** (🔘 rokpa.org), runs a winter soup kitchen and a home for street children.

Early morning and dusk are the **best times** to be here, when an otherworldly cacophony of ritual music drifts from the houses and monasteries that ring the stupa, and monks, locals and devout pilgrims all perform *kora* together, strolling, shuffling and prostrating their way around the dome. At other times, the souvenir shops and cafés in the tall houses that ring the stupa can seem intrusive, and the brick-paved piazza is filled with more tourists than Tibetans. And if you follow either of the two lanes heading **north of the stupa**, the romance evaporates in short order: this is Boudha the boomtown, an unplanned quagmire of garbage-strewn lanes, unlovely new buildings, schools and businesses.

Brief history

Traditions differ as to the stupa's origins. A **Tibetan text** relates how a daughter of Indra stole flowers from heaven and was reassigned to earth as a lowly poultryman's daughter, yet prospered and decided to use some of her wealth to build a stupa to honour a mythical Buddha of a previous age. She petitioned the king, who cynically

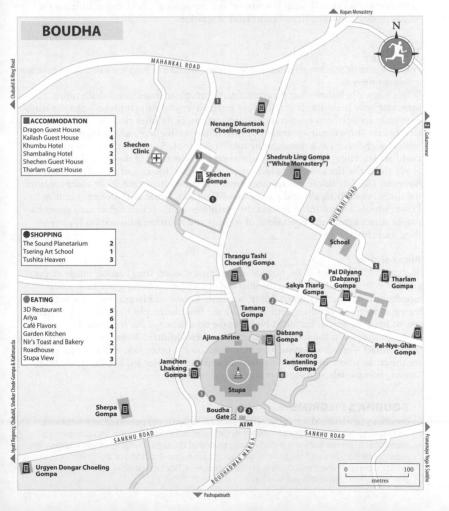

BOUDHA

Kopan Monastery

MAHANKAL ROAD

ACCOMMODATION
Dragon Guest House	1
Kailash Guest House	4
Khumbu Hotel	6
Shambaling Hotel	2
Shechen Guest House	3
Tharlam Guest House	5

SHOPPING
The Sound Planetarium	2
Tsering Art School	1
Tushita Heaven	3

EATING
3D Restaurant	5
Ariya	6
Café Flavors	4
Garden Kitchen	1
Nir's Toast and Bakery	2
Roadhouse	7
Stupa View	3

Nenang Dhuntsok Choeling Gompa

Shechen Clinic

Shechen Gompa

Shedrub Ling Gompa ("White Monastery")

PHULBARI ROAD

Gokarneswar

Chabahil & Ring Road

School

Thrangu Tashi Choeling Gompa

Pal Dilyang (Dabzang) Gompa

Tharlam Gompa

Sakya Tharig Gompa

Tamang Gompa

Dabzang Gompa

Ajima Shrine

Pal-Nye-Ghan Gompa

Jamchen Lhakang Gompa

Kerong Samtenling Gompa

Stupa

Boudha Gate

ATM

Sherpa Gompa

Hyatt Regency, Chabahil, Shekhar Chode Gompa & Kathmandu

SANKHU ROAD

SANKHU ROAD

Urgyen Dongar Choeling Gompa

BOUDHADWAR MARGA

Pranamaya Yoga & Sankhu

0   100

metres

Pashupatinath

N

2

granted her only as much land as could be covered by a buffalo hide. Undaunted, the woman cut the hide into thread-thin strips and joined them end to end to enclose a gigantic area.

The **Newari legend** has a firmer historical grounding, involving a drought that struck Kathmandu during the reign of the early Lichhavi king, Vrisadev. When court astrologers advised that only the sacrifice of a virtuous man would bring rain, Vrisadev commanded his son Mandev to go to the royal well on a moonless night and decapitate the shrouded body he would find there. Mandev obeyed, only to find to his horror that he had sacrificed his own father. When he asked the goddess Bajra Yogini of Sankhu how to expiate his guilt, she let fly a bird and told him to build a stupa at the spot where it landed, which was Boudha.

Whatever its legendary origins, it's possible that the core of the stupa dates as early as the fifth century AD, and it's almost certain that it encloses **holy relics**, perhaps parts of the Buddha's body (bones, hair, teeth) and objects touched or used by him, along with sacred texts and other ritual objects. The stupa has been sealed for centuries, of course, so no one knows exactly what lies within, but the relics are held responsible for the stupa's power, and its ability to command veneration.

The stupa

Foreigners are charged Rs250 for entry into the stupa plaza and surrounding area; pay at the main gate or at one of the checkpoints on the smaller roads into the plaza

While less embellished than Swayambhu, the **stupa** at Boudha exudes a more muscular holy presence. It is also more interactive: you can climb up onto the stupa's base from its northern end, and children sometimes fly kites from it. The dome is elevated on three twenty-cornered plinths of decreasing size, which reinforces the notion of the stupa as a mandala, or meditation tool. As usual, the primordial Buddha's searching blue eyes are painted on the four sides of the central spire, and above them rise the thirteen golden steps to *nirvana*. Instead of five *dhyani* Buddhas, however, 108 (an auspicious number) much smaller images are set in niches around the dome, describing a broad pantheon of Buddhas, lamas and protector deities. Prayer wheels are mounted around the perimeter wall – it's said that each spin of a prayer wheel here is the equivalent of reciting the mantra embossed on it eleven thousand times.

Ajima shrine

The small **Ajima shrine** at the far side of the stupa shelters the ghoulish image of the goddess Ajima literally sucking the guts out of a corpse, reflecting her malevolent aspect as the bringer of disease. More popularly known as Harati, she was a much-feared abductor of children until, it is said, the Buddha taught her a lesson by stealing one of her own brood. Buddhist Newars take care to propitiate her suitably, however; in return she acts as the revered protectress of their children. Next door is a room-sized prayer wheel – all are welcome to spin it – and on the other side of the shrine you'll see the tanks where whitewash is mixed during festivals. Behind lies the newly built **Tamang gompa**, whose balcony makes a good vantage point.

BOUDHA'S PILGRIMS

Boudha's stupa is famed throughout the Himalayan region for its powers of wish fulfilment and blessing. You'll see **pilgrims** repeatedly circumambulating the stupa, and doing endless sequences of prostrations in a secluded area on one of the upper terraces. Prayer wheels, heavy silver jewellery and rainbow-striped aprons are better indicators of a pilgrim's Tibetan origins than facial features, as Nepali Bhotiyas, people of Tibetan ethnicity, and Tamangs from the central hills also visit Boudha in force.

BOUDHA'S DHARMA SCENE

Boudha's **Western community** is well established, though to become a part of it you need either an introduction or a lot of time, as serious Western students of *dharma* tend to regard tourists as spiritual interference. But as those in the know say, if you're ready you will find a teacher here. Some will go on to warn enthusiastic newcomers that there are good teachers and bad, and Buddhism is big business in Boudha. Still, many Westerners rate it as the best place in the world to **study** Tibetan Buddhism. All four sects are well represented, and the main alternative, **Dharamsala** in India, arguably has a politically rather than spiritually charged atmosphere.

A good way to start is to stay at a **gompa guesthouse** (most monasteries operate them, and they are open to all), to check restaurant or guesthouse notice boards, or to sample some of the alternative treatments on offer everywhere – from massage to Tibetan medicine. You could also go straight to a monastery: *puja* ceremonies are open to all, and most rinpoches (or "respected teachers") at Boudha give occasional open **talks** – with or without English translation. Many also agree to one-on-one meetings to those who show a keen interest.

Some monasteries are particularly oriented towards Westerners; the following are worth checking out. Note that some of the more popular, better-funded monasteries operate grander **satellite institutes** in the countryside.

TEACHING GOMPA IN BOUDHA

Jamchen Lhakhang Gompa The Sakya school is represented at Boudha by this monastery, headed by the English-speaking Shabdrung Ngawang Kyenrab Rinchen Paljor; the monastery sponsors the Boudha-based International Buddhist Academy (winternational buddhistacademy.org), which offers an annual ten-day retreat in September, and four- and eight-week Buddhist philosophy and Tibetan-language courses.

Shechen Gompa wshechen.org. The death in 1991 of the revered Dilgo Khyentse of Shechen Tennyi Dargyeling, the "Bhutanese Monastery", left a large gap, but it is being filled by his grandson, the current abbot, Shechen Rabjam Rinpoche, who teaches courses in English.

Shedrub Ling Gompa (aka the "The White Monastery") wshedrub.org. Perennially popular among the *dharma* set, the Ka Nying Shedrub Ling Gompa holds a regular Saturday morning talk in English, and every November the English-speaking abbot Chökyi Nyima Rinpoche runs ten-day seminars. The monastery is affiliated to Kathmandu University for longer degree programmes (wryi.org).

Shelkar Chode Gompa 400m west of the stupa, facing the Hyatt Regency Hotel wlamawangdu.org. Lama Tsering Wangdu Rinpoche holds open sessions most mornings (around 7.30–11am); visitors can also attend the remarkable Chöd ritual, a tantric, symbolic offering of the body performed on the 10th and 25th of the Tibetan month.

Thrangu Tashi Choeling Gompa wrinpoche.com. Thrangu Rinpoche attracts many Western students, though usually to his grand-scale temple and teaching complex at Namobuddha (see p.182), rather than this relatively modest monastery in Boudha itself.

TEACHING GOMPA AROUND BOUDHA

Kopan Monastery 3km north of Boudha wkopan-monastery.com. One of the most welcoming monasteries to Westerners, with a full schedule of courses and teachings, including daily teachings at 10am, seven- and ten-day residential courses aimed at beginners, and a well-regarded month-long intensive course in November.

Pulahari Gompa Further along the ridge from Kopan wjamgonkongtrul.org. A major centre for long-term Western Buddhists, with frequent ten-day programmes.

The gompa

Where Swayambhu (see p.78) was traditionally sacred to Newar Buddhists, Boudha has always been essentially **Tibetan** in culture. Since the Chinese invasion, what was once a pilgrimage site has become the second pole of Tibetan religion, alongside Dharamsala in India. Over the last 35 years or so, Western donations and canny business ventures have laid down the foundations of considerable wealth in the Tibetan community, and much of it piously appeared above ground in the shape of *gompa*, or **monasteries**. There are some twenty scattered around the neighbourhood (a complete map is painted on a wall near the Ajima shrine). Most are named after *gompa* in Tibet that were destroyed by the Chinese, and preserve the same lineage of teachers and reincarnate lamas. While all four of the major Tibetan Buddhist sects are represented (see p.402), the majority belong to the Nyingma-pa, the oldest order of Tibetan Buddhism – and that of Nepal's ethnic Tamangs, who still own much of the land around Boudha.

Visiting Boudha's gompa

Only a few **gompa** keep their doors open throughout the day – but if the door is open you can go in. Most welcome spectators during their cacophonous morning and pre-dusk *puja*, or prayer ritual. On arrival, just slip off your shoes outside the main door, salute with a *namaste* palms-pressed-together-over-the-breast gesture, and sit on the floor – avoid the monks' benches. The interior of the main *lhakang* (assembly hall) is typically dominated by gilded statues of Buddhas and *bodhisattvas* and decorated with silk brocade hangings and polychrome murals depicting fearsome guardians of the faith, symbolic deities and cosmological patterns.

ARRIVAL AND INFORMATION   BOUDHA

By bus Crowded minibuses and microbuses (every 10–15min; around 30min), all numbered #2, depart from Kantipath near NAC (the Nepal Airlines office, often referred to as RNAC).

By taxi Taxis cost around Rs500 from central Kathmandu. You'll be dropped off on the Ring Road outside the main gate.

By bike Quite simply, don't: the road here is one of the valley's busiest and most polluted.

Services All the usual tourist facilities, including moneychangers, photo and phone shops, internet cafés, and travel/ticket agents, can be found in the immediate vicinity of the stupa. There are several ATMs just outside the main Boudha gate, including a 24hr Standard Chartered one.

ACTIVITIES

Alternative therapies There are many Tibetan medicine clinics in Boudha, but Shechen Clinic, opposite Shechen Gompa (Sun–Thurs 9am–4.30pm; ☎01 448 7924, ⓦkaruna-shechen.org), is perhaps the most useful: as well as Tibetan treatments, it offers homeopathy, acupuncture and Western/drug-based medicine. It uses a proportion of the consultation fees to subsidize health care for local

people, and the adjacent hospice. The Sound Planetarium (see opposite), meanwhile, offers singing-bowl therapies.

Yoga The excellent Pranamaya Yoga (☎980 204 5484, ⓦpranamaya-yoga.com) runs a range of daily classes (Rs700), as well as three-day retreats: the studio is a 5min walk east of the main Boudha gate, on an alley opposite a big pipal tree.

ACCOMMODATION

You pay a premium to stay in Boudha, but it's worth it to enjoy the place at its dusk and early-morning best. Most guesthouses are within easy walking distance of the stupa. Those attached to **monasteries** are perhaps the most colourful, but expect early-morning wake-up calls courtesy of horns, drums and chanting monks. It's worth calling ahead to **reserve**, as popular places fill up, especially around the time of festivals, enthronements of lamas and so on.

Dragon Guest House Mahankal ☎01 447 9562, ⓔdragon@ntc.net.np. Comfortable hotel in a quiet area, run by a family from Mustang, and which attracts lots of returnees. Decently furnished rooms (the cheaper with shared bathrooms) are stacked up in a tall tower – upper rooms are airier. A 5min or so walk from the stupa. **Rs850**

Kailash Guest House Phulbari Rd ☎01 491 5741. This Sherpa-run place is something of a dive, but if budget is the priority it's decent enough, and you can pay a small premium for slightly fresher rooms and private bathrooms. Overlooks a *gompa* on the noisy main lane leading north from the stupa – but the back rooms are quieter. **Rs500**

Khumbu Hotel Beside the stupa ☎01 446 5241, ⓦkhumbuhotel.com.np. A narrow entrance on the stupa plaza leads through to this professional, though overpriced,

hotel. All rooms give onto common balconies, and have wood panelling, parquet floors, TVs and proper bathrooms (and sometimes a fair bit of dust). Tibetan murals and mannequins in the common areas give it character, and there's a terrace restaurant and small spa. **US$30**

Shambaling Hotel Off Phulbari Rd ☎01 491 6868, ⓦshambaling.com. Located a 10min walk from the stupa, this smart, eco-aware hotel has plenty in the way of character and comforts (including kettle, minibar and slippers in the en suites). There's a good garden restaurant, and massages (from Rs2500/hr) are available. **US$98**

★**Shechen Guest House** Shechen Gompa ☎01 447 9009, ⓦshechenguesthouse.com.np. Tucked away in a quiet area, with simple but perfectly acceptable rooms livened up by oddments of Tibetan fabrics. It's owned by

BOUDHA FESTIVALS

If you want an extra helping of Tibetan culture, go to Boudha during the festival of **Losar** in February or March, when the community hosts the biggest Tibetan New Year celebration in Nepal. Other busy times are **Buddha Jayanti** (the Buddha's birthday), held on the full moon of April–May, when an image of the Buddha is paraded around the stupa aboard an elephant, and the **full moon of March–April**, when ethnic Tamangs – the original guardians of the stupa – converge here to arrange marriages, and hundreds of eligible brides are sat around the stupa for inspection. Full-moon and **new-moon days** in general attract more pilgrims, since acts of worship earn more merit on these days.

2

the adjacent Shechen monastery, so you pay a little extra for the networking – there are often visiting monks taking tea in the well-tended gardens and restaurant. Good breakfasts, with home-made bread. Rs1420

Tharlam Guest House Phulbari ☎ 01 449 6878, ⊛ tharlammonastery.com. Newish three-storey building, with good-value, large and spotless rooms set in distinctly grand surroundings. These belong to the monastery behind, for which it acts as a kind of gatehouse – which inevitably means an early-morning *puja* call. Suites and rooms with kitchenettes are also available. Rs800

EATING

A handful of **restaurants** around the stupa plaza target day-trippers, with rooftop seating and standard tourist menus. Most are lacklustre, but stick to Tibetan food and enjoy the view and you can't go far wrong. Other, more authentic Tibetan places – with trademark curtained doors and windows – are tucked away in the back lanes and on the main road. Most places shut at around 9pm, but will close earlier on quiet nights – or stay open if there's a big group in.

3D Restaurant Off the stupa plaza. The dark, gloomy cafeteria setting isn't appealing, but the *Triple Dorjee*, or "3D", has a solid local reputation for Tibetan food that's fresh, authentic and inexpensive. Veg or meat *momos* and *thukpa* cost around Rs75–125. Daily 7/8am–8pm.

Ariya Stupa plaza. This tiny café has a minimalist feel with just five tables and little in the way of decor. The breakfast options (breakfast burritos Rs280–320), Illy coffee (Rs130–160) and sweet and savoury snacks are all good, though. Daily 8am–8pm.

Café Flavors Stupa plaza ☎ 01 449 8748. Sophisticated establishment set back from the plaza, with a peaceful courtyard filled with pot plants and black-and-white-checked tables. There are twenty types of coffee (Rs90–180), including a "tiramisu latte", plus a good range of beers (including several Belgian options for Rs500–550) and the usual, extensive international menu (mains Rs320–540). Daily 7.30am–9pm.

★ **Garden Kitchen Restaurant** Phulbari. A gate in a back alley leads to a real oasis: a spacious terracotta-floored courtyard surrounded by greenery, hung with paper lanterns, and thronging with the *dharma* crowd working up a spiritual appetite over coffee, cakes and reasonably priced, homely food. Good breakfast options, plus Nepali, Indian and Chinese mains (Rs75–215). Daily 8am–9pm.

Nir's Toast and Bakery Alleway off Phulbari Rd. This simple, courtyard café, tucked away at the end of an underground arcade, is great for coffee, cake and tapping into the Buddhist scene – there's a thriving notice board with courses, sessions and expats advertising for flatmates. Also does decent veg and non-veg main meals (Rs135–555). Profits go to schools in eastern Nepal. Daily 7/8am–9pm.

Roadhouse Stupa plaza ☎ 01 491 6446. Boudha's offshoot of this smart, mini-chain – there are also branches in Thamel and Patan – offers excellent though pricey food, notably wood-fired pizzas (from Rs475). It's also a good spot for a sunset cocktail (from Rs450). Daily 9am–9pm.

Stupa View Stupa plaza ☎ 01 491 4962. Long-running vegetarian restaurant, with (as you'd expect from the name) suitably impressive vistas of the stupa. The menu features several vegan options and is fairly imaginative: from masala potato wedges to Mustang apple gratin – a confection of cream, plums and cinnamon. Mains Rs385–595. Daily 9am–9/10pm.

SHOPPING

Run-of-the-mill **souvenirs** at Boudha are notoriously overpriced, but this is the place to come if you're seeking genuinely obscure items. Keep an eye out for tea tables, jewellery, flasks, butter-tea churns, singing bowls and prayer-flag printing blocks, not to mention some genuine, high-quality **thangka**. It's also a good place to buy prayer flags, brocade banners, Tibetan incense, *chuba* (Tibetan wraparound dresses) and maroon monks' garb, not to mention meditation CDs and DVDs. For books in English you're better off in Kathmandu's Thamel, though a few places sell traditional wood-block printed texts in Tibetan.

HIKING AND BIKING AROUND BOUDHA

Boudha makes a good springboard for several walks and bike rides in this part of the valley.

Pashupatineth The twin poles of Hinduism and Tibetan Buddhism in Nepal, Boudha and Pashupatinath, lie 2.5km apart – an intriguing half-hour's walk through the ordinary, domestic Kathmandu that few tourists see. From Boudha's main gate, cross the road and follow the lane that slopes slightly downhill past open-fronted shops and houses set amid the few remaining fields. You don't need to turn until you see the pine-clad slopes of Pashupatinath's Kailash Hill; turn right onto the main road just short of Gauri Ghat and follow the main road from there. Route finding is just as simple in reverse.

Kopan Monastery Occupying a ridge about 3km due north of the stupa, Kopan Monastery is an easy target, and is something of a pilgrimage destination for its astoundingly richly decorated "thousand-Buddha stupa", so named for the inordinate number of holy relics it contains. You can take a taxi all the way, but it's a pleasant walk.

Pulahari Monastery Half an hour's walk further to the east of Kopan (beyond the giant temple of the Amitabha Foundation), Pulahari Monastery sits atop the ridge like the superstructure of an enormous container ship; its huge new prayer hall is perhaps the most richly and exquisitely decorated in Nepal. Both monasteries are usually open to visitors in daylight hours unless there's a ceremony on.

Nagi Gompa From either Kopan or Pulahari, it's a strenuous two- to three-hour hike north up a wooded ridge to the nunnery of Nagi Gompa, though you probably shouldn't go without help finding the way. From here you can continue up into Shivapuri National Park (see p.139).

Gokarneswar Three kilometres northeast of Boudha (and 2km downhill from Pulahari on a paved road) lies Gokarneswar, where an imposing Shiva temple gazes across the Bagmati River to the peaceful Gokarna Forest – which encloses the luxury *Gokarna Forest Resort*, golf club and spa (see p.105). Frequent mini- and microbuses run from here back to Boudha and Kathmandu, along the main road from Sundarijal, the trailhead for Helambu treks (see p.334).

The Sound Planetarium Off Phulbari Rd, beside Shedrub Ling Gompa ☏ 984 134 8879, ⓦ sound planetarium.com. Tibetan singing bowls have long had mystical connotations, but this little boutique shop, with its therapy rooms behind, takes it to an extreme by finding "planetary alignments" and personality matches to the sound frequencies. The therapies, which use the bowls' vibrations to relax the body and heal the mind, feel rather amazing – but are not cheap, at Rs2200–2500 an hour. Singing bowls are also on sale in the shop. Daily 9am–5/6pm.

Tsering Art School Shechen Gompa ☏ 01 449 6097, ⓦ shechen.org/cultural-preservation/art-school. This offshoot of the adjacent Shechen *gompa* does most of its business with local monasteries, so it's an excellent place to learn about what you're buying. The shop mostly sells high-quality *thangka*, and would-be *thangka* artists can study here. Daily 8/9am–5/6pm.

Tushita Heaven Handicraft Stupa plaza ☏ 01 447 8546, ⓦ thangkatushita.com. This cooperative of *thangka* artists, some of whom can be seen at work in the shop, is one of the longer-standing and more serious of Boudha's outlets. You could commission your own piece, at least in terms of colour and theme – artists will only work within proper iconographical norms. Daily 8/9am–5/6pm.

Sankhu

The paved road beyond Boudha – one of the old trade routes to Tibet – rolls eastwards as far as **SANKHU**. It's still one of the valley's larger traditional Newari towns, but its location, in a rural corner hard up against the forested hills, gives it a pleasant backwater feel. There's an old bazaar area to the east of the main north–south road, but the area is worth visiting mainly for its temple to **Bajra Yogini**, whose gilded roof glints from a grove of trees on the wooded hillside north of town. Snack food can be found in the bazaar but there's nothing oriented towards tourists.

The Bajra Yogini temple

2km from Sankhu • Daily dawn–dusk • Free • Follow the main road through the arch at the town's north end, then bear left after 400m on a cobbled path. If you have a car/bike, continue for another 1km until the road peters out. The last 30min or so is a stiff climb

Bajra Yogini is the eldest of a ferocious foursome of **tantric goddesses** specially venerated in the Kathmandu Valley. To Buddhist Newars – her main devotees – she is identified with Ugratara, the wrathful, corpse-trampling emanation of Tara, one of the female aspects of Buddhahood. Hindus identify her as Durga (Kali), the most terrifying of the eight mother goddesses. She's also known as Khadga Yogini, for the sword (*khadga*) held in her right hand.

The current **Bajra Yogini temple** dates from the seventeenth century, though the smaller building next to it is more ancient: indeed, its natural stone dome may well be the original seventh-century object of worship at this site. The stone just to the right of the temple door is a *nag* (snake) shrine.

The pilgrim's rest-house

Steps lead up, past scurrying troupes of monkeys, to a picturesque, Rana-era **pilgrim's rest-house**, set around a courtyard. The wing nearest the temple houses a subsidiary shrine to Bajra Yogini, tucked away on the first floor. Touching the goddess herself is forbidden, so this gilt copper copy was created for the annual **jatra** procession down to Sankhu (held for nine days from the full to the new moon of March–April); as a mother goddess, she is flanked by her two children.

On the ground floor, a seventh-century **Buddha head** and an enormous overturned **frying pan** are displayed. These belong respectively to Vrisadev, whose decapitation led to the founding of Boudha (see p.131) and to an ancient king who offered his own body as a daily sacrificial fry-up to Bajra Yogini. According to legend, the goddess would restore him to life and endow him with supernatural powers; when a rival tried to copy the trick, the goddess accepted his flesh, with no resurrection, and then turned over the frying pan to indicate that she would require no more sacrifices. Blood sacrifices are now performed only in front of the triangular stone of **Bhairab**, Bajra Yogini's consort, which guards the path some hundred-odd steps below the temple; on the average day it gleams darkly with fresh blood.

The caves

In the back wall of the compound, a small square opening indicates a meditation **cave**. Another cave just behind the *pati* west of the compound (recognizable by the faint Tibetan inscription of the Avalokitesvara mantra over the door) is known as Dharma Pap Gupha: those who can squeeze through the opening into the inner chamber demonstrate their virtue (*dharma*); those who can't, their vice (*pap*).

ARRIVAL AND DEPARTURE	SANKHU
By bus Buses (every 10–15min; 1hr) run from Kathmandu's City Bus Park.	(just east of Boudha). With a mountain bike, you can continue on to Nagarkot (see p.176): head north from the
By bike It's possible to cycle from Kathmandu to Sankhu, though there's heavy industrial traffic until beyond Jorpati	old bazaar area on the main road. Other, rougher trails ascend the ridge to Changu Narayan (see p.167).

Budhanilkantha

A paved road leads 8km north from Kathmandu to **Narayanthan**, a roadside village centred on **BUDHANILKANTHA**, the site of a monolithic and hugely impressive sleeping Vishnu statue. A visit can be combined with a **hike** or **mountain-bike** ride up to the thickly forested peak of **Shivapuri** (see p.139), from where there are some of the finest Himalayan views anywhere in the valley. The road from Kathmandu to Budhanilkantha is busy at first, but a quieter route heads north to Tokha then cuts across east.

"OLD BLUE-THROAT"

Budhanilkantha's name has been a source of endless confusion. It has nothing to do with the Buddha (*budha* means "old", though that doesn't stop Buddhist Newars from worshipping the image). The real puzzler is why Budhanilkantha (literally, "Old Blue-Throat"), a title that unquestionably refers to Shiva, has been attached here to Vishnu. The myth of **Shiva's blue throat**, a favourite in Nepal, relates how the gods churned the ocean of existence and inadvertently unleashed a poison that threatened to destroy the world. They begged Shiva to save them from their blunder and he obliged by drinking the poison. His throat burning, the great god flew up to the range north of Kathmandu, struck the mountainside with his trident to create a lake, Gosainkund, and quenched his thirst – suffering no lasting ill effect except for a blue patch on his throat. The water in the Sleeping Vishnu's tank is popularly believed to originate in Gosainkund, and Shaivas claim that a reclining image of Shiva can be seen under the waters of the lake during the annual Shiva festival there in August, which perhaps explains the association. Local legend maintains that a mirror-image statue of Shiva lies on the statue's underside.

Nonetheless, the Budhanilkantha sculpture bears all the hallmarks of Vishnu or, as he's often called in Nepal, **Narayan**. It depicts Vishnu floating in the ocean of existence upon the endless snake Shesh; from his navel will grow Brahma and the rest of creation.

The Sleeping Vishnu

Daily dawn–dusk; *puja* daily 9–10am & 6–7pm • Free

The valley's largest stone sculpture, the 5m-long **Sleeping Vishnu** (Jalakshayan Narayan) at Budhanilkantha, reclines in a recessed water tank like an oversized astronaut in suspended animation. Carved from a type of basalt found miles away in the southern hills, it was apparently dragged here by forced labour during the reign of the seventh-century monarch Vishnugupta, who controlled the valley under the Licchavi king Bhimarjunadev, much as the Ranas ruled in the name of the Shah dynasty in the early twentieth century. According to legend the image was lost and buried for centuries, only to be rediscovered by a farmer tilling his fields.

Hindus may enter the sanctum area to perform *puja* before the Sleeping Vishnu; others may only view it from between concrete railings. Priests and novices continually tend, bathe and anoint the image but the bustle of religious activity is at its height at morning and evening *puja*. Each year the god is said to "awaken" from his summer slumber during the Haribondhini Ekadashi **festival** in late October or early November, an event that draws thousands of worshippers.

Historically, one person who would never put in an appearance here was the king of Nepal. Some attribute this absence to a seventeenth-century curse; others to the fact that the monarchs were held to be reincarnations of Vishnu and should never gaze upon their own image.

ARRIVAL AND DEPARTURE
BUDHANILKANTHA

By bus Microbuses (every 5–10min; 45min) leave Kathmandu from opposite the Nepal Airlines office (NAC, also often referred to as RNAC) on Kantipath, heading north on Kantipath past the Kaisher Mahal, just east of Thamel at Lainchaur. Some services head on to the Shivapuri National Park gate, 2km north, but you may have to walk.

ACCOMMODATION AND EATING

The **bazaar** surrounding the Sleeping Vishnu supports a lively trade in sweets, snacks and tea, as well as religious paraphernalia. If you're looking for something more substantial to eat, head to one of the hotel restaurants.

Park Village Resort ☏ 01 437 5280, ⊛ ktmgh.com. Located just off the main road, around 200m short of the Sleeping Vishnu, this country-club-style resort has extensive, bird-filled grounds with an infinity pool, tennis court, ping-pong tables and spa. The restaurant serves good food, and the en suites and cottages are spacious. A pleasant, semi-rural retreat for those who want to stay near Kathmandu but not in it. Rooms US$96, cottages US$112

Shivapuri Heights Cottage ⊕984 137 1927, ⓦshivapuricottage.com. This pair of attractive, traditionally designed cottages lies a 5–15min drive off the road (depending on your vehicle and road conditions), on the edge of the Shivapuri forest, a short way west of Budhanilkantha. The place has great valley views and is a popular weekend retreat for expats – dinner and breakfast are included in the rates, and they can arrange cocktails, massages, guides and more. Staying here also allows you to get an early start for the dawn hike to the summit of Shivapuri (see below). **US$100**

2

Shivapuri National Park

Park gate 2km north of Budhanilkantha • Daily 8am–4.30pm; ticket office closes around 2pm • Rs250, bicycles Rs1000; campers pay Rs100/tent at the park gate • Microbuses from Kathmandu to Budhanilkantha (every 5–10min; 45min) occasionally continue as far as the park gate, but you may have to walk

At 2732m, **Shivapuri** (or Sheopuri) is the second highest point on the valley rim. It lies within the forested **Shivapuri Nagarjun National Park**, designed to protect the valley's water supply and offering visitors superlative Himalayan views.

By far the most rewarding **route to the peak** from the park gate, 2km north of Budhanilkantha, isn't the direct but masochistic ascent up the largely unshaded, giant-scale **stone staircase**, but instead starts with a walk east along a dirt road (usually navigable on a 4WD or motorbike in decent conditions) to **Nagi Gompa**, a former Tamang monastery gifted to the renowned lama Urgyen Rinpoche, and now occupied by nuns – along with the occasional Western *dharma* student sent up from Boudha. (If you're interested in Buddhism, ask to stay in the simple guesthouse here.) It's a pleasant walk of an hour or so, climbing and contouring eastward through the forest. From Nagi Gompa, it takes anything from two to three hours up to the peak (when in doubt, bear left). Just short of the top you'll pass **Baghdwar**, where the holy Bagmati River gushes forth from the mouth of a tiger's head, and a Hindu hermitage.

The total vertical gain – nearly 1200m – shouldn't be taken lightly: pack food and sufficient water. Clouds tend to move in by lunchtime but if you're up early enough you should have superb views of the Himalayas, from Jugal and Ganesh Himal out to Himalchuli, and eastwards from Langtang Lirung to Dorje Lakpa. To be sure of the views, you can **camp** on the flat, grassy summit.

A direct descent route leads west to a minor col a short distance from the summit, and from there down the well-made but relentless stone staircase; the trail can either

---

HIKING AND BIKING IN SHIVAPURI NATIONAL PARK

There are numerous **walking** and **biking** routes in Shivapuri National Park, and Nagi Gompa makes a good place to start. The rough road contours from the nunnery all the way along the southern side of the park to its easternmost point, offering various ways to drop down to the valley. One good, bikeable route descends from a fork some 500m east of the nunnery, following a lovely ridge-line south to Gokarna (see p.136) or Kopan (see p.136); this is also an attractive (if long) route up to Shivapuri peak

From the Tamang village of **Mulkharka**, 10km east of Nagi Gompa, along the road, walkers can descend to the small town of **Sundarijal** in less than half an hour; from here plentiful buses run back to Boudha and Kathmandu. Alternatively, you can trek northwards and upwards through the middle of the park from Mulkharka (where there's basic accommodation) to the pass at Borlang Bhangjang (roughly 3hr), from where you descend to **Chisapani**, at the park's northeastern side (1hr); this is traditionally the first day of the Helambu Circuit (see p.334).

From Mulkharka, you can also take a classic **mountain-bike** route, heading east on the rough road all the way to the park gate at Jhule, and continuing south from there to Nagarkot or Sankhu; you could even turn north and carry on all the way round the fringe of the park to Chisapani. Budhanilkantha to Chisapani would be an all-day ride of 30km (count on 8hr). Between Mulkharka and Jhule, walkers can descend directly south to Sankhu, via the Bajra Yogini temple (see p.137).

return you to the main gate or to the road roughly halfway between Budhanilkantha and the park gate.

Nagarjun Ban and around

The valley's northwestern fringe is its most congested. Kathmandu sprawls right to the very edge of the basin, while the main road to Trisuli (see p.188) heaves itself smokily out of the valley. The wooded hillside of **Nagarjun Ban** provides a pleasant swathe of green, however, and just outside its boundaries – it is part of the Shivapuri–Nagarjun National Park – lie the curious Sleeping Vishnu at **Balaju** and the rustic temple of **Ichangu Narayan**. It's true that Nagarjun's forest is no match for Shivapuri, that the Vishnu plays second fiddle to the one at Budhanilkantha, and that the temple is distinctly ordinary compared to the similarly named Changu Narayan, but they're all handily close to the city centre.

Balaju Water Garden

2km northwest of Thamel along the Trisuli road · Daily 7am–7pm · Rs5 · From Kathmandu, frequent microbuses run from outside NAC (Nepal Airlines) on Kantipath, heading to Balaju via Jamal and Lainchaur, on Kantipath, and Lekhnath Marg, in north Thamel; Balaju is also within easy cycling distance of Thamel

The Water Garden at **BALAJU** is really a suburban picnic park just beyond the Ring Road. The official name of Baisdhara Garden comes from the open water tank feeding 22 (*baais*) stone spouts (*dhara*). It heaves with bathing worshippers during the **festival** of Lhuti Punhi, observed on the day of the full moon of March–April. The park's chief attraction, however, is a **Sleeping Vishnu** statue that was once thought to be a copy of the more famous and much larger seventh-century image at Budhanilkantha (see p.137), but may actually antedate it. The iconography is obscure, but the god appears to be holding a conch and mace in his two left hands, and ashes and a rosary in his right (attributes of Vishnu and Shiva respectively), making the figure a **Shankar-Narayan** or half-Vishnu, half-Shiva. If so, this may reflect the balancing act of the early Gupta rulers, who introduced Vaishnavism but continued to honour the more ancient, popular worship of Shiva.

Nagarjun Ban

Park gate 2km from Balaju · Daily 8am–4.30pm; ticket office closes around 2pm · Rs250, bicycles Rs1000 · Frequent microbuses (every 10min or so; around 45min) run from Nepal Airlines (NAC) on Kathmandu's Kantipath, to Balaju via Jamal and Lainchaur, on Kantipath, and Lekhnath Marg, in north Thamel. Ask to be let off at Machha Pokhari Chowk – an obvious major junction

Two kilometres up the road from Balaju stands the park gate to **Nagarjun Ban** (also known as Rani Ban), a large and surprisingly wild forest reserve. An unpaved road winds from the park gate to the *chaitya*-topped summit of 2096m **Jamacho**, but you can hike more directly up the ridge along a 5km trail (allow at least two hours on foot). You'll pass numerous limestone **caves** with Buddhist legends attached.

The gate is the only official entrance to the reserve, but various **trails** thread through the forest and exit at a number of points around the perimeter. Perhaps the most useful route cuts down from the main Jamacho road due south towards Ichangu Narayan, but at the time of writing it was blocked off by a police checkpost. There are also a number of good **mountain-bike** routes (see p.139). If you want to walk for long in the forest, and especially if climbing Jamacho peak, it would be wise to come as part of a group, as **robberies** have been reported here in recent years.

You can eat in pleasant surroundings at a few outdoor **cafés** along the main road beyond the forest entrance.

Ichangu Narayan

3km northwest of Swayambhunath • Daily dawn–dusk • Free • A roughish road leaves the Ring Road immediately opposite
Swayambhunath's western tip; there's no bus, but taxis wait at this junction, or you can hike or bike up through the suburb of Halchok
towards a small notch in the ridge behind a big Buddhist monastery; from here an increasingly rough road descends into the Ichangu
valley to reach the temple after about 3km

According to tradition, a Narayan temple occupies each of the four cardinal points
of Kathmandu Valley. The western one, **Ichangu Narayan**, is rustic rather than
distinguished, but it nestles in a surprisingly pleasant rural side valley at the southern
base of Jamacho. Just east of the temple, a road breaks off to the south beside a quarry;
from here mountain bikers could head westwards to Bhimdhunga and on to Thankot,
astride the westbound Prithvi Highway.

Kirtipur

Once-proud **KIRTIPUR** ("City of Glory") occupies a long, low battleship of a ridge 5km
southwest of Kathmandu. Commanding a panoramic – not to mention strategic –
view of the valley, the well-preserved old town is vehicle-free and great for a morning
or afternoon's wandering. It also conceals, deep within its miniature maze of brick and
stone streets, one of the best Newari **restaurants** in the valley (see p.143).

In modern times, Kirtipur's hilltop position has proved more of a handicap than an
asset. The commerce all takes place at the foot of the hill, in **Naya Bazaar**, the "New
Market" (with its Thai-style Theravada Buddhist temple). It's here, too, that you'll
notice the throngs of resident students from the adjacent **Tribhuwan University** –
Nepal's chief centre of higher education, and a hotbed of political activism in recent
years. The old, upper town is splendidly preserved, thanks to a conservation project

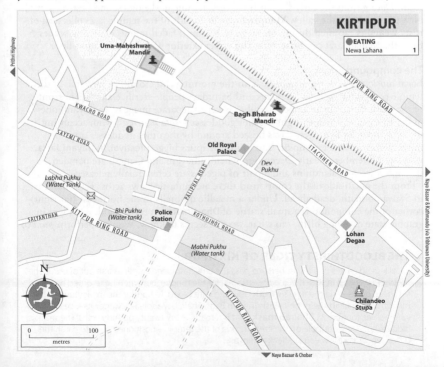

that furnished the streets with fine stone paving and restored many of its temples. Despite the clean-up, it preserves an authentically old-world atmosphere: many residents of the old town are Jyapus, from the Newari farming subcaste, and they still work the fields surrounding town. In spring and autumn, the streets are full of sheaves being threshed and grain being stored. In a typically Newari arrangement, the northwestern end of town is predominantly Hindu, the southeastern Buddhist, but everyone shares the same festivals.

Brief history

Established as a western outpost of Patan in the twelfth century, Kirtipur had gained nominal independence by the time Prithvi Narayan Shah began his final conquest of the Kathmandu Valley in 1767. The Gorkha king considered the town to be the **military linchpin** of the valley and made its capture his first priority. After two separate attacks and a six-month siege, with no help forthcoming from Patan, Kirtipur surrendered on the understanding it would receive a total amnesty. Instead, in an **atrocity** intended to demoralize the remaining opposition in the valley, Prithvi Shah ordered his troops to cut off the noses and lips of every man and boy in Kirtipur. Supposedly, only men skilled in the playing of wind instruments were spared. The rest of the valley fell within a year.

Bagh Bhairab Mandir

Purano Kirtipur • Daily dawn–dusk • Free

The road from the university switchbacks to the saddle of Kirtipur's twin-humped ridge and deposits you in a square outside the prodigious **Bagh Bhairab Mandir**, which serves double duty as a war memorial and a cathedral to Bhairab in his tiger (*bagh*) form. Dating from the early sixteenth century, it's one of the oldest and best-preserved Newari pagodas in the valley. Mounted on the outside of the temple is a collection of rusty **weapons** captured during the siege of Kirtipur; faded murals depicting scenes from the Mahabharat can be seen on the upper exterior walls of the ground floor.

The compound

Local musicians perform *bhajan* early in the morning and around dinnertime in the temple compound, and on Tuesdays and Saturdays people sacrifice animals in front of the main shrine. In an upper chamber is kept a separate image of Indrayani, one of the Kathmandu Valley's eight mother goddesses (*ashta matrika*), who, according to one Cinderella-like legend, was bossed around by the other goddesses until she miraculously turned a pumpkin into gold. Kirtipur's biggest **festival, Indrayani Jatra**, is in late November or early December, when Indrayani and Ganesh are paraded through town on palanquins and a pair of pigeons are ceremonially released.

From the north side of the compound there are fantastic views across Kathmandu to Swayambunath, dead ahead. Under a metallic umbrella in the northeast (far right) corner of the compound is a small statue of **Dhartimata**, an earth goddess, shown in a graphic state of giving birth – to what, no one seems to know. Women perform *puja* to

---

THE BLOODTHIRSTY TIGER OF KIRTIPUR

Local legend relates that a shepherd, to pass the time, fashioned a tiger image out of burrs. The shepherd went off in search of a poinsettia leaf for the tongue, but when he returned he found his sheep gone – and the tiger's mouth dripping with blood. To honour the miraculously bloodthirsty Bhairab, the people enshrined in Bagh Bhairab Mandir a clay tiger, its face covered with a silver, tongueless **Bhairab mask** that is remade every twenty or thirty years. The mask is hidden, but a tiny porthole on the eastern side of the temple – positioned so as to catch the dawn sun – may allow you to sneak a glimpse.

this statue to safeguard against problems during pregnancy and childbirth. At the opposite, southern end, on the left of the gate as you go in, a small pagoda shrine dedicated to Ganesh houses an ancient – possibly pre-Lichhavi (pre-fourth century) – statue of a standing **Shiva**, half-armless but equipped with a potently erect penis. Along the back wall of this shrine sit five tiny mother-goddess statues associated with five sheep that escaped the tiger; they're thought to date from the fifth century.

Uma-Maheshwar Mandir

2

Purano Kirtipur • Daily dawn–dusk • Free

At the top of the northern, Hindu hump of the city stands the elephant-guarded **Uma-Maheshwar Mandir**, whose temple bell is a copy, cast in the unlikely setting of Croydon, England. The original bell tolled the hours in the old Kathmandu clock tower for many years before the structure collapsed in the earthquake of 1934. Long unfinished, the wooden struts under the lowest pagoda roof were finally adorned with the traditional carvings in 2008.

The erotic scenes on the lowest level are supposed to have less to do with *Kamasutra*-style sexual gymnastics and more with local tantric and fertility traditions; that said, the artist does seem to have let his imagination off the leash.

Chilandeo Stupa

Heading southeastwards from the Bagh Bhairab temple first brings you to the Lohan Degaa, a stone *shikra* shared by both Hindu and Buddhist worshippers. Beyond, the atmospheric **Chilandeo Stupa** crowns the southern hill, its exposed brickwork lending a hoary antiquity generally lacking in better-maintained stupas. Chilandeo (also known as Chilancho Bahal) is popularly supposed to have been erected by Ashoka. The ridge that rears up so impressively to the southwest is Champadevi (see p.145), one of the high points along the valley rim.

ARRIVAL AND DEPARTURE   KIRTIPUR

By bus Microbuses and minibuses (every 5–10min; around 30min) leave from Kathmandu's City Bus Park for Naya Bazaar, from where it's a 10min walk up to the village.
By bike The ride to Kirtipur from Kathmandu is relatively enjoyable – once you're free of the city – and a bike is useful for exploring the countryside beyond, towards Chobar and Dakshinkali, perhaps (see p.147). The main route travels via Tribhuwan University, off the Dakshinkali road (turn right at the red-brick gate and take the left fork 1km later). Other paths lead to Kirtipur from the Prithvi (Kathmandu–Pokhara) Highway, the Ring Road and Chobar.

EATING

★Newa Lahana Thambahal ✆984 138 9797. This authentic community-run restaurant occupies a rooftop in an otherwise undistinguished house hidden in the little maze of old Kirtipur (follow the sign at the junction just west of the Bagh Bhairab Mandir). You sit on wicker mats with the welcoming locals and enjoy an incredible menu of tapas-like Newari duck, chicken and buffalo meat dishes – the latter running from tongue to tail via the spinal cord. All are served in brass bowls or on proper *sal* leaf plates. Alternatively, there are pizza-like *woh* pancakes, sweet-sour dishes such as *aloo tama* (potatoes and bamboo shoots), and *daal bhaat*. *Raksi* is distilled in the basement, and poured from traditional brass vessels. Dishes cost Rs35–300. Daily 8am–10pm.

The Dakshinkali road

One of Nepal's moodiest tantric sacrificial shrines, Dakshinkali (*dakshin* or "southern" Kali), lies at the end of the Kathmandu Valley's longest and most varied road. As it snakes its way along a fold in the valley rim towards the shrine, the **Dakshinkali road** passes a fine succession of Buddhist and Hindu holy places, offering an intense, half-day

2

TEARING THROUGH TO THE TERAI

A number of roads pick their way through the hills south of Kathmandu. The so-called **Kanti Highway** (though it's no such thing) heads south from Patan down the Bagmati Valley via Tika Bhairab to Thingana, where it turns west for Hetauda (though it will one day carry on due south to Nijgadh, making a new "fast track" route to the Terai).

The more useful routes are the two that break off the Dakshinkali Road – though both are still only paved in parts, and can become temporarily impassable during the monsoon. For now, they're traversed by large, roof-racked "Tata Sumo" jeeps, which wait at the Balkhu junction, on the Ring Road where it crosses the Bagmati River, ready to depart as soon as they're full of passengers. The 65km Dakshinkali route, known as the **Madan Bhandari Highway**, is more reliable and paved for longer sections (buses usually make it to Sisneri, 1hr from Dakshinkali). The higher, slightly shorter **Pharping route** can be quicker, and has the advantage of crossing the picturesque Kulekhani Reservoir dam. Both roads meet just below the Kulekhani Reservoir then descend via the picturesque bazaar town of Bhimphedi to join the Tribhuwan Rajpath at Bhainse, 11km north of Hetauda (see p.284), in the Terai. By either route, the journey costs around Rs400–500 per head and takes three to four hours, and the traffic is light enough to make mountain biking an attractive option (see p.378).

---

snapshot of Nepal's religious culture. The road begins at the busy Balkhu junction of the Ring Road, at the southwest corner of Kathmandu, just short of Kirtipur (which would make a fine side trip; see p.141). From Balkhu, it's possible to take a 4WD taxi south through the hills, descending to the Terai at Hetauda (see p.284). All Kathmandu–Dakshinkali **buses** pass through Chobar, Shesh Narayan and Pharping.

Chobar

The village of **CHOBAR**, 3km south of the Ring Road, caps the top of a deceptively tall hill overlooking the main road and Bagmati River winding below. From the bus stop, an apparently endless stone stairway leads up through the forest to the huddle of old-fashioned houses and hilltop **Adinath Mandir**. (Cyclists should take the paved road that breaks right from the main road a little further south.) The temple's front is festooned with kitchen utensils, offered to Lokeshwar, the temple's deity. Explanations for this curious custom are various: newlyweds say it ensures a happy union, others claim it's a rite for the departed. Lokeshwar is worshipped here in the form of a red mask, which bears a close resemblance to Patan's Rato Machhendranath.

Chobar Gorge

When Manjushri drained the Kathmandu Valley of its legendary lake, **Chobar Gorge** was one of the places he smote with his sword to release the waters. As the Bagmati River slices through a wrinkle in the valley floor, 1km south of Chobar and just beside the Dakshinkali road, it really does look like the work of a neat sword stroke. To see it, you can get off the bus either beside the sign for **Manjushree Park** at the top of the hill and walk down, or at the cluster of shacks at the bottom and walk back up.

The best gorge vantage point, at the upstream end, is free to view. The twitchy suspension **footbridge**, custom-cast by an Aberdonian foundry and assembled here in 1907, stands beside a new road bridge that cuts through towards Patan and the Bungmati road. Immediately upstream stands the seventeenth-century **Jal Binayak** temple. The tip of its rocky outcrop is worshipped as Ganesh, and women sell leaf-plates of the god's favourite foods – meat, milk, soybeans, banana, ginger, pickles – to offer as *puja*.

Manjushree Park
Daily 7am–6.30pm • Rs50

Manjushree Park is a kind of rockery garden spread out over the hillside that allows you to wander its concrete stairways and descend part way into the gorge itself. The gorge is impressively sheer but the stench of the foaming Bagmati as it vomits forth from the valley rather detracts from the experience. The park ticket offices can sell you a guided tour of the Chobar Gupha caves (see below).

Chobar Gupha
Guided 1hr tour (longer tours can be arranged) Rs700; buy tickets at Manjushree Park ticket office

The **Chobar Gupha** cave system features more than 3km of passages – among the largest in South Asia. Even on a one-hour tour there are plenty of tight corners to squeeze through and holes to scramble down: wear old clothes. Guides have some spare torches.

2

CHAMPADEVI HIKES

The southwestern rim of the Kathmandu Valley rears up in a prominent fishtail of twin peaks, the highest visible parts of the **Chandragiri range**. The eastern summit is known as **Champadevi**, after the resident goddess.

THE HAATIBAN ASCENT ROUTE

Perhaps the simplest ascent route follows the rough dirt road that skirts the **Dollu valley** (the one immediately north of Pharping) up to the *Haatiban Resort* (see p.147). From the resort, a well-trodden track leads northwest up (and sometimes down) through pine forest, and then along the grassy ridgetop to the stupa-marked summit (2249m). A return trip from the resort should take around three hours. If you walk up from the Dakshinkali road it might take four to six hours, so bring food and water.

ALTERNATIVE ASCENT ROUTES

A good alternative ascent route begins just after the Dakshinkali road makes an abrupt bend beyond **Taudaha**, climbing westwards along dirt roads through fields towards the edge of forest; at the trees, the trail turns southwards, and the last part of the route climbs steeply up through the forest to gain the ridge above *Haatiban Resort*, at about 2000m.

Another route approaches from the south, following a dirt road up the northern side of the **Pharping valley** before turning off up the small Sundol valley; you can follow any of a number of trails up from here – all lead directly north to the summit of Champadevi. To avoid the road section of this Pharping route, however, you could also ascend the forested ridge that divides Dollu from Pharping; the trail begins at the monastery immediately west of the **Bajra Yogini** temple – it's a bit tricky at the start as you have to find your way through a profusion of prayer flags and paths.

BEYOND CHAMPADEVI

From the summit of Champadevi, you can continue down and up to the unnamed **western peak** of the fishtail – which is actually slightly higher, at 2286m. You can then continue west along the ridge for an hour or so, following a well-made path down to a saddle and then up to a higher peak (2509m). From here, another ridge tracks south for another hour or so up to the highest peak of the range, **Bhasmesur** (2622m) – said to be the ashy remains of a demon tricked by Vishnu into incinerating himself. West of the Bhasmesur spur, a path turns north off the ridge (though the actual ridge-line is confused around here – and the illegal charcoal-burning pits don't help), descending a steep and seemingly endless stone staircase down to the village of **Machegaon** (90min descent) from where various trails and roads lead back to Kirtipur.

If you had the requisite time, weather, guide (or good map and route-asking skills) and fitness, you could also trek west along the ridgetop from the Bhasmesur spur to a col at Deurali, and then on west to another pass at Chitlang Bhanjyang, from where a dirt road descends to Thankot, on the busy Prithvi Highway (the Pokhara road); it would be a very long day.

Taudaha pond

Daily 10am–5pm • Rs25; pay entrance fee at the gate

Two kilometres south of Chobar, the road passes the **Taudaha pond**, a watering hole for winter migrant birds, including many different duck species and nationally threatened birds such as the oriental darter, falcated duck and Baillon's crake. According to legend, when Manjushri drained the Kathmandu Valley he left Taudaha as a home for the snakes, and the serpent king Karkatnag still lives at the bottom, coiled around a heap of treasure. A row of **café shacks** and picnic spots winds around the far side of the water.

Shesh Narayan

From Taudaha pond, the road ascends steadily for another 6km to its highest point, a little beyond Pikhel. Two kilometres beyond the high point, the quiet and shady **pools** of **Shesh Narayan** crouch under a wooded hillside. Hindus worship Vishnu here as the mighty creator who formed the universe out of the cosmic ocean; the snake Shesh (or Ananta), the "remainder" of the cosmic waters after Vishnu's creation, is symbolized by the four pools. A sculpture depicting Surya riding his twelve-horse chariot stands half-submerged in the semicircular pool.

Steps from the pools lead to Narayan's **temple** at the base of a limestone overhang, whose serpentine stalactites are said by Vaishnavas to be the "milk", or blessing, of Shesh. To the left of the temple is another hunk of eroded limestone known as Chaumunda – you're supposed to put your ear to it to hear the sound of running water.

Yanglesho

To the right of the Narayan temple, a doorway conceals a cave that Buddhists call **Yanglesho**, where Padma Sambhava, the eighth-century founder of Tibetan Buddhism, is supposed to have wrestled with a horde of *nag (serpents)* and turned them to stone. The story probably refers to the saint's struggle to introduce his brand of tantric Buddhism from India.

Pharping

A few hundred metres beyond Shesh Narayan, **PHARPING** is an unexpectedly large and lively community for this distant corner of the valley. The original Newari village is now overshadowed by a Tibetan Buddhist boomtown, with upwards of a dozen monasteries and retreat centres taking advantage of the clean air. The wooded ridge above is festooned with strings of brightly coloured prayer flags, while the valley extends back into rich farmland, locally famous for its cucumbers, *naspati* (Asian pear) and *lapsi* (an indigenous, sweet-sour yellow-green fruit that is usually cooked in pickles or made into sweets). The best way to see Pharping is to act like a Buddhist pilgrim – of which there are many – and **walk the sacred circuit**.

The sacred circuit

Walking the **sacred circuit** can be done in a leisurely hour. Turning off the ever-more-noxious junction with the main road, overlooked by a giant Buddha statue, you walk up past a 3.5m-high golden **statue of Guru Rinpoche** in a giant glass case – a sign of things to come.

The Green Tara

Passing a cluster of cafés and houses, and the ornate, white-and-gold, bell-like chorten of the Sakya Tharik Gompa, you come to a set of steps, just before the road rises and turns to the right. These lead up to a cluster of monastery buildings and a small **shrine room** where butter lamps burn in honour of a "self-arisen" image of the Buddhist deity **Green Tara**, who protects from danger. The miraculous image turns out to be a hand-sized figurine standing out from the naked rock in bas-relief. A Hindu Ganesh statue sits incongruously alongside, while other rocky pimples to the right are supposed to be further Taras in the process of emanation. A duty monk recites the Green Tara *puja* at all hours of the day and night.

The Asura Cave

From the Green Tara shrine, steps continue upwards to the **Asura Cave**, a narrow fissure filled with votive offerings to the irrepressible Padma Sambhava, aka Guru Rinpoche, who is said to have achieved enlightenment here. His two footprints and (less obvious) clawing hand-marks are apparently signs of the cosmic power he realized at that moment.

Pharping Bajra Yogini temple

From the Asura Cave, the trail turns back towards the main road, passing through other monastery buildings before, after about ten minutes, starting to descend towards the golden-roofed **Pharping Bajra Yogini temple**, one of the valley's four tantric temples dedicated to the angry female aspect of Buddhahood. The first-floor sanctum conceals two prancing images of Bajra Yogini, each holding a skull-cup and knife.

Steps lead down from here directly to the main Pharping road, just above the Guru Rinpoche statue. Above, a path leads up the ridge towards the peak of Champadevi (see box, p.145).

ACCOMMODATION AND EATING   **PHARPING**

Apart from aspiring Buddhists, most people visit Pharping as part of a day-trip to Dakshinkali. That said, the village offers the best base for deeper exploration of the area, including hikes up Champadevi (see box, p.145). **Staying overnight** also means you can take an early visit to the Dakshinkali shrine, when it's at its liveliest. There's also one appealing hilltop resort, *Haatiban Resort*, which is a destination in itself.

Dakchhinkali Village Inn Dakshinkali Rd, near Pharping ☎ 01 471 0053, ⓦ dakchhinkali.com. Set just back from the ornamental gateway that stands astride the main road just before it descends towards the Dakshinkali shrine, this is a decent resort-in-miniature, with balconied brick bungalows set around grassy gardens. It's nothing special, but well kept, and makes a useful overnight stop if you want to get to the action at the shrine early. US$50
Family Guesthouse Pharping ☎ 01 471 0412 or ☎ 981 33729, ⓔ familyguesthouse@yahoo.com. This unprepossessing brick pile in the bazaar area of Pharping has gloomy concrete rooms, but it's the only inexpensive (non-monastery) option around here, and the management is youthful and friendly – if not actually a family. Rs600
Haatiban Resort Pharping, Haatiban ☎ 01 691 6140 or ☎ 01 437 1537, ⓦ nepalluxurytreks.com. This isolated, somewhat overpriced resort (sometimes known as the *Himalayan Height Resort*) sits astride a pine-clad ridge, roughly halfway up Champadevi. It offers great

views, especially from the stunning terrace restaurant (on weekdays, lunch must be pre-booked, unless you're staying). The rooms are in pleasant, well-appointed chalets dotted around the gardens. The signposted but very rough road up to the resort breaks off the Dakshinkali Road at the lovely green valley of Dollu, 2km short (east) of Shesh Narayan. US$150
Himalayan Restaurant Pharping. The best of the homely, Tibetan-oriented restaurants in the middle of the bazaar area of Pharping – 200m up from the Dakshinkali road junction, right opposite the path to Bajra Yogini. Serves inexpensive Tibetan food – *thukpa* and *momos* for under Rs200 – and a few basic Western dishes. Daily 8am–7pm.
Rigdzin Phodrang Gompa Pharping. The chief reason to stay in Pharping itself is to study at a monastery. Most have their own inexpensive guesthouses, but this monastery, run by the respected Ralo Rinpoche, is perhaps the most open to uninitiated visitors seeking shorter-term retreats. Rs400

Dakshinkali

The best and worst aspect of **Dakshinkali** is that everything happens out in the open. The famous **sacrificial pit** of "Southern Kali" – the last stop for hundreds of chickens, goats and pigs every week – lies at the bottom of a steep, forested ravine, affording an

2

> ## SACRIFICIAL CHICKENS AND TANTRIC GOATS
>
> If orthodox Indian Hindus are very much of the "pure veg", non-violent persuasion, their tantrically inclined Nepali cousins have a more bloodthirsty bent. At least, the thirst is on the part of **Kali**, Nepal's fearsome – yet strangely popular – mother goddess who demands blood sacrifice in return for her favours.
>
> Nepalis are curiously gentle in their worship: they lead their offerings to the slaughter tenderly, often whispering prayers in the animal's ear and sprinkling its head with water to encourage it to shrug in assent; they believe that the death of this "unfortunate brother" will give it the chance to be reborn as a higher life form. Chickens, goats or, most expensively, buffaloes can be sacrificed, but only uncastrated males, preferably dark in colour, are offered.
>
> At **Dakshinkali**, men of a special caste slit the animals' throats and let the blood spray over the idols. Brahman priests oversee the butchering and instruct worshippers in all the complex rituals that follow. However, you don't need to speak Nepali to get the gist of the explanations.

intimate view of Nepali religious rituals. The spectacle makes many people feel uncomfortable – if it's not squeamishness, it'll be the sense of prying. That said, the public bloodbath is quite a sight, and attracts busloads at the holiest times: Saturday and, to a lesser extent, Tuesday mornings. Asthami, the eighth day after a new or full moon, draws the largest crowds of all.

Dakshinkali is as much a **picnic area** as a holy spot. The sacrifice done, families make for the pavilions that surround the shrine and merrily cook up the remains of their offerings. If you didn't sacrifice anything, you can get fried snacks from the "fast-food" stalls near the gate to the shrine.

The shrine
From the bus stop, a path leads through a small bazaar of stalls selling food and sacrificial accessories to the **shrine** directly below, positioned at the auspicious confluence of two streams. Tiled like an abattoir (for easy hosing down) and covered with a gilt canopy, the sacred area consists of little more than a row of short statuettes, Kali being the heavily decorated one under the canopy. Before the sacrifices, you'll see devotees pouring water all over their goat's head; they're waiting for it to shake its head – a sign of the god's acceptance of the offering.

From the back of the shrine, it's a ten-minute walk up stone steps through a pine wood to a small promontory where there's a **subsidiary shrine** to Mata, Kali's mother, and good views across to Pharping. The sacrifice here is less off-putting: people bring pigeons, and set them free.

ARRIVAL AND DEPARTURE
DAKSHINKALI

By bus Buses depart from Kathmandu's City Bus Park as soon as they are full – roughly every 15min (1hr).
By taxi Taxis from Kathmandu to Dakshinkali cost about Rs1600–2000 return, on a half-day basis.
By bike The outward (upward) leg to Dakshinkali will take at least 2hr from Kathmandu, even with a mountain bike,

but you'd be advised to put your bike on the roof of the bus – you'll need to pay a small tip.
On foot The walk from Pharping to Dakshinkali takes 20min; the footpath comes out in Dakshinkali at the stone steps by the road just above the shrine.

Bungmati and around

BUNGMATI, 5km south of the Ring Road, could almost be a Tuscan village. This brick huddle atop a hillock, centred on a sunny central square, is one of the better-preserved Newari towns in the valley. It is also one of the least-visited, so if you prefer your

CLOCKWISE FROM TOP DAKSHINKALI (P.147); BHAKTAPUR (P.154); SADHU, KATHMANDU VALLEY >

2

AGRICULTURE IN THE KATHMANDU VALLEY

Even as the capital's swelling population threatens to fill the Kathmandu Valley in lot after lot of detached, blockhouse, commuter concrete, the Jyapus, indigenous Newari farmers, continue to live in huddled-up, brick-built towns, digging their fields by hand in the time-honoured fashion: with a distinctive two-handed spade called *kodaalo* (*ku* in Newari). The valley's soil repays such labour-intensive care: it is endowed with a fertile, black clay called *kalimati*, a by-product of sediment from the prehistoric lake, and is low enough in elevation to support two or even three main crops a year. **Rice** is seeded in special irrigated beds shortly before the first monsoon rains in June, and seedlings are transplanted into flooded terraces no later than the end of July. Normally women do this job, using their toes to bed each shoot in the mud. The stalks grow green and bushy during the summer, turning a golden brown and producing mature grain by October.

At **harvest time** sheaves are spread out on paved roads for cars to loosen the kernels, and then run through portable hand-cranked threshers or bashed against rocks. The grain is gathered in bamboo trays (*nanglo*) and tossed in the wind to winnow away the chaff, or, if there's no wind, *nanglo* can be used to fan away the chaff. Some sheaves are left in stacks to ferment for up to two weeks, producing a soft food known as *hakuja*, or "black" rice. The rice dealt with, terraces are then planted with **winter wheat**. Unfortunately, for tourists, the period of planting, when the soil looks bare and brown, coincides with the peak tourist season. The wheat is harvested in April or May, after which a third crop of pulses or maize can often be squeezed in. Vegetables are raised year-round at the edges of plots or, in the case of squashes, festooned along fences and on top of shrubs and low trees.

Most Kathmandu Valley farmers are tenants, and have to pay huge proportions of their harvests in rent. But their lot has improved in the past generation: **land reform** in the 1950s and 1960s was relatively diligently implemented near the capital, helping to get landlords and moneylenders off the backs of small farmers, and the Maoist government has also forced landowners to break up and sell off larger holdings. However, the traditional Newari system of **inheritance**, in which family property is divided up among the sons, means that landholdings actually get smaller with each generation. That presents a contrasting problem: farms that are too small to make mechanical equipment worthwhile, necessitating labour-intensive methods and keeping productivity low.

temples without a side serving of droning electronic Om tracks, and without offers of help from persistent guides, this is the place to come. Bungmati is also a renowned centre for woodcarving: open workshops house artisans at work, and it's always possible to buy direct.

The central square

Plunge down any of the narrow, brick alleys leading downhill to the west, and you'll soon find your way to the broad, teeming **central square**, dominated by the whitewashed *shikra* of **Machhendranath**, whose more ancient Newari name is Bunga Dyo ("God of Bunga"). According to legend, Bungmati marks the spot where Machhendranath, having arrived in the valley in the form of a bee to save it from drought, was "born" as the valley's protector-rainmaker. Each summer at the end of Patan's Raato Machhendranath festival, the god's red mask is brought to the Bungmati temple for a six-month residency, but every twelfth year it is kept here through the winter and then pulled by lumbering chariot all the way to Patan (see p.86).

In the southeast corner of the square, a smaller, more traditional temple is dedicated to **Bhairab** in his angry form. This god demands blood sacrifices, and is rarely disappointed. You can climb the steps to peek through the door at his extravagantly fierce gold repoussé mask, and the large skull-bowl on the floor where he receives sacrifices.

Khokana

One kilometre north of Bungmati, **KHOKANA** resembles its neighbour in many ways, but lacks its character as it was largely rebuilt after the 1934 earthquake. It's locally renowned for its mustard oil, and in season the presses run full tilt. Khokana's pagoda-style **Shekali Mai Mandir**, a massive three-tiered job, honours a local nature goddess. Midway between Khokana and Bungmati stands the poorly maintained **Karya Binayak**, another of the valley's four Ganesh temples.

ARRIVAL AND DEPARTURE   BUNGMATI AND AROUND

By bus Buses (every 20min; around 45min) from Kathmandu's Ratna Park run to the bus park on the eastern edge of Bungmati, and then on to Khokana. There are no services between the two, but it's an easy enough walk.

The Chapagaun road

The road due south of Patan's Lagankhel bus park serves two traditional, brick-built Newari towns: **THECHO**, 8km south of Patan, and **CHAPAGAUN**, 1km further south. More attractive than either is the seventeenth-century **Bajra Barahi Mandir**, secreted in a small wood 500m east along a track from Chapagaun, and dedicated to the goddess Kali. The main road continues south for another 4km to **Tika Bhairab**, an abstract mural of the god Bhairab, painted on a wall at the junction of two small streams. If you're on a mountain bike, however, the more picturesque route from Chapagaun to Tika Bhairab takes you east then south, via the Lele Valley (see p.376); it's also possible to cut through to the Godavari road (see p.376), and the hardy can even continue right through to Hetauda and the Terai (see p.378).

Godavari and around

The greenest, most pristine part of the valley lies at its southeastern edge, around **GODAVARI** (pronounced Go-*dao*-ri). Nestling at the foot of forested Phulchoki, the highest peak of the valley rim, are the pleasant **National Botanical Garden**, the temple at **Naudhara** and the shrine of **Bishanku Narayan**, hidden in a gorgeously rural side valley.

En route to Godavari, the road passes through **HARISIDDHI**, a traditional Newari town 4km south of Patan, with a sinister legend. Its pagoda-style **Bal Kumari Mandir** – reached by walking straight up a stepped path where the main road jinks left – was once said to have been the centre of a child-sacrifice cult. Beyond Harisiddhi, the road quietens as it climbs, ending at Godavari.

Naudhara

Daily dawn–dusk • Free • Head south from the Godavari bus park; the temple complex lies to the left of the road opposite a marble quarry, just beyond the Jesuit-run St Xavier School and the entrance to the local Community Forest

The temple complex of **Naudhara** lies a short walk south of Godavari's bus park; its name means "nine spouts" and that's exactly what you'll find, along with worshippers and local women washing clothes. The site is especially holy to the Silwar caste, who come here in huge numbers to worship their ancestral god in the full moon of the month of Bhadau (Aug–Sept). Just left of the spouts stands a small temple, said to represent the feet of the local mother goddess **Phulchoki Mai**. (Pilgrims eager to ascend to Phulchoki Mai's "head", or principal shrine, can take the trail that starts directly behind here to the top of Phulchoki peak; see p.152.) The shrine is kept locked to protect the sacred (but withered) tree stump inside from Buddhists who, hunting for relics, were chipping away at the holy wood.

National Botanical Garden

1km from Godavari bus park • Daily: Feb–Oct 10am–5pm; Nov–Jan 10am–4pm • Rs200 • From the Godavari bus park, head east (straight across from the Patan road) down the paved road and left again just before a clump of restaurants to reach the main gate

Rudyard Kipling wrote that "the wildest dreams of Kew/Are the facts of Kathmandu", and the **National Botanical Garden** might seem to be the obvious place to put his theory to the test. The garden is in fact more a peaceful picnic spot than anything else (as well as a popular location for local pop videos), but there is a resplendent orchid house and of course some fine trees. The labelling is inadequate, but the book *Enjoy Trees*, sold in most Kathmandu bookshops, makes a good stand-in.

Godavari Kunda

800m east of the Godavari bus park • No fixed opening hours • Free

A little short of the gate to the National Botanical Garden, just to the right of the road, the otherwise inconspicuous spring-fed water tank of **Godavari Kunda** hosts a big *mela* every twelve years during the month of Bhadra (mid-Aug to mid-Sept; the next is in 2015). The adjacent **Buddhist retreat centre**, which must have one of the most fabulous back gardens in the world, is an offshoot of Than *gompa*, in Pharping, and only for serious seekers of enlightenment: the minimum stay is three years.

Phulchoki

Phulchoki (2762m) is the highest of the forested peaks that guard the Kathmandu Valley. Its name in Nepal means "flower-covered", and you'll see orchids, morning glories, corydalis and, in spring, endless rhododendrons. The mountainside also preserves the native **primary forest** better than any other in the valley, and as you climb from subtropical base to temperate summit you pass through mixed stands of *chilaune* (*Schima wallichii*), *katus* (*Castanopsis indica* or Nepal chestnut) and holly, with Nepali alder in the ravines; higher up there are evergreen oaks, laurel and, of course, rhododendron. Its pristine, luxuriant state means that the forest is one of the best places in Nepal for butterfly-spotting and **birdwatching** – a trained eye is supposed to be able to spot a hundred or more bird species in a day.

All walks in the Phulchoki forest should only be undertaken in a group, as there have been numerous **robberies** in recent years. Be wary of making off-trail excursions through the forest, too, even if you're chasing down a rare sighting: the Maoists laid anti-personnel mines during the conflict in this area (especially on the westward side, towards Lele), and it's impossible to be sure that they have all been found and removed.

Ascending the peak

Getting to the top of Phulchoki involves a tough walk of at least four hours, with 1200m of ascent. The trail begins behind Naudhara (see p.151), which represents the feet of mother goddess **Phulchoki Mai**. You soon rejoin the switchbacking **summit road**, which continues all the way to the top. The road might allow a less energetic ascent if you can find a 4WD vehicle or a taxi driver willing to commit his car (the latter is unlikely).

If the **summit** isn't wreathed in clouds, you'll have a magnificent view of a wide range of the Himalayas and practically the entire Kathmandu Valley (smog permitting). The effect is only slightly marred by the presence of an army base and microwave relay station, but the ragged prayer flags that festoon Phulchoki Mai's shrine do help.

With a good map, and possibly advice from soldiers at the army base at the summit, it would be possible to make a – long, tough – circular walk by breaking off the dirt road about halfway down (just below a long left-hand bend), then descending along a

THE NEWARS

The **Newars** are a special case. Their stronghold is a valley – the Kathmandu Valley – which, while geographically located within Nepal's hill region, has its own distinct climate and history. Newars are careful to distinguish themselves from other hill peoples, and although they're an ethnic minority nationally, their majority presence in the pivotal Kathmandu Valley has enabled them to exert a cultural influence far beyond their numbers. An outsider could easily make the mistake of thinking that Newari culture is Nepali culture.

Many anthropologists believe that the root stock of the Newars is the **Kirats**, a clan who legendarily ruled the Kathmandu Valley between the seventh century BC and the second century AD. However, Newari culture has been in the making for millennia, as waves of immigrants, overlords, traders and usurpers have mingled in the melting pot of the valley. These arrivals contributed new customs, beliefs and skills to the overall stew, but they weren't completely assimilated – rather, they found their own niches in society, maintaining internal social structures and traditions and fulfilling unique spiritual and professional roles. In time, these *thars* (clans) were formally organized into a Newari caste system that mirrored that of the Baahun–Chhetris and, still later, became nested within it. Thus Newari society is a microcosm of Nepali society, with many shared cultural traits and a common language (Newari), but also with an enormous amount of diversity among its members.

RELIGION AND CULTURE

Newari **religion** is extremely complex (see p.402); suffice to say that individual Newars may identify themselves as either Hindu or Buddhist, depending on their *thar*'s historical origin, but this makes little difference to their fundamental doctrines or practices. **Kinship** roles are extremely important to Newars, and are reinforced by elaborate life-cycle rituals and annual feasts; likewise, each *thar* has its role to play in festivals and other public events. A uniquely Newar social invention is the *guthi*, a kind of kinship-based Rotary club which maintains temples and rest-houses, organizes festivals and, indirectly, ensures the transmission of Newar culture from one generation to the next. *Guthi* have been in serious decline since the 1960s, however, when land reform deprived them of much of their income from holdings around the valley.

CITIES AND VILLAGES

With so great an emphasis placed on **social relationships**, it's little wonder that Newars like to live so close together. Unlike other hill peoples, they're urbanites at heart. Their cities are masterpieces of density, with tall tenements pressing against narrow alleys and shopfronts opening directly onto streets. In the past couple of centuries, Newar traders have colonized lucrative crossroads and recreated their bustling bazaars throughout Nepal. Even Newari farmers build their villages in compact, urban nuclei (partly to conserve the fertile farmland of the valley).

ART AND ARCHITECTURE

Centuries of domination by foreign rulers have, if anything, only accentuated the uniqueness of Newari art and architecture. For 1500 years the Newars have sustained an almost continuous artistic flowering in stone, wood, metal and brick. They're believed to have invented the pagoda, and it was a Newari architect, Arniko, who led a Nepali delegation in the thirteenth century to introduce the technique to the Chinese. The pagoda style of stacked, strut-supported roofs finds unique expression in Nepali (read Newari) temples, and is echoed in the overhanging eaves of Newari houses.

TRADITIONAL CLOTHING

Newars are easily recognized. Traditionally they carry heavy loads in baskets suspended at either end of a shoulder pole (*nol*), in contrast with Nepali hill people who carry things on their backs supported by a tumpline from the forehead. As for clothing, you can usually tell a Newari woman by the fanned pleats at the front of her sari; men have mostly abandoned traditional dress, but some still wear the customary *daura suruwal* and waistcoat.

path that follows the Tribeni Danda ridge-line north (heading in the direction of Lakuri Bhanjhyang, a minor pass on the Patan to Panauti road). As the trail emerges from the forest, about a third of the way to Lakuri Bhanjhyang, you take a left turn at a junction, taking the zigzagging jeep track that descends east towards the National Botanical Garden at Godavari.

Bishanku Narayan

3km north of Godavari bus park • Taxis cost around Rs300, or it's roughly 1hr on foot: start on the dirt road that turns sharply left, and continue along paths across the Bishanku valley floor and up the ridge. You can also get there from the western (back) entrance of the Botanical Garden, and from Badegaun, halfway between Harisiddhi and Godavari on the Patan–Godavari road

The sheltered, southwest-facing side valley of **Bishanku** is one of the Kathmandu Valley's most idyllic and unspoilt corners. In a notch in the partly forested ridge on the far northwest side, the shrine of **Bishanku Narayan** overlooks the paddy and mustard fields that line the valley floor. One of the valley's four main Narayan (Vishnu) sites, Bishanku is not a temple – rather, it's a small **cave** reached by a set of precarious steps. A chain-mail curtain protects the god's image inside the cave. If you're thin enough, you can descend through another narrow fissure; according to popular belief, those who manage to squeeze through it will be absolved of past sins.

ARRIVAL AND DEPARTURE

By bus Microbuses (every 10–15min; 45min–1hr) depart from Patan's Lagankhel bus for the Godavari bus park.

GODAVARI AND AROUND

There's usually no onward transport, but most of the sights are just a short walk away.

ACCOMMODATION

Godavari Village Resort Amarabati, Taukhel, Godavarai ☎ 01 556 0675, ⓦ godavariresort.com.np. This pricey resort, about 2km north of Godavari, is chiefly oriented towards conferences and wealthy weekenders. It has a pleasantly landscaped rural setting and sympathetic Newari-style cottages, plus a pool and health club. Beyond the resort, a quiet unpaved road leads westwards through farm country to the Bajra Barahi Mandir and Chapagaun. __US$180__

Bhaktapur

In the soft, dusty light of evening the old city of Bhaktapur, with its pagoda roofs and its harmonious blend of wood, mud-brick and copper, looked extraordinarily beautiful. It was as though a faded medieval tapestry were tacked on to the pale tea-rose sky. In the foreground a farmhouse was on fire, and orange flames licked like liquescent dragon's tongues across the thatched roof. One thought of Chaucer's England and Rabelais's France; of a world of intense, violent passions and brilliant colour, where sin was plentiful but so were grace and forgiveness …

Charlie Pye-Smith *Travels in Nepal*

Kathmandu's field of gravity weakens somewhere east of the airport; beyond, you fall into the rich atmosphere of **BHAKTAPUR** (also known as **BHADGAUN**). Rising in a tight mass of warm brick out of the fertile fields of the valley, the city looks something like Kathmandu must have done before the arrival of the modern world. During the day, tour groups and persistent "student" guides mill about enthusiastically in the main squares, but after hours, or in among the maze of backstreets, it would be hard not to feel the pulse of this quintessential Newari city. In among Bhaktapur's herringbone-paved streets and narrow alleys, women wash at public taps, men in traditional dress lounge in the many *sattal*, or covered loggias, peasants squat by the road selling meagre baskets of vegetables, and worshippers assiduously attend neighbourhood shrines. And everywhere the burnt-peach hue of bricks is offset by the deep brown of intensely carved wood – the essential materials of the Newari architects.

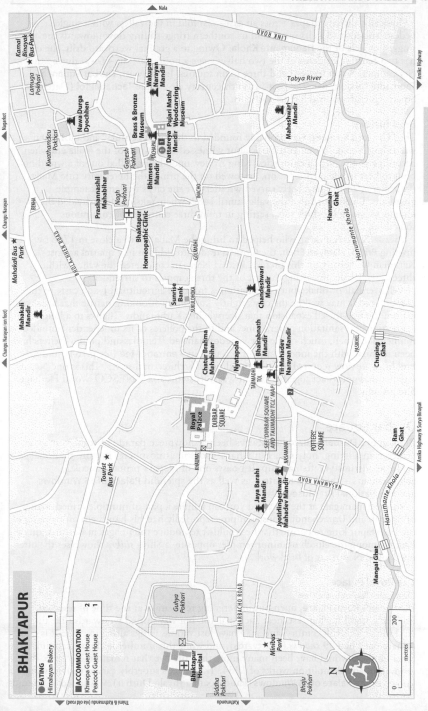

BHAKTAPUR

● EATING
Himalayan Bakery 1

■ ACCOMMODATION
Khwopa Guest House 2
Peacock Guest House 1

Nala

LINK ROAD

Tabya River

Amniko Highway

Kamal
Binayak
Bus Park

Lamuga
Pokhari

Wakupati
Narayan Mandir

Nawa Durga
Dyochhen

Brass & Bronze
Museum

Pujari Math/
Woodcarving
Museum

Maheshwari
Mandir

Kwathamdcu
Pokhari

Ganesh
Pokhari

PACHPALI

Bhimsen
Mandir

Dattatreya
Mandir

TINACHO

Prashannashil
Mahabihar

Nag
Pokhari

GOLMADHI

Bhaktapur
Homeopathic Clinic

Mahakali Bus
Park

Sunrise
Bank

Chandeshwari
Mandir

SUKULDHOKA

Mahakali
Mandir

Hanuman
Ghat

Hanumante Khola

Chuping
Ghat

PASIKHEL

Bhairabnath
Mandir

Til Mahadev
Narayan Mandir

Chatur Brahma
Mahabihar

Nyatapola

TAUMADHI
TOL

Royal
Palace

DURBAR
SQUARE

SEE 'DURBAR SQUARE
AND TAUMADHI TOL' MAP

2

Tourist
Bus Park

KHAUMA

NASMANA

Jaya Barahi
Mandir

POTTERS'
SQUARE

Ram
Ghat

Jyotirlingeshwar
Mahadev Mandir

NASAMANA ROAD

Hanumante Khola

Amniko Highway & Surya Binayat

Guhya
Pokhari

BHARBACHO ROAD

Minibus
Park

Bhaktapur
Hospital

Siddha
Pokhari

Bhaju
Pokhari

N

0   200
metres

Thimi & Kathmandu (via old road)

Kathmandu

Nagarkot

Changu Narayan

Changu Narayan (on foot)

BHOLACHHEN ROAD

BERKHA

NASMANA ROAD

Physically, the city drapes across an east–west fold in the valley, with a single pedestrianized road as its spine, and its southern fringe sliding down towards the sluggish waters of the **Hanumante Khola**. Owing to a gradual westward drift, the city has two centres (residents of the two halves stage a boisterous tug-of-war during the city's annual Bisket festival) and three main squares. In the west, **Durbar Square** and **Taumadhi Tol** dominate the post-fifteenth-century city, while **Tachapal Tol** (Dattatreya Square) presides over the older east end.

Brief history

The "City of Devotees" was probably founded in the ninth century, and by 1200 it was ruling Nepal. In that year Bhaktapur witnessed the launch of the **Malla era** when, according to the Nepali chronicles, King Aridev, upon being called out of a wrestling bout to hear of the birth of a son, bestowed on the prince the hereditary title Malla ("wrestler"). To this day, beefy carved wrestlers are the city's trademark temple guardians. Bhaktapur ruled the valley until 1482, when Yaksha Malla divided the kingdom among his three sons, setting in train three centuries of continuous squabbling.

It was a Bhaktapur king who helped to bring the Malla era to a close in 1766 by inviting **Prithvi Narayan Shah**, the Gorkha leader, to aid him in a quarrel against Kathmandu. Seizing on this pretext, Prithvi Narayan conquered the valley within three years, Bhaktapur being the last of the three capitals to surrender.

Well over half of Bhaktapur's population is from the agricultural Jyapu caste of the Newars, and it may well be the city's tightly knit, inward-looking nature that has saved it from the free-for-all expansion that overwhelms Kathmandu. Thanks to a long-term restoration and sanitation programme, and to the policies of its independent-minded municipal council, much of the city is **pedestrianized**. Temples and public shelters have been restored with the money raised from the city's **entrance fee** (see p.164), and new buildings are now required to follow traditional architectural styles. This is one Nepali city that has got its act together, and it wears its status as a UNESCO World Heritage Site proudly.

Durbar Square

Bhaktapur's **Durbar Square** has always been a showpiece parade of regal monuments rather than a living, holy site. But what it lacks in atmosphere, it more than makes up for in virtuoso craftsmanship. It boasts one of Nepal's proudest artistic achievements – the **Golden Gate** – as well as the splendid **Palace of 55 Windows** and the **National Art Museum**.

Near the main gate at the west end you can admire a pair of multiple-armed statues of **Bhairab** and **Ugrachandi**, whose sculptor reportedly had his hands cut off by order of the Bhaktapur king to ensure that he wouldn't reproduce the images in Kathmandu or Patan. Among the clutch of minor temples opposite, a Shiva *shikra* showcases the often overlooked Newar art of brickwork.

The Royal Palace

Durbar Square • Daily dawn–dusk • Free

Bhaktapur's **Royal Palace**, open but undergoing renovation at the time of research, originally stood further east, near Tachapal Tol, but was shifted westwards (like the city) in the fifteenth century, and may have lost various wings along the way. It is said to have once had 99 *chowks* (courtyards), and while this number is almost certainly fanciful, there would have been many more than the five that remain today since the renovation and demolition works of 1934. The palace's superbly carved eastern wing, known as the **Palace of 55 Windows** (Panchapanna Jhyale Durbar), was raised in around

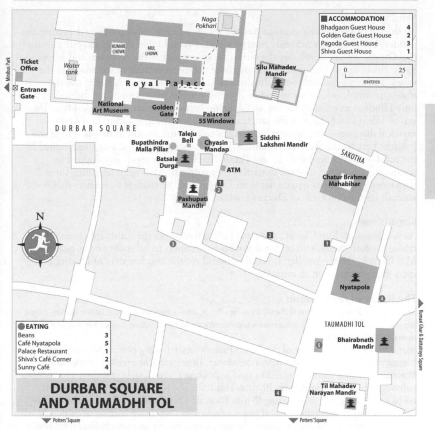

ACCOMMODATION

Bhadgaon Guest House	4
Golden Gate Guest House	2
Pagoda Guest House	3
Shiva Guest House	1

EATING

Beans	3
Café Nyatapola	5
Palace Restaurant	1
Shiva's Café Corner	2
Sunny Café	4

DURBAR SQUARE AND TAUMADHI TOL

1700 by Bupalendra Malla, Bhaktapur's great builder-king, whose *namaste*-ing figure kneels on a stone **pillar** opposite. Note the serpent coiled around the lotus base – and the tiny bird atop its head.

The Golden Gate

While the **Golden Gate** (Sun Dhoka) probably wouldn't be so famous if it were made of wood or stone – it is, in fact, gilt copper repoussé – its detail and sheer exuberance have ensured its current renown. The *torana* above the door features a squat, winged Garud (see p.397) and a ten-armed, four-headed Taleju, the Mallas' guardian deity, but to locals the most powerful figures are those of Bhairab and Kali, situated chest-high on either side of the gate. These alone among the statues are covered in red *abhir* and yellow *keshori* powder, showing that they are still worshipped today.

Naga Pokhari

Entering the palace through the Golden Gate, you follow an outdoor passage around the building. Towards the right, a doorway leads through to **Naga Pokhari** ("Snake Pond"), a regal bathing tank dating from the early sixteenth century. The extraordinary waterspout writhes with images of thirsty animals in gilt copper, overlooked by two sinister gilt *nag* figures standing clear of the water.

Mul Chowk

To the left of the palace's outdoor passage stands an impressive doorway depicting the goddess **Taleju** and her heavenly host in wood. Beyond it lies the ornate, polychrome **Mul Chowk**, which is probably the oldest surviving part of the complex, and is regarded by art historians as one of the most exquisite palace courtyards in the whole of the valley. You can peek in through the door to catch tantalizing glimpses of the riotously elaborate metalwork, carvings and wall paintings, but photographs are forbidden, and only Hindus can enter to see the metal *kalash* (vessel) representing the goddess. The actual Taleju idol hidden in the sanctum in the south wing – said to be a *yantra*, or mystical diagram – may be seen by initiates only. South Indian in origin, Taleju was brought here by the fourteenth-century king Harisinghadev, and was also adopted by the royal houses of Kathmandu and Patan. She was never much worshipped by commoners, however, and the dynasties that patronized her are long gone. Those who worship her today equate her with Durga, and she receives a sacrifice of 108 animals on the ninth day of Durga's festival, Dasain.

Kumari Chowk

As you peer into Mul Chowk, the door facing you across the courtyard closes off the fabled **Kumari Chowk**, said by the few who have seen it to be as old and as beautiful as Mul Chowk, though smaller. It is only opened on the four key days of Dasain, and even then remains shut to outsiders.

The National Art Museum

Durbar Square • Mid-Jan to mid-Oct Mon 10.30am–2.30pm, Tues–Sun 10.30am–3.30pm; mid-Oct to mid-Jan Mon 10.30am–2.30pm, Tues–Sun 10.30am–4.30pm • Rs150, includes admission to Woodcarving Museum (see p.162) and Brass and Bronze Museum (see p.162); camera Rs100 • ☎ 01 427 1478

Stone friezes at the entrance of the Royal Palace's western wing portray Vishnu Varahi and Narasimha, Vishnu's boar and man-lion avatar. They guard the excellent **National Art Museum**, which is chiefly devoted to tantric **poubha** (Newari-style painting) and *thangka* paintings of the fierce local gods Bhairab and Kali. The former is seen in many of his 64 bloodcurdling forms, including White Bhairab, Lion-faced and Fire-breathing. The collection also includes illuminated pages of religious texts going back as far as the eleventh century, a few erotic miniatures, some historic stone images and inscriptions from the Malla dynasty and, by the main entrance, examples of the Nawa Durga masks (see p.163).

Upstairs, a series of **royal portraits** above the staircase ends, pointedly, with Dipendra – and an empty nail where, presumably, Gyanendra briefly hung. In the adjacent gallery, an eighteenth-century *poubha* labelled "Gorkha Palace" acts as a wonderful botanical-zoological-topographical map of Nepal, stretching from the Terai to cranes soaring over the Himalayas. The high-ceilinged **main hall**, at the end of the first-floor galleries, houses a fine, seventeenth-century depiction of Nritaswor, the dancing, copulating tantric union of Shiva and Shakti (coyly labelled "Dancing Shiva"), and the curious *Sata Chakra Darsan (*labelled *"Yogapurush"*), showing the location of the seven power points (*chakra*) of the human body.

Pashupati Mandir and around

In the entire square, only the fifteenth-century **Yaksheswar** or **Pashupati Mandir** at the eastern end receives much in the way of reverence. The oldest structure in Bhaktapur, it houses a copy of the exalted Pashupatinath *linga*, and its roof struts sport some wildly deviant erotic carvings. In front of it stands the mid-eighteenth-century **Batsala Durga** temple whose *shikra* design is distinctively North Indian, but whose stone guardian creatures, flanking the stairs to the shrine, are probably a sign of Chinese influence. In front of the *shikra*, facing the palace, hangs the improbably huge **Taleju Bell**, plus a smaller replica known generally as the "**Bell of Barking Dogs**", so called because its toll evidently inflicts ultrasonic agony on local canines.

Chyasin Mandap

The **Chyasin Mandap**, the Pavilion of the Eight Corners, immediately opposite the Palace of 55 Windows, was probably used by Bhaktapur's kings to watch festivals and processions. It's actually an exact, 1990 replica of an eighteenth-century structure destroyed in the 1934 earthquake, lacking only the original carved roof struts, which have adorned the entrance archway leading into Kathmandu's New Road since 1934.

Siddhi Lakshmi Mandir and around

Marking the eastern edge of Durbar Square proper, the pale stone shikra of the **Siddhi Lakshmi Mandir** thrusts upwards from the wide, stepped plinth, where pairs of warriors and fierce animals guard access to the holy of holies above. Beyond, in the offshoot square to the east, a pair of steadfast stone lions still stand guard, though the three-tiered pagoda temple that once stood here has vanished. The **Silu Mahadev** temple, overlooking them, only has its plinth and guardian animals – the little white domed sanctuary plonked incongruously on top was supposed to be a temporary replacement for the destroyed original.

Chatur Brahma

Rare for predominantly Hindu Bhaktapur, the well-preserved **Chatur Brahma Mahabihar**, a few steps east of Durbar Square, attracts Buddhist as well as Hindu worshippers, and is a gathering place for neighbourhood metalsmiths in the evening. You might hear *bhajan* hymn singing, with its languorous accompaniment on harmonium and tabla.

BISKET: NEW YEAR, BHAKTAPUR STYLE

While many Nepali festivals have their origins in religious myth, Bhaktapur's high-spirited **Bisket** festival is based on a fairy tale. Similar fables appear in Zoroastrian myth and in the biblical Apocrypha's Book of Tobit. According to the local version, a Bhaktapur king wanted to marry off his daughter, but each time he made a match, the groom would turn up dead in the marital bed the next morning. One day a stranger came to town and learned of the situation from his host, whose son was due to be the next groom, and offered to take the son's place. Forcing himself to stay awake after doing the act with the princess, the stranger watched as two deadly serpents slithered out of her nostrils. The hero slew the snakes, broke the spell and won the undying gratitude of the people, who now celebrate his deed with an annual festival. The festival's Newari name, Biska, is a contraction of two words meaning "snake" and "death".

Bisket also differs from most Nepali festivals in that its date is reckoned by the solar calendar, not the lunar one, which means it always starts on April 9 or 10. It kicks off with a raucous **tug-of-war** in Taumadhi Tol, in which residents of the upper and lower halves of the city try to pull a creaky, three-storied chariot containing the image of Bhairab to their respective sides; you can usually see the chariot's wheels lying beside the Bhairab temple. On the fourth day – the day before Nawa Barsa (Nepali New Year) – Bhairab and another smaller chariot are pulled to the sloping open area above Chuping Ghat. When the chariots are in place, men of the city struggle to raise a 25m-high **ceremonial pole** with a crossbeam to which are attached two banners representing the two slain snakes – an exciting and sometimes dangerous operation.

The pole stays up until the next afternoon, when residents again take up a tug-of-war, this time trying to pull the mighty pole down to their side. (This is an even more dangerous performance: on one or two occasions people have been killed by the falling pole.) The pole's plunge marks the official beginning of the **new year**. Bisket continues for another four days, with a wild parade of *khats*, or gorgeous palanquins for deities, in the eastern part of the city, a candlelight procession to Dattatreya Square, an all-city display of temple deities, and a final tug-of-war over Bhairab's chariot.

2

Taumadhi Tol

All the life and energy of the western part of Bhaktapur seems to flow away from Durbar Square and down the alleys that lead to **Taumadhi Tol**, 100m to the southeast. This is the true nerve centre of Bhaktapur's Newari culture, especially at night when men sing *bhajan* hymns and street vendors sell *momos* and other snacks from their mobile stalls; full-moon nights are particularly vibrant. In mid-April this square serves as the assembly point for **Bisket**, Nepal's foremost New Year celebration (see box, p.159).

Nyatapola

Dominating Taumadhi and all of Bhaktapur, the graceful, five-tiered **Nyatapola** is Nepal's tallest and most classically proportioned pagoda. So obscure is its deity, a tantric goddess named Siddhi Lakshmi, that she apparently has no devotees, and the sanctuary has been barred to all but priests ever since its completion in 1702. Perhaps that's why the temple is named not for a deity but, uniquely, for its architectural dimensions: in Newari, *nyata* means "five-stepped" and *pola* means "roof". The Nyatapola's five pairs of **temple guardians** – the Malla-era wrestlers Jaimala and Patta, elephants, lions, griffins and two minor goddesses, Baghini (Tigress) and Singhini (Lioness) – are as famous as the temple itself. Each pair is supposed to be ten times as strong as the pair below.

Bhairabnath Mandir

The heavy, thick-set **Bhairabnath Mandir** is as different from the slender Nyatapola as one pagoda could possibly be from another. The most peculiar thing about this heavy-set building, in fact, is the tiny Bhairab idol mounted on a sort of mantel on the front of the temple (several other figures are kept inside, including the larger mask that leads the Bisket parade). A story is told that Bhairab, travelling incognito, once came to Bhaktapur to watch the Bisket festivities. Divining the god's presence and hoping to extract a boon, the priests bound him with tantric spells, and when he tried to escape by sinking into the ground they chopped off his head. Now Bhairab, or at least his head, gets to ride in the Bisket parade every year – inside a locked box on board the chariot. The *kinkinimali*, or golden metal fringe at the very top of the temple, is held to be particularly fine.

Til Mahadev Narayan Mandir

Hidden away on the southeast side of Taumadhi Tol, the seventeenth-century **Til Mahadev Narayan Mandir** displays all the iconography of a Vishnu (Narayan) temple: a gilded *sankha* (conch), *chakra* (wheel) and Garud are all hoisted on pillars out in front. The temple's name, it's said, derives from an incident involving a trader from Thimi who, upon unfolding his wares here, magically discovered the image of Narayan in a consignment of sesame seeds (*til*).

Kumari Ghar

A block northeast of the Bhairabnath Mandir stands Bhaktapur's **Kumari Ghar**. An image of the goddess is kept upstairs and is only displayed publicly during Bisket. The living goddess herself, who is regarded as a manifestation of Durga, normally lives in another building north of Tachapal Tol, but resides here in October for the ten days of Dasain – her own festival, celebrating her victory over the buffalo demon.

West from Taumadhi

Like a brick canyon, Bhaktapur's main commercial thoroughfare runs from Taumadhi west to the city gate. Roughly 150m along, you'll reach a kind of playground of sculptures and shrines, and a *shikra* that rejoices in the name of **Jyotirlingeshwar Mahadev Mandir**, freely translatable as "Great God of the Resplendent Phallus" – a reference to a myth in which Shiva challenges Brahma and Vishnu to find the end of his organ (they never do). Further west, the broad **Jaya Barahi Mandir** – one of many whose face-lift was paid for by the tourist entrance fee – commemorates the *shakti* (consort) of Vishnu the boar; you have to stand well back to see its pagoda roofs.

Potters' Square

Dark, damp alleys beckon on either side of the main road by Jaya Barahi Mandir – north towards Durbar Square and south to the river. An obligatory destination in this area is Kumale Tol, the **Potters' Square**, a sloping open space just southwest of Taumadhi Tol. Until recent years, Bhaktapur's potters (*kumal*) used to crank out simple water vessels, stovepipes, disposable yogurt pots and so on, but as imported plastic has undercut local pottery, and as tourist numbers have swollen, the square has shifted its output to piggy banks, miniature elephants and the like. Workaday pottery is now produced in more obscure corners of Nepal, such as in neighbouring Thimi, but the tourist trade keeps the craft alive. You'll see the potters kneading their clay by hand, and a few still form their vessels on hand-powered wheels. The finished creations are set out in soldierly rows to dry in the sun for a few days before firing, which turns them from grey to brick red.

Tachapal Tol (Dattatreya Square) and around

From Taumadhi, the eastern segment of Bhaktapur's main artery snakes its way to the original and still-beating heart of the city, **Tachapal Tol** (**Dattatreya Square**). Here again a pair of temples loom over the square, older than those of Taumadhi if not as eye-catching. More notably, though, Tachapal conceals Nepal's most celebrated masterpiece of woodcarving, the Pujari Math's Peacock Window, and a superb **woodcarving museum**. You'll also find the finest woodwork studios in Nepal here, which are well worth a browse, even if you haven't got room in your rucksack for an 2.5m-high, Rs100,000 peacock-window reproduction.

Just north of Tachapal, a second open space around **Ganesh Pokhari** is equally busy with *pasal* (shops) and street vendors. **South of the square** is also good for exploring, as Bhaktapur's medieval backstreets spill down the steep slope to the river-like tributaries.

Dattatreya Mandir

The **Dattatreya Mandir** is one of Bhaktapur's oldest structures, rearing up behind an angelic pillar-statue of Garud, and the same pair of wrestlers that guard the Nyatapola temple (see opposite). It was raised in 1427 during the reign of Yaksha Malla, the last king to rule the valley from Bhaktapur. Like the Kasthamandap of Kathmandu, which it resembles, it was once a *sattal*, a three-storey loggia and public meeting place, and is similarly reputed to have been built from the wood of a single tree. Dattatreya, a sort of one-size-fits-all deity imported from South India, epitomizes the religious syncretism that Nepal is famous for: to Vaishnavas, Dattatreya is an incarnation of Vishnu, while Shaivas hail him as Shiva's guru and Buddhists even fit him into their pantheon as a *bodhisattva*.

Bhimsen Mandir

Bhimsen Mandir, the oblong temple across Tachapal Tol from Dattatreya Mandir, belongs to the patron saint of Newari merchants, whose territory Tachapal is. As usual for a Bhimsen temple, the ground floor is open – making a popular meeting place – and the shrine is hidden upstairs.

2

The Pujari Math

Behind and to the right of the Dattatreya temple stands the sumptuous eighteenth-century **Pujari Math**, one of a dozen priests' quarters (*math*) that once ringed Tachapal Tol. Similar to Buddhist *bahal*, these *math* typically sheltered communities of Hindu devotees loyal to a single leader or sect. Like *bahal*, most have now also been converted to other, secular uses. Given the nature of the caste system, it's not surprising that the grandest houses in the city traditionally belonged to priests. The Pujari Math's awesome windows can be seen on two sides; the often-imitated **Peacock Window**, overlooking a narrow lane on the building's far (east) side, has for two centuries been acclaimed as the zenith of Nepali window lattice carving.

The Woodcarving Museum

Pujari Math, Tachapal Tol • Mid-Jan to mid-Oct Mon 10.30am–2.30pm, Tues–Sun 10.30am–4.30pm; mid-Oct to mid-Jan Mon 10.30am–2.30pm, Tues–Sun 10.30am–3.30pm • Rs150, includes admission to the National Art Museum (see p.158) and the Brass and Bronze Museum (see below)

The small **Woodcarving Museum**, on the upper floors of the Pujari Math, offers an exquisite taste of a fine Newar house's interior, and gets you closer to exquisite temple carvings than is otherwise possible. On the third floor, protected by a glass case, a highlight of the collection is the alluring fifteenth-century Nartaki Devi (labelled "dancing goddess"), with her classically exaggerated hourglass figure and smile. A large, waist-up Bhairava (Bhairab) dates from the seventeenth century, and there are several magnificent steles and *torana*, and various abstractly weathered temple struts. The tiny **courtyard** is a lavish, almost oppressive, concentration of woodcarving virtuosity – arguably the finest in the country.

The Brass and Bronze Museum

Tachapal Tol, directly opposite the Pujari Math • Mid-Jan to mid-Oct Mon 10.30am–2.30pm, Tues–Sun 10.30am–4.30pm; mid-Oct to mid-Jan Mon 10.30am–2.30pm, Tues–Sun 10.30am–3.30pm • Rs150, includes admission to National Art Museum (see p.158) and Woodcarving Museum (see above)

The **Brass and Bronze Museum** gathers together an interesting selection of domestic and ritual vessels and implements. Their craftsmanship is superb, and their esoteric uses give a good insight into just how complex traditional Nepali culture can be – every last dish and ladle and lamp has its own very specific purpose.

Wakupati Narayan Mandir

East of Tachapal is the **Wakupati Narayan Mandir**, where local Jyapus (members of the Newari farming subcaste) worship Vishnu as a harvest god. The temple displays no fewer than five Garuds mounted on pillars in a line.

Nawa Durga Dyochhen

North of Tachapal, the **Nawa Durga Dyochhen** honours the nine Durgas, or manifestations of Parvati, Shiva's consort. According to legend, they used to eat solitary travellers, turning the area east of Bhaktapur into a Bermuda triangle until a priest managed to cast a tantric spell on them. The Nawa Durga occupy a special place in Bhaktapur's spiritual landscape: the city is said to be delimited by symbolic Nawa Durga stones (*pith*), and most *tol* (neighbourhoods) have adopted one of the nine as their protector goddess.

The temple here is the point of origin for one of Nepal's darker **festivals**. Over a period of a month, in the lead up to Dasain, in October, a buffalo is housed and fed in a dark room, ready to play its role as the demon Mashishasura – over whom Durga was victorious at Bijaya Dasami, the tenth day of Dasain. On the evening of the ninth day of the festival, the buffalo is force-fed beer then chased drunkenly through the streets to Brahmayani Pith, beside the waters of the Hanumante Khola. Here it is sacrificed, and its blood used to bring the **Nawa Durga masks** to life as deities, ready for their dance on the morning of the **Bijaya Dasami** (see box opposite).

THE NAWA DURGA DANCERS

The **Nawa Durga dancers** draw their members from the caste of flower sellers. Each wears a **painted clay mask** which, empowered by tantric incantations, enables the wearer to become the very embodiment of the deity. Every September a new set of masks is moulded from local clay and the ashes of last year's masks, then painted according to strict iconographical rules. There are actually thirteen masks in all – the Nawa Durga plus four attendant deities – but only seven are carried by dancers. On the morning of **Bijaya Dasami**, the "victorious tenth day" of Dasain (usually early Oct), the dancers and accompanying musicians re-enact the legend of Durga's victory over the buffalo demon, beginning at Brahmayani Pith, beside the Hanumante Khola, and processing to Bhaktapur's Durbar Square through the day. The troupe continues to perform at designated places on days determined by the lunar calendar throughout the winter and spring wedding and festival seasons. In the month of Bhadau (Aug–Sept) their masks are formally (but privately) retired and burned, along with accompanying sacrifices. You can buy miniature reproductions all over town.

West of the Nawa Durga Dyochhen, the **Prashannashil Mahabihar**, distinguished by its pagoda-style cupola, is another of Bhaktapur's few Buddhist institutions.

Along the Hanumante Khola

The **Hanumante Khola** is Bhaktapur's humble tributary of the River Ganga, its name derived from the monkey god Hanuman who, locals like to think, stopped here for a drink on his way back from the Himalayas after gathering medicinal herbs to heal Ram's brother in an episode of the Ramayana. Like all rivers in the valley, it's pretty disgusting, but **Hanuman Ghat**, located straight downhill from Tachapal Tol where two tributaries join, manages to transcend the stink. Morning *puja* and ablutions are a routine for many, while old-timers come here just to hangout. The area is reached by passing between two jumbo *shivalinga* hoisted on octagonal plinths. Behind the left-hand one is the Ram temple that gives the ghat its Hanuman association: a statue of the monkey god outside the sanctum pays tribute to his master sheltered within. Another Hanuman, painted orange, keeps watch over a clutter of small Shiva *linga* scattered around the confluence area.

Chuping Ghat temple complex

Downhill from Taumadhi Tol, **Chuping Ghat's** temple complex has been partially restored and taken over by Kathmandu University's Department of Music, and sometimes offers short courses in Nepali music. The long, sloping area above the ghat is the focal point on New Year's Day (Nawa Barsa) in April, when a 25m-high *linga* pole is ceremonially toppled by the throng (see box, p.159). This area is inhabited mainly by members of the sweeper caste, so much of Bhaktapur's rubbish ends up nearby.

Ram Ghat and Mangal Ghat

Ram Ghat, below Potters' Square, has little to offer beyond a run-of-the-mill Ram temple. **Mangal Ghat**, further downstream, boasts a more atmospheric selection of neglected artefacts, and by following the trail of *linga* across the river you'll end up at a forbidding Kali temple in one of Bhaktapur's satellite villages.

ARRIVAL AND DEPARTURE   **BHAKTAPUR**

By bus Handiest of the buses to Bhaktapur is the "Express" minibus service (every 30min; 30min) from Kathmandu's Bhaktapur Bus Park (on Bagh Bazaar, 20m east of the junction with Durbar Marg, at the northeast corner of Ratna Park). The bus arrives in Bhaktapur – after a journey along the six-lane section of the Arniko Highway – at the minibus park next to Siddha Pokhari, a 5min walk west of Durbar Square. You could also take one of the frequent

Banepa-, Dhulikhel- or Barhabise-bound buses from the City Bus Park, which drop you on the Arniko Highway about 10min walk south of town – you can also pick these up at Surya Binayak, the main junction 300m south of Ram Ghat. Local buses from Nagarkot terminate at Kamal Binayak, 5min northeast of Tachapal.

By private tour bus If you come on a private tour bus you'll be deposited at the Tourist Bus Park, just north of Durbar Square.

By taxi Taxis (Rs800 or more from Kathmandu) will take you only to the nearest city gate.

By bike Only a desperado would cycle to Bhaktapur on the main road from Kathmandu. Once beyond the airport, however, it's possible to turn off the busy trunk road (either just before or just after the Manchara River) and head up to join the old road which leads past Thimi (see p.170) to Bhaktapur.

INFORMATION

Entrance fee Westerners are charged US$15 (or the equivalent in Nepali rupees – roughly Rs1500) to enter Bhaktapur, and you may be asked to show your ticket as you walk around town. Note that you only need to pay once, however long your stay: make your intentions clear when you buy your ticket at the entry gate. If you intend to visit the city more than once, the ticket can be extended to become a pass covering the length of your stay in Nepal. For this you'll need to bring two passport photos and a photocopy of the main pages of your passport (including the page with your Nepali visa).

Banks and exchange ATMs can be found on Durbar Square, next to *Shiva Guest House*; on the main road between Durbar Square and Tachapal Tol; and at Surya Binayak, on the junction with the main road to Kathmandu.

Hospitals and clinics Bhaktapur's hospital is not a great place to have to go in an emergency. There is the Western-staffed Bhaktapur Homeopathic Clinic, at Nagh Pokhari (☎ 01 661 3197, ☯ homeopathynepal.com), but it's better, arguably, at spreading preventative health messages than treating real disease.

ACCOMMODATION

Most guesthouses in Bhaktapur are small and exceptionally well located in the area around Taumadhi and Durbar Square (though this means that early morning *puja* bells may prevent a lie-in). As a rule, **prices** are significantly higher than for comparable lodgings in Kathmandu, but it's worth it to stay here. The city doesn't have that many beds, so book ahead in busy times, or arrive as early as possible in the day. Most guesthouses can **book tourist buses** and even domestic flights, saving you a trip to Kathmandu, and may be able to find you a rental **bike** if you want to explore the area.

Bhadgaon Guest House Taumadhi Tol ☎ 01 661 0488, ☯ bhadgaon.com.np; map p.157. A little pricey, but the friendly staff give this place a professional feel. There's a range of rooms: those on the higher floors (one with its own terrace) are attractive, comfortably appointed and boast great views; there are more in the relatively drab annexe. Also has a calm central terrace area, a good rooftop restaurant and a *Himalayan Java* (see p.166) outlet. US$45

Golden Gate Guest House Off Taumadhi Tol ☎ 01 661 0534, ☯ goldengateguesthouse.com; map p.157. The justifiably popular *Golden Gate Guesthouse* is a relatively large brick-and-concrete block with simple, somewhat faded rooms. It's clean, friendly, pleasantly secluded and has good views from the roof and upper (more expensive) rooms. Rs800

Khwopa Guest House Bolachhen ☎ 01 661 4661, ☯ khwopa-guesthouse.com.np; map p.155. Homely place with cosy (if rather dark), low-ceilinged rooms piled up over three floors. Furnishings are simple but the communal areas are attractive, with wooden fittings and terracotta tiles. It suffers a little from road noise, so bring earplugs. US$18

★**Pagoda Guest House** Taumadhi Tol ☎ 01 661 3248, ☯ pagodaguesthouse.com; map p.157. Friendly, family-run place with creeper-festooned balconies overlooking a small front court and the Nyatapola. Only the more expensive rooms have private bathrooms and (in some cases) views, but they're all clean and well furnished, and the place attracts lots of return visitors. There's newer, smarter accommodation (think terracotta floor tiles, bamboo furniture, carved wood windows and lots of cream linen fabrics; US$44) in the neighbouring "Newa" annexe. US$13

Peacock Guest House Tachapal Tol ☎ 01 661 1829, ☯ peacockguesthousenepal.com; map p.155. This is one of the few guesthouses on the eastern side of the city, and thus removed from the city's more touristy side. You enter through a busy woodcarving atelier on the historic square, then go through to a traditional, characterfully low-ceilinged house on an inner courtyard. The smart rooms were renovated in 2014, and the owners also run the on-site *Himalayan Bakery* (see p.166). US$45

2

KING CURD

Bhaktapur's culinary speciality, famed throughout Nepal, is **juju dhau**, or "king of curds". Made from naturally sweet buffalo milk, it is boiled up in an iron pot along with cloves, cardamom, coconut and cashew – sugar, properly, isn't added at all – and then cooled slowly, with the addition of an older batch to introduce the lactobacillus that makes it curdle. Most tourist restaurants serve it, at a price, but you can find it anywhere you see the painted, cartoon sign of a full bowl. A number of inexpensive shops on the main road between the minibus park and Durbar Square serve it in the traditional clay *bhingat* bowls. There's no added water, and it shouldn't pose any health risk. Whether or not you're getting the real, natural product, or a fake made using powdered milk, sugar and a freezer, can't be guaranteed, however. One test is said to be to upend the bowl: real king curd won't fall out.

Shiva Guest House Durbar Square ☎ 01 661 3912, ⓦ shivaguesthouse.com; map p.157. This was the first guesthouse in Bhaktapur, and it has a classic location overlooking the Pashupati Mandir. It's unexceptional but reasonably cheerful inside, with helpful management and good food, too (see below). There's a range of rooms, from simple ones with shared bathrooms to en suites ($28) with views of the square. If you're booking in advance, make sure you stay here, and not in the less well-situated annexe (*Shiva Guest House 2*) to the east. **US$12.50**

EATING

Most of the guesthouses have their own **restaurants** with fairly unimaginative tourist menus. Meanwhile, several cafés overlooking the various squares cater mainly to day-trippers: they're pricey but great places to soak up the atmosphere, and some offer a few Newari dishes.

Beans Just off Durbar Square; map p.157. Appealing, low-key café with just four tables: the coffee (Rs80–200) is the star of the show, but there are also good smoothies, milkshakes and cakes ranging from coconut Danish pastries to chocolate brownies. Daily 8am–7/8pm.

Café Nyatapola Taumadhi Tol ☎ 01 661 0346; map p.157. The prices are hugely inflated, but the location, in a former temple in Taumadhi Tol, is irresistible, and the atmosphere is fairly smart. Apart from the luxurious three-course *daal bhaat* (Rs1045), the food is mostly snacky, with omelettes, chips and Newari meat and egg side dishes, and drinks (from Rs120) from *lassis* to cappuccinos. Daily 8am–7pm.

Himalayan Bakery Tachapal Tol ☎ 01 661 1829; map p.155. This charming bakery-café is a little pricey, but the Illy coffee (Rs150–220) and cakes (Rs70–120) are undeniably good. Muffins are a speciality: try the walnut and apple flavour, or the cinnamon and pumpkin. Daily 7am–9pm.

Palace Restaurant Durbar Square ☎ 984 120 4577; map p.157. The long and atmospheric dining room is the main attraction, hidden behind ancient windows and feeling almost like a train carriage, though there's little life to observe at this side of the square. The menu is very small and on the pricey side (the Nepali set lunches, for example, cost Rs645–710) but it's good for coffee and drinks. Daily 10am–8/9pm.

Shiva's Café Corner Durbar Square ☎ 01 661 3912; map p.157. One of the better guesthouse restaurants, with the interior made cosy by a big wooden bar and beams above, and views through the window onto Durbar Square. The food is surprisingly good for a menu that runs the gamut from steak to spaghetti, with, of course, Nepali, Chinese and Indian dishes too. Prices are fairly reasonable, with mains Rs240–800. Daily 7am–8.30pm.

Sunny Café Taumadhi Tol ☎ 01 661 6094; map p.157. The location is the thing here, with a south-facing roof terrace right next to the Nyatapola. Prices (mains Rs190–715) are relatively uninflated for fair-enough food: Mexican, Italian, Chinese, Indian, Nepali and Newari dishes all feature on the menu. Daily 7.30am–8.30pm or later.

SHOPPING

Bhaktapur offers a relatively modest selection of most of the tourist-oriented goods you can buy in Kathmandu, usually at similar prices. The best buys are perhaps **woodcarving** and the renowned Nawa Durga **puppets** and papier-mâché **masks** (see p.163). And of course you can pick up cheap **pottery** at Potters' Square: animal figures, planters, candlestick holders, ashtrays, piggy banks (onomatopoeically called *kutrukke*) and so on. Nepalis recognize Bhaktapur for its traditional **textiles**, such as black-and-red *pataasi* material and the formal *Bhadgaonle topi* headgear. There are plentiful woollens and pashmina shawls for sale, along with quality *thangka* and watercolours of local scenes, painted locally. **Metal** pieces such as incense holders and traditional ritual objects are also produced here.

Changu Narayan

Perched at the abrupt end of the ridge north of Bhaktapur, the tranquil temple complex of **CHANGU NARAYAN** commands a fine view of the valley in three directions. "One remembers all the wealth of carving of the rest of the valley," wrote Percival Landon in 1928, "but when all is recalled it is probably to the shrine of Changu Narayan that one offers the palm." Landon wasn't wrong, and once you've run the gauntlet of the souvenir stalls in the little village, you'll find a site that retains its palpably holy, ancient atmosphere – not to mention the finest collection of statues outside the National Museum.

A single, stone-paved pedestrian street stretches west from the **entrance booth**, where you pay a fee (see p.170), along the ridgetop, towards the temple at its apex. It's lined with souvenir stalls for much of its length, or simple shops selling soft drinks and the like.

Changu Museum

Halfway to the temple, 200m west of the bus park • Daily 8am–6pm • Rs200

The small and eccentric **Changu Museum**, set in an old-fashioned Newari townhouse, offers a beguiling display of traditional utensils, swords and musical instruments. The owner leads you up and down narrow wooden staircases, from the family kitchen and prayer room on the top floor to the rice storage cupboard and *raksi* still at ground level. Also on show are a collection of Nepali coins – including a medieval one claimed to be the world's smallest – a bowl of 220-year-old rice, a holy, hairy cow's gallstone and other curiosities.

The temple complex

A few steps up the hill from the museum stands the **temple complex**, a hushed cluster of rest-houses and pilgrims' shelters with a grand quadrangle at its heart.

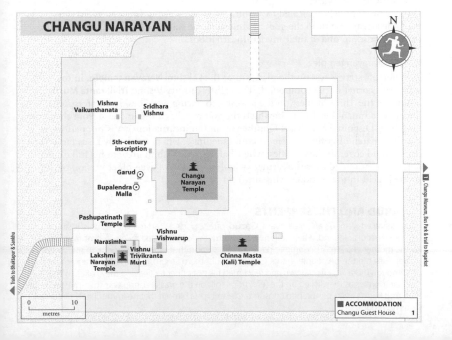

It is the valley's oldest Vaishnava site, with a documented history running back to the fifth century AD – the same date as the original stone image of Vishnu, covered in a seventh-century gilt sheath, which is kept hidden inside the sanctuary from profane view. From time to time, the statue is said to sweat miraculously, indicating that Vishnu is battling with the *nag* spirits, and the cloth used to wipe the god's brow is considered a charm against snakebites. On the north and west side, 108 stone steps – a sacred number – descend through the forest towards the scattered series of hamlets.

Changu Narayan temple

The main temple building was reconstructed around 1700. The repoussé work on the front of the building is as intricate as any you'll find in Nepal, as are the carved, painted struts supporting the roofs. A measure of the temple's ritual importance, meanwhile, is the exaggerated size of the four traditional emblems of Vishnu – the wheel (*chakra*), conch (*sankha*), lotus (*padma*) and mace (*gada*) – mounted on two pillars at its western corners. The base of the *chakra* pillar bears the **oldest inscription** in the valley: dated 454 AD and attributed to the Lichhavi king Mandev, it relates how Mandev, upon the death of his father, dissuaded his mother from committing *sati*, saying "what use are the joys and pleasures of this world without you?"

The face of the celebrated **statue of Garud** is thought to be a portrait of Mandev. Probably dating from the sixth century, it kneels before the main doorway, looking human but for a pair of wings. He used to be mounted on a pillar, the broken base of which is lying just to his right. The statues inside a screened cage next to Garud commemorate **King Bupalendra Malla** of Bhaktapur and his queen Bubana Lakshmi, who ruled during the late seventeenth and early eighteenth centuries. The king's gold-plated image was stolen in September 2001, only to be discovered by a cowherd the next day, half buried in a nearby field.

The temple courtyard

If the main temple is dedicated to Vishnu, then the surrounding **courtyard** is a veritable artistic hymn to the god, as almost all the statues show him, or his faithful carrier, Garud, in one of their myriad incarnations.

Lakshmi Narayan temple

Two notable statues rest on the platform of the **Lakshmi Narayan temple**, in the southwest corner of the compound. The eighth-century **Vishnu Trivikranta Murti**, Vishnu of the Three Strides (on the lowest step, facing west, beside a waterspout), illustrates a much-loved story in which the god reclaimed the universe from the demon king Bali. Disguised as a dwarf (another of his ten incarnations), Vishnu petitioned Bali for a patch of ground where he could meditate, which need only be as far as the dwarf could cover in three strides; when Bali agreed, Vishnu grew to his full divine height and bounded over the earth, sky and heavens. (An even older version of this statue is held in the National Museum.)

GARUD AND THE SERPENTS

In Nepali art, Vishnu's angelic servant, **Garud**, often sports a scarf made of cobras. It stems from a peculiar legend, which tells how his mother was kidnapped by his stepmother, Kadru, the mother of all snakes. Garud appealed to his stepbrothers, the *nag* serpent-spirits, to free her. They did this on condition that Garud brought them ambrosia from Indra's heaven. Although Indra later flew down and reclaimed his pot of nectar (leaving the snakes to split their tongues as they licked up the few drops spilt on the grass), Vishnu was so impressed that Garud hadn't been tempted to consume the ambrosia himself that he immediately hired him as his mount.

The adjacent eleventh- or twelfth-century image – also covered in red *abhir* powder, an indication that worship is very much alive – depicts Vishnu in yet another of his incarnations, that of the furious man-lion **Narasimha**; he carries across his lap the demon Hiranyakasyapu. The story here is that the demon's pious son had acknowledged Vishnu as supreme, omnipresent deity over his own father. In scorn and fury, Hiranyakasyapu asked his son, "Where is this Vishnu of yours? Here in this pillar?", and broke a column open – whereupon Vishnu promptly appeared. It was said that the demon could be killed by neither man nor animal, by night nor day, in earth nor in space, indoors nor out, and by neither living weapons nor inanimate ones. Vishnu therefore appeared at twilight, as the man-lion, taking the demon across his lap and tearing him apart with his fingernails – as is vividly depicted.

Vishnu Vishwarup

The eighth-century image of **Vishnu Vishwarup** ("Vishnu of the Universal Form"), immediately to the east of the Lakshmi Narayan temple, is an awesome composition, even if it has lost its top-right corner. In its lower portion, it shows Vishnu reclining on the snake of infinity in the ocean of existence; above, he rises from the waters before a heavenly host, his thousand heads and arms symbolizing sheer omnipotence. The latter image is borrowed from an episode in the Mahabharata in which the warrior Arjuna loses his nerve and Krishna (an incarnation of Vishnu) appears in this universal form to dictate the entire Bhagavad Gita by way of encouragement.

Vishnu Vaikunthanata

At the northwest corner of the compound, the twelfth- or thirteenth-century **Vishnu Vaikunthanata** shows a purposeful Vishnu riding Garud like a true cosmic traveller. Nearby, underneath a jasmine bush, stands a **Sridhara Vishnu** of the ninth or tenth century, an early example of what has since become the standard Nepali representation of Vishnu.

Chinna Masta (Kali) temple

One of the smaller temples in the compound is dedicated to **Chinna Masta**, a local version of the bloodthirsty Kali – note the nearby post used for tethering sacrificial animals. Some scholars speculate that she is the mother goddess who was worshipped at this site in prehistoric times, though she has been transformed into a tantric goddess of destructively sexual power – she is usually depicted holding aloft her own severed head. Her cult endures: the gold on the roofs and doors is in good condition, and a Chinna Masta Mai chariot procession is held here for five days after *aunshi* – the new moon night of the Nepali month of Baisaakh (April–May).

WALKS FROM CHANGU NARAYAN

You can hike the 10km from **Nagarkot to Bhaktapur** via Changu Narayan (see p.178 for more details). It's also possible to walk or mountain bike from Changu Narayan to **Sankhu** (see p.136), 5km to the northeast. This trail begins along the dirt road heading northeast from the Changu bus park (take the first fork on the left), though without a guide you may need to ask local help finding the way, and if the temporary bridge is down you'll have to cross the Manohara River on foot – easy in the dry season, impassable after rain. A short cut leads down directly from the steps descending from the west side of the temple, then heads 1km north across the fields (make for the mobile phone mast) to the Sankhu road, via a footbridge over the river; frequent buses run along this road between Kathmandu and Sankhu.

2

By bus From Bhaktapur, minibuses (every 30min or so; 30min) depart from the Mahakali bus park – little more than a wide place at the junction of the Changu road with the main tarmac road that passes the north side of the city.

By taxi Taxis from Bhaktapur cost upwards of Rs800.

By bike If you're cycling you'll need a mountain bike; coming from Bhaktapur the last 2km or so are very steep.

On foot From Bhaktapur, take one of the two roads that set off from the north side of town, immediately west of the main motor road to Changu Narayan (a sign for *Hotel Planet* on the main road shows the way); these soon converge and become a pleasant trail that passes through

rural villages (you're a third of the way there at Jhaukhel) before a steep ascent to reach the west side of the temple after 5km. It'll take up to 1hr 30min on foot, and it's easy to find your way – keep heading north towards the Changu ridge. There are plenty of people to ask if you get stuck. If you're walking back to Bhaktapur, descend the stone steps on the west side of the temple compound, and turn left at the bottom, past a stone waterspout.

Entrance fee A fee of Rs100 is charged at the gate by the bus park (6am–6pm). The money goes to the Village Development Committee.

ACCOMMODATION

Changu Guest House ☏ 01 509 0852 or ☏ 984 165 2158, ⊛ changuguesthouse.com. Situated below the temple steps, this annexe to a Brahmin family home has six simple rooms, some with balcony views across the valley towards Bhaktapur. The mother makes you welcome, the knowledgeable son acts as temple guide (for a reasonable donation) and there's a modest rooftop restaurant. **US$10**

Thimi and around

THIMI, the valley's fourth-largest town, spreads across a minor eminence 4km west of Bhaktapur. The name is said to be a corruption of *chhemi,* meaning "capable people", a bit of flattery offered by Bhaktapur to make up for the fact that the town used to get mauled every time Bhaktapur picked a fight with Kathmandu or Patan. Little has changed: caught between Kathmandu's rampant development and Bhaktapur's careful spirit of conservation, Thimi has rather lost out. Recently the town has revived its ancient name of **MADHYAPUR** ("Middle Place") – which says it all.

The town itself is grotty and oddly sullen. The main north–south lane is dotted with chortens and modest temples for its full 1km length. The only sight of note, the sixteenth-century pagoda temple of **Balkumari**, comes just short of its southern end. Childless couples come here to pray to the "Child Kumari" – represented by an unmistakeable, vulva-like gilt slit – presenting her with coconuts as a symbol of fertility. The temple is bespattered with pigeon droppings and has been protected by a steel cage since its precious peacock statue was stolen in 2001; the current figure, atop its tall pillar, is a reproduction. The temple is the focus of the **Sindoor Jatra** festival for Nepali New Year (in April), when dozens of deities are ferried around on palanquins, and red powder (red being the colour of rejoicing) is thrown like confetti.

THIMI POTTERY AND PAPIER-MÂCHÉ

Thimi's main attraction is its tradition of open-air **pottery** production. Some potters may have moved on to electric wheels and kerosene-fired kilns, but in the maze of the town's back alleys and courtyards you can still see barrow-loads of raw clay and potters spinning their wheels by hand with long sticks. Most extraordinary are the open-air kilns: huge heaps of sand and charcoal belching smoke from carefully tended vents. The main pottery quarter lies in the smoky heart of town: turn west at Chapacho, the cluster of small temples halfway down the high street, opposite the Community Health Clinic.

Thimi is also known for **papier-mâché masks**, which originated with the local Chitrakar family, famed for generations as purveyors of fine festival masks. They still produce them in a range of sizes and styles, notably snarling Bhairab, kindly Kumari and elephant-headed Ganesh.

Bode

A small, tight-knit Newari community, **BODE** is built on a bluff overlooking the Manohara River, 1km north of Thimi. The village's main shrine, the **Mahalakshmi Mandir**, stands at the northwest corner of the village, a modest and not particularly well-maintained two-tiered pagoda. The goddess of wealth, Maha (Great) Lakshmi is feted during a three-day **festival** beginning on New Year's Day (here called Baisaakh Sankranti, meaning the first day of Baisaakh – April 13 or 14). The highlight of the proceedings comes on the second day, when a volunteer has his tongue bored with a thin steel spike and, thus impaled and bearing a disc-shaped object with flaming torches mounted on it, accompanies the goddess as she's paraded around the village. Volunteers believe that they won't bleed if they've followed a prescribed three-day fast and have sufficient faith, and that by performing this act they'll go directly to heaven when they die.

2

ARRIVAL AND DEPARTURE   THIMI AND AROUND

By bus Any bus between Kathmandu and Bhaktapur (see p.163) will drop you off at the southern end of Thimi. Sporadic minibuses (every 30min–1hr; 20min) between Bhaktapur and Kathmandu ply the old road, which runs parallel to the main Arniko Highway, passing the northern sides of both Thimi and Bhaktapur; at the Kathmandu end,

they stop at Koteswor, on the Ring Road.
By bike Once you're clear of the Ring Road at Koteswor, you can cycle in along the old road to Bhaktapur, which skirts the town to the north – Thimi's main street runs due south from a small temple with two yellow roofs.

The Central Hills

NAMOBUDDHA

The Central Hills

It's only when you leave it that you appreciate just how extraordinary the Kathmandu Valley is, surrounded by a 700km band of jumbled foothills that offer barely enough flat land to build a volleyball court. Only half a dozen roads fight their way out of the valley, but they are enough to make the Central Hills the most accessible area in the largely roadless hill country – though not necessarily the most travelled. To the northeast, the Arniko Highway follows the old Kathmandu–Lhasa trade route through broad valleys and misty gorges to the Tibet border; northwestwards, the Trisuli road snakes its way down into a subtropical valley nearly 1000m lower than Kathmandu; while west and then south, the Tribhuwan Rajpath, Nepal's first highway, takes a wildly tortuous route on its way to the Terai. The scenery in this area is a shade less dramatic than you'll encounter further west, but the land is nonetheless varied, rugged and only partially tamed by defiant terraces.

The majority of places in this chapter are easy overnights from anywhere in the Kathmandu Valley. The most popular are those that involve mountain views: **Nagarkot** and **Dhulikhel**, with well-developed lodgings, are both acknowledged classics; while the former has slightly better vistas, the latter boasts some interesting Newari architecture. The village of **Daman** has the most comprehensive views, but requires a little more effort to reach. These vantage points can't compare with what you'll see on a trek, but they do provide a taste of the Himalayas and can also serve as springboards for hiking and mountain-biking trips. The **Tibet border area**, meanwhile, has big appeal for **adventure-sports** enthusiasts: a handful of resorts in this area offer a wide range of activities including canyoning, whitewater rafting, kayaking and one of the world's highest bungee jumps.

Although cultural attractions are relatively few outside the Kathmandu Valley, **Panauti** is among Nepal's most intriguing small towns – all the more so because it is so seldom visited – with fascinating temples, bathing ghats and pilgrims' houses. In the northwest of the Central Hills, the peaceful village of **Nuwakot** is also a worthwhile destination, with a superb fortress and a lovely hillside location.

To an extent, the boundaries of this chapter are dictated by **travel formalities**: towns and day hikes are described here, while longer backcountry treks are covered in detail in our "Trekking" chapter (see p.302). Many of the places described in this chapter could even be strung together with destinations in the Kathmandu Valley to create one long quasi-trek or mountain-bike ride.

Widespread destruction was caused to Nuwakot district during the **April 2015 earthquake** (see box, p.6), which took place just as this book was going to press.

PANAUTI

Highlights

❶ **Nagarkot** An expansive view of the Himalayas, less than two hours from Kathmandu, with some great mountain-wbiking and hiking opportunities. **See p.176**

❷ **Panauti** Beautifully preserved small town with a perfect miniature pagoda complex at the holy confluence of two rivers. **See p.179**

❸ **Dhulikhel** See the sun rise over the Himalayas from the hilltop Kali shrine above this friendly Newari town. **See p.180**

❹ **Namobuddha** One of the holiest Tibetan Buddhist pilgrimage sites in the Himalayas, a gentle day hike away from Dhulikhel. **See p.182**

❺ **The Bhote Koshi** The whitest water of all, charging down from the Tibet border and offering some of the world's best rafting, as well as a 162m-high bungee jump. **See p.186**

❻ **Tribhuwan Rajpath** Nepal's first road, built in the 1950s, stretches from the Kathmandu Valley to the Terai and remains the best and toughest cycle route of all. **See p.189**

HIGHLIGHTS ARE MARKED ON THE MAP ON P.176

Nagarkot

Set on a ridge northeast of Bhaktapur, **NAGARKOT** (1950m) has a classic panorama of the Himalayas. While the view isn't as expansive as from Daman, and the area not as interesting as Dhulikhel, Nagarkot is easy to get to from Kathmandu and you don't have to stay in an expensive hotel to get a fantastic vista from your window.

The first tourists to visit here are thought to have been a troop of Punjabi mercenaries recruited to defend the Valley against Prithvi Narayan's troops. Stationed at the now-vanished ridgetop fort, they quickly succumbed to the "mountain air", proving drunkenly incapable when the Gurkha invaders finally arrived. Since then, numerous guesthouses have sprouted along some two kilometres of ridge. Taking in the sunrise and sunset views is the standard activity, though there's also a wealth of **hiking** and **biking** opportunities (see box, p.178).

The view tower

Most hotels in Nagarkot have good views, but they're even better from the **view tower** at the highest southern point of the ridge (2164m), an hour's walk from the centre along a tarmac road. When you get here you'll understand why Nagarkot has been the site of a fort (*kot*) since Rana times: this hilltop controlled the eastern entrance to the Kathmandu Valley and the vital trade route to Tibet. There's still a large army training base here, though relations with the community are strained after a drunken soldier killed eleven locals in 2005.

The view is dominated by the Langtang range, which on good days looms alarmingly close above a wall of dark rock. Haze usually obscures anything west of Ganesh Himal, though you can sometimes see Himchuli and even Annapurna. The view to the east is even more weather-dependent, and the mountains of Khumbu rarely appear as more than a rose-tinted dawn haze. On a good day, Everest can be seen, but only from high up, near the view tower: it's the second peak left of the rounded M-shaped mountain.

On peak-season mornings the area becomes something of a tourist circus; for more peace, and equally good views, stop off at one of the grassy mounds just short of the tower. Nearer to the hotel area, there are good views from the tiny **Mahakali shrine**,

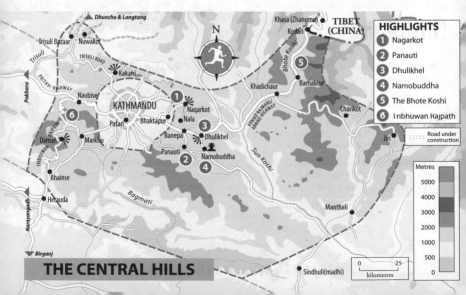

from where the only obstructions are the ever-growing towers of *Hotel View Point* and *Peaceful Cottage*: good viewpoints themselves, they are accessible to non-guests, generally for free.

ARRIVAL AND DEPARTURE   NAGARKOT

By bus Two daily minibuses (2hr) travel between Nagarkot and Kathmandu's City Bus Park; there are also regular buses between Nagarkot and Bhaktapur (every 30min; 1hr).
By taxi A taxi from Kathmandu or Dhulikhel costs

Rs2500–3500.
By bike The easiest route up is along the main road from Bhaktapur. It's consistently steep for the last 12km but paved all the way and relatively traffic-free.

ACCOMMODATION

Nagarkot's sobriquet of "Thamel-on-the-Hill" isn't quite deserved, but the boom in hotel construction here certainly resembles that in the famed Kathmandu district. The **view** is the major selling point, but just a few hotels boast a complete panorama. Only the smarter places are heated, so it's worth bringing a sleeping bag in the colder months.

Hotel Country Villa North of the Mahakali Shrine ☎01 470 0305, ⓦ hotelcountryvilla.com. Large en suites with high ceilings, colourful rugs, pinewood panelling and TVs. If you tire of the views, the hotel can help arrange plenty of activities, including pony trekking and birdwatching. US$130

Eco-Home Northeast of the bus stop ☎01 668 0180, ⓦ ecohomenagarkot.com. The warmest welcome in town, complete with nice touches such as hot-water bottles at night. Delightful rooms have futons, prayer flags, masks, photos, lamps fashioned from mini tree trunks, and pristine private baths, though no real views. US$35

★**The Fort Resort** Northeast of the bus stop ☎01 668 0069, ⓦ mountain-retreats.com. A well-run top-end hotel, located where the ridgetop fort used to stand, with traditional architecture, attractive en suites and cottages, a lovely garden, a top restaurant and unbroken views. The bigger deluxe rooms are much better value at US$150. Booking recommended. US$111

Hotel Galaxy View Tower Northeast of the bus stop ☎01 668 0122, ⓦ hotelgalaxyviewtower .com. There's no tower, and the views (from the terrace) aren't as special as the name suggests, but the sizeable rooms are clean and pretty comfortable, with private bathrooms (with tubs); the better ones also have TVs and balconies. US$10

Hotel Green Valley Northeast of the bus stop ☎01 668 0078, ⓦ hotelgreenvalley.com.np. The standard rooms, with attached bathrooms, are plain, the "deluxe" ones a touch smarter, but the real selling point is the stunning panoramic view from both types of room. Chocolate cake and apple pie are also on offer in the restaurant. US$55

Himalayan Guesthouse 150m northwest of the bus stop ☎985 117 7018, ⓔ rajuwaiba97@yahoo .com. The best of a line of inexpensive guesthouses just up from the centre of town, with clean, homely rooms, the cheapest of which have no bathrooms.

Bigger deluxe rooms upstairs (Rs1000) have a pleasant terrace with fairly good mountain views. Rs600

Hotel at the End of the Universe Near the Mahakali Shrine ☎01 668 0011, ⓦ endoftheuniverse.com.np. Up a steep series of steps, this lodge has a range of rooms including cheapies with cold water, rustic huts, en-suite options with good views (US$60) and cottages suitable for families or groups. There's a nice restaurant and a bar, and staff can help arrange volunteering opportunities. US$10

Nagarkot Farmhouse Resort Nearly 1.5km north of the Manakali Shrine ☎01 620 2022,

3

NAGARKOT

■ EATING
Berg House Café 2
Hotel New Dragon ... 1

Mahakali Shrine

Information boards & maps

Bus Stop

ATM

Army Gate

Bus Stop

Sankhu & 1 — Hiuwapati

Bhaktapur

Hiuwapati

View Tower & Nala

■ ACCOMMODATION
Hotel Country Villa 3
Eco-Home 7
Hotel at the End
  of the Universe 6
The Fort Resort 5
Himalayan Guesthouse ... 10
Hotel Galaxy View Tower ... 8
Hotel Green Valley 9
Nagarkot Farmhouse 1
Peaceful Cottage 4
Unkai Resort 2

3

CYCLING AND HIKING FROM NAGARKOT

There are some excellent mountain-biking, hiking and motorcycling opportunities around Nagarkot. Probably the most popular goes via **Changu Narayan** (see p.167) to **Bhaktapur**, three or four hours on foot, or half that on a mountain bike or motorcycle. The route follows the main road to Phedi, from where you take a dirt road to Changu Narayan. It's another 6km down to Bhaktapur.

The descent to **Sankhu** (p.136) is favoured by mountain bikers. The route forks just beyond *Nagarkot Farmhouse*: the left-hand route is steep, rutted and good fun; the right-hand one is smoother and longer.

A longer two-day trek to **Shivapuri National Park** (p.139) initially follows the latter route, then bears north on a rough motorable road to the watershed. Most hikers spend a night in Bhotechaur, near Jhule. It's then an easy day's walk to Sundarijal or Nagi Gompa (see p.139), and an optional hard third day up to the summit of Shivapuri and back to Kathmandu via Budhanilkantha. You can't ride up to the summit, but cyclists can make it from Nagarkot to Nagi Gompa or further in a day, and to Kakani (see p.188) in two days.

Heading to **Nala** (see opposite), continue south from the view tower, from where it's a stiff 700m descent along any of three different routes. The road that bears right around the tower is tarmacked and continues down to the main road between Banepa and Bhaktapur. The other two trails, via the villages of Tukucha and Ghimiregaun, descend from a track heading left from the tower and end up in Nala. Yet another option is to descend eastwards to **Hiuwapati**, deep down in the valley of the Indrawati River.

A decent **map** makes all of these excursions much easier, although they are possible without one. The best are the 1:25,000 sheets by HMG/FINNIDA, available in Kathmandu bookshops, but Himalayan Map House equivalents will suffice.

ⓦnagarkotfarmhouse.com. Under the same management as Kathmandu's excellent *Hotel Vajra* (see p.105), this red-brick lodge has compact rooms (with either shared or private bathrooms), restful grounds and massage treatments. Staff can help organize a range of walks, too. US$50

Peaceful Cottage Just north of the Mahakali Shrine ⓣ01 668 0077, ⓦpeaceful-cottage.com. In a fairly secluded location despite encroaching development, *Peaceful Cottage* feels as if it's about to be consumed by the forest. There's a rooftop viewing tower with a vast four-person suite (US$70), as well as smaller rooms and cottages; most (though not the cheaper ones in the annex) have great vistas and intricately carved wooden beds. US$35

★ **Unkai Resort** North of the Mahakali Shrine ⓣ01 668 0178, ⓔanniett@mos.com.np. This wonderfully situated hotel has some of Nagarkot's best views, both from its terrace and the more expensive en-suite rooms. A tranquil place, frequented mainly by Japanese travellers, *Unkai* also has a good restaurant. US$22

EATING

Though some of the expensive hotels have pretty good restaurants, **food** at the budget guesthouses usually doesn't live up to expectations. If you eat dinner out, take a **torch** for the dark walk back to your hotel.

Berg House Café Just south of the bus stop ⓣ01 668 0061. A step ahead of the other traveller cafés in the area – despite the glacially slow service – with an array of sugary breakfast items (Rs70–230), plus a sprinkling of Indian and Chinese dishes and a decent *daal bhaat* (from Rs230). Generally open daily 6.30am–9pm.

Hotel New Dragon Opposite Eco-Home ⓣ984 172 5365. The usual mix of Nepali, Indian and Chinese dishes (Rs200–400), but produced with a little more flair than the norm; the *momos* are particularly good. The sunny terraces are good spots to enjoy a cold beer (Rs300–325). Generally open daily 6am–10pm.

The Arniko Highway

Leaving the Kathmandu Valley through a gap at its eastern edge, Nepal's only road to the Tibet border is the **Arniko Highway** (or Arniko Rajmarg). Constructed by the Chinese in the mid-1960s – to long-standing rival India's great distress – the highway is a busy conduit for lorry-loads of Chinese goods by way of Lhasa, as well as tourists heading to the **adventure resorts** along its northern end. The first stop along the highway is **Banepa**, which together with **Nala** and **Panauti** once comprised a short-lived independent kingdom east of the Kathmandu Valley. Just east is the Newari town of **Dhulikhel**, a day's hike from the Tibetan pilgrimage site of **Namobuddha**.

Banepa and around

BANEPA, 26km east of Kathmandu, was for centuries an important staging post to Tibet, and is now – such is progress – an unattractive pit stop for buses heading up the Arniko Highway. From the first roundabout north of the highway, a road leading northeastwards to Panchkhal (p.184) first passes by the **Chandeshwari Mandir**, which overlooks a set of cremation ghats. The restored three-tiered temple commemorates Bhagwati who, according to Hindu scripture, slew a giant called Chand here, earning her the title Chandeshwari ("Lord of Chand"). Chandeshwari's image is the object of a local chariot festival coinciding with the Nepali New Year (April 13 or 14).

From Banepa, an unpaved road heads 3km northwestwards to **NALA**, a village with a seventeenth-century pagoda. From here you can continue west, passing a Lokeshwar temple en route, to reach Bhaktapur in 10km. Three quite rough tracks branch off from it ascend to Nagarkot (see p.176).

3

ARRIVAL AND DEPARTURE	BANEPA
By bus The bus park is located just to the south of the main road, with frequent buses to and from Kathmandu (from Rathna Bus Park; every 5–10min; 45min); minibuses also	run to Kathmandu (from City Bus Park; every 10min; 45min). Change at Banepa for Dhulikhel (every 10–15min; 10min) and Panauti (every 10min; 15min).

Panauti

Built on a single stratum of rock, **PANAUTI** is said to be the safest place in these parts to be when the next big earthquake hits. The best-preserved Newari town after Bhaktapur, it's an enticing enough place at any time, leading a self-sufficient existence in its own small valley 7km south of Banepa. Its centre is a perfect nugget of extended family dwellings, temples and public meeting houses, all built in the Newars' signature pink brick and carved wood; a cluster of riverside temples and ghats lies at the bottom end.

Wedged between the Punyamati and Roshi streams, Panauti forms the shape of a triangle, with a serpent (*nag*) idol standing at each of its three corners to protect against floods. Buses pull up at the newer northwest corner, but the oldest and most interesting sights are concentrated at the streams' confluence at the east end of town, approached through a distinctive entry gate.

Khware

The shrine area at the sacred confluence, known as the **Khware** or **Tribeni Ghat**, is a tranquil spot. The large *sattal* (pilgrims' house) here sports an eclectic range of frescoes depicting scenes from Hindu (and sometimes Buddhist) mythology: Vishnu in cosmic sleep, Ram killing the demon king Ravana, and Krishna being chased up a tree by a pack of naked *gopi* (milkmaids). Krishna is the featured deity of the pagoda temple next door, too, where he's shown serenading his *gopi* groupies with a flute. Other small shrines dotted around the complex are dedicated to just about every deity known to Hinduism.

The Khware has been regarded as a *tirtha* (place of sacred power) since ancient times, and on the first day of the month of Magh (usually Jan 14), it draws hundreds for ritual bathing. Beside the river, the tombstone-shaped ramps set into the ghats are where dying people are laid out, allowing their feet to be immersed in the water at the moment of death. Orthodox cremations are held at the actual confluence, but local Newars are cremated on the opposite bank, apparently to prevent their ghosts troubling the town.

Indreshwar Mahadev Mandir

Just west of the Khware, the massive **Indreshwar Mahadev Mandir** stands in the middle of a lovely walled quadrangle. The temple is dedicated to Shiva, the "Lord of Indra" in several myths, who is represented by a magnificent brass four-faced *linga*. Some authorities believe this to be the original temple (albeit restored since a 1988 earthquake) that was raised here in 1294, which would make it the oldest surviving pagoda in Nepal. Sharing the compound is the smaller, rectangular temple of Unmatta Bhairab, distinguished by three carved wooden figures occupying its upstairs windows. "Unmatta" refers to Bhairab's erotic form, in which he is depicted as a terrifying, red-bodied demon with a prominent erection.

ARRIVAL AND DEPARTURE   PANAUTI

By bus Frequent buses leave for Panauti from Kathmandu's Rathna Bus Park (every 5–10min; 45min), while minibuses depart from the capital's City Bus Park (every 5–10min; 45min) via Banepa.

By bike The most pleasant way of reaching Panauti is to cycle from Lubhu (see p.376), Banepa (see p.179), Dhulikhel (see below) or Namobuddha (see p.182).

ACCOMMODATION

Hotel Panauti Just off the main road south, 200m along from the bus park ☎01 166 1055, ✉hotelpanauti@yahoo.com; map p.182. Easily the best of Panauti's limited selection of hotels, this place has a range of clean, economical rooms with either shared or private bathrooms (the latter twice the price). Staff are very friendly and can advise about local trekking opportunities, and there are good views from the roof-terrace restaurant. **Rs500**

Dhulikhel

DHULIKHEL is justly famous as a well-preserved Newari town, mountain viewpoint, and hiking and biking hub, though its popularity is waning as modernization takes its toll. Located 5km east of Banepa, just beyond the Kathmandu Valley rim, it sits at the relatively low elevation of 1550m, and is now something of a boomtown. It's home to **Kathmandu University** and one of Nepal's best public hospitals; meanwhile, its location on the new 158km route to **Sindhulimadi** (also known as Sindhuli) and the eastern Terai seems likely to turn the place into one of Nepal's principal transport junctions.

Old Dhulikhel

Old Dhulikhel starts immediately to the west of **Mahendra Chowk**, the main square at the newer, east end of town. A traditional Newari settlement, this area is comprised almost exclusively of four- and five-storey brick mansions, many with ornate wooden lattices in place of glass windows, some affecting Neoclassical detailing imported from Europe during the Rana regime. The older buildings, held together only by mud mortar, show some serious cracks from the infamous 1934 earthquake; Dhulikhel also experienced damage during a 1988 quake centred near Dharan in the Terai.

Highlights include the central square of **Narayanthan**, containing a temple to Narayan and a smaller one to Harisiddhi (both emanations of Vishnu), and the **Bhagwati Mandir**, set at the high point of the village and with partial mountain views.

The sunrise walk

The most popular activity in Dhulikhel is hiking to the high point southeast of town in time for a **sunrise over the peaks**. To get to the top, take the road leading east from Mahendra Chowk for about 1km, passing a big recreation area on the left, and then turn right at the next fork. Cyclists will have to stay on this graded road, but hikers can climb the more direct flights of steps. On foot, allow about 45 minutes from Dhulikhel to the top, as well as plenty of time for gawking at the numerous birds and butterflies – lookout for the racquet-tailed drongos and turtle doves. The **summit** (1715m) is

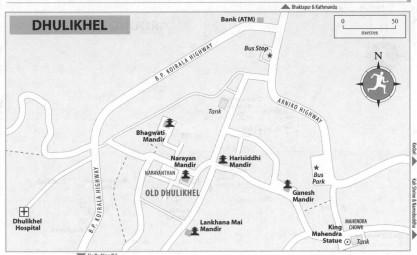

marked by a small **Kali shrine** and, unfortunately, a small military base and a microwave tower; a viewing platform, a couple of guesthouses and a café are close by. The peaks from Ganesh Himal to Everest are visible from here, and the view of Dhulikhel's old town is pretty wonderful, too.

On the way back down you can call in at a small, mossy Shiva temple complex, hidden down a flagstone path that angles off to the left just past the *Snow View Guest House*. The main temple, known as the **Gokureshwar Mahadev Mandir**, contains a large bronze *linga*.

ARRIVAL AND DEPARTURE   DHULIKHEL

By bus Services to Dhulikhel depart from Kathmandu's City Bus Park (every 5–10min; 1hr 10min–2hr) and equally regularly from Bhaktapur (1hr) or Banepa (10min).
By taxi A taxi from Kathmandu or Nagarkot costs around

Rs3000–4000.
By bike On a bike, it's best to come on one of the back ways: via Lubhu–Panauti, Bhaktapur–Nala or Nagarkot–Nala.

ACCOMMODATION AND EATING

Dhulikhel used to get more independent travellers, but nowadays most of its **accommodation** is outside the centre and geared towards tour groups. The more expensive places may offer substantial discounts to walk-in customers. Apart from the hotels and guesthouses, which all have decent if not particularly exciting **restaurants**, there are clusters of inexpensive restaurants serving Nepali food near the bus station and in the bazaar area.

Dhulikhel Lodge Resort Just off the highway ☎ 01 149 0114, ⓦ dhulikhellodgeresort.com; map p.182. The oldest resort in town, with attractive decor and tasteful rooms (all with views, though they're a bit overpriced, even with breakfast included). An organic plot provides ingredients for the restaurant and there's a bucolic garden. **US$127**
Dwarika's Resort Dhulikhel 1.5km east of Mahendra Chowk ☎ 01 149 0612, ⓦ dwarikashimalayanshangrila .com; map p.182. Sister of the exemplary *Dwarika's* in Kathmandu (see p.105), this luxury resort is spread across the hillside below the Kali shrine and seems hermetically sealed from the real world outside. It focuses on health and holistic treatments, and boasts sumptuous en suites with

high ceilings and huge windows, peaceful grounds, a pool, spa, three restaurants and a bar. **US$430**
★ **High View Resort** On a side road 600m off the highway ☎ 01 149 0048, ⓦ highviewresort.com; map p.182. Along a winding path and up a steep flight of steps, *High View* has neat, good-value en suites, with little private balconies, all with great views, even from the showers. The restaurant often hosts barbecues in the summer, and rates include breakfast. **US$80**
★ **Nawaranga Guest House** 300m east of Mahendra Chowk ☎ 01 149 0226, ⓔ nawaranga@hotmail.com; map p.182. The last of the town's budget guesthouses is just about clinging on, maintaining a chilled hippy vibe. Dilapidated and

3

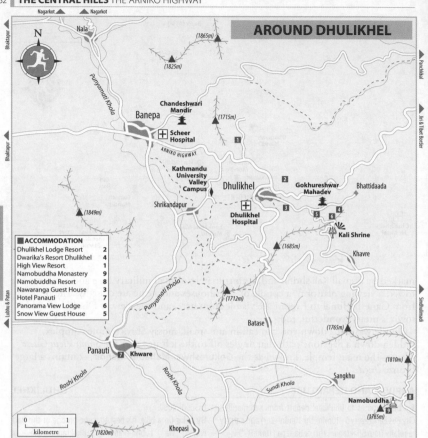

AROUND DHULIKHEL

ACCOMMODATION

Dhulikhel Lodge Resort	2
Dwarika's Resort Dhulikhel	4
High View Resort	1
Namobuddha Monastery	9
Namobuddha Resort	8
Nawaranga Guest House	3
Hotel Panauti	7
Panorama View Lodge	6
Snow View Guest House	5

ramshackle with threadbare but clean homely rooms with shared or private squat toilets, it also has a small art gallery, book exchange, and partial views from the roof. The owner Purna (and his family), have been running this place since 1972, and he has some stories to tell. **Rs500**

Panorama View Lodge Near the Kali temple ☎ 01 168 0786, ⓦ panoramaviewlodge.com.np; map above. Dynamite views, splendid isolation and simple rooms (somewhat overpriced, but you're paying for the best views

in town) with small private bathrooms. A taxi from town should cost around Rs500. **Rs1200**

Snow View Guest House 1km east of Mahendra Chowk ☎ 9841 482 487; map above. While it lacks the traveller buzz of *Nawaranga*, *Snow View* has slightly more comfortable – though still pretty basic – rooms, some en suite. The owner is extremely welcoming and there are decent views from some of the rooms at the front (Rs1000) and the roof terraces. **Rs500**

Namobuddha

Resting on a red-earth ledge near the top of a jungly ridge, **NAMOBUDDHA** (or **Namura**) is one of the three holiest Tibetan pilgrimage sites south of the Himalayas. Similar in spirit to Boudha, it is something of a Tibetan Buddhist boomtown (or boom-village at least), particularly during the February/March pilgrimage season.

The **stupa** celebrates the compassion of a young prince (in some versions, the previous incarnation of Buddha himself) who encountered a starving tigress about to devour a small child, and offered his own flesh instead – a sacrifice that ensured

THE NAMOBUDDHA CIRCUIT

Although the scenery isn't spectacular, the **Namobuddha circuit** is a pleasant day hike or a (much quicker) bike ride from Dhulikhel, with some interesting stop-offs en route. It's worth trying to combine Namobuddha with a sunrise walk to the Kali shrine (see p.181).

The route follows the road beyond the Kali shrine, passing through **Khavre** village, crossing the Sindhuli Highway after 2.5km, and contouring close to the crest of a ridge for another 7km (the first 4km paved) to an intersection at a small saddle. True off-the-beaten-path bike riding can be found down any of the tracks off to the left in this section, particularly the one at this last junction (see the HMG/FINNIDA map series for details). For **Namobuddha**, though, bear right, and after a further 2km you'll arrive in the village.

From Namobuddha, the road descends to **Sangkhu**, where a right fork leads to Batase and eventually back to Dhulikhel along various roads or trails. However, it's about the same distance (9km) to Panauti (see p.179), and this is a preferable alternative if you have the time to spend the night there. From Panauti you can return to Dhulikhel a number of different ways by foot, bike or bus.

3

his canonization as a *bodhisattva*. The Tibetan name of the stupa, **Takmo Lujin** (Tiger Body Gift), links it explicitly to the well-known legend; it's believed that half the prince's skeleton lies within it. According to one Tibetan scribe, the name Namobuddha ("Hail to the Buddha") came into popular usage in the seventeenth century, when the superstition took hold that the site's real name should not be uttered.

Among the homes and teahouses surrounding the stupa is a scruffy little Tamang *gompa*. Since the 1980s, however, the main Buddhist population at Namobuddha has been Tibetan. A steep path leads up to the **ridge** behind, which is festooned with *chaitya* and prayer flags; in a small shelter near the top is a famous stone relief sculpture of the prince feeding his flesh to the tigress. There's also a collection of Tibetan retreats and lesser stupas, as well as an atmospheric **monastery**.

ARRIVAL AND DEPARTURE
NAMOBUDDHA

By taxi A taxi to Namobuddha from Dhulikhel should cost around Rs1500–2000.

On foot or by bike The walk from Dhulikhel is just over

11km and takes a day; you can bike the route much quicker. See box above for details.

ACCOMMODATION

Namobuddha Monastery On the ridge behind the village ☎ 984 901 4446, ✉ TTy1@gmail.com. The most memorable accommodation in Namobuddha is a basic cell at the monastery. Don't expect great comfort, late nights or a lie-in. Full-board per person $\underline{Rs1000}$

Namobuddha Resort A 25min walk north of the Namobuddha stupa ☎ 01 691 2212, ⌨ namobuddha resort.com; map p.182. This peaceful place is

surrounded by an organic farm, and has cosy wooden cabins with great Himalayan views. You can hike, mountain bike, relax in the sauna or even use the yoga hall or flotation tank (which is supposed to aid meditation). There's a great bakery, and a restaurant which serves only vegetarian and organic food. The cheapest cabins have outside showers. $\underline{€50}$

The Arniko Highway: the route to Tibet

When travelling to the **border**, you should disabuse yourself of any visions of high, snowy passes into Tibet. The **crossing point** itself – the **Friendship Bridge** – sits at the bottom of a deep valley, with nary a yak in sight. Its low elevation isn't as extraordinary as it might seem, though: the main Himalayan chain, which the border generally follows, is breached in several places by rivers that are older than the mountains themselves. The border here was actually shifted further south after an ill-advised war with Tibet in 1792.

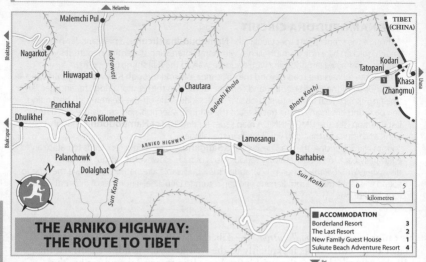

3

THE ARNIKO HIGHWAY:
THE ROUTE TO TIBET

■ **ACCOMMODATION**
Borderland Resort	3
The Last Resort	2
New Family Guest House	1
Sukute Beach Adventure Resort	4

Tour groups bound for **Tibet** follow the **Arniko Highway** to **Kodari**, the only official border crossing from Nepal, and some individual travellers make the trip up to the border just to see it. Rafting, canyoning and bungee-jumping parties also pass this way en route to trips on the Sun Koshi River, or to the adventure resorts on the Bhote Koshi River. Trekkers on their way to **Jiri**, the main trailhead for the Everest region, follow the Arniko Highway for most of its length before heading off on a spectacular side road.

Dhulikhel to Dolalghat
From Dhulikhel, the Arniko Highway descends 600m into the broad Panchkhal Valley, a lush, irrigated plain cultivated with rice paddy, sugar cane and tropical fruits. So-called **Zero Kilometre**, little more than a collection of snack stalls, just beyond the village of **Panchkhal**, is a minor gateway to the Helambu trekking region: a paved road, served by two daily local buses, heads north past **Hiuwapati** to the trailhead at Malemchi Pul. Meanwhile, a rough road to the south leads 9km to **PALANCHOWK**, home of the famous black-stone **Palanchowk Bhagwati**, which draws pilgrims seeking protection; three buses bounce down it daily.

The Arniko Highway reaches its lowest point 29km beyond Dhulikhel at **DOLALGHAT** (634m), a small market town clumped at either end of the bridge across the Indrawati River. This is the put-in point for many rafting trips on the Sun Koshi, which joins the Indrawati just around the corner. A paved side road forks left just beyond Dolalghat to reach **Chautara** (1400m), an obscure trailhead for Helambu treks, after 25km. A Bhimsen temple at a high point of the ridge 3km further up the road offers good views.

The Sun Koshi Valley
The scenery begins to change beyond Dolalghat, as the highway bends northeastwards up the deep, terraced **Sun Koshi Valley**. Nepal's terraces, while marvellous feats of engineering, are a sign of agricultural desperation: with so little flat land available and a growing number to feed, hill people have no choice but to farm ever steeper and less productive slopes.

Having built the Arniko Highway, China has poured much of its aid to Nepal into infrastructure projects along the route. The first of these to come into view is a hydroelectric diversion, whose spillway and powerhouse are located just beyond the

turning for Jiri at Khadichaur. Human impact on the valley is much in evidence for the next couple of kilometres to **Lamosangu** (740m), which is distinguished by a defunct magnesite processing plant.

The Bhote Koshi

A few kilometres upstream of **Lamosangu**, the highway proceeds up the larger of two tributaries, the **Bhote Koshi**, or Tibet River, passing after 8km **Barhabise** – the last town of any size before the border. Taking advantage of both the highway and the river is a series of safari-style **adventure resorts** (see box below), offering rafting and a host of other activities.

Tatopani

After passing a series of hydroelectric plants, the road approaches **TATOPANI** (1530m), which until the mid-1980s enjoyed a small following among Westerners, who came to gaze into forbidden Tibet and soak in the village's **hot springs** (daily 5am–8pm; Rs20) at the northern end of the village (*taato paani* means "hot water"): the red water splashes out of pipes into a concrete pool and is used strictly for washing. Now Tibet is open again, Tatopani has fallen out of fashion. The village stretches along the highway

---

ADVENTURE RESORTS ON THE BHOTE KOSHI

The raging Bhote Koshi's reputation as one of the most extreme **rafting** rivers in Nepal, and the fact that there's actually only about a day's worth of rafting to be done, attracts a young, thrill-seeking crowd. The big rafting operators have been quick to develop the trend and, as well as the classic rafting trip, now offer **mountain biking, trekking, bungee jumping** and **canyoning** expeditions.

Three major companies base their operations in attractive tented **resort camps** that – even if you're not intent on throwing yourself downriver on a raft, or off a 162m-high suspension bridge attached to an elastic rope – make excellent bases for exploring the valley or just chilling out. Camps come with luxuriant gardens, flush toilets, showers, hammocks, restaurants and bar areas. They also regularly host **adventure events** such as mountain-bike races and the Nepal International Kayak Rodeo (held annually in Nov). Many overseas rafting and kayak groups now go straight from the Kathmandu airport to one of these riverside resorts.

Prices usually come as part of packages including activities, transport and meals. Expect to pay around US$50–60 per person for an overnight stay with full board (but no activities), US$50 for a day's rafting and US$60–70 for a one-day canyoning trip.

Borderland Resort At the bottom of the gorge 9km north of Barhabise ☎01 470 1295, ⓦ borderlandresorts.com; map p.184. Ultimate Descents' well-established resort is a sedate, relaxing place with three classes of thatched tents, a pool and nice gardens. Offers canyoning, rafting, kayaking, trekking and mountain biking. Rate per person per night from US$55

★ **The Last Resort** ☎01 470 0525, ⓦ thelastresort .com.np; map p.184. Furthest north of the Bhote Koshi adventure resorts, Ultimate Rivers' Last Resort has the most spectacular location, accessed by a footbridge suspended 160m above the gorge. The bridge also serves as the launching point for their bungee jump, one of the world's highest (€82 including transport and lunch, €70 for guests staying at the resort, €105 package including accommodation and a jump). If the bungee doesn't sate your appetite, you

can always try the canyon swing (same price as bungee). This is the funkiest of the three resorts, with the smartest tents, beautifully landscaped grounds, sauna, plunge pool (free) and massage (€22/hr) options, plus a sociable bar. Rate per person per night full board from €47

Sukute Beach Adventure Resort ☎01 435 6644, ⓦ equatorexpeditionsnepal.com; map p.184. Equator Expeditions' Bhote Koshi resort specializes in canoeing, rafting and kayaking, and is one of the closest to Kathmandu, sitting alongside a wide, relatively gentle stretch of the Sun Koshi between Dolalghat and the Balephi bridge. They provide a mix of safari tents and rooms overlooking a sandy stretch of the riverbank, and there's an attractive swimming pool and restaurant. It's much more of a party scene than the other upmarket resorts. Rate per person per night full board from US$50

> ## TAMANGS
> **Tamangs**, Nepal's largest ethnic group, make up around twenty percent of the population and dominate the Central Hills between elevations of around 1500m and 2500m. With their origins in Tibet (Tamang means "horse trader" in Tibetan), the group follow a form of Buddhism virtually indistinguishable from Lamaism, though most also worship clan deities, employ shamans and observe major Hindu festivals. Despite their numbers, they remain one of Nepal's most **exploited** groups, a situation dating back to the Gorkhali conquest in the late eighteenth century. Much of their land was appropriated, leaving them as tenant farmers, bonded labourers or woodcutters, or stuck in menial jobs. The Tamangs today remain an underclass, locked into low wage or exploitative jobs, or simply locked up (surveys suggest a disproportionate number are in prison).

for almost a kilometre. Tamangs (see box above) are in the majority at this altitude, and they maintain a modest **gompa** a five-minute walk above the southern bazaar. Just before Tatopani is a police checkpost, and from here up, the Bhote Koshi forms the **border** – Tibet is just across the river.

Kodari and the Tibetan border
Around 3km from Tatopani is the bustling, fly-bitten village of **KODARI** (1640m), the lowest point along the Nepal–Tibet border, and long used by traders travelling between Kathmandu and Lhasa. You pass a scruffy agglomeration of shops and lodges before coming to the border and its associated checkpoints. If you have time to kill, a twenty-minute walk up the stone steps by the Nepali customs checkpoint will bring you to **Liping Gompa**, a small Buddhist (and generally deserted) monastery, from where there is a great view down the valley.

The Tibetan border itself is marked by the so-called **Friendship Bridge**, which spans the Bhote Koshi at the top end of town. Up at the head of the valley, 600m higher than Kodari, the Chinese buildings of **Khasa** (or **Zhangmu**) cling to the side of a mountain – that's the extent of the view of Tibet from here. Be very careful about **taking photos** of Tibet: Chinese border guards (often in plain clothes) are very sensitive and have snatched and broken cameras in the past.

ARRIVAL AND GETTING AROUND
THE ROUTE TO TIBET

By bus The best way to travel along the Arniko Highway to Kodari is on one of the six daily private express services from Kathmandu (bookable through travel agents). Alternatively, public buses run regularly between Kathmandu's Old Bus Park and Kodari (hourly until around 5pm), though travel times are up to double those of the private express bus times listed below; note that you may have to change at Barhabise for Kodari. All buses travel via Banepa (1hr 15min), Dhulikhel (1hr 30min), Dolalghat (2hr), Khadichaur (2hr 30min), Barhabise (3hr) and Kodari (4hr). All timings are approximate and dependent on road and weather conditions and stops. All buses leave Kathmandu and Kodari before 5pm.
By taxi A taxi between Kathmandu and Kodari costs around Rs4000–5000, though you'll have to bargain hard.

By bike The route from Kathmandu to Kodari is great by mountain bike; ask at one of the Thamel operators (see p.99) for details.

TO TIBET
You can't officially enter Tibet (China) from Nepal without a Tibetan visa, and you must also be part of an official organized tour. Rules are strictly enforced: you have no chance of getting in without the correct paperwork (see p.96). If you're entering Nepal from Tibet, it's best to set off early from Khasa if you plan to make Kathmandu. Visas are easily available at Nepali immigration, but watch out for overcharging. Tibet is two hours and fifteen minutes ahead of Nepal.

ACCOMMODATION AND EATING
Although you're unlikely to be stuck in **Kodari**, there are a couple of bare-bones places to stay, as well as a number of snack bars with dubious levels of hygiene. **Tatopani**, 3km down the road, is a better bet, as accommodation is around half the price.

New Family Guest House Tatopani ☎ 01 169 0245. Although a little overpriced, this lodge is clean and friendly – balconies and even the toilets boast good river views. It also has a reasonable restaurant serving the usual mix of Nepali, Tibetan and Chinese food. Rs1000

The Trisuli road

The **Trisuli road** was constructed in the mid-1960s as part of a hydroelectric project on the Trisuli River, northwest of Kathmandu. That's the official story, anyway: the road probably owes its existence at least partly to historical nostalgia, as it retraces the triumphal approach of Prithvi Narayan Shah, Nepal's founding father, from his fortress of Nuwakot to the Kathmandu Valley. The majority of travellers passing this way are only concerned about getting to Dhunche and Syabrubesi for the Langtang and Gosainkund treks (see p.334), but **Nuwakot** and **Kakani** are both well worth visiting. **Trisuli Bazaar** flourished for a time as the trailhead for Langtang treks, but nowadays most trekkers just pass through en route to Dhunche and Syabrubesi, and there is little to see, although there is an ATM and plenty of mid-range accommodation if you're stuck.

Kakani

KAKANI, Kathmandu's closest mountain viewpoint, straddles the valley's northwestern rim. It's less developed than Nagarkot, Dhulikhel or Daman, and the views are somewhat inferior, but it's very peaceful. There's not much here apart from a very eclectic mix of low-key sights: the former British Resident's bungalow (it's the yellow building next door to the *Tara Gaon* resort); a UN peacekeeper training college; the Scientology-run Narcanon centre; and, occupying a high point further to the east, the **Kakani Memorial Park**, which honours those who died in a 1992 Thai airliner crash north of here. The western end of the forested **Shivapuri National Park** (see p.139) lies near Kakani, and a pleasant **day walk** through the forest can be organized through the *View Himalaya* (see below); the park entrance fee and a guide costs Rs1500 per person.

ARRIVAL AND DEPARTURE   KAKANI

By bus Buses from Kathmandu to Trisuli Bazaar drop you off at a gap in the valley rim, 24km from the capital (every 30min; 1hr–1hr 30min), from where it's a 4km walk up a paved side road to Kakani; local minibuses also ply this route, and both leave from Machha Pokhari Bus Station (aka Bypass Bus Station), just west of Kathmandu's Gongabu Bus Park.

ACCOMMODATION AND EATING

In addition to the hotels reviewed below, the rather more expensive *Tara Gaon* resort also has a reasonable **restaurant**. Fresh trout and strawberries are among the area's specialities.

Hotel Prince Almost at the end of the main road ☎ 984 159 9751. The only budget lodging in the village, with small rooms that offer no views but are clean and comfortable enough. Also has an attached restaurant with the cheapest food in town. En suite will cost you Rs200 more. Rs800

View Himalaya Almost at the end of the main road ☎ 01 691 5706. A good choice, with comfortable, clean rooms and the best views in the village. The small, cheapest rooms are in an annex and lack views; if you want to see the mountains you'll have to splash out on one of the pricier, much nicer, rooms (Rs2500/3500). Staff are friendly and can organize hiking in the Shivapuri National Park (see p.139), and there's also an economical restaurant. Rs1500

Nuwakot

Despite having one of Nepal's proudest historical monuments, the tiny village of **NUWAKOT** remains relatively untouristed, which is odd considering that it has some decent Himalayan views to boot. Prithvi Narayan Shah's abandoned **fortress** looms like a forgotten shipwreck on a ridge above Trisuli, casting a poignant, almost romantic spell over the settlement. It was from this command centre that the unifier of Nepal directed his dogged campaign on the Kathmandu Valley from 1744 to 1769. In his determination to conquer the valley, Prithvi Narayan had three other towers built in the name of the three valley capitals, perhaps hoping to bring about their downfall by a kind of voodoo; the Kathmandu and Patan towers share the main compound, while the crumbling Bhaktapur tower stands on a rise just outside.

The fortress
On the right as you head up from Nuwakot main square • Museum Nov 2–Jan 29 Tues–Sat 10.30am–3pm, Sun 10.30am–2pm; Jan 30–Nov 1 10.30am–4pm, Sun 10.30am–3pm • Rs150

Nuwakot's **fortress** consists of three brick towers rising like Monopoly hotels in and around a walled compound; much of the surrounding area is now occupied by the army. The tallest tower has been turned into a **museum**, and although it contains few exhibits the views from the top-floor windows are stupendous, looking out on Ganesh Himal and the pastoral Trisuli and Tadi valleys.

The Bhairabi Mandir
Nuwakot's old main street runs south from the fortress along the spine of the ridge and suddenly comes to a dead end, the land falling away to reveal a lovely panorama of the Tadi and Trisuli valleys. Several ornate old brick-and-wood buildings remain here, including the **Bhairabi Mandir**. During the Bhairabi **festival** here, in March–April, the priest, under the influence of divine powers, drinks the blood of an entire buffalo straight from its severed neck. He immediately vomits it back up; not so many years ago it was the custom for worshippers to drink the vomited blood as a sacrament.

ARRIVAL AND DEPARTURE   NUWAKOT

By bus Three daily morning buses (2hr 20min) travel between Machha Pokhari Bus Station (aka Bypass Bus Station), just west of Kathmandu's Gongabu Bus Park, and Nuwakot. Alternatively, take a bus from the same bus station to Trisuli Bazaar (every 30min; 2hr), from where you can walk up to Nuwakot in around an hour, or charter a minivan for RS1000.

ACCOMMODATION

★ **The Famous Farm** Left above the main square and about 500m ☎ 01 470 0426, ⊛ himalayanencounters .com. This tranquil Himalayan Encounters-run guesthouse is surrounded by bucolic grounds and has superb vistas. Atmospheric accommodation is provided in restored 100-year-old farmhouse buildings. The guesthouse also supports a nearby school for children with speech and hearing difficulties. Rates include full board. US$120

Sunset Lodge Left above the main square and about 150m ☎ 984 154 8932. First of a new wave of budget accommodations in Nuwakot, this place has basic rooms with clean outside bathrooms. The owner is a teacher in the nearby school for children with speech and hearing difficulties, and also runs a restaurant in town which serves good *momos* and *daal bhaat*. There's a homestay next door too. Rs500

Tribhuwan Rajpath: Kathmandu to Hetauda

Nepal's most magnificent and hair-raising highway, the **Tribhuwan Rajpath** (usually just called the Rajpath, meaning "King's Way") heads west out of the Kathmandu Valley and then hurls itself, through an astounding series of switchbacks, straight over the Mahabharat Lek to the Terai. En route it passes through lush stands of rhododendrons (which bloom in April), and takes in superb views of the Himalayas, especially from **Daman**.

Built by Indian engineers in the mid-1950s, the Rajpath was the first highway to link Kathmandu to the outside world. At the time, India was on the brink of war with China and preferred to make any route through Nepal as inconvenient as possible to

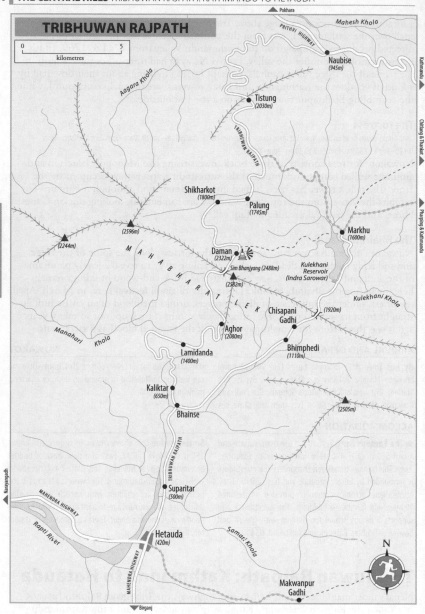

TRIBHUWAN RAJPATH

reduce the risk of invasion. Since the faster Mugling/Narayangadh route was completed, the road has become something of a backwater, which makes it perfect for **mountain biking** (see p.368) or motorcycling.

For its first 26km, the Rajpath follows the Prithvi Highway towards Pokhara, leaving the Kathmandu Valley through its ugliest, most industrial corridor. At **Naubise** (945m) the Rajpath leaves the Prithvi Highway and begins its relentless 30km climb to Tistung

(2030m), before descending 9km to **Palung** (1745m). **Daman** is another 12km on, beyond which the Rajpath crosses the **Sim Bhanjyang pass** (2488m) where it begins a 2000m descent through jungle, forest and finally terraced farmland to the **Bhainse**. **Hetauda** (see p.284) is 10km further on.

GETTING AROUND	TRIBHUWAN RAJPATH: KATHMANDU TO HETAUDA
By bus The Rajpath is poorly served by public transport, with infrequent buses travelling in the morning between Kathmandu and Hetauda (4–6 daily; around 6hr). There are	also two daily minibuses (around 4hr) that run each way between Kathmandu and Hetauda, which also both depart in the morning.

Daman

DAMAN (2322m) is the most comprehensive of the Himalayan viewpoints surrounding Kathmandu. Sitting below the Rajpath's highest point, the hamlet overlooks the peaceful Palung Valley towards a magnificent spread of peaks. However, the mountains will probably be in clouds when you arrive: an overnight stay is obligatory to see them in their best morning light.

The viewing tower
No fixed opening hours • Rs50

The focal point of the village is an enclosed **viewing tower** that looks as if it might have been built for air-traffic control. Operated by the *Daman Mountain Resort*, the tower offers views of seven 8000m peaks, along with the closer 7000m peaks of Himalchuli, Ganesh Himal and Langtang. A couple of high-powered **telescopes** give awesome close-ups: the magnified view of Everest (otherwise just a smudge on the horizon, and generally only visible in the winter) is almost identical to the one you get from Kala Pattar, ten days into the Everest trek. An even more sweeping vista can be had from the *Everest Panorama Resort*, a thirty-minute walk up the Rajpath passing a small Buddhist **gompa**; treating yourself to an early breakfast on the resort's terrace is money well spent.

ARRIVAL AND DEPARTURE	DAMAN
By bus A handful of morning buses (4 daily; 4hr) travel direct between Kalanki, on Kathmandu's outskirts, and Daman. More frequent buses to and from Hetauda (6 daily;	last bus 2pm; 1hr 30min–2hr) pass through, though you'll struggle to get a seat.

ACCOMMODATION AND EATING

Hotel Daman & Lodge Daman ☎ 984 507 0549. One of a handful of family-run, shoestring places on the north side of the village, *Hotel Daman & Lodge* provides no frills (and no English sign; it's opposite the *Everest Lodge*) but has a chilled vibe and clean-enough rooms – though they can get pretty chilly. Food-wise, there's plenty of *daal bhaat* on offer, but little else. **Rs700**

Daman Mountain Resort Daman ☎ 01 443 8023. This aged hotel is well overdue a spruce up, but has friendly staff and is a reasonable choice, offering a mixture of cottages and rooms, the latter rather tired, the cheapest have no windows, so a room with a view here will cost you Rs1500. **Rs700**

Everest Panorama Resort 2.5km south above Daman ☎ 05 762 1480, ⊚ everestpanoramaresort.net. The top hotel in town, with comfortable (and heated) en suites and cute "honeymoon cottages", plus a good, though expensive, restaurant. The steam bath can warm you up if it's cold and the price includes breakfast. **US$126**

The Western Hills

TANSEN

The Western Hills

The Western Hills are Nepal at its most quintessentially, outstandingly Nepalese. There are roaring gorges, precariously perched villages and terraced fields reaching to improbable heights, and some of the most graceful and accessible peaks of the Himalayas for a backdrop. Yet in this, Nepal's most populous hill region, people are the dominant feature. Magars and Gurungs, the most visible ethnic groups, live in their own villages or side by side with Tamangs, caste Hindus, Newari merchants and Tibetans. Life is traditional and close to the land, but relatively prosperous: houses are tidy and spacious, and hill women are festooned with the family gold.

The chief destination of the Western Hills is the laidback lakeside resort of **Pokhara**, a hub for trekking – the Annapurna range lies immediately to the north – paragliding, yoga and almost everything else. Many visitors are understandably intent on heading straight for Pokhara, but it's well worth sidestepping from the road to visit a trio of hilltop sights: the historic fortress of **Gorkha**, the pilgrimage site of **Manakamana** and the lofty old bazaar of **Bandipur**. Continuing on to Pokhara from all of these by public bus along the **Prithvi Highway** is an experience in itself, and easily bearable given the short distances involved. Beyond Pokhara, on the magnificent **Siddhartha Highway** to the Indian border, the charming town of **Tansen** lies at the southern edge of the hills.

Along the Prithvi Highway to Pokhara

The **Prithvi Highway** – the road from Kathmandu to Pokhara – offers many visitors to Nepal their first vision of the middle hills. It remains a fabulous vision, even if it is through a bus window clouded by the grit-laden exhaust smoke of the overloaded lorry in front. Once you've struggled out of the Kathmandu Valley through the notch in the rim at **Thankot**, the first shock is the epic scale and steepness of the hills beyond. The second is the evident danger of the road, which for its first half is also the main trunk route between Kathmandu and India.

From Thankot, the long, switchbacking descent to **Naubise** – where the Tribhuwan Rajpath breaks off – continues down to the **Trisuli River** at **Baireni**, one of several put-in points along this popular rafting river. From here, the road mostly follows the valley bottoms: keep an eye out for spidery suspension bridges, precarious ropeways, and funeral pyres on the sandy banks. You can't miss the scores of lorries parked in the riverbed; they're used for collecting stones, which are broken up by hand by families of workers attracted by

Highlights

❶ **Manakamana** Swoop up to this lofty, wish-fulfilling temple via Nepal's only cable-car system. **See p.197**

❷ **Gorkha** Soak up the views – and the history – at Gorkha's gorgeously carved temple-palace, perched high on a ridge above the town. See p.198

❸ **Bandipur** A charming Newari hamlet, with beautiful architecture and breathtaking views of the Himalayas. **See p.202**

❹ **Pokhara** Relax by the serene lake and trawl the bazaar of Lakeside in this tourist hub. See p.206

❺ **Paragliding** Soar like a bird from Sarangkot, a world-famous spot for paragliding. **See p.216**

❻ **Sarangkot to Naudaada** Get a taste for trekking, and a classic panorama of the Annapurna range, on this easy ridgetop amble. See p.226

❼ **Tansen** The stunning but little-used back road out of Pokhara leads past this thriving bazaar town. **See p.231**

❽ **Rani Ghat** A glorious day hike from Tansen leads to this romantically crumbling palace at the bottom of the Kali Gandaki gorge. See p.235

HIGHLIGHTS ARE MARKED ON THE MAP ON P.196

The Western Hills – specifically Gorkha district – was the epicentre of the massive **earthquake** of April 25, 2015 (see box, p.6), which struck as this book went to press. There was an appalling loss of life in the region, and many remote areas were cut off for several days. Some seventy percent of the homes in Gorkha district were destroyed and many villages were wiped off the map. The Manakamana Devi temple, the Gorkha Durbar and Tansen's Rani Durbar were among the historic sites that suffered serious damage, though the full extent of the impact was unclear at the time of writing.

the chance of earning a couple of dollars a day. There are rice terraces and sugar-cane plantations to gaze at, perhaps complete with local farmers ploughing or harvesting by hand. The scraps of forest are mostly heavily pruned for fodder or firewood, though you can spot the odd, stately *simal*, the symmetrically branching silk-cotton or kapok tree, which produces red flowers in early March and pods of cotton-like seeds in May.

Most tourist buses make a mid-morning pit stop for *daal bhaat* at resorts en route; Greenlines Tours halts at **River Side Springs Resort** (see p.198), which is easily the most attractive accommodation along the road. Public buses break for lunch at **Mugling**, a ghastly crossroads at the junction of the Trisuli and Marsyangdi rivers that exists mainly to provide *daal bhaat* and prostitutes to long-distance drivers.

Traffic bound for the Terai turns south here for the gradual 34km descent to Narayangadh, while the Prithvi Highway crosses the Trisuli and heads upstream along the **Marsyangdi**, passing the massive **Marsyangdi Hydroelectric Project** powerhouse. The spur road to **Gorkha** (see p.198) leaves the highway at **Abu Khaireni**, 7km west of Mugling, while **Dumre**, 11km beyond, is the turning for two side roads: one north to Lamjung's **Besisahar**, the starting point of the Annapurna Circuit, and one south to **Bandipur** (see p.202). **Damauli**, 8km west of Dumre, is marked out by its position overlooking the confluence of the Madi and Seti rivers. In reverence of this union, there is a complex of shrines set back from the road, and to the left of them is **Byas Gupha**, a cave where Byas (or Vyasa), the sage of the Mahabharat, is supposed to have been born and lived.

After crossing the Madi, the Prithvi Highway rises and then descends gradually to rejoin the broad Seti Valley, finally reaching Pokhara's ever-spreading conurbation. **Lakes Begnas and Rupa** are off to the right of the highway on the approach to Pokhara (see p.229).

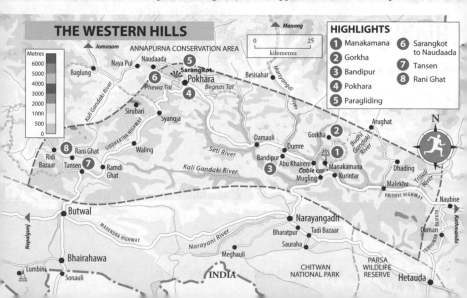

Manakamana

Just about every Nepali has either been to **MANAKAMANA** or hopes one day to go.
Located on a prominent ridge high above the confluence of the Trisuli and Marsyangdi
rivers, the village is home to Nepal's famous wish-granting **temple**. Each year more
than half a million people make the journey, the wealthier of them speeding up the
hillside to Manakamana with a bird's-eye view from the swish **cable car**. Sadhus, poorer
pilgrims and the odd, more contemplative tourist still toil up the walking route on the
other side of the hill, starting from Abu Khaireni. If you're here in the November and
December season, be sure to buy the famous local oranges. Their green skins are not a
sign of unripeness, but entirely natural in the subtropics: oranges need almost frosty
temperatures to acquire the colour that northerners are used to.

The cable car

Daily: March–Sept 9am–noon & 1.30–5pm; Oct–Feb 8am–noon & 1.30–5pm • US$20 return • ☏ 064 460 044 , ⊛ chitawoncoe.com.np
/manakamana/html/cablecar.html

Completed in 1998, at a cost of US$7.5 million, the Manakamana **cable car** remains
the only one in Nepal – a statement of intent from the country that still longs to be the
Switzerland of Asia. It survives on the patronage of middle-class Nepali tourists and
Indian pilgrims. Saturdays are the liveliest days, for religious reasons, so be prepared for
long queues. The gondolas are international-ski-resort standard, and whisk you up the
2.8km line in just ten minutes – thrilling, but barely long enough to enjoy the views.
Regular maintenance checks mean it's worth confirming that the cable car is running
in advance: closures are well advertised in the press, and most guesthouses will be aware
of the latest situation.

Manakamana Devi temple

From the cable-car station, a path leads between stalls of Hindu souvenirs, toys and
snacks up to the famous **Manakamana Devi temple**, set in a square and overlooked by
a huge sacred champ tree, a kind of magnolia whose flowers are intensely perfumed.
Tradition has it that the goddess Bhagwati rewards those who make the pilgrimage to
her shrine by granting their wishes; she's especially popular with Newari newlyweds,
who pray for sons. The evening *aarti* ritual (around 6pm) is particularly lovely, as
priests pass a plate of candles and flowers around the assembled pilgrims, for
blessing, as bells ring and devotees chant hymns. But the temple really goes into
overdrive on **Saturday mornings**, when the vast majority of pilgrims come to perform
animal sacrifices; locals raise goats, chickens and pigeons specifically for this. The
festivals of **Dasain** (Sept–Oct) and **Nag Panchami** (July–Aug) bring even greater
numbers of celebrants.

MANAKAMANA MOUNTAIN VIEWS

In addition to its temple, Manakamana is also famous for its **mountain views**: from various
high points around the village you can see a limited panorama from Annapurna II and
Lamjung Himal across to Peak 29 and Baudha of the Manaslu Himal. The nearest **viewpoint** is
the new bus park, a fifteen-minute walk up from the temple. If you're game for more, you can
continue 45 minutes further up the ridge to another temple, the **Bakeshwar Mahadev
Mandir**, and then another fifteen minutes to **Lakhan Thapa Gupha**, a holy cave near the
highest point, from where the views are tremendous on clear mornings. The cave is named
after the founder of the Manakamana temple, a seventeenth-century royal priest whose
descendant is still the chief temple *pujari* today.

4

ARRIVAL AND DEPARTURE

By cable car Tourist buses between Kathmandu and Pokhara (or indeed any bus plying the Prithvi Highway) will drop you at the turning for the cable-car base station, marked by a big brick archway just off the highway, halfway between Kurintar and Mugling. It's a 3hr journey from either Kathmandu or Pokhara.

By bus For those not taking the cable car, local buses to Manakamana depart from Abu Khaireni, a busy junction town on the Prithvi Highway at its junction with the road to Gorkha, beside the Marsyangdi Khola. The steep, scenic but painfully slow stop-start journey takes up to 2hr, turning off the Gorkha road after 7km at the village of Syauli, where the 14.5km climb to Manakamana begins; buses stop beside the road, 15min walk below the main temple. To move on from Manakamana, board any local bus plying the Prithvi

MANAKAMANA

Highway at the cable-car base station or Abu Khaireni – it's only three bearable hours to either Kathmandu or Pokhara.

By jeep You can get a ride in a shared jeep from either the foot of the cable-car station or from Abu Khaireni (see p.197). It costs around Rs500–600 per person one-way from the base station, and takes less than an hour.

On foot Walking up to Manakamana takes about three hours from Abu Khaireni, which is the most popular of the pilgrim routes. The broad trail starts beside the Dharaundi Khola, an obvious stream, and is more steady than steep – though it is a fairly relentless 1000m. To walk to Gorkha from Manakamana, there's a more ambitious hike (4hr) along the old porters' path that bends north along the ridge from the Bakeshwar Mahadev Mandir; it can be hard to follow, so consider taking a guide (ask at your guesthouse).

ACCOMMODATION

Dozens of **lodges** vie for pilgrims' business, which means you're unlikely to have any trouble finding a room, except on Friday or Saturday nights, when prices can almost double. There's nothing much oriented towards Western tourists.

River Side Springs Resort Kurintar, 3km east of Manakamana cable-car base station ☎ 056 540 129, ⓦ rsr.com.np. Appealing resort with its own, palatial, spring-fed swimming pool (closed Wed), pleasant thatched cabins and row of tents right beside the Trisuli River. Decent restaurant too. Tents US$43, cabins US$$74

Sunrise Home Manakamana Hill Station-3, Gorkha

☎ 064 460 055, ✉ hotelsunrisehome@gmail.com. In a good location 300m up from the cable-car station and just 100m below the temple, this is one of the better hotels in the village. Rooms are spacious, with clean quilts and sheets, smart (if garish) paintwork and TVs – though not all have Western-style attached toilets. The rate quoted here is for Fri/Sat; prices drop at other times. Rs1500

EATING AND DRINKING

Both the hotels listed above do good *daal bhaat* and Indian foods, and the village is dotted with inexpensive Nepali **bhojanalayas**, and Marwadi restaurants specializing in Indian vegetarian food.

Manakamana Café Manakamana cable-car base station, near Kurintar ☎ 064 460 044. This is the big, official cable-car restaurant, with traditionally styled architecture and a cafeteria ambience. It offers the biggest range of food hereabouts (mains around Rs150–400), from chow mein to burgers, and of course *daal bhaat*. Whether you're desperate for a steak sizzler or a *masala dosa*, you'll

find it here. Daily 8am–7/8pm.

Monsoon Restaurant 150m below the temple. Little thatched cabins set among flower gardens in an orange orchard make this a lovely place to lunch. It offers mostly snack foods like chips, soups, *momos* and pakoras, but you can also find a good egg biryani, fried rice and a generous chicken *daal bhaat* (dishes Rs90–300). Daily 8am–8pm or later.

Gorkha

Despite its status as the cradle of the nation, **GORKHA** remains strangely untouristed, even though the 24km paved road up from Abu Khaireni makes it a relatively painless half-day's ride from Pokhara, Kathmandu or Chitwan, and even quicker from Bandipur. Conscious of its tourist potential, the government has spruced up Gorkha's main monuments, but the lower town remains a fairly ordinary roadhead bazaar.

As the ancestral home of the Nepali royal family, Gorkha occupies a central place in Nepali history. Hunched on the hilltop above the bazaar is its link with that splendid past, the **Gorkha Durbar**, an architectural tour de force worthy of the flamboyant Gorkha kings and the dynasty they founded. Unless you're setting straight off on a trek or just finishing one, you'll have to spend the night here. The Durbar and its agreeable

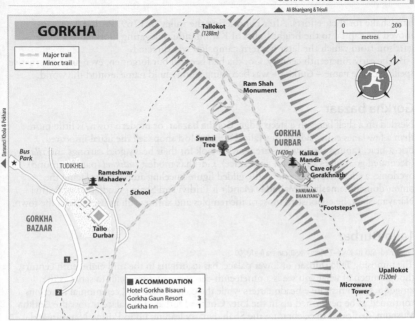

surroundings can easily soak up a day, and hikes around the area could keep you busy for another couple.

Brief history

In a sense, Gorkha's history is not its own. A petty hill state in medieval times, it was occupied and transformed into a Himalayan Sparta by outsiders who used it as a base for a dogged campaign against Kathmandu and then, having won their prize, restored Gorkha to obscurity. Yet during those two centuries of occupation, it raised the nation's most famous son, **Prithvi Narayan Shah**, and somehow bred in him the audacity to conquer all of Nepal.

Prithvi Narayan's ancestors came to Gorkha in the mid-sixteenth century, having been driven into the hills from their native Rajasthan by Muslim invaders, and soon gained a reputation as a single-mindedly martial lot. His father launched the first unsuccessful raid on the Kathmandu Valley in the early eighteenth century, and when Prithvi Narayan himself ascended to the throne in 1743, at the age of twenty, he already had his father's obsession fixed in his mind. Within a year, he was leading Gorkha in a war of expansion that was eventually to unify all of present-day Nepal, plus parts of India and Tibet. Looking at the meagre terraces of Gorkha today, you can imagine what a drain it must have been to keep a standing army fed and supplied for 27 years of continuous campaigning. The hardy peasants of Gorkha got little more than a

---

WHY PRITHVI NARAYAN DIDN'T CONQUER THE WORLD

As a young man, **Prithvi Narayan Shah** is said to have prayed to the guru for success, and was answered in a dream by an old man (some say he came in person, and at this spot) who offered the young prince a bowl of curd. Haughtily, Prithvi Narayan let it fall to his feet (though some say he spilled it by accident), whereupon Gorakhnath revealed himself, saying that the future king would conquer everywhere he set his foot. If he had accepted and eaten the curd, the guru admonished, he would have conquered the world.

handshake for their efforts. After conquering the valley in 1769, Prithvi Narayan moved his capital to the bright lights of Kathmandu, relegating Gorkha to a mere garrison from which the later western campaign was directed.

By the early nineteenth century, Gorkha had been all but forgotten, even as an alternative spelling of the name – **Gurkha** – was becoming a household name around the world.

Gorkha bazaar

Nestled on a shelf beneath a steep ridge, **Gorkha bazaar**, or modern town, is little more than a few lanes either side of the Tallo Durbar. Most shops sell the usual imported bric-a-brac, though the jewellers are worth a look for their heavy gold earrings and *tilari* (decorated gold tubes strung on a necklace). Gorkha's modest *tudikhel* (parade ground) overlooks a small temple precinct: the gilded figure kneeling atop a pillar facing the onion-domed **Rameshwar Mahadev Mandir** is Prithvi Pati Shah; grandfather of Prithvi Narayan Shah, he established most of the temples and shrines still in use around the town.

Tallo Durbar

Mon & Wed–Sun 10.30am–2.30pm • Rs50, camera fee Rs200

The imposing **Tallo Durbar**, or lower palace, has its origins in the mid-eighteenth century, though much of what you see is a nineteenth-century structure, built to serve as the kingdom's administrative headquarters while the court's ritual and ceremonial functions continued to be performed up in the lofty Gorkha Durbar. The palace is now the **Gorkha Museum**, dedicated to celebrating the Shah dynasty leading up to Prithvi Narayan and beyond. There are paintings of historical scenes, musical instruments, old coins, weights and measures, and weapons – including a large eighteenth-century cannon by the entrance – but the chief draw is simply wandering about the palace, and its landscaped gardens.

The Gorkha Durbar

Daily: Feb–Oct 6am–6pm; Nov–Jan 7am–5pm • Rs50, camera fee Rs200

It's a half-hour-plus 300m slog up a stone stairway to the **Gorkha Durbar** from Pokharithok, the junction just east of Tallo Durbar. With a 4WD vehicle, it is possible to drive most of the way up, circling round via the western side, but the walk is half the pleasure – and provides a properly testing approach. After a landmark *swami* (weeping fig) tree, the path forks: the most direct route ascends steeply through the old, pleasantly rural village, where there are opportunities to buy cold drinks and cups of tea; the longer, gentler left fork leads towards the ridgetop a short distance to the west of the palace.

The twin buildings of the palace sit atop the steepest, highest point of the ridge, buttressed by serried ranks of stone walls, and approached by a royal staircase worthy of any prince. It must have cowed visiting vassals into submission – a neat trick for a tin-pot realm that could barely muster 150 soldiers at the time of Prithvi Narayan's first campaign. Entrance to the Durbar is through a doorway towards the western side, reached by a path to the left of the retaining wall. No leather is allowed in the compound.

The Kalika Mandir

Conceived as a dwelling for kings and gods, the fortress remains a religious place, and first stop in any visit is the revered **Kalika Mandir**, occupying the left (western) half of the Durbar building. Its interior is closed to all but priests – who say that any others would die upon beholding Kali's terrible image. Sacrifices are made in the alcove in front of the entrance daily except on *ekadasi* (which falls every fourteen days, following the lunar calendar). After the observance of *astami* (again, twice monthly on the lunar month), which is celebrated with special gusto in Gorkha, the paving stones are sticky with blood. Most worshippers arrive cradling a trembling goat or chicken and leave swinging a headless carcass. Chait Dasain, Gorkha's biggest annual **festival**, brings processions and more blood-letting in late March or early April, as does the tenth day of Dasain in October.

The palace

The right (east) wing of the Durbar is the historic **palace**, site of Prithvi Narayan's birthplace and, by extension, the ancestral shrine of the Shah kings. Though pre-dating the Gorkhali conquest of Kathmandu, the exceptional eighteenth-century brick- and woodwork palace bears the unmistakeable stamp of Newari craftsmanship. You can peer through the latticework of the door at the eastern facade and see the flank of what is claimed to be Prithvi Narayan's **throne**.

The cave of Gorakhnath

The space within the fortress walls is fairly littered with other Hindu shrines. By the eastern exit is a small temple built around the holy **cave of Gorakhnath**, the centre for worship of the shadowy Indian guru who gave Gorkha its name and is regarded as a kind of guardian angel by the Shah kings. Sadhus of the Gorakhnath cult are known as *kaanphata* ("split-ears"), after an initiation ceremony in which they insert sticks in their ear lobes – a walk in the park compared to some of the other things they get up to in the name of their guru. *Kaanphata* priests sometimes administer ashen *tika* (mark on the forehead) from the shelter above the cave.

Gorakhnath's footsteps

The views are good from the Durbar, but carry on along the ridge for much better ones. Exit the compound through the eastern door and walk down a few yards to **Hanuman Bhanjyang** (Hanuman Pass), a small notch in the ridge named after the valiant monkey king whose image guards the popular shady rest stop. Cross the main trail (a branch of the old Pokhara–Trisuli porter route) and follow a steep path up for just a couple of minutes to an awesome vantage point where you can stand in a pair of stone **"footsteps"** (ascribed to Gorakhnath or – by Buddhists – Padma Sambhava) and, weather allowing, snap a picture of the Durbar and the mountains to the north. The Himalayas seen from here stretch from the Annapurnas (and even Dhaulagiri, which from this angle is to the right of Annapurna I and Machhapuchhre) to Ganesh Himal, with the pyramids of Baudha and Himalchuli occupying centre stage. Come early to catch the sunrise.

Upallokot and Tallokot viewpoints

From Hanuman Bhanjyang it's a thirty-minute hike to **Upallokot** (Upper Fort – though it's now more like a hut), a 1520m eyrie at the highest, easternmost point of

---

WALKS AROUND GORKHA

The obvious destination from Gorkha is **Manakamana** (see p.197). The old walking trail is increasingly ignored, now there's a road, but you can still find the trail, starting from the unpaved side road off the main Gorkha road, 7km down from the town. It takes four hours to walk to Manakamana, and it's possible to return via the cable car and bus the same day. The trail can, however, be difficult to follow, so consider hiring a guide (your hotel can help you find one).

Longer routes can be found by taking the high trail through **Hanuman Bhanjyang** – this is the traditional start of the Manaslu Circuit trek. From the little pass, you descend gently for about ninety minutes to **Ali Bhanjyang** (where you can find tea and snack food); from here you can ascend along a ridge with fabulous views to **Khanchok** (about 2hr 30min). This would be about the limit for a day hike, but given an early start you could continue down to the subtropical banks of the Budhi Gandaki at **Arughat**, a long day's 20km from Gorkha – and a third of the way to Trisuli. A rough road connects Arughat to the town of **Dhading**, which is 21km up a surfaced side road from Malekhu, on the Prithvi Highway.

the ridge. To get to it you have to walk through a fenced microwave relay facility. At the other, western end of the ridge stands **Tallokot**, another watch post with limited views. You can easily stroll there from the Durbar, passing a small Ganesh shrine and a new monument to **Ram Shah**, the seventh-generation ancestor of Prithvi Narayan Shah who is reckoned by some to have been the progenitor of the Shah title. The views from this monument are also excellent.

ARRIVAL AND INFORMATION
GORKHA

By bus From Kathmandu or Pokhara, it's easiest to take a tourist bus to Abu Khaireni and then a local bus from there (every 30min; 30–45min). In addition, direct bus, minibus and microbus services connect Gorkha with Kathmandu (every 30min; 4–6hr) – the minibuses are quicker than the big buses and safer than the microbuses. Minibuses connect to Pokhara (3–4 daily; 4hr), with departures in the morning, both ways. All buses terminate at Gorkha's modest bus park just west of the bazaar.

By bike If you're pedalling, bear in mind it's a 900m ascent from Abu Khaireni to Gorkha, and it gets steeper as you go.

Banks and exchange Manaslu Bikas Bank, on the main road beside the bus park, has an ATM and exchange facilities.

ACCOMMODATION AND EATING

There's little choice of accommodation in Gorkha. For those on a real budget, there is a collection of cheap, mostly grubby guesthouses close to the bus park. The best restaurants are found in the smarter guesthouses.

Hotel Gorkha Bisauni Gorkha Bazaar ☎ 064 420 107. A promising start, with neat terraces overlooking the road and a warm welcome from a uniformed ex-Gurkha, is let down by shabby, run-down rooms – though a couple of the larger ones (Rs1000) at the front are a slight improvement. <u>Rs500</u>

Gorkha Gaun Resort A 20min drive southeast of town, beyond Laxmi Bazaar ☎ 980 101 0557 or ☎ 980 108 4605, ⊕ gorkhagaun.com. Brand-new, eco-friendly lodge in a tranquil, hilltop location outside town, with lush grounds and stunning views in every direction. The attractive but simple en-suite stone cottages have bamboo furniture, high ceilings and terraces. Advance bookings are essential. <u>US$60</u>

Gurkha Inn Pokharithok ☎ 064 20206 or ☎ 984 609 8375. The best option in the town itself, with spruce rooms that have nice details like painted beams, stencils or Tibetan rugs. The hotel keeps its back to the road, so its balconies overlook a charming garden and a fine view. Welcoming staff, and a decent menu. <u>US$40</u>

Bandipur

The miniature bazaar of **BANDIPUR** perches improbably on a ridge, beneath steep limestone peaks that rear up romantically, as if they'd tumbled out of a Chinese brush painting, and facing breathtaking views of the Himalayas. Originally a simple Magar village, it was colonized in the 1800s by Newars from Bhaktapur and became a prosperous centre for garment-making and a trading stop along the India–Tibet route. The eradication of malaria from the Terai in the 1950s, and the completion of the Prithvi Highway in 1973, strangled business, however, and today the town is little more than a single, sleepy high street where children play and unhurried locals sell imported goods. Still, the town's nineteenth-century mansions, with their grand Neoclassical facades and shuttered windows, speak of past glories, and tourism is providing a new economic mini-boom – the town has become a popular tourist stopover between Kathmandu and Pokhara, and there are numerous **boutique hotels** and **homestays**.

Bandipur bazaar

The **bazaar** proper is one long street, handsomely paved with stone, that runs along the ridgetop in classic Newari fashion and is oriented broadly east–west. At its eastern end stands the elegantly carved Padma Library, a former *pati* or rest shelter that is now run as a community centre, and the modest **Bhindebasini Mandir**. To the west is the dusty bus park; a long-running battle to keep traffic off the main street means it now bypasses town on a little-used dirt road on the northern side, 200m below.

The temples

Several temples and shrines surround the bazaar. The largest, the **Khadga Devi Mandir**, is reached by heading up the steps at the north end of the main street. It houses a holy sword supposedly given by Shiva to the Magar king Mukunda Sen of Palpa, who ruled this part of Nepal in the sixteenth century. The relic is displayed on the seventh day of Dasain but bound in cloth because locals believe that anyone looking at the blade hidden beneath will die instantly, as if struck down by a sword. The miniature pagoda of the **Mahalaxmi Mandir**, reached via stone steps behind the information centre (see p.204), has some finely carved roof struts. A third holy place lies some ten minutes' walk east of the bazaar (take the right fork behind the library), where the three snake-shaped waterspouts of the **Tin Dhara** pour onto smooth flagstones. It's a great place to do your washing, and locals will happily lend you some soap.

The tudikhel

The most dramatic point on the ridge-line immediately north of the bazaar is the **tudikhel**, the former parade ground that's now chiefly a cherished flat spot for schoolboys to play football, or for politicians to hold rallies. It is perched exhilaratingly on a rock outcrop 500m from the main street (continue beyond the steps for the Khadga Devi Mandir). To the north and east are sheer drops, while a stately promenade of fig trees and *chautaara* (see box, p.209) shades the western side. The **view** to the north is stunning: you're looking at a map of the eastern half of the Annapurna Circuit, with the Marsyangdi valley straight ahead and the Annapurna and Manaslu ranges behind.

Gurungche Daada

The steepest of the limestone hills that frame Bandipur is **Gurungche Daada**, which rears up west of the bazaar. There's a well-maintained but occasionally giddy footpath that leads up and over the spine. It takes about twenty minutes to climb to the wooded shrine of **Thani Mai**, Khadga Devi's "sister"; it's little more than a concrete shelter festooned with spooky animist rags, but the views north to the Himalayan peaks are thunderously good.

Siddha Gupha and around

Daily 8am–5pm • Rs50; guides around Rs100–150

Incredibly, Nepal's biggest cave chamber, **Siddha Gupha**, was discovered only in 1987. It's 10m wide, 400m long and full of stalactites, not to mention a sizeable bat population. You'll need to bring your own torch/flashlight, and it gets chilly, so take a

---

HIKES TO AND AROUND BANDIPUR

The historic **trail** to Bandipur was immortalized in a poem by King Mahendra, who observed how remarkably long and steep it was. In fact, it takes two to three hours, beginning 500m east of the main Dumre intersection, and climbing through shady forest punctuated by very civilized rest shelters and waterspouts. It arrives at the *tudikhel* (if you're heading down, note that the path drops to the left of the *tudikhel's* avenue of trees as you approach from the bazaar). An alternative route starting from Bimalnagar, on the Prithvi Highway 1km east of Dumre, takes you past the Siddha Gupha cave complex (see above) after about half an hour.

Other, longer hikes go through pretty, cultivated hills and traditional Magar villages, and are worth considering as alternatives to leaving Bandipur by bus. The Magar village of **Rankot**, two hours' hike from Bandipur, is one of the most scenic, with its wooden balconied houses – and even a few, rare thatched roundhouses. You can walk on to **Damauli** via the pilgrimage place of Chabda Barahi Mandir, two hours from Ramkot – with panoramic views of the Annapurnas from the crest of the hill along the way. The last hour to Damauli is on a paved road.

jumper; note that there are no handrails. You may be able to hire a guide on the spot, but it's better to bring one from your guesthouse – this would also help in route-finding, as the signs sometimes disappear. It takes about ninety minutes to walk down to the cave from the bazaar, or a tough half-hour to walk up to it from the Prithvi Highway at Bimalnagar, 1km east of Dumre.

Close by Siddha Gupha, the sheer-to-overhanging 70m section of the limestone cliff, known as **Chun Pahara**, attracts rock climbers. You'll need your own kit, but in Bimalnagar you may find local enthusiasts who will show you the routes – try asking for Lal Kumar Shrestha in the *Helen and Rocky Land Restaurant and Lodge* (☎065 580 155 or ☎984 602 8298). Dedicated cave visitors could also walk for two hours from Siddha Gupha to the so-called **Patale Dwar**, or "gateway to paradise". Entering is supposed to wash away sins, but the experience is not as impressive as at the main cave.

ARRIVAL AND DEPARTURE

BANDIPUR

By bus, microbus and jeep From Pokhara, Kathmandu or Narayangadh, take any bus heading along the Prithvi Highway and get off at Dumre, from where you can pick up a ride in a crowded jeep or minibus (every 30min; 25min). Book ahead and the more expensive hotels will pick you up from the roadhead. Moving on, you can walk or it's easy to get a lift down to Dumre in a shared jeep. From Dumre, shared jeeps and microbuses shuttle to and from Pokhara (1hr 30min), and Kathmandu (3–5hr). The smarter hotels will provide transfers.

INFORMATION AND ACTIVITIES

Information centre Next to the library, a small information centre is open for most of the daylight hours, albeit somewhat sporadically, and can advise on modest local sights, such as the silk farm, an easy half-hour walk from the town.

Paragliding Bandipur is becoming a popular place to paraglide; Blue Sky Paragliding (☺blue-sky-paragliding .com) has options for all levels of experience.

ACCOMMODATION AND EATING

Guesthouses are springing up all the time in Bandipur, many of them in atmospheric old buildings. The bazaar area is filled with identikit **guesthouse restaurants**, each serving a multi-cuisine menu (most mains Rs100–300) and cold beer. The restaurants at the smarter hotels – notably *Old Inn* and *Guan Ghar*, which also have great Himalayan views – are more accomplished (and more expensive).

Gaun Ghar Bandipur Bazaar ☎065 520 129, ☺gaunghar.com. The smartest boutique hotel in town, with rooms tucked in all sorts of corners in a stunningly restored historic townhouse, filled with dark, carved wood, brass sinks, objets d'art and soft lighting – there's even a carp pond. What you gain in professional, uniformed service, however, you lose in the local touch. US$185

Heritage Guest House Bandipur Bazaar ☎065 520 041 or ☎984 606 7421. Squeezed into one of the original crumbling mansions at the western end of the bazaar, this budget guesthouse is surprisingly small and utterly traditional inside – with undersized doors and windows, lino floors and basic rooms with shared facilities. The welcome is friendly though. Rs600

Ke Garne Café Opposite the Old Inn, Bandipur Bazaar. A charming little café with a semi-outdoors open-sided balcony on the sunny south side of the village, with views over to Rani Ban. Serves coffee, drinks and a short menu of simple food (Rs100–450), from a good breakfast to sandwiches and roast chicken. Daily 9am–8pm.

Kriti Home Bandipur Bazaar ☎065 520 107 or ☎984 608 7378. This family home, above a general shop on the main bazaar, offers a couple of simple bedrooms (with shared or private bathroom) at the front. There's a friendly welcome, hot (or rather warm) water most of the time, and good *daal bhaat*. Rs500

★**Old Inn** Bandipur Bazaar ☎065 520 110 or ☎01 470 0426, ☺himalayanencounters.com. Superbly run by respected local travel agency Himalayan Encounters, this romantic place at the eastern end of the bazaar has beautifully atmospheric rooms – all traditional beams and windows, slate floors and little balconies. The courtyard garden restaurant faces out towards the mountains, and twinkles with candles at night. Dinner (the food is excellent), transport and guide costs are included in the full-board price, and they can arrange inexpensive local homestays, volunteering activities and treks. US$80

Mountain Ridge Depchedara, just outside Bandipur ☎984 120 5843, ☺mountainridge-bandipur.com. Located in a small community just outside Bandipur, this popular

guesthouse has three attractive, en-suite rooms, each one with a different theme ("Tibetan","Floral" and "Ethnic") and a private balcony, plus a suite ($70). The food's good too. US$45

Pradhan's Family Guesthouse Bandipur Bazaar ☎ 065 520 106. Simple house in the middle of the bazaar,

with budget rooms that have been given a basic version of the Bandipur boutique makeover – a few carved doors and beams, fresh lino on the floors, and a decent shower/toilet outhouse off the balcony out back. R600

Pokhara

The Himalayas make the greatest rise from subtropical valley floor to icy summit of any mountain range on earth, and the contrast is stunningly apparent at the tourist hub of **POKHARA**. Basking beside its verdant lakeshore, on clear mornings it boasts a nearly unobstructed view of the 8000m-plus Annapurna and Manaslu ranges, looming almost touchably 25km to the north.

Pokhara's tourist scene lolls beside **Phewa Tal** (Phewa Lake), which turns an indifferent back to the modern Nepali city of Pokhara – in fact, if it wasn't for the smog that increasingly obscures the mountains on most afternoons, you'd hardly know the city was there. "Lakeside", as it's known, may not be the rustic travellers' haven it once was, but it remains Nepal's little tourist paradise: carefree and culturally undemanding, with a steaks-and-cakes scene that almost rivals Thamel's, and a pocket version of the same nightlife to match. It's significantly more laidback than Thamel, however – and relatively horizontal, if you've come up from North India.

Pokhara is the first place many travellers venture to after Kathmandu. It may be short on A-list sights, apart from the lake itself, but it's very long on activities: for **trekkers**, it's the gateway to Nepal's most popular trails; for **rafters** and **kayakers**, it's Nepal's river-running headquarters; for **paragliders** and **mountain bikers** it's one of the best spots on earth. The **climate** is balmy: at 800m above sea level it's both cooler than the plains in summer and warmer than Kathmandu in winter. (It may be significantly wetter than the capital, but most of the rain falls outside the tourist season, so the only sign of water many visitors see is the lake, and the lush subtropical greenery.)

Phewa Tal (Phewa Lake)

Pokara's shining lake, **Phewa Tal**, is cherished by Nepalis with the kind of fervour that is normally reserved for holy shrines. Stretches of tranquil, shining water are rare in the Western Hills – and they'll one day be rarer still. Phewa owes its present size to the construction of **Pardi Dam** in 1967, which brought electricity and irrigation to the valley, and gave Damside its name. The dam also restricted the through-flow of sediment from the tributary Harpan Khola, however, and the western third of the lake's former surface is already silted up. One day, Pokhara's verdant valley will probably be no more watery than Kathmandu's. A more immediate problem is the water hyacinth,

---

THE LEGEND OF THE LAKE

According to a local legend, **Phewa Tal** covers the area of a once-prosperous valley, whose inhabitants one day scorned a wandering beggar. Finding only one sympathetic woman, the beggar warned her of an impending flood: as the woman and her family fled to higher ground, a torrent roared down from the mountains and submerged the town – the "beggar" having been none other than the goddess Barahi Bhagwati. The woman's descendants settled beside the new lake and erected the island shrine of **Tal Barahi**.

The geological explanation is that the entire Pokhara Valley, like the Kathmandu Valley, was submerged about 200,000 years ago when the fast-rising Mahabharat ridge dammed up the Seti Nadi. Over time, the Seti eroded an ever-deeper outlet, lowering the water level and leaving Phewa Tal and several smaller lakes as remnants.

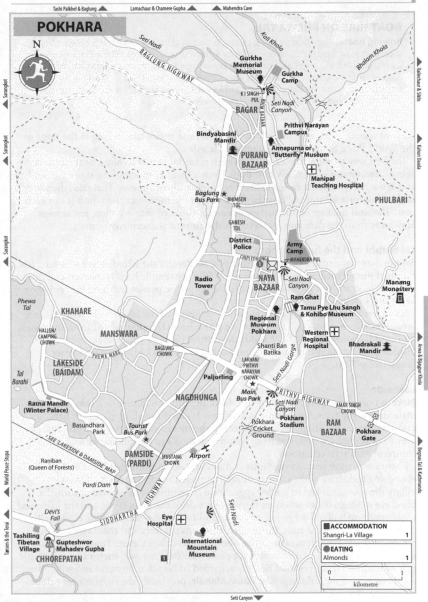

which first appeared on the surface of the lake in the 1990s. Locals now organize regular clearing sessions.

Activities on the lake

An embanked **path** now runs along much of the length of the eastern shore; this has seen a return of some of Lakeside's once-fabled lake views, which had been obscured in the 1990s and 2000s by illegal construction. In around five to eight hours, depending

---

BOAT HIRE ON PHEWA TAL

Rowing boats, which hold six easily, can be rented all along the eastern shore. Prices are supposed to be fixed (Rs350/hr or Rs800/day if you row yourself; Rs400/hr with someone to row for you) but "discounts" are possible for longer trips. Life jackets cost extra (Rs10/hr or Rs30/day). Fibreglass and wooden **sailboats** are available from *Hotel Fewa*, south of the fishery, and some rafting companies (see p.214) rent out **kayaks** (around US$30/day). Pedalos are also available. Motorized boats aren't allowed on the lake.

---

on your route, it's possible to walk right around the entire lake, taking in the ridge of the World Peace Stupa (see p.224) on the far side.

The best way to enjoy Phewa Tal, however, is undoubtedly to **hire a boat** (see box above). **Swimming** is definitely best done from a boat, as much of the shore is muddy, and sewage seeps from some of Lakeside's hotels and restaurants. That said, the water is fairly clean for a subtropical lake, largely because the monsoon rains flush it out each year. The stuff floating on the surface at certain times of year is pollen, not sewage. Stay away from the dam area, however, as the **current** is deceptively strong.

Tal Barahi and the further shore

An obvious first destination on a boat trip is **Tal Barahi**, the island shrine located a few hundred metres offshore from the palace. While the temple itself is modern and not much to look at, it's a popular spot with Nepali picnic parties and local lads enjoying beers and snacks.

It's a twenty- to thirty-minute row to the far shore of the lake which, with dense jungle, manic monkeys and few places to put ashore, is best observed from the water. You could, however, make for **Anadu**, the diffuse Gurung village that covers the hillside directly opposite Lakeside, and perhaps walk back via the World Peace Stupa (see p.224).

Lakeside

Next to boating, or perhaps eating and drinking, promenading along **Lakeside**'s main drag is the favourite pastime in Pokhara. It's an astonishing parade of bars, café-restaurants and shops selling everything the tourist might require, from domestic beer to imported olive oil, and from folk dance shows to paragliding expeditions complete with trained hawks.

First-timers, travellers up from India and trekkers down from the hills often find the easy-going hedonism of the scene exciting, but there's no doubt that the Lakeside is killing the goose that laid its golden eggs. Local government has allowed or turned a blind eye to illegal construction on the western side of the main street, and the balconied wickerwork cafés of old are giving way to neon-lit shopping-and-nightlife mini-malls.

There are few sights as such, though impressive pipal trees and **chautaara** (see box opposite) shade key intersections. The one at the so-called Centre Point is particularly impressive, while immediately south (opposite the *Busy Bee bar)* there's a characteristic pair of bar and pipal trees, traditionally regarded in Nepal as husband and wife. The southern part of the strip begins at **Ratna Mandir**, previously the royal **Winter Palace**.

LAKESIDE FESTIVALS

Basundhara Park, Lakeside's biggest patch of open space, is the venue for the annual **Annapurna Festival** (usually held in April), a cultural event featuring music, dance and food. Every year, from 28 December to 1 January, Lakeside is invaded by an infinity of food stalls for the Street festival. Various cultural events take place for the **New Year** under the name of the Phewa Festival: there are more food and handicraft stalls, plus fairground rides and street dancing and singing.

CHAUTAARA

A uniquely Nepali institution found in every hill village, the **chautaara** is a resting place that serves important social and religious functions. The standard design consists of a rectangular flagstoned platform, built at just the right height for porters easily to set down their *doko*, or basket, while two trees provide shade.

Chautaara are erected and maintained by individuals as an act of public service, often to earn religious merit or in memory of a deceased parent. Commonly they'll be found on sites associated with pre-Hindu nature deities, often indicated by stones smeared with red *abhir* and yellow *keshori* powder.

The trees, too, are considered sacred. Invariably, one will be a **pipal**, whose Latin name (*Ficus religiosa*) recalls its role as the *bodhi* tree under which the Buddha attained enlightenment. Nepalis regard the pipal, with its heart-shaped leaves, as a female symbol and incarnation of Lakshmi, and women will sometimes fast and pray for children in front of one. It's said that no one can tell a lie under the shade of a pipal, which makes the trees doubly useful for village assemblies. Its "husband", representing Shiva Mahadev, is the bar or **banyan** (*Ficus bengalensis*), another member of the fig genus, which sends down Tarzan-vine-like aerial roots that, if not pruned, will eventually take root and establish satellite trunks. A *chautaara* is incomplete without the pair; occasionally you'll see one with a single tree, but sooner or later someone will get around to planting the other.

At the northern edge of the palace grounds, a road leads down to the lake and **Barahi Ghat**, the main launching site for boats to Tal Barahi. South again lies **Basundhara Park**, a worn-out patch of green that's a popular strolling and picnicking place for Nepalis.

The focus of the northern part of the strip is **Hallan Chowk**, universally known as **Camping Chowk**, after the municipal campground that has long stood there. This is one of the few places in Lakeside where you can feel the presence of Pokhara city, which leaks into the tourist enclave down busy Phewa Marg. North of here, Lakeside slowly peters out. In the area known as **Khahare**, the lake again becomes visible from the main road, which you can follow along the attractive and less developed northern shore. Side trails lead up to Sarangkot (p.225) from there.

Pokhara city

Until it was linked to the outside world by the Prithvi Highway in 1973, **Pokhara Bazaar** was a small Newari market town along the trade route from Butwal to Mustang. The once-tight bazaar has now spread into a city of some 265,000, with traffic and all the rest, but its proliferation of gardens and green setting in the valley mean that it rarely feels congested. Most of Pokhara was destroyed in a fire in 1949, but some remnants of the old town can still be seen in the **Purano Bazaar**, which runs from Bhimsen Tol up to Bagar. The centre of the bazaar area of the city is **Mahendra Pul**, named after the nearby bridge.

Bindhyabasini Mandir

Perched on a hillock in the middle of the old bazaar area is the **Bindhyabasini Mandir**, where the views are arguably more interesting than the shrines. The featured deity, Bindhyabasini, is an incarnation of Kali, the mother goddess in her bloodthirsty aspect. Animal sacrifices are common, particularly on Saturdays and the ninth day of Dasain in October. Bindhyabasini has a reputation as a bit of a prima donna: in one celebrated incident, her stone image began to sweat mysteriously, causing such a panic that the late King Tribhuwan had to order special rites to pacify the goddess. The 1949 fire allegedly started here, when an offering burned out of control.

Annapurna or "Butterfly" Museum

Prithvi Narayan Campus, Bagar • Sun–Thurs 10am–1.30pm & 2–5pm, Fri 10am–1.30pm & 2–3pm • Free

Tucked away inside the Prithvi Narayan University Campus at the northeastern part of town, the **Annapurna Museum** offers a cartoonish treatment of Nepal's natural history that's really meant for local schoolkids. The draw, and its local name, **Butterfly Museum**, comes from its astounding collection of 500-odd Himalayan specimens, perfectly pinned in their glass cases, which are kept inside stacks of wooden drawers. An adjacent **information centre**, maintained by the Annapurna Conservation Area Project (ACAP), contains some enlightening exhibits about wildlife, geology, ethnic groups and culture in the ACAP area.

Gurkha Memorial Museum

Near K.I. Singh Pul • Daily 8am–4.30pm • Rs200 • ☎ 061 441 762, ⓦ gurkhamuseum.org.np

The **Gurkha Memorial Museum**, beside the British Gurkha Camp, would simply be a stuffy exhibition of uniforms and regimental history, were it not for the extraordinary achievements of the Gurkhas themselves. Photographs of the many Nepalese winners of the Victoria Cross line the walls, attached to short paragraphs of no-nonsense prose that describe act after extraordinary act of old-fashioned courage performed by individual Gurkha soldiers in British service. There's also a well-labelled display of traditional utensils from the Western Hills, together with photographs of them in use.

Regional Museum Pokhara

Nayabazaar • Feb–Oct Mon 10am–2.30pm, Wed–Sun 10am–4.30pm; Nov–Jan Mon 10am–2.30pm, Wed–Sun 10am–3.30pm • Rs30

South of Mahendra Pul, the **Regional Museum Pokhara** is a worthy if not thrilling survey of the ethnic groups of the Western Region. Exhibits show traditional dress of various ethnicities, along with jewellery, farming and cooking utensils, and musical instruments. There's also a basic mock-up of a traditional Gurung roundhouse, and a Hindu wedding ceremony enacted by dummies.

THE GURKHAS

An elite Nepali corps within the British and Indian armies for almost two centuries, the **Gurkha regiments** have long been rated among the finest fighting units in the world. Ironically, the regiments were born out of the 1814–16 war between Nepal and Britain's East India Company: so impressed were the British by the men of "Goorkha" (Gorkha, the ancestral home of Nepal's rulers) that they began recruiting Nepalis into the Indian Army before the peace was even signed.

In the century that followed, Gurkhas fought in every major British military operation, including the 1857 **Indian Mutiny**. More than 200,000 Gurkhas served in the two world wars (often earmarked for "high-wastage" roles – sixteen thousand have died in British service), earning respect for their bravery: ten of the one hundred **Victoria Crosses** awarded in World War II went to Gurkhas. Following India's independence, Britain kept four of the ten regiments and India retained the rest. More recently, Gurkhas have distinguished themselves in Iraq and Afghanistan and as UN peacekeepers. In 2011 Sergeant Dipprasad Pun was awarded the Conspicuous Gallantry Cross for single-handedly fighting off two dozen Taliban fighters.

Recruits hail mainly from the Magar, Gurung, Rai and Limbu ethnic groups, from Nepal's middle hills. Most boys from these groups have traditionally dreamt of making it into the Gurkhas, not only for the money, but also for a rare chance to see the world and return with prestige and a comfortable pension. Those who fail can always try in the lower-paid Indian regiments; the Nepali army is considered the last resort.

Gurkhas used to be Nepal's major source of foreign remittances, sending home millions of dollars annually, but the achievement of **pension equality** and, in 2009, the final acceptance of the right to reside in the UK, have changed the long-standing and culturally influential lifestyle pattern. Many Gurkha families have now moved to the UK, and in addition, the Gurkhas' long and faithful service to Britain is winding down. The only remaining **training centre** is in Pokhara, where thousands of would-be recruits still try out for places. It remains to be seen how the removal of the Gurkhas' cash injection will affect the economy of cities like Pokhara and Dharan, though the increase in other work migration (mostly to the Middle East) has made up for the remittance shortfall, at a national level at least.

The Seti Nadi gorge

The eastern fringe of Pokhara is defined by the dramatic course of the **Seti Nadi**, the "white river", which gets its name from the thick glacial deposits that the water carries in suspension down from the mountains. As it passes the city, it alternately cuts through plungingly narrow canyons and stretches of gorge marked by broad, stony shallows. The best place to see the widest stretch of the **Seti Nadi gorge** is just north of the ugly main bus park: head north from Prithvi Narayan Chowk for 400m, then turn right along the fence of the forested Shanti Ban Batika park. At the end of this road, after another 500m or so, are two gates: one leads into the forest park (a popular picnic spot); the other leads down via stone steps to a riverside promontory, offering fine views of the gorge's great sweep and its crumbling cliff walls. Paths thread north from here, through the woods of the west bank, towards the cremation point of Ram Ghat.

The Seti Nadi canyons

In other parts of Pokhara, the Seti Nadi plunges through single-metre-narrow canyons where it almost seems the bedrock has been split by a giant axe blow. The easiest place to see this phenomenon is on the main bridge carrying the Prithvi Highway into town, but the traffic makes this unappealing. It's better to make for Mahendra Pul, near the centre of the bazaar, or K.I. Singh Pul, near the city's northern limits, beside the British Army Gurkha Camp. At the latter, there's a small, litter-strewn park (Rs20 entry fee) where you can peer 50m down into the **Seti canyon**, or you can just loiter freely on the bridge itself. If you can't quite see the river thundering below, you'll certainly hear it. Other canyon viewpoints can be found to the north of the International Mountain Museum.

Tamu Pye Lhu Sangh and Kohibo Museum

Shaktighat • Daily 10am–4pm • Rs30

Pokhara's most esoteric cultural attraction, the **Tamu Pye Lhu Sangh,** or Gurung religious and cultural centre, sits on the eastern bank of the gorge, opposite Ram Ghat (it's best reached by the small, low-slung bridge immediately south of Mahendra Pul). The ambitiously curving modern building is a scaled-up, four-pronged version of the *kaindu*, the cone of rice powder that plays such a prominent role in Tamu (the Gurung word for Gurung) rituals. On the ground floor is a temple, situated here for proximity to the ghats on the riverbank. On the first floor, the **Tamu Kohibo Museum** gives an introduction to Gurung religion – which sits somewhere between animism and Tibetan Bön, with a heavy dose of Nepali shamanism. Even though there's not much to see, you might find yourself a traditional healer here, or perhaps procure an invitation to a ritual.

International Mountain Museum

Tatapaira • Daily 9am–5pm • Rs400, garden Rs20 • ☎ 061 460 742, ⓦ internationalmountainmuseum.org

At the extreme southern end of the city, just below the airport, the worthwhile **International Mountain Museum** houses an exhibit of historical mountaineering equipment with mannequins of renowned climbers, giant-scale model peaks, and plentiful information on the culture, geology, flora and fauna of the Himalayas and other mountain ranges – including a life-size model yeti. There's a peak-shaped, 21m-high artificial climbing wall and a somewhat smaller model of Machhapuchhare that you can walk or scramble up (unlike the real thing, of course, which remains a sacred and forbidden summit).

Chhorepatan

The ramshackle bazaar of **Chhorepatan**, about 2km west of Damside, spreads along the Siddhartha Highway on the west side of the Pardi Khola, the stream that drains Phewa Tal. Most visitors are heading on up to the World Peace Stupa, perched on the forested ridge immediately northwest, but a trio of intriguing sights – a waterfall, a cave-shrine and a Tibetan settlement – makes it worth exploring for an hour or two.

Devi's Falls

Daily 6am–6pm • Rs30

At **Devi's Falls** the Pardi Khola abruptly plummets into a veritable crack in the earth. In the autumn immediately following a strong monsoon it can be frighteningly impressive; in the winter less so. The spot is perhaps more interesting as a source of pop mythology: known to locals as **Patale Chhango** (roughly, "Waterfall to the Underworld"), the sinkhole's name is supposed to be a Nepalification of Devin, the name of a Swiss woman said to have drowned while skinny-dipping with her boyfriend in 1961 (though other accounts make the victim "David" or even a "Mrs Davis"). The name "Devi" may be a casualty of the transliteration system, or possibly part of the Nepali propensity to deify anything that moves – *devi* means "goddess". The whole story sounds like a fabrication to warn local youth to shun promiscuous Western ways.

Gupteshwor Mahadev Gupha

Daily 6am–7pm • Rs30, or Rs100 with Falls viewpoint • ⓦ gupteshworcave.com

On the opposite side of the highway to Devi's Falls, a signposted path leads for a few metres between houses and curio stalls to **Gupteshwor Mahadev Gupha**, a cave-shrine dedicated to Shankhar, who incorporates both Shiva and his consort Parbati as male and female halves of one figure. Guided by a dream vision, a priest discovered the idol in 1992, since when the cave has attracted increasing numbers of devotees. Enshrined in a large womblike chamber, the black Shankhar figure is a natural rock form dolled up with a carved *nag* (snake) crown. In the winter dry season, a tunnel leads through to the downstream side of Devi's Falls – even more impressive here, seen from underground.

Tashiling

The modest Tibetan settlement of **Tashiling** overlooks Chhorepatan. Walk to the far end of the compound, past the school, *gompa* and curio stalls, to reach the community's small carpet-weaving hall; a short walk beyond brings you to an abrupt drop and a glorious panorama of the valley of the Phusre Khola.

ARRIVAL AND DEPARTURE
POKHARA

By plane Frequent flights to and from Kathmandu are an option for anyone in a hurry – and the mountain views are stupendous. At the time of writing, a taxi from the airport to central Lakeside was Rs400 and takes around 10–15min. There are very limited food and drink facilities at the airport, while the registered moneychanger usually offers fairly decent rates. A new international airport is planned for the outskirts of town.

Destinations Jomosom (3–4 daily; 25min); Kathmandu (14–17 daily; 40min); Manang Humde (1 weekly; 25min).

By tourist bus Tourist buses arrive at their own bus park near Damside, with the exception of Greenline buses, which run directly to the office at the southern end of Lakeside. Greenline (☎061 464 472, ⓦ greenline.com.np; US$23 to Kathmandu, US$17 to Sauraha, Chitwan) is the premier, a/c service, with Golden Travels its nearest rival. Other than lack of a/c, there's nothing wrong with the less expensive buses, which charge around half the price and may offer a bigger range of departures: Blue Sky (☎061 462 435, ⓦ blue-sky-tours.com) has a good reputation. It's a pretty easy walk from the tourist bus park to most lodgings, but the touts, who are problematic here as nowhere else in Pokhara, make

this tricky. Don't be surprised if they insist that your guesthouse burned down last week or if your driver tries to earn commission by taking you to a different one. If you do allow a tout to entice you with an offer of a free taxi ride, expect to pay more for the room – if you don't the fare will be inflated by several hundred rupees, depending on your destination and bargaining skills.

By public bus Public buses terminate at the main bus park east of Prithvi Chowk. A taxi to Lakeside should cost around Rs300. Onward transport to trekking trailheads is covered separately, in our "Trekking" chapter (see p.302).

Destinations (day buses) Baglung (frequent; 3hr); Bartun for Tansen (17 daily; 5hr); Begnas Tal (every 20min; 45min); Beni (8 daily; 4hr); Besisahar (4 daily; 5hr); Birgunj (8–9 daily; 8hr); Butwal for Sonauli (every 30min; 7–8hr); Gorkha (3–4 daily; 4hr); Jagatpur (2 daily; 8hr); Janakpur (1 daily; 11hr); Kakarbhitta (1 daily; 14hr); Kathmandu (every 20min; 6–7hr); Narayangadh for Chitwan (every 30min; 4–5hr). There are also microbuses to Kathmandu (every 10min; 4–5hr), though these have a worse accident record than the bigger buses.

Destinations (night buses) Birgunj (2 daily; 10hr); Butwal

for Sonauli (3 daily; 10hr); Dhangadhi for Bardia (1 daily; 15hr); Janakpur (1 daily; 12hr); Kakarbhitta (3 daily; 16hr); Kathmandu (6 daily; 6–7hr); Mahendra Nagar (1 daily; 16hr); Nepalgunj (1 daily; 14hr).

GETTING AROUND

By bus Few visitors bother with Pokhara's ailing and slow local transport system: taking a taxi, cycling or walking makes more sense.

By bike A bicycle, rentable all over Lakeside and Damside, increases mobility tremendously. Boneshakers go for about Rs300/day. A mountain bike (from Rs500) is more practical for exploring the valley, although the ones for rent on the street aren't very good. You'll pay in the region of Rs1000–2500 to hire a serious, Western-made mountain bike from specialists such as the Pokhara Mountain Bike Club (see p.216).

By motorbike There are come-and-go motorbike rental places all over Lakeside, but the main cluster is on Phewa Marg, leading east from Hallan/Camping Chowk (around *Mamma Mia* restaurant). In Lakeside, prices range from Rs600/day (not including fuel) for something basic to over Rs1500 for the biggest, newest bikes.

By taxi Taxis wait at several spots along Lakeside's main drag, notably at junctions. They're more expensive than in Kathmandu, and drivers are very reluctant to use meters.

By private vehicle For day-trips around the valley it makes sense to hire a taxi for the day, which should cost about Rs3000–3500 for a full day including petrol – let someone at your guesthouse do the negotiations. For longer trips in private cars, you'll pay a hefty premium because the car (and driver) have to return to Pokhara. Fares to trekking trailheads are covered separately, in our "Trekking" chapter (see p.302).

INFORMATION

Tourist information Guesthouse staff are the best sources of up-to-the-minute information; they can book anything, charging commission no higher than travel agents.

Travel agent Adam Tours and Travels (☎061 461 806, ⓦadamtravels.com). Right in the centre of Lakeside, next to *Punjabi Restaurant*, this is an efficient and reliable agency for booking tickets, arranging vehicles and so on.

Maps The standard tourist maps of Pokhara, sold in most bookshops, are detailed and mostly accurate. If you're touring the valley, the 1:50,000 *Around Pokhara* (Nepal Maps) is very useful, and includes a detailed map of Lakeside.

Newspapers International newspapers and magazines are available in bookshops. The English-language Nepali papers mostly arrive around noon, on the morning flights from Kathmandu.

TREKKING, RAFTING AND OTHER ACTIVITIES

Pokhara is the outdoor recreation and adventure sports capital of Nepal. It's the gateway to some of the best **treks** in the world, and an ever-growing centre for **rafting**, **kayaking**, **paragliding**, **mountain biking** and ultralight flights. In recent years, **skydiving**, **bungee jumping** and **zip lining** have been added to the list of thrills.

TREKKING COMPANIES

Our "Trekking" chapter (see p.302) has full details on trekking preparations, routes and agencies. As a rule, it's misleading to recommend budget trekking companies

---

ORGANIZING A TREK FROM POKHARA

Pokhara is within a few hours' drive of all the main **Annapurna trailheads**, which can be reached via taxi or public bus, as detailed in our "Trekking" chapter (see p.302). You could also hike straight in from Lakeside, via **Sarangkot** (see p.225), from Begnas Tal (see p.229), or even by hiring someone to row you up the lake to a point below Naudaada.

There are scores of **trekking agencies** in Pokhara, but you don't need one to trek in the Annapurna region unless you're doing something unorthodox, and **guides** and **porters** (see p.311) can be hired through any agency, equipment shop, or guesthouse. You'll sometimes see messages at Lakeside notice boards from people looking for potential trekking partners, but you'll certainly meet tons of people as soon as you start walking. Pokhara's selection of **rental trekking equipment** is as good as Kathmandu's, and you'll pay for fewer days by renting locally.

The required **TIMS permit** (US$10 if you're trekking with a guide, US$20 if trekking independently) and **Annapurna Conservation Area or ACAP fee** (US$20) can both be bought in the Nepal Tourism Board building, just south of Rastra Bank Chowk in Damside (ACAP counter daily 10am–5pm; TIMS counter Sun–Fri 10am–5pm). Bring two passport photos per permit (there are a couple of shops nearby where you can have photos taken), and note that you have to pay in rupees.

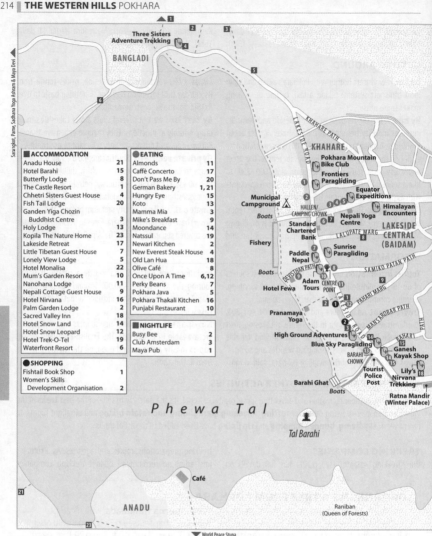

Saratighat, Pame, Sadhana Yoga Ashram & Maya Devi

Three Sisters
Adventure Trekking

BANGLADI

KHARARE PATH

LAKESIDE ROAD

KHAHARE

Pokhara Mountain
Bike Club

Frontiers
Paragliding

Equator
Expeditions

Municipal
Campground

HALLEN/
CAMPING CHOWK

Boats

Himalayan
Encounters

Nepali Yoga
Centre

Standard
Chartered
Bank

LALUPATE MARG

LAKESIDE
CENTRAL
(BAIDAM)

Fishery

Sunrise
Paragliding

Paddle
Nepal

DEVISTHAN PATH

SAMIKO PATAN PATH

Boats

Hotel Fewa

Adam
Tours

CENTRE
POINT

PAHARI MARG

MANSAROBAR PATH

Pranamaya
Yoga

High Ground Adventures

Blue Sky Paragliding

BARAHI
CHOWK

PAHARI PATH

Ganesh
Kayak Shop

Lily's
Nirvana
Trekking

Tourist
Police
Post

Barahi Ghat

Boats

Ratna Mandir
(Winter Palace)

■ ACCOMMODATION
Anadu House	21
Hotel Barahi	15
Butterfly Lodge	8
The Castle Resort	1
Chhetri Sisters Guest House	4
Fish Tail Lodge	20
Ganden Yiga Chozin	
Buddhist Centre	3
Holy Lodge	13
Kopila The Nature Home	23
Lakeside Retreat	17
Little Tibetan Guest House	7
Lonely View Lodge	5
Hotel Monalisa	22
Mum's Garden Resort	10
Nanohana Lodge	11
Nepali Cottage Guest House	9
Hotel Nirvana	16
Palm Garden Lodge	2
Sacred Valley Inn	18
Hotel Snow Land	14
Hotel Snow Leopard	12
Hotel Trek-O-Tel	19
Waterfront Resort	6

● SHOPPING
Fishtail Book Shop	1
Women's Skills	
Development Organisation	2

● EATING
Almonds	11
Caffè Concerto	17
Don't Pass Me By	20
German Bakery	1, 21
Hungry Eye	15
Koto	13
Mamma Mia	3
Mike's Breakfast	9
Moondance	14
Natssul	19
Newari Kitchen	2
New Everest Steak House	4
Old Lan Hua	18
Olive Café	8
Once Upon A Time	6,12
Perky Beans	7
Pokhara Java	5
Pokhara Thakali Kitchen	16
Punjabi Restaurant	10

■ NIGHTLIFE
Busy Bee	2
Club Amsterdam	3
Maya Pub	1

4

P h e w a   T a l

Tal Barahi

Café

ANADU

Raniban
(Queen of Forests)

World Peace Stupa

– the quality of their service can vary so much from trip to trip, and much depends on the individual guide – but the two local trekking operations listed below are long-standing and reputable outfits.

Lily's Nirvana Trekking Sacred Valley Inn, Lakeside Marg, Lakeside South ☏061 461 792, ⓦsacred valleyinn.com; map pp.214–215. Run by the owners of *Sacred Valley Inn*, this is a long-standing, reputable agency that employs experienced local guides.

Three Sisters Adventure Trekking Khahare, Lakeside ☏061 462 066, ⓦ3sistersadventure.com; map pp.214–215. This innovative, energetic agency nabbed a *National Geographic* ecotourism award for their efforts at empowering

women and helping local people develop tourism in remote areas. Run by three Chhetri sisters, it's almost unique in being able to arrange (in-house-trained) female guides and porters – for which it's best to book in advance. They can also arrange rock climbing on the cliffs behind the office.

RAFTING AND KAYAKING

Pokhara is within striking distance of no fewer than four rafting rivers: the Kali Gandaki, Trisuli, Seti and Marsyangdi. The Kali Gandaki is probably the most popular trip out of Pokhara; the Trisuli is better done out of Kathmandu, since the starting point is closer to there and the river flows towards Pokhara. The Seti is best known as the venue for

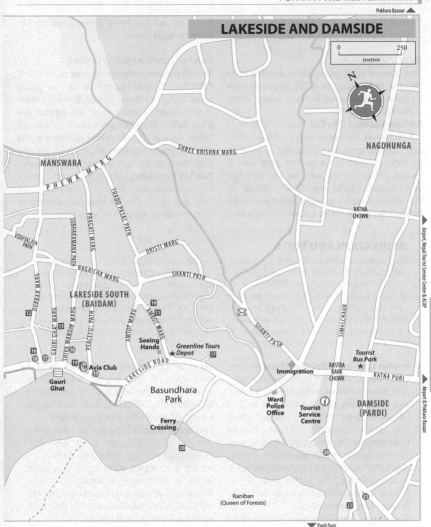

Pokhara Bazaar ▲

LAKESIDE AND DAMSIDE

0   250
metres

NAGDHUNGA

SHREE KRISHNA MARG

MANSWARA

PHEWA MARG

RATNA
CHOWK

THADO PASAL PATH

PRAGATI MARG

SUBRAHMANYA PATH

VIDHYALAYA
PATH

DRISTI MARG

BAGAICHA MARG

SHANTI PATH

DURBAR MARG

SHIVA MANDIR MARG

GAURI GHAT MARG

PEACEFUL PATH

AMBOT MARG

AMROT MARG

LAKESIDE SOUTH
(BAIDAM)

SHANTI PATH

SIMALCHAUR

10

11

12

13

16
18

17

Seeing
Hands

16

19

Avia Club

19

LAKESIDE ROAD

Greenline Tours
★ Depot

17

Tourist
Bus Park
★

Immigration

RASTRA
BANK
CHOWK

RATNA PURI

Gauri
Ghat

Basundhara
Park

Ward
Police
Office

Tourist
Service
Centre

(i)

DAMSIDE
(PARDI)

Ferry
Crossing

20

20

21

22

Raniban
(Queen of Forests)

▼ Pardi Dam

Airport, Nepal Tourist Service Centre & ACAP ▶

Airport & Pokhara Bazaar ▶

4

---

kayak clinics, which are organized by several companies; kayaks can be rented from most of the rafting and kayaking companies (around Rs1000/day). The "Rafting and kayaking" chapter (see p.354) has more detail about rivers, rafting and kayaking, while the "Kathmandu" chapter (see p.99) has full reviews of the big rafting companies, all of which have branches in Lakeside Central.

Equator Expeditions Phewa Marg, 400m east of Hallan Chowk, opposite Hotel Mountain Villa, Lakeside ☎ 061 465 999 or ☎ 975 609 999, ⓦ expeditionsnepal.com; map pp.214–215. Pokhara branch of the Kathmandu-based operator (see p.99).

Ganesh Kayak Shop Barahi Chowk, Lakeside Marg,

Lakeside Central ☎ 061 462 657; map pp.214–215. Specialist operator offering kayaking clinics on the Seti, kayak hire, hydrospeeds, equipment and excellent advice.

Himlayan Encounters Phewa Marg, 500m east of Hallan Chowk, beside Hotel Mountain Villa, Lakeside Central ☎ 061 461 954, ⓦ himalayanencounters.com; map pp.214–215. Hugely professional adventure company with strong UK links. Offers rafting as well as trekking, trips to Bandipur and more.

Paddle Nepal 50m north of Centre Point, Lakeside Marg, Lakeside Central ☎ 061 465 730, ⓦ paddlenepal .com; map pp.214–215. This rafting company is actually based in Pokhara, rather than in Kathmandu. As well as all the usual rafting trips, it offers kayaking clinics on the Seti, kayak hire and kayaking guides, as well as canyoning trips.

MOUNTAIN BIKING

Local mountain-biking possibilities are described in our "Mountain biking" chapter (see p.366), and possible routes are also indicated throughout the "Pokhara Valley" section of this chapter (see p.223).

Pokhara Mountain Bike Club Khahare, 200m north of Hallan Chowk, Lakeside ☎ 061 466 224 or ☎ 980 413 4788, ⓦ nepalmountainbike.com; map pp.214–215. It's surprisingly hard to hire good mountain bikes in Pokhara, but this excellent outfit can help; they have serious mountain bikes for around Rs1000–2500/day. The club also offers more than twenty guided rides in the Pokhara Valley, Tansen, and the Annapurnas (from Rs3000/

day all-in), and give free professional mountain-bike training to Nepali children.

PARAGLIDING AND SKYDIVING

Pokhara's paragliding companies all charge around US$100 for the basic 20–30min tandem flight from Sarangkot, or around US$135 for a 45min–1hr flight. Most offer a wealth of other options, including jumps from Bandipur (see p.202), flights with trained eagles or vultures, and a range of courses. The Nepal Open Paragliding championship takes place every year between December and January, attracting pilots from all over the world. Skydiving is now also on offer.

Blue Sky Paragliding Khahare, 400m north of Hallan Chowk, Lakeside ☎ 061 464 737, ⓦ paragliding-nepal .com; map pp.214–215. This Nepali-Swiss joint venture offers an exciting range of cross-country adventures.

MEDITATION AND YOGA

Many **spiritual centres** last only a season or two in Lakeside, and your best bet is to get personal recommendations from people who've just come back from a retreat (while bearing in mind that people seek very different kinds of experiences in this area). **Courses** can easily be found by checking notice boards or online, and yoga enthusiasts are fairly easily found in Lakeside's chatty guesthouses and cafés – especially if you head north towards **Khahare**, where many of the more serious meditation centres are found. There's little doubt that some Lakeside places are fairly commercial, but then that's true of many yoga centres back home, too. Introductory classes are sometimes free.

Ganden Yiga Chozin Buddhist Centre Khahare, Lakeside ☎ 061 462 923, ⓦ pokharabuddhistcentre .com. A peaceful and serious Buddhist facility with its own modest prayer hall. It's a short walk north of Lakeside, set up and back from the main drag – albeit in an area where construction is fast taking away the rural atmosphere. They run regular three-day weekend courses (starting on Fri afternoons; Rs6500), as well as daily meditation and yoga classes (Rs400), and simple accommodation (see p.219). Buddhist monks come up in season from Kopan monastery, outside Kathmandu, to run teachings and meditations.

Nepali Yoga Centre Phewa Marg, Lakeside ☎ 984 604 1879. Run by Devika Gurung, a yoga teacher originally from Jomosom, in the Annapurna region, this small, friendly, female-staffed and central Lakeside place offers well-regarded hatha yoga classes mornings and afternoons (90min; Rs400), as well as longer residential courses.

Pokhara Vipassana Centre Pachabhaiya, Lekhnath-11, Kaski ☎ 061 691 972, ⓦ pokhara .dhamma.org. In a stunning, utterly tranquil setting in the woods that rise steeply out of Begnas Tal's southern bank, 15km east of Pokhara and close to *Begnas Lake Resort* (see p.231), this rustic complex of buildings is taken over for ten-day courses (starting on the 1st of

every month) and day-long courses (on the last Sat of every month). It's highly regarded, but not for the tentative: the day starts at 4am and the rules designed to keep minds focused include no reading, no talking, no drinking and no sex. Relies entirely on donations.

Pranamaya Yoga Jiva Spa, just off Lakeside Rd, near the Busy Bee bar ☎ 980 204 5484, ⓦ pranamaya-yoga.com. Overlooking the lake, this excellent place offers a wide range of daily classes (Rs700) in everything from Ashtanga to vinyasa. Massages and an array of spa treatments are on offer, and there's a café too. Pranamaya has three other branches in Thamel, Patan and Boudha.

Sadhana Yoga Ashram Sedi Bagar, north of Lakeside ☎ 061 694 041 or ☎ 984 607 8117, ⓦ sadhana-asanga-yoga.com. This four-storey, no-frills building sits atop a hillock fifteen minutes above the Lakeside road, close to the path up to Sarangkot. The owners run popular ashram-style residential yoga courses – bells ring to keep you on your toes, hour by hour; you'll have "karma yoga" domestic chores to do, and it's more about breathing than anything athletic. You pay a premium for the secluded location and international reputation: US$440 for a four-day, five-night stay. Longer stays, cookery courses and sunrise tours up Sarangkot are also on offer.

Frontiers Paragliding Lakeside Central ☎061 466 044, ⓦnepal-paragliding.com or ⓦparahawking.com; map pp.214–215. One of the most innovative companies, offering the incredibly exciting parahawking option, in which a trained vulture guides you to thermals, and wheels and swoops around you ($210). Some money goes to vulture conservation projects, from where the "rescue birds" come, though some birders frown on anything that encourages the commercial use of endangered species. You can also drop by the *Maya Devi* village restaurant and learn to handle the birds.

Pokhara Skydive Amrit Marg, Thamel, Kathmandu ⓦnepalskydive.com. Tandem ($650) and solo ($350) skydives are offered, as well as multi-day courses. Much more expensive sky dives in the Everest region can also be arranged, if you have US$25,000–35,000 to spare.

Sunrise Paragliding 50m north of Centre Point, Lakeside Central ☎061 463 174, ⓦsunrise-paragliding .com; map pp.214–215. The original paragliding company, offering jumps (from Rs8500) from Bandipur and other sites. Qualified jumpers can try out para-treks, which involve hiking up to various local summits and floating back down.

BUNGEE JUMPING AND ZIP LINING

Two of the latest additions to Pokhara's adventure sports repertoire are bungee jumping and zip lining (Rs6490 for either; discounts available if you do both). Both are offered by High Ground Adventures, which also has plans for a large-scale adventure sports park outside Pokhara.

High Ground Adventures Lakeside Central ☎061 466 349, ⓦhighgroundnepal.com; map pp.214–215. Offers a range of different activities, most notably bungee jumping from a 70m-high tower and a 1.8km zip line (dubbed the world's "most extreme"); book directly with them or via your guesthouse.

SPORTS AND RECREATION

Golf *Fulbari Resort and Spa* (4km south of the airport; ☎061 432 451, ⓦfulbari.com) has a nine-hole course. The eighteen-hole *Himalayan Golf Course* (☎061 521 882, ⓦhimalayangolfcourse.com; US$50 for 18 holes) was set up by an ex-Gurkha major on the banks of the Bijayapur River gorge; sheep keep the fairways trim and the fourth hole, famously, is on an island.

Motorcycling Hearts and Tears Motorcycle Club, based at the *Busy Bee*, Lakeside Marg (☎984 602 0293, ⓦheartsandtears.com) rent out 1950s-vintage Royal Enfield Bullets (prices start at US$50 a day, including a thorough backup service; a bike recovery service is also possible). They also offer guided tours for experienced riders (from US$130/day, all in), which can take you on exciting roads towards and beyond Tansen.

Pony trekking Pony trekking in Pokhara is chiefly a matter of child-focused rides beside the lake. Most agents or hotels can help you book (around US$20/half-day). For anything more extreme, you'll have to talk to trekking guides or agencies about hiring horses in the Annapurna region – which is easily enough done, as they're commonly used for evacuating injured trekkers.

Swimming Hotel Barahi (see below), the *Castle Resort* (see p.218) and *Shangri-La Village* (see p.219) allow nonresidents to use their pools (for a fee).

Tennis Nonresidents can play at the *Hotel Barahi* in Lakeside (see below).

Ultralight flights If you want a sensational closer look at the Annapurnas, you can fly with Avia Club Nepal, 100m south of Centre Point, Lakeside Marg (☎061 462 192, ⓦaviaclubnepal.com), which takes off many times every morning from the airport (roughly 6.30–10am). Their ultralight aircraft can carry one passenger at a time: a 25min trip costs US$90, but it's worth spending US$130 for a 50min flight that takes you unforgettably close to the mountains.

ACCOMMODATION

Pokhara is glutted with **inexpensive** and moderately priced accommodation options, the majority with clean rooms, friendly staff and good breakfasts; some of Nepal's classiest **luxury hotels** are also found here (see p.219). Just about all independent travellers stay in **Lakeside** but if you're looking for the chilled-out vibe that made Pokhara's name, consider shifting a few minutes north towards **Bangladi**, which is still partly rural. In general, the views are better the further south you stay, though the competitive building of new storeys by hoteliers means that views can disappear from one season to the next. **Rates** vary according to season and the kind of room; rooms with balconies, attached bathrooms, views or on upper floors attract premiums. If you're booking, make sure you know what you're getting, but be prepared for things to switch around, as bookings are pretty fluid. Our listings start with the most popular accommodation area, which we've divided into Lakeside Central and Lakeside South. These are not actual place names (the official name for the whole area is **Baidam**), but correspond to areas with distinctive personalities.

LAKESIDE CENTRAL

With its strip of high-rise guesthouses, restaurants and trekking and rafting agencies, the central portion of Lakeside Marg, the main street, is like a relaxed, spread-out version of Kathmandu's Thamel.

Hotel Barahi Barahi Path, Lakeside ☎061 460 617, ⓦbarahi.com; map pp.214–215. One of the better smarter hotels in Lakeside itself, this professional yet friendly place offers Western-style rooms. The handful of standard-class rooms are a bit disappointing for the price, and overlook the pool – which can be noisy. Rooms ($178) in the new stone wing have a/c and more character; those on the upper floors have mountain views. There's also a modest swimming pool. **US$97**

Butterfly Lodge Lakeside ☎061 461 892, ⓦbutterfly-lodge.org; map pp.214–215. Set around a spacious garden, this solid, mid-range hotel has sparkling – though slightly overpriced – rooms with TVs; the more expensive en-suite options with balconies and a/c are the best value ($80). Profits from the hotel support local charitable projects, and staff can organize volunteer placements. **US$60**

Little Tibetan Guest House Lakeside ☎061 461 898 or ☎984 602 6166, ⓔlittletibgh@yahoo.com; map pp.214–215. Set back behind a quiet garden, on a side road off busy Phewa Marg, this Tibetan-run guesthouse offers big rooms nicely furnished with Tibetan bedspreads and carpets. **Rs1000**

Nepali Cottage Guest House Lakeside ☎061 461 637, ⓔkushwaha_3@hotmail.com; map pp.214–215. This intimate budget hotel, run by two friendly and helpful brothers, offers a few large rooms in a small building shoehorned into the thick of the action, at the end of a narrow little garden. Good value. **Rs600**

Hotel Snow Land Lakeside Marg, Lakeside ☎061 462 384, ⓦhotelsnowlandpokhara.com; map pp.214–215. Large, efficient hotel right in the heart of the strip, with views of the lake, a/c and satellite TV in the "deluxe" and "super deluxe" rooms ($74–86). The standard rooms are comfortable enough, but less desirable. **US$37**

LAKESIDE SOUTH

Things get quieter south of the Ratna Mandir and you can actually see the lake from the strip – the mountain views are better too. The flipside of all this is that there are fewer restaurants, bars and shops, so you may find yourself trekking up to the central portion of Lakeside a couple of times a day.

Holy Lodge Lakeside Marg, Lakeside ☎061 463 422, ⓦholylodge.com.np; map pp.214–215. Set back from the main lakeside drag, this long-running, peaceful place has space enough for a big garden stocked with papaya, lemon and mango trees, and a thatched seating area with fireplace in winter. The rooms are big and fairly well maintained, and the owners – a family – are friendly. **Rs800**

Lakeside Retreat Off Lakeside Marg, Lakeside ☎061 464 226, ⓦlsrpokhara.com; map pp.214–215. Swish hotel, set well back from the main road, with attractive en suites and cottages (all with a/c, TVs, telephones and fridges) set around a peaceful garden. There's a good restaurant and various spa options are available. Rooms **US$65**, cottages **US$105**

Mum's Garden Resort Ambot Marg, Lakeside ☎061 463 468, ⓦmumsgardenresort.com; map pp.214–215. Finally, a boutique hotel with a feel for design. Here you get beautifully cut stone walls and floors, inside and out, set

around a courtyard garden. A professional but welcoming place that justifies its relatively high price. **US$65**

★**Nanohana Lodge** Ambot Marg, Lakeside ☎061 464 478, ⓦnanohanalodge.com; map pp.214–215. The lively owner ensures this place stays in all the guidebooks (so book early) by redecorating every year. The spotless rooms have particularly comfortable beds and big, pleasant balconies overlooking a small garden; the more expensive ones ($20 upwards) have mountain views. Free airport pick-ups. **US$12**

Hotel Nirvana Ambot Marg, Lakeside ☎061 463 332, ⓔnirvanapkr@wlink.com.np; map pp.214–215. Huge, thoughtfully decorated and spotless rooms overlooking spacious, flower-strewn balconies and a garden – it feels like a real sanctuary, if not quite nirvana. The management is friendly, knowledgeable and open to negotiation, and the owners also run a good trekking agency, Lily's Treks. **US$20**

★**Sacred Valley Inn** Lakeside Marg, Lakeside ☎061 461 792, ⓦsacredvalleyinn.com; map pp.214–215. Owned by the same people as *Hotel Nirvana* (see above), this has large, very clean rooms, the priciest with balconies and views ($30), in a spacious building in a great location – close enough to the action, but on the quiet side of town. Bishnu and his team are friendly and very knowledgeable and can arrange treks. Hugely popular, so book early. **US$15**

Hotel Snow Leopard Durbar Marg, Lakeside ☎061 466 144, ⓦhotelsnowleopard.webs.com; map pp.214–215. This professionally run, mid-range hotel is set back from the main drag. Although the decor is a little garish – think pink walls – the rooms themselves are comfortable, and those on the upper floors boast decent views. **Rs1500**

Hotel Trek-O-Tel Gaurighat, Lakeside ☎061 464 996, ⓦacehotelsnepal.com; map pp.214–215. Look beyond the eccentric name and the tight-packed cluster of octagonal buildings and you'll find a classy hotel that's popular with international aid agencies for its quiet but central location and uniformed, very polite staff. Rooms are well furnished, with terracotta floors, a/c and sparkling bathrooms. **US$70**

KHAHARE AND BEYOND

Khahare, the area north of Hallan/Camping Chowk, has long attracted long-term travellers, yoga enthusiasts and anyone looking for the kind of rural retreat Pokhara used to be. It's developing fast, however, and the southerly parts of this area are turning into a less commercialized, more thinly populated extension of Lakeside. Taxis from the airport can get to any of the guesthouses listed here, but they'll charge more than the standard fare to Lakeside.

★**The Castle Resort** Above Khahare ☎061 461 926, ⓦpokharacastle.com; map pp.214–215. The 15min walk up is worth it for this fantastically turreted miniature castle, perched on a ridge above Khahare. It offers a beautiful view, lush rural surroundings amid gardens and terraced fields and a small pool (open to nonresidents for a modest charge). The rooms are in the turrets or romantic, traditionally styled cottages, and the Irish and Portuguese owners preside over the welcoming Irish pub-cum-restaurant, providing good food, wine and company. There is also road access from above, for those arriving the easy way. US$58

Chhetri Sisters Guest House Khahare, Lakeside ☎061 462 066, ⊛3sistersadventure.com; map pp.214–215. This smart and ever-expanding guesthouse is run by three famous sisters, pioneers of trekking for women (see p.214). Rooms are light, airy and well kept, with shared or private bathrooms, and paintings of local scenes. Plenty of single female visitors use the guesthouse to meet like-minded travellers (and potential trek partners), but it takes all-comers. US$30

Ganden Yiga Chozin Buddhist Centre Khahare, Lakeside ☎061 522 932 or ☎061 462 923, ⊛pokharabuddhistcentre.com; map pp.214–215. Suitably basic accommodation is provided in the modest annexe of this miniature meditation retreat centre (see p.216) – which has its own prayer room and giant prayer wheel. Daily meditation and yoga classes, and regular (silent) retreat and study sessions (Fri–Sun). Rs400

Lonely View Lodge Lakeside Marg, Khahare, Lakeside ☎984 602 3090, ⊛homestaypokhara.wordpress.com; map pp.214–215. Pleasant little guesthouse with five very simple, low-cost rooms, all with fans and a shared bathroom. The "apartment" (Rs500) also comes with basic cooking facilities, a fridge and a TV. Rs300

Palm Garden Lodge Khahare, Lakeside ☎984 629 4890, ⊛palm-garden-lodge.com; map pp.214–215. This large budget lodge is set among pleasant gardens above the main Lakeside road in the still rural area to the north – though the construction of lodges such as this one is rapidly changing the atmosphere of Khahare. Friendly, with a good sense of what travellers are looking for. Rs500

Waterfront Resort Lakeside Marg, Khahare, Lakeside ☎061 466 304, ⊛ktmgh.com; map pp.214–215. A new hotel from the long-established Kathmandu Guest House Group, *Waterfront Resort* has a tranquil location, smart and spacious en suites with private balconies overlooking the lake, two good restaurants and a delightful swimming pool. US$150

DAMSIDE

Damside, or Pardi, to give it its proper Nepali name, is more of a suburb than a tourist zone these days, but a few hotels and restaurants cling to what's left of the hotel trade. On the upside, it's peaceful, and the mountain views are good.

Hotel Monalisa Damside ☎061 463 863; map pp.214–215. Decent mid-range place in a good location overlooking the neck of the lake, with the mountains behind. The net curtains and brown coverlets and carpeting feel drab rather than characterful, but the welcome is friendly and sincere, and the rooms are pretty good

(though a/c costs US$20 extra). US$30

ACROSS THE LAKE: ANADU

Directly across the lake from Lakeside, Anadu is not one of Nepal's friendliest villages, but it's peaceful and there's a certain bohemian attraction to staying in a place that can only be reached by boat. (Actually, you can walk to Anadu from the highway on the other side of the ridge behind, but let's not spoil the illusion.) Furthermore, the views from here are better than they are from anywhere in Lakeside, the water is clean and there's a great hike (to the Peace Stupa) right outside your back door. Most of the places can be reached after about twenty minutes' rowing from the palace area of Lakeside.

★**Anadu House** Anadu ☎061 464 599 or ☎980 661 2556, ✉manadu22@gmail.com; map pp.214–215. Stunning and pleasingly eccentric private house on the Anadu hillside, set above stone steps leading up from the water and built by traditional craftsmen. The German long-term-resident owner, Manner, rents out the whole house (sleeping up to six), and you can enjoy his Himalayan art collection, the views, and the full shopping, cooking and cleaning service provided by the in-house butler. Minimum three-night stay; longer rents are possible. Three nights US$440

Kopila The Nature Home Anadu ☎061 621 369, ⊛facebook.com/kopilatnh; map pp.214–215. There's not much competition, but this is the best of the cheaper places in Anadu: awesome views, shady (though unkempt) and indescribably peaceful grounds amid the forest, tended by the Japanese-Nepali owners. The restaurant, and hot water, are both a bit patchy, though, and the decor a little tired – in general, it feels as if it's fallen off since busier days. Rs1000

RESORT HOTELS

Though Pokhara's resort hotels do provide a bit of welcome luxury and a lovely environment for relaxing and maybe swimming in the pool, don't expect perfection. Offers and discounts mean that prices can be significantly lower in practice than the tariff rates quoted. If you're in the market for this kind of accommodation, consider also *Begnas Lake Resort and Villas* (see p.231) and *Waterfront Resort* (see above).

Fish Tail Lodge Opposite Lakeside South ☎061 465 071, ⊛fishtail-lodge.com; map pp.214–215. This is Lakeside's original deluxe hotel – the dated styling and rooms housed in polygonal buildings dotted about the (fabulous) grounds give the feel of a Bond villain's lair. It has a pool and an unrivalled view of the lake, though, with the classic profile of the mountains behind – which is how they get away with the prices. Access by punt or rope ferry. US$145

Shangri-La Village 1.5km south of the airport ☎061 462 222, ⊛hotelshangrila.com; map p.207. Well-designed complex of deluxe Nepali houses scattered through expensively landscaped grounds. The serene pool

4

is open to all. Service is slow and ground-floor rooms disappointing, though. US$185

★**Tiger Mountain Pokhara Lodge** 5km east of Pokhara ☎01 436 1500 or ☎061 691 887, ⓦtigermountainpokhara.com; map p.224. Seriously

classy outfit along the ridge some 5km due east of Pokhara, offering fine views, superb service and attractive rooms in stone bungalows, plus a pool. All meals, activities and transportation to and from Pokhara are included in the price. US$310

EATING

Pokhara has an exceptional number of **restaurants** and, while there's not much nightlife after around 10.30pm, when many places stop serving, the congenial restaurants and cafés around the lake are easy places to make friends and find trekking partners. Candlelight (often imposed by load-shedding) adds to the romance. Most tourist restaurants offer a more or less standard menu, featuring an implausible selection of improvised **non-Nepali** dishes and local fish prepared umpteen different ways. For something much cheaper, try one of the myriad **momo** shacks (there's a good cluster in the vicinity of *Hotel Barahi*) and, for a real change of scene, head for Pokhara Bazaar, which has a number of **Indian** restaurants – *Almonds* is the classic. The usual basic diners serving Nepali or **Tibetan** food are scattered throughout the city – just head up any back road away from the strip. Watch out for the **juice** sellers: they'll dilute the juice with (unsafe) water and sugar behind the scenes. **Mini-supermarkets** along the main Lakeside road anticipate your every need: chocolate, tinned food, bread, cheese, wine, spirits, toiletries, batteries and the like. Shops in Mahendra Pul (the centre of the bazaar area of the city) are of course much cheaper.

LAKESIDE CENTRAL

★**Almonds** Lakeside Marg ☎061 460 271; map pp.214–215; second branch overlooking B.P. Chowk ☎061 530 176; map p.207. Perhaps the best restaurant for Indian food on Lakeside, and popular with locals. The butter chicken is popular, but it's better to explore the wide range of curry dishes (Rs230–350) or order a complete *thali* (Rs310–430). The Chipledhunga branch in the main city bazaar (overlooking the busy B.P. Chowk crossroads) is even better – and worth the trip for a taste of Nepali rather than tourist Pokhara. Service isn't always as good as it should be. Daily 9am–10.30pm or later.

Hungry Eye Lakeside Marg ☎061 463 096; map pp.214–215. This large and faintly flashy place is aimed at groups, but does offer one of the better (if noisier) culture shows on the strip, featuring genuine, and well-performed Nepali songs and dances (7am–9pm). The Continental-Indian-Chinese-Nepali menu is implausibly comprehensive (most mains Rs310–550) but perfectly respectable. Daily 7am–10pm.

Koto Lakeside Marg ☎061 463 414; map pp.214–215. From its partly open-air, first-floor terrace, this renowned restaurant serves about the best Japanese food you'll find in Pokhara, including *yakitori* and *teriyaki* dishes, udon and donburi noodles, sticky rice and even smoked salmon sushi. Excellent set menus (from Rs395). Daily 11.30am–3pm & 6–9pm.

Mamma Mia Phewa Marg ☎061 464 810; map pp.214–215. One of the best Italian restaurants, with a relaxed wicker interior open to the street. Serves surprisingly good home-made pasta with fresh sauces, such as garlic and olive oil spaghetti, and real, crispy-crusted wood-oven pizzas (Rs305–605). Happy hour 5–8pm. Daily 7am–11pm.

Mike's Breakfast Devisthan Path ☎061 463 151; map pp.214–215. *Mike's* has fallen off since its heyday, when it was in glorious isolation on this side of the strip, but this café still has the closest seating to the lake, and serves the famous breakfasts (Rs437–510), with large portions of authentic American-style waffles, eggs Benedict, *huevos rancheros*, apple pancakes and the like. Daily 6.30am–9pm.

Moondance Lakeside Marg ☎061 461 835; map pp.214–215. The epicentre of Lakeside eating, with a glamorous interior defined by a curving mezzanine level and a huge fire with a showpiece copper chimney. Service can be slow on busy nights, but they offer dishes you won't easily find elsewhere, such as British-style sausage and mash (Rs732) and barbecued spare ribs (a whopping Rs1722), as well as good pizzas (from Rs320). Good for chilled after-dinner drinking and a game of pool, too. Daily 8am–10.30pm or later.

★**Newari Kitchen** Near Camping Chowk, Lakeside Marg ☎061 462 633; map pp.214–215. The nicely recreated traditional Newari atmosphere is boosted by the company of swallows – there's a nest inside the premises – and the views down to the lake from the little terrace. They offer European and pan-Asian food, but go for the Newari specialities: the set meals (Rs475–735), the potato and bamboo-shoot soup or the *juju dhau* sweet curd. Daily 7am–10pm.

New Everest Steak House Phewa Marg; map pp.214–215. This restaurant serves reputedly the best (and perhaps the biggest) steaks in town (Rs495–1400), with every conceivable sauce. The sizzlers are the classics, and a few chicken and other beef dishes are also on the menu. Daily 9am–10pm.

Olive Café Lakeside Marg ☎061 462 575; map pp.214–215. Owned by *Moondance* (see above), this restaurant aims high; the atmosphere is relaxed, with a few outdoor

tables on the street, European café-style. Try the tabbouleh (Rs467), or the zingy fresh Mediterranean platter, complete with real olives and hummus. It bustles at night too, with a taverna-like atmosphere (happy hour 4–6pm). Drinks include imported Belgian beers (Rs800), cocktails and a delicious mint lemonade (Rs154). Daily 6.30am–11pm.

Once Upon A Time Lakeside Marg ☎061 461 881; map pp.214–215. One of the nicest central café-restaurants, overlooking a spreading fig tree and preserving a flavour of old Lakeside with its open wickerwork balcony upstairs. Good pizzas, Mexican food and generous Indian *thalis* (mains from Rs545). There's another branch just east of Camping Chowk. Daily 8am–11pm.

Perky Beans Lakeside Marg ☎984 615 3975; map pp.214–215. This cute little wooden-floored café offers fine Nepali-grown organic coffee (you can even get a decent flat white; coffee Rs90–250), breakfast options, sandwiches, cakes, pastries and cookies. There are only five tables, but takeaway options are available. Daily 8am–8pm.

Pokhara Java Phewa Marg ☎061 123 456, ⓦpokharajava.com; map pp.214–215. Breezy coffee shop with wicker chairs and very welcome ceiling fans. The coffee options (Rs95–225) range from ristrettos to caramel machiattos, and you can even get soya milk. Sandwiches, cakes and snacks are also available. Daily 6.30am–8/9pm.

Punjabi Restaurant Lakeside Marg ☎984 602 5937; map pp.214–215. Authentic, pure vegetarian Indian restaurant, offering delicious Punjabi and South Indian dishes (Rs215–400) in a cosy, faintly festive atmosphere, with wicker chairs and warm, coloured lighting. Service can be sluggish. Daily 8am–11pm.

LAKESIDE SOUTH

Caffè Concerto In front of the Ratna Mandir, Lakeside Marg ☎061 463 529; map pp.214–215. Authentic Italian dishes (pasta Rs400–595, pizza Rs430–660) in a mellow, jazz-infused atmosphere. Their tiramisu and home-made ice cream are the real McCoy, and the pizzas feature inventive toppings such as rocket and prosciutto. Tolerable wine. Daily 8am–10.30pm.

Natssul Lakeside Marg, Lakeside ☎061 229 198, ⓦnatssul.com; map pp.214–215. One of the last open-air garden restaurants in Lakeside, with little thatched roofs over tables and, rare thing, a view of the lake. Passionately run by a Korean couple known as April (her) and October (him), this place will reawaken the most Lakeside-jaded palate (mains Rs330–825). Try the *bulgogi* hot-stone pot stew, the *kimboh* sushi or the delicious pork barbecue dishes (after 5pm). Generally noon–10pm, though sometimes opens slightly earlier and closes later.

Old Lan Hua Gaurighat, Lakeside Marg ☎061 463 797; map pp.214–215. This is as good a Chinese restaurant as you'll find in any Chinatown, and very popular with locals and Chinese tourists – ask one to help you navigate the more recherché corners of the vast menu (double-cooked gizzard?), or go for a classic duck with ginger or shredded pork. Portions are huge (dishes from Rs125). Daily 11am–10pm.

Pokhara Thakali Kitchen Gaurighat, Lakeside Marg ☎061 206 536; map pp.214–215. Thakali food is a sign of quality for Nepalis, and this place doesn't disappoint, with its sumptuous *daal bhaat*, and excellent, richly spiced, meaty Newari dishes such as chillied Mustang potatoes and *sukuti* (dried meat). The interior is smartly but cosily done up in traditional Nepali style with dry-stone walls and red/white plastering, and in winter you can sit round the big circular fire. *Thalis* and set meals cost Rs220–715. Daily 10am–10pm.

DAMSIDE

Don't Pass Me By Damside, Pardi; map pp.214–215. Unbeatable location, with flower-framed gardens running down to the lake's final finger, and wooded slopes just opposite. Better for breakfast or a simple lunch (from Rs300), as insects can be troublesome at night. Daily 9am–8.30pm.

German Bakery Damside, Pardi ☎061 463 175; map pp.214–215. Tolerable croissants, good set breakfasts and a genuinely enticing cake display (from Rs45), as well as simple main dishes such as *thukpa* noodle soup. There is another branch just north of Camping Chowk. Daily 6am–9pm.

NIGHTLIFE

Pokhara's **nightlife scene** is second only to Thamel's, but it's distinctly more laidback, with little of the aggro, and fairly strictly observed closing times – not much happens after 11pm. Almost all bars feature **happy hours** – which usually means most of the afternoon up to 5–7pm. The **music** scene consists of Nepali rock bands playing covers earlier in the evening, and sometimes DJs playing the usual dancefloor-filling Western tunes later on, but you can occasionally find Bollywood nights, jazz bands or more interesting fusion groups – you'll have to follow your ears. Over dinner, the *Hungry Eye*, *Hotel Barahi* and a few other tourist restaurants put on free folk music and dance performances by local troupes.

Busy Bee Lakeside Marg, Lakeside North; map pp.214–215. Spacious, partially open-air bar that's as lively as the name suggests, with a group rocking every night (8–11pm), pool and table football, a long cocktail list (happy hour 3–7pm) and a buzzing garden area down by the lake complete with a water-feature and a little bridge. Popular chiefly with young Westerners. Daily noon–1am.

Club Amsterdam Lakeside Marg, Lakeside North; map pp.214–215. Popular pub-like venue with a well-stocked bar (beer from Rs450; happy hour 2–8pm), pool table, massive satellite TV, live music (blues or rock almost nightly, sometimes jazz) and a small dancefloor that's fairly well used later on. Daily 10am–midnight or later.

Maya Pub Lakeside Marg, Lakeside North; map pp.214–215. A popular bar-restaurant with a legendary Australian manager. Good for after-house lounging with beer (from Rs300), cocktails and music. Serves good, moderately priced pastas, sizzlers and vegetarian dishes, too. Daily 9am–11pm or later.

SHOPPING

You can buy the entire range of Nepali **souvenirs** in Pokhara, from cute woollens to *khukuri* knives, and from *thangka* paintings to Tibetan jewellery – most of it at slightly higher prices than in Kathmandu, from where it's often imported. **Local specialities** include batiks (dyed wall hangings), wooden flasks, dolls in ethnic dress and fossil-bearing *shaligram* stones from the Kali Gandaki – which are often carved. The best place to buy handicrafts is the long strip of shanty-shops opposite the Ratna Mandir, in Lakeside South. Kashmiris have colonized Lakeside, with boutiques touting "Asian" art, mainly high-priced carpets and cheap papier-mâché and soapstone widgets. **Tibetan carpets** are probably best bought at the Tibetan villages, while for anything manufactured you're best off in the Mahendral Pul area of the city, around B.P. Chowk.

Fishtail Book Shop Opposite Maya Pub, Lakeside Marg ☎061 462 368; map pp.214–215. There's no standout bookshop in Pokhara (along the lines of Pilgrims in Kathmandu), but this is one of the biggest and best, with a good selection of new and secondhand books (including some Rough Guides), and very helpful management. Daily 8am–9.30pm.

Women's Skills Development Organization Just south of Fishtail Book Shop, Lakeside Marg ☎980 281 5100; map pp.214–215. A fair trade, nonprofit shop selling attractive handmade products – including hand-woven bags, cushion covers and clothes, as well as a small selection of metalwork – produced by economically and/or socially disadvantaged Nepali women. Daily 9am–9pm.

DIRECTORY

4

Banks and money Standard Chartered, just south of Hallan/Camping Chowk, Lakeside Marg, handles foreign exchange (Sun–Thurs 9am–4pm, Fri 9am–1pm). There are ATMs up and down the main Lakeside road.

Hospitals, clinics and pharmacies Several pharmacies in Lakeside and Damside do stool tests, though incorrect diagnoses are common. One or two also offer ayurvedic medicine. In an emergency head for the Manipal Teaching Hospital, in Phulbari, on the east bank of the Seti Nadi towards the northern end of the city (☎061 526 416); it is well resourced and has a staff of Indian-trained doctors. Slightly closer to hand, but much less preferable (and still on the opposite side of the Seti, at Hospital Chowk, near the Bhadrakali Mandir) is the Western Regional Hospital (☎061 520 066), also known as the Gandaki Hospital – its ER looks terrible, but quite a few Western-trained doctors work there.

Laundry Most lodges take laundry for a few rupees per item, and laundries with machines can be found all over Lakeside.

Massage Seeing Hands, Lakeside Marg (☎061 465 786, ⓦseeinghandsnepal.org) has a good reputation, and is certainly ethical, as it trains and employs blind therapists – their salon is opposite Basundhara Park, just north of the Greenline office. They offer a range of services – including deep tissue work for aching trekkers (massages from Rs1800/hr). Barbers, who mostly come from India, are well versed in traditional head massage, and usually offer neck, back and full-body too.

Police The tourist police post on the south side of Barahi Chowk, Lakeside Marg, is the best first port of call. For anything serious, you're best getting the help of your hotel – or embassy.

Post Tourist book- and postcard shops sell stamps. Many shops and hotels will take mail to the post office; they're mostly trustworthy.

Visa extensions Visa extension procedures were changed in mid-2014: you now need to apply online first (at ⓦnepalimmigration.gov.np) and then take the email response with you to Pokhara's immigration office in Damside (Sun–Thurs: summer 10am–4pm; winter 10am–3pm; ☎061 465 167); your visa should be ready later the same day. Passport photos are available from photo shops around Lakeside.

The Pokhara Valley

Day-trips around the **Pokhara Valley** make excellent training for a trek. Start early to make the most of the views before the clouds move in and the heat builds, and bring lunch and water. If you're feeling adventurous, you can **stay overnight** at Sarangkot, Tashi Palkhel or Begnas Tal.

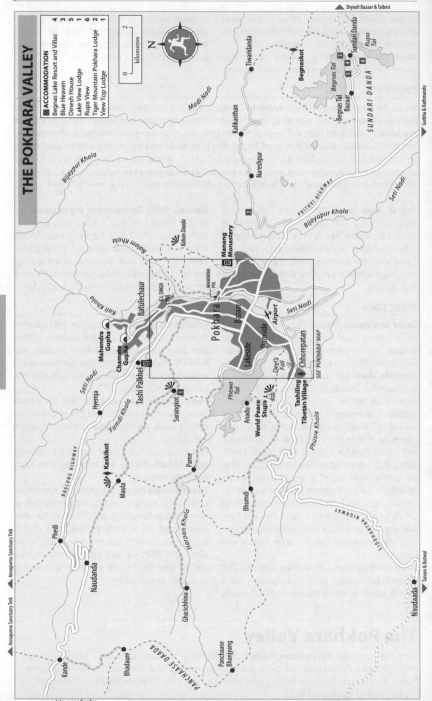

THE POKHARA VALLEY

ACCOMMODATION
Begnas Lake Resort and Villas	4
Blue Heaven	3
Dinesh House	5
Lake View Lodge	1
Rupa View	6
Tiger Mountain Pokhara Lodge	2
View Top Lodge	1

0 2
kilometres

4

TREKKING: THE WORLD PEACE STUPA AND BEYOND

The easiest approach to the World Peace Stupa is by trail **from Damside**. Cross the river on a footbridge just downstream of the dam, then follow the path as it bears left and passes a small shrine before beginning a gradual ascent up the back (south) side of the ridge. Don't take all your valuables or walk alone, and check with locals before leaving as there have been reports of robberies in the forest here. The way is somewhat obscure at first, but soon becomes a fine wide path through chestnut forest until the final ascent. The climb is steeper **from Anadu**, the village across the lake (reached by boat from Lakeside; Rs500/boat one-way). If descending this way, you should have no trouble getting a canoe back to Lakeside.

To make an easy day-trip of the walk you can **loop around Phewa Tal**. From the stupa, keep walking along the ridge-line past Rani Ban Retreat and along a rough road to the village of Bhumdi, where another road descends to the highway and a trail leads down to the sluggish Harpan Khola at Pame, 3km upstream of Phewa Tal. For a longer hike, continue further west beyond Bhumdi to the end of the road before descending to the Harpan Khola.

A superb two-day trek offering supreme views climbs on from Bhumdi up to **Panchaase Daada**, the prominent forested ridge west of Phewa Tal. From the top of the path, a trail follows the ridge northwest to Panchaase Bhanjyang, where you can stay at one of a handful of basic **lodges**. The next morning, continue up to the high point of the ridge (2509m) and on north to Bhadaure and the Baglung Highway, where you can pick up a bus past Naudaada back to Pokhara. Very few foreigners venture into this area, so a good map or knowledgeable guide is recommended.

The World Peace Stupa

The **World Peace Stupa**, a local landmark that crowns the ridge across the lake at an elevation of 1113m, provides one of the most satisfying short hikes in the Pokhara Valley. The views from the top are phenomenal, and since there are several routes up and back (see box above), you can work this into a loop that includes boating on the lake and/or visiting Chhorepatan. A basic up-and-back trip can be done in two to three hours, so you can leave after breakfast and be back in time for lunch.

Standing more than 40m tall, the stupa (sometimes entirely erroneously called the **pagoda**) looks as if it has been cross-bred with a lighthouse. It seems rather grandiose for a religious shrine, but the **view** from here is just about the best wide-angle panorama you can get of this part of the Himalayas, and certainly the only one with Phewa Tal and Pokhara in the foreground. Over on the far left you'll see the towering hump of Dhaulagiri and its more westerly sisters, in the middle rises the Annapurna Himal and the graceful pyramid of Machhapuchhare, and off to the right are Manaslu, Himalchuli and Baudha. Small **cafés** provide refreshment, and the Japanese Buddhist organization that funded the monument's construction maintains an adjacent monastery.

Sarangkot

From the peaklet of **Sarangkot** (1590m), the high point of the ridge that rises north of Phewa Tal, the Himalayas spread themselves in a stomach-lurchingly splendid panorama – it almost feels as if you could reach over across the green gulf of the Seti Nadi, at your feet, and touch them. The lake views behind you are pretty special too, making this the most popular mountain viewpoint around Pokhara. Not quite as many peaks are visible here as at the World Peace Stupa, but they feel bigger and closer. Dominating the skyline, in beauty if not in height, is the 6997m summit of Machhapuchhare ("Fish-Tailed"), so named for its twin-peaked summit, though only one peak is visible from Pokhara.

Many people hike up (see p.226) in the afternoon, spend the night in one of the lodges that cling to the slopes ten minutes below the top, then catch the dawn views.

HIKING UP SARANGKOT

The best **hiking route up Sarangkot** heads straight up from Pokhara's Lakeside, a long, steep climb with no mountain views until the very top – if you're running late you might miss them altogether. Follow the road north from Lakeside; 2km beyond Hallan/Camping Chowk the trail, marked by a painted stone, forks off to the right; when in doubt, stay on the flagstoned path and keep heading generally towards the summit. You'll be doing well to make it from the trailhead to the top in less than two and a half hours.

The easier alternative (especially if you take a taxi) is to follow the paved road that starts near the Bindhyabasini Mandir, which brings you to the "Sarangkot parking" turnaround point, half an hour's walk short of the summit. The final hike is steep enough to be tiring, but not frighteningly so, and the steps are crowded for most of the way with lodges and curio-sellers.

The Rs25 **admission fee** is payable at a booth beside the path, above Sarangkot parking. (Taxis pay a separate fee lower down.)

Others get up in the dark, take a taxi up to the car park and then walk the final half-hour to the summit. Others still come to **paraglide** (see p.216), taking in the panorama then circling down to the lakeshore in the later morning.

ARRIVAL AND DEPARTURE   SARANGKOT

By bus Buses for Sarangkot depart from Pokhara's Baglung bus park (4 daily; 45min–1hr).

By taxi A taxi from Pokhara costs around Rs1200.

ACCOMMODATION AND EATING

Several **lodges** line the path up to the top, all with (fairly basic) **restaurants** and some with excellent views. With the persistent ridgetop winds, Sarangkot feels a fair bit colder than Pokhara, so come prepared. If you're looking for somewhere really inexpensive, the best place to look is along the dirt road to Kaskikot and Naudaada – places and standards really come and go here, so it's a matter of seeing what you can find. At the time of research, the Kathmandu Guest House group (@ ktmgh.com) was building a new top-end hotel here.

Lake View Lodge Sarangkot-3, Kaski ☎ 980 589 0135, @ sarangkothotel.com. A big, well-established lodge right under the Nepal Television tower – it does indeed have lake rather than mountain views, but it's spacious and well kept, and one of the closest places to the summit viewpoint, just five minutes above. Rooms with attached bathrooms cost double. US$8

View Top Lodge Sarangkot-3, Kaski ☎ 974 606 4324, @ bikithapa@gmail.com. Just below the *Lake View Lodge* and the final steps to the summit viewpoint, this solid, comfortable place offers relatively good (but still partial) views from its large glass windows. Rooms are homely enough and food is available. Rs1500

Routes beyond Sarangkot

A road connects Sarangkot with Naudaada, about 10km further west on the Baglung Highway, making all sorts of longer trips beyond Sarangkot possible. A few villages are located along the way, notably **Maula**, the starting point of a flagstoned path up to **Kaskikot**, seat of the kingdom that once ruled the Pokhara Valley, perched on a craggy brow of the ridge with views as big as Sarangkot's. A stone enclosure and a house-like Kali temple are all that remain of the citadel of the Kaski kings, which fell to the Gorkhalis without a fight in 1781. **Naudaada** is another 4.5km west of Maula, and the first place from which Machhapuchhre's true fishtail profile can be seen. Two or three simple but attractive **lodges** offer trekking-style accommodation along the road between Maula and Naudaada. You'll probably catch a bus from Naudaada back to Pokhara, but other interesting variations are possible, including walking down from Maula to Pame or heading west along the main road from Naudaada to Kande, and then taking the foot trail south up to Panchaase Daada (see p.225).

Tashi Palkhel (Hyemja)

4km northwest of the north end of Pokhara Bazaar on the Baglung Highway; the entrance is clearly marked • Buses run from the Baglung bus park, or take a taxi (around Rs700)

With up to a thousand residents, eighty of them monks, **TASHI PALKHEL** (commonly known as **Hyemja**) is the largest and the least commercial of Pokhara's Tibetan settlements (see box below). On arrival, a footpath leads past curio-sellers straight to the community's large **gompa** (monastery), where resident monks usually gather for chanting at 6am and 3–4pm, and all day during festivals. The *gompa* is of the Kagyu-pa sect, under Shangpa Rinpoche and Dupsing Rinpoche, and portraits either side of the Buddha statue inside the hall depict the Dalai Lama and the Kagyu leader, the seventeenth Karma Lama. Smaller figures behind represent the 1008 Buddhas believed to exist during the present age.

Behind the monastery, steps lead up through a small Nepali **shantytown** – ironically, Nepalis fleeing conflict and poverty in the hills are the new refugees here – to the *or*, or holy place, where prayer flags flutter over a hillock and small chorten. The community also has a school to which Tibetan children from all over Nepal come as boarders, an old people's home, and a Tibetan medicine clinic, which is happy to treat foreigners – the physician speaks English, as indeed do many of the monks.

The carpet workshops

Opposite the monastery, a broad quadrangle is the last remnant of Tashi Palkhel's once-thriving **carpet industry**, which in the glory days used to employ scores of women, but can now keep fewer than half a dozen in work, due to undercutting by foreign competitors. You can still watch them at work on their looms, and even specify your own designs, which can be turned into a workable pattern and woven within a fortnight – ready for when you come back from that trek. Other traditional handicrafts can be purchased at the cooperative shop in the guesthouse compound, whose profits support community projects, as well as from private shops and freelance vendors.

4

TIBETANS IN EXILE

Thirty years ago, travel writer Dervla Murphy worked as a volunteer among **Tibetan refugees in Pokhara**, and called the account she wrote about her experiences *The Waiting Land*. Pokhara's Tibetans are still waiting: three former **refugee camps**, now largely self-sufficient, have settled into a pattern of permanent transience. Because Pokhara has no Buddhist holy places, many older Tibetans have remained in the camps, regarding them as havens where they can keep their culture and language alive.

At the time of the **Chinese invasion** of Tibet in 1950, the Tibetans now living in Pokhara were mainly peasants and nomads inhabiting the border areas of western Tibet. After the Dalai Lama fled Tibet in 1959 and the Chinese occupation turned violent, thousands streamed south through the Himalayas to safety. They gathered first at Jomosom, but the area soon became overcrowded and conditions desperate, and three **transit camps** were established around Pokhara.

The first five years in the camps were marked by rationing, sickness and unemployment. Relief came in the late 1960s, when the construction of Pardi Dam and the Prithvi and Siddhartha highways provided work. A second wave of refugees arrived around the same time, after the United States' detente with China ended a CIA operation supporting Tibetan freedom-fighters based in Mustang. Since then, the fortunes of Pokhara's Tibetans have risen with the tourism, carpet-weaving and Buddhism industries – the last of these is a big earner, due to foreign donations. A small but visible minority have become smooth-talking curio salespeople, plying the cafés of Lakeside and Damside, but whereas Tibetans have by now set up substantial businesses in Kathmandu, opportunities are fewer in Pokhara, and prosperity has come more slowly.

The Pokhara settlements – **Tashi Palkhel**, **Tashiling** and **Paljorling** – are open to the public, and a wander around one is an experience of workaday reality that contrasts with the otherworldliness of, say, Boudha or Swayambhu. You'll get a lot more out of a visit if you can get someone to show you around.

Batulechaur and around

Pokhara's conurbation spreads north up the valleys of the Seti Nadi and Kali Khola. Some 5km from the city centre lies **BATULECHAUR**, a village locally famous for its **gaaine** – wandering minstrels who earn their crust by singing ballads to the accompaniment of the *sarangi* fiddle. "I have no rice to eat/let the strings of the *sarangi* set to", runs the *gaaine*'s traditional opening couplet. There's little to see – the minstrels are wandering, after all – but 1km beyond the village lie two of the more interesting of the Pohara Valley's many **cave systems**, all created by water percolating through the local limestone bedrock.

Mahendra Gupha

Around 1km beyond Batulechaur (signed) • Daily 6.30am–6pm • Rs20 • To get here from Pokhara, pass K.I. Singh Pul (Bridge) at the top end of town, heading uphill north past the Gurkha camp for 2km; a taxi charges about Rs700

The stalactites that were once the chief attraction of **Mahendra Gupha** (Mahendra Cave) have mostly been stolen, leaving only a few surviving **stalagmites** daubed with *abhir* (red tikka powder) and revered as *shivalinga* because of their resemblance to phalluses. Most visitors now are Indian pilgrims, walking along a fairly well-lit path for five minutes to the internal Siddha Binayak shrine, where a pallid resident priest performs *puja*.

Chamere Gupha (Bat Cave)

Around 500m beyond Batulechaur • Daily 6.30am–6pm • Rs20, plus around Rs50–100 for a guide • To walk from Mahendra Gupha, a little under 1km, take the easy side road; alternatively, it's around 4km northwest of Pokhara Bazaar

The most impressive cave trip in these parts is to **Chamere Gupha** (which means **Bat Cave**, and is often called as much). There are no handrails or concrete footpaths here, so bring a torch (or rent one from the ticket seller) and take on one of the young guides – for all that they're fairly pushy and know little about bats. Most of the thousands of winter residents here are thought to be from two agile, insect-eating horseshoe species, but the valley is home to eighteen or more bat species, and roost sites are often shared. In season (approximately late Oct–April) thousands hang from the ceiling; out of season you'll only see a few stragglers. Guides will show you how to manage the tight, 3m vertical scramble up out of the main chamber: wear old clothes, and don't carry a big bag that you'll have to take off.

Kahun Daada

The view from **Kahun Daada**, the hill east of Pokhara, may be a shade less magnificent than Sarangkot's, but the trails leading up are totally uncommercialized – and the view takes in the Seti Nadi and its tributaries, which tumble out of the Annapurna Himal clouded with dissolved limestone (*seti* means white) and split the valley floor below with their broad gorges and dark canyons. The easiest **route up** starts behind Pokhara's Manipal Teaching Hospital, climbing north onto the east–west ridge-line and then straight up to the view tower (1442m).

The Manang Monastery trail

The most interesting starting point for climbing up to Kahun Daada is arguably the **Karma Dhubgyu Chokhorling monastery**, also known as Manang Gompa, which stands on a hill 2km east down the main road from Pokhara's Mahendra Pul. This large, seventy-monk monastery occupies a breezy spot at the top of a breathless couple of hundred steps, with valley views east and west. Near the *gompa*, on a hill a ten- to fifteen-minute walk away, is the Newari temple of Bhadrakali, an angry aspect of the goddess Parvati; the temple is rustically surrounded by bougainvilleas. From the *gompa*, it takes about ninety minutes to walk up to the top of Kahun Danda, along tracks that lead through several traditional villages collectively known as **Phulbari**. There are numerous possible routes, but if you keep heading towards the view tower, which is visible most of the way, and ask wherever possible, you won't go far wrong.

GURUNGS AND MAGARS

Once active trans-Himalayan traders – the Chinese occupation of Tibet put paid to that – **Gurungs** are a common sight around Gorkha and Pokhara, where many have invested their Gurkha pensions in guesthouses and retirement homes. The majority of Gurungs who don't serve in the military keep sheep for their wool, driving them to pastures high on the flanks of the Himalayas, and raise wheat, maize, millet and potatoes.

Traditional pursuits such as hunting and honey-gathering are being encroached upon by overpopulation, while the Gurung form of shamanism is coming under pressure from the advance of Hinduism and Buddhism. Gurungs employ shamans to appease ghosts, reclaim possessed souls from the underworld, and guide dead souls to the land of their ancestors – rituals that contain clear echoes of "classic" Siberian shamanism and are believed to resemble those of pre-Buddhist Tibet.

A somewhat less cohesive group, **Magars** are scattered throughout the lower elevations of the Western Hills and in some parts of the east. A network of Magar kingdoms once controlled the entire region, but the arrival of Hindus in the fifteenth century brought swift political decline and steady cultural assimilation. After centuries of coexistence with Hindu castes, most Magars employ Baahun priests and worship Hindu gods just like their Chhetri neighbours, differing only in that they're not allowed to wear the sacred thread of the "twice-born" castes. Despite the lack of unifying traits, group identity is still strong, and will probably remain so as long as Magars keep marrying only within the clan.

Bhalam Khola valley

The tidily terraced side valley of the **Bhalam Khola**, immediately north of Kahun Daada, is well worth exploring. To get there directly from the view tower, it's better to backtrack towards the monastery until you pick up the first main northbound trail. It's also accessible by a rough (bikeable) track heading northwards on the east bank of the Seti Nadi.

Begnas and Rupa Tal

With Lakeside so overdeveloped, it's strange that **Begnas Tal** and **Rupa Tal**, the smaller but still lovely twin lakes 15km east of Pokhara, haven't taken off as tourist destinations. Local belief has it that the lakes are husband and wife, and that an object thrown into one lake will eventually appear in the other. Begnas Tal, the bigger of the two, is framed by meticulously engineered paddy terraces, while Rupa, behind the ridge, remains pristinely hidden in a bushy, steep-sided valley. Come prepared to spend the night: several lodges can put you up, and trails open up a wealth of outstanding walking opportunities.

Begnas Tal

From the bus park at the dumpy hamlet of Begnas Tal Bazaar, the serene lake of **Begnas Tal** is less than five minutes' walk. Turn left at the top end of the bus park, walking past the concrete holding tanks of the government **fish farm**. Fishing is big business here, with the Chinese carp, native *sahar* and *mahseer* supplying Lakeside restaurants – those that the white egrets and ospreys don't get, at any rate. Just beyond the fish farm, the dam stretches away to the left, and there's a stretch of grubby shoreline where Phewa-style **boats** are rented out (Rs350/hr, but you could probably negotiate a discount for a half-day). With tent-shaped Annapurna II for a backdrop, the paddling here is scenic, and you'll often have the lake to yourself – it's a lovely place to swim, as long as you keep well away from the dam. A good destination is the wooded peninsula at the north side of the lake, which is a **bird sanctuary**. There are a few modest cafés on the far bank, too, where you could get a drink and a basic meal.

Rupa Tal

The paved road leads north from the far end of the bus park at Begnas Tal Bazaar and climbs steeply up the side of the ridge of **Panchbaiya Danda**. Hikers can turn left up to the ridgetop after about twenty minutes; cyclists and buses (just) stick to the road.

HIKES FROM BEGNAS TAL

About 1km beyond **Sundari Danda**, on an increasingly rough road, a trail leads off to the right, descending south past the muddy northern end of Rupa Tal and the village of Talbesi and then climbing steeply east to the hilltop of **Rupakot** (around 6hr round-trip from Sundari Danda). There are fine lake views, but for stunning views of the Annapurnas head north instead, along a trail which leads to the slightly higher grassy ridgetop of **Begnaskot** (also known as Kotbari; about 4hr round-trip from Sundari Danda); this latter route is part of the Royal Trek (see p.332). From Begnaskot you can descend due west to make a circuit of Begnas Tal, which would be a long day's hike, or continue about two hours north via the village of Tiwaridanda, where you could pick up a ride back to Pokhara along an impressive, partly ridgetop road.

Begnas Tal is visible first, on the left (steep, jungly paths lead down to the water), and then **Rupa Tal** comes into view after the highest point is passed (about 40min walk from the bus park). The things that look like fences peeping above the water are more fish farms – Rupa Tal is said to be particularly rich in nutrients, but it's not such a good choice for swimming, as the lake margins are choked with mud and water hyacinths. In another ten minutes or so the trail rejoins the road as it descends to the half-dozen shops of the village bazaar called **Sundari Danda**. Boats can usually be picked up by the Begnas Tal shore below here, taking you back to the dam area (around Rs400–500).

The Siddhartha Highway

The **Siddhartha Highway** (Siddhartha Rajmarg) offers the most direct route from Pokhara to the Indian border at **Sunauli**, 180km away. It's a relentlessly twisting road, however, so most buses and lorries travel via Narayangadh, to the east, and traffic is deliciously light – cyclists and motorbikers in particular will relish it. The scenery is certainly dramatic. After the first climb from Pokhara southwest to Naudanda (confusingly, not the Naudanda that lies northwest of Pokhara), the road clings to the side of the Adhi Khola valley. Around the old-fashioned town of **Syangja**, the valley closes in and the hills rear up spectacularly; west of here, the Gurung village of **Sirubari** offers organized homestays (see box below). Beyond **Waling**, the Siddhartha Highway descends to the deep, steamy gorge floor of the mighty Kali Gandaki, first passing the access road to the vast **Kali Gandaki "A" Hydropower Project** – which is now the finishing point for rafting trips on the river. Crossing the river at **Ramdi Ghat**, the site of many caves, the highway climbs almost 1000m to its highest point just short of the turn-off for Tansen at Bartung. From there it's a 35km, hour-long, brake-testing descent to

SIRUBARI HOMESTAYS

In the peaceful hills west of Syangja, south of Pokhara on the Siddhartha Highway, lies the delightful Gurung village of **Sirubari**. Amid terraced fields and patches of woodland, this cluster of traditional houses, most of them with wood-tiled roofs, was the first in Nepal to run organized **homestay programmes**, allowing visitors to stay in villagers' homes and join in cultural events. It attracts only a few dozen visitors each year, but it's well organized and, nowadays, open to individual travellers rather than just those buying package tours through travel agents. If you just turn up you may not benefit from all the activities – you won't be met by a welcome party of squealing folk musicians, for instance, nor Gurung women proffering flower garlands. Even if you don't book through a travel agent in Pokhara, your stay will be organized by the Village Development Committee, and just being there is much of the point (though there's also a fine Himalayan viewpoint, Thumro Juro, less than two hours' walk from the village). To get to Sirubari independently, you can drive all the way from Pokhara, some of it on rough roads (it takes half a day). It's arguably more appealing to take a bus on the Siddhartha Highway to Helu Lamachaur, 50km south of Pokhara, then walk up for two hours (or drive for considerably less in a shared jeep) to the village of Arjun Chaupari, from where it's a further two hours' hike.

Butwal and the Terai (see p.259), on a landslide-prone stretch, then a further 24km to the border crossing of Sunauli – 180 glorious kilometres from Pokhara.

ARRIVAL AND DEPARTURE

By bus Local buses, every 15min from the main bus park in Pokhara, take up to an hour and tend to be crowded. Every hour or two, buses from Begnas Tal Bazaar crawl along the mostly paved road that leads along Sundari Danda.

By taxi A taxi to Begnas Tal costs about Rs1300 one-way from Pokhara. A taxi from Begnas Tal Bazaar to Sundari

BEGNAS AND RUPA TAL

Danda will cost about Rs500.

By bike The first stretch from Pokhara along the Prithvi Highway is horribly polluted and fairly terrifying. After 10km, turn left at the signpost, and it's a pleasant 3km ride down a straight road to Begnas Tal Bazaar.

ACCOMMODATION AND EATING

There's surprisingly little **accommodation** around Begnas Tal, given how bloated Pokhara has become: just a half-dozen simple guesthouses and one luxury resort. **Food** served by the guesthouses is pretty unexciting compared to what's on offer in Pokhara, although you can usually get a few tourist items as well as the Nepali standards – which might well include fresh fish from the lakes.

Begnas Lake Resort and Villas Sundari Danda, Begnas Tal, Lekhnath-11, Kaski ☎ 061 560 030, ⓦ begnaslakeresort.com; map p.224. Seriously posh resort, whose rooms and stone cottages ($150 for the latter) spread down through the forested southeastern shore of Begnas Tal. It has a small landscaped swimming pool (not that you'll need it), a health spa and a decent restaurant. A steep stone staircase path leads down from the Panchbhayia ridge road, just short of Sundari Danda, but most guests come by boat from the Begnas dam – which is lovely in itself. Book online for the best deals. US$130

Blue Heaven Lekhnath-11, Panchbhaiya, Kaski ☎ 984 626 1384; map p.224. Set on a heavenly little grassy promontory below Sundari Danda, sloping down to the southeastern shore of Begnas Tal, this welcoming family guesthouse offers a couple of very simple rooms under a tin roof, but it's lovely at night with its lake view and friendly owners. Eggs come from the chickens you see pecking about, fish from the lake. You can get a boat here from the

Begnas Tal dam, or walk down from the road. Rs500

Dinesh House Lekhnath-11, Panchbhaiya, Kaski ☎ 984 953 9439, ⓦ dineshhouse.com; map p.224. A basic bolt-hole, near the top of the Panchbhaiya ridge (to the left of the road, roughly 2.5km beyond Begnas Tal Bazaar). They have just a handful of simple rooms (most with shared bathrooms) with mud floors and tin roofs – the garden is a tad unkempt, but it's a peaceful spot, and just a 15min walk from Begnas Tal. Rs500

★**Rupa View** Lekhnath-11, Panchbhaiya, Kaski ☎ 061 622 098, ⓦ sites.google.com/site/rupaview; map p.224. This welcoming family guesthouse marries delightful traditional style with smart modern facilities. It's located in a tranquil spot, a couple of minutes' well-signposted walk off the Panchbhaiya road, some 2km beyond Begnas Tal Bazaar. Some rooms have gorgeous mountain views, others lake views, and Rupa Tal lake is a 15min walk away. The family cooks up delicious food from their own plots. Hiking, mountain biking and horse-riding trips are all available (Rs1000–3000). Rs750

Tansen

Once the seat of a powerful kingdom, the hill town of **TANSEN** (Palpa) now seems little more than a bazaar town stranded in the hills. Tourism comes a low second to trading, yet slowly, almost reluctantly, Tansen yields its secrets: clacking *dhaka* looms glimpsed though doorways; the Himalayan view from Srinagar Hill; the fine day hikes and bike rides in the surrounding countryside. If you're coming from India, Tansen makes a far more authentic introduction to Nepal than Pokhara, and at an altitude of 1370m, it's usually pleasantly cool after the heat of the plains. From Pokhara, the 120 tortuous kilometres of the **Siddhartha Highway** (see opposite) provide a splendid show-opener.

Brief history

Under its old name of **Palpa** (by which many Nepalis still refer to it today), Tansen was one of the seats of the Sen princes, who may have been a local Magar clan or possibly Rajput princes fleeing the Muslim invasions of India. Either way, it was from his base in

Palpa that the dynasty's fabled second king, Mukunda Sen, raided Kathmandu in the early sixteenth century. He is said to have carried off two sacred Bhairab masks, only to be cut down by a plague sent by the Pashupatinath *linga*. After Mukunda Sen's death, in around 1533, his kingdom was divided between his sons, and weakened. Successors formed an alliance with Gorkha, which bought them breathing space when the latter began conquering territory in the mid-eighteenth century. Aided by the friendly Indian rajah of Oudh, to which it held itself feudally subject, Palpa staved off the inevitable until 1806, when it became the last territory to be annexed to modern Nepal. Tansen remains the headquarters of Palpa District, however, and retains a strong sense of its own dignity.

The bazaar

Tansen spills down Srinagar Hill, the southernmost flank of the Mahabharat range. The main road winds up through town from the **bus park** on the lowest, newest level, but you can cut straight up a steep path to the central **bazaar** area, around the palace. Established by Newari merchants from the Kathmandu Valley to take advantage of the trade route between India and Tibet, it now exists to retail Indian-manufactured goods to the local Magar people.

Tansen Palace

The showpiece centre of town is the **Tansen Palace**, built by British architects from Kolkata at the end of the nineteenth century – and rebuilt in 2011 and 2012 after it was destroyed

4

TANSEN

Srinagar Hill

Rani Ghat — Monument — Helipad & Viewing Tower

Kailash Nagar & Ridi

Ridi

Rani Ghat & Ghorabanda

Rani Ghat & Ghorabanda

■ACCOMMODATION	
City View Home Stay	2
Horizon Home Stay	3
Hotel Srinagar	1
Hotel The White Lake	4

●EATING	
Nanglo West	1

Ganesh Mandir

Mosque

GETUP Palpa

Shitalpati

TUNDIKHEL ROAD

Bhagwati Mandir

Baggi Dhoka

ATM

Amar Narayan Mandir

ASON ROAD

ASON ROAD

Tansen Palace

BANK ROAD

B.P. CHOWK

BARTUN

Municipality Office

Buddhist Monastery

Bus Park

Tudikhel

BAZAAR ROAD

BAZAAR ROAD

SIDDHARTHA HIGHWAY

Pokhara

Buses & Jeeps

Butwal

0 — 200 metres

THE PATTERNS OF PALPA

In Tansen's bazaar, keep an eye out for **dhaka weavers**, who work at wooden treadle looms shaped like upright pianos. They are the creators of the repeating geometric patterns that are the archetypal fabric for *dhaka* or *Palpali topi*, the garish, brimless crowning glory of Nepal's national dress. You can pick up a ready-made *topi* or "Nepali cap" for as little as Rs100 – or around Rs500 for a made-to-measure version (though you can pay significantly more for better quality material). Tansen is also known for **thailo**, a woman's purse made from *dhaka* with two coloured pairs of drawstrings, and **karuwa**, heavy, bulbous brass water vessels.

by fire during one of the most dramatic skirmishes of the Maoist conflict years. On the evening of January 31, 2006, thousands of fighters of the People's Liberation Army (PLA) launched parallel attacks on the barracks on Srinagar Hill and the town below. The palace was a particular target because it housed the district's government offices and police station. By the middle of the night, the pride of the Palpali was gutted by fire, and the Maoists had taken full control of the town's heart – though in classic guerrilla style, they returned to the hills at dawn, taking with them many hostages from the police and army. Only one civilian died in the battle, but the palace's semi-destruction left a deep scar in the town's psyche. Reconstruction was resolved upon almost immediately, though at the time of writing it was still undecided what the palace will be used for when it is finished.

Shitalpati and around

Shitalpati, the hub of the busy bazaar, is centred on a curious octagonal marble rest-house built by Khadga Shamsher, the Rana-era governor of Palpa. It is overlooked by a reminder of Tansen's grand past, the **Baggi Dhoka** or **Mul Dhoka** (main gate) – tall enough for elephants and their riders to pass through for grand processions, and reputedly the biggest of its kind in Nepal. It too was blown up by a Maoist bomb, but has been rebuilt – only to be adorned with a banner wishfully proclaiming the Magar Autonomous State, sign of the (new) times.

West of Shitalpati lie Tansen's oldest neighbourhoods, with lovely, quirky old houses, and the undistinguished modern **Bhagwati Mandir**, which enshrines the hostess of Tansen's biggest festival, the Bhagwati Jaatra (late Aug to early Sept). The cobbled lane going east from Shitalpati leads down to the nineteenth-century **Amar Narayan Mandir**, a pagoda-style temple that's the stopping place for sadhus on their way to Janai Purnima festivities at Muktinath in late July or early August.

Srinagar Hill

The best **Himalayan views** are from **Srinagar Hill**, immediately north of the bazaar. The most direct route to the top, which takes about half an hour on foot, starts from the small Ganesh Mandir above Shitalpati – but you have to zigzag a bit to get to the temple itself. From *Hotel Srinagar* it's an easy twenty-minute walk east along the ridge. The top (1525m) is planted with thick pine forest – catch the view from the helipad or the open area west of *Hotel Srinagar*. The peaks appear smaller and hazier from here than they do from Pokhara, but the Dhaulagiri and Annapurna ranges are still impressive, and Machhapuchhare's true "fishtail" profile is visible from this angle. On the southern side, beyond Tansen, lies the luxuriant Madi Valley, layered with paddy fields owned by Tansen's Newari landlords, and often obscured by a blanket of low cloud.

ARRIVAL AND DEPARTURE . **TANSEN**

By bus Local buses serve the Siddhartha Highway, very slowly, between Pokhara and Butwal, stopping at Bartun, the village at the start of the 3km Tansen spur road; note that the last buses leave at 1pm, both ways. At Bartun, jeeps and buses shuttle almost nonstop from the roadside to Tansen, leaving as soon as they're full. To move on from Tansen, note that there is a single, early-morning direct express bus to Pokhara and another Pokhara-bound express that can be picked up at Bartun, otherwise you're on local buses from Bartun. There are also direct services to

Bhairahawa, from where it's a short step to Lumbini; and a single early-morning service to Kathmandu, which stops at Narayangadh, for Chitwan.

Destinations Bhairahawa (3 daily; 3hr); Butwal (every 30min; 2hr); Kathmandu (1 daily; 10–11hr); Pokhara (local bus every 30min; 5–6hr; express bus 2 daily; 4hr).

INFORMATION AND TOURS

Information Perhaps the single best tourist information service in Nepal, the Group for Environmental and Tourism Upgrading (GETUP Palpa), is enthusiastically run by Man Mohan Shrestha and his friends, who can organize pretty much anything from transport to homestays in Tansen and the surrounding area. The office (10am–5pm – just ring the bell if the door is shut; ☎ 075 521 341 or ☎ 984 702 8885, ✉ getup@ntc.net.np) also provides well-produced leaflets on local hikes and excursions, complete with excellent maps, and with a day's notice can get you into Ghorabanda, 3km north of Tansen, to see the last of the famously drunken potters (members of the Kumal ethnic group) throwing their almost spherical water jugs on heavy clay flywheels. They can also arrange car or jeep hire.

Banks and money Nepal Investment Bank, Bank St (Sun–Thurs 10am–2pm, Fri 10am–noon), can change money and has an ATM.

ACCOMMODATION AND EATING

Tansen's **accommodation** is generally more expensive than Pokhara's, and hot water and electricity are always intermittent. Don't settle for the lodges near the bus park, which are noisy and a steep slog from the centre. The usual swarms of *daal bhaat* and snack stalls can be found all around town, and the hotel restaurants are respectable enough, but Tansen has one standout **eating** option: *Nanglo West* (see below).

City View Home Stay Thadogalli ☎075 520 563 or ☎ 984 702 8885, ✉ shrestha.manmohan@gmail.com. Next door to the GETUP information office, and run by the same friendly manager, this place has two simple but well-maintained rooms in a Nepali home. The nicest is on the rooftop, with its own terrace and bathroom. Guests are invited to eat *daal bhaat* with the family. **Rs400**

Horizon Homestay Bhagwati Tol, Shitalpati ☎075 522 728, ✉ homestayhorizonpalpa@yahoo.com. This justifiably popular, economically priced guesthouse has charming and very helpful owners, spick and span rooms (many of which have great views), an attractive terrace and good home-cooked food. **Rs400**

★ **Nanglo West** Bhagwati Tol, Shitalpati ☎075 520 184, ⌨ nanglo.com.np. A culinary oasis in these parts, this sophisticated restaurant stands right opposite the Mul Dhoka. Indoors, there are low tables and floor cushions, or you can sit in the lovely courtyard garden. They serve a range of Western dishes (Rs150–400), such as fried wings and sizzlers, and home-baked cakes (except on Sat), but the highlight is the superb, authentic Newari food: the set meal is excellent. Daily 10am–8.30pm.

Hotel Srinagar Srinagar Hill ☎075 520 045, ⌨ hotelsrinagar.com. The rooms in this multi-storey hotel, with a great location on Srinagar Hill, are the best you'll find in town – a kind of Nepali imitation of a chain hotel. Facilities and service aren't so great for the inflated price, though, especially if you pay the official tariff. It's a good 20min above town, so call ahead to arrange transport. **US$46**

Hotel The White Lake Tansen bazaar ☎075 521 932, ✉ thewhitelake502@yahoo.com. The best hotel in the bazaar area, and used to dealing with foreigners. Rooms in the old block are pretty decrepit, but the "deluxe" ones in the new wing behind are reasonable. Decent *daal bhaat*. **US$20**

Around Tansen

The best thing about Tansen is getting out of it to explore the outlying **hill country** and **Magar villages**, where people still greet visitors with delighted smiles and the full palms-together *namaste*. The paths around Tansen all pass through farmland and are heavily used by villagers, so it's fairly easy to find your way with just enough Nepali to ask directions. You may prefer to take a guide – ask your innkeeper – or the excellent maps provided by the GETUP Palpa information service (see above). Numerous other **hikes** are possible from Tansen, including taking the old trading route to Butwal, which passes the ruins of the old Sen palace at Nuwakot in one long day's walking (the path is not well maintained these days, though, so you'd need a guide). You can also follow the airy ridge-line east of Srinagar Hill through Bagnaskot to Arya Bhanjyang (11km; 2–3hr), on the Siddhartha Highway – where you can pick up transport back to town; on clear days you can see the Himalayas along the way.

Rani Ghat

The most rewarding day-trip from Tansen is to **RANI GHAT**, the site of a fantastically derelict palace set atop a rocky outcrop overlooking the turquoise Kali Gandaki. Rani Ghat is the site of occasional cremations, and has a couple of *chiya pasal* that offer basic food and lodging, but the main attraction is the porticoed, columned and romantically crumbling palace of **Rani Durbar**. It was built in the late nineteenth century by a Rana commander, Khadga Shamsher, who was exiled to Palpa after a failed coup against his brother, and feels like a place of melancholy isolation. You get a great view of it from the alarmingly long (222m) **suspension bridge** that crosses the river here – the second longest in Nepal. If you need to stay overnight, there's a very simple **lodge** immediately below the palace.

The hike to Rani Ghat

To get to Rani Ghat, you can hire transport on a dirt road (via Chandi Bhanjyang and Baugha Gumha), but at the time of writing it still stopped ninety minutes' walk short, at Chherlung. In any case, the 14km (4–7hr) **hike** is superb. The route begins at Kailash Nagar, on the ridge just beside *Hotel Srinagar,* and descends a ridge before following the sometimes jungly Barangdi valley (bring a torch if you want to visit the narrow, stalactite-hung Siddha Gupha cave, beyond Aule, about a third of the way along) to the Kali Gandaki. You can make a longer circuit walk (22km; 7–9hr) by heading out via Gorkhekot, on the Srinagar ridge a short way east of town (you can get there from a path leading behind the United Mission Hospital), and descending through an immensely satisfying landscape of farmland, trailside hamlets and sections of airy ridge, before the final switchback down to the Kali Gandaki and Rani Ghat.

4

Ridi Bazaar

With an early start, or an overnight stay, you could continue west from Rani Ghat to **RIDI BAZAAR**, following the fine trail along the southern flank of the Kali Gandaki gorge to Argeli, 11km away. From Argeli you have to follow the paved road for about 6km to Ridi Bazaar – buses are fairly frequent if you want to avoid this last tarmac stretch.

Set on the banks of the Kali Gandaki, Ridi is considered sacred because of the wealth of **shaligrams** – ammonite fossils associated with Vishnu – found in the river here. It was said that if a person were cremated at Ridi and his ashes sprinkled into the river, they would congeal to form a *shaligram*, making the devotee at one with his god. Pilgrims come for ritual bathing, especially during the **festival** of Magh Sankranti (mid-Jan). The colourful commercial end of town lies across a stream that joins the Kali Gandaki here, while the sixteenth-century **Rishikesh Mandir** is south of the stream, just above the bus stop.

To head back, it's a 30km journey from Ridi to Tansen along the road. It is also possible to walk back to Tansen by leaving the Tansen–Ridi road at a sharp right-hand hairpin and climbing up the handsome valley of the Kurung Khola to the village of Chandi Bhanjyang, from where it's about 45 minutes on a dirt road until you rejoin the main paved Ridi road a few steps west of *Hotel Srinagar*. It's no more difficult to follow this route in reverse, from Tansen. Allow four hours one-way on foot.

Palpa Bhairab

The temple of **Palpa Bhairab**, up a short path from the pretty Newari village of **Bhairabsthan**, 8km west of Tansen on the road to Ridi, is often compared with that of Dakshin Kali in the Kathmandu Valley. Its much-feared Bhairab image is kept in a small chamber at the far corner of the compound, and animal sacrifices are made to him in great quantity, especially on Saturday and Tuesday mornings. The gilded *trisul* (trident) here is claimed to be the biggest in Asia, and pilgrims have left hosts of smaller replicas at its base.

The Western Terai

LUMBINI

5

The Western Terai

A narrow strip of flatland extending along the length of Nepal's southern border, the Terai was originally covered in thick, malarial jungle. In the 1950s, however, the government identified the southern plains as a major growth area to relieve population pressure in the hills, and, with the help of liberal quantities of DDT, brought malaria under control. Since then, the jungle has been methodically cleared and the Terai has emerged as Nepal's most productive region, accounting for more than fifty percent of its GDP and supporting about half its population.

The jungle barrier that once insulated Nepal from Indian influences as effectively as the Himalayas had guarded the north, making possible the development of a uniquely Nepali culture, has disappeared. An unmistakeable **Indian** quality now pervades the Terai, as evidenced by the avid mercantilism of the border bazaars, the chewing of *betel*, the mosques and orthodox Brahmanism, the jute mills and sugar refineries, and the many roads and irrigation projects built with Indian aid.

Fortunately, the government has set aside sizeable chunks of the **Western Terai** in the form of national parks and reserves, which remain among the finest **wildlife and bird havens** on the subcontinent. Dense riverine forest provides cover for predators like tigers and leopards; swampy grasslands make the perfect habitat for rhinos; and vast, tall stands of *sal*, the Terai's most common tree, shelter huge herds of deer. Of the region's wildlife parks, the (maybe too) popular **Chitwan** is the most accessible and rich in game, but if you're willing to invest some extra effort, **Bardia** and **Sukla Phanta** further to the west make much quieter, and better, alternatives. The region's other claim to fame is historical: the Buddha was born 2500 years ago at **Lumbini**. Nearby, important archeological discoveries have also been made at **Tilaurakot**.

Four **border crossings** in the Western Terai are open to foreigners. As it's on the most direct route between Kathmandu and Varanasi, and fits in well with visits to Lumbini and Chitwan, **Sonauli** is the most heavily used. Less popular are the crossing points south of **Nepalgunj** and **Burgunj**, both of which are prime candidates for the least appealing place in Nepal. Alternatively, on the far western frontier is **Mahendra Nagar**, only around twelve hours from Delhi; although it's an arduous journey to Kathmandu, it does give you the opportunity to see the less visited parts of the West Terai.

The **weather** in the Terai is at its best from October to January – the days are pleasantly milder during the latter half of this period, though the nights and mornings can be surprisingly chilly and damp. However, wildlife viewing gets much better after the thatch has been cut, from late January, by which time the temperatures are starting to warm up again. It gets really hot in April, May and June. From July to September, the monsoon

CHITWAN NATIONAL PARK

Highlights

❶ **Ghatgain, Chitwan** Watch the sun go down over the teeming jungle from your guesthouse on the banks of the Rapti River. **See p.248**

❷ **Chitwan National Park** Spot the endangered Asian one-horned rhino among the grasses or, if you're lucky, an elephant or tiger. **See p.249**

❸ **Bis Hajaar Tal, Chitwan** Away from the tiger- and rhino-spotting crowds, the swampy "20,000 Lakes" are home to hundreds of exotic birds. **See p.256**

❹ **Devghat** Devout Hindus come to die at this holy confluence, spanned by a dramatic suspension footbridge and surrounded by temples. **See p.258**

❺ **Lumbini** Visit the birthplace of the Buddha, arguably Nepal's most important historical site, with archeological finds dating back to the third century. **See p.261**

❻ **Bardia National Park** Take a guided walk into the jungle, with no one else around to disturb the animals – it's your best chance to see tigers in Nepal. **See p.271**

HIGHLIGHTS ARE MARKED ON THE MAP ON PP.240–241

5

THE THARUS

Two great mysteries surround the Terai-dwelling **Tharus**, Nepal's second largest ethnic group: where they came from and how they became resistant to malaria. Some anthropologists speculate that they originally migrated from India's eastern hills, which would account for their Hindu-animist beliefs, but doesn't fully explain the radically differing dialects, dress and customs of different Tharu groups. Isolated by malarial jungle for thousands of years, bands of migrants certainly could have developed their own cultures, but then why would the name "Tharu" survive with such consistency?

Further confusing the issue are the **Rana Tharus** of the far west, who claim to be descended from high-caste Rajput women sent north by their husbands during the Muslim invasions – the husbands never came for them, so they ended up marrying their servants. (There is some circumstantial evidence for this: Rana Tharu women are given extraordinary autonomy in marriage and household affairs, and the Tharu stick dance has parallels in Rajasthan.)

In terms of the malarial resistance, red blood cells seem to play a part – the fact that Tharus are prone to sickle-cell anaemia may be significant – but little research has been done. At least as significant, Tharus boost their immunity by common-sense precautions, such as building houses with tiny windows to keep smoke in and mosquitoes (and ghosts) out.

Skilled hunter-gatherers, Tharus have in modern times become farmers and livestock raisers, fishing rivers, clearing patches in the forest and warding off wild animals. Their famed whirling **stick dance** evokes their uneasy, but respectful, relationship with the forest spirits. Their homes are made of mud and dung plastered over wood-and-reed frames, giving them a distinctive ribbed effect. In the west, half a dozen families or more often still live in the traditional communal longhouses.

The Tharus have fared poorly in recent years, reduced largely to sharecropping. Their distinct culture remains strong in the far west, but in other areas is being drowned out by dominating influences from elsewhere in Nepal and India. Like indigenous people throughout the world, the Tharus' traditional skills and knowledge of the environment seem to count for little these days.

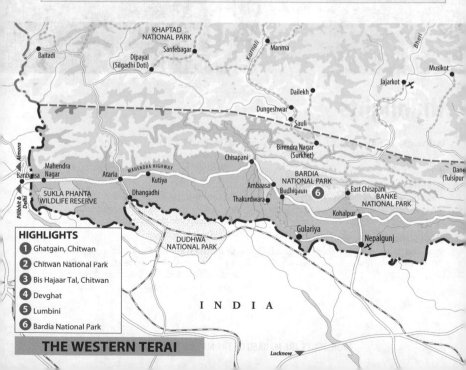

HIGHLIGHTS
1. Ghatgain, Chitwan
2. Chitwan National Park
3. Bis Hajaar Tal, Chitwan
4. Devghat
5. Lumbini
6. Bardia National Park

THE WESTERN TERAI

brings mosquitoes, malaria and leeches, and makes a lot of the more minor, unpaved roads very muddy and difficult to pass, and some rivers burst their banks.

Chitwan

Chitwan is the name not only of Nepal's most visited national park but also of the surrounding *dun* valley and administrative district. The name means "Heart of the Jungle" – a description that, sadly, now holds true only for the lands protected within the park and community forests. Yet the rest of the **valley** – though it's been reduced to a flat, furrowed plain – still provides fascinating vignettes of a rural lifestyle. Truly ugly development is confined to the wayside conurbation of **Narayangadh/Bharatpur**, and even this has left the nearby holy site of **Devghat** so far unscathed.

The best – and worst – aspects of **Chitwan National Park** are that it can be visited easily and inexpensively. It is high on the list of "things to do in Nepal", so unless you go during the steamy season you'll share your experience with a lot of other people; the park has over 130,000 foreign visitors a year. If you want to steer clear of the crowds, and don't mind making a little extra effort, try avoiding the much-touted tourist village of **Sauraha** and base yourself in one of two villages along the park's northern boundary, just west. **Ghatgain** and **Meghauli** are much quieter and less developed than Sauraha, but also have guesthouses, guides, elephants and entry checkposts (though jeeps are more difficult to come by). You can also do a jungle trek (see p.251) from Sauraha to either village.

Sauraha

Spectacularly situated on the banks of the Rapti River, opposite a prime area of jungle, **SAURAHA** (pronounced *So*-ruh-hah) is one of those unstoppably successful destinations

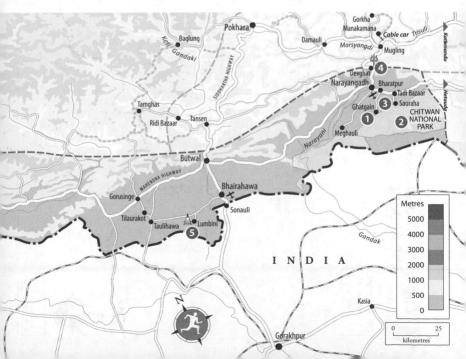

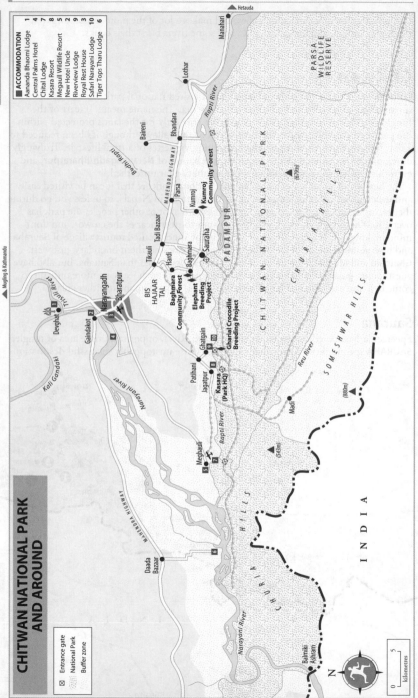

CHITWAN NATIONAL PARK AND AROUND

ACCOMMODATION
Ananda Bhaomi Lodge 1
Central Palms Hotel 4
Chital Lodge 7
Kasara Resort 8
Megaull Wildlife Resort 5
New Hotel Uncle 2
Riverview Lodge 9
Royal Rest House 3
Safari Narayani Lodge 10
Tiger Tops Tharu Lodge 6

Entrance gate
National Park
Buffer zone

5

BUDGET SAFARI PACKAGES TO CHITWAN NATIONAL PARK

The best advice is: avoid them! A two-night, three-day Chitwan safari **package**, booked via any Kathmandu or Pokhara travel agency, gives you only a day and a half in the park, and you'll have little control over the programme of activities. You'll be locked into a lodge that has little incentive to work for your business (and every incentive to cut corners), you'll be served inferior set meals, and you probably won't get to choose your guide. Additionally, a US$200 per person (minimum) package is likely to be much more expensive than doing the same thing on your own, and saves you hardly any trouble since Chitwan is incredibly easy to visit independently. If you must be bound by an itinerary, at least book directly with the lodge itself.

A package tour of Chitwan can also be combined with a **raft trip** on the Trisuli River, bookable through rafting operators in Kathmandu and Pokhara, but, for the reasons set out above, it's still a bad idea to book the Chitwan stay as part of the raft trip. And a raft won't take you all the way to the park no matter what the agent says: Narayangadh is normally the end of the line.

at which Nepal seems to excel. In some lights it looks like the archetypal budget safari village, with its lodges spread out along dusty roads at the edge of the forest; at other times, you could half-close your eyes and imagine yourself in a mini Thamel. While there's still a lot to recommend it, not least the ease of access into the park, each year Sauraha loses a little more of what once made it so enjoyable: buildings are springing up at an alarming rate. The fast-changing cluster of shops and hotels that make up Sauraha "**village**" constitutes most of the action, though there's little to do there except shop, eat and plan excursions.

Just after Christmas, the five-day **Chitwan Elephant Festival** takes over Sauraha, and features elephant races, elephant football and an elephant beauty contest, among other events. Read the box on p.252 about the ethics of elephant-based tourism before deciding whether or not to attend.

The hattisar (elephant stables)
Northwestern edge of Sauraha • Free

The majority of Chitwan's elephant workforce is housed at the government **hattisar** (elephant stables), on the northwestern edge of Sauraha. The best time to visit is mid-afternoon, when the elephants are around for feeding time. The elephants are kept chained up while not working in the countryside.

Elephant bathtime
In the Rapti River near *River Bank Inn*, Sauraha • Daily around 11am • No charge for watching, Rs150–200 if you want to join in

During **elephant bathtime**, some of Sauraha's elephants are taken down to the Rapti River for a good scrub down, and tourists can join in the experience for a small fee. For most tourists elephant bathtime is great fun – you sit on the elephant's neck while the mahout encourages it to spray you with cold river water – and very popular. Not everyone will appreciate it, however, especially if you have concerns about elephants being used in tourism (see box, p.252). If you join in, remember to wear appropriate (and modest) clothing, and take a change of clothes; take care, too, as these huge animals can inadvertently hurt you.

Tharu Cultural Museum
A 15–20min walk east of Sauraha bus park • Daily 6am–6pm • Rs50

The **Tharu Cultural Museum** holds an interesting collection of exhibits and paintings, including agricultural, fishing and clothing items, and displays on dance, religion and festivals. If this whets your appetite and you want to get more of a flavour of Terai village life, find yourself a **bicycle** and put as much distance between you and Sauraha as the heat allows (see box, p.247).

5

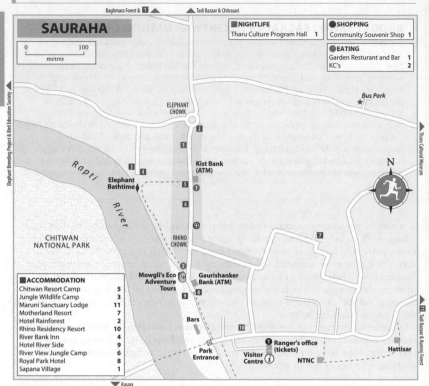

SAURAHA

0   100
metres

Baghmara Forest & ▲   ▲ Tadi Bazaar & Chitrasari

Elephant Breeding Project & Bird Education Society

■ NIGHTLIFE
Tharu Culture Program Hall   1

● SHOPPING
Community Souvenir Shop   1

● EATING
Garden Resturant and Bar   1
KC's   2

Bus Park ★

ELEPHANT CHOWK

Rapti River

Kist Bank (ATM)

Elephant Bathtime

CHITWAN NATIONAL PARK

RHINO CHOWK

@

N

Mowgli's Eco Adventure Tours

Gaurishanker Bank (ATM)

Bars

Park Entrance

Visitor Centre ⓘ

Ranger's office (tickets)

NTNC

Hattisar

Kasara

Tharu Cultural Museum

Tadi Bazaar & Kumroj Forest

■ ACCOMMODATION
Chitwan Resort Camp	5
Jungle Wildlife Camp	3
Maruni Sanctuary Lodge	11
Motherland Resort	7
Hotel Rainforest	2
Rhino Residency Resort	10
River Bank Inn	4
Hotel River Side	9
River View Jungle Camp	6
Royal Park Hotel	8
Sapana Village	1

Elephant Breeding Project

Some 4km west of Sauraha • Daily 8–10am & 4–6pm • Rs100

Baby elephants are the main attraction at the **Elephant Breeding Project**, which you can cycle or take a jeep tour to from Sauraha. Just inside the entrance is a small room with photos and nuggets of information about elephants, including verbal commands: for example *mail* means "stand up", while *baith* means "sit down".

Until the mid-1970s, Nepal's Parks Department commonly bought its elephants from India, where they were captured in the wild then trained in captivity. As the wild population shrank, this procedure became increasingly unaffordable, so the government began to breed and train its own elephants. In 1988, it established this facility, where elephants can mate in peace and mothers and babies can receive special attention. At any given time the project is home to a couple of breeding bulls, ten to fifteen cows, and usually a number of calves.

ARRIVAL AND DEPARTURE   SAURAHA

By plane Bharatpur (see p.257), about 20km away, has daily flights to Kathmandu.

By bus (Sauraha) Twelve daily tourist buses (around Rs550) run to Sauraha's bus park from Kathmandu (6–7hr); minibuses and the comfortable Greenline Tours bus (daily 7.30am; ☎056 560 267, ⓦgreenline.com.np; US$20, including lunch) cost more. Greenline also has a bus from Pokhara to Sauraha (daily 9.15am; 5hr 30min; US$20), a route also served by four slower public buses. Public buses

also run from Sauraha to Sonauli via Bhairahawa (7am; 3–5hr). Lodges in Sauraha can arrange tickets for a small commission. When you arrive at Sauraha bus park, touts will offer to take you by jeep to their guesthouse. Otherwise a lift into town costs around Rs75.

Destinations Kathmandu (13 daily; 6–7hr); Pokhara (5 daily; 5hr 30min).

By bus (Tadi Bazaar) There are more frequent public buses to and from Tadi Bazaar, on the Mahendra Highway

ASIAN ELEPHANTS

In Nepal and throughout southern Asia, **elephants** have been used as ceremonial transportation and beasts of burden for thousands of years, earning them a cherished place in the culture witness the popularity of elephant-headed Ganesh, the darling of the Hindu pantheon.

With brains four times the size of humans', elephants are reckoned to be as **intelligent** as dolphins. What we see as a herd is in fact a complex social structure, consisting of bonded pairs and a fluid hierarchy. In the wild, **herds** typically consist of fifteen to thirty females and one old bull, and are usually led by a senior female; other bulls live singly or in bachelor herds. Though they appear docile, elephants have strongly individual personalities and moods. They can learn dozens of commands, but they won't obey just anyone; as any handler will tell you, you can't make an elephant do what it doesn't want to do.

Asian elephants are smaller than those of the African species, but still formidable. A bull can grow up to 3m high and weigh four tons, although larger individuals are known to exist. An average day's intake is 200 litres of water and 225kg of fodder – and if you think that's impressive, wait till you see it come back out again. All that eating wears down teeth fast: an average elephant goes through six sets in its lifetime, each more durable than the last. The trunk is controlled by an estimated forty thousand muscles, enabling its owner to eat, drink, cuddle and even manipulate simple tools (such as a stick for scratching). Though up to 2.5cm thick, an elephant's skin is still very sensitive, and it will often take mud or dust baths to protect against insects. Life expectancy is about 75 years and, much the same as with humans, an elephant's working life can be expected to run from its mid-teens to its mid-fifties.

The issue of the ethics of elephant-based tourism in Nepal is discussed in the box on p.252.

6km north of Sauraha. Hotel touts offering rides often meet buses at Tadi during the day, but you can instead get an electric or auto rikshaw (roughly Rs350 for up to four people) or jeep (roughly Rs600 for up to four people) into Sauraha. Public buses also leave Tadi for Narayangadh/Bharatpur (where there's an even greater selection of onward services – see p.257) every 15min or so.

Destinations Kathmandu (every 30min–1hr in the mornings; 6hr–7hr); Narayangadh/Bharatpur (every 15min; 30min); Pokhara (5 daily; around 5hr); Sonauli via Bhairahawa (hourly; 3–5hr).

GETTING AROUND

By bike Bikes of varying qualities can be rented on the main strip in Sauraha for about Rs200/day.

Maps Chitwan maps are helpful if you're planning to do any unguided excursions outside the park: Mappa/Karto Atelier's map is the best.

INFORMATION

Tourist information The national park visitor centre (daily 6am–6pm; ⓦ chitwannationalpark.gov.np) has a modest and slightly mouldering but informative display on the ecology of the park and the local Tharu culture. It's also a place to find independent guides (around Rs1800 for a whole day). Staff at many lodges are also good sources of information.

Park permits Daily park entry permits (Rs1500; see also p.256) are sold at the ranger's office (daily 6am–6pm), next to the visitor centre.

THARU VILLAGE TOURS

Guided **Tharu village walks** out of Sauraha can be rather voyeuristic, especially when you consider how many tourists have trooped through the homes before you. For cultural tours with more sensitivity, try Mowgli's Eco Adventure Tours, who organize homestays in **Madi** – an authentic Tharu village towards the Indian border – and other villages. You can also **cycle** through a number of Terai villages from Sauraha (see p.247).

Mowgli's Eco Adventure Tours Just south of Rhino Chowk ☎ 984 505 5836, ⓦ mowgliecoadventure .com. This company, which gives 25 percent of its profits to local conservation and education programmes, runs jungle walks through the park to Madi, a Tharu village near the Indian border, where you can participate in a homestay. They also organize interesting treks and homestays in the Chepang Hills.

5

Banks and exchange There are several ATMs, including ones operated by Kist Bank and Gaurishanker Bank, both near Rhino Chowk; they're not the most reliable of machines, but there are also ATMs in Tadi Bazaar and Narayangadh (see p.257). Sauraha also has several moneychangers, though rates are a couple of percent lower than what you can get in a bank.

Pharmacies and hospitals There's a pharmacy on Rhino Chowk and a private clinic in Tadi Bazaar. If you're really ill, make for the hospital in Bharatpur (see p.257) or the better one at Kolhalpur.

Post office The post office is at the intersection east of the bus stand, but bookshops will take letters there for franking.

ACCOMMODATION

Most hotels are strung along the village's main north–south strip, which is handy for restaurants and the park entrance, though relatively noisy and crowded. Those overlooking the river, east of the park entrance, and out in the countryside are obviously more peaceful. Most **budget lodges** are pretty similar, offering rooms in concrete bungalows with thatched roofs arranged around subtropical gardens. The majority have mosquito nets; use them and have any holes sewn up. Competition is fierce in this category, so **prices** drop dramatically when occupancy is low, and discounts can often be negotiated, especially if you don't book ahead. While price isn't always an indicator of quality in Sauraha, the moderate and expensive lodges listed here are a cut above the budget pack: they get by mainly on expensive package business, but will usually take you on an accommodation-only basis if you just show up. The best bargains are to be had by finding somewhere not listed in the guides or online – typically they will be half the price of more established accommodations.

Chitwan Resort Camp North of Rhino Chowk ☎056 580 082, ⓦchitwanresortcamp.com. A series of bungalows with green corrugated iron roofs, set around a neatly tended garden featuring communal areas shaded by thatched-roof "umbrellas". Inside are smallish, cosy, carpeted rooms with private bathrooms and TVs. Rs1000

Jungle Wildlife Camp Southwest of Elephant Chowk ☎056 580 093, ⓔjunglewildlifecamp.com. This place has a selection of tasteful rooms in a peppermint-coloured building, a good restaurant, and a peaceful riverside location offering great views. Keep an eye out for the rhinos on the opposite bank in the morning. Rs1000

Maruni Sanctuary Lodge A couple of kilometres east of Sauraha ☎056 580 160, ⓦktmgh.com. The highlight of this peaceful lodge, run by Kathmandu Guest House Group, is its nature trail and pond, which attracts birds and sometimes crocodiles. The bungalow-style rooms are simple affairs featuring a/c and beds with impressively carved wooden frames. Price includes breakfast. US$98

Motherland Resort East of Rhino Chowk ☎056 580 183, ⓔbidari20@yahoo.com. About 300m east of the main drag. Typical of the new crop of guesthouses and camps, this peaceful place is located in the paddy fields east of Rhino Chowk and offers good-value clean rooms in a quiet, green environment. A/c rooms are available for Rs700 more. Rs500

Hotel Rainforest Elephant Chowk ☎056 580 007, ⓦhotelrainforest.com.np. Amiable owner and modern rooms with a/c, TVs and verandas/balconies, as well as nice views across to the Himalayas (and the hotel's elephant) from the rooftop terrace. Also has a nice green garden and solar-heated hot water. US$30

Rhino Residency Resort Near the park entrance ☎056 580 095, ⓦrhino-residency.com. The carpeted en suites, decorated with bird pictures and featuring flat-screen TVs, are probably the smartest centrally located rooms, though starting to look a bit faded. There's a pool and plenty of lime trees, and dragon statues in the garden. Rates include breakfast. US$60

★ **River Bank Inn** Southwest of Elephant Chowk ☎056 580 450, ⓦriverbankinn.com.np. In a pretty spot overlooking the river, this comfortable, well-run lodge has large, modern rooms with fans or a/c (though the latter have no river view), as well as three elephants. The welcoming owner is a fount of local knowledge (particularly regarding birds) and can organize volunteer placements, while the restaurant serves excellent Nepali food. Rs1000

Hotel River Side Just north of the park entrance ☎056 580 009, ⓔhriverside1@hotmail.com. A professional hotel with a wide range of rooms; the cheaper options (with fans and private bathrooms) are in the main building, while the more expensive "cottage-style" ones (US$45) offer lovely river views from private balconies and terraces. Rs1500

River View Jungle Camp North of Rhino Chowk ☎056 580 096, ⓦrvjcnepal.com. The deluxe rooms next to the river are the big draw here (US$65); they come with nice interiors, great bathrooms and balconies overlooking the water. Standard rooms are fine, too – red-brick with corrugated iron roofs, shaded by rows of tropical trees – but you'll have to rely on the lookout tower for the river view. Rates include breakfast. US$45

Royal Park Hotel North of the park entrance ☎056 580 061, ⓦroyalparkhotel.com.np. Cute buildings with terraces and lattice dividers sit in ample grounds, which also feature a tiny (and not always full) plunge pool. Opt for the (no more expensive) second-floor rooms with high ceilings and extra space. Rates include breakfast. US$35

★ **Sapana Village Lodge** 1.5km northwest of

Saaraha village ☎056 580 308, ⊛sapanalodge.com. Backed by a Dutch development project, *Sapana* aims to support the local Tharu community, both through employment opportunities and by giving visitors an insight into Tharu life via cooking classes, fishing trips, volunteering opportunities and homestays. The hacienda-style lodge, in a sedate riverside location, has delightful rooms with plenty of local touches. Rates include breakfast. <u>US$45</u>

EATING

Guesthouse dining rooms are generally not particularly exciting, while the handful of restaurants in and around the so-called **Rhino Chowk** serve a mix of fresh fish, Indian and Nepali dishes, and variable attempts at Western fare. You could also visit one of the classier lodges or go for inexpensive local food at one of the *bhatti* on the main drags.

Garden Restaurant and Bar Main Road. Family-run outdoor restaurant serving good Nepali and Indian food including a great *dal bhaat* (Rs220/330), served under bamboo and grass-thatch umbrellas. They also do barbecued meats (Rs710–2750). Not a bad place for a drink either: they have cocktails, beers and French or Indian wine by the glass (Rs440). Daily 7am–10pm.

★ **KC's** Rhino Chowk ☎056 580 309. The best restaurant in town, with a wonderful garden that leads down to the river. The menu features dishes from around the world, but the North Indian food (cooked using a proper *tandoor*) is the standout, with the fish tikka masala (Rs615) particularly good; most other mains cost Rs200–600. Generally open daily 8/9am–10/11pm.

NIGHTLIFE AND ENTERTAINMENT

Most of Sauraha's restaurants have happy hours (lasting most of the evening) and are good for **drinks**, but nothing stays open very late. At **sunset**, head to the "beach" on the riverbank by the park entrance, where a few shifting bars spring up

---

CYCLING THROUGH THE TERAI

A good way to learn about real Terai village life is to hop on a **bike** and just get lost on the back roads to the east and west of Sauraha. Stopping at any village and asking "chiya paunchha?" (where can I get a cup of tea?) will usually attract enough attention to get you introduced to someone.

In November, when the rice is harvested, you'll be able to watch villagers cutting the stems, tying them into sheaves and threshing them; or, since it's such a busy time of year, piling them in big stacks to await threshing. January is thatch-gathering time, when huge bundles are put by until a slack time before the monsoon allows time to repair roofs. In early March, the mustard, lentils and wheat that were planted after the rice crop are ready; maize is then planted, to be harvested in July for animal fodder, flour and meal. Rice is seeded in dense starter-plots in March, to be transplanted into separate paddy fields in April.

EAST OF SAURAHA

From Sauraha, the most fertile country for exploration lies to the **east**: heading towards Tadi Bazaar along the eastern side of the village, turn right (east) at the intersection marked by a health post and you can follow that road all the way to **Parsa**, 8km away on the Mahendra Highway; en route many side roads head off to villages, including **Kumroj**, gateway to the Kumroj Community Forest (see p.254). Given a full day and a good bike or motorcycle, you could continue eastwards from Parsa along the highway for another 10km, and just before Bhandara turn left onto a track leading to **Baireni**, a particularly well-preserved Tharu village. From **Lothar**, another 10km east of Bhandara, you can follow a trail upstream to reach the waterfalls on the Lothar Khola, a contemplative spot with a healthy measure of birdlife.

WEST OF SAURAHA

For a short ride **west** of Sauraha, first head north for 3km and take the first left after the river crossing, which brings you to the authentic Tharu villages of **Baghmara** and **Hardi**. If you're game for a longer journey, pedal to Tadi Bazaar and west along the Mahendra Highway to Tikauli. From there, the canal road through Bis Hajaar Tal leads about 10km through beautiful forest to **Gita Nagar**, where you join the Bharatpur–Jagatpur road, with almost unlimited possibilities.

A good route is to continue due west from Jagatpur on dirt roads all the way to **Meghauli**, though you may have to ford a river on the way, impossible on a motorbike from June/July until at least late November. Don't overlook the possibility of an outing to Devghat, either (see p.258).

5

THARU STICK DANCE

Sauraha's trademark entertainment is the **Tharu stick dance**, a mock battle in which participants parry each other's sticks with graceful, split-second timing. The original purpose of the dance, it's said, was simply to make a lot of racket to keep the wild animals away at night, although it is possible that it was carried with the Tharus from Rajasthan in the thirteenth century (see p.240). It still forms a traditional part of Tharu celebrations of Phaagun Purnima (the full moon of Feb–March), but the version you're likely to see is a more contrived tourist show put on for package groups at Sauraha lodges.

---

every season serving beers, cocktails and snacks on the sandy shore. Watching the sun go down over the jungle is one of Chitwan's more relaxing activities, but you'll have to get away from the bars to enjoy it in peace.

Tharu Culture Program Hall South of Elephant Chowk. Nightly culture shows, regional music and dance for tourist consumption (Rs60). Some of the smarter lodges host similar performances, often included in the package price. Daily 7pm.

SHOPPING

Small shops and stalls stock **food** and other items (beer, chocolate, batteries, toilet paper, postcards, crafts and so on), and there are a handful of decent secondhand **bookshops**. The town's **curio shops** sell mainly items from elsewhere, but if you search around you can find some locally produced Tharu handicrafts.

Community Souvenir Shop Opposite the park visitor centre. Useful books and maps, as well as mementos including Tharu handicrafts. Generally open daily 10am–4pm.

Ghatgain

The sleepy village of **GHATGAIN**, on the north bank of the Rapti River 16km west of Sauraha, holds a handful of simple lodges, a smart resort and little else. It's much quieter than Sauraha, and you're more likely to spot wildlife from your guesthouse here. Close by is a good patch of jungle, two interesting lakes (Lami Tal and Tamar Tal) and the Kasara park headquarters (see p.250), 4km downriver. The **park** itself starts on the other side of Rapti River from the village: guides (who guesthouses can provide) take you across by dugout canoe and you pay your entry fee, if you don't already have a ticket (see p.246).

ARRIVAL AND INFORMATION

By bus Take any bus for Jagatpur and ask to be let off at Patihani (if that doesn't ring a bell, ask for *Safari Narayani*). It's then a 15min walk south to Ghatgain. Destinations Kathmandu (1 daily; 7hr); Narayangadh (roughly hourly until mid-afternoon; 1hr); Pokhara (2 daily; 5hr).

Park permits You can get permits (Rs1500; see also p.256) for Chitwan National Park from the Kasara headquarters, 4km away (daily 6am–6pm).

ACCOMMODATION

Most locals will be able to point you towards any of the four budget **lodges**, which are close together in the heart of the village, making the most of the stunning river view. Near the Kasara park headquarters is the luxury *Kasasa Resort*.

Kasara Resort 2km from Kasara ☎ 01 443 7571, ⊛ kasararesort.com; map p.242. With a bit more modern style than "traditional" places, this tranquil resort boasts very comfortable rooms, each with their own private enclosed garden. Also has a nice pool, a yoga area and no TVs. Rate for two people, full board, including all activities US$468

Riverview Lodge ☎ 984 506 9589; map p.242. The pick of Ghatgain's budget options, *Riverview Lodge* has neat, clean rooms, a well-tended garden overlooking the river, friendly owners and good *daal bhaat*; the newer rooms are more comfortable, though twice as expensive. Rs500

Safari Narayani Lodge ☎ 01 553 7372, ⊛ safari narayani.com.np; map p.242. This smart package-only hotel boasts a giant pool, comfortable en suites and a palm-filled garden. Book via the website to get a twenty percent discount. Rates include full board, safaris and park and guide fees. Per person US$209

Meghauli

Some 19km west of Ghatgain, **MEGHAULI** sits opposite Bhimle, an area of the park just across the Rapti River, which boasts superb rhino and tiger habitat and birdwatching. Meghauli used to host the Elephant Polo Championships until the event moved to Bardia (see p.271); locals hope it will return to Meghauli, or they plan to organize their own competition.

ARRIVAL AND INFORMATION

MEGHAULI

By bus Local bus #5a from Narayangadh runs to Meghauli (roughly every 30min; about 2hr), stopping at the easternmost end of the village.
On foot Meghauli is a two-day trek from Sauraha.

Park permits The Bhimle guard post, where you can pay the park entrance fee (permits Rs1500; see also p.256), is 3km into the park; you'll need to hire a guide (via your guesthouse) to ferry you across the river.

ACCOMMODATION

Chital Lodge Beyond the airstrip (follow the signs) ☎ 984 515 5667; map p.242. This lodge has a lovely location, a knowledgeable owner and beautiful starfruit trees in the garden. The little wooden huts are poorly maintained, dusty and suitable only for very hardy travellers, but newer rooms with bathrooms are only Rs300 more. Rs500
Meghauli Wildlife Resort A 5min drive from Meghauli ☎ 056 620 134, ⓦ meghauliresort.com; map p.242. Aimed mainly at package tourists but open also to independent travellers, this hotel has a peaceful location

overlooking the river, pleasant grounds and a medicinal herb garden, plus comfortable (if twee) rooms with private bathrooms. US$40
Tiger Tops Tharu Lodge West of Meghauli ☎ 01 441 1225, ⓦ tigertops.com; map p.242. Luxury resort with architecture inspired by the traditional Tharu longhouse and an emphasis on cultural activities outside the park, as well as wildlife-viewing and safaris. Daily rate for two people, full-board, including all activities but excluding park fees US$492

Chitwan National Park

Whether **CHITWAN NATIONAL PARK** has been blessed or cursed by its own riches is an open question. The coexistence of the valley's people and wildlife has rarely been easy or harmonious, even before the creation of the national park. In the era of the trigger-happy maharajas, the relationship was at least simple: when Jang Bahadur Rana overthrew the Shah dynasty in 1846, one of his first actions was to make Chitwan a private hunting reserve. The following century saw some truly hideous **hunts** – during an eleven-day shoot in 1911, a visiting King George V killed 39 tigers and 18 rhinos.

Still, the Ranas' patronage afforded Chitwan a degree of protection, as did the presence of malaria. But in the early 1950s, the Ranas were thrown out, the monarchy was restored, and the new government launched its **malaria-control programme**. Settlers poured in and **poaching** went unpoliced – rhinos, whose horns were (and still are) valued for Chinese medicine and Yemeni knife handles, were especially hard hit. By 1960, the human population of the valley had trebled to 100,000, while the number of rhinos had plummeted from 1000 to just 200.

With the Asian one-horned rhino on the verge of extinction, Nepal emerged as an unlikely hero in one of conservation's finest hours. In 1962, Chitwan was set aside as a **rhino sanctuary** (becoming Nepal's first national park in 1973); and, despite the endless hype about tigers, rhinos are Chitwan's biggest attraction and its greatest triumph. Chitwan now boasts over 500 **rhinos**, and the park authorities have felt confident enough to relocate some to Bardia National Park. A number were killed by poachers during the Maoist conflict, but now that the soldiers are back at their posts in the park (and nationally) the problem has virtually disappeared, with zero known poaching in 2010/11 and 2013/14, and just one rhino lost since then.

There are thought to be over 120 **tigers** in the park. Chitwan also supports at least 400 **gaur** (Indian bison) and provides a part-time home to as many as 45 wild **elephants**, who roam between here and India. Altogether, 68 mammalian species are found in the park, including sloth bear, leopard, langur and four kinds of deer.

5

CHITWAN: A SEESAW BATTLE FOR SURVIVAL

While Chitwan's forest ecosystem is healthy at the moment, **pollution** from upstream industries is endangering the rivers that flow into it: gangetic dolphins have disappeared from the Narayani, and gharial crocodiles hang on thanks only to human intervention (see p.251). With more than 300,000 people now inhabiting the Chitwan Valley, human **population** growth represents an even graver danger in the long term. **Tourism** has picked up again, after dropping off considerably during the civil war – the key issue will be to ensure that the resultant development is handled in a sensitive, sustainable manner.

The key to safeguarding Chitwan, everyone agrees, is to win the support of local people, and there's some indication that this is happening. Several organizations run awareness-raising programmes, particularly targeting children, but there has been little government action in this regard. Another pressing problem for the area – and the country as a whole – is a lack of investment in infrastructure, notably roads.

Communities living in the 750 square kilometres around the park receive some state financial support, and compensation is paid for damage caused by wild animals. Safety has improved but one or two villagers are still killed each year. The **National Trust for Nature Conservation** (ⓦwww.ntnc.org.np), funded by several international agencies, is active in general community development efforts such as building schools, health posts, water taps and appropriate technology facilities, as well as in conservation education and training for guides and lodge owners. They have also been instrumental in helping set up **community forests** (see p.254) around Chitwan, and the prospect of collecting hefty entrance fees from these is turning local people into zealous guardians of the environment.

Chitwan is also Nepal's most important sanctuary for **birds**, with 544 species recorded, and there are also two types of **crocodile** and more than 150 types of **butterfly**.

Kasara and around

Chitwan National Park's headquarters lie at **KASARA**, about 15km west of Sauraha. Jeep tours generally pass through, taking in the crocodile breeding project, but it's not somewhere you'd go out of your way to visit.

Kasara Durbar

Museum daily 9am–5pm, though you may have to find someone to unlock it • Free

Kasara Durbar, which overlooks a small army base, was constructed in 1939 as a royal hunting lodge, and now serves as the park's administrative headquarters. A meagre **museum** holds a collection of skulls and school-project-like displays. Baby rhinos, orphaned by poachers, can sometimes be seen roaming freely and begging for food near here, pending relocation.

Gharial Crocodile Breeding Project

Daily 9am–5pm • Rs200

A well-used signposted track leads about 300m west from Kasara Durbar through light forest to the **Gharial Crocodile Breeding Project** (see box opposite), which is Kasara's only real attraction. The project gives you the chance to see baby crocodiles close-up, and – from a distance – bigger crocs a few years' old, just before they're released into the wild. Injured – or dangerous man-eating – tigers are sometimes kept in cages nearby. A few turtles can also be seen at the centre.

Chitwan Park activities

Visitors can only enter the national park accompanied by a **guide** (see p.256), and guides for activities such as jungle walks and elephant rides vie for your attention once you arrive in the vicinity of the park. Note, however, that promises of "safari adventure" in Chitwan can be misleading. While the park's **wildlife** is astoundingly concentrated, the dense vegetation doesn't allow the easy sightings you get in the savannahs of Africa

5

(especially in autumn, when the grass is high). Many guides assume that everyone wants to see only tigers and rhinos, but there are any number of birds and other animals to spot which the typical safari package may not cover, not to mention the many different ways simply to experience the luxuriant, teeming jungle: **elephant rides, jeep tours**, **canoe trips** and **jungle walks** each give a different slant.

The following **activities** are most commonly done inside Chitwan National Park, so you'll need to add the cost of an entry permit (see p.256) to the prices quoted. All activities can, and in most cases should, be arranged through your lodge, or via a guide service in Sauraha. Book the night before, or even earlier during the cut-throat months of October, November and March.

Guided walks

A morning's walk costs Rs700–1000/person (depending on the guide's level of experience and the number of clients). A full day costs Rs2000–2500

Guided walks allow you to appreciate the smaller attractions of the jungle at your own pace: orchids, strangler figs, towering termite mounds or tiger scratchings. You are virtually guaranteed to see a **rhino**, and deer and monkeys are easy to spot, but tiger sightings are rare: maybe one or two a week. Note that a full-day walk doesn't necessarily increase your chances of seeing game – most of the rhinos hangout close to Sauraha – but it gets you further into the park so you don't run into other parties every two minutes. In cool weather some guides lead all-day walks in the **Churia Hills**, where you may see gaur (Indian bison) as well as deer, monkeys and a huge number of bird species (look for parakeets, Indian rollers, paradise flycatchers, kingfishers, hornbills, cranes and literally hundreds of others).

The best season for walking is **spring**, when the grass is shorter, though at other times of year you can compensate by spending more time in the *sal* forest and riverine habitats. The region is also an important stopover spot for migratory birds in December and March; the **Bird Education Society** (see p.257) is an excellent source of information. No matter when you go, carry lots of water.

Jungle treks

The cost of a jungle trek is simply the guide's daily rate (Rs2000–2500/person), plus his and your food and lodging

To get well clear of the Sauraha crowds you need to walk for two or more days, overnighting en route outside the park – think of it as a **jungle trek**. Itineraries are limited by the fact that camping is not allowed inside the park. The next best thing to camping is to spend a night in an observation tower in one of the community forests (see p.254). There's a "teahouse" route in the park, plus any number of other possibilities

---

GHARIAL CROCODILES

The world's longest crocodile – adults can grow to more than 7m from nose to tail – the **gharial** is an awesome fishing machine. Its slender, broom-like snout, which bristles with a fine mesh of teeth, snaps shut on its prey like a spring-loaded trap. Unfortunately, its eggs are regarded as a delicacy, and males are hunted for their bulb-like snouts, believed to have medicinal powers.

In the mid-1970s, there were only 1300 gharials left. Chitwan's Gharial Crocodile Breeding Project was set up in 1977 to incubate eggs under controlled conditions, thus upping the survival rate – just 1 percent in the wild – to as high as 75 percent. The majority of hatchlings are released into the wild after three years, when they reach 1.2m in length; more than five hundred have been released so far into the Narayani, Koshi, Karnali and Babai rivers. Having been given this head start, however, the hatchlings must then survive a growing list of dangers, which now include not only hunters but also untreated effluents from upstream industries and a scarcity of food caused by the lack of fish ladders on a dam downstream in India. Counts indicate that captive-raised gharials now outnumber wild ones on the Narayani, which suggests that without constant artificial augmentation of their numbers they would soon become extinct.

5

THE ETHICS OF ELEPHANT RIDES

Elephant rides are available in most of the lowland national parks in Nepal, and there has been concern from some readers about the treatment of the animals. In the last few years some tour operators have also started to question the ethics of elephant rides, and in 2014, both STA Travel and Intrepid announced that they were removing elephant rides from all their tours worldwide; Intrepid's decision came after considering a three-year study into the welfare of captive elephants in Asia by charity World Animal Protection. It's a thorny issue, and one that you should consider before making the decision to go on an elephant ride or attend an event such as elephant polo. We've laid out some of the facts below so that you can decide for yourself.

TRAINING AND CONTROL

There are around 150–170 wild elephants in Nepal and around an equal number in **captivity**. The majority of the latter work in and around the national parks, involved either with conservation work or in giving tourists rides. Most of these are bred in captivity, and are forcibly taken away from their mothers at the age of two, when they are joined to a **mahout** (elephant handler) who will remain with the elephant for life – some compare it to a marriage.

Despite their long history of working with humans, elephants are not domesticated; they are wild animals, so must be trained to make them safe. The "**breaking in**" process can be brutal (as plenty of videos on the internet show), but to their mahouts it is considered necessary. These elephants (especially the bulls) are large, dangerous animals, which can easily kill humans. There have been ways of training elephants (and many other wild animals) developed in the West which do not use violence, but these are expensive and beyond the means of the Nepalese.

There are four ways an elephant is **controlled**. The basic way in which the mahout steers an elephant is by using their **toes** to poke behind its ears. If this doesn't work, then a short **stick** is used to hit the animal's head, although since an elephant's skull is centimetres thick, this does not harm it in any way. If the stick doesn't work (or if it's a young bull), the mahout may use the **anksi** (a small sickle) with which he can cut the elephant's ears, or the **bancheri** (small axe), used in emergencies only; both of these certainly do hurt the animals, though they are rarely used.

LIFE IN CAPTIVITY

Elephants are not designed to carry **heavy loads**, and the chairs strapped onto their backs, designed to carry many tourists at a time, can give them long-lasting spinal injuries. When not giving tourists rides, which they typically do for three to six hours a day, elephants are generally kept chained up in their stable (**hattisar**), unless they are collecting food. An elephant eats over 200kg of food a day, for which many owners receive a rice subsidy from the government, although owners sometimes sell this in the market if they're short of money. As with any captive animal, there are good owners and **bad owners**, and the economics of the business mean that bad owners can make more money by working the elephants harder and giving them less food – indeed, one elephant died of malnutrition in Chitwan in 2014.

INCOME AND CONSERVATION

On the positive side, many mahouts treat their elephants very well, and elephant rides bring **employment** and **income** to the locals. Elephants are used as cranes and bulldozers in rural areas, and also aid in forest **conservation** and in patrolling for **poachers**. In 2014 UK-based travel agency Responsible Travel announced that Nepal's national parks would be exempt from its policy of not promoting elephant rides or offering trips promoting them, stating that "Chitwan National Park in Nepal is one example where elephant rides (are) a positive force for conservation." The national park entrance fees generated by elephant rides allow investment in the conservation of Chitwan and its rare and endangered wildlife – and the wider income generated by tourism encourages local communities to help safeguard the park. One final consideration is that there is really no **space** for more elephants in the wild (they are in conflict with humans even in the national parks, killing around a dozen people a year), so simply letting them free is not an option.

READ MORE

PETA ⓦ action.peta.org.uk
Responsible travel ⓦ responsibletravel.com/holidays/elephant-conservation/travel-guide
World Animal Protection ⓦ worldanimalprotection.org.uk

if you stay in private homes. The Churia Hills are best for birds, while the teahouse route is excellent for animals. There's a fair chance of seeing bears in the Maadi Valley.

The **teahouse route** follows the forest road from **Sauraha to Kasara** and on **to Meghauli**, or vice versa. It takes two days of roughly equal length, or you could just do one half or the other. The Sauraha–Kasara leg is more commonly trekked, and is also the route taken by jeep tours out of Sauraha. There are of course no teahouses inside the park, but you can spend nights at Meghauli (see p.249) and Ghatgain (see p.248).

It's also possible to carry on trekking for a further two days (you could also start from Meghauli), overnighting at **Madi** in a beautiful valley just outside the park's southern boundary, and then returning to Sauraha. This allows you to get to less-visited parts of the park's interior, such as Tamar Tal, which is excellent for birdwatching. You can return to Sauraha by local bus or arrange to have a jeep take you back. Go with a guide who's done this trek before – most haven't.

Elephant rides

Safaris run in the early morning or late afternoon • Rides in the community forests cost Rs1500/person for 90min. Rides on privately owned elephants inside the park cost Rs2500/person/hour. Rates don't include park entry permit fees

The park's own elephants are not available for rides, and all **elephant safaris** are with privately owned elephants. The majority of elephant rides are in the **community forest** (see p.254), although the chance of seeing any wildlife on these is small. The safaris **within the park** give you a much better chance of seeing wildlife, although they are much more expensive and are often booked up well in advance; they can be arranged though hotels with their own elephants.

Riding on an elephant is the safest way to get around in the grasslands – especially in summer and autumn – and it's the best way to observe rhinos, since the elephant's scent masks your own; read the box opposite about the ethics of elephant rides before deciding whether or not to arrange one. Note that elephants don't work on major holidays, such as the eighth and ninth days of Dasain, and Lakshmi Puja.

Canoe trips

Short canoe trip to Elephant Breeding Project (3hr) Rs2000/person. Long canoe trip to Kasara (5hr) Rs2800–4000 (depending on number, up to 3 people). The hourly rate for longer trips is from Rs1000 per person

Floating down either of the Sauraha area's two rivers in a dugout **canoe** gives you your best shot at seeing **mugger crocodiles** (which, unlike the pointier-snouted gharials, prefer such marshy areas), and is also a relaxing way to watch birds and look for occasional wildlife on the shore. It's best done in winter, when the water is cool and the muggers sun themselves on the gravel banks; ruddy shelducks may be seen in profusion at this time, too. In hot weather, the outing is less rewarding, though you'll be assured of plenty of birds.

The standard short **itinerary** is to depart from near the Baghmara Community Forest (just west of Sauraha) and float for 45 minutes down the Budhi Rapti (Old Rapti) River to the Elephant Breeding Project (see p.244), then walk or catch a jeep back to your lodging. A longer trip runs all the way to Kasara and includes a visit to the Gharial Crocodile Breeding Project as well as a one- to two-hour jungle trek. The trips aren't actually within the park itself, but a park permit is still required.

The time spent on the water is relatively brief, and if you're not in the first couple of canoes that morning or afternoon you may not see much. Slightly longer trips on the main Rapti River are more worthwhile, though there's a tendency to pack too many people into one boat.

Jeep rides

Jeep tours generally cost Rs1700/person, including a guide. Hiring a 7-seater jeep yourself costs around Rs12,000 for a half-day, Rs15,000 for a full day

Hiring a **jeep** (or more often a battered army surplus vehicle) for half a day gives you the chance to get deep into the jungle, but is relatively disruptive. If you can't get a

5

STAYING ALIVE IN THE JUNGLE

Lodge owners and guides often play down the risks associated with tracking wildlife, but **safety** is a serious issue in Chitwan, and rarely a year goes by without one or two fatalities in the park. There are no emergency medical facilities in or near the park – the closest hospital is in Bharatpur, a minimum two-hour evacuation when you add up all the stages, which means that if there's major bleeding the patient is essentially out of luck.

The greatest danger comes from **rhinos**, which have a tendency to charge at anything they perceive to be a threat. If a rhino is about to charge it lowers its head and takes a step back; if it does charge you, try to run in a zigzag path and throw off a piece of clothing (the rhino will, hopefully, stop to smell it), or hide behind – or better yet, climb – the nearest big tree. **Sloth bears** can also be dangerous if surprised. If a bear charges, climb a small tree . Never run from a **tiger**: stare it straight in the eyes, hold your ground and make yourself more terrifying by pulling faces and shouting. With any of these animals, don't get anywhere near a mother with young ones.

The best safety tip is to get an experienced **guide**, but even they can't guarantee invulnerability. Most guides are young and gung-ho, and in their eagerness to please will sometimes encourage tourists to venture too close to animals. No matter how competent, a guide can't know where all the animals are, nor, in an emergency, assist more than one person at a time. For this reason most reputable guides will limit **group size** to four clients, and there should be two guides for every group.

group together, sign up for a half-day **jeep tour**, which can be pretty cramped as eight or nine people may be packed in. The **best months** are from February to April, after the grass has been cut and the new shoots attract the deer.

For big game, you're limited to what you can see through the dusty wake of the jeeps in the mid-morning or afternoon, which pretty much means **deer**, and often **rhinos** too. The standard jeep tour includes a stop at **Lami Tal** (Long Lake), which should be a prime spot for watching **birds** and **mugger crocodiles**, but things get pretty sleepy in the heat of the day. The tour continues to the Gharial Crocodile Breeding Project and Kasara Durbar.

The community forests

Large patches of jungle still exist outside the park in Chitwan's heavily populated buffer zone, albeit in a less pristine state. The areas designated as **community forests** were originally conceived to reduce the need for residents of this critical strip to go into the park to gather wood, thatch and other resources, but the forests are now nearly as rich in flora and fauna as Chitwan itself. Two forests, **Baghmara** and **Kumroj** on the outskirts of Sauraha, offer alternatives to entering the park itself, and the **elephant rides** here (see p.252) are an integral part of the Chitwan tourist conveyor belt.

Another community forest, the **Bis Hajaar Tal** wetland area, is one of the best areas – inside or outside the park – for **birdwatching**, though the growth of water hyacinth has reduced bird numbers. There are plenty of animals, but it's one of the few areas of jungle that can be visited independently with relative safety – though, as always, you'll probably get more out of it in the company of a good guide.

Baghmara and Kumroj community forests

Chitwan National Park entry tickets (Rs1500) are valid on the same day, or the following one, in the community forests

Closest to Sauraha, **Baghmara Community Forest** is a good place to see rhinos and birds; you can also combine your visit with a trip to Bis Hajaar Tal (see p.256), which it borders, or the Elephant Breeding Project, just south (see p.244). Its main entrance is 1km west of Sauraha.

Kumroj Community Forest (also written as Kumrose Community Forest), 2km east of Sauraha, is further away from most lodges and you'd probably only visit it on an

5

PARK PEOPLE

A procession of bicycle-toting locals crossing the Rapti at dusk, wading or being ferried across the river before disappearing into the trees of the national park on the far side, was once a familiar Sauraha scene.

In the late 1990s, more than 20,000 people lived within the park boundaries, mainly in **Padampur**, the area immediately opposite Sauraha. Inevitably, villagers were forced to compete with the park's animal population for forest resources and the ever-increasing number of wild animals would regularly raid farmers' crops, causing widespread damage and even deaths. The situation became increasingly unsustainable, and the government finally decided to **relocate** Padampur's villagers from the park itself to Saguntole, around 10km north of the national park, which extends from Bis Hajaar Tal towards the hills of the Mahabharat Lekh. This programme has now left Chitwan itself free of human settlement.

This has inevitably raised troubling issues. Foremost is that people have been forced to leave their homes to make way for animals and the tourists who come to see them. Although the villagers got a good deal financially (many have sold their new land at inflated prices), the community has been weakened and with it a great deal of knowledge has been, if not lost, then undoubtedly threatened.

elephant ride, though the route from Sauraha is partially forested. As in the national park, a guide is required to enter either of the community forests on foot, and you will also need a park entry permit (see below).

Bis Hajaar Tal

Chitwan National Park entry tickets (Rs1500) are valid on the same day, or the following one, in the community forests

Nepal's second largest natural wetland, the **Bis Hajaar Tal** ("Twenty Thousand Lakes") area, provides an important corridor for animals migrating between the Terai and the hills. The name refers to a maze of marshy oxbow lakes, many of them already filled in, well hidden among mature *sal* trees. The area teems with birds, including storks, kingfishers, eagles and the huge Lesser Adjutant. The forest starts just west of Baghmara and the Elephant Breeding Project and reaches its marshy climax about 5km northwest of there. You'll need a guide to enter Bis Hajaar Tal on foot, as well as a park entry permit (see below).

INFORMATION   CHITWAN NATIONAL PARK

Chitwan is by far the most popular of Nepal's national parks, although how busy it actually gets depends heavily upon the climate. **October** and **November** are relatively cool (though still pleasantly warm), but the most popular activities can get booked up, the tall grass makes sightings much rarer, and there's something depressing about your main confrontation with wildlife being another trained elephant topped by tourists. Tourist numbers tail off in **December** and **January**, but after the grass is cut (usually in late Jan), visitors flock in to take advantage of the easy sightings, particularly in **March**. From **April** onwards, the park gets almost unbearably hot – particularly in the steamy **monsoon** months of July, August and September – but at least you'll have the place to yourself.

ENTRY AND PERMITS

There are no formal park entrances to Chitwan, as the boundary is formed by the river, but you do need a park entry permit (Rs1500) – one for each day you are in the park, as there are no discounts for longer visits. Permits also allow you access to the community forests (see p.254) on the same day, and the following day as well. Once you have your permit, your guide will take you across the river and into the park by canoe or, in low water, by wading.

Sauraha Permits are sold at the ranger's office (daily 6am–6pm), next to the visitor centre.

Ghatgain Permits are available from the Kasara

headquarters (daily 6am–6pm).

Meghauli There's no ranger's office at Meghauli; once across the river your guide will help you buy one from the Bhimle guard post on the other side.

GUIDES

For safety reasons (see box, p.254), visitors are not allowed to enter the park on foot without a certified guide. For the most part, Sauraha's guides are keen and personable, and some are among Nepal's finest. Most are well versed in what tourists want to know, while the best are more than capable of explaining the park's animals, birds, butterflies, trees, plants and indeed its entire ecosystem in competent English. Their knowledge of species (especially birds) can be encyclopedic. **Fees and experience** The best (most experienced) guides are generally attached to lodges; they can usually put together a group, which lowers the per-person cost. There are also numerous qualified (though typically younger and less experienced) freelance guides who have set up shop around Sauraha; ask other travellers if they've found someone they can recommend. It's also possible to hire a guide at the national park visitor centre in Sauraha (see p.245). Fees will

depend on the activity and, to some extent, on the experience of the guide, though start at around Rs1500–1800. Note that less experienced guides are apt to speak less English. (If your guide yells *look*, that means "hide" in Nepali!)

The Bird Education Society Northwest of Elephant Chowk ☎ 056 580 113, ✉ besnepal@wlink.com.np. This office can put you in touch with excellent, committed guides who tend to specialize in birds. Every Saturday they run free early-morning birdwatching tours (donation appreciated); contact them in advance to book a place.

ACCOMMODATION

Luxury lodges The luxury lodges and tented camps inside Chitwan National Park were all kicked out in 2012, and there is now no accommodation at all within the park. The high-end lodges and camps have relocated to the buffer zone, and all only sell overpriced packages; two of the better ones are listed in the Ghatgain (see p.248) and Meghauli (see p.249) accounts.

Observation towers Both Baghmara and Kumroj

community forests have concrete machan (observation towers) where you can spend the night – good for nocturnal viewing if the moon is out. As in the park, a guide is required to enter either of the community forests on foot: guides charge around Rs1500 (excluding entry fees, food and drinks) for an overnight trip, and you'll have to pay Rs1000/person for sleeping.

Narayangadh/Bharatpur

It's hard to travel far in Nepal without passing through **NARAYANGADH**: the Mugling–Narayangadh highway has made it the gateway to the Terai and the country's busiest crossroads. What was once a far-flung intersection is now a kilometre-long strip of diesel and *daal bhaat* (and a hotbed of prostitution). Narayangadh's sister city, **BHARATPUR**, continues to the east without a visible break, though as the headquarters of Chitwan District it's tangibly more upmarket, and fast becoming an educational hub, boasting a university and two medical colleges as well as an airstrip. Unappealing as all that may sound, you may have occasion to pause in the area, and the side trip to the sacred confluence of **Devghat** (see p.258), 5km upstream of Narayangadh, makes for a refreshingly cultural outing from Chitwan.

ARRIVAL AND GETTING AROUND

NARAYANGADH/BHARATPUR

By plane Yeti Airlines run one daily flight at 11.30am to Kathmandu (10.50am in the other direction) from Bharatpur's airstrip, just south of the Mahendra Highway.

By bus Buses serving the northward Mugling Highway (to and from Pokhara, Gorkha and Devghat) have their own bus park (commonly known as the Pokhara bus park) at the north end of Narayangadh. All other express buses serving the Mahendra Highway stop at the fast-food parade just east of Pulchowk (the intersection of the Mugling and Mahendra highways). There are two additional bus parks for local services: buses and minibuses to Tadi Bazaar (for Sauraha) and eastern Chitwan District start from Sahid Chowk, about 500m east of Pulchowk; minibuses to Meghauli and Jagatpur

start from just north of Sahid Chowk – walk north for 50m, take the first right down a small lane, and it's on the left after 200m. Buses to Kathmandu all leave in the morning, and you should reserve the day before to be sure of a seat.

Destinations Bandipur (2–3 daily; 5hr); Birgunj (10–12 daily; 4–5hr); Butwal/Bhairahawa (hourly; 3–5hr); Gorkha (hourly; 2hr 30min–3hr); Jagatpur (hourly; 1hr); Kathmandu (every 30min–1hr in the mornings; 4–5hr); Meghauli (every 30min–1hr; 1hr); Pokhara (every 30min; 4hr).

By car A car (around Rs1500) to Sauraha can be organized through your hotel.

By rikshaw Rikshaws should take you anywhere within Narayangadh and Bharatpur for Rs100–150.

ACCOMMODATION AND EATING

Narayangadh has a decent range of slightly overpriced **hotels**, and although Bharatpur does have some more upmarket resorts, the chances are you're only here for the night so you're better off staying near the bus connections in Narayangadh. Food **stalls** can be found all around Pulchowk in Narayangadh, though hygiene isn't always the highest priority, while many of the so-called **restaurants** in this area are little more than whisky shacks. The restaurants at the smarter hotels are a safer bet.

5

Central Palms Hotel New Rd, 500m south of Pulchowk, Narayangadh ☎ 056 571 185, ⊛ central palms-hotel.com.np; map p.242. Despite being down a road badly in need of repair, *Central Palms* is probably the nicest hotel within the town centre, fairly quiet with swish contemporary en suites, a pool and one of the best restaurants in town. Rs3690
New Hotel Uncle West of Narayani bridge, Narayangadh ☎ 056 501 352; map p.242. Head to this riverside lodge for peaceful, economical (but decent) fan

rooms that have private bathrooms with hot showers – the Rs1500 a/c rooms also have balconies overlooking the river, and there's a pleasant, if twee, garden. Rs800
Royal Rest House Pulchowk, Narayangadh ☎ 056 571 442; map p.242. A reasonable choice above an economical restaurant. The cheapest rooms can be a bit grubby but better ones (Rs800) with private facilities – including bathtubs – are clean enough, though some lack natural light; a/c rooms cost Rs1200. Road noise can be an issue, so bring your earplugs. Rs300

Devghat

DEVGHAT (or Deoghat), 5km northwest of Narayangadh, is many people's idea of a great place to die. An astonishingly tranquil spot, it stands where the wooded hills meet the shimmering plains, and the Trisuli and the Kali Gandaki **rivers** merge to form the Narayani, a major tributary of the Ganga (Ganges). Some say Sita, heroine of the Ramayana, died here. The ashes of King Mahendra were sprinkled at this sacred *tribeni* (a confluence of three rivers: wherever two rivers meet, a third, spiritual one is believed to join them), and scores of *sunyasan*, those who have renounced the world, patiently live out their last days here hoping to achieve an equally auspicious death and rebirth. Many retire to Devghat to avoid being a burden to their children, to escape ungrateful offspring, or because they have no children to look after them in their old age and perform the necessary rites when they die. *Pujari* (priests) also practise here and often take in young candidates for the priesthood as resident students.

Dozens of small shrines lie dotted around the village, but you come here more for the **atmosphere** than the sights. Vaishnavas (followers of Vishnu) congregate at Devghat's largest and newest temple, the central *shikra*-style **Harihar Mandir**, founded in 1998 by the famed guru Shaktya Prakash Ananda of Haridwar. Shaivas (followers of Shiva) dominate the area overlooking the confluence at the western edge of the village.

The confluence

To reach the confluence, turn left at a prominent *chautaara* at the top of the path leading through the village: **Galeshwar Ashram**, on your right as you walk down the steps, and **Aghori Ashram**, further downhill on the right, are named after two deceased holy men. One of them, the one-armed Aghori Baba, was a follower of the extreme Aghori tradition (see p.128) and was often referred to as the "Crazy Baba", claiming to have cut off his own arm after being instructed to do so in a dream. Various paths lead upstream of the confluence, eventually arriving at **Sita Gupha**, a sacred cave that is closed except on Makar Sankranti, and **Chakrabarti Mandir**, a shady temple area housing a famous *shaligram* that locals say is growing. At the confluence keep an eye out for black pebbles (usually flecked with white), which are believed to be literally parts of a Vishnu, from a Vishnu *onkar* upstream.

THE DEVGHAT PILGRIMAGE

A huge **pilgrimage** is held at Devghat on Makar Sankranti (Jan 14 or 15), while Shiva Raatri, falling on the new moon of February–March, brings many Indian devotees. At other times, sadhus and pilgrims perform *puja* at the point where the rivers meet – cremations are also held here – and old-timers meditate outside their huts in the sun. Be sensitive to the residents, and don't disturb them or touch anything that might be holy: many are orthodox Baahuns and your touch is considered polluting.

ARRIVAL AND DEPARTURE

By bus Buses shuttle every couple of hours between the Pokhara bus park in Narayangadh and Devghat (30min); the last bus leaves Devghat around 6pm.

On foot Head north from Narayangadh's Pokhara bus park along the main highway to Mugling, and turn left under an arch after 1km onto a paved road – Devghat is at the end of the road, about 5km through forest. Either way, you cross the Trisuli by a dramatic suspension footbridge,

DEVGHAT

immortalized in the classic Nepali film *Kanchhi*, in which the heartbroken lover attempted suicide from it. From the far side of the bridge, bear left up and into the village. You can also cross the river further downstream by inflatable raft (Rs100) – for the return trip, the ferryman, if he thinks he can be spared from his duties, might even consent to take you all the way back to Narayangadh for a suitable fee (a negotiable Rs250–300).

ACCOMMODATION

Aananda Bhaomi Lodge On the left immediately across the bridge ☎ 984 189 0271; map p.242. The only place to stay in Devghat, this homestay has just one en-suite double, and one small four-person dorm. It's run

by Ramesh, a retired development officer, who travelled for forty years across Nepal and is a font of knowledge. Rooms are basic but clean, *dal bhaat* is available (Rs150/250) and there are views of the river. Dorms Rs300, room Rs500

Lumbini Terai

Hordes of travellers hurry through **Lumbini Terai**, an ancient part of the Terai west of Chitwan, but few take the time to look around. It's best known, unfairly, for **Sonauli**, the main tourist border crossing between Nepal and India. Yet just 20km away is one of Nepal's premier destinations, **Lumbini**: birthplace of the Buddha and the site of ruins going back almost three thousand years.

Butwal

Crouching uninvitingly at the point where the Tinau River spills out onto the plains, **BUTWAL** is an ugly modern town of convenience. It's the hub of the Lumbini administrative zone: north lies Pokhara; south is Sonauli and the Indian border; to the west, the Mahendra Highway barrels along towards Nepalgunj and Nepal's western border; and to the east, the Mahendra Highway runs 110km to Narayangadh, passing heavily used forest, cultivated fields and a jungle-cloaked spur of the Churia Hill.

Placed at the start of an important trade route to Tibet as well as the pilgrim trail to Muktinath, the **tax post** at Butwal was for centuries a tidy little earner for Palpa (Tansen) and then Kathmandu. Much later, it came to be a staging post for Gurkha soldiers. In the early nineteenth century, Nepal and the East India Company fell into a dispute over the territory around Butwal. In the subsequent two-year **war with Britain** (see p.384), Nepal scored several improbable early victories but was eventually forced to surrender. Under the resulting treaty, the Terai territories from Butwal west were ceded to the British (though Nepal struck a deal to get the disputed land around Butwal back the same year).

ARRIVAL AND DEPARTURE

By bus Express services are based at the bus park, to the south of town on the main Sonauli road (the Siddhartha Highway). Many of the buses to Sonauli via Bhairahawa stop off at "Trafik Chowk", a busy crossroads 500m north on the same highway. The bus park has a reputation for petty theft, so keep an eye on your belongings. Some local buses use the old bus park, four blocks to the west of Trafik Chowk.

BUTWAL

Destinations Bhairahawa (every 10min; 45min–1hr); Birgunj (1 night bus; 7–8hr); Dangadhi (1 day bus and 1 night bus; 9hr); Kathmandu (hourly; 7–8hr); Mahendra Nagar (1 day bus and 1 night bus; 11–12hr); Narayangadh (every 10min; 3–4hr); Nepalgunj (1 day bus and 1 night bus; 7–8hr); Pokhara (1 day bus and 1 night bus; 6–8hr); Sonauli (every 10min; 1hr–1hr 15min); Tansen (2 daily; 2hr 15min).

5

ACCOMMODATION AND EATING

Butwal has some ghastly highway dives, but there are a few fairly professional **hotels** – Bhairahawa (see below), however, is a much better place to stay. *Darcy's International Hotel* (see below) has a decent **restaurant**, and there are a few *bhojanalaya* (local Nepali diners) around Trafik Chowk.

Darcy's International Hotel Just east of the bus station on Darcy's Rd ☎071 550 700, ⚲darcys internationalhotel.com. This solid mid-range hotel has comfortable a/c rooms with private bathrooms, TVs and very soft beds. There's also a decent attached restaurant and bar. Rs2250

Hotel Manish One block west of Trafik Chowk ☎071 549 801. Not a bad budget choice, and conveniently close to the bus station, this place has neat, clean, en-suite

fan rooms as well as a few overpriced a/c ones for Rs1000 more. Most of the rooms are surprisingly quiet, but check first. Rs600

Nanglo West Around 2km north of the bus park on the main road ☎071 544 455. Inconveniently located, but worth a visit for its tasty Nepali and Newari food, including a very good *dal bhaat* (Rs370–460). They also do decent tandoori dishes (Rs150–550), including very fine naan bread. Daily noon–10pm.

Bhairahawa (Siddhartha Nagar)

Thirty minutes' south of Butwal by bus and just 4km from the border, **BHAIRAHAWA** (or **SIDDHARTHA NAGAR**) is less frenetic than Butwal, and a better place to stay than Sonauli. Its **bazaar** supports a sizeable minority of Muslim traders and, like so many border towns, exists primarily to peddle imported goods to acquisitive Indians.

Bhairahawa's three main streets form an upright triangle: the eastern side is the Siddhartha Highway (which continues north to Butwal and south to the Indian border), Bank Road runs along the south, and Narayanpath along the west. *Hotel Yeti* stands on a roundabout at the southeastern apex of the triangle and is a handy landmark; rikshaws and shared jeeps bound for Sonauli wait here. The road to Lumbini breaks west from the highway about 1km north of *Hotel Yeti*, just north of the triangle's northern apex.

ARRIVAL AND DEPARTURE   BHAIRAHAWA (SIDDHARTHA NAGAR)

By plane Bhairahawa Airport (also known as Gautam Buddha Airport), 10km north of town, has four daily flights to Kathmandu and one to Pokhara.

By bus The bus park, for all express services, lies 500m south of *Hotel Yeti* on the main Siddhartha Highway. Some local buses, however, still drop-off and pick up in town, at the main crossroads by *Hotel Yeti*. There are frequent buses to Kathmandu and Pokhara, as well as slightly more comfortable (and expensive) minibuses. Golden Travels operate a couple of tourist buses to Kathmandu (daily 7.30am & 8.30am). Services to Lumbini and Taulihawa depart from the bus station but also stop off for passengers

at the start of the westbound road to Lumbini, just outside town.

Destinations Birgunj (2–3 daily; 8–9hr); Butwal (every 15min; 30min–1hr); Kathmandu (every 10–30min; 8–9hr); Lumbini (every 30min; 1hr); Narayangadh (2–3 daily; 3–5hr); Pokhara (4–5 daily; 7–9hr); Taulihawa (for Tilaurakot; roughly hourly; 1hr 30min–2hr).

By car Cars and jeeps can be rented by the day (Rs2000 plus petrol), or for the journey to Lumbini (about Rs2500 one-way) or Tilaurakot (about Rs3500 return) – arrange through the better hotels or a central travel agent.

ACCOMMODATION AND EATING

Hotel Glasgow Bank Rd ☎071 523 737, ✉hotelglasgow@gmail.com. A portrait of Queen Elizabeth II greets you in the lobby of this well-run mid-range hotel, which offers homely en suites with TVs, writing desks and fans. There are also some a/c options for Rs800 or so more. The restaurant here is worth considering. Rs1000

Pawan Misthan Bhandar Main Rd, just south of Bank Rd. A bustling local joint serving inexpensive South Indian food like *dosas* and all manner of fried, sticky and sugary

delights (mains less than Rs100). There's no real menu and you may have to share a table, but that's all part of the fun. Daily 6am–8pm.

Hotel Yeti On the corner of the border highway and Bank Rd ☎071 520 551, ✉hotelyeti@ntc.net.np. This monolithic hotel, with an eye-catching pink exterior, has spacious a/c en suites that are the best in town, professional staff, and a good restaurant and bar. It's popular with package-tour groups, so book ahead. US$49

Sonauli (Belahiya)

The little border scrum of **SONAULI** (technically the Nepali side is known as **BELAHIYA**) is the most popular border crossing between Nepal and India. While it's not quite as awful as Raxaul/Birgunj (see p.285), there's no need to linger.

ARRIVAL AND DEPARTURE   SONAULI (BELAHIYA)

Transport connections All the main transport connections are in Bhairahawa, 5km north (see p.260). Rikshaws charge around Rs80 for the ten-minute journey, or there are cheaper (around R15) local buses, microbuses and jeeps, which depart almost continuously.

TO INDIA

Border hours The border at Sonauli is open daily 6am–10pm. Figure on a total of thirty minutes to get through Nepali and Indian border formalities unless you're crossing with a vehicle; appalling traffic jams on the Nepali side mean this can take hours. Nepal is fifteen minutes ahead of India.

Visas Nepali visas are available at the border, but Indian visas have to be obtained in advance (see p.96).

Onward transport in India Leaving Nepal is simple enough: get off whatever transport brought you here from Bhairahawa, and walk across the border. South of Indian

immigration, an easy 200m walk from the Nepali side, buses depart almost hourly to Gorakhpur (3hr) between about 5am and 11am. From Gorakhpur you can make broad-gauge train connections throughout India; it also has an airport. There's generally a daily tourist bus to Varanasi (10–12hr), as well as fairly regular public buses. Buses also run to Lucknow (12hr).

Onward transport in Nepal If you're entering Nepal, make straight for Bhairahawa (see p.260), the starting point for all buses to elsewhere in the country; local buses, microbuses and jeeps make the ten-minute journey almost continuously (around R15); a rikshaw costs about Rs80. Note that there are no a/c tourist buses to Kathmandu, whatever agents in Gorakhpur may say. A smart alternative is to continue on past Bhairahawa to nearby Lumbini. If you're coming from Varanasi, set off as early as possible if you want to carry on into Nepal the same day.

INFORMATION

Tourist office Though all the main tourist facilities are in Bhairahawa, Sonauli has a small tourist office, right on the Nepali side of the border (Sun–Fri 10am–5pm).

Banks and money Indian currency is readily accepted in Sonauli, and sometimes in Bhairahawa, but not beyond.

There are several government-approved moneychangers at the border, all keeping long hours, and numerous banks in Bhairahawa. If changing Nepali into Indian rupees, make sure the moneychanger doesn't off-load torn notes on you as these are hard to pass in India.

Lumbini

After I am no more, Ananda, men of belief will visit with faithful curiosity and devotion to the four places – where I was born … attained enlightenment … gave the first sermons … and passed into Nirvana.

The Buddha (c.543–463 BC)

For the world's one billion Buddhists, **LUMBINI**, 22km west of Bhairahawa, is where it all began. The **Buddha's birthplace** is arguably the single most important historical site in Nepal – not only the source of one of the world's great religions but also the centre of the country's most significant **archeological finds**, dating from the third century BC. With only modest ruins but powerful associations, it's the kind of place you could whizz round in two hours or rest in for days, soaking up the peaceful atmosphere of the wooded park and its monasteries, founded by countries from all over the Buddhist world.

Non-Buddhists might find the area a little contrived and slightly soulless – perhaps because the Buddha has long been a prophet without much honour in his own country, and the area around Lumbini is now predominantly Muslim. The main local **festival** is a Hindu one, commemorating the Buddha as the ninth incarnation of Vishnu – it's held on the full moon of the Nepali month of Baisaakh (April–May). Celebrations of **Buddha Jayanti** (the Buddha's birthday) are comparatively meagre because, as the local monks will tell you with visible disgust, Buddhists from the high country think Lumbini is too hot in May.

5

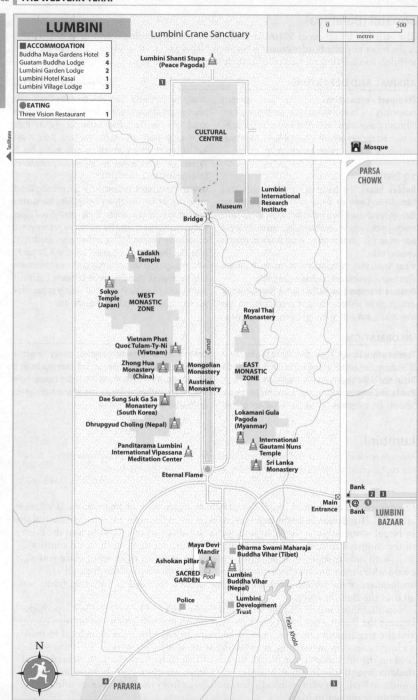

LUMBINI

ACCOMMODATION
Buddha Maya Gardens Hotel	5
Guatam Buddha Lodge	4
Lumbini Garden Lodge	2
Lumbini Hotel Kasai	1
Lumbini Village Lodge	3

EATING
Three Vision Restaurant	1

0   500
metres

Lumbini Crane Sanctuary

Lumbini Shanti Stupa
(Peace Pagoda)

Tautlihawa

Bhairawa

Mosque

PARSA
CHOWK

CULTURAL
CENTRE

Lumbini
International
Research
Institute

Museum

Bridge

Ladakh
Temple

Sokyo
Temple
(Japan)

WEST
MONASTIC
ZONE

Royal Thai
Monastery

Canal

Vietnam Phat
Quoc Tulam-Ty-Ni
(Vietnam)

Zhong Hua
Monastery
(China)

Mongolian
Monastery

Austrian
Monastery

EAST
MONASTIC
ZONE

Dae Sung Suk Ga Sa
Monastery
(South Korea)

Dhrupgyud Choling (Nepal)

Lokamani Gula
Pagoda
(Myanmar)

Panditarama Lumbini
International Vipassana
Meditation Center

Eternal Flame

International
Gautami Nuns
Temple

Sri Lanka
Monastery

Bank

Main
Entrance

@

Bank

LUMBINI
BAZAAR

Maya Devi
Mandir

Ashokan pillar

SACRED
GARDEN

Pool

Dharma Swami Maharaja
Buddha Vihar (Tibet)

Lumbini
Buddha Vihar
(Nepal)

Police

Lumbini
Development
Trust

Telar Kholo

N

PARARIA

Indian Border

THE LIFE OF THE BUDDHA

The year of the Buddha's **birth** is disputed – it was probably 543 BC – but it's generally accepted that it happened at **Lumbini** while his mother, Maya Devi, was on her way to her maternal home for the delivery. He was born Siddhartha Gautama ("he who has accomplished his aim"), the son of a king and a member of the Shakya clan, who ruled the central Terai from their capital at Tilaurakot (see p.268). Brought up in his father's palace, Prince Siddhartha was sheltered by his father from the evils of the world, until, at the age of 29, he encountered an old man, a sick man, a corpse and a hermit: old age, sickness and death were the end of life, he realized, and contemplation seemed the only way to understand the nature of suffering.

Siddhartha revolted against his former life of pleasure and fled the palace, leaving behind his wife, child and faithful servant – not to mention his horse, which another legend says promptly died of a broken heart. Passing through the east gate of the palace, he shaved his head and donned the yellow robe of an ascetic. He spent five years in this role before concluding that self-denial brought him no closer to the truth than self-indulgence. Under the famous *bodhi* tree of Bodhgaya in India, he vowed to keep meditating until he attained **enlightenment**. This he did after 49 days, at which time Siddhartha became the Buddha, released from the cycle of birth and death. He made his way to Sarnath (near Varanasi in India) and preached his **first sermon**, setting in motion, Buddhists believe, *dharma*, the wheel of the truth. Although he is said to have returned to Kapilvastu to convert his family (and according to some stories he even put in an appearance in the Kathmandu Valley), the Buddha spent most of the rest of his life preaching in northern India. He **died** at the age of eighty in Kushinagar, about 100km southeast of Lumbini, saying "all things are subject to decay. Strive earnestly".

Pilgrims used to stick to the more developed Indian sites of Bodhgaya, Sarnath and Kushinagar, but in the 1970s the government, with the backing of the UN, authorized a hugely ambitious **master plan** for a **religious park** consisting of monasteries, cultural facilities, gardens, fountains and a tourist village. After a glacially slow start, the plan is finally taking shape under the direction of (or perhaps in spite of) the Lumbini Development Trust (ⓦlumbinitrust.org); at the time of research 18 monasteries and meditation centres had been built (out of a target of 42), with a further 12 in the pipeline. Of course, there's ample cause for scepticism, not least when it comes to the nakedly commercial aspirations of the Nepali government (although the local people are still mired in poverty), but if the remaining plans come off, Lumbini could grow to be quite a cosmopolitan religious site. Japanese tour groups have already added it to their whirlwind tours of Buddhist holy places.

Roads enter the master-plan area from several directions, with the **main entrance gate** at the southeastern edge. A road leads from there to the **Sacred Garden**, which contains all the archeological treasures associated with the Buddha's birth. North of the Sacred Garden, two "**monastic zones**" are filled by an international array of temples, overlooked by the grand Shanti Stupa, or Peace Pagoda. Alongside, a miniature wetland reserve has been established for the endangered sarus crane, and 600,000 trees have been planted throughout the site, attracting many birds and animals.

The Sacred Garden

The **Sacred Garden**, where the Buddha was reputedly born, was by all accounts a well-tended grove in his day. Consecrated soon after his death, at least one monastery was attached to it by the third century BC when Ashoka, the great North Indian emperor and Buddhist evangelist, made a well-documented pilgrimage to the spot. Ashoka's patronage established a thriving religious community, but by the time the intrepid Chinese traveller Hiuen Tsang visited in the seventh century it was limping, and must have died out after the tenth century.

5

Brief history

The garden was lost for at least six hundred years, and its **rediscovery**, in 1896, solved one of the last great mysteries of the Orient. Europeans had been searching in earnest for the site since 1830, but it wasn't until 1893, when a Nepali officer on a hunting expedition claimed to have found a related Ashokan relic some miles to the west, that the first solid clue came to light. The race was on. Each of two main rivals – **A.A. Führer** of the Archeological Survey of India, and Austin Waddell, a British military doctor serving in Calcutta – pursued various trails based on their interpretations of the writings of Hiuen Tsang and other early pilgrims to Lumbini. In the end, the site was found more by chance than by science. In 1896, Führer's Nepali escort, **General Khadga Shamsher Jung Bahadur Rana**, suggested they rendezvous in Pararia before proceeding to the intended dig site. While awaiting Führer's arrival, the general was led by locals to an ancient pillar near the village and had his peons begin excavating it. The pillar was already known to at least one British official in the area, who had investigated its visible inscriptions and dismissed them as "medieval scribblings", but no one had ever bothered to dig below the surface. When Führer saw the much older inscription revealed by General Rana's excavations, he immediately recognized the pillar as the one described by the early travellers, and claimed credit for the find in his reports. Although he was later stripped of his credentials for his falsifications, he continues to be known as the discoverer of Lumbini.

The Maya Devi Mandir

Daily 7am–7pm, though times change regularly • Rs200 • No photos

Centrepiece of the Sacred Garden, the **Maya Devi Mandir** contains brickwork dating back to 300 BC, making it the oldest known structure in Nepal. A restoration project was completed in 2003, surrounding the original bricks by a simple building, which you can walk around if you remove your shoes.

Excavations in the course of the restoration confirmed earlier speculation that the known Gupta-period temple (fourth to sixth centuries AD) sat atop foundations from the earlier Kushana and Maurya periods. In fact, the lowest foundation seems to indicate a **pre-stupa structure** of a kind that existed at the time of the Buddha, suggesting that the site was venerated well before Ashoka's visit and adding further weight to Lumbini's claim as the Buddha's birthplace. Near the lowest level, archeologists also found a reddish-brown, 70cm-long stone that some believe is the "**marker stone**" Ashoka is reputed to have placed at the precise location of the Buddha's birth. In a sign of the times, it is now covered by a bullet-proof glass case.

The excavation and restoration of the Maya Devi Mandir has been something of a botched chapter in the annals of archeology. Launched in 1990, the project was originally conceived as a simple "renovation", which was supposed to mean trimming back a large **pipal tree** whose roots had been interfering with the temple for many years. But with little public consultation, the Japan Buddhist Federation, the organization leading the effort, unilaterally launched a full-scale excavation and cut down the tree, which had been regarded by many as a living link with the Buddha's day.

The temple derives its name from Maya Devi, the Buddha's mother. It houses a famous bas-relief **sculpture** (the so-called nativity scene) depicting her and the newborn Buddha in the Mathura style (from the fourth or fifth century AD). The sculpture's features are so worn, due to the flaky quality of the sedimentary stone used to make it, that archeologists at first dismissed it as Hindu because locals were worshipping the image as the wish-fulfilling goddess Rumindei (believed to be a corruption of "Lumbini Devi").

The Ashokan pillar

West of the temple is the **Ashokan pillar**, the oldest monument in Nepal. While not much to look at – it resembles a smokestack – its inscription, recording Ashoka's visit in 249 BC, is the best available evidence that the Buddha was born here. Split by

5

lightning sometime before the seventh century, its two halves are held together by metal bands. Pillars were a sort of trademark of Ashoka, serving the dual purpose of spreading the faith and marking the boundaries of his empire: this one announces that the king granted Lumbini tax-free status in honour of the Buddha's birth. The carved capital to this pillar, which early pilgrims describe as being in the shape of a horse, has never been found; the weathered stone lying on the ground beside the pillar is the lotus- or bell-shaped "bracket" upon which it would have rested.

The pool and around

The square, cement-lined **pool** just south of the Ashokan pillar is supposed to be where Maya Devi bathed before giving birth to the Buddha. Heavily restored **brick foundations** of buildings and stupas around the site, dating from the second century BC to the tenth century AD, chart the rise and fall of Lumbini's early monastic community. The two mounds north and south of the garden aren't ancient, but rather archeological debris removed during amateur excavations in the 1930s led by Field Marshal Kesar Shamsher Rana.

The Monastic Zones

A walk northwards from the Sacred Garden soon hits the highlights of the slowly unfurling master plan. An elevated path passes through what's supposed to be a reflecting pool encircling the Sacred Garden, and beyond burns an **eternal flame**, a symbolic remembrance of the "Light of Asia".

From here you can follow the kilometre-long central canal past the East (Theravada) and West (Mahayana) **Monastic Zones**, where 42 plots have been set aside for temples and monasteries representing each of Buddhism's major sects and national styles of worship. Many have already been built, and some are quite impressive – highlights include the Burmese (Myanmar) **Lokamani Gula Pagoda**, done in the style of Rangoon's famous Shwedagon temple, the Chinese **Zhong Hua Monastery**, a sort of mini Forbidden City featuring a big Buddha statue, and the eye-catching white **Royal Thai Monastery**. There seems to be more than a little religious one-upmanship going on here, however, and some say it's turned the area into a Buddhist Disneyland crossed with a construction site. However, it's still interesting to see so many different manifestations of Buddhism assembled in one place.

Several of the monasteries offer meditation sessions, courses and retreats, including – for serious students – the **Panditarama Lumbini International Vipassana Meditation Centre** (☎071 580 118, ⓦpanditarama-lumbini.info).

Lumbini International Research Institute and museum

Daily except Tues 10am–5pm • Rs50

The central canal ends at what is billed as Lumbini's **Cultural Centre**, which at the time of writing was decidedly lacking in culture, or for that matter, any real sign of life, with the planned restaurants and shops remaining stubbornly on paper – best guess is that construction may be finished by 2017. The tubular buildings of the Japanese-built **Lumbini International Research Institute** and **museum** are at least complete; the museum houses terracotta, religious manuscripts, coins and sculptures. It's well worth hooking up with one of the Lumbini Development Trust's archeologists, who sometimes freelance as guides – try asking at the research institute.

Lumbini Shanti Stupa (Peace Pagoda)

Daily 6am–6pm • Free

North of the Cultural Centre, the white-and-gold **Lumbini Shanti Stupa** (Peace Pagoda) soars 41m over the parkland. The impressive monument was finally completed in 2001 by Nippozan Myohoji, a Japanese Buddhist organization that is also responsible for the Peace Pagoda in London's Battersea Park, as well as around seventy other stupas across the world.

Lumbini Crane Sanctuary
Near the Peace Pagoda • Open 24hr • Free

The **Lumbini Crane Sanctuary** is one of the last refuges of the beautiful sarus crane, the world's tallest flying bird, and one of its most endangered. As many as 90 of Nepal's 200 to 300 sarus cranes reside here from time to time, along with storks, egrets and other arboreal birds. The area around the Lumbini site is itself something of a bird sanctuary, thanks to its wetlands and forests, with over 210 species recorded.

ARRIVAL AND DEPARTURE   LUMBINI

By bus If you're travelling between Kathmandu and India, it's easy to stop in Lumbini along the way. Three daily buses run to and from Kathmandu (6–7.30am; 9–11hr). Local buses (every 30min; 1hr) trundle between the transport hub of Bhairahawa and Pararia, the village immediately south of the site, stopping at the main east gate and Lumbini Bazaar on their way round the park. The last bus

from Bhairahawa leaves around 6pm; from Lumbini the final one departs about 5.30pm.
By jeep A car or jeep from Bhairahawa or Sonauli costs around Rs2500 one-way or Rs4500 for a return trip with an hour or two's waiting time. Consider having your driver take you first to Tilaurakot (see p.268), dropping you in Lumbini on the way back (about Rs5000).

INFORMATION AND TOURS

Tours Most hotels and lodges can organize bike trips (around Rs1000/person for 2–3hr including bike) to nearby villages where you can see local life first-hand. Good places to visit include Tenuhawa, which has a mosque; Ekala's Shiva temple; and Madhuvani, for a glimpse of Biraha culture.
Services Nepal Credit and Commerce (NCC) Bank,

Siddhartha Development Bank and Everest Bank, are all clustered close to each other in Lumbini Bazaar, on the corner of the main road. Each has an ATM and foreign exchange facilities. Buddha Nagar has several cyber cafés offering slow access including Community Multimedia Centre, next to the banks.

ACCOMMODATION AND EATING

Staying overnight is highly recommended. Lumbini is much more enjoyable in the early morning or late afternoon, when it's cooler and more peaceful. If you only see it in the heat of the day, with tour groups and school parties trooping around and the sounds of construction emanating from the temples, you'll probably be disappointed. Lumbini's accommodation is spread thinly over a wide area. The pleasant village of **Lumbini Bazaar** (or Mahilwar), strung along a side road near the main eastern gate, offers a cluster of budget guesthouses, while a number of luxury hotels have opened around the park. To really get close to the spirit of the area, stay in one of the **monasteries**: the Nepali (Theravada), Korean and Tibetan monasteries, among others, shelter pilgrims informally for a modest donation, but sorely lack things like bedding. There are plenty of inexpensive **places to eat** dotted around the entrances to the religious park and in Lumbini Bazaar, and all the guesthouses and hotels have restaurants.

Buddha Maya Gardens Hotel Near the southeast corner of the complex ☎ 071 580 220, ⓦ ktmgh.com. Part of the Kathmandu Guest House Group stable, *Buddha Maya Gardens* has the appearance of a modern palatial villa, offering smart a/c en suites, ample tree-lined grounds, a meditation "grotto", and a good restaurant and bakery. Rates include breakfast. US$106
Guatam Buddha Lodge Just south of the bus stand in Pararia ☎ 071 580 138, ⓔ guatambuddha200899 @yahoo.com. A bit less touristy than most other options in Lumbini, this Hindu-run place has basic but clean rooms and is the only accommodation in this fairly poor, dusty village. An authentic Tharu experience, warts and all. Rs500
Lumbini Garden Lodge Lumbini Bazaar ☎ 071 580 146, ⓔ lumbinigardenlodge@gmail.com. The exposed concrete in the hall and stairway is a bit off-putting, but the rooms with shared or private (Rs200 more) bathrooms are fine, although a little barren – some overlook the fields.

The friendly owner speaks English and the family are charming. Rs300
Lumbini Hotel Kasai Near the Shanti Stupa ☎ 071 404 036, ⓦ lumbinihotelkasai.com. Japanese-owned top-end hotel with smart yet understated en suites with wooden floors and furnishings, a/c and fridges, as well as a fine restaurant that uses produce from the hotel's organic farm. US$187
★**Lumbini Village Lodge** Lumbini Bazaar ☎ 071 580 432, ⓔ lumbinivillagelodge@yahoo.com. Clean, straightforward rooms with pink interiors and private baths – though the a/c ones on the top floor (Rs1800) are overpriced. There's also a dorm, internet café and bikes for rent. The owner is well attuned to travellers' needs, speaks good English and can organize local tours. Dorms Rs280, rooms Rs650
Three Vision Restaurant Lumbini Bazaar ☎ 984 999 1108. The current traveller hangout, this restaurant has an

5

economical menu (mains Rs60–280) of veg and non-veg Nepali, Indian and Chinese dishes, as well as rough approximations of Western dishes served in a dingy interior, or better, out on the street. The *momos* (Rs80–110) are very popular. Daily around 6am–10pm.

Tilaurakot and around

The ruins of **TILAURAKOT**, 24km west of Lumbini, are believed to be the remains of ancient **Kapilvastu**, seat of the ancient Shakya kingdom and the childhood home of Prince Siddhartha Gautama. Tilaurakot gets far fewer visitors than Lumbini, yet its ruins are at least as interesting, and its history arguably even more so. Shaded by mango, *kusum* and *karma* trees, the ruins have a serenity that Lumbini has begun to lose.

The remains include a couple of stupa bases, thick fortress walls and four gates. Looking out across the ruins from the **eastern gate** could hardly be a better opportunity for a moment's meditation, as it's said to be from here that the Buddha walked out on nearly thirty years of princely life to begin his search for enlightenment. It's doubtful this is literally the ruins of the palace of King Suddhodana, the Buddha's father, for the style of bricks used isn't thought to have been developed until the third century BC, but it may well have been built on top of it; assuming the earlier structure was made of wood, no trace would remain. Indian archeologists argue that Piprahwa, just south of the border, is the true site, but excavations at Tilaurakot in 2000 uncovered potsherds and terracotta beads contemporaneous with Buddha's lifetime, helping to corroborate the Nepali claim. A new Anglo-Japanese-Nepali excavation team started work in 2014, and plans to make the site more accessible.

The museum

Opposite the start of the side road to the site • Daily except Tues 10am–5pm • Rs50

The Tilaurakot **museum** displays some of the three thousand coins found in the area (including one bearing the Shakya name), together with pottery spanning three distinct periods and a thousand years. Even older pottery discovered in caves near Jomosom, high in the Himalayas, is for some reason also exhibited here, as are many photographs of Buddhist sites in India, perhaps because the museum was paid for by the Indian government.

Archeological sites around Tilaurakot

Tilaurakot is just one of several archeological sites, dating to the time of the Buddha, that are scattered around the town of **Taulihawa**, 3km from Tilaurakot. **Niglihawa**, around 8km northeast of Taulihawa, is the location of a broken Ashokan pillar associated with one of the mythical Buddhas of a previous age. **Sagarhawa**, 4km further northwest, contains an ancient water tank identified as the site of a notorious Shakya massacre. The Ashokan pillar and brick stupa at **Gotihawa**, 5km southwest of Taulihawa, commemorate where another previous Buddha gained enlightenment, while the *pokhari* at **Kudan**, 3km southwest of Taulihawa, is said to be where the Buddha returned after his enlightenment to preach the *dharma* to his father and young son.

ARRIVAL AND DEPARTURE   **TILAURAKOT**

By bus Irregular buses (roughly hourly; 2hr) make their way from Bhairawa to Taulihawa, 22km beyond Lumbini on the same road; you can flag these down at Lumbini's Parsa Chowk, but don't expect to get a seat. From the centre of Taulihawa, rikshaws are usually available to take you the last 3km along the main northbound road to an obvious intersection where the museum is on the left and a paved road on the right leads 400m to the site.

By jeep The easiest way to get to Tilaurakot and surrounding sites is by jeep from Bhairahawa (Rs5000 or so return, with waiting time), which enables you to visit Lumbini en route. Don't get locked into a rushed half-day tour of Lumbini and Tilaurakot – negotiate plenty of waiting time, and consider staying over at Lumbini on the way back.
By bike On a bike it takes around two hours to get from Lumbini to Tilaurakot.

INFORMATION

Admission Admission to all the excavation sites is free.
Guides This is one place where getting a knowledgeable guide (you can find one from a tour operator in Lumbini) is a good idea, as still not much is labelled, and the site makes little sense without some explanation. The guards will probably be happy to give you a tour around the grounds (although their English isn't great) for a donation of up to Rs150.
Tours Tours can be organized in Lumbini for around Rs700–1000/person (around 4hr), either by bicycle or jeep.

ACCOMMODATION AND EATING

Hotel Gautam Buddha (Golden Buddha) Taulihawa, on the road to Tilaurakot ☎071 560 029. The best lodgings in town, with en-suite fan rooms that are clean and comfortable but overpriced, plus identical a/c rooms which at just Rs300 are great value. <u>Rs1200</u>

The far west

Nepal's remote **far west**, linked to the rest of the country by the Mahendra Highway, is slowly opening its doors to travellers. It's still a hell of a haul to get here from Kathmandu, but Delhi is just twelve hours by bus from the far western border crossing, and the relatively smooth, fast road between Kathmandu and Delhi passes two of Nepal's richest wildlife parks, **Bardia National Park** and **Sukla Phanta Wildlife Reserve**. The partly Muslim city of **Nepalgunj**, the largest city in the west, is the hub for flights to several remoter airstrips.

The Mahendra Highway makes good time to Nepalgunj, 250km west of Butwal, crossing the Duduwa Hills (350m ascent) and following the green and pleasant valley of the Rapti River (no relation to the river of the same name in Chitwan). North of here lies **Dang**, home of the white-clad Dangaura Tharus, and fine cycling country.

Nepalgunj

The industrial and transport hub of the far west, **NEPALGUNJ** is also Nepal's most Muslim city. The presence of Muslims in the Terai is hardly surprising, since the border with India, where Muslims comprise a significant minority, was only determined in the nineteenth century. Until just prior to the 1814–16 war with the British, this area belonged to the Nawab of Oudh, one of India's biggest landowners; after Nepal's defeat it was ceded to the East India Company and only returned to Nepal as a goodwill gesture for services rendered during the Indian Mutiny of 1857. A fair few Muslims fled to Nepalgunj during the revolt – Lucknow, where the most violent incidents occurred, is due south of here – and others filtered in during the Rana years, seeing chances for cross-border trade. The resulting permanent Muslim community is self-contained, but maintains business and family links with India. Indeed, the entire city feels Indian.

In the heart of the sprawl is **Tribhuwan Chowk**, the lively but dilapidated intersection of the city's two main shopping thoroughfares, south of which the Indian-style Janaki Mandir sits in the middle of the road like a toll booth. The **Muslim quarter** lies northeast of Tribhuwan Chowk and is worth a wander. The mosques in this area are disappointingly modern, though, and out-of-bounds to nonbelievers. Hindu worship and trade centres around the nondescript **Bageshwari Mandir**; behind the temple is a large pool with a jaunty, kitsch statue of Mahadev (Shiva) in the middle.

ARRIVAL AND INFORMATION   NEPALGUNJ

By plane Nepalgunj's airport is 6km north of town, a Rs500 taxi ride away.
Destinations Bajura (2 weekly); Jufal/Dopla (4 weekly); Jumla (1 weekly); Kathmandu (4–5 daily); Rukum (1–3 weekly); Simikot (April–Aug 4 weekly; Sept–March 1 daily); Talcha (2 weekly).
By bus The bus park is inconveniently situated at the extreme northeast end of Nepalgunj, a 20min walk (or

5

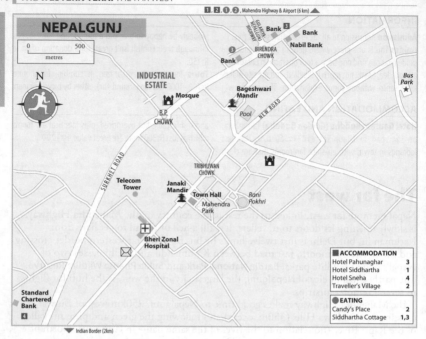

NEPALGUNJ

0 — 500
metres

N

INDUSTRIAL ESTATE

Mosque

B.P. CHOWK

1, 2, 1, 2, Mahendra Highway & Airport (6 km)

GUJAL PATH NEPALGANJ HIGHWAY

Bank 3   Bank

BIRENDRA CHOWK   Nabil Bank

3

Bank

Bageshwari Mandir

Pool

NEW ROAD

Bus Park ★

SURKHET ROAD

TRIBHUWAN CHOWK

Telecom Tower   Janaki Mandir   Town Hall   Rani Pokhri

Mahendra Park

Bheri Zonal Hospital

Standard Chartered Bank

4

▼ Indian Border (2km)

◼ ACCOMMODATION	
Hotel Pahunaghar	3
Hotel Siddhartha	1
Hotel Sneha	4
Traveller's Village	2

● EATING	
Candy's Place	2
Siddhartha Cottage	1,3

Rs50 by rikshaw) from the centre. Westbound bus services are frequent, and depart from the main road north of the bus park. Fewer, but still regular, buses head east, mostly travelling at night because of the distances involved. Several day buses and innumerable night ones run to Kathmandu (most leave 5.30–6pm), though it is better to break the journey up along the way. Two local buses leave at around 11.45am and 3.30pm for Thakurdwara/Bardia National Park.

Destinations Butwal (hourly; 7–8hr); Dhangadhi (hourly; 6hr); Kathmandu (frequent; around 13hr); Mahendra Nagar (hourly; 5–7hr); Pokhara (2–4 daily; 13–14hr); Thakurdwara (for Bardia National Park; 2 daily; 4hr).

By car A car or jeep to Bardia (2hr 30min) costs around

Rs4000–5000. Try one of the travel agents strung along the main road, and negotiate hard.

TO INDIA

The border crossing of Jamunaha, 6km south of Birendra Chowk, is open to tourists and you can get there by rikshaw (around Rs120–150).

Border hours The border is open daily 6am–10pm. There's little there besides immigration and customs offices. Nepal is fifteen minutes ahead of India.

Visas Nepali visas are available at the border, but Indian visas have to be obtained in advance (see p.96).

Onward transport Buses connect Rupaidia, the town on the Indian side of the border, with Lucknow (7hr).

ACCOMMODATION

Hotel Pahunaghar Surkhet Rd, near Birendra Chowk ☎ 081 522 358, ✉ kedarnathgupta89@yahoo.com. Solid budget choice with compact marble-floored rooms with TVs, fans, showers and squat toilets. More expensive a/c rooms with Western toilets (Rs1350) are also available in the garden building behind. Those at the back of the building are partially shielded from the road noise, though the generator is also in the garden. **Rs385**

Hotel Siddhartha Around 2.5km northeast of town towards the airport on Ratna Rajmarg ☎ 081 551 200, ⓦ siddharthabiz.com. This smart business-traveller-oriented hotel has good (though not luxurious) en suites

with TVs, phones and a/c, plus a swimming pool, a fine restaurant (see p.271) and a bar. **Rs1850**

Hotel Sneha South of the centre ☎ 081 520 119, ✉ hotel@sneha.wlink.com.np. This long-standing hotel, popular with NGO staff, is set back from the main road, behind well-tended gardens. The a/c en-suite rooms, housed in a whitewashed building, are comfortable, but could do with sprucing up. There's also a mini casino, and a pool. **US$56**

Traveller's Village Around 3km northeast of town towards the airport, just east off Ratna Rajmarg ☎ 081 550 329, ✉ travil@wlink.com.np. Near the UNICEF compound, *Traveller's Village* has a vaguely Mediterranean feel, with shady gardens, climbing plants, decorative portraits of Nepal's varied ethnic groups, and decent en suite a/c rooms. There's also an excellent Western restaurant (see below). US$44

EATING AND DRINKING

Nepalgunj's busiest eating areas, around Birendra Chowk and Tribhuwan Chowk, hold scores of *dhabas* and a few sweet shops. In the evenings, vendors in the **bazaar** dish up curd and *raabri*, a local speciality made from sweetened cream flavoured with cardamom and saffron. Several **restaurants** between B.P. Chowk and Birendra Chowk have almost identical menus – a mix of Chinese, Indian and (vaguely) Italian dishes.

★**Candy's Place** In Traveller's Village hotel, 4km northeast of town towards the airport ☎ 081 550 329, ✉ travil@wlink.com.np. Owned by Candy, a chatty American, this restaurant is the place to head to if you're feeling homesick; it does really good American food. The menu features delicious pancakes with maple syrup (Rs220–270), hygienic salads, steaks (Rs460–615), burgers (Rs310–615) and lemon meringue pie (Rs200; not available during monsoon). Generally daily 6.30am–9.30pm.

Siddhartha Cottage Behind the main street between B.P. Chowk and Birendra Chowk, plus a second branch at Hotel Siddhartha. "Sid's Place", as it's known to local expats, serves up mid-priced North Indian food (mains Rs220–400) and popular Nepalese set meals (Rs250–600), which you can enjoy in the pleasant garden at the back. The branch at *Hotel Siddhartha* is a bit smarter. Generally daily 8am–10pm.

Bardia National Park

With Chitwan becoming increasingly mass-market, **BARDIA NATIONAL PARK**, northwest of Nepalgunj and the largest area of undisturbed wilderness left in the Terai, beckons as an unspoiled alternative. Budget lodging is widely available, but there's nothing like Chitwan's commercialism, and the distance from Kathmandu is likely to shield the park from the masses for many years to come. The area was particularly badly affected during the civil war, and Bardia district had the highest rate of "**disappearances**" in the whole country.

Ecologically, Bardia spans a greater range of habitats than Chitwan, from thick riverine forest and *sal* stands to *phanta* (isolated pockets of savannah) and dry upland slopes. The **Geruwa**, a branch of the awesome **Karnali River**, forms the park's western boundary and major watering hole, and the density of wildlife and birds along this western edge is as great as anywhere in Asia. The **Babai River** drains the core area to the east of **Thakurdwara**, forming a sanctuary-like *dun* valley teeming with game, but it is out of bounds to visitors.

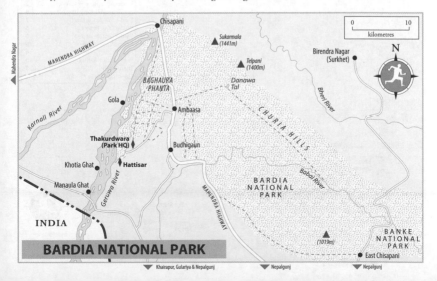

BARDIA NATIONAL PARK

5

Bordering Bardia to the west is **Banke National Park**, which was created in 2010 and stretches over 550 square kilometres. Together the two parks now form the biggest **tiger** conservation area in Asia, and have the highest density of tigers in the world. Tourism has not yet developed at Banke, but may well do so in the future.

The **Elephant Polo Championships**, formerly held in Meghauli (see p.249), are currently held in November each year at the *Tiger Tops Karnali Lodge* (⊕elephantpolo .com); read the box on p.252 about the ethics of elephant-based tourism before deciding whether or not to attend.

Thukurdwara and around

A sleepy collection of Tharu farming settlements, **THAKURDWARA** is archetypal Terai. The main centre is a kind of village green where local buses stop, encircled by a small bazaar known locally as the "mandir" because of its temple. Most visitors never stray this far from the **park headquarters**, however, which lie about 1km west of the bazaar. There are few facilities for either locals or tourists; most guesthouses have electricity, but few village homes are similarly equipped.

The small **mandir** near the bus stop is the focus of a modest *mela* (religious fair) held on the first day of the month of Magh (mid-Jan). A few other park-related points of interest are scattered in and around the leafy headquarters compound, but most of the action is inside the park. In short, it's a lot like Sauraha was in the good old days: quiet, remote and adventurous. Tourism will inevitably change Thakurdwara, but conservationists are already taking steps to ensure it doesn't repeat Sauraha's mistakes, and the National Trust for Nature Conservation is working to ensure that local people benefit from the park.

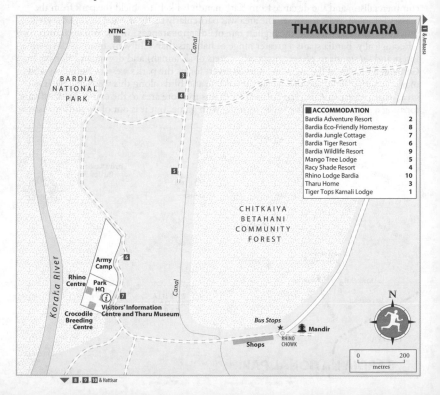

THAKURDWARA

NTNC

Canal

BARDIA
NATIONAL
PARK

Korata River

ACCOMMODATION
Bardia Adventure Resort	2
Bardia Eco-Friendly Homestay	8
Bardia Jungle Cottage	7
Bardia Tiger Resort	6
Bardia Wildlife Resort	9
Mango Tree Lodge	5
Racy Shade Resort	4
Rhino Lodge Bardia	10
Tharu Home	3
Tiger Tops Karnali Lodge	1

CHITKAIYA
BETAHANI
COMMUNITY
FOREST

Army
Camp

Rhino   Park
Centre   HQ

Crocodile   Visitors' Information
Breeding   Centre and Tharu Museum
Centre

Canal

Bus Stops

RHINO   Mandir
CHOWK

Shops

N

0   200
metres

▲ 1 & Ambassa

▼ 8 , 9 , 10 & Hattisar

The park headquarters

1km west of the bazaar • **Visitors' Information Centre** Daily 7am–sunset • **Tharu Museum** Daily 10am–4pm • **Crocodile Breeding Centre** Daily 10am–4pm • **Rhino Centre** Daily sunrise–sunset • Joint ticket including the hattisar (see below) Rs125

While you're at the **park headquarters**, stop by the **Visitors' Information Centre**, with its interesting displays on the park's flora and fauna, and the **Tharu Museum**, which provides a basic introduction to local culture. Also here is the **Crocodile Breeding Centre**, where gharials, mugger crocodiles and black turtles are raised from eggs before being released into local waters, and the **Rhino Centre**, home to Vikram, a (fairly) tame, almost blind rhino who was orphaned as a calf; he used to roam freely around the complex until (accidentally) knocking over and killing an elderly local man.

The hattisar

3km south of the park headquarters • Visit in late afternoon; at other times the elephants are likely to be working in the park or being trained • Rs50

To watch Bardia's hardest-working employees enjoying some downtime, visit the **hattisar** (elephant stables), outside the park, a forty-minute walk from the park headquarters. There are often baby elephants here, and sometimes you are allowed to feed them.

Manaula Ghat and Khotia Ghat

From the hattisar, the road continues southwards along the river and through dusty villages, remaining outside the park and ending up after a few kilometres at **Khotia Ghat**; **Manaula Ghat** is a few kilometres further on. Khotia Ghat is a good place to look for dolphins, and is also the location for the annual **elephant football competition**, which takes place during the Dasain festival (Sept/Oct); read the box on p.252 about the ethics of elephant-based tourism before deciding whether or not to attend. The football has replaced a game from before the Maoist uprising called *hattile sungur*

BARDIA'S WILDLIFE

Bardia was once hailed as a conservation success story: **rhinos**, hunted to extinction here in the early twentieth century, were reintroduced in the mid-1980s and numbered about fifty at the turn of the century. However, with a reduced army presence in the park during the civil war, poaching became a serious problem again (and a number of ex-army personnel were implicated). Security is now much tighter, and there are thought to be somewhere between 26 and 30 rhinos in the park. The **tiger** population was also badly affected by poaching; numbers are believed to have dwindled to 50–55. Although you still need some luck to spot a tiger – it's said that a tiger is a hundred times more likely to see you than you are to see it – sightings are still more common here than at Chitwan due to Bardia's smaller area. Because of its remoteness, and minimal human disturbance, tiger experts regard Bardia as the most promising place in Nepal in which to maintain a viable breeding population. For the same reasons, the park has also become an important sanctuary for over a hundred migratory **wild elephants**.

The Geruwa River is one of the few places anywhere where you may be able to get a peep at rare **gangetic dolphins** (see p.292); seven to nine still survive in the river's deep channels. You can also fish for huge **mahseer**. By 1989, the mugger and gharial **crocodile** populations in the river were reduced to fewer than a dozen of each species, but a successful project to release juveniles raised from hatchlings means they can now be easily spotted in winter. Five species of **deer** – spotted, sambar, hog, barking and swamp – are abundant, along with **langurs** and **wild pig**. Nilgai ("blue bull"), bovine-looking members of the antelope family, roam the drier upland areas, while more than two hundred graceful, corkscrew-horned **blackbuck** survive in an unprotected grassland area south of the park. More elusive are sloth bear, leopard and other nocturnal creatures, as well as the endangered hispid hare. The park is also home to over 472 bird species, three of which – the Bengal florican, the lesser florican and the sarus crane – are endangered. The commonest sight of all around Bardia are sandy-coloured **termite mounds**, which reach their greatest height – up to 2.5m – in the *sal* forest here.

5

kuchna, which roughly translates as "elephant stamping on piglet game". This was played with much gusto for about twenty years, and was as complicated – and gruesome – as it sounds.

Activities in the park

Bardia's menu of **activities** is similar to Chitwan's, and you'll find lengthier descriptions in that section (see p.249). Although you are less in danger from rhinos here than in Chitwan, it would nonetheless be foolhardy (not to mention illegal) to enter the park without a **guide** (see p.256).

Walking safaris

A day's walk with a guide (see p.256) costs Rs1000–1500/person, excluding park entry fee. Two-day/three-night trekking, camping, rafting and jeep ride trips cost at least Rd6000/person per day, excluding guide fee. A night in a machan costs Rs500/person, excluding guide fee

Most walks inside the park take a northerly bearing from Thakurdwara, roughly paralleling the Geruwa River through mixed grassland and jungle. Some of the best rhino habitat, as well as areas favoured by wild elephants, is found in the riverine corridor between Thakurdwara and **Gola**. Tigers, bears, boars, nilgai and dolphins may be sighted, and you're assured of seeing deer, monkeys and all manner of birds. The track to **Baghaura Phanta**, 7km northeast of Thakurdwara, is a prime birdwatching route.

Camping is only allowed at three spots inside the park, which limits the scope for longer hikes. However, guides have developed several routes that incorporate trekking, camping, rafting and jeep rides, which are typically two days and three nights. Another possibility for a nocturnal experience is to arrange with a guide to sleep out in a **machan** (tower) in Chitka Community Forest; don't forget to bring a mosquito net.

Elephant rides

Rs2500/person per hour, excluding park entry fee; reserve rides 1 day in advance, or even more during peak periods

You can arrange **elephant rides** yourself at the HQ ticket office, or have your guesthouse do it for you. Of the lodges, only *Tiger Tops* has its own elephants, but they are limited to the community forest. Departures are in the early morning and late afternoon from a platform at the far end of the HQ compound. Read the box on p.252 about the ethics of elephant rides before deciding whether or not to arrange one.

Jeep trips

Trips generally run 7–11am & 2–6pm • Rs3000–3500/person per half-day, including park entry, driver and guide fees; a full day costs around Rs8000

While a **jeep** allows you to penetrate the more remote parts of the park where the animals aren't as wary of humans, the vehicles are also likely to disturb much of the wildlife you've come to see. Most trips are confined to the network of tracks in the park's western sector, which take you through *sal* forest and the grasslands of **Baghaura Phanta** and give access to pristine stretches of river and rich wildlife habitat. Given more time you could continue north to Chisapani to look for gharials and dolphins. From Ambaasa, you can follow a track eastwards to **Danawa Tal**, a wetland at the base of the foothills where rhinos and elephants are sometimes spotted.

Nepal's only herd of blackbuck antelope congregates around a big *phanta* well south of the park at **Khairapur**, 32km from Thakurdwara by road and most easily reached by vehicle. From Thakurdwara, drive north to Ambaasa, then 3km south along the Mahendra Highway to Budhigaun, and then take the road south from there – look for the herd on your left as you approach Gulariya. Blackbucks were thought to be extinct until three were sighted here in 1973; now the herd is estimated at more than two hundred. Most lodges can organize trips here.

Raft trips

Around Rs4000–5000/person per day, including park entry, transport and guide fees

Once on the River Geruwa, you've got just as good a chance of seeing dolphins, muggers, monkeys and birds as you would on foot, and you may even be lucky enough to glimpse an elephant or tiger. A couple of lodges have **rafts**, and others will book you on one if places are available.

Fishing

Fishing permits cost Rs1000/day and you must also pay a Rs1000 conservation fee – both can be obtained from the ticket office at Park HQ

Many lodges can provide fishing gear, but if you're at all interested in angling you'll want to bring your own – and strong tackle. The Karnali/Geruwa is renowned for its **mahseer**, a sporting fish related to carp and weighing up to 40kg. If you catch one, release it: the *mahseer* population is declining due to pollution, dams, barriers and a general lack of headwaters protection. The Babai is superb for *mahseer* and *goonch*, another huge fish. Be alert for crocodiles. Fishing is allowed everywhere on the Karnali and Geruwa rivers (you can fish as part of a raft trip); on the Babai, it's restricted to the waters below the dam (the Mahendra Highway crossing).

Bike rides

Some guesthouses in Thakurdwara rent bicycles for Rs200 per day

Renting a **bicycle** opens up a host of possibilities for exploring the surrounding countryside. Two dirt roads head south from Thakurdwara and take you through numerous traditional Tharu villages. The one past the *hattisar* and on along the riverbank to Khotia Ghat (see p.273) gets far more tourist traffic. Cycling north along the road to Ambaasa is also a possibility; given more time and a packed lunch, you could conceivably cycle to Chisapani or other spots normally only reached by jeep. Neither of these routes is advisable alone, due to the presence of wild animals.

Tharu village tours

Tours cost around Rs1000–1500 (free for guests at some lodges)

It might be worth joining a guided **tour** to learn more about local Tharu culture, if you can get past the human-zoo aspect of it. Lodges can also organize **Tharu cultural performances** (including the special Bardia *chokara* dance), which are sometimes included in the package price.

ARRIVAL AND DEPARTURE   BARDIA NATIONAL PARK

By plane From Kathmandu, the quickest way to get to Bardia is to fly to Nepalgunj (see p.269) and travel on by bus or car.

By bus From Kathmandu and Pokhara, night buses to Dhangadhi or Mahendra Nagar pass by Ambaasa, the tea-shack turning for Thakurdwara, between around 4am and 6am; both take around 14hr. There's also generally a daily night bus direct from Kathmandu to Thakurdwara (15hr) during the dry season. It is advisable, however, to break up the journey from Pokhara or Kathmandu with an overnight stay. Regular buses between Nepalgunj and Mahendra Nagar/Dhangadhi pass by Ambaasa. There are also two direct local services from Nepalgunj to Thakurdwara (11.45am & 3.30pm; 4hr). Heading away from Bardia, buses to Kathmandu pass by Ambaasa at around 7am and 2pm; services to Pokhara travel past at roughly 3am and 5am. If you're heading west just flag down any bus going

past Ambaasa in that direction. There is a direct dry season bus to Kathmandu (4pm) from Thakurdwara, and two local services to Nepalgunj (7am & 9am). Lodges can help you buy tickets.

Destinations from Thakurdwara Kathmandu (1 daily in dry season; 15hr) Nepalgunj (2 daily; 4hr).

Destinations from Ambaasa Kathmandu (2 daily; 14hr); Mahendra Nagar (9–10 daily; 2hr); Nepalgunj (9–10 daily; 2hr); Pokhara (2 daily; 14hr).

By jeep Guesthouse jeeps wait at Ambaasa to ferry tourists the final 13km to Thakurdwara. This should be free if you stay at their lodge for a night (or have booked ahead); otherwise it's a steep Rs800. A car or jeep to or from Nepalgunj costs around Rs7000 (2hr 30min–3hr).

By raft You can also raft down the Karnali River (see p.364) to Bardia.

5

INFORMATION

Entry and permits All access to the park is via the main headquarters entrance in Thakurdwara. Entry permits cost Rs1000/day; buy them from the ticket office inside the headquarters compound, or have your guesthouse do it for you.

Guides Legally, you must be accompanied by a guide on any trip into the park. Although Bardia guides tend to speak less English and have less training than their Chitwan counterparts, they know the territory and can keep you out of harm's way. Guides can be hired through your lodge and

charge Rs1000–1500/person for a full day, excluding park entry fee. Alternatively, hire one at the park headquarters via the United Guide Office at the main entrance (☎974 110 8988, ✉ unitedguideoffice@yahoo.com; Rs2500–4000 for a full day for up to 5 people, excluding park fees).

Services Many guesthouses can change money informally, but there are no ATMs and the closest is 42km away, west on the highway at Lamki. There's a local health post and pharmacy near the bus stop; the nearest decent hospital is 72km away in Kohalpur, near Nepalgunj.

ACCOMMODATION AND EATING

Most of Bardia's lodgings are within walking distance of the park headquarters at **Thakurdwara**. The lodges here are all very similar, and all are acceptable. The formula (pioneered in, and steadily disappearing from, Sauraha) is simple: mud-and-thatch huts arranged around a garden, with a simple dining pavilion serving *daal bhaat* and approximations of Western dishes. A few places have more hotel-like concrete bungalows, and most have hot (or at least warm) water. All can arrange access to jeeps, fishing rods, guides, elephants and the like. Many lodges offer **packages**, but as in Chitwan, these provide little benefit for their added cost (see p.243). There are no **restaurants** in Thakurdwara, just a couple of snack stalls in the bazaar. Most people eat at their own lodge, or drop in at a neighbouring place if it's looking lively (that said, the lodges do advise guests not to walk around after dark without a guide because elephants and rhinos sometimes escape from the park).

Bardia Adventure Resort Near the NTNC complex ☎084 402 023, ✉ bar_bardia@wlink.com.np. A mix of rustic mud-and-thatch cottages and more modern bungalows with a green colour scheme; both types have private bathrooms, though not all have mosquito nets. There's also a lookout tower that's good for wildlife-spotting. **Rs500**

Bardia Eco-Friendly Homestay Banugau Village, 1.5km east of the hattisar ☎084 690 412, ✉ shardul .bhattarai@gmail.com. One of several homestay options around Thakurdwara, located in a very peaceful, untouristed spot among the rice paddies. Rooms are basic but homely (a couple have bathrooms, for Rs300 more), and the family speak English and are very friendly (as is the dog). *Dal bhaat* (Rs200) and rice wine is available. **Rs400**

Bardia Jungle Cottage Opposite the park HQ ☎084 402 014, ⊛ bardiajunglecottage.com.np. Thakurdwara's original budget lodge, owned by a knowledgeable former assistant park warden. Cross a humped-back bridge to find rustic cottages offering both basic and more comfortable accommodation, as well as a nice dining area propped up by exposed tree trunks. **Rs500**

Badia Tiger Resort Close to park HQ ☎084 402 002, ⊛ bardiatigerresort.com. This new mid-range lodge has a great range of neat and tidy rooms of varying levels of comfort: fan or a/c (Rs200 more) dorm beds, fan rooms and more luxurious a/c rooms (Rs3200, or opt not to use your a/c and pay Rs1800). There's a pleasant garden and they have a fund for the families of wildlife victims. Dorms **Rs400**, rooms **Rs1000**

★**Bardia Wildlife Resort** Between the park HQ and the hattisar ☎084 402 041, ⊛ bardiawildliferesort.com.

One of a few similar camps along this stretch of river, this friendly place is run by a husband-and-wife park guide team (in fact she's the only female guide in Bardia), and has the standard set-up, with en-suite Tharu mud huts, and more expensive and comfortable deluxe rooms for Rs700 more. Free village tour for guests. **Rs500**

★**Mango Tree Lodge** By the canal ☎974 802 1383, ⊛ mangotreelodge.com. Run by a pair of helpful Nepali and English naturalists, this recently renovated lodge has clean Tharu-style en-suite rooms with nice decorative touches and stylish showers, with the more expensive ones (US$36) nicer than the standard rooms at *Tiger Tops*. The larger rooms are ideal for groups or families, and some have bucolic views of the surrounding fields. Rates include breakfast. **US$24**

Racy Shade Resort By the canal ☎974 800 4002, ⊛ racyshade.com. This Franco-Nepali-owned lodge has smarter than average rooms and a lively atmosphere. The grass-thatched rooms have hat stands and wardrobes, and some even boast four-poster beds, all pleasingly done in a Tharu style. **Rs1500**

Rhino Lodge Bardia 3km south of park HQ ☎084 690 489, ⊛ rhinolodgebardia.com. In a secluded location close to the *hattisar*, *Rhino Lodge* has a tree-filled garden and a proper bar in its dining room. Its concrete cottages with a/c, modern baths and interiors display a little more flair than the budget lodges. **Rs3000**

Tharu Home By the canal ☎084 690 482, ⊛ bardiatharuhomeresort.com. This Tharu-run lodge has simple, economically priced rooms, a garden with shaded tables and a badminton court. Rates include a traditional Tharu evening meal, and there are also locally brewed spirits and beer on offer. **Rs600**

THE KARNALI BRIDGE AND DAM

The Mahendra Highway emerges from Bardia National Park to vault the mighty **Karnali River**, surging out of a gap in the rugged foothills, on what is reputed to be the longest single-tower **suspension bridge** in the world. The exotic design of this World Bank-funded structure appears to have been dictated mainly by the foreign contractors' need for a showcase project, but it's an impressive sight as you rush along the tarmac. Lookout for gharial crocodiles basking on the rocks as you pass over.

An even bigger showcase project is in the pipeline for the Karnali with the construction of a mammoth dam, the 900 MW **Upper Karnali Hydro Power Project**, upstream of the bridge. The dam, planned to be operational by 2021, is to be built by an Indian company, and (typically of the region's politics) its interconnection point to the Nepalese power grid will be located in India, thus giving the Indians complete control over the power to be generated.

Tiger Tops Karnali Lodge ☎01 436 1500, ⓦtigermountain.com. The lodge sits outside the park in a serene location, with stylish but not luxurious standard rooms, although the more expensive signature rooms are the best in town (if horribly overpriced). Rates include all activities. Per person US$307

West of the Karnali River

The "far west" of Nepal, west of the **Karnali River**, is a foreign land for most Nepalis – a remote, underdeveloped region long neglected by the Kathmandu government. In fact, Delhi is closer than the Nepali capital by bus and, until the completion of the Karnali bridge in the mid-1990s, the region was literally cut off altogether in the monsoon, the Karnali effectively forming Nepal's western border. The region makes for some great off-the-beaten-track travelling, though there's a distinct lack of facilities and communicating with local people can be difficult.

The westernmost section of the Mahendra Highway was finally completed in 2000, after a twitchy Indian government insisted on replacing the Chinese who were originally contracted to do the job. Twenty-two major bridges (many of which were subjected to Maoist attacks during the civil war) carry just 215km of asphalt, but the road now at least lives up to its alternative name of the East–West Highway, bringing new trade and industry to the region. The little-visited **Sukla Phanta Wildlife Reserve**, which lies just outside the relatively laidback border town of **Mahendra Nagar**, is an excellent destination for the adventurous traveller – foreign visitors number only in the hundreds here annually.

Mahendra Nagar

The Mahendra Highway ends at **MAHENDRA NAGAR**, a border town with a good deal of spark thanks to day-tripping shoppers from India. Its bustle is only a border aberration, however, for the outlying region is one of the more traditional parts of the Terai. Rana Tharu (see p.240) sharecroppers work the fields, maintaining an apparently happy symbiosis with their old-money landlords, and their villages, scattered along dirt tracks north of the Mahendra Highway, still consist of traditional communal longhouses. Mahendra Nagar is laid out in an unusually logical grid south of the highway. Walk south from the bus park, at the northwestern end, for 500m and you come to a roundabout: to the left (east) is Main Road, the street with the bazaar; to the right (west) is the road to the airstrip (3.5km) and Sukla Phanta Wildlife Reserve.

ARRIVAL AND INFORMATION
MAHENDRA NAGAR

By plane At the time of writing there were no scheduled flights from Mahendra Nagar airport; the closest airport, in Dhangadhi 50km away, has daily flights to Kathmandu.
By bus Three morning buses and three night buses travel to Kathmandu (16–17hr), and a couple make their way to Pokhara (around 16hr). Services also run to Nepalgunj (9–10 daily; 4hr) and Butwal (6–8 daily; 11hr).
Banks and exchange Rastriya Banijya Bank, 250m south of the bazaar on the third lane, changes Indian rupees and US dollars, but other currencies may be beyond its abilities.

5

Indian currency is readily accepted – and unofficially exchanged – everywhere in Mahendra Nagar.

TO INDIA
The border begins 6km west of Mahendra Nagar, and is reached by shared tempo (Rs20–25), rikshaw (Rs50), or bus (Rs20). A rough road traverses the 1km no-man's-land between the Nepali and Indian immigration posts.

Border hours The border is officially open daily 6am–10pm, but vehicles can only be brought through at certain times (6–7am, 1–2pm and 6–7pm). Nepal is fifteen minutes ahead of India.

Visas If you're entering Nepal, visas are available at the border; tourists are sometimes overcharged here. To avoid this, check the visa price beforehand, bring the exact money in US dollars and be firm if anyone tries to swindle you. Indian visas have to be obtained in advance (see p.96).

Onward transport From Indian immigration you can catch a rikshaw across the wide Mahakali River along the top of a huge flood-control/irrigation barrage and then a further 4km to Banbaasa, the first Indian town. Banbaasa is relatively friendly for a border town, but accommodation is poor, and since crossing the border can be fairly time-consuming, you'll want to make an early start from Mahendra Nagar to avoid being stuck there. Buses connect Banbaasa to Bareli (the nearest broad-gauge rail station; 2hr 30min), Almora (6hr), Nainital (7hr), Haridwar (9hr) and Delhi (10hr). Narrow-gauge trains from Banbaasa are slow and infrequent, so you're better off taking a bus.

ACCOMMODATION AND EATING

Several *dhabas* with inexpensive flea-pit **lodges** (under Rs500) attached are concentrated mainly along the road just east of the bus station, and serve a fair range of Nepali and Indian **food**.

Hotel Gangotri Plaza North of the bus park ☏ 099 520 397, ✉ jagdishmission2Q@gmail.com; map p.279. A convenient option if you're arriving late or leaving early, this hotel has perfectly fine en-suite fan rooms, which are much cleaner than the other budget options near the bus park. It also has a good, clean restaurant serving Nepali, Indian and Chinese food. Rs700

Hotel Opera Near the main chowk ☏ 099 522 101, ⓦ operahotelnepal.com.np; map p.279. Reassuringly well-run hotel, with good-value and comfortable rooms; all come with private bathrooms, and the more expensive also boast tubs, TVs and a/c. There's a good restaurant-bar, and staff can organize day-trips, including to Sukla Phanta. Rs1350

Sukla Phanta Wildlife Reserve

The great tracts of natural grassland (*phanta*) in Nepal's extreme southwest could almost be mistaken – albeit on a smaller scale – for the savannahs of East Africa. SUKLA PHANTA WILDLIFE RESERVE, south of Mahendra Nagar, is dotted with them, and touring the reserve is, for once, really like being on safari. Always hard to reach, Sukla Phanta was even more cut off during the civil war, and as a result attracts barely a trickle of visitors, just a few hundred a year. The **best time to visit** is after the *phanta* is burned back in mid-November; after April it's too tall to see anything.

The park is home to one of the world's largest populations of **swamp deer** – sightings of a thousand at a time are common – as well as a number of **wild elephants** and several rhinos. The **tiger** population has declined dramatically from 20–50 in 2005 to an estimated 17 in 2014 as a result of poaching, though numbers are slowly rising again thanks to local conservation efforts. Sukla Phanta remains astonishingly rich in **birds**, with over 470 species having been counted. Rare species include the Bengal florican and the giant hornbill.

Exploring the reserve

Several tracks crisscross the reserve, making itineraries flexible, but the first stop is bound to be the **Sukla Phanta** at the southwestern end, a rippling sea of grass that turns silvery-white in October (*sukila* means white in the local Tharu dialect). You're virtually guaranteed **swamp deer** here, and in quantity – make for the view tower in the middle and scan for them with binoculars. As *barasingha* ("twelve-pointer"), the swamp deer was one of Kipling's beloved *Jungle Book* animals – "that big deer which is like our red deer, but stronger" – and common throughout the plains and hills. Today it's an endangered species, finding safety in numbers in the *phanta* and particularly the boggy parts where seasonal fires don't burn off the grasses.

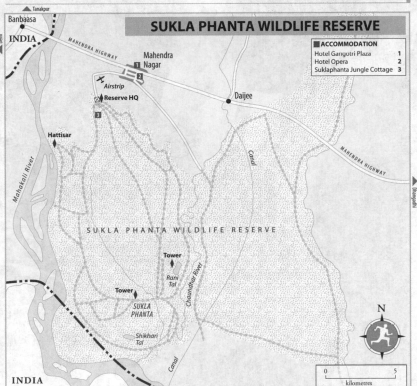

SUKLA PHANTA WILDLIFE RESERVE

ACCOMMODATION	
Hotel Gangotri Plaza	1
Hotel Opera	2
Suklaphanta Jungle Cottage	3

Having seen your obligatory *phanta*, make a beeline for **Rani Tal** (Queen's Lake), near the centre of the reserve. Surrounded by riotous, screeching forest, the lake – a lagoon, really – is like a prehistoric time capsule, with trees leaning out over the shore, deer wading shoulder-deep around the edges and crocodiles occasionally peering out of the water-hyacinth-choked depths. In the early morning, the **birdlife** is amazing: a dazzling display of cranes, cormorants, eagles and scores of others. You can watch all the comings and goings from a tower by the western shore. Nearby is an overgrown **brick circle**, 1.5km in circumference, which locals say was the fort of Singpal, an ancient Tharu king (Rani Tal is said to have been his queen's favourite spot).

ARRIVAL AND INFORMATION

SUKLA PHANTA WILDLIFE RESERVE

Entry and admissions The Reserve HQ is 5km southeast of Mahendra Nagar, past the airstrip (rikshaw Rs100/person, jeep Rs200/person). There's an Rs1000 entry fee, plus an Rs2000 vehicle fee.
Guides Guides are obligatory and available at the Reserve

HQ (Rs1000 for 5hr for 1–4 people).
Jeep tours A full day's drive into the jungle (10am–4pm) by jeep costs RS2000 for 1–4 people excluding park and guide fees.

ACCOMMODATION

Shuklaphanta Jungle Cottage 500m past the Reserve HQ ☎099 524 693, ✉suklaphantantajc @gmail.com. Currently the only place to stay independently near the reserve, this new camp has clean

fan and a/c en-suite rooms and can organize all your reserve activities, including an overnight camping safari (from Rs6000–13,000/person). Rates include full board. <u>Rs1200</u>

The Eastern Terai and hills

The Eastern Terai and hills

Lusher and more tropical than the west, the Eastern Terai – the southern flatlands east of Chitwan – are also more populous, more industrial and more Indian. Although the foothills are usually within sight, the main east–west highway sticks to the plains, where the way of life is essentially identical to that of Bihar and West Bengal just across the border; in many parts of this region, Nepali is the second or even third language, after Maithili, Bhojpuri and other North Indian dialects.

Most travellers only flit through on their way to the border crossings of **Birgunj** (for Patna) and **Kakarbhitta** (for Darjeeling); outside these places, there's little tourist hype. The cities are generally unappealing, with one outstanding exception: **Janakpur**, a famous Hindu pilgrimage centre. Birdwatchers, meanwhile, can check out **Koshi Tappu Wildlife Reserve**, straddling the alluvial plain of the mighty Sapt Koshi River.

While the few visitors that reach the **eastern hills** tend to be trekkers bound for the Everest or Kanchenjunga massifs, or rafters running the Sun Koshi, the area also offers great day-hiking. It's served by just two all-weather roads: one climbs to the lovely Newari town of **Dhankuta** and rowdier **Hile**, the other crawls up to **Ilam**, Nepal's tea-growing capital. **Tourist facilities** are minimal, but the **haat bazaars** (weekly markets) are well worth looking out for.

The Tribhuwan Rajpath: Hetauda to Birgunj

For centuries – before the advent of air travel – the only developed corridor through the Terai, the gentler southern section of the **Tribhuwan Rajpath**, served as every foreigner's introduction to Nepal. A narrow-gauge railway used to run from Raxaul, the last Indian station, as far as Amlekhganj, from where dignitaries were transported by elephant over the first band of hills to Hetauda, then carried the rest of the way to Kathmandu by donkey or sedan chair. Those few who made the journey during Nepal's pre-1951 isolation did so only by invitation of the prime minister or king. The construction of the Rajpath in the 1950s eliminated the need for elephants and sedan chairs, but the railway wasn't decommissioned until the 1970s.

If you're arriving from **India**, the Rajpath makes an exhilarating introduction to Nepal, particularly if coupled with an overnight stay in Daman, from where there's a superb Himalayan panorama. The dramatic northern section of the Tribhuwan Rajpath, including Daman, is covered separately in our "Central Hills" chapter (see p.172).

> The majority of the Eastern Terai escaped the worst of the **April 2015 earthquake** (see box, p.6), which occurred just as this book went to press, though Janaki Mandir in Janakpur was damaged.

Highlights

❶ Janakpur Join the pilgrims in this fascinating holy Hindu city, which features prominently in the Ramayana but not on most tourist itineraries. **See p.286**

❷ Janakpur Women's Development Center Learn about and buy eye-catching Maithili folk art at this nonprofit artists' cooperative – a great place to pick up ethical gifts. **See p.289**

❸ Koshi Tappu Wildlife Reserve Ride in a dugout canoe through the sandy, estuary-like river channels of this reserve, which is alive with waterbirds. **See p.292**

❹ Hile Airy, frontier-like bazaar town, populated by different ethnic groups who come here from the surrounding region to trade and drink hot millet beer from a traditional *tongba*. **See p.298**

❺ Ilam A trip to Nepal's finest tea gardens, perched among the steep, green hills below Kanchenjunga, give magnificent views along the road above, plus the chance to head to more remote locations such as the sacred pond at Mai Pokhari. **See p.299**

HIGHLIGHTS ARE MARKED ON THE MAP ON PP.284–285

Hetauda

Clumped around the junction of the Mahendra Highway and the Rajpath, **HETAUDA** is still a staging post on the India–Kathmandu route. It's a restless place, where trucks and buses rumble through at all hours, and prostitution is common, though you're unlikely to see it. Among Nepalis, Hetauda is probably most famous for its cement plant and industrial estate, responsible for much of the country's prodigious beer production. In fairness, though, Hetauda's roads are brightened up by lines of deep-green *ashok* trees, and much of the surrounding area is dominated by *sal* forest. The centre of Hetauda is **Mahendra Chowk**, a four-way intersection where the Mahendra Highway comes in from the west and the Rajpath from the north.

ARRIVAL AND GETTING AROUND   HETAUDA

By bus From the bus park, 150m southwest of Mahendra Chowk, regular buses head to Kathmandu along the main road. There are also regular buses to Birgunj and a few to Janakpur, though you're best off changing at Pathalaya if you're heading east.
Destinations Birgunj (hourly; 2hr); Daman (5 morning buses; 1hr 30min–2hr); Janakpur (every 3hr; 5hr); Kathmandu (every 2hr; around 6hr).

By jeep If you're heading to or from Kathmandu, slightly cheaper and much more interesting than the bus are 4WD jeeps, which take the short cut through the mountains via Bhainse.
By bike There are several cycling routes around Hetauda; LifeCycle Nepal (☎01 552 1120, ⍟lifecyclenepal.com) runs good trips.

ACCOMMODATION

★**Motel Avocado & Orchid Resort** 500m north of Mahendra Chowk ☎057 520 235, ⍟orchidresort.com. Hetauda's top hotel has a range of rooms suitable for most budgets – from boxy budget rooms in the annex to deluxe

a/c suites for US$56 – as well as an orchid garden and a grove of avocado trees planted by displaced Californians when this was the USAID guesthouse. US$10

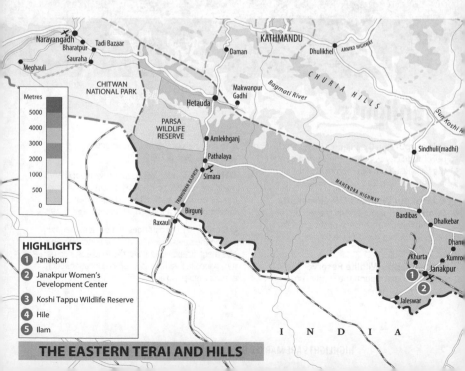

HIGHLIGHTS

1. Janakpur
2. Janakpur Women's Development Center
3. Koshi Tappu Wildlife Reserve
4. Hile
5. Ilam

THE EASTERN TERAI AND HILLS

The Rajpath south to Birgunj

Heading south over the low **Churia Hills**, the Rajpath enters a strange landscape of stunted trees and steeply eroded pinnacles. These hills are the newest wrinkle in the Himalayas, heaved up as the thirty-million-year collision between the Indian and Asian continental plates ripples southwards. Less than half a million years old, they're so young that the surface sediments haven't yet been eroded to expose bedrock.

Leaving the hills, the road passes **Amlekhganj**, the former rail terminus (now Nepal's main fuel depot), and, 4km further on, the entrance to **Parsa Wildlife Reserve**, an annexe of Chitwan National Park that provides secondary habitat for many of its sub-adult tigers. It's possible to visit the park (entrance Rs1000), but facilities are very limited and fewer than a dozen people make the effort each year. There are a couple of ponds 10km from the park entrance, just off a track that leads to Chitwan, and although the chance of seeing tigers is small, elephants and other wildlife are relatively common.

The Mahendra Highway branches off east at **Pathalaya**, while **Simara** heralds a dreary succession of factories and fields that continues all the way to Birgunj.

Birgunj

Ask a Nepali to name the worst place in Nepal, and **BIRGUNJ** will likely top the list of anyone who's been here. Chaotic, crowded, dirty, dusty and smelly, it manages, amazingly, not to be as bad as **Raxaul**, its even more evil twin across the border. The town has exploded in the last decade on the back of cross-border trade with India; its population has almost tripled since 2001. Unless you have business interests, there's no reason to come here except to cross the border to or from Varanasi or Kolkata. Even then, you're better using Sonauli (see p.261) because of its better connections within Nepal. You could probably kill an hour in the market area around **Maisthan**, a mother-goddess

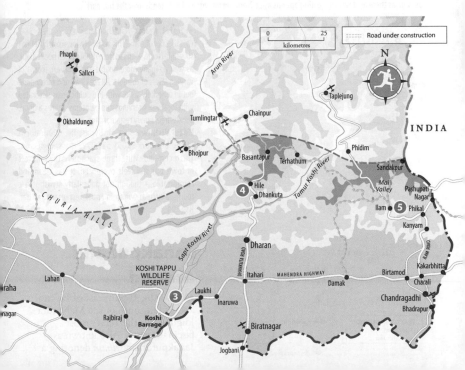

temple just east off the main drag. The **Adarsh Nagar** area, just south of the clock tower, is the nicest part of town and holds the majority of the better accommodation.

ARRIVAL AND INFORMATION

By plane The nearest airport is in Simara, a Rs1000 taxi ride away, and has regular flights to Kathmandu (6 daily; 15min).

By bus The chaotic bus park is an open area of dust or mud (depending on the weather) almost 1km east of the clock tower. There are frequent services to Kathmandu day and night, as well as to Janakpur. Less regular services run to Pokhara and other destinations, departing mainly in the morning and early evening, with most deluxe services leaving after 8pm. Rikshaws and *tongas* provide transport to and from town (Rs30–40).

Destinations Bhairahawa (1–2 daily; 8–9hr); Biratnagar (4–5 daily; 8–9hr); Janakpur (every 30min–1hr; 5hr); Kakarbhitta (1–2 daily; 9hr); Kathmandu (every 15min; around 9hr; buses travel via Narayangadh, 3–4hr); Pokhara (2–3 daily; 10–11hr).

Banks and exchange The Adarsh Nagar area holds numerous banks with ATMs, including Himalayan Bank.

Most businesses accept Indian rupees at the official rate.

TO INDIA

The border is 2km south of Birgunj, and Raxaul, the Indian border town, sprawls for another 2km south of it. Horrendous traffic jams are a regular occurrence – if you're driving it can take hours to get through, and that's leaving aside the paperwork.

Border hours The border is open daily 6am–10pm.

Visas If you're entering Nepal and don't have a visa, make sure you have the correct change in cash (US dollars). Indian visas are not available at the border.

Transport Rikshaws charge about Rs100–120 (Rs60–70 Indian) to ferry passengers from Birgunj through to Raxaul's train station. Raxaul Junction has trains to Delhi (2 daily; around 24–28hr), Mumbai (2 weekly; around 38hr) and Kolkata (1 daily; around 18hr). Buses depart for Patna (8hr) several times a day.

ACCOMMODATION AND EATING

Most of Birgunj's **accommodation** is aimed at Indian business-travellers, but there are a string of grubby budget options (Rs400–600) along the road between the bus station and the clock tower. All the hotels have **restaurants**, which is just as well, as there are few other eating options aside from the unhygenic food stands near the bus park.

★**Hotel Kailas** Adarsh Nagar ☎051 522 384, ⓦkailashotel.com. This relatively low-cost hotel has six single rooms with fan from Rs650 (often booked up), as well as many more double and twin a/c rooms of varying levels of comfort. All are clean and nicely done out in a homely style, with the public areas decorated with local woodcarvings and paintings. There's a good, smoke-free, family restaurant too. Rs1470

Hotel Vishuwa Just off Bypass Rd, 300m north of the bus park ☎051 527 777, ⓦvishuwa.com. This green-and-white three-star hotel is the smartest in town but still feels overpriced. It has clean and comfortable – though not paticularly stylish – a/c rooms, a circular swimming pool, restaurant and bar. Rs4294

Janakpur and around

JANAKPUR, 165km east of Birgunj and 25km south of the Mahendra Highway, is the Terai's most fascinating city. Also known as **Janakpurdham** (*dham* denoting a sacred place), it's a holy site of the first order, and its central temple, the ornate **Janaki Mandir**, is an obligatory stop on the Hindu pilgrimage circuit. Possessing a strong Indian influence, the city is small and manageable: motorized traffic is limited to two-wheelers in the centre, and tourist hustle is largely absent.

Despite the absence of ancient monuments to confirm its mythic past – no building is much more than a century old – Janakpur remains an attractive city. Religious fervour seems to lend an aura to everything; the skyline leaves a lasting impression of palm trees and the onion domes and pyramid roofs of local shrines. Most of these distinctive buildings are associated with **kuti** – self-contained pilgrimage centres and hostels for sadhus – some five hundred of which are scattered throughout the Janakpur area. The city's other distinguishing feature is its dozens of **sacred ponds**, which here take the place of river ghats for ritual bathing and *dhobi*-ing.

The **countryside** surrounding Janakpur is inhabited by Hindu castes and members of the Tharu and Danuwar ethnic groups, and features some of the most meticulously kept farmland you'll ever see. During the cooler months you can take bike rides along several roads radiating out from the city.

Brief history
Hindu mythology identifies Janakpur as the capital of the ancient kingdom of **Mithila**, which controlled a large part of northern India between the tenth and third centuries BC.

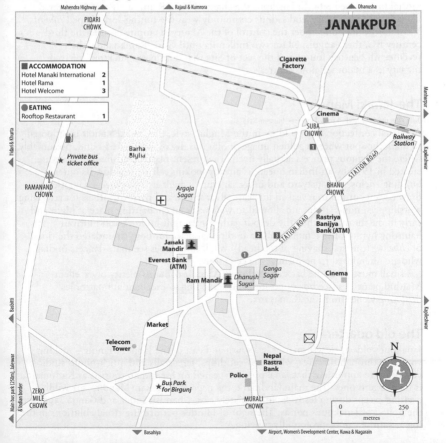

6

JANAKPUR'S FESTIVALS

Janakpur's atmosphere is charged with an intense devotional zeal. New shrines are forever being inaugurated and idols installed, while loudspeakers broadcast religious discourses and the mesmerizing drone of *bhajan* (devotional song). Pilgrimage is a year-round industry, marked by several highlights in the festival calendar:

Parikrama As many as 100,000 people join the annual one-day circumambulation of the city on the day of the February/March full moon, many performing prostrations along the entire 8km route. The pilgrimage coincides with the festival of Holi, when coloured water is thrown everywhere and on everyone.

Ram Navami Ram's birthday, celebrated on the ninth day after the March/April full moon, attracts thousands of sadhus, who receive free room and board at temples.

Chhath Women bathe in Janakpur's ponds and line them with elaborate offerings to the sun god Surya at dawn on the third day of Tihaar (Diwali) in October/November. Women in the villages surrounding Janakpur paint murals on the walls of their houses.

Biwaha Panchami The culmination of this five-day event – Janakpur's most important festival – is a re-enactment of Ram and Sita's wedding at the Janaki Mandir, which draws hundreds of thousands of pilgrims on the fifth day after the new moon of November/December.

The city features prominently in the Ramayana: it was here that **Ram** – Vishnu in mortal form – wed **Sita**. In Janakpur the chant of "Sita Ram, Sita Ram" is repeated like a Hindu Hail Mary, and sadhus commonly wear the tuning-fork-shaped *tika* of Vishnu. Mithila came under the control of the Mauryan empire around the third century BC, then languished for two millennia until Guru Ramananda, the seventeenth-century founder of the sect of Sita that dominates Janakpur, revived the city as a major religious centre.

The Janaki Mandir

Daily 24hr; rituals generally 8am & 4pm • Free, museum Rs15

A palatial confection of a building in the Mughal style, the **Janaki Mandir** is supposed to mark the spot where a golden image of Sita was discovered in 1657 and, presumably, where the virtuous princess actually lived. The present plaster-and-marble structure, erected in 1911 by an Indian queen, is already looking a little mouldy. Its outer building encloses a courtyard and inner sanctum, where at least twice a day priests draw back a curtain to reveal an intricate silver shrine and perform rituals for attending worshippers; non-Hindus are allowed to watch. It's an enchanting place at night and early in the morning, when the devout gather in lamplit huddles and murmur haunting hymns. The temple is also a traditional place for boys to undergo the ritual of *chhewar* (the first shaving of the head); you'll sometimes see male dancers in drag, who are often hired to perform at the ceremony.

A small **museum** at the back of the Janaki Mandir contains plenty of excellent Maithili paintings (see box opposite), and some not-so-excellent animatronics depicting scenes from the Ramayana.

The old quarter

Janakpur's oldest, closest quarter lies south and east of the Janaki Mandir – making your way through this area, with its sweet shops, *puja* stalls and quick-photo studios, you begin to appreciate that Janakpur is as geared up for Indian tourists as Kathmandu is for Western ones. The main landmark, the pagoda-style **Ram Mandir**, isn't wildly exciting except during festivals. Immediately east, **Dhanush Sagar** and **Ganga Sagar** are the holiest of Janakpur's ponds. The sight of Hindus performing ritual ablutions in the fog at sunrise can be profoundly moving.

Ramanand Chowk

On the highway a short walk west of the Janaki Mandir

The nucleus of many of Janakpur's *kuti*, **Ramanand Chowk** is a major sadhu gathering place during festivals. A four-way arch bearing a statue of Guru Ramananda, the saint responsible for Janakpur's modern fame, marks the intersection that bears his name. Two well-known establishments, Ramanand Ashram and Ratnasagar Kuti, are located west of here but, like most *kuti*, they are closed to non-Hindus.

6

Janakpur Women's Development Center (JWDC)

3km south of Janakpur • Sun–Thurs: mid-Feb to mid-Nov 10am–5pm; mid-Nov to mid-Feb 10am–4pm • ☏ 041 521 080, ⊛ jwdconline .com • Free • 15min by rikshaw (Rs100) from Janakpur; if walking or cycling, head south towards the airport, turn left 1km after Murali Chowk, and bear right after 200m, passing through the well-kept village of Kuwa – the centre is on the right after 500m. Ask directions frequently as it's easy to get lost; just ask for "JWDC"

Hindu women of the deeply conservative villages around Janakpur are rarely spared from their household duties, and, once married, are expected to remain veiled and silent before all males but their husbands. Fortunately, their rich tradition of folk art (see below) offers them an escape. Set in a walled compound, the nonprofit **Janakpur Women's Development Center** (*Nari Bikas Kendra*) provides a space for women from nearby villages to develop. Founded in 1989, with assistance from several international NGOs, the artists' cooperative helps its forty-odd members turn their skills into income – and the fact that some have gone on to start their own companies is a sure sign of the project's success. But more importantly, the centre empowers women through training in literacy and business skills, and support sessions in which they can share their feelings and discuss their roles in family and society.

MAITHILI PAINTING

For three thousand years, Hindu women of the region once known as Mithila have maintained a tradition of **painting**, using techniques and motifs passed from mother to daughter. The colourful images can be viewed as fertility charms, meditation aids or a form of storytelling, embodying millennia of traditional knowledge.

From an early age **Brahman girls** practice drawing complex symbols derived from Hindu myths and folk tales, which over the course of generations have been reduced to mandala-like abstractions. By the time she is in her teens, a girl will be presenting simple paintings to her arranged fiancé; the courtship culminates with the painting of a **kohbar**, an elaborate fresco on the wall of the bride's bedroom, where the newlyweds will spend their first nights. Depicting a stalk of bamboo surrounded by lotus leaves (symbols of male and female sexuality), the *kohbar* is a powerful celebration of life and creation. Other motifs include footprints and fishes (representing Vishnu), parrots (symbolic of a happy union), Krishna cavorting with his milkmaids, and Surabhi, the Cow of Plenty, who inflames the desire of those who milk her. Perhaps the most striking aspect of the *kohbar* is that, almost by definition, it is ephemeral: even the most amazing mural will be washed off within a week or two. Painting is seen as a form of prayer or meditation; once completed, the work has achieved its end.

Women of all castes create simpler **wall decorations** during the autumn festival of Tihaar (Diwali). In the weeks leading up to the festival they apply a new coat of mud mixed with dung and rice chaff to their houses and add relief designs. Just before Lakshmi Puja, the climactic third day of Tihaar, many paint images of peacocks, pregnant elephants and other symbols of prosperity in order to attract a visit from the goddess of wealth. Until Nepali New Year celebrations in April, the decorations are easily viewable in villages around Janakpur.

Paintings on paper, which traditionally play only a minor part in the culture, have become the most celebrated form of Maithili art – or Madhubani art, as it's known in India, where a community-development project began turning it into a marketable commodity in the 1960s. More recently, the **Janakpur Women's Development Center** (see above) has helped do the same in Nepal, making Maithili paintings a staple of Kathmandu tourist gift shops. Many artists concentrate on traditional religious motifs, but a growing number depict people – mainly women and children in domestic scenes, always shown in characteristic doe-eyed profile.

Initially specializing in Maithili paper art, the centre now has separate buildings for sewing, screen-printing, ceramics and painting. Visitors are welcome to meet the artists and learn about their work and traditions. A **gift shop** sells crafts made on the premises at very reasonable prices, as well as the booklet *Master Artists of Janakpur*, which explains the life stories of some of the women. The paintings (Rs300–5600) make great gifts, as do the bed sheets, mirrors, cups and bags. The centre can arrange postage, and now even sells online.

6

The Janakpur Railway

Janakpur's **narrow-gauge railway** was built in the 1940s to transport timber to India from the now-depleted forest west of Janakpur, and ran 29km to Jainagar just inside India. The railway is currently being upgraded to broad-gauge and is closed at the time of writing, so ask around for the latest information. The old narrow-gauge railway was an excellent way to get out into the country, and on a misty winter's morning, the ride past sleepy villages and minor temples was nothing short of magical; whether it will remain such a fabulous journey on broad-gauge is unclear. This is the first stage of a planned Nepalese rail network that will stretch from Kakrabhitta in the far east of the country to Gaddachaucki in the west.

Villages around Janakpur

Dozens of villages dot the land around Janakpur, each with its own mango grove and a pond or two. Subsistence farming – livestock, grains, vegetables and fish – is virtually the only occupation. You can explore south towards **Nagarain**, west to substantial **Khurta**, or there are also several picturesque villages on either side of the main road that connects Janakpur to the Mahendra Highway; the loveliest is **Kumrora**, on the right about 4km north of Pidari Chowk, a tidy Brahman settlement with particularly expressive wall murals.

ARRIVAL AND INFORMATION JANAKPUR

By plane Buddha Air, Agni Air and Yeti Airlines fly daily to and from Kathmandu. Rikshaws charge about Rs150–200 from the market to the airport, 2.5km south of the centre – it takes up to 25min due to the bad road.

By bus The main bus station is an easy rikshaw ride (around Rs100–150) southwest of the centre, though most private services drop-off and pick up by the ticket offices just north of Ramanand Chowk. Plenty of day and night buses head to and from Kathmandu, Biratnagar and Kakarbhitta; services to Birgunj leave from a separate bus station just south of the market.

Destinations Biratnagar (hourly; 6hr); Birgunj (hourly; 5hr); Kakarbhitta (hourly; 11hr); Kathmandu (12 daily; no services 7am–5pm; 10hr).

Banks and exchange Nepal Rastra bank, at the southern end of town, can exchange US dollars but not travellers' cheques. Everest Bank, near the Janaki Mandir, and Rastriya Banijya Bank, on Station Rd, both have ATMs.

ACCOMMODATION AND EATING

Standards at Janakpur's few **lodgings**, which are aimed more at Indian pilgrims than Western visitors, are dispiritingly low. Keep a distance from the *kuti* around the Janaki Mandir, as their loudspeakers create a hell of a racket. While the scarcity of accommodation normally doesn't present a problem, you need to **book** well ahead during the big festivals. Numerous inexpensive places to eat around the Janaki Mandir offer pure veg food, while a host of *mithai pasal* (sweet shops) in the same area sell sugary Indian-style sweets. The **restaurants** attached to the hotels below are all reliable too.

Hotel Manaki International Just off Station Rd ☏041 521 540, ✉hotelmanaki2010@hotmail.com. One of the town's top hotels, though starting to fray at the edges. It's popular with UN and NGO staff and has an extravagent white exterior and bright Maithili paintings in the lobby. Drab but clean rooms come with TVs, phones and fan; a/c rooms with baths cost roughly double. Rs1495

Hotel Rama Near Suba Chowk ☏041 520 059. Although the hallways are dark and musty, this is the best budget option in town as the rooms are clean and

OPPOSITE YOUNG BLACK-NECKED STORK, KOSHI TAPPU (P.292) >

comfortable and come with attached bathrooms, TVs, phones and fans; you can pay Rs1000 more for a/c. They also have a decent restaurant. Rs700

Hotel Welcome Station Rd ⓣ041 520 646, ⓦnepalhotelwelcome.com. Recently moved into a new building, this hotel has the most modern rooms in town; more luxurious rooms with a/c cost Rs1200 extra. Service is friendly, and they can provide you with a leaflet guide to the area. The hotel restaurant is one of the best in Jakakpur for Indian food. Rs2000

Rooftop Restaurant Station Rd ⓣ041 522 840. Smarter than most of the town's other restaurants, this dimly lit place has a large menu with tasty Indian, Nepali and Chinese vegetarian, meat and fish dishes (all Rs80–260), as well as so-so burgers and pizzas. In terms of snacks, the tasty *momos* are Rs120, and you can also get a very cold beer (from Rs350). Daily 9am–9.30pm.

6

Koshi Tappu Wildlife Reserve

Straddling a floodplain of shifting grassland and sandbanks north of the Koshi Barrage, **Koshi Tappu Wildlife Reserve** is the Terai's smallest park, and one of the least visited and most expensive, too. There are no tigers or rhinos, nor even any jungle, but **birdwatchers** can have a field day: it's not unheard of to spot over 150 species in a single day. Koshi Tappu is among the subcontinent's most important wetlands, and thanks to its location just downstream from one of the few breaches in the Himalayan barrier, it's an internationally important area for waterfowl and waders.

Some 501 **bird** species, many of them endangered, have been counted here. Flocks of up to fifty thousand ducks used to be seen in winter and spring, though numbers have been lower in recent years. Most of Nepal's egrets, storks, ibises, terns and gulls are represented, as are at least five globally threatened species, including the black-necked stork, red-necked falcon, swamp francolin and the impressive lesser adjutant, one of the world's largest storks. November and December are the optimum months to see winter migrants, while mid-February to early April are best for the late migratory species.

The reserve was established to protect one of the subcontinent's last surviving herds of **wild buffalo**, believed to number around 450 animals. However, there are concerns about the number of domestic buffalo getting into the reserve and mating with the wild ones. **Mugger crocodiles** and many species of **turtle** and **fish** are also present, as well as wild boar, langur and spotted deer. Between the channels of water, a number of semi-permanent islands of scrub and grassland are the main stomping ground for **blue bull**. (*Tappu* means "island" in Nepali, an accurate description of this floodplain in the wet summer months.) Blue bulls are big animals with sizeable horns; they normally run away at the first scent of humans, but you have to make sure not to threaten them or block their escape route.

NEPAL'S RIVER DOLPHINS

Nepal's susu, or **gangetic dolphins**, belong to one of only three species of freshwater dolphins in the world and, like their cousins in the Amazon and Indus, are highly endangered. Revered in myth as "messenger kings", the animals are practically blind, using echo-location to navigate.

Before 2008 – when the Sapt Koshi broke its embankment, resulting in a disastrous flood that cut the eastern Terai in two – dolphins used to cavort openly in the outflow of the **Koshi Barrage**, less than a dozen kilometres from Koshi Tappu Wildlife Reserve; since then spottings have been less frequent. Another small, isolated population survives in the far west of Nepal, downstream of the **Chisapani gorge** in the Karnali River. Whether the dolphins return to Nepal's rivers in numbers, or go the way of the now-extinct Yangtze Dolphin, remains to be seen.

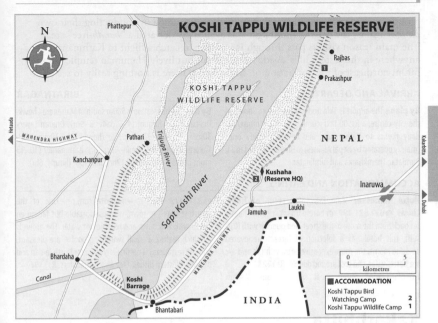

KOSHI TAPPU WILDLIFE RESERVE

Phattepur

Rajbas

Prakashpur

KOSHI TAPPU
WILDLIFE RESERVE

N E P A L

Hetauda

MAHENDRA HIGHWAY

Pathari

Kanchanpur

Trijuga River

Kushaha
(Reserve HQ)

Inaruwa

Sapt Koshi River

Jamuha   Laukhi

MAHENDRA HIGHWAY

Bhardaha

Canal

Koshi
Barrage

Bhantabari

I N D I A

0   5
kilometres

■ ACCOMMODATION
Koshi Tappu Bird
 Watching Camp   2
Koshi Tappu Wildlife Camp 1

Kakarbhita

Dahabi

6

INFORMATION AND ACTIVITIES

Park office The park office is in Kushaha (☎ 985 205 5405, @ iswar.khadka@gmail.com), 10km northeast of the Koshi Barrage, and signposted down a track through the fields 2.5km west off the Mahendra Highway at the village of Jamuha.

Entry fee Entry costs Rs1000/day.

Guides With no rhinos or large carnivores, Koshi Tappu is comparatively safe to enter on foot with a guide (Rs2000/

KOSHI TAPPU WILDLIFE RESERVE

day), though wild elephants have been known to maraud in this area, and kill around two local villagers annually.

Activities Elephant rides (Rs2500/hr) and canoe and rafting trips (Rs2000–2500 for 6hr) can be arranged. Read the box on p.252 before deciding whether or not to arrange an elephant ride.

ACCOMMODATION

Most of the few travellers who visit Koshi Tappu come on fairly expensive **package tours**, and the reserve is not really developed for independent travellers; however, there is a park campsite not far from the park HQ (Rs1000/person), as well as a few grubby guesthouses 30km east in Inaruwa. Both the camps listed here can organize transport from Biratnagar (for a price).

Koshi Tappu Birds Watching Camp Outside the park, close to the park office ☎ 980 736 8484, ⓦ koshitappu .net. This locally owned camp is slightly cheaper than its rivals. Accommodation is in safari tents on a small island on the river, or in basic mud rooms (same price). Rate per person, including full board and safaris US$184, full board only Rs4000

Koshi Tappu Wildlife Camp At the village of Prakashpur, within the buffer zone ☎ 01 422 6130, ⓦ koshitappu .com. This long-standing camp, organized from Kathmandu, has been running since 1993 and is focused primarily on birdwatching; it even has a bird-hide nearby. It offers twelve atmospheric safari tents, as well as a decent restaurant and bar. Rate per person, including full board and safaris US$201

Biratnagar

BIRATNAGAR, Nepal's second largest city, is an industrial place close to the border and pretty much devoid of any charm. Industry here was deeply shaken by the Madhesi movement; in 2009, protests and *bandhs* (strikes) by various minorities and political groups reached such an extreme that industrialists reacted by conducting their own *bandhs* against the *bandhs*; Biratnagar was declared a "*bandh*-free" area. The main reason visitors pass through is in order to catch a flight to Kathmandu or anywhere in the eastern hills. Aside from a small but lively Hanuman temple, around 500m northeast of the bus station on Main Road, there is nothing really to see or do.

6

ARRIVAL AND DEPARTURE   BIRATNAGAR

By plane The airport is 3km north of Mahendra Chowk in the city centre, a Rs500 taxi journey. There are numerous daily flights to Kathmandu, and several weekly ones (mainly operated by Nepal Airlines) to Bhojpur, Lamidanda, Rumjatar, Thamkharka and Tumlingtar.

By bus The bus station is 500m south of Mahendra Chowk. Destinations Birgunj (4–5 daily; 8–9hr); Dharan (every 30min; 1hr–1hr 30min); Hile (hourly; 3hr 30min–4hr); Kakarbhitta (every 30min–1hr; 3hr); Kathmandu (10–15 night buses daily; around 12hr); Janakpur (hourly; 6hr).

ACCOMMODATION AND EATING

Hotel Namaskar Main Rd, 100m south of Traffic Chowk ☎021 521 199, ⓦhotelnamaskar.com. Quietly set back from the noise of the street, and popular with NGO staff, this hotel has a selection of recently renovated en-suite rooms; the more expensive ones with TVs and a/c are better value and cost around double. **Rs1223**
Hotel Xenial 500m west of the bus station

☎021 472 950, ⓦxenialhotel.com.np. One of the smartest hotels in town, with comfortable but fading en suites with TVs, safes and reliable hot water. The grounds – which feature a small swimming pool – are pleasant, and the restaurant is particularly good for North Indian and pseudo-Western dishes. Free airport transfers. **Rs3396**

Kakarbhitta

Once-sleepy **KAKARBHITTA** is the municipal capital of Nepal's easternmost district. It's mainly a gateway, and most of those using it are Indians, hopping over from Darjeeling for some shopping, or heading to Biratnagar for business. The villages situated on both sides of the border also receive more dangerous legal migrants just passing by: **wild elephants**. Every year a few people are trampled to death and houses get destroyed by the pachyderms, who liberally help themselves to the grain stock.

If you have some time on your hands, you can hike out to the pleasantly green **Satighata tea estate**, just ten minutes' walk south of Kakarbhitta; a Buddhist **monastery** run by Tamangs can be visited on the way. Don't be afraid: the chances you'll meet any marauding elephants are very slim.

ARRIVAL AND DEPARTURE   KAKARBHITTA

By plane The closest airport, at Bhadrapur 19.5km southwest, has several daily flights to Kathmandu. A taxi

costs around Rs1300 and takes under an hour.
By bus The bus station is in the town centre. Numerous

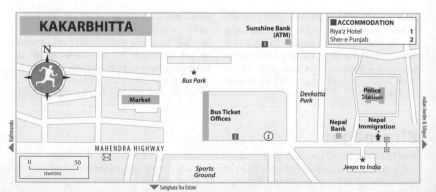

KAKARBHITTA

Sunshine Bank (ATM)

ACCOMMODATION
Riya'z Hotel   1
Sher-e Punjab   2

N

Bus Park

Market

Devkotta Park

Police Station

Bus Ticket Offices

Nepal Bank

Nepal Immigration

MAHENDRA HIGHWAY

0   50
metres

Sports Ground

Jeeps to India

Satighata Tea Estate

buses to Kathmandu leave in staggered intervals between 4–6am and 3–5pm, but book at least a couple of hours ahead to be sure of a good seat. Local buses travel direct to Hile, though there are more frequent departures from Itahari, which is the junction for Hile on the East–West Highway. Likewise with Ilam, it's best to take any bus west and change at Birtamod for a local connection.

Destinations Biratnagar (every 30min–1hr; 3hr); Birtamod (every 15–30min; 20min); Dharan (hourly; 3hr); Hile (2–3 daily; 5hr); Janakpur (hourly; 11hr); Itahari (every 30min; 2hr 30min); Kathmandu (frequent between 4–6am & 3–6pm; 14–15hr).

TO INDIA

The wide Mechi River forms the border with India, about 500m east of Kakarbhitta.

Border hours Formalities are pleasantly relaxed, and Nepali immigration is open daily 7am–7pm. Nepal is fifteen minutes ahead of India.

Visas Nepali visas are available at the border; US dollars, Indian rupees and even euros are accepted. Indian visas have to be obtained in advance (see p.96).

Onward transport If you're entering India here, chances are you're heading for Darjeeling, Sikkim or Kolkata. For any of these destinations, you're best off taking one of the host of shared jeeps clustered just outside of Nepalese immigration. Most shuttle to Siliguri, where the toy train to Darjeeling and bus services to Gangtok and Kalimpong all originate. At New Jalpaiguri you can pick up train services to Kolkata and Delhi, or make your way to the Bagdogra airport, with flights to Kolkata and Delhi. Other jeeps run all the way from Kakarbhitta to Darjeeling, Gantok and Kalimpong.

INFORMATION

Tourist information The tourist office, near the border (Sun–Thurs 10am–5pm, Fri 10am–2pm; ☎023 562 252), may be able to advise on onward travel.

Banks and exchange Moneychangers and lodges will swap Nepalese and Indian rupees at the market rate, but to

change hard currency you'll have to use the Nepal Bank, just west of the immigration building. There's only one ATM in town, at the Sunshine Bank, just around the corner from the *Riya'z Hotel*.

ACCOMMODATION AND EATING

Hotel New Sher-e Punjab South side of the bus station ☎023 562 008. Good budget choice, with tolerable standard rooms, or for Rs300 more, bigger and much more comfortable deluxe rooms which are particularly good value – as is the attached restaurant. Its location by the bus station means that earplugs may be

needed in some rooms. Rs500

Riya'z Hotel 50m northeast of the bus station ☎023 562 384. Probably the pick of the town's hotels, the *Riya'z* is a solid mid-range option with pretty comfortable en-suite fan and a/c rooms – the latter Rs1000 more expensive. The restaurant is pretty good too. Rs1200

The Dhankuta road

Call it development, or colonialism by another name, but the big donor nations have staked out distinct spheres of influence in Nepal. Despite the closure of the Gurkha Camp at **Dharan**, the bustling gateway to the eastern hills, almost half the British Army's Gurkha recruits still come from the area, and the old ties are strongly felt. Britain's aid programme, based in **Dhankuta**, has been handed over to the Nepalese government, but agriculture, forestry, health and cottage industries are still in operation. The biggest and most obvious British undertaking is the **road** to Dharan, Dhankuta, Hile and beyond, which was constructed with £50 million of British taxpayers' money. While there are few grand monuments or temples, this region is a bastion of traditional Nepali hill culture. The bazaar towns of **Hile** and **Basantapur**, in particular, give a powerful taste of what lies beyond the point where the tarmac runs out.

Dharan and around

From the Mahendra Highway, the Dhankuta road winds languidly through forests as it ascends the Bhabar, the sloping alluvial zone between the Terai and the foothills. **DHARAN**, 16km north of the highway, sits a slightly cooler 300m above the plain. Dharan hit world headlines in 1988 when an **earthquake** killed seven hundred people and flattened most of the town. Another crisis came in 1989, when the **British Army**

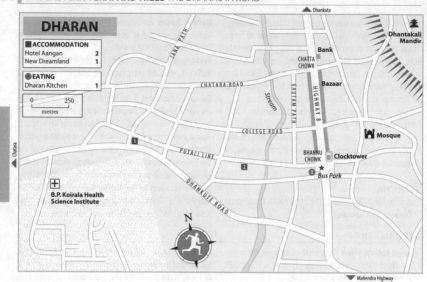

pulled out of the town and handed its Gurkha Camp back to the government. Would-be recruits must now travel to Pokhara (see p.206), though there are still plenty of institutes in town training them for the Gurkha test – you may see trainees in the area doing endurance training, such as jogging backwards up the hills. Fortunately, Dharan has bounced back smartly: the city's western half has grown into a neat little enclave of retired Gurkhas' bungalows, and the Gurkha Camp is now a fancy medical institute.

The bazaar

Dharan's **bazaar**, which runs the length of the main street between Chatta and Bhannu *chowks*, remains as earthily Nepali as ever. For many people throughout the eastern hills this is still the proverbial Bright Lights, where they come to sell oranges by the sackload. In the area northeast of central Bhanu Chowk, you'll see hill women investing the family fortune in gold ornaments, and shops selling silver coins to be strung into necklaces.

Dantakali Mandir and beyond

An easy path leads up from Dharan bazaar to the modest **Dantakali Mandir**, on a low ridge just east of the bazaar (where they hold the burnt remains of the goddess Sati's upper left jaw), and continues upwards after a couple of kilometres to two other temples, Buddhasubbha and Bindyabasini. They lie just within the tiny (free) **Panchakanya National Park**, a pleasantly wooded hill with several paths winding round it.

Chatara and Barahakshetra

Chatara, 15km west of Dharan, is the finishing point for rafting trips on the Sapta Koshi, although it's only accessible on a bad road by walking or 4WD, and often not at all during monsoon. Head 10km north of Chatara (on an even worse road) and you'll reach the sacred confluence of **Barahakshetra**, site of an atmospheric temple to Vishnu incarnated as a boar (Barahi) and an annual pilgrimage on the day of the full moon of October–November. Plans are afoot, however, to renovate the road here from Dharan, so check locally for the current state of play.

THE PEOPLE OF THE EASTERN TERAI

In addition to the mysterious Tharu (see p.240), the Eastern Terai is also home to the **Danuwars**, who are widely distributed across the region, and the **Majhis**, who live in riverside settlements between the Bagmati and the Sun Koshi. Both groups traditionally rely more on fishing than hunting or farming. Most of the Terai's **Hindu** caste families are first- or second-generation immigrants from India, and maintain close cultural, linguistic and economic ties with their homeland. In addition, a significant number of **Muslims** inhabit the Western Terai, especially around Nepalgunj, where they're in the majority.

6

ARRIVAL AND INFORMATION

DHARAN

By bus There are regular services from the bus park to Biratnagar, Kakarbhitta and Birgunj, as well as three night and six morning buses to Kathmandu. Buses to Dhankuta and points north depart from the eastern side of Bhannu Chowk and are chronically overcrowded; shared jeeps are faster, more comfortable and only slightly more expensive. Destinations Biratnagar (every 30min; 1hr–1hr 30min);

Birgunj (hourly; 9hr–10hr 30min); Dhankuta (every 30min; 3hr); Kakarbhitta (every 30min; 3hr); Kathmandu (9 daily; 15hr).

Banks and exchange You'll find an ATM in the Tamu complex, next to the bus park, and in Nabil Bank further north.

ACCOMMODATION AND EATING

Generally speaking, **accommodation** in Dharan is fairly poor, and made worse by bus-park noise. However, there are several reasonable **restaurants** in town, and all the hotels offer food too.

Hotel Aangan Putali Line ☎ 025 520 640. This hotel run by a "family" of orphans is – by the standards of most lodges in Dharan – reasonably quiet. Rooms are clean and pretty comfortable; it's worth paying Rs300 more for one with a private bathroom. **Rs500**

Dharan Kitchen Opposite the clock tower ☎ 025 521 580. Relaxed rooftop restaurant offering tasty Nepali and Indian dishes, and more variable attempts at Western options. Mains are Rs150–500, with *daal bhaat* Rs300.

Generally open daily 10am–10pm.

★**New Dreamland** Dhankute Rd, near the Koirala Institute ☎ 025 525 024. Far from the bus station, in a quiet suburb that shows the enduring influence of Britain on former Gurkha soldiers, *New Dreamland* is a good choice for a bit of peace, with comfortable rooms for all budgets, the cheapest of which have fans and outside toilets. A/c rooms are triple this price. **Rs790**

Dhankuta and around

From Dharan the road switchbacks dramatically over a 1420m saddle at Bhedetar, then descends to cross the Tamur Koshi at Mulghat (280m) before climbing once again to **DHANKUTA**, stretched out on a ridge at 1150m. Though you'd never guess, this is the administrative headquarters for eastern Nepal.

Dhankuta is a small, predominantly Newari town, with a friendly, well-to-do feel. Steps lead up from the bus park to the main **bazaar**, which climbs north along the ridge. The lower half of the bazaar, up to the police station, is paved and reasonably active; the upper half is quieter and more picturesque, lined with whitewashed, tiled and carved Newari townhouses. The outlying area is populated by Rais, Magars and Hindu castes, who make Dhankuta's **haat bazaar**, on Thursdays, a tremendously vivid affair.

Although you can't see the Himalayas, the area makes for fine **walking**. In **Santang**, about 45 minutes southeast of town, women are seen embroidering beautiful shawls and weaving *dhaka* (see p.233). You can walk to Hile (see p.298) in about two hours by taking short cuts off the main road: stick to the ridge and within sight of the electric power line.

Dhankuta Museum

Near the top of the bazaar • Daily except Tues 10am–5pm • Rs50 • To get there, walk up the flagstoned bazaar to the four-way intersection of Bhim Narayan Chowk, marked by a statue, then follow the road to the right around and down for 250m – the museum is above the road on the left, signposted in Nepali

If you have a free half-hour or so, it is worth paying a visit to the **Dhankuta Museum**, which has a small collection of cultural and archeological artefacts from across the eastern region of Nepal, although there's little information in English.

ARRIVAL AND DEPARTURE	DHANKUTA AND AROUND

By bus There are three night buses to Kathmandu 17–18hr), as well as daytime services every 30min to Dharan (3hr) and Hile (30min).

6

ACCOMMODATION AND EATING

Hotel Suravi On the main road, near the hospital ☎ 025 520 204. This central lodge is the best option in town. While there's little in the way of frills, the rooms are clean and simple; rooms with private bathrooms cost an extra Rs400, and have harder beds. There's also a good restaurant. Rs400

Hile and around

Most buses to Dhankuta continue as far as **HILE**, 15km beyond Dhankuta and 750m higher up along the same ridge. This spirited little settlement is one of the most important staging areas in eastern Nepal. Poised over the vast Arun Valley, Hile's bazaar strip straggles up the often fog-bound ridge, drawing in to trade Tamangs and Sherpas from the west, Newari and Indian traders from the south, and Rais from their heartland of the roadless hillsides all around. The most visible minority group, however, are **Bhotiyas** (see p.339) from the northern highlands, who run a number of simple lodges. One of the most exotic things you can do in Nepal is sit in a flickering Bhotiya kitchen sipping hot millet beer from an authentic **tongba** (miniature wooden steins with brass hoops and fitted tops unique to the eastern hills). They do like a tipple in Hile, as demonstrated by the fact that the municipal statue as you enter town is of a 4m-high *tongba*.

The only thing to do in town is browse the bazaar: Hile's **haat bazaar**, on Thursday, is lively, but smaller than Dhankuta's. Some landowners in the area cultivate tea: take a look at the organic **Guranse tea estate** (🌐 guransetea.com.np), whose main entrance is just down the road from the bazaar.

The Hattikharka trail

Most visitors are here to **trek**, and magnificent **views** can be had just a half-hour's walk from Hile – as long as you're up early enough to beat the clouds. Walk to the north end of the bazaar and bear right at the fork up a dirt lane; after 100m a set of steps leads up to join the **Hattikharka trail**, which contours around the hill. The panorama spreads out before you like a map: to the northwest, the Makalu Himal floats above the awesome canyon of the Arun; the ridges of the Milke Daada zigzag to the north; and part of the Kanchenjunga massif pokes up in the northeast.

Basantapur

For a day-trip from Hile, catch a bus to **Basantapur**, a dank, almost Elizabethan bazaar 21km northeast, where there are also a couple of lodges. En route you get tremendous views of the Makalu massif, while in town you can sample Hinwa, one of Nepal's few **fruit wines**, which is made from golden raspberries (around Rs450 a bottle).

ARRIVAL AND INFORMATION	HILE

By bus Hile's small bus park offers regular services to Dhankuta and Dharan, plus three night buses to Kathmandu. Most buses from Dhankuta rumble on to Basantapur. Cheaper microbuses also ply the route up to Basantapur, leaving when full (usually around every 15–25min).

Destinations Basantapur (every 15–30min; 2hr 30min); Dhankuta (every 30min; 30min); Dharan (every 30min; 3hr 30min); Kathmandu (3 daily; 17–18hr).

By jeep and 4WD A handful of jeeps make their way via Basantapur to the beautiful Newari towns of Chaipur and Tumlingtar (both 4–6hr). There are ongoing plans to expand the road from Basantapur to Ilam, though currently only 4WDs occasionally make the trip; ask locally for updates.

Banks and exchange The Rastriya Banjiya bank, opposite the small *gompa* at the southern end of the bazaar, can change cash and travellers' cheques.

ACCOMMODATION AND EATING

Half a dozen Bhotiya **lodges** in the bazaar charge around Rs400–500 for basic digs; look at a few before making a choice. Many **stalls** at either end of the bazaar offer inexpensive Nepali/Tibetan meals.

Hotel Makalu View At the top of the bazaar on the left ☎ 984 245 5775. The only mid-range option in Hile offers more formal accommodation than the lodges down in the bazaar, though it's slightly overpriced and not quite as atmospheric. The rooms aren't anything special, but they are at least clean, with better beds than anywhere else in town, and the restaurant serves more than just *daal bhaat*. **Rs1300**

6

The Ilam road

Like the Dhankuta road, the **Ilam road** keeps getting longer: originally engineered by the Koreans to connect the tea estates of Kanyam and Ilam with the Terai, it now goes all the way to Taplejung, the most common starting point for Kanchenjunga treks. The road is in excellent shape as far as Ilam, but it's extremely steep and entails a couple of monster ascents.

After traversing lush lowlands, the road begins a laborious 1600m ascent to **Kanyam**, where you can visit a tea factory (see box below). At Phikal, a few kilometres further on, a pitched side road leads steeply up for 10km to **Pashupati Nagar**, a small bazaar at 2200m just below the ridge that separates Nepal and India. Shared jeeps wait at the turn-off at Phikal, from where the road descends 1200m in a series of tight switchbacks to cross the Mai Khola before climbing another 700m to Ilam (1200m).

Ilam and around

To Nepalis, **ILAM** means **tea**: cool and moist for much of the year, the hills of Ilam district (like those of Darjeeling, just across the border) enjoy the perfect conditions for growing it. The bazaar is fairly shabby – though it does contain some nice old wooden buildings – and there are no mountain views. There are, however, plenty of **hikes** and some good **birdwatching**. Settled by Newars, Rais and Marwaris (a business-minded Indian group with interests in tea), Ilam was eastern Nepal's main centre of commerce at one time, and the Thursday **haat bazaar** here still draws shoppers from a wide radius.

Ilam district was badly affected by the earthquake on September 18, 2011, with around 10,000 people displaced from their homes.

TIME FOR TEA: THE KANYAM TEA FACTORY

The **tea factory** at **Kanyam**, built using British aid money in 1985, is the largest in the district. Once inside you're likely to be welcomed with a short **tour** (daily 10am–5pm; free) and a cup of tea – you'll have an opportunity to buy some before you leave. The plucked leaves are loaded into "withering chutes" upstairs, where fans remove about half their moisture content. They're then transferred to big rolling machines to break the cell walls and release their juices, and placed on fermentation beds to bring out their flavour and colour. Finally, most of the remaining moisture is removed in a wood-fired drying machine, and the leaves are sorted into grades. Ilam's premium tea compares favourably with Darjeeling's, and indeed most of it is exported to Germany to be blended into "Darjeeling" teas. Kanyam is an hour and a half from Ilam by jeep, bus or microbus.

6

ILAM

■ ACCOMMODATION
Danfe Guest House **2**
Green View Guest House **1, 3**

Tea Gardens

BIRENDRA
CHOWK

Haat
Bazaar

Old Tea
Factory

Bus
Park

N

Playing
Field

0   100
metres

Biblete, Phidim & Mai Pokhari ▲

◀ Sanumba

Maibeni ▶

◀ Sanumba

Mahendra Highway ▶

▼ Bindyabasini Mandir

Ilam tea gardens

Ilam's **tea gardens** carpet the ridge above town and tumble down its steep far side. Between April and November, you can watch the pickers at work. The tea estate – Nepal's first – was established in 1864 by a relative of the prime minister after a visit to Darjeeling, where tea cultivation was just becoming big business. Marwaris soon assumed control of the plantation, an arrangement that lasted until the 1960s when the government nationalized this and six other hill estates. In 1999, however, the government sold the estates to an Indian company. As a result, the 140-year-old tea factory in Ilam town was closed and workers lost their pensions, but production increased.

Mai Valley

The **Mai Valley**, which Ilam overlooks, is renowned for its **birds**: the dense, wet habitat and abundant undergrowth provide cover for some 450 species. To see anywhere near that number, you'll need a guide (you can hire one locally, or beforehand in Kathmandu, Chitwan or Koshi Tappu; around Rs2000/day). Lowland species such as drongos, bulbuls and flycatchers are best observed in the Sukarni forest southwest of Ilam, below the Soktim tea estate. Temperate birds inhabit the oak-rhododendron forest of the upper Mai Valley to the northeast, from Mabu up to **Sandakpur** on the Indian border, at elevations of 2000m to 3000m. There are three daily jeep departures (early morning, noon, and late afternoon) which struggle up from Ilam up to Sandakpur, where there is basic lodge accommodation.

ARRIVAL AND DEPARTURE ILAM AND AROUND

By bus There are buses to Birtamod (hourly; 3–4hr), Dharan (3 daily; 6hr) and Phidim (2 daily; 2hr), plus a single night bus to Kathmandu (27–28hr). Birtamod has more frequent bus services to points in the Eastern Terai. Services can be very crowded.

By jeep You can also take a shared jeep to Birtamod; these are somewhat quicker than the buses, but are often full.

WALKS AROUND ILAM

Rewarding **walks** set off in several directions around Ilam. From the tea gardens, you can contour westwards and cross the **Puwamai Khola**, ascending the other side to **Sanrumba**, site of a Tuesday market, with views of Kanchenjunga from further along the ridge. A trail heading east from Ilam descends to cross the **Mai Khola**, where the annual Beni Mela attracts thousands of Hindus on the first day of Magh (mid-Jan), and continues on to **Naya Bazaar**.

Atop a wooded ridge north of Ilam, the sacred pond of **Mai Pokhari** (considered the sacred abode of the goddess Bhagawati) can be reached by walking or hitching 6km along the road towards Phidim and turning right at a signpost (and map of the area) 2km from the **Biblete** bazaar. From there it's another 11km ascent (around 2–3hr) along a very rocky road, passing through rhododendron and magnolia forest, as well as beautifully kept villages and a couple of tea estates. Once at the top, you can spend an hour strolling through the moist pine forest that surrounds the pond, where there are also a couple of small temples. There's a clean, basic **lodge**, as well as a few *chai* shops opposite the entrance. Although there's only one daily scheduled jeep between Mai Pokhari and Ilam (coming down in the morning and returning late afternoon), it's fairly easy to hitch up or down – as long as you don't mind the bone-juddering ride or sitting on a sack of flour.

6

ACCOMMODATION

Danfe Guest House Near Ilam centre ☎ 027 520 048. Rooms in this classic bare-bones trekking inn are spartan, but acceptable for a night or two. The owners are a friendly family and the location among the tea bushes is superb. *Daal bhaat* is available at mealtimes. **Rs300**

Green View Guest House Ilam centre ☎ 027 520 103.

The most comfortable lodge in town, *Green View* now has two buildings. The cheaper old building has spacious rooms with private bathrooms (with hot water) and TVs; try to get one with a balcony overlooking the tea gardens. The new building is closer to town and has much swankier fan rooms for Rs1500, and a/c rooms for Rs3000 . **Rs850**

Trekking

THORUNG LA, ANNAPURNA CIRCUIT

Trekking

The soaring Himalayas are, to many travellers' minds, the chief reason for visiting Nepal. The country tumbles precipitously down from the 800km stretch of the Himalayan battlements that forms its northern border, and can claim no fewer than eight of the world's ten highest peaks – including, of course, Everest, the highest of them all. The mountains are more than just physically stupendous, however. The cultures of highland-dwelling Nepalese peoples are rich and fascinating, and the relaxed, companionable spirit of trekking life is an attraction in itself. The Himalayas have long exerted a powerful spiritual pull, too. In Hindu mythology, the mountains are where gods go to meditate, while the Sherpas and other mountain peoples hold certain summits to be the very embodiment of deities.

Most visitors to mountain areas stick to a few well-established **trekking routes**. They have good reasons for doing so: the classic trails of the Everest and Annapurna regions are popular because they offer close-up views of the very highest peaks, dramatic scenery and fascinating local cultures. Lodges on the main trails make it possible to go without carrying a lot of gear, learning Nepali or spending too much money. There are also plenty of less-developed routes, of course, and simply going out of season or taking a side route off the main trail makes a huge difference.

Almost two-thirds of trekkers make for the **Annapurna region**, north of Pokhara, with its spectacular scenery, ease of access and variety of treks. The **Everest region**, in the near east of the country, is one of Nepal's most exciting areas and attracts roughly a quarter of trekkers, although altitude and distance from the trailheads make shorter treks less viable. The **Helambu** and **Langtang** regions are less dramatic but conveniently close to Kathmandu, attracting fewer than ten percent of trekkers. This leaves vast areas of **eastern and far western Nepal** relatively untrodden by visitors. To walk in these areas you'll need either to be prepared to camp and carry your own supplies, and live like a local, or pay to join an organized trek with tents and accept the compromises that go along with that. With a good agency, you can go just about anywhere. A Great Himalayan Trail now runs the length of highland Nepal – though it will be many years, if ever, before such a route will be fully serviced by lodges.

AMA DABLAM, KHUMBU

Highlights

❶ The Annapurna Sanctuary One of the most popular treks, and for good reason: the trail penetrates a steep, wooded gorge, emerging into a secret high-mountain cirque. **See p.323**

❷ Foothill approaches Many trekkers come for the mountains, but they go away with powerful memories of the terraced hills, Nepal's cultural heartland. **See p.326 & p.344**

❸ Mustang Hiding in the rain shadow of the Annapurna massif, this restricted area is a perfect slice of Tibet. **See p.329 & p.353**

❹ The Manaslu Circuit As the Annapurna Circuit is diminished by the road, Manaslu is

emerging as the awe-inspiring and still underdeveloped replacement. **See p.333**

❺ Khumbu Even if it wasn't capped by Everest, the lofty and colourful Buddhist Sherpa country of Khumbu would be one of the highlights of a trip to Nepal. **See p.339**

❻ Pangpema Base camp for the north face of Kanchenjunga, deep in a protected wilderness – you can't get more remote than this. **See p.349**

❼ Going off-piste Whether you do it with the help of a guide, an agency or simply a willingness to embrace truly local accommodation, just stepping off the main trail is one of the most rewarding things you can do. **See p.351**

HIGHLIGHTS ARE MARKED ON THE MAP ON PP.306–307

TWELVE MONTHS OF DISASTERS

Nepal suffered three terrible natural disasters in just over twelve months in 2014 and 2015, each of which seriously impacted the country's trekking and mountaineering communities. On April 18, 2014, at the start of Everest's annual climbing season, sixteen Sherpas were killed in an **avalanche** in the Khumbu Icefall. It was the single deadliest accident on the mountain, which was closed for the rest of the season, and the disaster inflamed long-standing pay and safety concerns. In October, at least 41 people died when **freak blizzards** and avalanches swept across the Annapurna region; over five hundred trekkers were airlifted to safety. In the wake of the disaster, the Nepali authorities announced several safety measures ahead of the 2015 trekking season: all trekkers will be required to hire a trained local guide, rent a GPS tracking unit, and register at checkpoints when entering and exiting trekking areas. The impact – and indeed longevity – of these measures remains to be seen, and there may well be more on the way.

  The inherent risks that come with trekking and climbing in the Himalayas were tragically reiterated by the April 25, 2015 **earthquake** (see box, p.6), which caused avalanches on Everest and flattened base camp, killing scores of people and leaving many more stranded.

7

When to go

Where you go trekking depends hugely on when you go. The following seasonal descriptions are generalizations: Annapurna is notoriously wetter than regions further east, and climate change – which is already hitting the Himalayas hard – is having unpredictable effects. There have been freak dry winters in Khumbu, and serious snowstorms in April, after the spring.

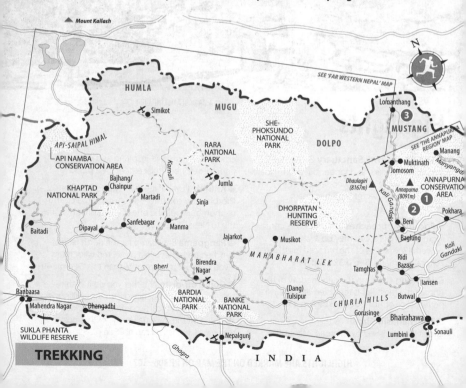

The peak seasons

Autumn (early Oct to early Dec) is the peak season: generally dry, stable and very clear, although there can be the odd shower or freak autumn storm. It gets progressively colder at night higher up, but the chill is rarely severe until December and daytime temperatures are pleasantly cool for walking; at low elevations it can be distinctly hot. The fine conditions mean that the main Annapurna and Everest trails will be busy: porters will charge top dollar, flights will be tight and guides will race ahead to book up lodges – forcing some independent trekkers to carry on up the trail to the next village to find a bed. The other drawback is the general lack of greenery on the freshly ploughed terraces in the Middle Hills. In general, autumn is a good time to think about getting off the beaten track.

After winter, temperatures and the snow line rise steadily during **spring** (Feb–April). The warmer weather also brings more trekkers, though not nearly as many as in autumn. The main factor that keeps the numbers down is a disappointing haze that creeps up in elevation during this period, plus the occasional sudden downpour (or freak snowstorm) and sometimes unpleasant afternoon winds. By April, you probably won't get good views until you reach 4000m or so, though this is also the time when the most colourful rhododendrons bloom, generally between 2000m and 3000m.

The off seasons

Winter (Dec–Jan) is for the most part dry and settled, albeit colder. When precipitation does fall, the snow line drops to 2500m and sometimes lower. Passes over 4000m (including the highest on the Annapurna Sanctuary and Circuit treks) may be impassable due to snow and ice, and some settlements described in trekking guidebooks may be uninhabited. High-altitude treks, such as Everest, require good gear and experience in cold-weather conditions, as temperatures at 5000m can drop below minus 20°C and heavy snow can fall. If you're up to it, however, this can be a magical time to trek: trekkers are much scarcer (some treks see something like twenty or thirty times the numbers of trekkers in autumn as in midwinter), and below 2000m temperatures can be quite spring-like, though valleys are often filled with fog or haze.

7

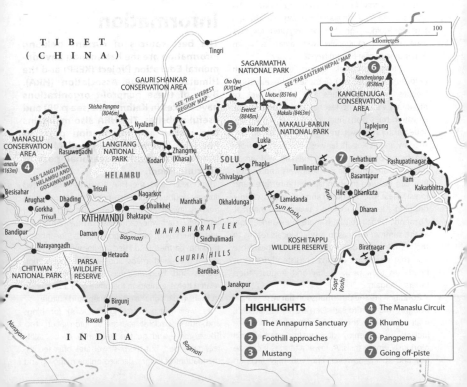

HIGHLIGHTS

1. The Annapurna Sanctuary
2. Foothill approaches
3. Mustang
4. The Manaslu Circuit
5. Khumbu
6. Pangpema
7. Going off-piste

7

CONSERVATION TIPS

Your impact, as a trekker, is heavier than you might imagine. It's not just a question of litter, sanitation and path erosion: outside conservation areas where wood-burning is prohibited, it's estimated that one trekker consumes, directly and indirectly, between five and ten times more wood per day than a Nepali. The following are suggestions on how to **minimize your impact** on the fragile Himalayan environment.

- Where the choice exists, eat at places that cook with kerosene, electricity or propane instead of wood. If trekking with an agency, complain if wood is being used.
- Bring plenty of warm clothes so you (and your porter) are less reliant on wood fires.
- Try to coordinate meal orders with other trekkers; cooking food in big batches is more efficient.
- Avoid hot showers except where the water is heated by electricity, solar panels or fuel-efficient "back boilers".
- Treat your own drinking water rather than relying on bottled or boiled. Plastic bottles are not recycled in Nepal.
- Use latrines wherever possible. Where there's no facility, go well away from water sources, bury your faeces and burn your toilet paper (or use water, as Nepalis do).
- Use phosphate-free soap and shampoo, and don't rinse directly in streams.
- Deposit litter in designated rubbish bins, where they exist. Elsewhere, carry back all non-burnable litter: tins, plastic bottles and especially batteries.

During May and June it gets hotter, hazier and increasingly unsettled. The warming Asian land mass has begun drawing air up from the south, ushering in the **pre-monsoon** – a season of erratic weather and increasingly frequent afternoon storms. The trails and lodges again begin to empty out. This is a time for going high, but be prepared for rain, especially in traditionally wet areas such as Annapurna and far eastern Nepal.

Few foreigners trek during the **monsoon** (mid-June to early Sept), because of the rain, mud, leeches, travel difficulties and general lack of mountain views. (The leeches along the middle-elevation trails won't hurt you, but are not for the squeamish.) However, treks in the Himalayan rain shadow and in Nepal's far west are sheltered from the brunt of the monsoon. Even in wet areas, mornings are often clear, wildflowers and butterflies can be seen in abundance, the terraces and forests are a luscious green and the soundscape – dripping leaves, roaring rivers – magical. Authentic Nepali culture is more in evidence, too, as the summer off-season is when locals return to their farming and other traditional activities. Note also that the monsoon isn't consistently rainy: it builds up to a peak in July and August, then tapers off again.

Conditions in the post-monsoon **harvest** season (roughly mid-Sept to early Oct) are hard to predict: it all depends on the timing of the rains. If you're lucky, you can enjoy clear, warm weather and gloriously empty trails. At lower altitudes it can be hot and sticky, however, and you may face an extended monsoon tail, with clouds obscuring the peaks and heavy afternoon showers or snow flurries higher up.

Information

The best sources of current trekking information are the Kathmandu Environmental Education Project (KEEP) and the Himalayan Rescue Association (HRA). Both of these nonprofit organizations have offices in Kathmandu (see p.98) and useful websites. The HRA also maintains two rescue and information posts at Pheriche (Everest region) and Manang (Annapurna), with a seasonal post at Thorung Phedi.

Both KEEP and the HRA have trekking-related libraries, logbooks full of comments from returning trekkers (invaluable for tips on routes and trekking agencies), staff who can advise on trail conditions and equipment, and notice boards for finding trekking partners and used equipment. KEEP also sells books and maps, iodine water-purification tablets and biodegradable and other trekking-related items; exhibits in the office give a primer on trekkers' impact on the environment and culture.

It's well worth searching the web for blogs and other specialist sources of information, too. These come and go too frequently to be safely recommended, but the best websites offer recommendations of lodges, detailed online mapping and notice boards where people just back from a trek share information and tips.

ONLINE RESOURCES

Ⓦ **everestnews.com** Expedition reports, climber profiles and extensive info on Everest and other major peaks.

Ⓦ **high-altitude-medicine.com** Good info on high-altitude health, with links.

Ⓦ **himalayanrescue.org** The Himalayan Rescue Association (HRA)'s site: the best information on health, altitude and helicopter rescue.

Ⓦ **ippg.net** The International Porter Protection Group builds shelters, provides warm clothing and medicine and offers excellent online guidelines on the ethical employment of porters.

Ⓦ **keepnepal.org** Tips on environmentally sensitive trekking from the Kathmandu Environmental Education Project (KEEP).

Ⓦ **mountainexplorers.org** The International Mountain Explorers Connection's website features trip reports and a newsletter, plus information on volunteer opportunities and on the Porter Assistance Project, which provides warm clothing to porters.

Ⓦ **nepalmountaineering.org** Information on expedition and trekking peaks from the Nepal Mountaineering Association, which runs the permit scheme as well as mountaineering courses.

Ⓦ **taan.org.np** Site of the Trekking Agents' Association of Nepal, with useful (if not always up to date) information on permits, fees and other bureaucracy.

Ⓦ **thegreathimalayatrail.org** Detailed site covering the country-length Great Himalaya Trail and trekking in Nepal in general –

with a good notice board for finding trek buddies.

Ⓦ **trekinfo.com** The leading general-purpose site, with a host of links and an excellent forum site (at trekinfo.com/forums/) which offers recent route descriptions, companion-finding and endorsements of (and warnings about) guides.

Ⓦ **trekkingpartners.com** Useful notice board site – better for finding partners than guides.

Books and maps

Although the **main trails** are generally pretty clear, this chapter is not intended to take the place of a detailed **guidebook** to an individual trek, still less a full-size, fold-out **map** with contour lines, minor trails and all the rest. Buying both would be a very good idea, for safety's sake alone, even when you have a guide with you.

All trekking **guidebooks** can be bought in Kathmandu, and most of them in Pokhara. You'll also find an increasing number of Nepalese-published guides: the *Himalayan Travel Guides* series is generally good. Given how infrequently most trekking guides can realistically be updated, it's worth going on the date of the last revision as much as your individual preference for the style. There is a list of specialist trekking guides in our bibliography (see p.426).

7

TREKKING LIFE: WHAT TO EXPECT

Many first-timers are surprised that most treks are not wilderness experiences. The Himalayas are incredibly well settled, for the most part, and typically it's only when crossing the highest passes, or on the final pull up to a base camp, that trails pass through barren, unpopulated country. This makes trekking **relatively safe**. That said, even in populated areas you are committed to walking for hours every day, sometimes in uncomfortably sweaty or frigid conditions, and occasionally on steep, slippery or alarmingly narrow trails. Some trekkers find suspension footbridges terrifying. Others find the bumpy journey by road to the trailhead – or the possibly bumpier flight to the airstrip – the worst bit (and these probably are the riskiest parts of any trek, objectively speaking).

Fitness is less of an issue than you might think, as you can walk at your own pace, ambling from one glass of *chiya* to the next. Most trekkers set off early each morning to make the most of the clear weather (clouds usually roll in around midday), which makes afternoons typically leisurely affairs, fitting in a short side trip or monastery visit around snacks, games of cards, reading, journal-writing and the rest. Evenings are usually cheerfully communal, as everyone tends to huddle in the relative warmth of the dining hall (or mess tent, if you're camping) ordering a steady stream of dishes and hot drinks. Bedtimes usually come early.

Everyone treks in their own way, but there are a few tips for how to get the best from a trip. Allow space in your schedule for **rest days**, weather and contingencies, and make sure you do at least one **side trip**. Some of the most fascinating or beautiful sights – monasteries, villages, waterfalls, glaciers – are tucked away up side valleys, and walking even a few steps away from the main trail can take you back virtual decades, in terms of development and commercialization. Instead of ordering pizza from a menu, you may find yourself sitting round the fire with a local family sipping a mug of *chhang*. Many trekkers find they enjoy these interactions with local people as much as they love the mountains.

Maps

Nepal's trekking regions are fairly well **mapped**, although you get what you pay for – and none currently shows an up-to-date road network. The best product for a particular trek will vary from year to year, as companies leapfrog past each other with new editions. Currently, the locally produced (and widely available) *NepaMaps* series is the clearest and is fairly up to date, although there are some howling errors and the maps can't be relied upon for off-trail route-finding. *National Geographic* do a similar job with their "Nepal Adventure Map" series, though they only cover the main regions. The pricier *Geo-Buch* ("Schneider") maps of the Everest and Langtang/Helambu areas have much more reliable contours and topographical details, though they're way out of date for villages and roads.

For more obscure treks, try the *HMG/FINNIDA* maps – they're superb and not too expensive, though they're not designed specifically for trekking, are terribly out of date in terms of new roads and are only patchily available in tourist bookshops.

Trekking independently

Trekking independently – making all your own arrangements, carrying your own pack and staying in lodges – saves money and may give you more freedom or flexibility on the trail. In terms of route choice, however, it's more limiting than an organized trek. In the wake of the 2014 Annapurna trekking disaster (see box, p.306), the Nepali authorities announced that all independent trekkers would be required to hire a trained local guide, although at the time of writing it was unclear whether this policy would be formally enacted.

Trekking independently gives you more **control** over many aspects of the trek: you can go at your own pace, stop when and where you like, choose your travelling companions and take rest days or side trips as you please. The downside is that you have to spend a day or three lining up bus or plane tickets, renting equipment, buying supplies and tracking down a guide (and perhaps a porter). Trekking to remote areas is also difficult (see p.347).

An independent trek is also likely to be less comfortable than one arranged through an agency. Lodges can be noisy and lacking in privacy, and there may be long waits for food of dubious quality. The active **social scene** in lodges goes a long way to compensating for this, however.

By not being part of a group, you're better placed to learn from Nepali ways rather than forcing local people to adapt to yours. Equally important, a high proportion of the money you spend goes directly to the local economy (whereas most of the money paid to trekking agencies goes no further than Kathmandu, and often finds its way overseas). However, as an independent trekker you must guard against contributing to **deforestation**. If you or your porters or guides order meals cooked over wood fires, you encourage innkeepers to cut down more trees. Fortunately, kerosene is replacing wood in the most popular areas.

FLIGHTS TO MOUNTAIN AIRSTRIPS

Flying to a **mountain airstrip** such as Jomosom or Lukla is one of the most thrilling things you can do in Nepal (possibly a bit too exciting in the case of the flight to Lukla, which is perilously short and, disturbingly, faces right into the mountainside). It's increasingly possible to book domestic flights online, but you might not want to expose your credit card in this way, so get your guide, guesthouse or any reputable trekking or travel agency to do it for you. **Prices** are standard, within a dollar or two. All mountain flights are subject to frequent **delays and cancellations**, usually due to clouds or high wind. If your flight is cancelled, your ticket remains valid, but you'll be put on a waiting list rather than on the next departure. Plan for delays, and always try to book the earliest flight available: if a weather window does open, you'll be the first through it. To or from Lukla, where there are three rounds of flights every morning, this means booking early and asking for "first flight, first round". If you have to cancel a booked flight yourself, make sure you get a **"cancellation stamp"** (from the ticket agent or at the airstrip), otherwise you'll be counted as a no-show and lose all your money; cancellations otherwise cost a third of the fare. Note that Nepal has a lamentable **air safety** record (see p.25), and there have been several accidents involving the mountain airstrips.

SEXUAL POLITICS IN THE MOUNTAINS

The vast majority of Nepali guides are meticulously respectful, but there are very occasional reports that guides have **sexually harassed** female clients. This may be partly the result of perceptions about Western sexual behaviour, and an unfortunate consequence of the fact that a number of women do hook up with Nepali boyfriends, leading to over-eager expectations. The best way to avoid problems is to follow the recommendations of people you trust, insist on meeting the guide before hiring, bring along a trekking partner, and nip any unwanted advances in the bud. You might also consider hiring a female guide (see p.214). If you do sleep with a guide, be aware that this may well not be their first time, and rates of HIV infection in Nepal are rising fast.

Costs

The biggest single cost, aside from permits and park fees (see p.313) is likely to be **transport**. Public buses to the major trailheads usually cost anything up to about Rs700, but if you choose to hire a taxi or, where it's possible, buy a seat in a shared jeep to get further up the trail, the costs can mount up. Single plane fares to mountain airstrips (see box, p.311) are almost all in the $90–150 range, though tickets to some of the very remotest airstrips can be a little more expensive, and if you need to touch down anywhere on the way, you have to buy a separate ticket.

Unless you seek out luxurious lodges, the cost of **lodging** is negligible (see p.314), and there's very little else to spend your money on besides a porter or guide and **food**. Provisions (for those camping) and basic, local meals are both inexpensive; if you're off the beaten track expect to spend around $20–25 a day. On the major Everest and Annapurna trails, however, food costs can add up, and the daily budget is more likely to be $30–35, and could easily rise if you choose rooms with attached bathrooms and order pizzas, chips, beer and the like. Beer in particular is expensive, and, like food, goes up in price as you ascend away from the road. Hiring a **porter** will add considerably to your daily cost (see below).

Guides

The best **guides** have detailed, impassioned knowledge of wildlife and local culture; the worst are city kids with a barely concealed contempt for rural life. Some may steer you to certain lodges, and restrict your contact with local people by conducting all negotiations on your behalf – you want to avoid this, as a good guide should act as a translator and facilitator. Some, but not all, guides are willing to carry gear as well. Many carry first-aid kits, and good ones know how to use them.

The **hiring** process is informal, so shop around: ask for recommendations from fellow travellers, people who have just returned from Nepal or online. You could also visit **KEEP** (see p.98) or go through an agency. Guesthouses almost always have guide contacts, too. Try to interview more than one candidate, and take the time to talk a while, maybe over tea or a meal, to get a feel for whether you'll get along. Trust your instincts and don't settle on someone you don't feel right about: you're going to be spending a lot of time together. A guide who's actually from the area you plan to trek in is often preferable to one who's not, because he or she will have family and friends along the way and will be respected by the local people.

Trekking agencies pay their guides a pittance of around $15–20 a day (which doesn't leave them much after costs) and are likely to charge you at least $30–40. If you're employing a guide directly, $30 would be a fair wage, with guides funding their own expenses. Guides on longer treks and those with good language skills or perhaps wildlife expertise may command slightly higher wages. Be clear whether or not any agreed amount includes food and drink (it may avoid problems if guides pay for themselves) and don't pay too much up front: fifty percent is pretty standard. Expect to give your guide a ten percent **tip**, assuming the work was well done, and bear in mind that their work is difficult and sometimes dangerous.

If you've never hiked in Nepal before, don't try to organize a trek off the well-trodden routes. Finding a guide familiar with a particular area will be hard, and transporting him with a crew of porters and supplies to the trailhead a major (and expensive) logistical exercise. Getting a trekking agency to do it might not cost much more.

Porters

Porters – with their characteristic *doko* baskets carried on a *naamlo*, or tumpline round the head – are an important part of the Himalayan economy. There's no shame in hiring one. With a porter taking most of your gear, you only have to carry a small pack containing the things you need during

7

ETHICAL EMPLOYMENT OF PORTERS AND GUIDES

The **responsibilities** of employing a porter or guide cannot be overstated. Porters, especially, are some of the poorest people in Nepal. Most do a back-breaking job only because they have no alternative, and the vast majority are illiterate and landless. They are typically able to get work for less than eighty days a year, and are at significant risk of injury or ill health. When hiring, don't over-negotiate: Rs100 a day is trivial to you, but can make a huge difference to your porter. You should also ensure that your porter has health and life **insurance**: agencies should do this as standard, and if you're hiring independently this can be easily and inexpensively arranged through an agency. For more information, speak to the International Porter Protection Group (IPPG) – contactable via the HRA (see p.98).

Several porters die needlessly each year, typically because their *sahib* (pronounced "sahb") thought they wouldn't mind sleeping outside in a blizzard. You must make sure your employees are adequately **clothed** for the journey – on high-altitude treks, this will mean buying or renting them good shoes and socks, a parka, sunglasses, mittens and a sleeping bag. Establish beforehand if something is a loan. You must check that they have proper **shelter**. If they get **sick**, it's up to you to look after them – including making sure they are not paid off and sent down without anyone checking on their fitness first. Since many porters hired in Kathmandu and Pokhara will know little about altitude-related problems, it's your responsibility to be aware of all the facts. It's also important not to **overload** porters. Some are capable of bearing wondrous loads, but 30kg is an accepted maximum; it may need to be reduced according to your porters' age and fitness.

---

the day; this can be a great relief at hot or high elevations, and it may be essential in remote mountain areas, where tents, cooking equipment and serious amounts of food may have to be brought in.

Hiring a porter is simple enough: just ask at your guesthouse, a reputable trekking agency or an equipment-rental shop. Hiring someone off the street is riskier, but it will save you money and the porter will end up better off too. If you start out without help and change your mind later, you will be able to hire a porter at one of the major trailside settlements, such as Namche and Manang.

A typical **wage** for a porter is about Rs1000 a day, though those hired through agencies or middlemen may cost significantly more, and porters higher on the Everest trail may charge Rs1200–1500. Porters generally pay for their own food and lodging; be aware that this can cost them Rs220–440 (Rs400–600 in the Everest region), so **tips** are crucial. You should tip anything from ten to twenty percent, and many trekkers also give spare gear or clothing at the end of the trek, or make donations to organizations like KEEP (see p.98).

Organized treks

Organized treks are useful for people who haven't got the time or inclination to make their own arrangements. Although they limit your freedom on the trail, they do have the advantage of taking you off the beaten track. Recommended organized trekking agencies are listed on p.22, p.98 and p.213.

If booked in Nepal, an organized trek will **cost** from around $60–70 a day (for a basic Annapurna or Langtang trek), to around $80–90 (for a basic Everest Base Camp trek), or more like $110–150 a day for more remote camping routes. Prices don't include **flights**, though, and vary considerably depending on the standard of service, size of the group and whether you're in tents or lodges. The price should always include a guide, porters, food and shelter, although cheap outfits often charge extra for things like national park fees and transport, and may cut other corners as well. The lower the price, the more wary you need to be.

A trek is hard work however you do it, but a good company will help you along with a few **creature comforts**: you can expect appetizing food, "bed tea" and hot "washing water" on cold mornings, camp chairs and a latrine tent with toilet paper. Depending on the size of your party, a guide, *sirdar* (guide foreman) or Western trek leader will be able to answer questions and cope with problems. Trekking groups usually sleep in **tents**, which, while quieter than lodges, may be colder and are certainly more cramped. The daily routine of eating as a group can get monotonous, and gives you **less contact** with local people. There's something to be said for safety in numbers, but trekking with a group imposes a somewhat **inflexible itinerary** on you, and if you don't like the people in your group, you're stuck.

In theory, organized treks are more **environmentally sound**, at least in the national parks and conservation areas, where trekkers' meals are supposed to be cooked with kerosene. Sometimes, however, cooks use wood so they can sell the kerosene at the end of the trek – and, worse still, for each trekker eating a kerosene-cooked meal, there may be two or three porters and other staff cooking their *bhaat* over a wood fire.

But the main advantage of organized trekking is it enables you to get **off the beaten track**. A number of companies now offer "wilderness" or "nature" treks, which forsake the traditional village-to-village valley routes for obscure trails along uninhabited ridgelines or through forested areas, often with experienced wildlife enthusiasts as guides. Shop around and you'll also find special-interest treks based around Tibetan Buddhism, birdwatching, rhododendron-viewing, and trail construction or clean-up. Many companies also run trips that combine trekking with rafting, cycling and wildlife-viewing.

Agents and operators

Trekking operators are notoriously hard to recommend: many are fly-by-night set-ups who represent themselves as trekking specialists when in fact they're merely agents, taking a commission and providing very little service for it. A few of the more established budget companies run scheduled treks, but again, usually only to the most popular areas. In this category, names change often and standards can quickly rise and fall. Kathmandu's **big operators** (see p.98) mainly package treks on behalf of overseas agencies, but they may allow "walk-ins" to join at a reduced price. They also offer camping treks specifically for the local market, typically priced at around $110–130 a day for camping treks in the Annapurna region, or $130–150 for Everest Base Camp. For customized treks to exotic areas, make contact several months in advance.

Booking through an **overseas agency** (see p.22) lets you arrange everything before you leave home, and may not cost all that much more: expect to pay upwards of $100 per day for a teahouse trek. Some agencies have their own Nepali subsidiaries in Kathmandu, others effectively subcontract. Overseas agencies will look after all your arrangements up until the time you leave your home country, and will also play a part in maintaining quality control in Nepal. Some may allow you to join up in Kathmandu at a reduced price.

Park fees and red tape

Trekking permits are no longer required for most areas, including all the standard routes in the Annapurna, Everest and Langtang/Helambu/Gosainkund areas. You will, however, need to register for a TIMS card – a kind of trekkers' register – and pay a national park or conservation area entry fee. Organized treks will do this for you.

Before setting off on any trek, **register** with your embassy in Kathmandu, as this will speed things up should you need rescuing. You can have KEEP (see p.98) or the HRA (see p.98) forward the details to your embassy.

National Park and Conservation Area fees

If your trek goes through any of the **national parks** or conservation areas, and almost all treks do, you'll

---

QUESTIONS TO ASK TREKKING COMPANIES

Trekking companies in Nepal speak the green lingo as fluently as anyone, but in many cases their walk doesn't match their talk. Here are some specific **questions** to ask to find out what they're actually doing to minimize their impact on the environment. You may not find a company able to answer every question, but the exercise should help establish which outfits are genuinely concerned.

• Do they carry enough kerosene to cook all meals for all members of the party, including porters?
• What equipment do they provide to porters? Tents, proper clothing, shoes, UV sunglasses?
• Do they carry out all non-burnable/non-biodegradable waste?
• How many of their staff have certificates from the Kathmandu Environmental Education Project's (KEEP) eco-trekking workshop? Have they attended courses with the Trekking Agencies' Association of Nepal (TAAN) or Nepal Mountaineering Association?
• Does the guide have certificated wilderness first-aid training?

7

FEES FOR REMOTE AREAS

Permits are required for treks that pass through certain **remote areas**, and these can only be arranged through registered agencies – which means going with a registered guide and, usually, on a fully equipped camping trek. The situation sometimes changes, so check for updates at the Trekking Agencies' Association of Nepal (Ⓦ taan.org.np) or at the Department of Immigration (Ⓦ nepalimmigration.gov.np).

- **Lower Dolpo, Kanchenjunga, and Gauri Shankar** (ie Dolakha district, just west of the Everest region) $10/week
- **Makalu** $10/week for the first four weeks and then $20/week
- **Chekampar and Chumchet** (below Ganesh Himal, north of Gorkha) Sept–Nov $35/8 days; Dec–Aug $25
- **Mount Kailash** (ie all of Humla District) $50/week, then $7/day
- **Manaslu** Sept–Nov $70/week, then $10/day; Dec–Aug $50/$7
- **Nar-Phu (near Manang)** Sept–Nov $90/week; Dec–Aug $75
- **Upper Mustang and Upper (Inner) Dolpo** $500 for the first ten days, then $50/day

---

have to buy an **entry ticket**. The proceeds go towards important conservation work, from tree nurseries and path maintenance to local education on sustainable lodge management. **Fees** for all **national parks** (except Shivapuri National Park, outside Kathmandu) are Rs3000; Langtang and Everest's Sagarmatha National Park fees are payable at the entry checkposts at Dhunche and Monjo, respectively. The **Annapurna Conservation Area Project**, **Manaslu Conservation Area** and **Kanchenjunga Conservation Area** charge Rs2000 entry, which you should pay in advance at the ACAP offices in Kathmandu (in the Tourist Service Center, Exhibition Rd, Bhikruti Mandap – see p.98) or Pokhara (in the Nepal Tourism Board, Damside – see p.213); bring your passport and a passport photograph. If you don't buy an ACAP permit in advance, you'll be charged double at the park gate. Children under ten receive free admission to all parks.

The TIMS card

Trekkers are obliged to buy a **TIMS** (Trekkers' Information Management System) card. It costs $20 to independent trekkers (known as FIT, or Free Independent Trekkers), or $10 to those booked on a group package; at the time of writing it was unclear how the new regulations proposed after the 2014 Annapurna trekking disaster (see box, p.306) would affect TIMS. The TIMS card is supposed to help the government know if anyone goes missing and to keep an eye on rogue companies; it's also a modest tourist tax. On organized tours it will be arranged for you by the agency. Independent trekkers can get their card from the Tourist Service Center offices in Kathmandu (see p.98) and at the Nepal Tourism Board in Pokhara (see p.213) –conveniently placed in the same building as the ACAP office, where you need to pay your park entry fee (see above) – or through TAAN, the Trekking Agencies' Association of Nepal, which has offices in Maligaon, Kathmandu, and Lakeside, Pokhara. You'll need your passport and two passport photos – the latter easily and inexpensively obtained in Thamel and Lakeside.

Accommodation

Trekking lodges are still sometimes called "teahouses" in guidebooks, though the traditional *bhatti*, or teashop with basic dormitory behind, is rare on the main trails. On all but the most remote routes, most lodges are efficient operations these days, with English signs, enticing menus, displays of flowers and usually an English-speaking proprietor.

Many are **family homes**, typically run by the matriarch with the help of local children, with a stone-and-wood annexe for lodging and a dining room off the family kitchen. In the Annapurna and Everest regions, however, fancy, purpose-built lodges are increasingly common: you'll find glazed sun terraces, electric lighting, kerosene heaters, telephones (satellite or otherwise, both with high per-minute prices), solar-powered hot showers, Western toilets and even wi-fi. An appealing alternative is the **community lodge**, set up on sustainable principles with the aim of spreading the benefits of tourism more widely.

Most lodges follow the Nepali tradition of providing inexpensive accommodation so long as you eat your meals in house – though note that while lodging (and food) **prices** in the Annapurna region are officially agreed, prices rise steeply as you gain altitude, and the Everest Base Camp route is relatively expensive. Lodges typically offer a basic wooden bed with a simple mattress or foam pad, a cotton pillow, and a blanket or quilt. On the main trails, many lodges now offer **private rooms**, though in busy seasons or at altitude these get full and you may find yourself sharing a **dormitory**. (Unroll your sleeping bag early to reserve your place, and relax: it's surprising how quickly most people adapt to shared sleeping space, and being physically tired helps hugely.) You'll find fewer comforts on less-trekked trails, where lodgings are likely to be basic teahouse dormitories, or even a bench by the kitchen fire, and meals are eaten amid eye-watering smoke.

Most lodges in the Annapurna and Everest regions have solar or electric-heated showers. Others will offer washing **water** that has been heated on a wood fire. Off the established routes or at higher elevations, you'll have to bathe and do laundry under makeshift outdoor taps or in a tin bucket, using freezing cold water. Most provide outdoor latrines (*chaarpi*), and a few even have indoor flush toilets, but don't be surprised if you're pointed to a half-covered privy hanging over a stream or basic pit.

There is little to be gained by recommending specific lodges in this chapter – in truth much depends on who is running the place on the day. It's best to ask advice from other trekkers coming back along your chosen route.

Food and drink

Trekking cuisine is a world unto itself. Although lodges' plastic-coated menus promise tempting international delicacies, such items may turn out to be "paindaina" (unavailable), and you'll notice that the spring rolls, enchiladas, pizzas and pancakes all bear more than a passing resemblance to chapatis.

But at any rate, eggs, porridge, muesli and noodles are reassuringly familiar, and the basic pasta and rice dishes always on offer are at least filling. Goodies like chocolate and biscuits are always available, too. In highland areas you'll be able to eat such **Tibetan dishes** as momo, thukpa and riki kur, and instead of porridge you might be served *tsampa* (see p.31). At lower elevations, *daal bhaat*, chow mein, packet noodles and seasonal vegetables are standard.

When **ordering**, bear in mind that the cook can only make one or two things at a time, and there may be many others ahead of you: simplify the process and save fuel by coordinating your order with other trekkers. *Daal bhaat* may be the most filling choice but also the slowest, as you may find yourself waiting till all the Western food orders are done. Most innkeepers expect orders to be placed several hours in advance, and there's usually a notepad floating around for keeping a tally of everything you've eaten; you pay on departure, or at breakfast. Eating dinner at a lodge other than the one where you're staying is very much frowned upon.

Tea and hot lemon are traditionally the main **drinks** on the trail, though coffee is found everywhere. Bottled soft drinks, bottled water and even beer are common along the popular routes, but the price of each bottle rises for each extra day it has to be portered from the nearest road. Don't miss trying *chhang*, *raksi* and *tongba* (see p.33), and the delicious apple cider and apple *raksi* sporadically available in the Everest and Jomosom regions.

Health

Guidebooks tend to go overboard about the health hazards of trekking, particularly altitude sickness. Don't be put off – the vast majority of trekkers never experience anything worse than a sore throat (common in high, dry air) and a mild headache. That said, trekking can be physically demanding, and may take you a week or more from the nearest medical facilities.

Children, seniors and people with disabilities have all trekked successfully, but a certain **fitness** level (or, failing that, bloody-mindedness) is required. Don't allow yourself to be talked into biting off more than you can chew or you'll have little fun and could get into trouble. It's certainly worth checking that your insurance policy doesn't exclude trekking, which may be listed as a hazardous sport. Check the policy on helicopter rescue as well.

Stomach troubles

The risk of **stomach troubles** is particularly high while trekking. Follow the general travel advice on fresh food and clean water (see p.38), and note that while innkeepers normally boil water and tea, it is not always for long enough, and at high altitudes the boiling point of water is so low that a longer boiling time is necessary. All running water should be assumed to be contaminated – almost wherever you go, there will be people, or at least animals, upstream. **Treating water** (see p.38) is not only the best line of defence against

7

FIRST-AID CHECKLIST

This is a minimum **first-aid kit**, and won't cope with serious injuries or emergencies. Most of the items can be bought inexpensively in Nepal. For self-diagnosis of diarrhoea or dysentery, and antibiotics and drugs to treat it, see the "Basics" chapter of this guide (p.39).

FOR INJURIES

Plasters/Band-Aids in large and small sizes
Vaseline Guards again friction blisters and chafing, and stops nostrils drying out in the cold
Gauze pads (or panty-liners), sterile dressing, steri-strips, surgical tape, swabs for wounds and large blisters
Moleskin or **"Second Skin"** synthetic adhesive padding for blisters
Elastic support bandages for knee strains and ankle sprains
Antiseptic cream for scrapes, blisters and insect bites
Tweezers, scissors

FOR ILLNESSES

Ibuprofen Pain relief for swollen joints and strained muscles
Throat lozenges Sore throats are common at high elevations
Diarrhoea tablets Blockers, such as Imodium, are useful; consider also bringing antibiotics for bacterial diarrhoea (see p.39)
Diamox Consider carrying this drug for treatment of AMS (see below)
Oral rehydration formula to replace fluids lost due to diarrhoea
Allergy tablets if you need them (especially in spring)

---

illness, it also reduces your reliance on boiled or bottled water, both of which cause significant environmental problems in mountain areas.

Minor injuries

Most minor injuries occur while walking downhill; **knee strains** are common, especially among trekkers carrying their own packs. If you know your knees are weak, bind them up with crepe (ace) bandages as a preventive measure, or hire a porter. Good, supportive boots reduce the risk of **ankle sprains** or twists, but the best prevention is just to pay careful attention to where you put your feet. A walking stick or hiking pole(s) can help, as can using Nepali technique: smaller, pitter-patter steps on steeper slopes.

It's hard to avoid getting **blisters**, but make sure your boots are well broken in. Some people swear by two pairs of socks. Airing your feet and changing socks regularly also helps: you can have one pair on while the other dries on the back of your pack. Apply Vaseline to rubbing spots and protective padding (moleskin is recommended) to sore spots as soon as they develop, making sure to clean and cover blisters so they can heal as quickly as possible.

Altitude

At high elevations, the combination of reduced oxygen and lower atmospheric pressure can produce a variety of unpredictable effects on the body – known collectively as acute mountain sickness (**AMS**) or, colloquially, "**altitude sickness**".

Barraged by medical advice and horror stories, trekkers all too often develop altitude paranoia. The fact is that just about everyone who treks over 4000m experiences some mild symptoms of AMS, but serious cases are very rare and the simple cure – descent – almost always brings immediate recovery. Up to around 4000m, very few people will experience anything worse than slowness, dizziness and headaches. That said, the syndrome varies hugely from one person to the next, and strikes without regard for fitness – in fact, young people seem to be more susceptible. It can be hard to monitor your own symptoms of altitude sickness, too: keep an eye on your trekking companions. For further advice on AMS, visit the Himalayan Rescue Association's aid posts at Manang (on the Annapurna Circuit) and Pheriche (on the Everest trek).

Prevention

The body can acclimatize to some very high elevations but it takes time and must be done in stages. The **golden rule** is don't go too high too fast. Above 3000m, experts recommend that the daily net elevation gain should be no more than 300–400m. Take mandatory acclimatization days at around 3500m and 4500m – more if you're feeling unwell – and try to spend them day-hiking higher. These are only guidelines, and you'll have to regulate your ascent according

THE THREE RULES OF ALTITUDE
- Know the early **symptoms** of acute mountain sickness (AMS) and be willing to recognize when you have them
- **Never ascend** to sleep at a higher altitude if you have any AMS symptoms
- If symptoms are worsening while at rest, **descend** immediately, no matter how late in the day

to how you feel. Trekkers who fly directly to high airstrips have to be especially careful to acclimatize.

Drink plenty of **liquids** at altitude, since the air is incredibly dry – unless you pee clear, you're probably not drinking enough. Keeping warm, eating well, getting plenty of sleep and avoiding alcohol will also help reduce the chances of developing AMS.

Symptoms

AMS usually gives plenty of warning before it becomes life-threatening. **Mild symptoms** include headaches, dizziness, racing pulse, nausea, loss of appetite, shortness of breath, disturbed sleep and swelling of the hands and feet. One or two of these symptoms is a sign that your body hasn't yet adjusted and you shouldn't ascend further until you start feeling better; if you do keep going, be prepared to beat a hasty retreat if the condition gets worse.

AMS is defined as **moderate** if the headache becomes severe and medication doesn't help, the nausea verges on vomiting, and coordination starts to suffer. At this point you want to start descending, as **severe AMS symptoms** can develop from moderate ones within hours; these can include all of the above, plus shortness of breath even while at rest, difficulty walking, mental confusion or lethargy, bubbly breathing or coughing, and bloody sputum. The worst case scenario is High Altitude Pulmonary or Cerebral Odema (HAPO/HACO), or potentially fatal build-up of fluids in the lungs or brain.

Descent and Diamox

The only cure for AMS is immediate **descent**. Anyone showing moderate or severe symptoms should be taken downhill immediately, regardless of the time of day or night – hire a porter or pack animal to carry the sufferer if necessary. Recovery is usually dramatic, often after a descent of only a few hundred vertical metres.

Acetazolamide (better known under the brand name **Diamox**) improves respiration at altitude, and can therefore accelerate acclimatization. (It also stimulates breathing, evening out the disturbing peaks and troughs of "periodic breathing" during sleep at altitude.) Some doctors recommend a preventive dose (125mg twice a day) for people trekking at high elevations, though note that

unpleasant side effects such as numbness, tingling sensations (Nepali guides call it *jhum jhum*) and light-headedness are not uncommon. To treat AMS, the dosage is 250mg every twelve hours. Note that Diamox is a diuretic, so it's all the more important to keep hydrated while taking it. And note too that while it can accelerate acclimatization, it won't stop AMS symptoms worsening if you keep on ascending.

Heat stroke, hypothermia and frostbite

Heat stroke is more common than you might think; drink plenty of water, eat something salty, wear a hat and rest. Other altitude-related dangers such as hypothermia and frostbite are encountered less often by trekkers, but can pose real threats on high, exposed passes or in bad weather. Common-sense precautions bear repeating: wear or carry adequate clothing; keep dry; cover exposed extremities in severe weather; eat lots and carry emergency snacks; and make for shelter if conditions get bad.

The symptoms of **hypothermia** are similar to those of AMS: slurred speech, fatigue, irrational behaviour and loss of coordination. Low body temperature is the surest sign. The treatment, in a word, is heat. Get the victim out of the cold, put him or her in a good sleeping bag (with another person, if necessary) and ply with warm food and drink.

Frostbite appears initially as small white patches on exposed skin, caused by local freezing. The skin will feel cold and numb. To treat, apply warmth (*not* snow!). Avoid getting frostbite a second time, as this can lead to permanent damage. **Snow blindness** shouldn't be a worry as long as you're equipped with a good pair of sunglasses. On snowy surfaces you'll need proper glacier glasses with side shields.

Emergencies

Serious trekking emergencies are rare, but illness, altitude sickness, storms, missteps, landslides and even avalanches can happen to anyone, as the Annapurna trekking disaster of 2014 tragically demonstrated (see box, p.306). In non-urgent

AVALANCHES

In the really well-trekked areas, **avalanches** are only a serious hazard in the Annapurna Sanctuary. Follow local advice and, if possible, ask for a crash course in how to recognize avalanche zones or gauge avalanche danger at one of the HRA posts.

7

cases, your best bet is to be carried by porter (around Rs2500 a day) or pack animal (around three times that) to the nearest airstrip or health post, although bear in mind that medical facilities outside Kathmandu and a few other major cities are very rudimentary. Locals are the best source of information as to the nearest and quickest way to access health care.

Where the situation is more serious, phone (or send word to the nearest village with a phone, satellite phone or police radio transmitter) to request a **helicopter rescue**. Write down and repeat your message as clearly as possible, indicating the severity of the problem as well as your location – ideally at the side of a large field for landing. Note that it could be 24 hours between an accident and a helicopter reaching you, partly because many helicopters can only fly in the early morning. Helicopter rescue costs in the region of US$2000 per hour, which means around US$2000 in the Annapurna region, or upwards of US$5000 if you're high on the Everest trail. Helicopters won't come until they're satisfied you'll be able to pay. This usually means finding a lodge owner willing to process your credit card, though it may also be possible if you have left a copy of your insurance documents with your embassy or trekking agency. Registering with your embassy will also speed the process of contacting relatives who can vouch for you.

Crime and personal safety

In terms of crime and personal safety, Nepal's hills are probably among the safer parts of the world. Travellers occasionally report luggage stolen or rifled on a bus to the roadhead, a tent or bedroom looted, or boots vanishing from outside a bedroom. With the end of the Maoist insurrection, and the return of police posts, violent crime is now relatively unusual, though inevitably every year there are a few muggings-with-menace and attacks (including sexual assaults).

Due to its accessibility and the volume of tourism, the **Annapurna region** has a slightly worse reputation than other areas, and there have been sporadic incidents in the **Birethanti–Ghandruk–Ghorepani** triangle. **Trekking alone** is likely to become a thing of the past in the wake of the Annapurna disaster (see box, p.306), but if solo trekking without a guide remains possible, note that trekking alone increases your risk of attracting unwanted criminal attention, and massively increases the potential seriousness of any injury. If for any reason you do end up walking alone, take a phone with you and leave information concerning your route ahead with lodges as you go. The simplest way to do this is to leave a note (with your full name) in the lodge's order book for meals – this also functions as the bill, so is kept carefully.

Equipment

Having the right equipment on a trek is obviously important, though when you see how little porters get by with, you'll realize high-tech gear isn't essential. Bring what you need to be comfortable, but keep weight to a minimum. Our checklist (see box, p.319) is intended mainly for independent trekkers staying in lodges. If you're planning to camp, you'll need more, and if you're trekking with an agency you won't need so much.

A **sleeping bag** is strongly recommended for all but the warmest seasons. Most lodges will supply quilts or blankets on demand, but you don't know who used the bedding last or what surprises might lurk therein – and if you're trekking a major route in peak season lodges can sometimes run out. A three-season bag is adequate for mid-elevation treks; above 4000m, or in winter, you'll need a four-season bag. A sleeping bag liner adds warmth, and makes cleaning much easier. **Camera** equipment involves a trade-off between weight and performance – and cold weather and stunning views can really eat up batteries. On the most popular trails, and often off them too, you can usually find somewhere with solar or other electricity to recharge camera batteries, often for a fee. Otherwise you'll need disposables or a portable solar charger (you can buy ones specifically designed to fit backpacks, for charging on the move). If you're taking an SLR body, be sure to bring a polarizing filter to cope with the Himalayan skies and snowfields.

By **renting** bulky or specialized items in Nepal, you'll avoid having to lug them around during the rest of your travels. Kathmandu and Pokhara both have dozens of rental places; if you're trekking in the Everest region, you can rent high-altitude gear in Namche. Even in Kathmandu, you might have trouble finding good gear of exactly the right size during the busy autumn trekking season. You'll be expected to leave a deposit. Inspect sleeping bags and parkas carefully for fleas and make sure zippers are in working order. You can also **buy** equipment quite cheaply.

Clothing and footwear

Clothes should be lightweight, versatile and breathable (cotton gets very sweaty), especially on long treks where conditions vary from subtropical to

---

WHAT TO BRING

All the items listed below can be bought in Kathmandu and Pokhara, though branded, top-quality clothing and gear is rarely much less expensive than at home. Kit marked (*) can be rented. If you're camping, of course, you'll need all the camping gear as well. If you're with an agency, you won't need some of the kit – for instance the medical kit, which guides should carry.

ESSENTIALS

Sunglasses – a good UV-protective pair, ideally with side shields if you expect to be in snow
Water bottle, plus **iodine** tablets or solution and/or a **water-purification system** – see p.38
Sleeping bag* – though you can get by with borrowed blankets on lower trails
Toiletries – including biodegradable soap/shampoo and toilet paper
Headtorch/flashlight – spare batteries are available on main trails
Backpack* – though if you're using a porter, any pack will do
Sunscreen, **lip balm** – at altitude you'll need a high factor
Medical kit – see p.316
Map and **guidebook**

FOOTWEAR AND SPECIALIST CLOTHING

Crampons and ice axes* – not needed on any standard treks, though should be considered, depending on season, for crossings of the Thorung La (Annapurna Circuit), Cho La (Everest) and other high, icy passes. Lightweight mini-crampons may be a good compromise if ice or snow is possible but unlikely
Waterproofs – breathable waterproofs are best, and provide crucial windproofing; you're unlikely to need waterproof trousers outside the wet season
Wool sweaters or **fleeces** – fleece dries quickly and stays warm when wet; close-fitting layers are much warmer than loose ones
Down jacket* – fantastic on high or late-autumn/winter treks; down overtrousers and booties are rarely needed

Thermals – warm, breathable (not cotton) long johns and vests are essential for high-altitude or winter treks
Gaiters* – if snow is likely on passes; can also help with leeches in the monsoon
Sun hat and **warm hat** – helpful at both low and high elevations
Bandana – to use as a handkerchief, sweatband or scarf
Hiking boots* – can be rented, but it's hard to find good ones
Mittens/gloves

OTHER USEFUL ITEMS

Telescoping hiking poles* – may be useful for keeping your balance and protecting the knees on descents
Stuff sacks – handy for separating things in your pack and for creating a pillow when filled with clothes
Plastic bags – a big one to cover your pack in the rain; small sealable ones for many uses
A book, journal or pack of cards – trekking days can be short, leaving long afternoons
Snack food – biscuits and chocolate can be bought along the way on the major treks
Sleeping mat* – for independent trekkers likely to sleep in basic accommodation
Umbrella – usually better than a coat in hot, often windless monsoon conditions
Mobile phone – for emergencies; coverage is patchy in the mountains
Toilet paper – refer to our "Conservation tips" (see box, p.308)
Daypack – if a porter is carrying your main pack
Whistle – for emergencies
Candles
Sewing kit

7

arctic. Many first-time trekkers underestimate the potential for heat especially. Be prepared for sun, rain, snow and very chilly mornings, and dress in layers for maximum flexibility. Note too that high-altitude trekking days are short, so you may spend many hours lounging around in the cold. Many Nepalis have conservative attitudes about dress (see p.40), and for minimum impact, avoid figure-hugging or otherwise revealing clothes. Women should avoid vest tops that show the shoulders; men might note that shorts traditionally indicate low status, though this isn't an issue nowadays along the popular trekking routes. Both sexes should wear at least a **swimsuit** when bathing, preferably a T-shirt too. For **footwear**, hiking boots are pretty essential, providing better traction, ankle support and protection than anything else; many hiking trainers have soles that just don't grip on Nepalese stone. A pair of trainers, sports sandals or flip-flops are useful for rest days and airing your feet; Croc-style plastic sandals are particularly lightweight and

can be bought cheaply in Kathmandu. Bring plenty of **socks**, because you'll be changing them often.

Trekking with children

The potential problems when considering whether to go trekking with children are obvious: will they walk? Will they let a porter carry them? What if they get sick? What if the weather is bad? Yet trekking with kids may be one of the best things you or they ever do – especially if there are lots of children together. Delights lie round every corner: chickens, goats, jingling donkey trains, frogs, bugs, waterfalls, caves, temples, prayer wheels – all that plus being the centre of attention everywhere they go.

TREKS AT A GLANCE

This list omits treks that require agency or extensive porter support. Note that the length in **days** quoted here does not include transport to and from the trailhead.

TREK	DAYS	BEST MONTHS	ELEVATION (M)
Jomosom/Kali Gandaki	5–7	Oct–April	1100–3800
Helambu	3–8	Oct–April	800–3600
Poon Hill	4–6	Oct–April	1100–3200
Macchapuchhare	5–7	Oct–April	1100–3700
Siklis	4–7	Oct–April	1100–2200
Rara	6–8	Oct–Nov, April–June	2400–3500
Langtang	7–12	Oct–May	1700–3750
Annapurna Sanctuary	8–12	Oct–Dec, Feb–April	1100–4130
Annapurna Circuit	12–21	Oct–Nov, March–April	450–5380
Everest (Lukla fly-in)	14–18	Oct–Nov, March–May	2800–5550
Manaslu Circuit	13–20	Oct–Nov, March–May	550–5100
Gosainkund	4–7	Oct–Dec, Feb–May	1950–4380
Everest (Shivalaya walk-in)	21–28	Oct–Nov, March–April	1500–5550
Everest (Eastern route)	28+	Nov, March	300–5550

7

Stick to easy **routes** and don't take a young child above 3500m due to the risks of AMS. The standard treks generally offer more comforts and easier access to emergency services, although a good agency can help you take children off the beaten track. Spending hours on winding mountain roads is a recipe for car sickness and misery; if possible, rent a more comfortable vehicle, or fly. The **pace** of your trek will depend on the age and sportiness of your youngest; plan on modest days, stopping by mid-afternoon. That said, many children are up for much longer walks than they might be willing to try at home. Consider a **porter** for each child. Almost all porters are great playmates/baby-sitters, despite the language barrier, and they can carry the child for all or part of the trek in a customized *doko*. Make sure any porter you hire is agile, conscientious and sober, and treat him or her well.

Trekking has most of the same **hazards** as a weekend camping trip. The extra concern is tummy bugs: teach kids to drink only boiled or purified water, keep hands and foreign objects out of mouths and wash hands frequently (sanitary wipes come in handy). Establish clear ground rules about not wandering off, not running, not venturing close to drop-offs, and staying clear of animals. Bathroom arrangements in the more primitive trekking inns may put children off.

When it comes to **food and drink**, familiar Western dishes are found on the main trails. Some kids love *daal bhaat* – they can eat it with their fingers – but of course many turn up their noses. A water-purifying travel cup is a handy device, or consider bringing neutralizing powder to remove the taste of iodine from purified water. Bring the same range of **clothes** for your child as for yourself, only more and warmer – and don't rely on renting locally. Bring a few lightweight games or **toys**; crayons are ideal. You probably won't need as many books as you might think, as bedtime comes early.

7

DIFFICULTY	COMMENTS
Easy to moderate	Spectacular, varied but commercial and somewhat undermined by the new road.
Moderate	Easy access, uncrowded, varied; only modest views.
Moderate	Easy access, excellent views; very commercial.
Moderate	Easy access; a little-trekked route through fields and forest.
Moderate	Easy access; uncrowded village trek.
Moderate	Fly in; must be prepared to camp; pristine lake and forest.
Moderate	Beautiful alpine valley close to Kathmandu.
Moderate to strenuous	Spectacular scenery, easy access; acclimatization necessary.
Strenuous	Incredible diversity and scenery; high pass requires care and acclimatization; jeep descent from Muktinath makes "half-circuit" possible.
Strenuous	Superb scenery; flights can be a problem; acclimatization necessary.
Strenuous	Spectacular, remote and still little-trekked due to its high pass, though it's becoming an increasingly popular alternative to the Annapurna Circuit.
Strenuous	Sacred lakes; usually combined with Langtang or Helambu.
Very strenuous	Wonderful mix of hill and high-elevation walking, but with a lot of up-and-down; can save time by flying one-way.
Very strenuous	Similar to above, but with an even greater net vertical gain.

The Annapurna region

The **ANNAPURNA REGION**'s popularity is well deserved: nowhere else do you get such a varied feast of scenery and hill culture and the **logistics** are relatively simple. However, the 2014 disaster (see box, p.306) provided significant pause for thought; it remains to be seen what impact this will have on trekking in the region. Treks can all start or finish close to Pokhara, which is a relaxing place to end a trek and a handy place to start one, with its clued-up guesthouses, equipment-rental shops and easy transportation to trailheads. With great views just two days up the trail, short treks in the Annapurnas are particularly feasible. Tourism is relatively sustainable, too, thanks to **ACAP**, the Annapurna Conservation Area Project. The inevitable consequence is commercialization. The popular treks in this region are on a well-beaten track, and unless you step aside from them you're more likely to be ordering bottled beer from a laminated menu than drinking home-brew with locals.

The **Annapurna Himal** faces Pokhara like an icy, crenellated wall, 40km across, with nine peaks over 7000m spurring from its ramparts and Annapurna I reigning above them all at 8091m. It's a region of stunning diversity, ranging from the sodden bamboo forests of the southern slopes (Lumle, northwest of Pokhara, is the wettest village in Nepal) to windswept desert (Jomosom, in the northern rain shadow, is the driest).

The *himal* and adjacent hill areas are protected within the Annapurna Conservation Area Project (ACAP), for which you have to pay an **entry fee** (see p.313). The aims of the ACAP, a quasi-park administered by a non-governmental trust, are to protect the area's natural and cultural heritage and ensure sustainable benefit for local people. To take the pressure off local forests, the project has set up kerosene depots and installed microhydroelectric generators, and supports reforestation efforts. Lodge owners benefit from training and low-interest loans, enabling them to invest in things like solar water heaters and efficient stoves. Safe drinking-water stations (bottled water is banned), rubbish pits, latrines, health posts and a telephone service have all been established on the proceeds of park entry fees. ACAP also sets **fixed lodge prices** (Rs300 for a double room, or Rs600 with attached bathroom), and agrees menu prices (which vary by area), to prevent undercutting and price wars; these prices should be respected rather than negotiated – though the system does seem to be breaking down, and lodge owners get around it by putting "special items" on their menus.

GETTING THERE   THE ANNAPURNA TRAILHEADS

TO PHEDI, NAYAPUL, BAGLUNG AND BENI

By bus Heading west from Pokhara, buses to Phedi (45min), Nayapul (2hr), Baglung (3hr 30min) and Beni (4hr 30min) all leave from the Baglung bus park, 4km from Lakeside. Departures are at least every 30min as far as Baglung; buses and microbuses through to Beni leave more like hourly, with the majority heading off in the morning. Buses to Phedi can also be picked up in Harichowk, Bagar, 5km from Lakeside.

By taxi Many trekkers commission taxis all the way to the roadhead, thus saving around a third of the travel time – depending on road conditions, and the driver. Taxi costs vary hugely with fuel prices, but are in the region of Rs1000–1200 to Phedi, Rs220–2500 to Nayapul and Rs4500–5000 to Beni.

TO JOMOSOM

By bus and jeep As you head up the rough road above Beni (see p.327) towards Jomosom, on the northwestern

side of the Annapurna range, transport prices will change dramatically depending on the road conditions. A bus service has been reliably established as far as Tatopani, but above there you may have to hop between different local bus and jeep companies, each fiercely guarding the right to ply their own segment of the road. Expect to pay in the region of Rs2000–2500 for the (very approximately) twelve-hour trip from Beni to Jomosom. Ask around in Pokhara before setting off, and be aware that this is one of the roughest and most alarming roads in Nepal.

By air The fast – and decidedly thrilling – alternative is to fly. From Pokhara there are flights to Jomosom (3–9 daily). Strong winds can mean flights are cancelled.

TO MANANG AND THE MARSYANGDI VALLEY

By bus, jeep or taxi To head towards Manang and the Marsyangdi valley, you'll use the main bus terminus at Besisahar, a bustling district centre with at least a dozen lodges, a bank, a hospital and so on. It's probably best reached by tourist bus to Dumre on the Prithvi Highway, on the way between Pokhara and Kathmandu; you can then pick up a bus (or hire a jeep) for the 43km (3hr by bus) north to Besisahar. There are also direct public buses from Kathmandu (7 daily; 6–7hr) and Pokhara (2–3 daily; 4–7hr) – slower, but you don't have the hassle of changing at Dumre. The quickest option, of course, is a direct taxi from Pokhara (3hr); expect to pay around Rs5000–5500. From Besisahar, frequent jeeps (and some public buses) can take you north; at the time of writing buses travelled as far as Bhulbhule and jeeps continued on the rough road as far as Syange (4hr).

By air Nepal Airlines operates flights from Pokhara to Manang (or rather, to the Humde airstrip, at least three hours below Manang) at most only two or three times a week in the high season, and often not at all; plus, if you start your trek this high you're asking for altitude problems. Strong winds at the airstrip can mean flights are cancelled.

The Annapurna Sanctuary

The **ANNAPURNA SANCTUARY** is the most intensely scenic short trek in Nepal, and one of the most well-trodden – there are lodges and tea stops at hourly intervals or less, until the highest sections at least. The trail takes you into the very heart of the Annapurna range, passing through huge hills in Gurung country with ever-improving views of the mountains ahead, then following the short, steep Modi Khola, before you pass into the most magnificent mountain cirque: the Sanctuary. Wherever you stand, the 360-degree views are unspeakably beautiful, and although clouds roll in early, the curtain often parts at sunset to reveal radiant, molten peaks.

The Sanctuary is usually an eight- to twelve-day round-trip from Pokhara. The actual distance covered isn't great, but **altitude**, **weather** and **trail conditions** all tend to slow you down. The trail gains more than 2000m from Ghandruk to the top, at 4100m, so you'd be wise to spread the climb over three or four days – and dress for snow. Frequent precipitation makes the higher trail slippery at the best of times, and in winter it can be impassable due to snow or avalanche danger.

There are two main approaches, both converging on the major village of **Chhomrong** (2170m) after two or three days' walk (though hardy types have made it in one exhausting day). At the time of writing, however, new roads were being built towards the largest villages, Ghorepani and Ghandruk, which will reduce the walk-in – though it may take some time for regular bus or jeep services to become established, and longer still for this area to become a tourist rather than a trekking destination.

The Phedi approach

Arguably the most satisfying approach route begins at **Phedi** (1160m), a mere twenty-minute taxi drive west of Pokhara. From here the trail ascends the wooded Dhampus ridge, climbing steeply up the last hour to Pothana (1900m), where you're rewarded with fine views of the mountains, including Machapuchare, the "Fish Tail" mountain. From the col at **Bhichok Deurali** (2080m), a well-paved trail descends again through thicker rhododendron forest, then contours and gently switchbacks through cultivated hillsides around the village of **Tolka** (1700m) before reaching **Landruk**, a substantial Gurung village with wonderful views of Annapurna South. From here the trail follows the Modi Khola upwards, crossing the river at **New Bridge** (1340m) and climbing very steeply above **Jhinu Danda** (near which there are good hot springs) to Chhomrong, with its smart lodges and its viewpoint at **Gurung Hill**, two hours above.

The Nayapul alternative

A slightly more direct approach leaves the Jomosom road at the **Nayapul** bridge, sloping down to the lively town of **Birethanti** (1050m), where you enter the Annapurna Conservation Area – sign in at the gate. From here, the trail pushes up the steep, terraced west bank of the **Modi Khola**. (A road already runs towards Ghandruk as far as Syauli Bazaar and Chane; permission to build a dam near New Bridge has been given, however, so expect more road building and disruption.) You can either climb to the major settlement of **Ghandruk** (1940m) – given those 900m of ascent, this is likely to

7

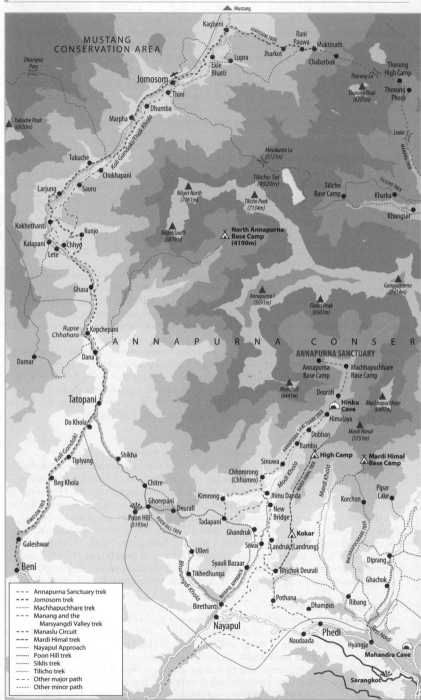

Map labels:

▲ Mustang

MUSTANG CONSERVATION AREA

Kagbeni
JOMOSOM TREK
Rani Pauwa
Muktinath
Lupra
Jharkot
Chababuk
Thorung High Camp
Ekle Bhatti
Thorung La
Dhampus Pass
Jomosom
Thini
Thorung Peak (6201m)
Thorung Phedi
Marpha
Dhumba
Ledar
Tukuche Peak (6920m)
Tukuche
Chokhapani
Mesokanto La (5121m)
Larjung
Sauru
Nilgiri North (7061m)
Tilicho Tal (4920m)
Tilicho Base Camp
Kharka
Kokhethanti
Kunjo
Tilicho Peak (7134m)
Khangsar
Kalapani
Chhyo
Lete
Nilgiri South (6839m)
North Annapurna Base Camp (4190m)
Ghasa
Annapurna I (8091m)
Ganggapurna (7454m)
Rupse Chhahara
Kopchepani
A N N A P U R N A   C O N S E R ... E R
Dana
Fluted Peak (6501m)
Damar
ANNAPURNA SANCTUARY
Annapurna Base Camp
Machhapuchhare Base Camp
Hiunchuli (6441m)
Deurali
Tatopani
Hinku Cave
Machhapuchhare (6997m)
Do Khola
Himalaya
Shikha
Dobhan
Mardi Himal (5553m)
Tiplyang
Bambu
Sinuwa
High Camp
Mardi Himal Base Camp
Beg Khola
Chitre
Chhomrong (Chhumro)
Kimrong
Jhinu Danda
Pipar Lake
Ghorepani
Deurali
Korchon
Poon Hill (3193m)
Tadapani
New Bridge
Galeshwar
Ghandruk
Kokar
Diprang
Beni
Ulleri
Siwai
Landruk (Landrung)
Ghachok
Syauli Bazaar
Bhichok Deurali
Tikhedhunga
Ribang
Birethanti
Pothana
Dhampus
Naudaada
Nayapul
Phedi
Hyangja
Mahandra Cave
Sarangkot

Legend:
- - - Annapurna Sanctuary trek
- - - Jomosom trek
······ Machhapuchhare trek
- - - Manang and the Marsyangdi Valley trek
- - - Manaslu Circuit
- - - Mardi Himal trek
······ Nayapul Approach
······ Poon Hill trek
······ Siklis trek
······ Tilicho trek
- - Other major path
····· Other minor path

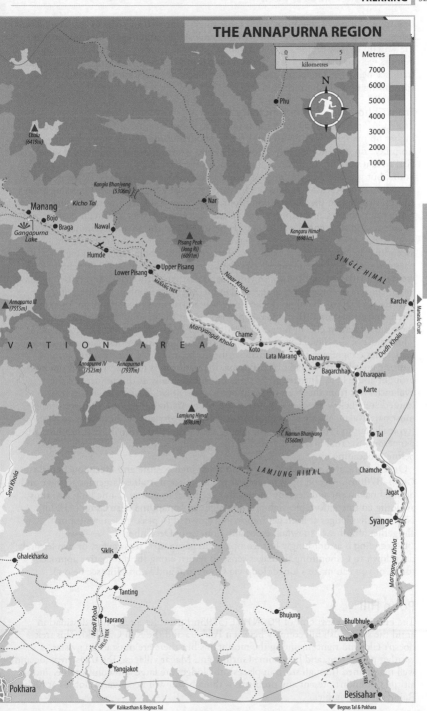

THE ANNAPURNA REGION

7

Phu

N

Metres	
7000	
6000	
5000	
4000	
3000	
2000	
1000	
0	

0   5
kilometres

Chulu
(6419m)

Kangla Bhanjyang
(5306m)

Manang   Kicho Tal   Nar

Bojo

Gangapurna   Braga   Nawal
Lake

Kangaru Himal
(6981m)

SINGLE HIMAL

Pisang Peak
(Jong Ri)
(6091m)

Humde

Upper Pisang

Lower Pisang   MANANG TREK

Naar Khola

Annapurna III
(7555m)

Karche

Manaslu Circuit

V A T I O N   A R E A

Marsyangdi Khola   Chame

Koto   Dudh Khola

Lata Marang   Danakyu

Annapurna IV   Annapurna II   Bagarchhap   Dharapani
(7525m)   (7937m)

Karte

Lamjung Himal
(6983m)

Tal

Namun Bhanjyang
(5560m)

Chamche

L A M J U N G   H I M A L

Jagat

Syange

Marsyangdi Khola

Ghalekharka   Siklis

Tanting

Madi Khola   Bhujung   Bhulbhule

Taprang   SIKLIS TREK   Khudi

MANANG TREK

Yangjakot

Pokhara   Besisahar

Kalikasthan & Begnas Tal   Begnas Tal & Pokhara

be enough for one day – or for a still more direct approach stay low in the Modi Khola valley, leaving the main road-cum-trail at Syauli Bazaar and bypassing Ghandruk on the way up to **New Bridge** and **Jhinu Danda** via **Siwai**. Leaving Ghandruk, the usual trail detours west to the crest of the fine **Komrong Danda** (2654m), joining the Ghorepani trail (see below) at **Tadapani** (2630m) before descending to **Kimrong** (1890m), then contouring up to Chhomrong.

From Chhomrong to the Sanctuary

The ACAP post at **Chhomrong** can inform you about weather and avalanche conditions higher up the trail. They'll also clue you up **about altitude**, which poses real danger from here on up – not least the danger that you won't reach the Sanctuary if you go too fast. Actual walking time from Chhomrong to the Sanctuary is in the region of twelve hours, but you should plan to spread the trip over three or four days. Be aware that in the autumn peak season, lodges can fill early, especially higher up, and trekkers often end up sleeping on the dining-room floor; make sure you have a warm sleeping bag.

The route above Chhomrong is simple and spectacular. After a difficult descent and re-ascent, and then another descent after **Sinuwa** (2360m) on a three-hundred-step stone staircase (which gets very slippery in the wet or snow), you start steadily ascending the west side of the deep and forested Modi Khola valley, making for a narrow notch between the sheer lower flanks of Machapuchare and Hiunchuli. There are no real villages past Sinuwa, so you ascend past regularly spaced (every two hours or so) clusters of cottage-like lodges at **Bambu** (2310m), Dobhan (2600m) and Himalaya (2920m). Bamboo thickets give way to oak and rhododendron, then to birch, and Annapurna III and Gangapurna loom at the head of the gorge. Note that there are no settlements or lodges at Kuldhigar or Bagar, as suggested on many maps.

Just short of the **Hinku Cave** (3170m), an overhanging rock where langur monkeys sometimes congregate, there's a small shrine in the middle of the path to a local Gurung guardian deity, Pojo Nim Baraha; the tradition is that meat should not be brought above here. The tree cover thins out substantially at this point, and the **avalanche risk** from the steep slopes above is at its worst – especially in the areas immediately below the cave and above and below **Deurali** (3239m), though for the most part avalanches are only something to really worry about after heavy snows (typically Jan to Feb), or during the spring melt (March and April). If conditions are dangerous, the trail may be diverted to the opposite bank or shut altogether – ask before proceeding up.

Once beyond this sanctuary "gate", you reach high pasture and **Machapuchare Base Camp** (3700m). A good tip is to sleep at the more comfortable, larger lodges here and do the final ascent and descent (alongside the glacial moraine) in one long day, thus avoiding an uncomfortable high-altitude night at **Annapurna Base Camp** (4100m). Note too that lodges at both get impossibly crowded in peak season, and shut altogether after heavy snowfall, especially from early December.

Descending is astonishingly fast, compared to going up – it's one fast or two leisurely days down to Chhomrong. It makes sense to return along the alternative approach route, or you can make a longer loop via Ghorepani and Poon Hill (see below).

Poon Hill

The Himalayan viewpoint of **POON HILL** (3193m) provides a tempting destination amid the steep, lush hill country between Pokhara and the Kali Gandaki. This trek doesn't take you right in among the mountains but there are outstanding vistas, weather permitting, and handsome Gurung and Magar villages. The **trails** are wide and well maintained (though steep in places), the lodges are large and comfortable, and the altitude shouldn't present any problems – though you will need **warm clothes** at night. Rain gear is advisable.

NAMES, PLACES AND PRONUNCIATIONS

The spelling and pronunciation of **Himalayan place names** has given many a traveller a headache. There are competing systems for transliterating from Nepali into English, and many names in mountain regions are taken from Tibetan dialects or even unwritten languages, so the possibilities can proliferate chaotically. When reading from maps and guides, or asking for directions, keep an open mind as to what might mean where. In general, we follow the most widely used spellings, but significant alternatives are given in brackets.

As regards **pronunciation**, there's not even agreement on what to call the country – or its mountains. Should it be Nuh-pawl, as it has been in English for a century or so, or Nay-paal, imitating Nepali pronunciation? Is the range a singular I li-maal-ee-yuh (reflecting the local word for mountain, *himal*) or Him-uh-lay-ers? Actually, that one's easy: the name derives from the Sanskrit *hima laya*, or "Abode of Snow", not *himal*, so the stress should be fairly even; and in English mountain ranges are usually plural, like "the Alps". Hee-maa-lay-ahs it is, then.

besi lower	**himal** mountain range
bhanjyang pass, col	**kosi** river
cho, **tso** lake	**khola** stream
chorten stone religious monument/ reliquary	**la** mountain pass
	lekh watershed range of hills, ridge
deurali meeting point, often of paths on the saddle or side of a hill	**mani** wall of stones inscribed with prayers
	phedi settlement at the foot of a hill
danda hillside	**pokhari** lake
gao village	**ri** peak
gompa monastery	**tal** lake

7

Most people do Poon Hill as a loop from Pokhara, starting at **Birethanti** (1050m), just below the roadside settlement of **Nayapul**. A dirt road has been built up the Bhurungdi Khola valley towards Ghorepani, but there's little traffic, and for most people it's still two shortish but relentlessly uphill days on foot via the handsome Magar village of **Ulleri** (1960m) and some fine rhododendron forest to **Ghorepani** (2860m) or, a little higher up, the thrumming cluster of lodges at **Ghorepani Deurali**. There's no need to set your alarm at either, as you'll be awakened at 4am by the daily stampede of Poon Hill sunrise-seekers. If clouds block your view, as they often do, it's worth hanging on for an extra day for the sight of Annapurna South apparently looming over Annapurna I, and the hump-shouldered pyramid of Dhaulagiri.

Beyond Ghorepani Deurali, the trail descends the thriving, terraced valley of the Ghar Khola, where a road is being built; coming down, you'll meet it near Shikha, though the trail stays off it and there's next to no traffic. The trail finally plunges down to cross the Kali Gandaki on a splendid suspension bridge and arrives at the busy townlet of **Tatopani** (1190m), a fairly demanding day's walk from Ghorepani. At Tatopani, there are banks (no ATMs as yet), restaurants, a health post and all the other facilities you might need, as well as the well-maintained hot springs beside the river, from which the town gets its name (it means "hot water" in Nepali). Frequent buses and jeeps head down to Beni and Pokhara.

For a slower return to Pokhara, head east from the old, lower village of Ghorepani, making for **Ghandruk** – one long or two short days' walk. The first section to the lonely little cluster of basic lodges at **Deurali** (not to be confused with the Deurali above/north of Ghorepani) is a fine ridge walk through rhododendron forest, with great views of Dhaulagiri and Machapuchare, especially from the lodges perched at **Ban Thanti** (3180m); the descent to **Tadapani** (2630m) is steep and slippery. At Tadapani you join the Ghandruk route described under the Nayapul approach to the Annapurna Sanctuary (see p.332), but you could easily make a longer loop, crossing to the east bank of the Modi Khola to rejoin the road at Phedi.

The Jomosom trek: the Kali Gandaki and Muktinath

The trek up (or down) the **Kali Gandaki** gorge from the pilgrim site of **Muktinath** and the Wild-West-style regional capital of **JOMOSOM** was for many years the classic Himalayan sampler, and the most developed stretch of trail in Nepal, with food and lodging closer to what you'd find in Thamel than the usual hill fare. Since the construction of an 83km road from Beni to Jomosom, on the west bank of the Kali Gandaki, many would-be trekkers are going elsewhere, though Indian pilgrims are replacing them (especially during festivals throughout auspicious seasons, notably April to June, and mid-August to mid-September – in the latter season, especially, guesthouses are full to bursting with tour groups). It's still perfectly possible to do the trek, however, following new trails on the steeper eastern side of the valley or paths that weave on and off the road. Guides can show you some fantastic **day hikes** and overnight trips up from the valley floor, too: little-trekked trails lead to North Annapurna Base Camp, the Dhaulagiri Icefall (way out west of Larjung) and the high-level Dhampus Pass (5182m), the key to Dolpo.

Many trekkers fly to Jomosom and walk up to Muktinath, then down again, but you'll have more sense of arrival (and acclimatize better) if you do the trek the hard way. The best approach route on foot is from Nayapul to Tatopani via **Poon Hill** (see p.326).

Tatopani to Jomosom

From Tatopani to Jomosom is typically three or four days' walk – or a tough, scary day in buses and/or jeeps. It's possible to avoid the road most or all of the way by following the **eastern bank**. That said, landslides are a perennial problem, meaning that the east-bank trails can be tricky or impassable in places – and information about the state of the route can be hard to come by. The main settlements (and most of the trekking lodges) are on the western side, and people there aren't exactly keen to see the foot traffic pass them by. Path maintenance on the eastern side isn't a priority for the same reason. Temporary wooden bridges make crisscrossing relatively simple in the dry season, but when the river is high, you may have to make strategic crossings at the permanent suspension bridges and resign yourself to walking on the road for longer stretches. Taking a guide who has walked the route recently will ease the logistics considerably.

Above **Tatopani** (1190m), where the trail from Poon Hill joins the road up from Beni, the route passes into the world's deepest gorge, the **Kali Gandaki**, with the 8000m hulks of Dhaulagiri and Annapurna towering on either side. Above Tatopani, you often

---

THE ANNAPURNA CIRCUIT

The legendary **Annapurna Circuit** – a world-class, though now very busy, circular trek which runs up the Marsyangdi valley, crosses the Thorung La pass and heads back down the Kali Gandaki valley – is not what it was, but it isn't as dead as the doom-mongers make out. The construction of roads on both sides of the circuit has certainly changed things: on the western half of the Annapurnas, roads now extend right up the Kali Gandaki gorge into Mustang (and Tibet, though the border is shut to tourists), and on the eastern side of the circuit a road penetrates the Marsyangdi valley to Manang. Yet the potentially deadly altitude of the Thorung La pass, at the crux of the circuit, makes the idea of future vehicle tours unlikely, and traffic remains very light as landslides and missing bridges regularly cut both roads. There is as yet no established bus service from Pokhara through to either Jomosom or Manang, either, and travellers are forced to walk between one bus or jeep drop-off point and the next pick-up further along, making as many as three or four changes.

The biggest change is that tens of thousands of Indian pilgrims now head up to Muktinath, chiefly in the monsoon months, bringing new touristic and spiritual life to the region. Many Western visitors are now doing a **two-week half-circuit**, walking up the Marsyangdi, crossing the Thorung La, then treating themselves to a jeep ride or a flight down from Jomosom to Pokhara. Others are treating Manang as the launch pad for exciting side trips to Tilicho Tal, or the high settlements of Nar and Phu.

have to stick to the west bank, and near the old Magar village of **Dana**, you enter the steepest, sheerest part of the gorge; there's a lookout point below the waterfall of Rupse Chhahara. The east-bank trail from Kopchepani, just above and opposite the falls, up to **Ghasa** (2010m) is relatively good.

At Ghasa, you enter **Lower Mustang** district and the homeland of the Buddhist Thakali people (see box, p.330) – from here on up, the river is known locally as the **Thak Khola**, and subtropical greenery starts to give way to alpine trees and shrubs. You usually have to stick to the west bank from Ghasa to the village of **Chhyo**, opposite Lete (2480m), but from there a good east-bank trail climbs up to Kunjo and the little lake of Titi Tal before dropping down, partly on a rough road, to the well-established trekking village of **Kokhetanti** (2545m), where you are usually forced to re-cross the river to Larjung, on the west bank – the east-bank route up to Tukuche via Sirkung and Sauru is particularly prone to landslides. The relatively large and prosperous village of **Tukuche** (2590m) is the place to cross back onto the east bank, heading up via Chimang, with its lovely Dhaulagiri views, and Chairo, a Tibetan settlement. It's usually possible to continue up the east bank directly to Thini, but it would be a pity not to cross over short of Dhumba to handsome, stony **Marpha** (2670m), which sits amid apricot and apple orchards – the cider and brandy are famous. The administrative centre of **Jomosom** (2720m), with its busy airstrip, looks like a stony Wild West settlement, but is useful for supplies, doctors, banks, police and so on, and great for those seeking respite – it has plenty of relatively fancy hotels.

Jomosom to Muktinath

Above Jomosom, the valley starts to level out, and you enter a dry and powerfully Tibetan-flavoured highland region. A few motorbikes and jeeps plug dustily up the rough road (Jomosom to Muktinath in a shared jeep takes two hours and costs roughly Rs710), though paths are easy enough to find, often on the stones of the valley floor. Beware the extraordinary late-morning and afternoon **katabatic winds**, however, which tear up from the south after about 11am, rushing to fill the void left by the hot air rising from the highlands above. The winds carry enormous amounts of grit and dust from the riverbed – and, nowadays, vehicle dust too – meaning that a scarf as a mask, a hat and sunglasses are vital. If you're heading into the wind, coming down, walking can be anything from severely trying to almost impossible.

At the romantic fortress town of **Kagbeni**, with its medieval buildings and terracotta Buddhist figures, you're on the very edge of the Tibetan plateau, and can gaze north into Upper Mustang. What with the expensive permit that's necessary to visit (see p.314), this really is a forbidden kingdom. Eastwards, however, it's an open-access, 1000m climb towards Muktinath, up a delightful, open side valley dotted with orchards and lined with dry-stone walls. The trail crisscrosses the road, and takes you through the impressive village of **Jharkot** (3550m), where there's a fine *gompa*. Jeeps can take you as far as **Rani Pauwa** (3710m), where dozens of hotels cater to the Indian pilgrim trade; from there you have to walk the last twenty breathless minutes to Muktinath, or buy a seat on the "Muktinath Express" – which means riding pillion on a motorcycle.

Muktinath

The Mahabharata mentions poplar-shaded **MUKTINATH** (3760m) as the source of mystic *shaligrams*, stone ammonite fossils found in the Kali Gandaki gorge. It is one of the most important religious sites in the Himalayas – and ever since the arrival of the road, a pilgrim boomtown. A priest will show you around the Vishnu temple, with its 108 waterspouts (where pilgrims bathe in the freezing water) and its shrine sheltering a tiny perpetual natural-gas flame hidden half-underground beside a little spring – a particularly holy combination of earth, air, fire and water. Yartung, a madly exotic **festival** of horseriding, is held at Muktinath around the full moon of August–September.

If you're **returning to Jomosom**, it's possible to take a dramatic, high-level side route over the shoulder of the hills to the southeast of Ranipauwa, descending on precipitous paths (and crossing the Panda Khola on temporary bridges – so ask before setting out) via the old-world Thakali village of **Lupra**. If you're heading up over the Thorung La to follow the Annapurna Circuit (see box, p.328) towards **Manang**, bear in mind that there are a couple of basic high-season-only teahouse lodges at **Chabarbuk** (4200m), also known as Phedi, just before the zigzagging, four-hour climb up the pass begins; sleeping here would get you an hour's head start in the morning.

Manang and the Marsyangdi valley

The **MARSYANGDI VALLEY**, which curls around the east side of the Annapurna range, was once the less commercialized half of the Annapurna Circuit (see box, p.328), trekked only by the hard-core few intending to cross the 5415m pass of the Thorung La and descend towards Jomosom. However, with the construction of a road up the valley, **Manang** – the end of the road – is now eclipsing Jomoson as a destination in itself, and is the base for some stunning side treks. At the time of writing, if you have your own vehicle, it was possible to drive all the way to Manang – subject to landslides and the usual roughness of road. Expect sections to be periodically buried and rebuilt.

The main **trailhead** for the Marsyangdi valley is at Besisahar; with a guide, you could also walk in two to three days from Begnas Tal, via Nalma Phedi and Baglungpani, to **Khudi**, just north of Besisahar.

The Upper Marsyangdi to Manang

Above the riverside settlement of **Syange**, the trail passes from terraced farmland into the gorge of the **Upper Marsyangdi**; it's three or four marvellous days' walk up to Manang, mostly through Buddhist country. The trail crosses astonishing suspension footbridges and passes along dramatic walkways blasted into the rock, all the time climbing through successive climatic zones: temperate forest, coniferous forest, alpine meadows and finally the arid steppes of the rain shadow. The walk from Chame to **MANANG** is spectacular and shouldn't be rushed. The sight of the huge, glacier-dolloped Annapurnas towering almost 5000m above the valley will stay with you forever. Manang's architecture, like that of all the older villages here, is strongly Tibetan.

The Thorung La

The **THORUNG LA** (5416m) is tricky to impossible from late December till early March, while the lower parts of the trek are uncomfortably warm from April onwards; the

---

THAKALIS AND MANANGIS

A small but economically powerful clan, **Thakalis** are the ingenious traders, innkeepers and pony-handlers of the Thak Khola in the Annapurna region. Their entrepreneurial flair goes back at least to the mid-nineteenth century, when the government awarded them a regional monopoly in the salt trade. When Nepal opened to the outside world, many branched out into more exotic forms of commerce, such as importing electronics from Singapore and Hong Kong, while others set up efficient inns in the western hills. Similarly, the **Manangis** (or Manang-pa) of the upper Marsyangdi, the next valley to the east of the Thak Khola, built early trading privileges into a reputation for international smuggling and other shady activities. Women have traditionally run most of the trekking lodges in both of these valleys, while their well-travelled husbands spent a lot of their time away on business. In recent years, the relaxation of import restrictions and currency controls has deprived these groups of their special status, and many traders have returned to their home villages. Both groups could arguably be classified as Bhotiyas (see p.339), but their languages are more akin to Gurung dialects than to Tibetan; Manangis are Buddhists, while Thakali religion blends Buddhism with Hinduism and shamanism.

October 2014 trekking disaster (see box, p.306) highlighted the danger that freak weather conditions can pose at other times of the year. Snow can block the pass at any time of year, so be prepared to wait it out or go back down the way you came. If you're going for it, you'll need proper boots, gloves, very warm clothes and a three- or, better, four-season sleeping bag; visit Manang's Himalayan Rescue Association post for information on weather conditions, AMS and suggested pacing of the route.

It's only six or seven hours to **Thorung Phedi** (4450m), the last cluster of lodges before the pass, but you should spread the ascent over at least two days – perhaps making day-trips from Manang (see p.330). Thorung Phedi and the worryingly high **Thorung High Camp** (4925m) are grotty places where you'll be woken up at 3am by trekkers who've been told (wrongly) that they have to clear the pass by 8am. Afternoons do get very windy, though, so an early start is advisable. The climb up the pass (where there's sometimes a teashop in high season), and the knee-killing 1600m descent down the other side to **Muktinath** (see p.328) is a tough but exhilarating day.

Short side trips from Manang

Manang makes a fine base for exploratory day hikes around the Upper Marsyangdi valley – ideal for acclimatizing if you're crossing the Thorung La, and worthy as destinations in their own right. The **gompa** at Manang, Bojo and Braga, all within half an hour of each other, are well worth visiting, and you could add on a short stroll from Manang to **Gangapurna Lake** and the fine viewpoint two hours above. **Kicho Tal** (4950m), an icy lake where *bharal* (blue sheep) have been sighted, makes a fine day hike.

Tilicho

The most enticing destination west of Manang is **TILICHO** (sometimes called Tilicho Tal or Tilicho Lake), not the highest lake in the world, as is often said, but beautiful and remarkable nonetheless. Getting there is two or three days' hard work: paths are scree-ridden and dicey, routes may be hard to find and lodges are often shut out of season. Take advice and an experienced guide.

The trail to the lake passes **Khangsar** (3734m), two tricky hours west of Manang; the highest permanent village in the Marsyangdi valley, it has a few lodges. From here the trail doesn't follow the landslide-prone Marsyangdi valley, but a higher northern route passing Kharka (also known as Srikharka or Shreechaur; there's a good guesthouse here) and a high col (4920m), descending to **Tilicho Base Camp** (4150m), some five hours from Khangsar. A second overnight at one of the two icy lodges at Tilicho Base Camp would make possible a steep day-trip the next day towards the astounding, often iced-over **Tilicho Tal** (4920m), a further three hours up (on snow, in parts, between November and May). There is currently just one very basic, seasonal teahouse (dorm room only) beside the lake, on the Manang side, but check if it's open before you head up without camping gear. Most people visit the lake as a day's round-trip from Tilicho Base Camp, but hardy trekkers can return to Khangsar (or even Manang) in one long day.

The Mesokanto La

Tilicho is not a trip for the inexperienced; still less is the high, snowy, dangerous route from Tilicho through to Jomosom (or Marpha). The lakeshore can't be circumnavigated (whatever maps may show), so the route demands either a roped-up crossing of the frozen lake (very roughly Nov or Dec–April, but make sure), or a high detour to the north across the Eastern Pass (5340m). After that you have to cross the watershed range, usually via the perilous **MESOKANTO LA** (5121m), sometimes called the Middle Pass (as there is a higher but supposedly easier one to the north). Only very strong walkers should expect to make it down to Jomosom (or even Thini) in one day from Tilicho Tal; ten hours would be fast, so it's better to camp at one of the two sites along the way.

Other Annapurna region treks

The following four treks have little in common with the well-serviced routes described above. You'll typically find only Nepali food and lodging, or will need to camp – and possibly stay in people's homes for at least some nights.

Of course, there are scores of possibilities beyond the treks described here. The **Khopra Lake** trek, on the shoulder of Annapurna South above Ghorepani and Tadapani, could one day rival Poon Hill in popularity, with its stunning views towards Dhaulagiri, and high point at the small, sacred Khayar Lake (4880m). There's no lodge at Khopra, but there is one at Dharamdanda, halfway between Tadapani and Khopra Danda; you can also stay at Swanta, above Chitre. Increasing numbers of trekkers are exploring west of the Kali Gandaki towards the **Dhaulagiri** massif and the little-visited **Dhorpatan Hunting Reserve**; beyond that, of course, there's Dolpo (see p.351).

The Machhapuchhare trek

One of the newer routes in the region takes a loop north of Pokhara, towards the south faces of Mardi Himal and **MACHHAPUCHHARE** (6997m), with fine views of the Annapurna wall. The usual approach route heads up the upper valleys of the Seti Khola, leaving a spur road just above **Hyangja** – twenty minutes by taxi from Pokhara – and passing through lush, terraced farmland around the Gurung villages of **Ghachok** and **Diprang** (1440m), where there's a community lodge and a natural hot spring nearby. A choice of steep paths lead up through forest (one passes **Pipar Lake**, prime pheasant habitat with a stunning view of Machapuchare, looming just to the north) to a high ridge dripping with rhododendrons and alive with birds, which you can follow up to the minor peak at **Korchon** (3682m), and potentially on up in the direction of **Mardi Himal Base Camp** (4120m). Most treks descend the ridge before dropping to the Mardi Khola at the village of Ribang. The trek takes five to seven days, and requires camping and supplies.

Mardi Himal trek

One ridge to the west of the Macchapuchhare trek is another fine camping route, the **MARDI HIMAL TREK**. The usual starting places are at Phedi or Kande, both on the road to Nayapul. From either, you climb on well-made trails to the villages of Pothana (1890m) and Bhichok Deurali (2100m). From here, you ascend the incredible ridge that drops south from Mardi Himal (5553m) between the Mardi and Modi Kholas. There are stunning views from the ridgetop, while rhododendron forests drop away on either side, and campsites appear every four hours or so: at Kokar (2550m), Low Camp (3050m) and High Camp (3900m). From High Camp, you can continue on up the ridge as high as you dare – it's snowy from around November. From Low Camp, a good, steep trail drops east through the forest towards Sidhing, on the Machhapuchhare Model Trek.

The Royal trek

The so-called **ROYAL TREK**, an undemanding if somewhat unexciting amble through lush countryside, gets its name from Prince Charles's visit in 1981. It was more enticing then, before the road was build east from Pokhara to Kalikasthan, and concrete houses started replacing traditional homes in places. It's usually done over three (sometimes four) days, staying in homestay-style lodges. The first day follows gradual ups and downs as you head eastwards from Kalikasthan to Lipeyani; the second takes you up to ridgetop Chisopani (the last section is steep, but never scarily so), where there are fine views of the mountains; the third takes you back to Rupa Tal (see p.229), from where you can pick up a bus to Pokhara.

The Siklis trek

The **SIKLIS TREK** probes an uncrowded corner of the Annapurna Conservation Area under the shadows of Lamjung Himal and Annapurnas II and IV – though you'll see more terraced fields than mountains and forests. The usual itinerary takes about a week, starting at Begnas Tal (see p.229) and heading north to Kalikasthan (first night) then following the river's west bank to Taprang (second night) and on up to well-preserved **Siklis** (1980m), Nepal's biggest Gurung village. The fourth day is hard work: you strike westwards over the thickly forested ridge that separates the Madi and Seti drainages to Tara Hill, where a small teahouse offers incredible views of Machhapuchhare; you then descend via **Ghalekharka** and the Sardikhola to the Seti Khola, returning towards Hyangja via Ghachok (see p.332) and the hot springs at Diprang. It's now possible to make this trek without camping or staying in local homes, but the lodges are still pretty basic.

The Manaslu Circuit

There's only one trek of note in the region east of the Annapurnas and north of Gorkha: the **MANASLU CIRCUIT**. It's some trek, however, passing through relatively unspoiled and hugely varied countryside, from rice terraces to spare Tibetan villages, and from rich forest to a 5100m pass. It takes two weeks (13–18 days) to walk the challenging route, and it's well worth considering if you were thinking of doing the Annapurna Circuit and were put off by the increased commercialization.

It is possible to trek the Manaslu Circuit by staying in lodges, without taking camping equipment, but the **facilities** are for the most part quite basic. Things are changing fast (⑩manaslucircuittrek.com is a good place to seek traveller reports and updates), but this is still *daal bhaat* and shared dormitories territory.

The trek traditionally starts in Gorkha (see p.198), passing right next to the royal palace and then through some very scenic and culturally rich country. Many people now shave off the first three days or so, however, by beginning at **Arughat**. Direct buses run from Kathmandu to Arughat (2 daily; 7hr), or you can get off the Prithvi Highway between Kathmandu and Pokhara at Malekhu, and catch frequent local buses or jeeps from there up the paved road to Dhading, a busy administrative centre, and then on up the rough road that continues to Arughat (and indeed beyond, as far as Arkhet or Sozti Khola).

The Manaslu Circuit route

From Arughat (530m), the first eight days or so climb steadily up the wooded, peaceful **Burhi Gandaki** valley. You're passing through deep Gurung country, where local women wear heavy gold jewellery, and working men carry the distinctive Gurung *bhangro*, a heavy, cream-coloured rough woollen cloak which is cross-tied around the waist and shoulders and doubles as a bag.

After three or, more likely, four days, you pass into the Manaslu Conservation Area at Jagat (1340m), where there's a checkpost (see box below), and the scenery becomes ever more spectacular. (A fascinating side trip would be east of Philim up to the stunning, forested and intensely Buddhist Tsum valley, which penetrates behind the 7000m peaks of **Ganesh Himal**.) Beyond **Deng** (1800m), one long or two short days above Jagat, the valley starts to turn west and you enter the high, strongly Tibetan-flavoured country of Nupri; it's three or, more sensibly, four days up through increasingly lofty, Buddhist country to the town of Samdo (3870m). It's worth taking your time to acclimatize, and Samdo, with its cluster of relatively comfortable lodges,

---

MANASLU CIRCUIT PERMITS

An authorized agency will need to arrange your special **permit** for the Manaslu Circuit trek (Sept–Nov $70 per person for a week, then $10 per day; Dec–Aug $50/$7), and you are obliged to take a guide. You don't need a TIMS card, because of the permit, but you will need park entry permits for both the Manaslu and Annapurna Conservation Areas (MCAP and ACAP; Rs2000 each), as the trail passes through both.

and possibility of a side trip towards the Lajyung La (which leads into Tibet), is a good place to take a rest day. If need be, porters can be hired here – at a price.

It's inadvisable, on acclimatization grounds as well as those of fatigue, to try to do one huge, ten-hour day from Samdo all the way over the pass of the **Larkya La** (5135m) and down to the lodges at Bimtang (3720m). The only alternative, if you're not camping, is the single lodge at Larkye La Phedi, also known as Larkye Dharamsala (4470m), three hours above Samdo; at the time of writing, however, there was a question over its future, as it was built illegally. The Larkya La itself, which clings to the very shoulder of Manaslu, takes four to five hours to ascend from Larkya Phedi, and can be windy and dangerous; in snowy conditions, which are common (and should be expected from November), guides should use a rope for the steepest hour or two of the descent. The views are sensational, even if they don't take in an 8000m peak – only Annapurna II, at a shade over 7900m.

The **descent** can be very fast: two to three steep days down the Dudh Khola to the Marsyangdi valley. At **Dharapani** (1860m), you enter the ACAP zone (permit needed) and relative civilization. You meet the road at Syange, where jeeps come up from Besisahar, but it might be preferable to walk to Bhulbhule (see p.323).

Langtang, Helambu and Gosainkund

Trekking **north of Kathmandu** is curiously underrated and relatively uncrowded. The most accessible of all the trekking regions, it's well suited to one- or two-week itineraries. What it lacks in superlatives – there are no 8000m peaks in the vicinity (unless you count Shisha Pangma, across the border in Tibet) – it makes up for in base-to-peak rises that are as dramatic as anywhere. Langtang, in particular, delivers more amazing views in a short time than any other walk-in trek in Nepal, with the possible exception of the Annapurna Sanctuary.

Two distinct basins and an intervening *lek* (ridge) lend their names to the major treks here; each stands on its own, but given enough time and good weather you can mix-and-match them. **Helambu** is closest to Kathmandu, comprising the rugged north–south valleys and ridges that lie just beyond the northeast rim of the Kathmandu Valley. North of Helambu, running east–west and tantalizingly close to the Tibet border, lies the high, alpine **Langtang valley**, which in its upper reaches burrows spectacularly between the Langtang and Jugal Himals. **Gosainkund** comprises a chain of sacred lakes nestled in a rugged intermediate range northwest of Helambu. One practical inconvenience is that the connections between these three treks aren't reliable – winter snow may block the passes between Helambu and the other two – and done on their own, the Langtang and Gosainkund treks require you to retrace your steps for much of the return journey. A grand tour of all three areas takes sixteen or more days.

CROSSING TO CHINA AT RASUWAGADHI

The road to Langtang, named the **Pasang Lhamu Highway** after the first Sherpa woman (that is, the first Nepali woman) to climb Everest, continues beyond the Langtang trailhead, heading all the way up the Bhote Koshi valley to Rasuwagadhi, at the Tibetan border. The border crossing is currently shut to vehicle traffic and foreigners, but it won't be for long: in 2015, China was due to complete construction on the second "**Friendship Bridge**". It is likely to transform the Langtang region of Nepal – and quite possibly Nepal's international relations, too. **Rasuwagadhi** (or Rasuwa, as it's also known) will always be beset by landslides and snowfall, but it is still likely to become the major route between Nepal and China. The Chinese government plans to extend the Lhasa railway from Shigatse to cover the mere 275km to Kerung, the Tibetan border town just 18km from Rasuwagadhi.

THE TAMANG HERITAGE TRAIL

Perhaps trying to compensate for the lack of celebrity peaks, many agencies arrange **cultural treks** in the Langtang area, with nights spent in village homes, visits to religious sites and monasteries, and evening "cultural shows" – which are generally much better than they sound. There's often a strong emphasis on wildlife-viewing and sustainable tourism. In all, these treks offer a refreshing change from the relentless altitude- and view-bagging mentality behind the big-name Annapurna and Everest trails. The area northwest of Syaphru Besi, in particular, has been developed as a **Tamang Heritage Trail**. The usual route is a four- to six-day circuit, via Gatlang, Tatopani, with its hot springs, and Briddim. The route may change, however, now the Chinese have completed a 16km road between Syaphru Besi and Rasuwagadhi, on the Tibet border.

Food and lodging here are less luxurious than in the Annapurna and Everest regions, but lodges are mostly perfectly comfortable. All these routes take you into **Langtang National Park**, for which there's a Rs3000 entry fee.

7

GETTING THERE   THE LANGTANG TRAILHEADS

To Syaphru Besi and Dunche Three buses daily from Macha Pokhari, near Kathmandu's Gongabu Bus Park, run to Syaphru Besi via Dunche, all leaving early in the morning (8–9hr).

To Sundarijal There are frequent buses from Kathmandu's Ratna Park (1hr–1hr 30min). Alternatively, taxis cost around Rs1200–1500.

To Melamchi Bazaar and beyond Take the Arniko Highway to Banepa (buses every 5–10min from

Kathmandu's Rathna Bus Park; minibuses every 10min from City Bus Park; 45min) or Dhulikhel (buses every 5–10min from Kathmandu's City Bus Park; 1hr 10min–2hr; taxis around Rs3000–4000), and change to one of the fairly frequent buses (2–3 daily; around 1hr 30min–2hr 30min) for Melamchi Bazaar. Jeeps and buses run north from Melamchi Bazaar to Thimbu and Sermathang, but can't be counted on as roads are frequently blocked.

Langtang trek

The **LANGTANG TREK** can be done in as little as a week, but day hikes in the upper valley should detain you for at least another two or three days, and given more time you'll want to add Gosainkund to the itinerary. Most people start at **Syaphru Besi** (1400m), a very "local", bumpy (and, at points, vertiginous), full day's bus ride from Kathmandu.

The first two days of the trek are spent climbing briskly up the gorge-like lower Langtang valley, probably overnighting at **Lama Hotel** (2470m) or **Ghoratabela** (2970m). Oaks and rhododendron give way to peaceful hemlock and larch forest; after ascending an old moraine, snowy peaks suddenly loom ahead and the gorge opens into a U-shaped glacial valley – prime yak pasture. Springtime is excellent for flowers here, and in autumn the berberis bushes turn a deep rust colour. Two Bhotiya villages occupy the upper valley: **Langtang** (3300m), the bigger of the two, makes a good place to spend an extra night and acclimatize, while **Kyanjin Gompa** (3750m) boasts a small monastery, a cheese "factory" (with fabulous yoghurt) and a cluster of chalet-lodges which fill up early in high season.

The **Langtang Glacier** is further up the valley – a long day's round-trip, as there are no lodges, though you may be able to hire a tent at Kyanjin Gompa if you want to overnight. From the rocky viewpoint of **Langshisha Kharka** (4100m), a little beyond the yak pasture at Numthang, you can see ice and moraine spreading up the high valleys, hemmed in by snowy peaks. Equally tempting are the ascents of either **Tsergo Ri** (4984m), a challenging, six- or seven-hour round-trip that offers an awesome white wilderness of peaks, or **Kyanjin Ri** (4773m), which stands a mere two hours or so above Kyanjin Gompa.

You can **return** by crossing into Helambu via the Kangja La route (see p.339), but most people go back down the valley, perhaps varying the last leg by turning off to Thulo Syaphru (where the trail to Gosainkund branches off) and down to Dhunche.

7

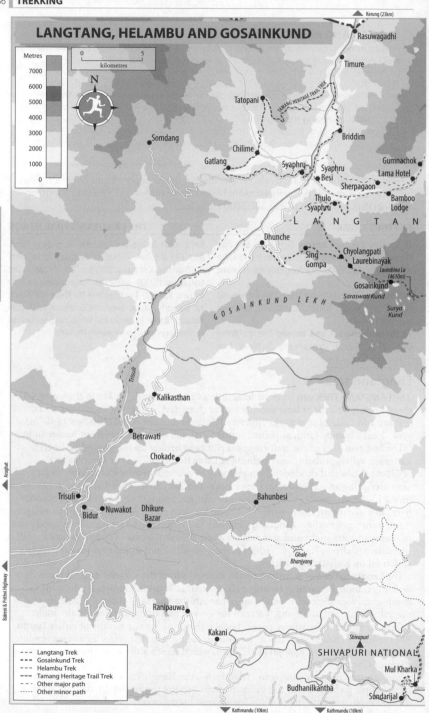

LANGTANG, HELAMBU AND GOSAINKUND

Metres
7000
6000
5000
4000
3000
2000
1000
0

N

0   5
kilometres

Kerung (23km)

Rasuwagadhi

Timure

Tatopani

TAMANG HERITAGE TRAIL TREK

Somdang

Chilime

Gatlang

Briddim

Syaphru

Gumnachok

Syaphru
Besi

Lama Hotel

Sherpagaon

Thulo
Syaphru

Bamboo
Lodge

L A N G T A N

Dhunche

Chyolangpati
Laurebinayak

Sing
Gompa

Laurabina La
(4610m)

Gosainkund

Saraswati Kund

Surya
Kund

G O S A I N K U N D   L E K H

Trisuli

Kalikasthan

Betrawati

Chokade

Trisuli

Bidur

Nuwakot

Dhikure
Bazar

Bahunbesi

Anghat

Baireni & Prithvi Highway

Ghale
Bhanjyang

Ranipauwa

Kakani

Shivapuri

SHIVAPURI NATIONAL

Mul Kharka

Budhanilkantha

Sundarijal

Kathmandu (10km)   Kathmandu (10km)

--- Langtang Trek
--- Gosainkund Trek
--- Helambu Trek
--- Tamang Heritage Trail Trek
--- Other major path
⋯ Other minor path

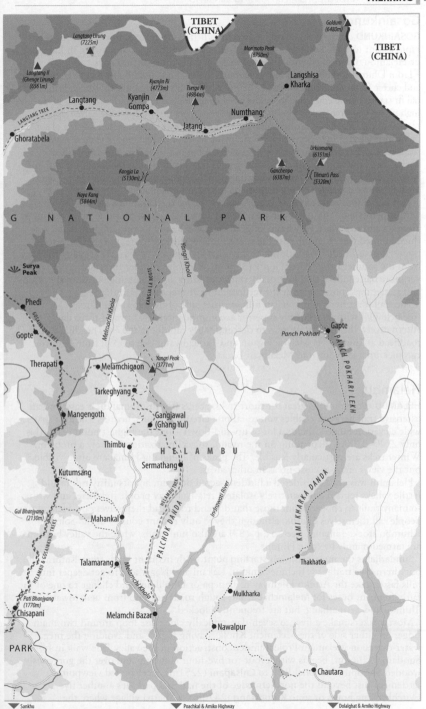

TIBET
(CHINA)

TIBET
(CHINA)

Goldum
(6480m)

Langtang Lirung
(7225m)

Morimoto Peak
(6750m)

Langtang II
(Ghenge Lirung)
(6561m)

Kyanjin Ri
(4773m)

Tserga Ri
(4984m)

Langshisa
Kharka

Langtang

Kyanjin
Gompa

Numthang

Jatang

LANGTANG TREK

Ghoratabela

Urkinmang
(6151m)

Kangja La
(5130m)

Ganchenpo
(6387m)

Tilman's Pass
(5320m)

Naya Kang
(5844m)

G   N A T I O N A L   P A R K

7

Surya
Peak

Yangri Khola

KANGJA LA ROUTE

Melamchi Khola

Phedi

GOSAINKUND TREK

Gopte

Gapte

Panch Pokhari

PANCH POKHARI LEKH

Therapati

Melamchigaon

Yangri Peak
(3771m)

Tarkeghyang

Mangengoth

Gangjawal
(Ghang Yul)

Thimbu

H E L A M B U

Kutumsang

Sermathang

KAMI KHARKA DANDA

Gul Bhanjyang
(2130m)

PALCHOK DANDA

MELAMCHI TREK

Mahankal

Indrawati River

HELAMBU & GOSAINKUND TREKS

Talamarang

Melamchi Khola

Thakhatka

Pati Bhanjyang
(1770m)

Mulkharka

Chisapani

Melamchi Bazar

Nawalpur

PARK

Chautara

▼ Sankhu   ▼ Poachkal & Arniko Highway   ▼ Dolalghat & Arniko Highway

Gosainkund

GOSAINKUND can be trekked on its own in as little as four days, but because of the rapid ascent to high elevation – 4610m – it's best done after acclimatizing in Langtang or Helambu. Combined with either of these, it adds three or four days.

From Dhunche, trails ascend steeply through mossy rhododendron forest to the monastery and cheese factory of **Sing Gompa** at 3250m. Above Sing Gompa, the trail ascends through tall fir stands before emerging above the tree line for increasingly panoramic views of the high peaks. **Laurebinayak** is a beautiful place to stop, before you enter the barren upper reaches of the Trisuli River, where glacial moraines and rockslides have left a string of some half-dozen lakes (*kund*). Several lodges sit by the shore of **Gosainkund**, the most sacred of the lakes and renowned among Nepali Hindus. A famous legend recounts how Shiva, having saved the world by drinking a dangerous poison, struck this mountainside with his *trisul* to create the lake and cool his burning throat. During the full moon of July–August, Janai Purnima, a massive Hindu **pilgrimage** is held at Gosainkund.

Two hours southeast of Gosainkund, you pass over the **Laurabina La** (4610m), a pass with superb views, though it can be tricky or impassable in winter due to ice and snow. You descend towards a very basic lodge at Bera Goth, and an only slightly better one three hours down from the pass (be sure to follow the low route, not the dangerous upper one) at Phedi (3630m); this is the usual starting point if you're crossing the pass from the southern side. After Gopte (3530m), a hamlet another three hours on, with yet more basic lodges, you eventually start ascending again, coming out onto the windy and sometimes snowy ridge at the settlement of **Therapati** (3510m).

The trail forks here, and you can follow either side of the Helambu Circuit (see below) – with its relatively superior accommodation – for two or three days. Alternatively, the quicker route is to descend fairly rapidly to the east, heading to the roadhead at **Thimbu** via Melamchigaon and Tarkeghyang (see p.339); from here you can pick up a jeep down to Melamchi Bazaar.

Helambu

HELAMBU (or Helmu) is great for short treks: access from Kathmandu is easy, and an extensive trail network enables you to tailor a circuit to your schedule. The area spans a wide elevation range – there's a lot of up-and-down – but the highest point reached is only 2700–3200m (depending on the route), so acclimatization is rarely a problem. Winter treks are particularly feasible. The peaks of Langtang Himal are often visible, but the views aren't as close-up as in other areas.

Helambu was once considered a hidden, sacred domain, and its misty ridges and fertile valleys remain comparatively isolated; relatively few people trek here, and with so many trails to choose from, those that do tend to spread themselves out. Helambu's people call themselves **Sherpa**, although they're only distant cousins of the Solu-Khumbu stock. Tamangs (see box, p.187) are also numerous, while the valley bottoms are farmed mainly by caste Hindus.

Sundarijal is the most common **starting point**, with frequent buses from Kathmandu, but alternative trailheads include Sankhu, Kakani and Nagarkot. To get deeper into the hills faster, take the Arniko Highway to Banepa or Dhulikhel, and change to one of the fairly frequent buses for **Melamchi Bazaar**; rough roads head up from here towards both Thimbu and Sermathang, but are frequently blocked.

Most trekkers make a five- to seven-day, typically clockwise loop around two main ridges on either side of the Melamchi Khola, staying high – and avoiding the mega water-diversion Melamchi Project under construction in the valley. The walk in from Sundarijal (1460m) begins with a four- or five-hour climb up and over the gorgeously wooded Shivapuri National Park to **Chisapani** (2251m), a celebrated viewpoint settlement just beyond the northern edge of the national park. It's another five switchbacking hours or so to **Kutumsang** (2470m), a Sherpa village where the

NEPAL'S MOUNTAIN PEOPLES

The inhabitants of Nepal's northernmost, highest-altitude regions are culturally close to their Tibetan cousins, on the other side of the range. While many have developed their own local identities, most famously the Lo-pa of Lo (better known as Mustang) and the Sherpas of Khumbu in the Everest region, Nepalis collectively call these peoples **Bhotiya**. This means, broadly, "Tibetan", but usually conveys an unfortunate derogatory sense of "hicks from the sticks".

Farmers, herders and trans-Himalayan traders, the highland peoples eke out a living in the harsh climate by growing barley, buckwheat and potatoes, and herding yaks and yak hybrids. Their villages vary in appearance: those in the west are strongly Tibetan, with houses stacked up slopes so that the flat roof of one serves as the grain-drying terrace of the next, while in the east houses are more likely to be detached and have sloping, shingle roofs. Like Tibetans, they traditionally take their tea flavoured with salt and yak butter, and married women wear trademark rainbow aprons (**pangden**) and wraparound dresses (**chuba**). That said, jogging pants with a fleece or down jacket is practically a uniform in tourist areas.

Almost all highland ethnic peoples are **Tibetan Buddhists**. Their **chortens** (stupa-like cremation monuments), **mani** walls (consisting of slates inscribed with the mantra **Om mani padme hum** – see p.397), *gompa* (monasteries) and prayer flags (**lung ta**: literally, "wind horse") are the most memorable man-made features of the Himalayas. Unencumbered by caste, highlanders have fewer restrictions than many Nepali people: women, in particular, play a more equal role in household affairs, speak their minds openly, are able to tease and mingle with men publicly, and can divorce without stigma. Trekkers are likely to encounter many highland women running their own tourist lodges and businesses while their husbands are off farming, yak herding or guiding.

7

Langtang National Park headquarters is based; there are settlements all the way up until Kutumsang, so the walk can be broken almost wherever you like. From **Kutumsang** the route continues north along the ridge for four or five hours, passing through lovely oak then rhododendron forest via Mangengoth (3390m) to **Therapati** (3510m).

From here, the circuit breaks east, taking in the fine villages of **Melamchigaon**, **Tarkeghyang** and **Sermathang**. The walk between the latter two is somewhat shadowed by a rough road, but is otherwise very rewarding, passing picturesque monasteries and contouring through forests of oak, rhododendron and *lokta*, whose bark is used to make traditional paper. From Sermathang, you can continue down the ridge towards Melamchi Bazaar, though jeeps and buses are available (condition of the road permitting). From Tarkheghyang, the faster alternative is to take a side trail down to the Melamchi Khola and Melamchi road at **Thimbu** (or, failing that, an hour or so below Thimbu) where you can pick up a jeep down to Melamchi Bazaar if the road is passable. Countless other trails strike west and east to villages that see few trekkers.

Gosainkund can be reached from Helambu by a long, high, rugged route from Therapati, via the **Laurabina La** (see p.338). The higher, still tougher alternative route to Langtang heads north from Tarkeghyang over the **Kangja La** (5130m), a serious three-day traverse for which you'll need a tent, food, crampons and ice axe (it may be impassable between Dec and March). From Tarkeghyang, lesser trails cut across the Indrawati basin and over to **Panch Pokhari** (3800m), a set of lakes two or three days to the east, and from there you could continue south to the Chautara road, which joins the Arniko Highway just above Dolalghat.

The Everest region

EVEREST is more a pilgrimage than a trek: a tough personal challenge with a clear goal at the end, it passes deep into Buddhist Sherpa country, among some of the world's most sublime peaks. In terms of popularity, the region runs second to Annapurna. That said, the majority of trekkers in **Solu-Khumbu**, the Everest region, are all heading up the same trail. From the alarming airstrip at **Lukla**, the trail leads north into mountainous **Khumbu**, the dizzyingly high Sherpa homeland. The trail forks above the Sherpa capital of **Namche Bazaar** (or Namche for short): one route leads to Everest Base Camp and the viewpoint of Kala Pattar; the other for the beautiful Gokyo Lakes. Both high points are about eight days from Lukla, and can be combined by crossing the high pass of the **Cho La**.

Relatively few trekkers now take the switchback hike from the roadhead at **Shivalaya** through **Solu**, the lower, greener, more populous and more ethnically diverse country to the south. It's a stunning route, and offers a great way to acclimatize, but the extra five to seven days' walking is too much for many people. You should leave slack in your schedule even if you're flying, though, as getting a place on a plane out of Lukla can be problematic if bad weather causes cancellations to stack up.

To get a good look at Everest, you'll have to spend at least four nights above 4000m and at least one at around 5000m. At these altitudes, there is a serious risk of developing **acute mountain sickness** (AMS) and you must know the signs (see p.316). Everest is also the **coldest** of the major treks, so you'll need a good sleeping bag, several layers of warm clothes, and sturdy boots that will keep out snow. The rental shops of Namche, in Khumbu, allow you to stock up on high-altitude gear and return it on the way back down. Because of weather, the **trekking "window"** is especially short in Khumbu – early October to mid-November, and late March to late April – and this, in turn, creates a seasonal stampede on the trails and at the Lukla airstrip. Winter isn't out of the question, but it's just that much colder.

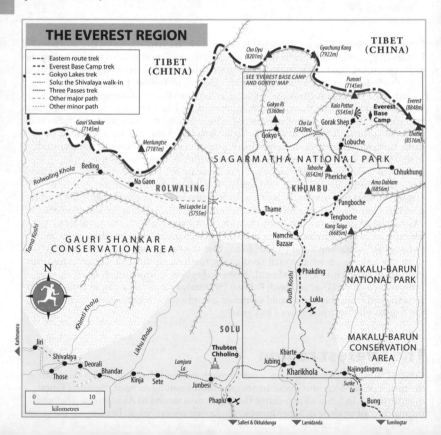

While Everest isn't as heavily trekked as Annapurna, its high-altitude **environment** is even more fragile. Khumbu, with less than four thousand inhabitants, receives anything from ten to twenty thousand trekkers a year, and probably twice as many porters. Lodge-building almost destroyed the Blue Pine and Silver Fir forests around Lukla, and the demand for firewood is many times the regeneration capacity of the area. Near trekking villages, up to half the juniper shrubs have vanished in smoke. The **Sagarmatha National Park**, which covers most of Khumbu, has done some fine work in reforestation (funded by the Rs3000 entry fee), but it can't be said often enough: have as little to do with wood-burning as possible.

The popular trails through Solu-Khumbu are well equipped with **lodges**, some basic, some fancy (and surprisingly expensive, until you consider the costs of portering in all supplies this far). Prices rise as you ascend; near the top, most lodges offer basic bunk beds only. The main Jiri–Lukla–Namche–Base Camp route is very straightforward, as is the alternative high-level spur to the Gokyo lakes, but a **guide** is advisable for pretty much anything else – and may be compulsory, if the new rules for independent trekking come into force. Solu-Khumbu is the easiest area in Nepal to hire a **woman porter** – a Sherpani – although few speak enough English to serve as guides.

7

GETTING THERE   **THE EVEREST TRAILHEADS**

Most trekkers fly to **Lukla** from Kathmandu, though the dedicated few walk from the nearest roadhead, at **Shivalaya**. It's also possible to fly to **Phaplu**, on the old Everest walk-in route. For accounts of the longer, eastern approaches to Everest, see "The eastern routes" (see p.346).
To Lukla Lukla airstrip is one of the world's most alarming – or thrilling, depending on your point of view: a distressingly short uphill runway apparently heading into the mountain halfway up the Dudh Koshi gorge. At least it's got tarmac these days and they've cleared away the plane wreckage that used to festoon it. There are up to 24 flights a day, in three "rounds" of flights, but the problems of cancellations because of bad weather and trekkers queuing to get out remain. Book early, and book the earliest possible flight in the day to have the best chance of

avoiding delays and cancellations.
To Phaplu There are almost daily flights to Phaplu, a couple of hours below Junbesi. It's not much cheaper than flying all the way to Lukla, three days further on, and not much more reliable, but you'd be walking a much less well-trodden route.
To Shivalaya All transport to Shivalaya departs from the City Bus Park in Kathmandu (see p.95), leaving very early in the morning. There's only one daily bus (12–14hr), though other buses stop a 3hr walk short of Shivalaya, at the old roadhead of Jiri. Tata Sumo jeeps are quicker (8–10hr), and some will take you on the rough road that now stretches beyond as far as Bhandar – potentially cutting the first day off the trek, though at the cost of at least three very uncomfortable hours.

Everest Base Camp

From **Lukla** (2840m), the trail powers north up the Dudh Koshi before passing into Khumbu and the Sagarmatha National Park (Rs3000 entry fee) at **Jorsale** (2740m), and bounding up to lofty **NAMCHE BAZAAR** (3450m) – **NAMCHE** for short – where Khumbu and the serious scenery start. Nestled handsomely in a horseshoe bowl, the Sherpa "capital" has done very well out of mountaineering and trekking over the years, and shops sell (or rent) absolutely anything a trekker could desire. There's also a bank (with an ATM), a post office, a bakery, a place calling itself "the world's highest bar", and even internet access. Try to make your trip coincide with the **Saturday market**, which draws Tibetans from the north and **Rais** from the south, or visit the national park **visitors' centre**, perched on the ridge east of town, which contains an informative museum. **Thame**, a beautiful few hours' walk west of Namche, makes an excellent side trip.

There are numerous possibilities **above Namche**, including passing through the relatively untouristy and unusually flat settlements of **Khumjung** (3780m) and Khunde. The main route contours to Sanasa (where the trail to Gokyo breaks off – see p.345), before descending to cross the genuinely milky-looking Dudh Koshi ("Milk River"), at **Phunki Tenga** (3250m). The trail veers northeast into a tributary valley and climbs steeply to **Tengboche** (3860m), where the wildlife-rich juniper forest has long been

7

SHERPAS

Nepal's most famous ethnic group, the **Sherpas** probably migrated to Solu-Khumbu four or five centuries ago from eastern Tibet; their name, locally pronounced "sharwa", means "People from the East". Until the arrival of the potato in the 1830s, whose calorific value meant that a settled lifestyle was possible, they were nomads, driving their yaks to pasture in Tibet and wintering in Nepal. (Sherpa potatoes today are famously delicious, eaten boiled in their skins, with a little salt and chilli.) Cross-border trade is now very much one-way, with everything from butter, noodles and meat to electronics, carpets and cement making its way south from Tibet.

Sherpas maintain the highest permanent settlements in the world – up to 4700m – which accounts for their legendary hardiness at **altitude**. From the 1900s, Sherpas worked as high-altitude expedition porters, gaining a reputation as "tigers of the snows" and learning climbing techniques. In 1953, **Tenzing Norgay** became one of the first two men to reach the top of Everest, achieving worldwide fame for his people. The break couldn't have come at a better time, for trans-Himalayan trade was soon cut short by the Chinese occupation of Tibet. Since then, Sherpas have deftly diversified into tourism, starting their own trekking and mountaineering agencies, opening lodges and selling souvenirs and equipment. Forty years ago, Namche Bazaar was a cluster of stone, wood and slate huts; now every single roof is metal, all windows are glazed and some lodges are palatial.

Canny commercialism doesn't mean that Sherpas aren't devout **Buddhists**, and most villages of note support a *gompa* and a few monks (or nuns). But there are a few animist elements as well: they revere Khumbila, a sacred peak just north of Namche, as a sort of tribal totem, and regard fire as a deity (it's disrespectful to throw rubbish into a Sherpa hearth). Sherpas eat meat, of course, but in deference to the *dharma* they draw the line at slaughtering it – they hire people of other groups to do that.

---

protected by the local lamas and there's a show-stealing view of everybody's favourite peak, Ama Dablam (6828m) – the "mother with a jewel box", as Sherpas call it. Tengboche's large monastery was lavishly rebuilt in the early 1990s, and has a fascinating permanent exhibition. Mani Rimdu (see p.36), the Sherpa dance-drama festival, is held here on the full moon of October–November.

The trail briefly descends through birch and fir forest to Deboche, a settlement with a nunnery, before ascending again to **Pangboche**, containing Khumbu's oldest *gompa*, where for a donation the lama will show you some yeti relics. (The higher trail leading west out of Pangboche allows you to cut across to the Gokyo trek, on the opposite side of the Dudh Koshi valley.) After crossing the Imja Khola, the trail follows the terraces of the valley floor to Pheriche (4250m), site of a Himalayan Rescue Association post (AMS talks are held most afternoons, and consultations are available). Above Pheriche, the stone and slate-roofed Sherpa settlements are strictly seasonal – trekking lodges aside.

The village of **Dingboche** (4360m), in the valley of the Imja Khola a little above Pheriche, is a slight detour from the fastest route up, but sitting right under Ama Dablam as it does, it has a more appealing situation than Pheriche, and offers some fine acclimatization side trips: to a *gompa* 400m above, or further up the Imja Khola to **Chhukhung** (4730m). This sensationally situated village is tiny, with only a few lodges, but can serve as a base for higher explorations still: on to Imja Tso (a glacial meltwater lake marooned in moraine that threatens to burst), up to the peak of Chhukung Ri (5546m) or ascending towards the Kongma La (see p.345).

The Dingboche route rejoins the trail up from Pheriche at **Dughla** (4620m), which is where acclimatization problems set in for many trekkers. Do not ascend with symptoms of AMS (see p.316). Immediately above the trail climbs the stony terminal moraine of the Khumbu Glacier, passing a series of monuments to Sherpas killed on Everest, to reach **Lobuche** (4930m). Another day's march along the grassy edge of the glacier's lateral moraine brings you to **Gorak Shep** (5180m), the last huddle of lodges – and a cold, breathless and probably sleepless night in uncomfortably crowded bunk rooms.

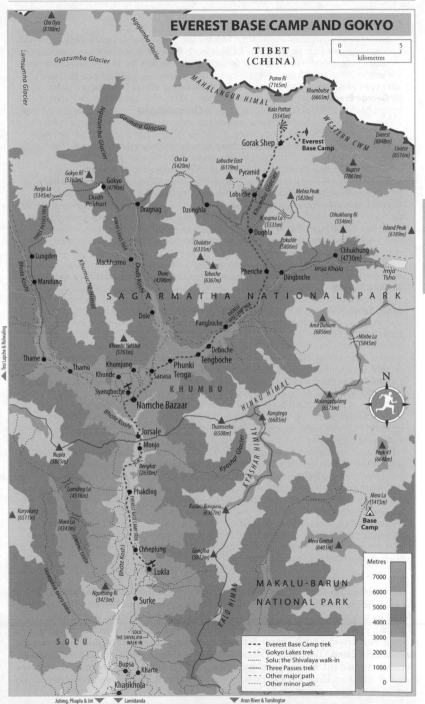

EVEREST BASE CAMP AND GOKYO

TIBET
(CHINA)

0 — 5
kilometres

7

SAGARMATHA NATIONAL PARK

KHUMBU

HINKU HIMAL

KYASHAR HIMAL

KALO HIMAL

MAKALU-BARUN
NATIONAL PARK

SOLU

N

Tesi Lapche & Rolwaling

Jubing, Phaplu & Jiri   Lamidanda   Arun River & Tumlingtar

Lumsumna Glacier
Gyazumba Glacier
Ngozumba Glacier
Gaunara Glacier
Cho Oyu (8188m)
Mahalangur Himal
Pumo Ri (7165m)
Khumbutse (6665m)
Kala Pattar (5545m)
Western Cwm
Everest (8848m)
Gorak Shep
Everest Base Camp
Lhotse (8516m)
Nuptse (7861m)
Gokyo Ri (5360m)
Gokyo (4790m)
Dudh Pokhari
Cho La (5420m)
Lobuche East (6119m)
Pyramid
Lobuche
Mehra Peak (5820m)
Chhukhung Ri (5546m)
Island Peak (6189m)
Renjo La (5345m)
Ngozumba Glacier
Dragnag
Dzonghla
Kongma La (5535m)
Dughla
Pokalde (5806m)
Chhukhung (4730m)
Three Passes Trek
Gokyo Lakes Trek
Lungden
Machhermo
Cholatse (6335m)
Thare (4390m)
Taboche (6367m)
Pheriche
Dingboche
Imja Khola
Imja Tsho
Marulung
Khumuche Himal
Dole
Pangboche
Ama Dablam (6856m)
Minbo La (5845m)
Bhote Koshi
Khumbi Yul Lha (5761m)
Deboche
Tengboche
Thame
Thamo
Khumjung
Phunki Tenga
Sanasa
Khunde
Syangboche
Namche Bazaar
Malangphulang (6573m)
Kangtega (6685m)
Everest Base Camp Trek
Jorsale
Monjo
Thamserku (6508m)
Kyashar Glacier
Peak 41 (6648m)
Nupla (5885m)
Bengkar (2630m)
Lumding La (4516m)
Phakding
Kusum Kanguru (6367m)
Mera La (5415m)
Base Camp
Karyolung (6511m)
Mora La (4343m)
Chheplung
Ganglha (5813m)
Mera Central (6461m)
Lukla
Ngothung Ri (3473m)
Surke
Bupsa
Kharte
Khatikhola
Solu: The Shivalaya Walk-In

Metres

	7000
	6000
	5000
	4000
	3000
	2000
	1000
	0

--- Everest Base Camp trek
--- Gokyo Lakes trek
····· Solu: the Shivalaya walk-in
····· Three Passes trek
--- Other major path
--- Other minor path

7

CLIMBING EVEREST

In 1841, while taking routine measurements from the plains, members of the Survey of India logged a previously unnoted summit which they labelled simply **Peak XV**. Fifteen years later, computations revealed it to be the world's highest mountain, at 29,002ft, or 8840m. The estimate was later revised upwards to 8848m, though two surveys in the last fifteen years have tried to change the figure again to either 8850m or 8844m. Take your pick; it's still the highest. The British named it after **Sir George Everest**, head of the Survey of India from 1823 to 1843, and it was decades before anyone troubled to find out the local, Sherpa name: **Chomolungma**. Usually translated as "Mother Goddess", this is actually a contraction of *jomo miyo langsangma*, one of five sister mountain gods, known to Sherpas for her agricultural bounty. There's also a Nepali name, Sagarmatha, from the Sanskrit for "Forehead of the Sky", but it was invented in the 1960s by a Hindu-nationalist Nepali government. The Chinese use the Sherpa name, rendered as "Zhumulangma".

Politically off-limits until the early twentieth century, the climb to the summit was first attempted from the Tibetan side in 1922 by a British party that included **George Mallory**, who famously justified his attempt on the mountain "because it is there". Two years later, Mallory and Andrew Irvine reached at least 8500m before probably falling to their deaths from the Second Step – a barrier that would likely have thwarted any attempt with the equipment of the day; a 1999 search found Mallory's remains. Several more attempts were made until World War II suspended activities, and the Chinese invasion of Tibet in 1950 closed the northern approach to mountaineers.

With the opening of Nepal in 1951, a race between Swiss and British teams was on. The mountain was finally scaled via the South Col by New Zealander **Edmund Hillary** and Sherpa **Tenzing Norgay** in a British-led expedition in 1953. Throughout the next two decades, increasingly big expeditions put ever greater numbers of men – and women, starting with **Junko Tabei** of Japan in 1975 – on the top. From the mid-1970s, smaller, quicker "alpine-style" ascents began to grab the headlines. **Reinhold Messner** was one of two climbers to reach the summit without oxygen in 1978, and in 1980 he made the first successful solo ascent of Everest.

After Messner's landmark achievements, climbing became a matter of finding new and ever-harder routes, or setting new records for youngest/oldest/fastest ascents, or descending on **skis** (Davo Karnicar in 2000), **snowboards** (Marco Siffredi and Stefan Gatt in 2001) or **paragliders** (Bertrand and Claire Bernier Roche; eight minutes from summit to base camp). Or indeed going up repeatedly: professional guide-climber **Apa Sherpa** had summited 21 times at the time of writing; on his penultimate ascent he unfurled a banner reading "You heard our voice, now raise yours – we can stop climate change in the Himalayas". Between the first ascent in 1953 and 1990, over four hundred people had climbed Everest. At the time of writing, the tally was well over four thousand.

Everest has most often hit the headlines in recent years due to **pollution** – well-climbed areas of the mountain are littered with old ropes, tents, oxygen canisters and even bodies – and a few notorious **tragedies**. One of the most controversial was the storm of 1996, chronicled in Jon Krakauer's *Into Thin Air* (see p.426), in which eight climbers died in a single day – partly due to the fixed ropes up the southeast ridge being so congested with clients on commercial expeditions that climbers were too slow getting up, and too late making their descent. In 2006, new controversy flared when it was revealed that a number of expeditions passed by the frostbitten and disoriented climber David Sharp without trying to rescue him. And then in 2014, the single most deadly accident on the mountain occurred, when sixteen Sherpas were killed in an avalanche (see box, p.306).

The payoff comes the next day, when you climb up the mound of **Kala Pattar** (5545m): the extra height provides an unbelievable panorama, not only of **Everest** (8848m) but also of its neighbours Lhotse (Nepal's third-highest peak, at 8516m) and Nuptse (7861m), as well as the sugarloaf of Pumo Ri (7165m), the "daughter mountain".

A separate day-trip can be made across the thrillingly ice-spired Khumbu Glacier to **Everest Base Camp**. The trail is well trodden by climbing expeditions and their yaks and porters, so you don't need any technical equipment beyond stout boots. Only the very fittest and best-acclimatized can manage Kala Pattar and Base Camp in one day; if you have to choose one over the other, make it Kala Pattar.

The Gokyo Lakes spur

You're that little bit further away from Everest, but the scenery is every bit as good at **GOKYO LAKES**, in the next valley to the west, and the lodges are much more appealing, with their glazed-in sun decks. The route breaks off the Base Camp trail at Sanasa, below Khumjung, following the Dudh Koshi north via Machhermo (where there's an HRA medical post) to **Gokyo**, a cluster of lodges set beside the Ngozumba Glacier – the biggest in Nepal. It can be done in a long day if you're fit and acclimatized; two or three if you're not – there are lodges at frequent intervals all the way up. Several jewel-blue lakes, dammed up by the glacier's lateral moraine, dot the west side of the valley above and below Gokyo. The high point is an overlook, **Gokyo Ri**, surveying a clutter of blue teeth – Cho Oyu, Everest and Lhotse are just the ones over 8000m – and the long grey glacier tongue.

The Three Passes

The fabulous, ambitious **"THREE PASSES" ROUTE** turns the otherwise up-and-down Everest trek into a true, high-level circuit. To attempt it, you'll need to be experienced, well equipped (though ropes and crampons are not usually needed, at least not in the early autumn and spring seasons) and be trekking with an experienced guide. The usual starting point is **Chhukhung** (the ascent from Dingboche is just too great), from where you have to get over the **Kongma La** (5535m) and down to Lobuche in one long, tough day.

From there, perhaps after a side trip to Everest Base Camp, you cross the strenuous **Cho La** (5420m) over to the Gokyo valley, in two days. There are a couple of simple lodges at unappealing Dzonghla (4910m), two to three hours from Lobuche, and at Dragnag (4700m) on the other side of the pass, four hours from Gokyo. But the high, middle section, crossing the pass, has to be done in one long day (unless you have tents): that's six to eight hours, or more in bad conditions or if you suffer from altitude problems – which is all too likely this high. The pass is usually snowy on the eastern side, where you have to cross onto a glacier, with some tricky and slippery sections. Don't attempt it if you're in any doubt about the weather, or your own condition, and team up with a group. In good autumn and spring conditions, full crampons aren't usually necessary, but mini-crampons are an excellent, lightweight idea, and an ice axe could be handy; an experienced guide with a thorough understanding of the route is essential.

From Gokyo, you head west over the **Renjo La** (5345m), to the basic rest-houses at Lungden (4350m) or Marulung (4200m), then on to Thame and Namche the next day. How long the route takes depends entirely on acclimatization and fitness. The ascent from Lukla should be spread over 6–8 days, and it would be dangerously taxing to attempt all three passes in quick succession. Count on no less than 14 days, then, and ideally 18–20, and note that the passes are typically shut between late November and early March.

Solu: the Shivalaya walk-in

The **SHIVALAYA WALK-IN** is one of the classic Middle Hill treks in Nepal, and the crowds flying straight in to Lukla don't know what they are missing. Cutting across the lay of the land, the trail dips and soars between tropical valleys as low as 1500m and alpine passes as high as 3500m, but the sense of excitement as you get closer to the mountains proper makes all the gruelling legwork worthwhile – not to mention the fitness and acclimitization you'll accrue. A few glimpses of peaks – notably Gauri Shankar (7145m) – urge you along during the first five or six days, although the lasting images of the Solu region are of tumbling gorges, rhododendron forests and terraced fields hewn out of steep hillsides. Expect to walk for six or seven days to reach Lukla, not counting side trips – but thereafter you'll be walking much faster than those flying in, skipping up to Namche Bazaar in a day from Lukla. The bulk of traffic through

7

THE FABLED YETI

The **yeti** ("man of the rocky places") has been a staple of Sherpa and Tibetan folklore for centuries, and takes three forms: the grey- or reddish-haired, man-like **drema**, who portends disaster; the huge, bear-like **chuti**, who preys on livestock; and the red or golden-furred **mite**, who sometimes attacks humans. Stories of hairy, ape-like creatures roaming the snowy heights first came to the attention of the outside world when explorers reported seeing mysterious moving figures and large, unidentified footprints in the snow. Captivated by the reports, an imaginative Fleet Street hack coined the term "abominable snowman", a wilful mistranslation of *metoh kang-mi*, or "man-bear snow-man", which was how a Sherpa guide described the creature during the 1921 Everest reconnaissance expedition. It wasn't until 1951, during the first British Everest expedition from the Nepal side, that climber Eric Shipton took **photographs** of supposed yeti tracks. Since then, several highly publicized **yeti-hunts**, including one led by Sir Edmund Hillary in 1960, and others led by Reinhold Messner in the 1990s, have brought back a wealth of circumstantial evidence – Messner claimed to have seen a yeti in Tibet himself in 1986 – but not one authenticated sighting, spoor or hair sample. Oversized footprints could be any animal's tracks, melted and enlarged by the sun. Meanwhile, "yeti" scalps kept at various *gompa* have been revealed to be stitched-together animal skins, while the skeletal hand at Pangboche is likely to be a human relic.

Messner eventually concluded that his yeti was simply a Himalayan black bear. Zoologists observe, however, that most sightings emphasize the redness of the creature's hair, which rather suggests that an **unknown primate** might indeed exist in the high Himalayas. The sadder conclusion is that yetis did exist, within human memory, but, like so many other Himalayan species, they're either so critically endangered as to be almost invisible, or extinct. For more on the wildlife of the high Himalayas, turn to "Contexts" (see p.419).

Solu consists of porters humping in gear for trekking groups and expeditions flying into Lukla, and this is reflected in the relatively no-frills **food and lodging** available.

There are a number of variations on the route, but essentially you're switchbacking over three passes, each bigger than the last. After the steamy, bustling riverside bazaar of **Shivalaya** (1770m) you climb over the pass at **Deurali** (2710m) – an alternative side route takes you higher, via the cheese factory at **Thodung** (3091m) – and down via the handsome village of **Bhandar** (2190m) to another settlement on the warm valley floor: **Kinja** (1630m). It is possible to get transport from Shivalaya to Bhandar, where the road ends, but you won't save much time and the road is slow and deeply uncomfortable.

Most people choose to break the monumental third climb that lies ahead into two parts by spending their third night at **Sete** (2575m), halfway up to the **Lamjura La** (3530m), a pass where you first taste the scale of the mountains ahead. From there, it's a long descent through forest to the idyllic quasi-alpine Sherpa village of **Junbesi** (2680m). Most trekkers are understandably impatient to get up to Everest, but a side trip to the powerfully Tibetan **Thubten Chholing Gompa**, north of Junbesi, is well worth it, and it's possible to spend many days in the area. The airstrip at Phaplu is just two hours south, and immediately below that is Solu-Khumbu's rarely visited capital, Salleri, a long strip of two-storey houses strung out on a green hillside, with a thriving Saturday bazaar at its bottom end.

Less than two hours above Junbesi, **Everest View** gives the first serious view of the Khumbu range, with Everest itself apparently subsidiary to the nearer peaks. The next pass, **Traksindho La** (3071m), finally takes you into the Dudh Koshi valley and, at **Jubing**, an attractively bamboo-festooned Rai village below, the trail bends north towards Everest. Two days later, it sidesteps Lukla and joins the well-trodden route to Khumbu.

The eastern routes

The **EASTERN ROUTES** to or from Everest are sometimes treated as an exit by trekkers who want to avoid the long backtrack to Shivalaya, but there's no reason why the itineraries can't be done in reverse, except perhaps that it's better to gain some confidence before tackling this less-trekked region. Another factor to consider is the **season**: try to do the lower section of the trek when it's cooler. The routes are equipped with **lodges** and a guide isn't needed, but don't expect many English signs or much fancy food.

From the Everest region, the most interesting **route** leaves the Shivalaya walk-in at **Kharte**, about a day south of Lukla, and heads southeastwards to reach Tumlingtar five to seven days later, crossing three passes over 3000m. Part of this stretch traverses the Makalu-Barun Conservation Area (see p.348), and the Rs3000 entrance fee may be required at a checkpost. The first half of the trek passes through tangled hills inhabited mainly by Rais; after reaching the last and highest pass, the Salpa Bhanjyang (3350m), it descends steadily to the deep, hot valley of the Arun – the traditional Rai homeland, though with a strong Hindu-caste presence. After crossing the river at a mere 300m, it's a short day to **Tumlingtar**, a busy bazaar overlooking the Arun River; from here there are flights twice daily or more to Kathmandu, or you can pick up a local bus for the tortuous journey back via Chainpur and Basantapur to Hile (see p.298).

Other routes head south from the Tragsindho La or, alternatively, Junbesi, to the **Phaplu** airstrip (see p.310), which is connected by road to the Terai. A full route description is included in our "Mountain biking" chapter (see p.366). Another southbound route aims roughly due south from Jubing down the Dudh Koshi, then bounds across the big hills on the eastern side of the valley and over to **Lamidanda** airstrip.

Remote and restricted areas

Treks in remote **far eastern** and **far western** Nepal are mostly restricted to two kinds of traveller, both adventurous in their own way. The majority come on **organized camping treks** with agencies – in fact, this is obligatory for those areas that require a permit (see p.314). The minority are **independent trekkers** prepared either to carry tents and food and negotiate with porters, or to seek food and lodging in local homes and basic lodges. Independent travel is difficult in the west, where food shortages, relatively low population and cultural barriers can be problematic. **Access** is a problem on both sides of the country. In the east, Basantapur, the principal trailhead, is some 24 hours by **bus** from Kathmandu. Journey times to the far west by road – where there *are* roads – don't even bear calculating. **Flights**, therefore, are worth looking into. Few cost much more than $100 one-way, though some remote areas require two flights to reach.

Far eastern Nepal

Ethnically, **EASTERN NEPAL** is even more diverse than the Annapurna region: Rais and Limbus (see p.349) are dominant in the hills, while Sherpas, Tamangs and other highlanders inhabit the high country, and Hindu castes the valleys. Makalu, Kanchenjunga and other big peaks provide stunning **views** from most high points. Flora and fauna are also of great interest to specialists, especially the **butterflies** and other insects of the upper Arun valley, and the **rhododendrons** of the Milke Daada. The east is relatively well-off, so in the settled areas, especially in the region around the Newari bazaar towns of Bhojpur, Chainpur and Khandbari, **food** and **lodging** is easy to come by – making fine country for adventurous trekkers who like exploring places that aren't written up in guidebooks. The serious mountain treks to Makalu and Kanchenjunga, however, require expedition-scale planning, official permits and agency support.

The Milke Daada
A long north–south ridge famed for its spectacular views and rhododendrons, the **MILKE DAADA** can be linked up with a visit to the bazaar town of Chainpur for a fine trek of

7

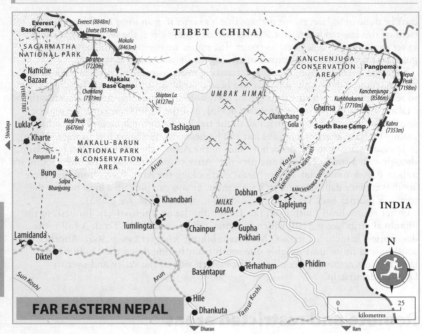

FAR EASTERN NEPAL

seven or so days, going no higher than 3500m. From Basantapur (p.347) the route heads north, initially following a rough road then continuing north on paths through the lush cloud forest of the Milke Daada, past the lakes at **Gupha Pokhari** (2890m). Various trails to **Chainpur** branch off to the west; from there you can hitch a jeep ride to the airstrip at Tumlingtar or return to Hile. Alternatively, you could head east from Gupha Pokhari to Taplejung airstrip. Both Tumlingtar and Taplejung airstrips have more frequent and reliable connections to Biratnagar, in the Eastern Terai, than to Kathmandu.

Basic **food and lodging** can be found along most of this route, but the absence of lodges north of Gupha Pokhari limits an independent trekker's ability to explore higher up the Milke Daada.

Makalu Base Camp

Much of the **MAKALU BASE CAMP** trek passes through the wild and remote **Makalu-Barun National Park** (Rs3000 entry fee) and the contiguous **Makalu-Barun Conservation Area**. Established in 1992, the park is intended to stem the growing human pressure around the base-camp area and preserve one of the most botanically diverse and wildlife-rich areas in the Himalayas. The usual starting point is the airstrip at **Tumlingtar**, though a marathon road trip could get you there (and even beyond, up to Khandbari) via Dharan, Hile and Basantapur. There are alternative routes on either side of the Arun for the first three or four days, but only one route above there for the next seven days or so (for which a tent and food are required) to the base camp, so you're obliged to retrace your steps most of the way back. The highest days take you over the Barun also known as the **Shipton La** (4127m), and into the remote Upper Barun valley, whose lofty beauty is often compared to the Annapurna Sanctuary.

Kanchenjunga

The most incredible trek in this part of Nepal is to the foot of **Kanchenjunga**, the third-highest peak in the world at 8586m, and arguably the most romantic.

RAIS AND LIMBUS

The traditional inhabitants of the eastern hills are the Kirati peoples, usually labelled either **Rai** or **Limbu**, though Rai is really an honorific title meaning "chief" and Rais and Limbus divide themselves into numerous *thars*, or clans. There are more than 24 Rai languages – an astonishing number in a population of around half a million. The orally transmitted myths and legends of the Rais and Limbus differ from clan to clan, but largely agree that each clan is descended from one of ten (or more, or less) "brothers" who took different routes as they migrated to Kirat, probably from the east. Rais traditionally occupy the middle-elevation hills between the Dudh Koshi and the Arun River. Limbuwan, the traditional Limbu homeland, lies further east, centred around the lower slopes of the Tamur Koshi valley.

Like the Magars and Gurungs of the west, members of these staunchly independent hill groups make up a significant portion of the **Gurkha regiments**, and army pensions have traditionally boosted the local, virtually subsistence economy. Rais and Limbus follow their own forms of nature- and ancestor-worship, combined with ingredients of shamanism, but increasingly also embrace **Hindu practices**. In recent years, some have joined the ranks of a Kirat revivalist sect founded by the late Guru Phalgunanda, which incorporates many orthodox Hindu practices – including abstinence from meat and tobacco. Such behaviour is somewhat alien to traditional Kirati culture, which seems to have set great store by the ritual raising – and sometimes, still, sacrifice – of pigs and other animals, and even greater store by the liberal drinking of home-brewed beer and distilled *raksi*. Unusually, Rais and Limbus bury their dead (cremation is the usual practice throughout the subcontinent), and Limbus erect distinctive rectangular, whitewashed monuments over graves.

7

Kanchenjunga is an expensive trek because it's officially restricted to agency-organized groups and, given its remote location in the extreme northeastern corner of the country, it involves up to three weeks' walking, or more if you plan to visit both south and north sides. There's a Rs2000 fee to enter the **Kanchenjunga Conservation Area**.

The starting points are either the roadhead at **Basantapur** (see p.347), initially following the trail up the Milke Daada, or, saving three days, the airstrip at **Taplejung** – which has occasional direct flights from Kathmandu but is more efficiently served via Biratnagar (see p.293), in the Eastern Terai.

The trek passes deep into Limbu country (see box above), forking a few days northeast of Taplejung, one trail going to the snowy and fabulously scenic North Base Camp at glacier-strewn **Pangpema**, the other rollicking up and down on the way to the South Base Camp and the Yalung Glacier. (The high passes connecting the two are distinctly tricky propositions, and not to be considered without experienced guides.) Both routes offer terraced hills, wildlife-rich forests and a serious taste of unspoiled Nepali hill culture, along with fabulous views. The northern trail takes you deeper into the high mountains for longer – up to a week longer, with all the problems and risks that entails.

Far western Nepal

West of Dhaulagiri, the Himalayas retreat north into Tibet, while the foothill zone broadens, the climate becomes drier and the people poorer. The northern third of the region, left in the rain shadow of the Himalayas, receives little monsoon moisture – in every way but politically, this highland strip is part of Tibet. Jagged Himalayan grandeur isn't so much in evidence, but there's a wildness and a vastness here, and the feeling of isolation is thrilling. Treks in the **FAR WEST** are well off the beaten track: they're a chore to get to, they require a lot of preparation and, with the exception of Rara Lake, you'll find that very few Westerners have gone before you. All that might appeal if you're an experienced trekker looking for new challenges, but if you're a first-timer without agency support, forget it. That said, as roads gradually penetrate into the far west, trekking is becoming easier.

7

Logistics make or break a trek in the far west. Given the distances involved, you'll probably want to **fly** to the starting point, but the usual problems of confirming bookings are generally worse in this area. **Food and lodging** are in uncomfortably short supply, so you'll need to bring a tent, cooking utensils and at least some provisions. You should be prepared to carry it all yourself, because **porters** here are a fickle lot and often can't be spared from their farmwork. **Guides** familiar with the area are also scarce. If you go on an **organized trek** you may not be entirely insulated from these inconveniences, and for this reason agencies may try to steer you towards more easterly destinations.

The treks described below are the most realistic possibilities.

Rara National Park

RARA NATIONAL PARK is the best known of the far western trekking areas. The usual itinerary is a loop that starts and ends at Jumla airstrip, three to four days' walk from the lake; most tours take about eight days for the trip. The country is a sea of choppy, mostly forested mountains, offering only glimpses of Himalayan peaks, but the highlight is Nepal's largest lake, a lofty blue jewel surrounded by a wilderness area of meadows and forests of blue pine and rhododendron.

To get to the trailhead you first have to **fly** to Nepalgunj and then from there to **Jumla**; flights are supposed to be daily in season, but are often cancelled. There is also an airstrip at **Talcha**, less than three hours from the lake beside Gumgarhi, the remote capital of Mugu district, but flights up from Nepalgunj are irregular and most people choose to walk from Jumla. The overland alternative is to head up from **Birendra Nagar** (Surkhet) towards Jumla, which is either a week to ten days' walk each way or a horrendously, unpredictably long bus journey – 48 hours isn't unrealistic – on the grandiously named Karnali Highway, via Dailekh, Kalikot and **Sinja**, where the ruins of the capital of the twelfth- to fourteenth-century Khasa dynasty can be viewed across the river. There are **lodges** in Jumla and a bunkhouse at the lake; in between, there are a few teahouses where you might be able to stay, but camping is more pleasant and certainly more reliable – especially as food can be in short supply. The **park fee** is Rs3000.

THE GREAT HIMALAYA TRAIL, AND THE LESSER ONES

For centuries, large areas of the high Himalayas were closed off due to border disputes, cultural sensitivities, military paranoia or simply the sheer difficulty of access. In 2002, however, Nepal at last resolved its disagreements with China over the Tibet frontier, and opened up new areas along the border to visitors. Few saw any. Then, in 2008 and 2009, the adventurer and trekking enthusiast **Robin Boustead** managed to stitch together a single high-level traverse of the entire breadth of Nepal, linking all the most fabled sections of existing treks with crossings of high passes, and creating four entirely new routes. At 160 days, or so, the **Great Himalaya Trail** really is the ultimate Himalayan trek, and few would attempt to do the entire thing. (The permits for remote areas alone cost thousands of dollars, in total.) It has stimulated new interest in otherwise unvisited areas, and inspired trekking agencies to look further afield. Boustead's book, *Nepal Trekking and the Great Himalaya Trail* details the route (see p.426), and the ⓦ thegreathimalayatrail.org website is lively and authoritative.

You don't have to don crampons and hit the high passes to do some exciting, **off-piste walking** in Nepal, however. The entire country is threaded with a vast network of paths, most of which never see a foreign visitor. Rural Nepali people are accustomed to travellers requesting food and lodging, too. So in Nepal's well-populated Middle Hills, there is nothing stopping any would-be adventurer striding off from village to village, and from family home to family home, making up their own Lesser Himalaya Trail as they go.

Technical difficulties aside, Rara makes a fair compromise between the popular treks and the really obscure ones, and in a way combines the best of both worlds: like the popular treks, Rara is given detailed route descriptions in the trekking books, so you can do it without an organized group (or even a guide, if the new trekking restrictions are relaxed), yet it's remote enough to ensure that you'll see few – if any – other foreigners. Starting at the airstrip at Jumla (2400m), the route crosses two 3500m ridges before reaching pristine **Rara Lake** at 3000m. The park is one of the best places in Nepal to see **wildlife**, including Himalayan black bear, tahr, goral, musk deer and the rare red (lesser) panda; the lake itself is home to many species of waterfowl. Autumn and spring are the best seasons, and Rara is particularly worth considering in May and June, when the weather elsewhere is getting too hot or unpredictable.

Dolpo and She-Phoksundo National Park

DOLPO (sometimes written Dolpa) is an enormous, isolated district northwest of Dhaulagiri and bordering Tibet, the western half of which has been set aside as **SHE-PHOKSUNDO NATIONAL PARK**, Nepal's biggest. The park protects an awe-inspiring region of deep valleys, unclimbed peaks, remote monasteries and rare fauna. The best **time to go** is September, with May, June, October and November close behind.

Dolpo was the setting of Peter Matthiessen's *The Snow Leopard* (see p.424), and for many years the book was as close as most foreigners were allowed to get to it. It's now open to organized trekking groups, although, unofficially, it might be possible to arrange a trekking permit for **Southern (Lower) Dolpo** through an agency and do everything else independently. The permit costs $10 per week, and a trek there will take a week to ten days. There are some lodges in Lower Dolpo, but it's a food-deficit area so you'll need to bring several days' worth of provisions. Guides and porters can be hired near the airstrip. The agency-trekking requirement for **Northern (Upper) Dolpo** is strictly enforced, and the permit is much more expensive: $500 for the first ten days, $50 per day thereafter.

Most people fly into **Juphal**, the airstrip for Dolpo District, from Nepalgunj. Flying into or out of **Jumla**, about five days' walk further west, is also possible. From Juphal the route heads east to Dunai and then north, entering the park after about a day (Rs3000 **entry fee**) and reaching the village of Ringmo and the stunningly blue **Phoksundo Tal** after another two days. There are plenty of day-hiking opportunities around the lake. Beyond lies Northern Dolpo.

Humla and Mount Kailash

Tucked away in the extreme northwestern corner of Nepal, **HUMLA** is high, dry and strongly Tibetan. Snowcapped peaks hem the district in on three sides and shut out most outside influences, including the monsoon. It's open only to organized groups, and the permit costs $50 for the first week, $7 per day thereafter. This area often experiences serious spring and early-summer famines, so it's essential to bring all the food you'll need – and then some. Most people do Mount Kailash as part of a Tibet package: you might pay about $4000 per person for a 22-day itinerary which takes you on to Lhasa, with a flight back to Kathmandu; or around $3500 for an 18-day trip returning on a jeep via Kodari.

7

TREKKING PEAKS AND MOUNTAINEERING

Thirty-three lesser summits, ranging in elevation from 5550m to 6654m, are designated as **trekking peaks**. They fill the gap between standard hikes and full-on mountaineering expeditions: some are little more than snowy, breathless plods, others technical, multi-day rock and ice climbs. You need to be especially fit and able to cope with very cold and potentially stormy conditions; previous climbing experience is preferable for the easier peaks, and essential for the harder ones. Above all, acclimatization is crucial: many agency expeditions don't allow enough time, and many clients fail to summit – or worse – as a result.

The most popular trekking peaks are in the **Everest** region. Imja Tse, aka Island Peak (6160m), is busy and relatively straightforward; Lobuje East (6119m) is a demanding ridge climb; Mera Peak (6654m) is the highest of all trekking peaks, and thus among the most dangerous – even if technically it's a walk. In the **Annapurna** region, popular peaks include Pisang (6091m), a moderately difficult peak with rocky sections near Manang; and Tharphu Chuli, aka Tent Peak (5663m), dramatically situated in the Annapurna Sanctuary.

There are two categories of peak: **"Group B"** peaks are the original eighteen trekking peaks; **"Group A"** mountains were only opened to climbing parties in 2002, and may offer more of a sense of breaking new ground. They're distinguished only by bureaucracy, with harder and easier climbs in both groups.

Climbing a trekking peak takes more time than most standard routes – three to four weeks is typical – and inevitably **costs** more. Contributing to the expense is the peak **permit**. Group B peaks cost $350 for a group of 1–4 people, with an extra $350 for 5–8 people, plus $40 per person, and an extra $510 for 9–12 people, plus $25 per person; Group A peaks cost $500 for up to 7 members, plus $100 per additional person, up to a maximum of 12 in the party. Fees are payable to the official Nepal Mountaineering Association (NMA) through a certified guide or authorized trekking or travel agency. You'll also have to pay the salaries of a NMA-certified **sirdar**, who will arrange logistics, and at least a few porters, and transportation and equipment for both trekkers and staff. Some peaks are located in restricted areas, for which an additional permit fee is payable. It will take several days to a week to organize a trekking peak expedition from scratch in Kathmandu.

Another hundred-odd higher peaks are open only to **expeditions**, which must comply with additional regulations and pay significantly higher fees, though there are deep discounts for small groups climbing out of season and some peaks in the mid- and far west are now royalty-free. Scores of agencies offer guided or organized trips, some arranged around mountaineering courses.

AGENCIES

Asian Trekking Thamel Northeast, Kathmandu ☏ 01 442 4249, ⓦ asian-trekking.com.
Explore Himalaya Thamel Northwest, Kathmandu ☏ 01 441 8100, ⓦ explorehimalaya.com.
Highlander Trekking and Expeditions Thamel, Kathmandu ☏ 01 470 0563, ⓦ highlandernepal.com.
Himalayan Glacier Thamel, Kathmandu ☏ 01 441 1387, ⓦ himalayanglacier.com.
Thamserku Trekking Baluwatar ☏ 01 400 0701, ⓦ thamserkutrekking.com.

INFORMATION

Nepal Mountaineering Association Nagpokhari, Naxal ☏ 01 443 4525, ⓦ nepalmountaineering.org.

Nepal Airlines **flies** from Nepalgunj to **Simikot** (Humla's district headquarters) most days of the week in season. The most popular trek from here heads west up the valley of the Humla Karnali Nadi, struggling over the 4580m Nara La before descending to the river again and the **Tibet** border at Hilsa; it's about six or seven days' walk. From Sher, on the Tibetan side, a jeep will take you to (and, if need be, right around) **Lake Manasarowar** and the starting point for the three-day-plus circumambulation on foot of sacred **MOUNT KAILASH**. (The Humla Karnali trail is in the long process of being turned into a road, which will one day make it possible to drive the entire way from Simikot; those who prefer to walk will still be able to take a high, northerly route via Talung Lake to the border.) In May and June, which is the **best time** to go, the wildflowers are out of this world.

Upper Mustang

UPPER MUSTANG, the high-desert headwaters of the Thak Khola, was closed to foreigners until 1992, and still retains much of its medieval Tibetan culture – even if its raja has now officially been deposed and Chinese goods now pour across the border (closed to foreigners). Thousands of tourists now visit each year, but **permits** to trek in Upper Mustang are expensive – $500 for the first ten days, $50 per day thereafter; they are no longer limited to agency-organized groups, but if you are trekking independently you will need to take a **guide**. It is possible to stay in lodges – often gloriously traditional family homes – rather than have to camp.

The restricted area officially begins at Kagbeni, and most visitors fly in and out of Jomosom (see p.328), just a half-day's walk to the south. From there up the high, desertified valley of the Thak Khola to **Lo Manthang** (3840m), the lofty, walled capital, it's about five days' walk, past wind-eroded cliffs in astonishing shades of sand, rust and grey. There's little traffic on the road, but it's bound to increase, so consider alternative routes avoiding the road, such as hiking southwest out of Lo Manthang, for instance, via the Chogo La and **Ghar Gompa** to rejoin the main trail at Ghemi.

This chapter was updated with the assistance of Ramesh Chaudhary.

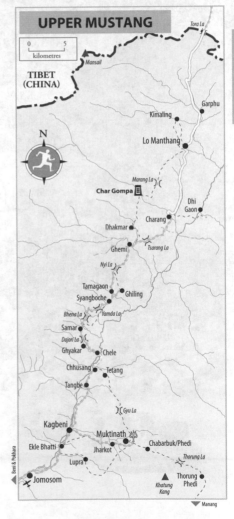

Rafting and kayaking

RAFTING ON THE MARSYANGDI RIVER

Rafting and kayaking

Thanks to the Himalayas, Nepal has some of the best, most scenic and most varied whitewater on earth. The shorter trips are hugely accessible, even for beginners, while a few of the longer trips are world classics, offering the experience of a lifetime. As well as the tranquillity of being deep in the countryside, away from towns and roads, rafting provides the thrills, laughter and companionship that comes from shooting rapids. Then there's the sheer escapism of life on the river: camping on white-sand beaches, bonfires under the stars, warm water (most rivers in Nepal are at lower, semitropical elevations), jungle-clad slopes, wildlife and birds. Some of the more remote trips, meanwhile, also involve mini-treks through little-visited areas just to get to the put-in point. Almost all rivers in Nepal are clean, and there are barely any nasty biting insects on the beaches (mosquitoes are very rare).

Your choice of **where to raft or kayak** will be largely dictated by what the operators are running during your stay. Within that context, consider what you're after in a river trip – thrills, scenery, culture, relaxation – as well as how much time and money you're willing to invest. Consider also that water levels at different times of year make a huge difference to a river's character. And remember that you don't have to return to base, and that some rafting trips open up parts of Nepal that you might not otherwise visit.

Note that a number of hydroelectric dams and diversions are either proposed or under construction; this may eventually shorten or eliminate some popular routes, and put more pressure on the remaining ones. Roads, on the other hand – which are often built to access new dams – can open up previously un-rafted river sections by creating new put-in and take-out points.

The descriptions that follow in this chapter are given roughly in order of popularity. Note that the stated grades are only a guideline, and river levels – and difficulties, therefore – can fluctuate dramatically at any time of year.

RIVER CLASSIFICATIONS

Below is a summary of the international classification system of rafting river difficulty.

Class 1 Easy. Moving water with occasional small rapids. Few or no obstacles.

Class 2 Moderate. Small rapids with regular waves. Some manoeuvring required, but easy to navigate.

Class 3 Difficult. Rapids with irregular waves and hazards that need avoiding. More difficult manoeuvring required but routes are normally obvious. Scouting from the shore is occasionally necessary.

Class 4 Very difficult. Large rapids that require careful manoeuvring. Dangerous hazards. Scouting from the shore is often necessary and rescue is usually difficult. Kayakers should be able to roll. Turbulent water and large irregular waves may flip rafts. In the event of a mishap, there is significant risk of loss, damage and/or injury.

Class 5 Extremely difficult. Long and very violent rapids with severe hazards. Continuous, powerful, confused water makes route-finding difficult, and scouting from the shore is essential. Precise manoeuvring is critical and for kayakers rolling ability needs to be 100 percent. Rescue is very difficult or impossible, and in the event of a mishap there is a significant hazard to life.

Class 6 Nearly impossible. Might possibly (but not probably) be run by a team of experts at the right water level, in the right conditions, with all possible safety precautions, but still with considerable hazard to life.

CAMP ON THE TAMUR RIVER

Highlights

❶ Kayak school How cool is it to say that you learned to kayak in the Himalayas? **See p.360**

❷ The Upper Kali Gandaki Fly to Jomosom, trek or take a jeep down the magnificent gorge of the Upper Kali Gandaki valley, and then raft your way towards the jungle lowlands. See p.362

❸ The Seti A tame, picturesque and easily accessible river, the Seti is warmed by geothermal springs. **See p.362**

❹ The Bhote Koshi A short adrenaline rush on the steepest and hardest of Nepal's raftable

rivers, which plunges down from the Tibetan border. **See p.362**

❺ The Marsyangdi A magnificent, technical stretch of river with a stunning mountain backdrop. **See p.363**

❻ The Sun Koshi The perfect introduction to rafting in Nepal: eight varied days through remote hill country. **See p.363**

❼ The Tamur Six days of challenging whitewater in the far east of the country, with the option of trekking to the put-in point through the beautiful eastern hills. **See p.364**

HIGHLIGHTS ARE MARKED ON THE MAP ON P.361

When to go

The time of year makes an enormous difference: water volume during the height of the monsoon (July to mid-Sept) is ten or more times greater than in February and March, making the major rivers off limits to all but experts. The water is more manageably exciting in mid- or late October to November, the peak rafting season, and becomes mellower (but colder) from December through to February. March through to May has rising water levels, when snowmelt and pre-monsoon storms begin to add to flows again.

Winter isn't as chilly as you might think, since most raftable river sections are below 500m elevation, but it's a slow time for tourism generally in Nepal, so many river operators don't run trips then. March and April are the **best months** for long, warm days and excellent birdwatching. However, different rivers are at their best at different times of the year – for example, the Sun Koshi is actually quite good starting in late September – so which river you go on will depend to a large extent on when you're in Nepal. Note that a given trip will take less time in high water than when the water is running more slowly.

Information, books and maps

You'll be able to get most or all of your questions answered by your rafting company, assuming you're going on an organized trip.

Independent rafters and kayakers, however, should get hold of a copy of *White Water Nepal* by Peter Knowles and Darren Clarkson-King (Rivers Publishing, 3rd edition Oct 2011); it provides comprehensive river descriptions (including detail on a host of little-rafted rivers not mentioned here), maps, and excellent advice on logistics.

For more information, updates and links to operators, visit Ⓦraftnepal.org. Himalayan Map House publishes rafting **maps** for the more popular rivers (such as the Sun Koshi and Trisuli), showing rapids, put-in points and so on. For other areas, trekking maps (see p.310) can keep you oriented.

Rafting operators and agents

A fairly sophisticated river-running industry exists in Nepal, with dozens of

NEPAL'S RIVERS AT A GLANCE

RIVER	CLASS	VOLUME	TOTAL DAYS
Trisuli	3+	Big	1–4
Upper Kali Gandaki	4-	Med	4
Seti	3-	Small	3
Upper Seti	3+	Small	2
Bhote Koshi	4+	Med	2
Upper Sun Koshi/Lower Bhote Koshi	3	Med	2
Marsyangdi	4+	Med	6
Sun Koshi	4-	Huge	8–10
Karnali	4	Huge	10
Tamur	4	Med	11
Bheri	3+	Med	8–10
Lower Kali Gandaki	2	Med	5

KEY

Volume Relative volumes are given – the actual flows vary enormously according to season.

Total days Days from Kathmandu or Pokhara and back.

Nepali and Western-associated rafting operators offering both scheduled and customized trips. Unless you're an experienced kayaker (see p.360) or are on some sort of a self-organized expedition, you'll go with one of these companies. The standards of most operators exceed international guidelines, but you get what you pay for, and Nepal has its share of sub-standard companies, too.

A few of the more **reputable Nepal-based operators** are listed in our accounts of Kathmandu (see p.99) and Pokhara (see p.214). These deal with bookings from overseas, but they'll also take walk-in clients, and if you can muster up a few friends you can arrange your own customized departure. Booking with an agency in your own country (see p.22) is more expensive, but guarantees arrangements – and in high season the best trips are fully booked months in advance.

Some of the cut-price outfits in Kathmandu and Pokhara aren't bad, but making recommendations would be misleading – companies come and go, and standards rise and fall (sometimes dramatically) from one season to the next. Shop around, and press operators hard as regards the criteria given below. Only use a company belonging to the **Nepal Association of Rafting Agents**, a trade body that sets safety standards, requires its members to employ only trained and licensed guides, and handles complaints.

Many places advertising rafting trips are merely **agents**, who usually don't know what they're talking about and who will add their own commission (low or high) to the operator's price, so you're strongly advised to **book directly** with the rafting operator. In that way, too, you can find out who else is booked on the trip, which might well influence your enjoyment.

Rafting costs

Rafting trips booked in Nepal cost $30 to $90 a day, depending on the river, number of people in the party and standard of service. For trips on the Trisuli and Kali Gandaki (the most popular rafting rivers), smarter companies typically charge $40–50 a day to a walk-in customer, which should include transport to and from the river by private bus, good, hygienic meals and a mat in a tent. Budget outfits offer these trips for around $30 a day, but at that price you can expect to travel by local bus and be served pretty unappetizing food – or even pay for your own bus tickets and meals. Other more remote rivers cost $15–40 or so a day extra.

RIVER DAYS	SCENERY/ WILDLIFE RATING	OVERALL RATING	ELEVATION (START/FINISH)
1–4	*	**	330m/170m
3	**	**	750m/500m
2	**	**	345m/190m
½	**	**	1050m/980m
1–2	**	***	1020m/760m
1	*	xx	730m/650m
4	***	**	850m/370m
6–8	**	***	625m/105m
8	***	***	560m/195m
6	**	***	635m/105m
6–8	***	***	770m/195m
4	**	**	370m/170m

KEY

Overall rating This is a subjective score of the river as a rafting trip, taking into account whitewater, scenery, logistics and cost:

*** = Highly recommended
** = Recommended
* = Specialist interest

These prices assume full rafts, which hold up to seven paying passengers each. Note that the most popular high-season trips with the most popular high-standard companies are often fully **booked up** months in advance.

When reckoning **cost per day**, bear in mind that a "three-day" trip is rarely three days of solid rafting: you may be travelling to the river most of day one, with just an hour spent on the river that afternoon, rafting for maybe four hours on day two, and then travelling back on your last day.

Rafting equipment

Most companies use paddle rafts, in which everyone paddles and the guide steers from the rear – lots of group participation and fun. On less exciting oar trips, the guide does all the work, giving the clients the chance to sit back and enjoy the scenery.

Your rafting company will advise on what to **bring**, but you'll definitely need a swimsuit, sunglasses, sunhat, sun cream, rubber-soled shoes or sport sandals, a change of clothes and shoes for camp, a towel, a head torch/flashlight and spare batteries. T-shirts and shorts are standard river wear, but if the weather is likely to be cold and/or wet, bring thermal tops and trousers; the better companies provide wetsuits, thermal tops and paddling jackets. Tents, foam mattresses and water-proof bags are normally supplied, but you need to bring your own sleeping bag (rentable in Kathmandu or Pokhara). Some companies provide waterproof barrels for **cameras**.

Kayaking

Nepal has taken off as one of the world's leading destinations for recreational kayaking, and is recognized as one of the best countries for whitewater multi-day trips. There are rivers for all abilities, including beginners.

Most visiting kayakers start by booking on a rafting trip for a **warm-up** – often on the Sun Koshi or Kali Gandaki rivers. If you book on as a kayaker, the rafting company will normally provide you free use of a kayak as part of the deal, or give you a discount if you have your own boat.

If you're thinking of **bringing your own kayak**, talk to others who've visited Nepal recently, as some

have ended up paying high excess-baggage charges on the way back. There's a wide selection of modern kayaks available for **rent** at around $20 a day in both Kathmandu and Pokhara – the latter has become quite a thriving centre for kayakers, with a couple of excellent rental outlets (see p.214). You'll need to leave a passport or a significant cash deposit. Kayak **guides** can be hired for around $20 a day. It's worth bringing all your own kayaking gear with you, but this is also available for rent if necessary.

Kayak schools are a recent development in Nepal, mostly operating out of Pokhara and offering a half-day introduction on Phewa Tal and another four-days' practice and paddling on the nearby Seti, with rafting support. The Seti is warmed by geothermal springs, making it a very pleasant place to practice rolling. Other kayak schools operate out of the riverside resorts on the Bhote Koshi and Upper Sun Koshi rivers, not far from Kathmandu. Typical prices for a five-day course start at around $300, which includes tuition, gear, food, transport, raft support and camping – that's great value.

While not so popular, another conveyance for enjoying Nepal's whitewater is the **hydrospeed**, a sort of boogie board for swimming down rivers. Pokhara's Ganesh Kayak Shop (see p.215) rents out hydrospeeds with wetsuits and helmets, as well as inflatable canoes (known as "**duckies**") and **catarafts** for those planning a do-it-yourself trip.

Safety and responsibility

By and large, rafting and kayaking are reasonably safe, with a much better accident rate than, say, mountain biking or skiing (or, for that matter, trekking). However, there are few government controls on Nepal's low-end operators and there have been fatalities in the past.

If you're rafting, make sure the company supplies life jackets (and not ancient ones), helmets and a full first-aid kit, and satisfy yourself that the rafts are in good running order and that there will be a safety demonstration. There must be a minimum of **two rafts**, in case one capsizes. In high-water conditions or on any river more difficult than class 2, the rafts should be self-bailing and there should be **safety kayakers** to rescue "swimmers".

Whether you're rafting or kayaking, **guides** must be trained, certified (including first-aid certified),

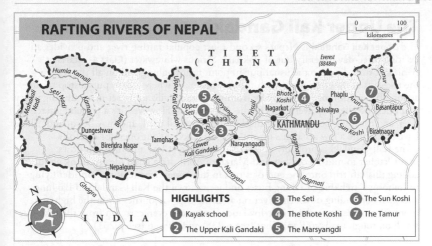

RAFTING RIVERS OF NEPAL

HIGHLIGHTS

1 Kayak school
2 The Upper Kali Gandaki
3 The Seti
4 The Bhote Koshi
5 The Marsyangdi
6 The Sun Koshi
7 The Tamur

have experience guiding on the stretch of river in question and speak adequate English – there should be an opportunity to meet guides before departure.

The more distant but potentially catastrophic safety concern is from **landslides** or rare **GLOF** or glacial lake outburst flooding (see p.417) events. If you hear an unusual, thunderous sound coming from upstream while you're on or beside the river, scramble for high ground. A big wave might be coming.

Your travel **insurance** policy should cover the proposed activity: if you're away from main roads then helicopter rescue may be needed, and no helicopter will take off without cash in hand or the assurance of repayment by an insurance company. Leave a copy of your travel policy with the operator, highlighting the emergency contact number.

Rafters and kayakers have the same responsibilities to **the environment** as trekkers, particularly regarding firewood, sanitation and litter (see p.308).

8

The Trisuli

Perhaps fifty percent of all raft trips are on the **Trisuli**, west of Kathmandu, and this is an obvious choice if you want whitewater with limited time or budget. Most itineraries are two or three days. The Trisuli has some rapids of medium difficulty (**Class 3+**) and good scenery, though it's hardly wilderness – the main road to Kathmandu follows it the entire way, and in October and November you'll have to share the river (and perhaps your beach campsite) with many other parties. Some operators have their own fixed campsites or lodges, ranging from private, green, semi-luxurious safari-style resorts to windblown village beaches complete with begging kids and scavenging dogs. Check out the camps and lodges carefully, especially with regard to how close a camp is to the noisy highway.

When booking, ask where the put-in point is: anything starting at Kuringhat or Mugling will, by and large, be a relaxing float. The **best whitewater** section is upstream of Mugling, from Charaundi to Kuringhat, and this can be done as a full-on half-day trip (perhaps as a break in the journey from Kathmandu to Pokhara).

The Trisuli lies between Pokhara, Kathmandu and Chitwan National Park, so it might make sense to incorporate your raft trip into your travel schedule. Your rafting company will normally be able to help you with logistics and look after your luggage. However, rafting all the way to Chitwan isn't allowed, so you'll have to travel from Narayanghadh to the park by vehicle.

The Upper Kali Gandaki

The **Upper Kali Gandaki** is Nepal's second most popular rafting river and provides an exciting three-day itinerary out of Pokhara. Serious whitewater (**Class 4-**) starts at Beni, and runs down to the usual put-in point near Baglung and on all the way to the take-out at the confluence with the Andi Khola – where a dam puts a stop to the action. This section of water is away from roads and civilization, set in a stunning valley that offers excellent upriver views of the Annapurnas. However, it's a popular stretch of river, and camping beaches are limited in number, well used, and may be squalid. There have been quite a few accidents on this river, so choose your operator carefully.

The Kali Gandaki is probably at its best for rafting at low and medium flows: mid-October to mid-December and March to April. It's a good idea to think about adding this raft trip onto the end of a trek in the Annapurna region. Consider flying to Jomosom, trekking or taking buses and jeeps down the Kali Gandaki to Baglung, and then continuing down the river on a rafting trip – a journey from the highest mountains on earth to the jungle lowlands. You could even carry on from the take-out south on rough roads to Rani Ghat (see p.235) and Tansen (see p.231).

The Seti

Another river easily reached from Pokhara, the **Seti** (or **Seti Nadi**) offers a gentler alternative to the Upper Kali Gandaki. It's a fairly tame (**Class 3-**) but very picturesque river, taking two or three days to float from Damauli to near Narayanghadh.

This is a better choice than a similar trip starting on the Trisuli, as it takes you away from the road and has a fine green "jungle corridor" in its lower section, and beautiful white-sand beaches for camping. It's a popular choice for birdwatching groups, who often schedule it into their itinerary from Pokhara to Chitwan. The water temperature is incredibly warm, making it a popular choice for winter trips and for kayak clinics.

The Upper Seti

During high water from September to early November the **Upper Seti** offers an action-packed ninety-minute whitewater trip (**Class 3+**) from just above Hyemja to the dam at Bajar, just above Pokhara (below here the river goes underground). It is only thirty minutes from Pokhara by road to the starting point and companies do this as a half-day trip.

The Bhote Koshi

The **Bhote Koshi**, which runs alongside the Arniko Highway to the Tibetan border northeast of Kathmandu, is probably the steepest and hardest commercial rafting river in Nepal (**Class 4+**). In low water it's like a pinball machine (and you're the ball); in medium flows it's more like being flushed down the U-bend of a toilet. A few companies specialize in this deviant experience, offering it as a one- or two-day trip out of Kathmandu (it's only a three-hour drive) using road support, empty rafts and safety kayakers. At higher flows in late October and November most companies run the Upper Sun Koshi (see p.363) on the first day as a warm-up and the Bhote Koshi on the second day. If you have previous rafting experience or are just looking for an adrenaline rush, then this is the one for you. It's a cold river, so if you are running it in the winter months between December and late February then look for a company that provides wetsuits and paddle jackets. An enticing option is a two-day trip, staying the night at one of the comfortable riverside resort camps (see box, p.186).

Note that a **dam** is under construction near the Tibet border; when it's complete, possibly in the lifetime of this guide, it may affect rafting on the Bhote Koshi.

Upper Sun Koshi (Lower Bhote Koshi)

Only two to three hours' drive from Kathmandu, the **Upper Sun Koshi** makes an easier alternative or a warm-up to the Bhote Koshi, especially at higher water levels (and it's sometimes referred to by companies as the Lower Bhote Koshi). There are two different sections: the top one is a fun **Class 3** whitewater run in peak season; the lower, below Sukute Beach, is a mellow, scenic, **flat-water** float. The river is clean and blue with green valley sides, and the nearby Arniko Highway is relatively quiet, so this stretch of river is an ideal choice for a half-day rafting trip close to Kathmandu, and makes a welcome escape from the city if you stay overnight at one of the resort camps on the riverside (see box, p.186). This is a popular river for kayak schools.

The Marsyangdi

The **Marsyangdi** is a magnificent, blue whitewater river with a spectacular mountain backdrop. Kayakers rave about it. It's a full-on, continuously technical river (**Class 4+**), like a large nonstop slalom, needing experienced river staff and shore support. Companies normally run it as a four-day trip from near Khudi or Bhulbule (along the Annapurna Circuit trek) down to the Kathmandu–Pokhara highway, and many combine this with a scenic three-day trek from Begnas Tal (near Pokhara) to Khudi. The river is particularly beautiful in November, when levels are reasonably low and the mountain views are usually clear. The **dam** at Phaliya Sanghu, some 14km by road south of Beisisahar has, sadly, broken the Marsyangdi into two sections of whitewater, separated by a short drive around the dam, and the road traffic along the bank is increasing (though it is still relatively small) – but it remains a classic.

The Sun Koshi

Widely acknowledged as one of the ten best rafting trips in the world, the **Sun Koshi** is the most popular of several longer floats in Nepal, and logistics are fairly easy, making it one of the cheapest in terms of cost per day. It's a six- to nine-day run, generally beginning at Dumja, three hours east of Kathmandu, and ending at Chatara, between Dharan (see p.295) and the Koshi Tappu Wildlife Refuge in the Eastern Terai (see p.292). If you're planning to go on from Nepal to Darjeeling, this raft trip cuts out most of the twenty-hour bus ride to the eastern border.

Relatively few companies run scheduled trips on the Sun Koshi, so you're less likely to see other parties, and the camping, on beautiful white-sand beaches, is great. The river traverses a remote part of the country, flowing through a varied landscape of jungle-clad canyons, arid, open valleys and sparse settlements. Unlike most rivers, which start out rough and get tamer as they descend, this one starts gently, affording a chance to build up experience and confidence prior to a steady diet of increasingly exciting whitewater (**Class 3–4**). This makes it an especially good choice for those doing their first river trip. It's at its best for rafting at medium to high flows – from mid-September to late October and in May and early June; from December to March much of the whitewater disappears.

The Karnali

Nepal's biggest and longest river, the **Karnali** provides perhaps the finest trip of its kind in the world. Way out in the remote far west, it requires a long bus ride to Birendra Nagar (many groups fly to Nepalgunj) and then about three hours' rough bus ride to the small village of Sauli. From here it is either a two-hour trek to the river or, if the road is in good shape, you can drive onto Dungeshwar right on the Karnali. Most rafting trips last eight days, with challenging, big-water rapids, superb canyons, pristine wilderness and plentiful wildlife. The biggest rapids (**Class 4**) come in the first three days, with the river gradually mellowing after that. You can raft the Karnali right into Bardia National Park, where wild elephants, tigers, crocodiles and rhinos may sometimes be seen from the river. Many parties take the opportunity to spend a few extra days watching wildlife in Bardia.

The Karnali is best run at low to medium levels – it's a particularly good choice in March and April, though the nature of the channel makes it lively at all times outside of high water. There are plentiful driftwood supplies for campfires, so this makes it a popular choice for overseas kayak groups around Christmas. It's also renowned as Nepal's premier fishing river, with giant **mahseer** (a freshwater perch) and catfish. Note that the Upper or **Humla Karnali**, from Simikot down to the Lower Karnali put-in, is a Class 5 terror for skilled, committed expedition kayakers only.

The Tamur

The **Tamur** offers six days of fabulous and challenging whitewater (**Class 4**) in a remote and scenic valley in eastern Nepal, coupled with a highly scenic trek. The river is at its best in medium flows – it would be a nightmare at high levels – with the optimum time (after a normal monsoon) being late October to late November. Note that the final day of the trip from Mulghat (where a highway crosses the river) can be added as an exciting extra day to a Sun Koshi trip.

The trip starts with a twenty-hour bus ride to Basantapur, via Dharan (see p.295) followed by a four-day walk in along a high ridge with wide panoramas of Kanchenjunga and the Everest peaks – often described as one of the most beautiful treks in Nepal (see p.339). It is possible to fly from Kathmandu to Taplejung, only a couple of hours' hike from the put-in point at Dobhan, but flights may be delayed by weather, so it's more reliable to fly to Biratnagar and then take a taxi or bus from there to the Basantapur trailhead. You can also drive via Ilam to Dobhan, but it's a wearyingly long journey on an unreliable road.

The Bheri

The **Bheri** offers a shorter and easier alternative (**Class 3+**) to the Karnali, of which it's a tributary. It's one of the most scenic rivers in Nepal, with golden cliffs, green jungle, crystal-clear green water, white-sand beaches, excellent fishing and good birdwatching, all coupled with a powerful current and sparkling rapids of moderate difficulty. Access is from the Nepalgunj–Birendra Nagar road, just short of Birendra Nagar – a total of about fifteen hours of bus travel from Kathmandu (via Nepalgunj). Few companies raft the Bheri at the moment, but it is likely to become more popular as the road improves. There's also a dirt road that creeps up the valley all the way to Jajarkot, which offers the attractive possibility of a higher put-in.

The Lower Kali Gandaki

The **lower** section of the **Kali Gandaki**, starting from Ramdi Ghat on the Siddhartha Highway, offers a longer alternative to the Seti. It's a medium-volume and relatively easy river (**Class 2**), with the same beautiful scenery as the Seti, and it flows through a completely unspoilt and seldom visited valley of pretty villages, small gorges and jungle-backed beaches. Although the river is easily accessible, it takes longer to get to than the Seti (5hr from Pokhara to the put-in at Ramdhi Ghat), making it less crowded – ideal as the perfect river for a relaxed, romantic, away-from-it-all break. Like the Seti, this is probably a good choice for a do-it-yourself trip in a "duckie" (inflatable canoe), rentable in Pokhara.

8

Mountain biking

THE ANNAPURNA CIRCUIT

9

Mountain biking

The best way to see Nepal, it has long been said, is to walk. Nowadays, however, mountain biking is a serious alternative. Decent mountain bikes are available to rent in Kathmandu and Pokhara, where you'll also find good route information and well-organized tours. Even if you're not planning an extreme off-road Himalayan MTB adventure, renting a bike is worth considering: they provide a more intimate experience than a speeding jeep or bus, and get you to places at a more exciting pace than trekking.

Despite Nepal's Himalayan mystique, it's not all **steep**: the Kathmandu Valley's slopes are generally easy, and the Terai region is just plain flat. The longer and more scenic routes do tend to require a high level of fitness, and there are monster ascents (and descents) for those who relish that sort of thing, but there are also plenty of relaxed village-to-village rambles and downhill rides. Mountain bikes are pretty much the only option: even major roads, where you could otherwise get away with a hybrid or robust tourer, have frequent potholes and damaged sections.

The **itineraries** in this chapter are grouped as being out of either **Kathmandu** or **Pokhara**, as these are the only places where you can rent a decent mountain bike. They also offer many of the best routes, as tour operators and bike-shop gurus are continually pioneering new off-road rides. On the downside, **traffic** is a serious problem near cities; in the Kathmandu Valley, especially, what were once pleasant rides may now be choked and frightening. It's always best to seek the latest information locally from someone in the know.

The pace of **road construction**, meanwhile, is producing an exponential increase in the possibilities. Many roads are no longer the one-way spurs they once were, making it possible to create exciting long loops, or find enticing back routes between, say, Kathmandu and Pokhara, or Trisuli and Gorkha. It would also be quite possible to devise some incredible **long-distance itineraries** within Nepal, exploring well beyond the bounds of this chapter. If riding further afield than the Pokhara or Kathmandu Valleys, seek expert advice (ask in a bike shop) and find the most up-to-date map possible – and even then, treat any map with a degree of scepticism. Rough roads become paved, trails turn into rough roads, and roads get longer (or shorter, after a bad monsoon) every season.

CYCLING TO EVEREST

Although Sagarmatha National Park itself continues to ban mountain bikes, it'll be possible one day – perhaps very soon – to **cycle to the gates of Everest**. The traditional approach road to Everest now slips and slides as far as Bhandar (see p.346). East of that, the giant Lamjura pass, with its endless stair of a walking trail, would put off all but the most dedicated of mountain bikers. Other, rough roads are steadily approaching from Dharan and the Arun valley, to the southeast, however, and a well-built road now approaches from the south. Breaking off the East–West Highway 37km east of the Janakpur turn off, this exciting new option threads north through huge and intensely populated hills to the thriving district capitals of Okhaldunga and Salleri, and to tiny Phaplu airstrip – which is just a few hours' walk south of the Everest walk-in trail at Junbesi (see p.346) – and Junbesi is just the other side of that huge Lamjura pass. Linking any of these routes as a loop, or with the trek north to the high Everest country, would currently require an off-putting amount of portage, but roads are changing fast in Nepal.

MOUNTAIN BIKING IN THE KATHMANDU VALLEY

Highlights

❶ Shivapuri National Park Unpaved but well-mapped roads thread through this delightful forest preserve in the Kathmandu Valley's northern reaches. **See p.373**

❷ The Tribhuwan Rajpath A classic monster climb and descent, with the possibility of some delightful return routes. **See p.375**

❸ Lhasa to Kathmandu Packages offering "the world's longest descent" usually give you two heart-lifting (and heart-and-lung-testing) weeks of Tibetan touring, including high-altitude Everest views, followed by the legendary 4000m descent from the Tibetan plateau into Kathmandu. **See p.376**

❹ Nagarkot descent On this classic tour trip, you get a pre-dawn (or previous evening) bus ride up to Nagarkot for the Himalayan sunrise view, which is followed by a thrilling 800m descent to Kathmandu along either 4WD trails or serious single-tracks. **See p.376**

❺ Begnas Tal This fine lake is the gateway to miles of pastoral back roads east of Pokhara. **See p.377**

❻ The Annapurna Circuit The controversial Annapurna roads may have given trekking a knock, but they offer the possibility of an amazing ascent to Manang, and a descent through the world's deepest gorge. **See p.378**

HIGHLIGHTS ARE MARKED ON THE MAP ON P.374

9

When to go

If you have a choice, go for October to December, when there's not much rain and visibility is good. It gets gradually cooler but never gets very cold at biking elevations – in fact, even in December and January the days can be sunny and even warm anywhere up to about 3000m, though snow may occasionally be encountered as low as 2000m.

December and **January** are also the most comfortable months for cycling in Pokhara and the Terai. The shortening days are a factor, though: by December you'll need to be off the roads or trails by 4.30pm or so.

From **January to March** the days lengthen and grow warmer. This too is a good time for biking. In April, May and the first part of June, the weather keeps getting hotter, the road conditions dustier, the air hazier – and afternoon showers become more common. On the plus side, you can take advantage of long daylight hours. The monsoon (**mid-June to late Sept**) is hot and damp; the mountains are usually hidden by clouds, and the trails are wet or muddy. This is prime riding time in Tibet and Mustang, however, both of which are shielded from the rains by the Himalayas.

Another seasonal consideration is the **race calendar**. Events run by different mountain-bike companies are held throughout the year, but some have a serious international profile. **Yak Attack** (Ⓦ theyakattack.com), organized by Dawn Till Dusk, usually takes place in early March, and takes serious competitors from Kathmandu west via Nuwakot and Gorkha (off the main roads) towards an incredible crossing of the Thorung La pass, in the Annapurna range. The **Trans Nepal race**, in December, follows a five-day route on 4WD trails from Kathmandu to Pokhara.

Information, books and maps

Bike shops in Kathmandu and Pokhara have up-to-date information on trails and roads, though of course they're in business mainly to sell tours, and won't divulge all their secret routes.

There is no dedicated mountain-biking **guidebook**, but James Giambrone's *Kathmandu Bikes & Hikes* gives reasonable if dated coverage of this area. A **map** is crucial, but shouldn't be relied upon absolutely – and maps go out of date fast in Nepal. Nepamaps does a 1:50,000 scale *Biking Around Kathmandu Valley* map, and a 1:75,000 *Biking Around Annapurna* map, both available in Kathmandu. Coverage of the former extends beyond the valley into the Central Hills, and bike trails are marked, if not always entirely accurately. Otherwise, you'll have to rely on trekking maps (see p.309).

Tours and cycling independently

Like trekking, mountain biking can be done independently or as part of a tour – which can simply mean teaming up with a guide and perhaps a couple of other clients for a day or more. With mountain biking, the specialized equipment involved and the difficulty of route-finding makes tours an attractive option.

Organized tours

An **organized bike tour** will save lots of pre-departure time and headaches, and maximize the chances that all will go more or less according to plan. The itinerary will be well planned, avoiding the dead ends and wrong turns that inevitably come with a self-organized trip. Decent bikes and all the necessary gear will be provided, and guides will take care of maintenance and on-the-spot repairs. Guides can also show you trails you'd never find on your own, keep you off (dangerous) paved roads and help interpret Nepali culture. On longer tours, a "sag wagon" will tote heavy gear, provide emergency backup, and whisk you past the busier or less interesting stretches of road.

A one-day guided trip will typically **cost** around $40–80, including bike hire, while longer excursions including vehicle support and accommodation work out at more like $130–170 per day. Generally, you get what you pay for – and it's worth checking exactly what you're getting. Many overseas companies offer mountain-bike tours, but almost all are actually organized by a few **operators** in

---

Many of the same **environmental do's and don'ts** for trekking (see p.308) also apply when mountain biking, especially if you're camping.

Kathmandu (see p.99), and you can save money by booking directly with them. They often require a minimum of four people for vehicle-supported tours, but shorter customized trips can be organized for just one or two people. Pokhara also has some good mountain-bike shops which double as tour operators (see p.216).

Cycling independently

Cycling independently takes a certain pioneering spirit and a greater tolerance for discomfort. It's up to you to rent or bring your own equipment and to arrange food and accommodation; if starting from Kathmandu, you'll need to organize transport out of the city or else put up with some ugly traffic. You'll definitely make mistakes finding your own way, which might mean spending more time than you'd intended, getting lost or having to backtrack, or spending more time on traffic-heavy paved roads and less time on trails. However, you'll have more direct contact with local people than you would with a group.

Day-trips in the Kathmandu and Pokhara valleys are the easiest to do on your own, since you can rent bikes in both cities. Though you probably won't find the more obscure trails, you'll no doubt stumble upon others. If you're riding **long-distance** without vehicle support, you'll have to tote your own gear and may find yourself spending nights in basic lodges where little English is spoken. This will be par for the course if you're on a long tour of the subcontinent, though, and the going is certainly easier in Nepal than in India: the roads, for the most part, are quieter, and there's less staring, hassling and risk of theft.

Equipment

Since good (and not-so-good) bikes can be rented in Nepal, you'll probably be better off not bringing a bike from home unless you plan to do a lot of riding. However, clothing and certain accessories are worth taking with you, especially if you can also use them when trekking or rafting.

Renting or buying a bike in Nepal

Chinese- and Indian-made bikes are available to rent from streetside vendors for a few hundred rupees per day. Superficially, they look the part – some even have suspension – but they're heavy and often uncomfortable, components are flimsy, maintenance may be poor, and they rarely come with a helmet. If you find such a bike in a fairly new condition, you could get away with using it for a day-trip or overnight loop but they're not really fit for rough roads. Don't ride this kind of bike further than you're prepared to walk back with it.

For hard or long-distance riding you'll need a **real mountain bike**, which can be rented from specialist bike shops/tour operators in Kathmandu and Pokhara (but nowhere else). A helmet and basic tool kit should come with the bike. Chinese-made bikes with V-brakes go for around Rs500 a day, but if you're doing anything more than pootling about it's worth paying for a Western bike: prices start at around Rs1000–2000, though you can expect to pay around Rs6000 for a top-end model. You'll be expected to leave a passport or something of value as security, and you'll generally have to pay for damage or above-normal wear and tear. Be sure to reserve these bikes as far ahead as possible, especially during busy times; choice is definitely limited in the peak season.

Whichever kind of bike you rent, it's your responsibility to check it over before setting off. **Check** brakes and pads, test spoke tension (they should all be taut), ensure that tyres have sufficient tread and are properly inflated (check inflation while sitting on the bike), test the chain for tautness, and work the bike through its gears to see that the derailleurs function smoothly. Check that there's a bell – you'll be using it a lot.

You may be able to **buy** a decent used bike from a departing traveller, especially towards the end of the autumn or spring seasons – check mountain-bike shop notice boards in Kathmandu or Pokhara or their websites. Alternatively, you could buy new and sell on yourself: good-quality bikes from manufacturers such as Trek or Commencal can be bought in Kathmandu and Pokhara, at prices similar to home.

Bringing a bike from home

Don't bring a bike unless you have the time, energy and commitment to use it a lot. **Airlines** (both international and domestic) now generally impose a 25kg weight limit, with extortionate rates for extra kilos, so check the costs and allowances when you book your ticket – and pack light. The specialist mountain-bike shops in Kathmandu and Pokhara offer re-assembly and full servicing. Before you

9

return home, make sure to clean off mud or soil to avoid problems at customs; a good local operator can wash, service and pack your bike post-tour. Soft bike bags are worth considering; you'll be expected to deflate the tyres and swivel the handlebars parallel with the frame. Nepali (and Chinese/Tibetan, if you're cycling that way) customs may want verbal assurance that the bike will be returning with you when you leave the country, but this shouldn't be a problem and should not cost money. Domestic airlines' willingness to accept bikes as baggage is always dependent upon available luggage space, so check in early.

Clothes and other equipment

Other than a helmet and water bottle, no special gear is necessary for day-trips, though enthusiasts may want to pack their own saddle, pedals and shoes, and if you're cycling in and around Kathmandu you'll definitely want a proper **face mask** against dust and pollution. Good (expensive) ones are sold in department stores; the cheaper ones only keep out the worst of the dust, not the dangerous particulates. Cycling **clothing**, shoes and gloves aren't easily obtainable in Nepal, nor is good waterproof/windproof outerwear. Note that tight Lycra clothing is embarrassing or offensive to many Nepalis, especially when worn by women, so unless you're sticking to the main Pokhara or Kathmandu trails, consider a pair of comfortable shorts over body-hugging bike gear.

A **helmet** and **water bottle** will come with a better rental bike. If renting a cheaper one, you could buy a helmet in a Kathmandu department store and carry your own water bottle – with something for water purification (see p.38). **Panniers** and racks can be rented from the better bike shops, and daypacks and waist-packs are sold all over tourist areas. You can pick up bungee cords in any motorcycle accessory or repair shop.

A good **lock** and cable are essential, especially if bringing a fancy bike from home. Local bike shops

sell cheap, less effective locks. Bring bikes inside at night. Puncture-repair places are everywhere on the roads, but travel with your own **patch kit**, inner tube(s), pump and basic tool kit, especially if riding off-road.

Repairs and service

Local bike **repair shops**, found in every town and crossroads, are equipped mainly to fix basic local bikes, but they can patch any sort of flat (puncture) and are often remarkably adept at performing improvised repairs and mini-tune-ups. Just be sure to ask the price first: a puncture repair should cost around Rs100 or so. The Kathmandu tour operators have **workshops** with trained bike mechanics, a full range of tools and even a stock of spare parts. A full service will cost in the region of Rs1000–1400.

Riding conditions

Given the incredible variety of the country, it's hard to generalize, but this section describes the major riding conditions you're likely to encounter.

Conditions on Kathmandu's **city streets** are downright awful. If it's not a vehicle that'll get you, it's a pedestrian or a pothole – or the dangerous levels of pollution. At roundabouts or junctions it can actually be dangerous to stop and wait for a space, as Nepali drivers tend to keep moving and find space where they can. Nights are particularly lethal: drink-driving is routine, and street lighting is patchy – or absent altogether in load-shedding hours.

Highways

The scarcity of **highways** in Nepal means that all heavy-vehicle traffic converges on those few roads. Add the lack of consideration or attention afforded

---

ROUTE-FINDING AND TIMING

Little English is spoken in the rural areas that are best for riding, so it's good to learn how to **ask directions** in Nepali (see p.430). Don't point when asking directions, as many people will say yes out of courtesy, even if they don't know – it's better to put your hands in your pockets and ask "Which way to?" Do this several times to be sure you've got the right answer. Don't ask how far it is to a given destination – rather, ask how long it takes to get there. The answer will be a rough walking time in hours; you'll somehow have to convert that to riding time. With so many **gradients** and variable **road conditions**, distances on the map bear little relation to actual time.

to cyclists by drivers and you'd be best advised to avoid busy roads altogether. Fortunately, the unpleasant stretches are limited mainly to the central Kathmandu–Pokhara and Mugling–Birgunj routes, and alternative routes are increasingly possible. Although highway cycling always entails dust and exhaust fumes, the traffic diminishes noticeably as you get further from Kathmandu; the eastern and particularly the far western portions of the Mahendra Highway can be delightfully rural.

If you want to skip a busy section or avoid backtracking, take a **bus** or a **taxi**. The latter come in especially handy in the Kathmandu Valley, where comparatively short lifts can get you past the urban blight. It's usually no problem to load your bike on the roof of a public bus, though you may need to tip Rs50–100 or so, depending on the distance and your negotiating skills. Tourist buses will charge slightly more. Lay the bike down flat and tie and lock it down securely (bungee cords are useful for this). Improvise padding (use your pack) to save your frame and derailleurs, and supervise the loading so that other luggage isn't laid on top.

Lesser roads and trails

Nepal's surprising number of paved and unpaved **secondary roads** mostly see very little traffic. There's also a burgeoning number of half-completed or half-washed-out jeep tracks, especially in the hills south of Kathmandu. With a good map to locate them, the possibilities are almost unlimited.

Although there are a multitude of **off-road trails**, most aren't suitable for mountain biking because they're too steep, stepped and heavily used by humans and animals. One notable exception is the **Annapurna Circuit**, a fair proportion of which is rideable; the controversial road around its western half opens up the amazing possibility of a flight to

Jomosom and a descent through the Kali Gandaki gorge to Pokhara. In the past, a few bikers have "ridden" trekking trails to Everest Base Camp and elsewhere, but the mountainous **national parks** (with the exception of the Annapurna Conservation Area) are now officially out of bounds for bikes.

There are some excellent **single-track rides**, but finding them is tricky without a tour guide. If you go off-road, give people and livestock **priority**, slow down around all signs of habitation and signal your approach by ringing your bell or yelling *"Saikal aiyo!"* ("Cycle coming!"). It will often be necessary to dismount. Maintain a watchful eye for children, who like to grab hold of the back of bikes and run alongside, or throw stuff at your spokes. Be careful around buffalo and other livestock because it's easy to send them stampeding down a narrow trail – or be knocked off. If you kill an animal you'll be liable for its replacement value.

Pedestrians and other hazards

Traffic culture in Nepal is communitarian and fatalistic: it's everyone's job to work their way around everyone else, hoping for the best. Horns and bells are integral parts of the system: sounding them sends the message, "I'm here". On a bicycle, you're near the bottom of the pecking order. Cars and buses will squeeze you off the road, motorbikes will approach head-on, and taxis will suddenly veer around obstacles with no apparent regard for your presence. It won't take you long to discover that there are few road rules. If you hit someone you'll probably be asked to pay compensation, whether it was your fault or not. The single saving grace is the **slow speed** at which most vehicles travel. However, smooth new highway surfaces are tempting many to go faster, especially young motorbike riders.

Rides in the Kathmandu Valley

Kathmandu is not the best place to be based if you're planning to do much biking around the valley. For rides towards the south, you'll make a cleaner escape from the traffic by staying in **Patan**. The highly rideable **eastern valley and rim routes** are best explored from Bhaktapur, Nagarkot, Dhulikhel or Panauti.

Shivapuri National Park

Park gate 2km north of Budhanilkantha • Daily 8am–4.30pm; ticket office closes around 2pm • Rs250; bicycles Rs1000; campers pay Rs100/tent at the park gate

Shivapuri National Park (see p.139), which afforests Kathmandu Valley's northern rim, offers some superb possibilities. The scarcely used network of dirt roads begins right at

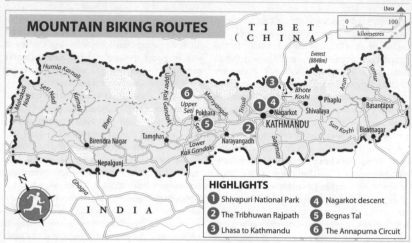

the **Budhanilkantha** entrance. The road to the left (west) snakes generally westwards for at least 15km, at which point the hill resort of **Kakani** (see p.188) is only about 2km further east along the ridge by a trail with some challengingly technical sections (some carrying required). This ride is more enjoyable from Kakani to Budhanilkantha. For a shorter loop starting and ending in Budhanilkantha, ride to the Tokha Hospital and then descend along a steep, sandy road.

The road to the right (east) of the Budhanilkantha gate contours and climbs out of the valley, passing the monastery of **Nagi Gompa** and reaching the watershed's easternmost point at Jhule after about 20km. From Jhule you can bike southwards to **Nagarkot**, or make a jarring, stone-paved descent to the valley floor at **Sankhu**, a ride of 45 to 60 minutes. Alternatively, you can stay on the park road for another 8km beyond Jhule, rounding the Shivapuri ridge and reaching **Chisapani**, a village on the main Helambu trekking trail, from where you can cycle the long way to Nagarkot. Along this route, **accommodation** is available in Mulkharka, Chisopani, Chauki Danda and, of course, Nagarkot (see p.176).

Trisuli, Kakani and Nuwakot

The **Trisuli Road** heads northwestwards out of the Kathmandu Valley, skirting the hill station of **Kakani** (see p.188) before plunging nearly 1500m to **Trisuli Bazaar** (see p.188) and the subtropical valley of the Trisuli River. Kakani is usually considered an overnight ride, since it has (limited) accommodation and mountain views that are best seen in the morning. A tough alternative route to Trisuli avoids the main vehicle road altogether, taking you steeply up through the northwestern side of **Shivapuri National Park** (see p.139), over the watershed, then along flatter or descending sections of rough track for about 30km, before a tough final 500m ascent to **Nuwakot** (see p.188), perched above Trisuli Bazaar. From Trisuli, rural roads and tracks extend for miles in several directions: east to the historic forts of Nuwakot and beyond, south and then east up the Tadi Khola, west up the lovely Samari Khola towards **Gorkha** (see p.198), and north up to the **Langtang trailheads** (see p.334).

Nagarjun Ban

Nagarjun Ban (see p.140), an annexe of Shivapuri National Park, offers wilderness-style riding under a beautiful canopy of trees – though there have been a few attacks on tourists, so solo riders are usually prohibited for safety reasons. Seek local advice before committing to the following rides through the park.

Entering via the southern gate, you embark on a challenging 18km ascent on a jeep trail; the last 2km increases in gradient to reach a final elevation of 2096m. The return trip to the north gate is an additional 12km via a less established trail.

A marvellous section of trail leads to Nagarjun's western entrance from **Sitapaila**, a village west of Swayambhu. Contouring high above the Mahesh Khola, this sometimes narrow single-track provides excellent riding for intermediate and advanced riders. The road beyond **Ichangu Narayan** (see p.167), a temple northwest of Swayambhu, links with this trail beyond the village of Baralgaun. Once in the forest park, keep to your left and you'll come out at the northern gate, on the main road to Kakani.

Another way to get to or from Nagarjun is via **Tokha**, a well-preserved village reached by trail from the Ring Road at Gongabu. From Tokha you can proceed in a north-northwest arc along excellent undulating dirt trails and through traditional villages all the way to the southern gate. Even if you skip Nagarjun, this is a great day on the bike, and can be extended all the way east through to Budhanilkantha (roughly 1hr 30min from the southern gate).

The Tribhuwan Rajpath

The spectacular and little-used **Tribhuwan Rajpath** racks up a total elevation gain of more than 1700m from Kathmandu to a cloud-forested pass through the Mahabharat Lek, before descending an even more dizzying 2300m to the Terai. There's a map and route account in the "Central Hills" chapter (see p.189).

For a classic two-days-plus loop out of Kathmandu, make for **Daman** (see p.191), a mountain viewpoint just below the pass. It's a very long day's ride up the Rajpath, taking between six and nine hours in the saddle, almost all of it climbing. Even if you're an expert you'll want to skip the first traffic-choked, oil-slicked 26km – put your bike on a bus as far as Naubise, where the Rajpath branches off from the main Kathmandu–Pokhara highway. After overnighting in Daman, you can return via Markhu, the Kulekhani Reservoir and **Pharping** (see p.146) in the southern Kathmandu Valley.

Dakshinkali, Pharping and the Kulekhani Reservoir

The sealed **Dakshinkali road** strings together some fascinating cultural sights (see p.143) and while the ride out is largely uphill, it's gradual. The return, of course, is a fine descent.

You can explore further – potentially as far as the Terai – on one of two roads (see box, p.378). The major route, now used by jeeps almost year-round, heads south from the Dakshinkali gate, making for Hetauda – 60km in all from Kathmandu. The slightly longer and rougher road is better for bikers. It heads broadly west and uphill from **Pharping** (see p.146), making for the dam on the **Kulekhani Reservoir**. From here you can take the road north along the eastern shore to **Markhu** (1600m), a small, newly built village (with lodges) at the reservoir's northern extremity. From Markhu, a rough spur road heads northeast for **Thankot**, on the Prithvi Highway; a longer but better-graded route heads 13km northwest on a good, pine-shaded road to join the Tribhuwan Rajpath 15km north of **Daman** (see p.191). From the dam, you can also climb a 1920m pass on the Mahabharat Lek range and head down a steep valley to the historic but now pleasantly bypassed town of **Bhimphedi** (where there's more accommodation); from Bhimphedi, a paved road descends to join the Tribhuwan Rajpath at **Bhainse**, some 8km north of Hetauda, in the Terai.

9

The Lele Valley

The **Bungmati**, **Chapagaun** and **Godavari** roads provide the backbones for some easy loops through the southern valley (see p.151). For something a bit harder and longer, head east from Chapagaun past the Bajra Barahi temple and onto the Godavari road, before striking south on a smaller road that crosses a steep, forested ridge and enters the **Lele Valley**. From there, you can choose from a number of trails heading south into little-visited hill country. Just south of **Tika Bhairab** (see p.151), a rough road ascends to more than 2000m at Tinpani Bhanjyang before descending via Bhattedanda and Makwanpurgadhi to Hetauda and the Terai. Conditions are highly variable, however, and there's no bridge over the Bagmati, so you won't be able to get right through during the monsoon.

The Lakuri Bhanjyang

The 30km road connecting Patan with Panauti is a superb intermediate-level ride that can be done in either direction. From Patan, ride out of town on the road past **Sundhara** and the Eastern Stupa. The first section to **Lubhu**, a brick-making and hand-loom centre 6km beyond the Ring Road, is busy and uninteresting, but the road climbs up before commencing a serious 500m switchback ascent to the **Lakuri Bhanjyang**. On a clear day, the view of the valley and mountains is splendid. The second half of the ride is a sweet descent through the rural valley of the **Bebar Khola** and its scattered Tamang, Chhetri and finally Newar settlements to **Panauti** (see p.179), where you can spend the night. From there you can link up with Dhulikhel and Namobuddha area rides (see p.182), on paved or dirt roads.

Dhulikhel, Namobuddha and Panauti

Dhulikhel is the traditional starting point of a very popular round-trip – the **Namobuddha circuit** (see box, p.183) – to the Buddhist stupa of Namobuddha, and (optionally) on to the Newar town of **Panauti** (see p.179). Panauti is perhaps the better starting point nowadays, given the increasing urbanization around Dhulikhel.

The Arniko Highway to the Tibet border

The **Arniko Highway** from Kathmandu to the **Tibet border** at Kodari is an adventurous three- to five-day round-trip. The road gets much quieter and better for cycling after heavy traffic turns off at Dhulikhel for the southward road to Sindhuli, Bardibas and the Terai – so consider approaching via Nagarkot, Nala or across the Lakuri Bhanjyang. From **Dhulikhel** (see p.180), the Arniko Highway descends 600m and then ascends more than 800m to the border. You can make a fascinating side trip by going uphill off the main highway to **Palanchowk** (see p.184), the gateway to further rides down to the Sun Koshi River.

If you want to **cross the border** on a bike, you'll have to join a tour (see p.370). Some companies offer adventurous excursions into and back out of Tibet, notably the so-called "Longest Downhill", an eleven-day round-trip from Kathmandu that allows you to spend time in **Lhasa** before you begin the epic drop from Yarle Shungla (Tibet) to Dolaghat (Nepal) – 4380m over 157km.

Around Nagarkot

From **Nagarkot** (see p.176) the options before you are almost unlimited. Rough roads and trails radiate in all directions: northwest to Sankhu; west to Changu Narayan; south to Nala and Banepa; east to Hiuwapati, Sipaghat and Panchkhal; and north to Chisopani and the Helambu trails. All these routes are described in the Nagarkot section of this guide (see p.178). However, there are endless forks, many of which lead to dead ends or treacherous descents, so don't bike alone.

Unless you're a very strong rider, the ascent from Kathmandu to Nagarkot will probably be all you care to do in a day, and in any case you'll want to spend the night for the views the next morning. Most bike tour operators run popular two-day trips, including transportation up, an overnight stay, and the amazing descent back to the Kathmandu Valley, taking more pleasant back roads.

Rides around Pokhara

The **Pokhara Valley** account (see p.223) gives more detail on roads and bikeable destinations in that area. A few recommended itineraries are given below, though you'll need patience, local advice and good map-reading skills to get the most out of them – hiring a guide is recommended. If you're planning on biking from **Kathmandu to Pokhara**, the Prithvi Highway can't be recommended because of the volume of trucks and microbuses and other vehicles. It would be better to put your bike on the roof of a bus – or plan an ambitious, multi-day (minimum five days) route via **Trisuli Bazaar** (see p.188), Dhading, Gorkha and the Marsyangdi valley.

Phewa Tal loops

A shortish day's circumnavigation of **Phewa Tal** (see p.206) is easily possible, heading out along the north shore and returning via Danda Kot and the World Peace Stupa – the last part takes you downhill along single-tracks through the forest, coming out just west of Damside. This loop will take most people around five hours. A more adventurous, slightly longer option heads out across the face of the hillside underneath Sarangkot – but you'll need a guide to find the mix of 4WD trails and single-track; the longer alternative would be to follow the Sarangkot ridge. To make a really full day-trip, you can extend the loop south of the Peace Stupa down the **Seti Nadi** (see p.362).

Sarangkot and beyond

The hilltop viewpoint of **Sarangkot** (see p.225) makes a great focus for an intermediate-level day-trip or overnight, and one that can be easily done without a guide. From the Bindyabasini temple in the bazaar, follow the paved road 8km westwards to Sarangkot town and lodges, where there's a junction: the hilltop viewpoint is another 3km along to the right, while the left-hand fork leads towards **Naudaada**. The first 10km of the Naudaada road contours pleasantly along the south side of the ridge through forest, terraced farmland and villages; at Naudaada you can head back to Pokhara on the busy Baglung Highway. A shorter, but more demanding alternative is to break off the Naudaada road at the saddle of Deurali, then descend steeply on off-road tracks via Kaskiot to Pame, a couple of kilometres west of Pokhara along the lakeshore.

Begnas Tal and Rupa Tal

A fine road, paved only in its earliest sections, follows a ridge between two beautiful lakes, **Rupa Tal** and **Begnas Tal** (see p.229), and then westwards to Besisahar. A network of trails developing in this region can offer one or several days' riding – enquire at Pokhara bike shops. A fairly tough, long day's route, involving some carrying, is known as the **Begnas Loop**: it takes you east of Pokhara (from the Bhadrakali Mandir), along the ridge road past *Tiger Mountain Pokhara Lodge* to Kalikasthan and Tiwaridanda; from here it's downhill, heading south on a rough road to Kotbari and Sundari Danda (see p.230), then back on the partially paved road between Begnas Tal and Rupa Tal. Heading east of Begnas Tal, it's a 40km three-day rough-road trip through Bhorletar and Sundaari Bazaar on the way to the paved road at Besisahar; from there you could

9

head on up the rough road up the **Marsyangdi valley** (the eastern side of the Annapurna Circuit) or return to Pokhara (with a side trip to Bandipur).

The Annapurna Circuit

Only the most committed mountain bikers take on the full, trekking-style **Annapurna Circuit**, carrying their bikes across the high pass of the Thorung La. Some tour companies offer the option of plane, bus and mule transport to the top, followed by an incredible downhill, but it's expensive. If the complete circuit is beyond most people's reach, it's increasingly possible to follow either of its arms upwards, then turn around and descend the same way. The **eastern side** is the more popular. Attractive roads lead to **Besisahar** (see p.322), from where you can cycle up the Marsyangdi valley all the way to Manang – though you may find yourself carrying your bike for up to a quarter of the ascent. The trip from Pokhara to Manang usually takes seven to ten days. The **western side** of the circuit is less varied, at first, though new roads being built will soon offer the possibility of a cut-through from Birethanti to Tatopani, via Ghorepani. Currently, however, it's 90km from Pokhara to Beni, and then a fairly relentless climb along the mostly unpaved 80km road up the Kali Gandaki from Beni to Jomosom. Above Jomosom, dusty, Tibetan-style and relatively flat roads beckon on towards Muktinath (and, with a special permit, Upper Mustang).

No special bike **permits** are needed for the Annapurna Circuit, but if you are entering the Annapurna Conservation Area (ACAP) you will need a TIMS card and park entry ticket (see p.313), just as trekkers do. At the time of writing it was unclear how the 2014 trekking disaster (see box, p.306) would affect mountain biking in the area.

The Seti Nadi

Unpaved roads head downstream along the churning **Seti Nadi**, with dramatic overlooks of the canyon and views of the mountains. The road on the south side of the canyon goes on for many easy, downhill miles, and leads to some more remote trails further to the southeast. One good loop from Pokhara follows a trail south from the main road to **Chhorepatan** (see p.211), stopping just short of Kristi Nachana Chaur, then turns east to Nirmal Pokhari; from here, you descend to the Seti, crossing at Dobila, below the huge *Fulbari Resort* – from where it's a relatively gentle ride up the Seti towards Lakeside.

To the Terai: Chitwan, Lumbini and the Mahendra Highway

The easiest route to **the Terai** is along the Prithvi Highway to Mugling and then south from there to Narayangadh, which is only a short hop from **Chitwan National Park**. It does get heavy traffic, but is mostly downhill and you can pedal it in a day.

A more adventurous and strenuous route follows the winding, scenic **Siddhartha Highway** southwards to Butwal, via **Tansen** (see p.231). This ride requires some long

---

CYCLING IN THE TERAI

From Hetauda, Kathmandu's gateway to the Terai, it's a half-day's ride west along the busy Mahendra Highway to **Chitwan National Park** (see p.249), where there are many flat village trails to explore by bike. Moving on to Pokhara requires travelling via Narayanghat and the Prithvi (Kathmandu–Pokhara) Highway – worryingly busy in the mornings, but nonetheless beautiful, especially between Mugling and Pokhara. Another option is just to put your bike on a bus. East out of Hetauda, the Mahendra Highway is sometimes interestingly rural, sometimes rather urbanized, and always flat. There's a good network of lovely rural tracks around **Janakpur** (see p.286).

stints in the saddle and several overnight stops. It's a fast downhill ride from Tansen to Butwal, and from there it's a flat and easy couple of hours to the Buddha's birthplace, **Lumbini** (see p.261).

An even more adventurous option would be to head west of Pokhara to Baglung, and from there follow the incredible, switchbacking **Tamghas Highway** south – either looping round southeastwards via **Ridi Bazaar** (see p.235) to Tansen (it's 80km from Tamghas to Tansen via Ridi), or continuing south and west from Tamghas via Sandhikarka, on 90km of rough roads, joining the Mahendra Highway at Gorusinge, 48km west of Butwal (and some 10km north of the Buddhist archeological site of Kapilvastu). West of Butwal, the **Mahendra Highway** leads through a beautiful *dun* valley towards the relatively undeveloped far west, the traffic lightening as you go.

YAK, EVEREST REGION

Contexts

History

For a backward Himalayan statelet, squeezed uncomfortably between India and China, Nepal has played a surprisingly pivotal role in Asian history. In its early days, the country reared the Buddha; much later, its remarkable conquests led it into wars with Tibet and Britain. Its name and recorded history go back nearly three thousand years, although it has existed as a nation for barely two hundred: before 1769, "Nepal" referred only to a kingdom based in the Kathmandu Valley. Some rural people still talk about it as such.

The rise of the Himalayas

All Nepal's history – its peoples, its politics and its development – is founded on its extraordinary **landscape**. The **Himalayas**, which march across the country's northern border, are a kind of cataclysmic, geo-scale crumple zone. Despite being astonishingly young – they began rising a mere 55 million years ago – they're already so high that they have created the desertified **Tibetan plateau**, parts of which lie within the northwestern borders of Nepal.

The body and cultural heart of Nepal – and its capital, Kathmandu – lies in the **Middle Hills**, or *pahaad*, a mightily upswelling belt of green created as much by water as plate tectonics. Beginning deep within Tibet, the Karnali, Kali Gandaki and Arun rivers have carved some of the world's deepest and grandest **gorges** through the country. Towards Nepal's southern edge, the geologically more recent uprising of the **Mahabharat Lek** and **Churia Hills** has formed a last barrier, forcing the great southbound rivers to make lengthy east–west detours before they flood out across the flat **Terai** region, and on into India.

Ancient migrations

According to the Newars, who it's believed have lived there longest of all, the Kathmandu Valley was once filled with a **primordial lake**. Geologists agree that a lake dried up some 100,000 years ago. Whether the valley itself was inhabited is uncertain, but hilltop shrines such as Swayambunath may once have existed to rise above the waterline. Archeologists have found simple stone tools in the Churia Hills, to the south, which date back at least 100,000 years.

Folk myths suggest that most of Nepal's current ethnic groups arrived as migrant hunter-gatherers. (Many preserved those ways of life until around the seventeenth century.) Semi-mythological genealogies talk about the warlike **Kiranti** (or Kirati) people who, by the sixth or seventh century BC were controlling the eastern hills – where they remain today – and the Kathmandu Valley. By this time, Hindus from the south were clearing the malarial jungle of the Terai, founding the city-states of

65 million years ago	100,000 years ago	30,000 years ago	c.400 BC
As the Indian tectonic plate collides with the Asian plate, the impact starts to lift the Himalayas.	The primordial lake in the Kathmandu Valley dries up.	Humans using tools live in the Kathmandu Valley.	Gautama Buddha is born at Lumbini.

Mithila (modern Janakpur), the scene of many of the events in the Ramayana epic, and Kapilvastu (now Tilaurakot), where the Buddha spent his pre-enlightenment years during the sixth century BC.

During the first millennium, the hills were populated from all sides. The **Khasas** steadily pushed eastward into what would become western Nepal, bringing their Indo-Aryan Nepali language and Hindu religion with them. From Tibet and the north came waves of migrants: first the **Tamangs**, then the **Gurungs**, in about 500 AD. At first these northerners were animists, practising nature worship and Shamanism; after Buddhism took root in Tibet, they reimported their version of the religion into its original homeland. Not counting modern-day refugees, the last Tibetans to cross the passes into Nepal as a distinct group were the **Sherpas**, from the 1530s onwards.

The ethnic groups of the hills largely kept themselves to themselves. The Kathmandu Valley, by contrast, acted as a giant ethnic mixing bowl. Even the Valley's "indigenous" **Newars** speak a language, Newari, whose Tibeto-Burman roots have come under strong Sanskrit (Indian) influences, and the Newars' genes seem to be as mixed as their language.

The Licchavis and Thakuris

In the second century AD, the **Licchavi** clan, of North Indian origin, overthrew the Kirants and established their capital and their dynasty at Deopatan (modern Pashupatinath), exploiting the valley's position as a trading entrepôt between India and Tibet. Although Hindus, the Licchavis endowed both Hindu and Buddhist temples and established Nepal's long-standing policy of religious tolerance. No Licchavi buildings survive, but Chinese travellers described "multi-storeyed temples so tall one would take them for a crown of clouds" – perhaps a reference to the pagodas that would become a Nepali trademark. Sculptors, meanwhile, ushered in a classical age of stonework, and Licchavi statues still litter the Kathmandu Valley.

The earliest stone inscription, dated 464 AD and still on view at Changu Narayan, extols the Licchavi king **Mandev** (often spelled Manadeva), the legendary builder of the Boudha stupa. The greatest of the Licchavi line, **Amsuvarman** (605–621) was said to have built a splendid palace, probably at present-day Naksal in Kathmandu. But by this time Nepal had become a vassal of Tibet, and Amsuvarman's daughter, Bhrikuti, was carried off by the Tibetan king. She is popularly credited with introducing Buddhism to Tibet as a result.

The Licchavi era came to a close in 879. The three centuries that followed are sometimes referred to as Nepal's **Dark Ages**, though Nepalese chronicles record a long list of **Thakuri kings**, who may have been puppets installed by the various powers controlling the Terai. Nonetheless, learning and the arts continued to thrive, and from the eleventh century onwards the Kathmandu Valley became an important centre of tantric studies (see p.401).

The Khasas and Mallas

From the twelfth century, the great regional power was based in Sinja, in the Karnali basin near modern-day Jumla. The **Khasa empire**, at its height, controlled the Himalayas from Kashmir to present-day Pokhara. The resurgence of the Kathmandu Valley – then known as "Nepal" – began when the Thakuri king of Bhaktapur, Arideva, took the title

First millennium AD	c.400	c.620
Migrants from the Tibetan plateau and Indian plains steadily populate Nepal.	The Licchavi dynasty begins ruling from Pashupatinath.	King Songtsän Gampo of Tibet (legendarily) weds the Licchavi princess Bhrikuti, thus bringing Buddhism to Tibet.

Malla, probably in the year 1200. The name came to be associated with three major dynasties across more than five centuries, presiding over a golden age of Nepali culture.

The early Mallas had to defend their nascent kingdoms against destructive raids by Khasas and, in 1349, Muslims from Bengal. Yet trade and the arts flourished. Arniko, the great Nepali architect, was even dispatched to teach the Ming Chinese to build pagodas. **Jayasthiti Malla** (1354–95) inaugurated a period of strong central rule from Bhaktapur, and legendarily imposed the caste system. Malla power reached its zenith under **Yaksha Malla** (1428–82), who extended his domain westwards to Gorkha and eastwards as far as present-day Biratnagar. Upon his death, the kingdom was divided among three sons, and for nearly three centuries the independent city states of Kathmandu, Patan and Bhaktapur (and occasionally others) feuded and competed, building ever more opulent palaces and temples in a battle of regal theatricality.

While the Kathmandu Valley flourished, new powers were arising in the west. A steady stream of Rajasthani princes fled the Muslim conquest of North India, seeking conquest or refuge in the hills, and by the early fifteenth century the Khasa empire had fragmented into a collection of petty provinces. Those in the Karnali basin came to be known as the **Baaisi Rajya** (Twenty-two Kingdoms), while those that ruled over subjugated Magar and Gurung states further east, in the Gandaki basin, became the **Chaubisi** (Twenty-four). Khasa peoples, meanwhile, began migrating eastward towards and into the Kathmandu Valley, laying down the ethnic foundations of Nepal's long-dominant **Parbatiya**, or caste-Hindu population.

Gorkha conquest

The Chaubisi and Baaisi confederacies were small, weak and culturally backward, but politically stable. Then **Gorkha**, the most easterly territory, began to have ambitions. Under the inspired, obsessive leadership of **Prithvi Narayan Shah** (1722–75), the Gorkhalis launched a campaign that was to take 27 years to conquer the valley kingdoms of "Nepal", and as long again to unite all of modern Nepal.

Prithvi Narayan hoped to create a single pan-Himalayan kingdom, a bastion of Hindu culture in contrast to North India, which had fallen first to the Mughals and then the British. He first captured Nuwakot, a day's march northwest of Kathmandu. From there he directed a ruthless twenty-year **war of attrition** against the valley. Kirtipur surrendered first, following a six-month siege. Its inhabitants had their lips and noses cut off as punishment for resistance. Desperate, the Kathmandu king, Jaya Prakash Malla, sought help from the British East India Company. It was to no avail: of the 2400 soldiers loaned by the Company, only eight hundred returned to India. On the eve of Indra Jaatra in 1768, Jaya Prakash, by now rumoured to be insane, let down the city's defences and **Kathmandu fell** to the Gorkhalis without a fight. Patan followed, two days later, and Bhaktapur the following year; by 1774 the Gorkhalis had marched eastwards all the way to Sikkim.

Suspicious of Britain's ambitions in India and China's in Tibet – he called his kingdom "a yam between two stones" – Prithvi Narayan closed Nepal to foreigners. The gates would remain almost entirely shut until the 1950s. Instead, Nepal turned in on itself, becoming embroiled in a series of bloody **battles for succession** which set the pattern for the next two hundred years. Yet when they weren't stabbing each

c.1200	From c.1200	1288–c.1340
Arideva of Bhaktapur inaugurates the glorious Malla dynasty, named after his love of wrestling.	Buddhism begins to decline in Nepal in the face of strong Hindu monarchies.	The Kathmandu Valley is repeatedly attacked by Khasas from the west, and Doyas from the Terai.

other in the back, the Shahs managed to continue the wars of conquest. Lured on by promises of land grants – every hill man's dream – the Nepali army became an unstoppable fighting machine, and by 1790 Nepal stretched far beyond its present eastern and western borders.

Expansion was finally halted first by a brief but chastening **war with Tibet** and then, in 1814, by a clash with **Britain**'s East India Company after Nepal annexed the Butwal sector of the Terai. It took Britain two years and heavy losses before finally bringing Nepal to heel. The 1816 **Treaty of Segauli** forced Nepal to accept its present eastern and western boundaries and surrender much of the Terai. Worst of all, it had to accept an official British "resident" in Kathmandu. Yet so impressed were the British by "our valiant opponent" that they began recruiting Nepalis into the Indian Army, an arrangement which continues today in the famed **Gurkha regiments** (see p.210). Britain restored Nepal's Terai lands in return for its help in quelling the Indian Mutiny of 1857.

Rana misrule

The intrigues and assassinations that bedevilled the Kathmandu court during the first half of the nineteenth century culminated in the ghastly **Kot massacre** of 1846, in which more than fifty courtiers were butchered in a courtyard off Kathmandu's Durbar Square. Behind the plot was a shrewd young general, **Jang Bahadur Rana**, who seized power and proclaimed himself prime minister for life. He later made the office hereditary, in a move that speaks volumes about the court: his title was attached to a grade of kingship, Shri Tin Maharaja (short for Shri Shri Shri Maharaja), or His Three-Times-Great Highness the King.

The Shah king may have had five Shris before his title but the Ranas held all the power. For a century, they remained authoritarian and isolationist, building almost no roads or schools, only overweening Neoclassical palaces. They kept on careful good terms with the British, but only allowed a handful of foreigners to actually enter Nepal – and usually only as far as Chitwan. Even the British resident was corralled within the Kathmandu Valley. The eastern and western tracts of the country were treated as colonies, the religious and land-tenure customs of the hill tribes subject to ever-greater "sanskritization" – meaning colonization by Parbatiya, or caste-Hindu, culture. Peasants migrated ever further eastward across the hills, and south into the Terai's jungle in search of ever-scarcer land. Slash-and-burn agriculture gave way to subsistence farming, while the Tibetan salt and trade networks were increasingly bypassed by the new British route via Darjeeling. Newar merchants fanned out across Nepal, meanwhile, establishing bazaars where they could sell imported goods. And from the early twentieth century, the population began to grow.

Chandra Shamsher Rana, who came to power in 1901 by deposing his brother, is best known for building the thousand-roomed Singha Durbar and (belatedly) abolishing slavery and the practice of *sati*, or widow-burning. He also built Nepal's first college and hydroelectric plant, along with suspension bridges on the hill trails and the celebrated **ropeway** connecting Kathmandu with the Terai. India's railway network was joined to Nepal in the inter-war years, but never penetrated more than a few miles into the Terai. Factories were established around Biratnagar in the 1930s, and Nepal's first airstrip arrived in 1942.

1383	After 1482	c.1490	1530s
1700 noblemen swear allegiance to Jayasthiti Malla, who is thus acknowledged as overlord of the entire Kathmandu Valley.	Kathmandu, Patan and Bhaktapur become three independent kingdoms.	Ratna Malla of Kathmandu allows Muslims to settle.	Sherpa people start to arrive in Solu Khumbu from Tibet.

The monarchy restored

The absurdly anachronistic regime could not hope to survive the geopolitical seismic shifts of the postwar era. In 1947 the British quit India. In 1949, the Communists took power in China – and within two years had taken over in **Tibet**. Seeking stability, Nepal signed a far-reaching **"peace and friendship" treaty** with India in 1950. Despite the upheavals that were to follow, it remains the contentious basis for all relations between the two countries.

In 1950, the **Nepali Congress Party**, which had recently been formed in Kolkata, called for an armed struggle against the Ranas. Within a month, King Tribhuwan had requested asylum at the Indian embassy and was smuggled away to Delhi. Sporadic fighting and political dealing continued for two months until the Ranas, internationally discredited, reluctantly agreed to enter into negotiations. Brokered by India, the so-called **Delhi Compromise** arranged for Ranas and the Congress Party to share power under the king's rule. Power-sharing squabbles between Ranas and Congress factions, however, ensured that the compromise was ineffective and short-lived. Tribhuwan himself died in 1955, and the promised Constituent Assembly, which was supposed to write a new democratic constitution, never came to fruition.

Crowned in 1955, **King Mahendra** pushed through a constitution which guaranteed him emergency powers, and ultimate control of the army. Long-delayed elections were eventually held in 1959, but this **"experiment with democracy"** was too successful. Under Prime Minister **B.P. Koirala** the Nepali Congress Party began bypassing palace control; in response, Mahendra banned political parties, jailed the Congress leaders and created the "partyless" **panchayat** system. His national assembly, elected ultimately from local village councils (*panchayat*), served in practice as a rubber stamp for royal policies and a conduit for corruption and cronyism. The regime only survived on **foreign aid** and by playing India and China off against each other.

King Birendra assumed his father's throne in 1972, immediately declaring Nepal to be a **Zone of Peace**, a Swiss-style neutrality pledge which won international plaudits – but antagonized India. Birendra made minor concessions towards political reform throughout his reign, and was widely admired, but it became clear in the 1980s that he could neither curtail ever-growing corruption – which involved his own family – nor keep the lid on simmering discontent.

Development under the Shahs

Under the three Shah kings, Nepal's **population** exploded: from 8.4 million in 1954 to 18.5 million in 1991. Much of that growth was absorbed in the flat Terai region, bordering India, where the jungle was cleared for farmland and malaria sprayed out of existence. But slowly, the land began to run out. So too did forest – a crucial fuel and fodder resource for farmers in the hills. Up to a third of Nepalis lacked sufficient food, and the majority of men would migrate in winter in search of paid employment. The Kathmandu Valley's population trebled to well over a million by 1991, and over a million more crossed the border into India. Piecemeal **development projects** failed to stimulate growth, instead bloating the bureaucracy and distorting the budget so that during the peak dependency era, in the late 1980s, forty percent of all government spending derived from foreign aid.

Royal rule was not entirely disastrous for Nepal. Literacy rates stood at a dismal forty percent by 1991 – but it was an improvement on the five percent rate of fifty

1553	1721	1768
King Mukunda Sen dies, leading to the break-up of the great but short-lived Palpa kingdom of the west.	Jesuit priest Ippolito Desideri is the first Westerner to visit the Kathmandu Valley and report back.	Kathmandu falls to Prithvi Narayan.

years earlier. In the same period, infant mortality fell from an appalling twenty percent to a merely shocking ten percent. Notwithstanding huge problems over tariff and trade agreements with India, industrial estates were established at Balaju, Birgunj and Hetauda, and **carpet-weaving**, a trade largely controlled by Tibetan refugees, employed up to 250,000 people by the mid-1980s. But **tourism** was perhaps the most conspicuously successful of Nepal's endeavours. The kingdom that once accepted a single British resident was welcoming 4000 visitors in 1960, 100,000 in 1976, at the close of the hippy era, and – due to a new kind of tourism cleverly marketed as **trekking** – 250,000 by the early 1990s.

Democracy and discontent

The **panchayat** government might have tottered on for many more years if it hadn't been for a trade and migration dispute with India, whose government punished Nepal with a virtual **blockade** through most of 1989. The government might still have ridden out the crisis had it not been for the inspiration provided by China's failed pro-democracy movement at Tiananmen Square, and the successful revolutions in Eastern Europe.

The banned opposition parties united in the **Movement to Restore Democracy**, calling for a national day of protest on February 18, 1990 – the anniversary of the first post-Rana government, a date already known as Democracy Day. Street clashes with police and the arrest of leading opposition figures did little to contain the desire for change, and the **Jana Andolan** ("People's Movement") gathered pace. On March 31, the Newari inhabitants of Patan took control of their city. On April 6, the king promised constitutional reform – but his move failed to placate the 200,000 people marching up Kathmandu's Durbar Marg towards the Royal Palace. After the army fired into the crowd, **killing** dozens, the king's hand was forced. He dissolved his cabinet, lifted the ban on political parties and invited the opposition to form an interim government.

Once again, calls for a constitution to be written by a Constituent Assembly were bypassed; and once again the king clung onto key powers as constitutional monarch – and Nepal remained officially a Hindu state, not a secular one. However, the old Rastriya Panchayat was replaced by a true bicameral parliament, and free **elections** were held in May 1991. Again, the Nepali Congress Party, under **Girija Prasad Koirala**, younger brother of B.P. Koirala, came out on top. The challenge from Nepal's several Communist parties, however, was strong: they maintained their traditional strongholds in the east and, incredibly, captured the Kathmandu Valley. For the next five years, power swung between Congress and the **Communist Party of Nepal–United Marxist-Leninist (CPN-UML)**. No matter who was in power, political infighting and horse-trading for the powers of patronage and the proceeds of corruption took precedence over the real business of government. The impoverished millions living outside the Kathmandu Valley seemed all but forgotten.

Maoists and massacres

Between 1990 and 2000, Nepal certainly developed. The road network doubled in size, phones proliferated, literacy rose by twenty percent (to 58 percent) and infant mortality improved substantially. But **growth** was quickly swallowed up by

1814	1846	1854
War with Britain: the Nepalese inflict several defeats, but are forced back to the Mahakali River.	Court official Jang Bahadur Rana massacres his political opponents, becoming de facto ruler of Nepal. King Rajendra Shah flees to Benares.	Prime Minister Jang Bahadur passes the Muluki Ain, enshrining the rigid caste system in law.

demographics, and hope was increasingly replaced by cynicism. By the end of the decade half a million young Nepalis were leaving school and seeking work each year, but few had any hope of finding employment. In the roadless hills, meanwhile, where three-quarters of the population lived, development still seemed a world away.

In February 1996, members of the **Nepal Communist Party (Maoist)** broke with what they considered to be Nepal's failed democratic system, launching a **"People's War"** from their base in the midwestern hill districts of Rolpa and Rukum. The Congress government paid little heed – a miscalculation that it would regret. The Maoists picked

THE ROYAL MASSACRE

The **royal massacre** of June 1, 2001 – in which **Crown Prince Dipendra** killed most of his family, including his father, the king – traumatized and ultimately transformed the nation. The Shah dynasty had created Nepal back in the eighteenth century, and the monarchy was seen as the very bedrock of national identity, holding dozens of ethnic groups and castes together in peaceful coexistence. The king was regarded as an incarnation of the god Vishnu, a supreme patriarch whose very existence proclaimed Nepal's uniqueness – as the last Hindu kingdom, when all of India had fallen to either the Mughals or the British.

Most monstrous of all, the alleged killer was the king's own son. In a culture where parents still command the highest respect from their children, and where murder is rare, such a crime was almost unimaginable. Nepalis felt grief, anger and deep shame at the egregious breaking of taboos. But above all they felt **disbelief**. Could the crown prince really have done it? Based on the testimony of survivors and palace employees, it's known that before an untypical family gathering, Dipendra was drinking whisky and smoking hashish laced with an unnamed "black substance" – presumably opium. Shortly after, he had to be helped to his room. A few minutes later, he entered the billiard room where the royal family was assembled, dressed in camouflage fatigues with an automatic weapon in each hand. He opened fire, coolly targeting the king first and then other members of his family. He then retreated to the garden where he apparently shot his mother, who had fled, and finally himself.

His motivations seemed oddly run-of-the-mill. Dipendra was apparently furious with the queen for opposing his plans to marry his girlfriend, **Devyani Rana**. He was also known to have a lethal temper, a fetish for weapons, a predilection for alcohol and drugs, and – observers concluded – a propensity for violent psychotic outbursts. It seemed clear cut. But the hastily produced **High Level Committee Report**, delivered just two weeks after the tragedy, was riddled with unanswered – indeed unasked – questions. Why was the first response of the royal aides de camp on duty that night to call a doctor, rather than to overpower the attacker, and why did it take them ten minutes to do that? Why were no post-mortems performed on the victims? Why did Dipendra, who was right-handed, shoot himself behind the left ear? Why did a soldier throw the weapon lying next to Dipendra's body into a pond?

Conspiracy theorists thought it no accident that Gyanendra, alone among the immediate family, was absent from the palace that evening, and that his unpopular son Paras, who was present, escaped unhurt. Others connected the killings with the Maoists – who in turn claimed it was a plot coordinated by the CIA and its Indian counterpart, RAW. Whoever did it, some said, killed Dipendra and replaced him with a stand-in wearing a lifelike mask (which would account for why Dipendra reportedly neither spoke nor showed any expression during the rampage). Others held that Dipendra was a patsy, drugged and given weapons by the real perpetrators and then bumped off afterwards. Whatever the truth, the damage done to the institution of the monarchy was severe – if not fatal.

1857	1921	1947
Jang Bahadur personally leads an army to help the British during the Indian Mutiny; he is rewarded with a knighthood and the return of the Western Terai.	From the Tibetan border, George Mallory is the first mountaineer to glimpse Everest's Nepalese face.	B.P. Koirala founds the Nepali Congress Party in exile in India.

off police stations and district offices one at a time, financing their operations by robbing banks and demanding protection money. Political enemies were intimidated or killed. Political friends were won by aggressive development programmes: schools, courts and health posts were run with renewed efficiency, land redistributed and programmes empowering women, lower castes and minorities launched. Five years later the rebels effectively controlled nearly a quarter of the country's 75 districts, and had infiltrated another half.

In 2001, Maoist leader Pushpa Kamal Dahal – better known by his nom de guerre **Prachanda** ("the Fierce") – issued his preconditions for peace: a Constitutional Assembly with seats for Maoists, and the abolition of the monarchy. Girija Prasad Koirala's government responded by creating a paramilitary **Armed Police Force** with broad powers to combat the rebels. As yet, parliament was unwilling to cross the political Rubicon by letting the army out of its barracks. It owed its loyalty to the king, after all.

The monarchy was soon to enter politics for a very different reason. On the evening of June 1, 2001, King Birendra, Queen Aishwarya and seven other members of the royal family were **massacred** in the Narayanhiti Royal Palace by the heir to the throne, Prince **Dipendra**, who then turned the gun on himself. Dipendra survived on a life-support machine for almost two days, during which time the country boiled with anxiety, speculation and conspiracy theories. When Dipendra's death and his uncle **Gyanendra's ascension** were finally announced, **riots** broke out.

Nepal in crisis: the royal regime

The royal massacre gave the Maoists a golden opportunity to tap into **anti-monarchist feelings**. Gyanendra was known to be sharper-nosed and harder-line than his brother, and his son Paras, now crown prince, was widely loathed. The Maoists stepped up their offensive, even bombing the hitherto safe Kathmandu Valley and successfully enforcing a general strike.

The Congress party, as ever, seemed more concerned with infighting than government. When **Sher Bahadur Deuba** took over from Girija Prasad Koirala in July 2001, his was the eleventh government in as many years. In November 2001, the new king proved his critics right by declaring a **state of emergency** in which he suspended civil liberties, began imprisoning thousands of dissidents, and mobilized Nepal's **army**. Aggressive "search and destroy" operations took Nepali troops deep into the hills. In response, the Maoist People's Liberation Army began to target dams, telecommunications facilities and other infrastructure. A regional insurgency by a fringe political party was escalating into **civil war**. By 2004, the Maoists were strong enough to be able to blockade Kathmandu for an entire week.

Before the war was over, it would kill some fourteen thousand Nepalis, leaving the economy in tatters, the tourist industry in ruins and the Kathmandu Valley straining at the seams with villagers fleeing the fighting in the hills. Nepalis had given up hope. The Maoists, it seemed, could not succeed in taking control of the capital and winning outright. The army could not militarily defeat a movement whose roots ran deep into the roadless hills. The government, meanwhile, was collapsing in a series of failed administrations, postponed elections and compromises with an ever-more interventionist Royal Palace.

6 November 1950	1951	1953
King Tribhuwan escapes his palace imprisonment under the Ranas and flees to India.	The Nepali Congress Party brings Tribhuwan back in triumph to Nepal, and the Rana regime is ended.	On May 29, Tenzing Norgay Sherpa and Edmund Hillary are the first to climb Everest – from the Nepalese side.

The Second People's Movement

In February 2005, Gyanendra snapped, **seizing power** and imposing martial law; as a result, the previously fractious political parties united against him. As the **Seven Party Alliance (SPA)**, the politicians signed an understanding with the Maoists: they would back Maoist demands for a Constituent Assembly and drop support for the monarchy; the Maoists, in return, would announce a ceasefire. Everyone would mobilize against Gyanendra's regime.

During the winter of 2005–06, the scale and belligerence of the protests, rallies and strikes grew – as did the aggression of the government response. Hundreds of political leaders were arrested and, once again, Nepalis died under government bullets. **Bandhs**, or complete shut-downs of the Kathmandu Valley, became commonplace. By early April it was like 1990 all over again – indeed, the movement became known as **Jana Andolan II** (Second People's Movement) though others preferred to call it the **Loktantra Andolan** (Democracy Movement). During April, hundreds of thousands of Nepalis came out onto the streets of Kathmandu day after day, in the face of aggressively enforced curfews. On April 21, Gyanendra played his last card, asking the leaders of the SPA to name a new prime minister. With Maoist guns behind them, the SPA could afford to call the king's bluff, and three days later parliament was duly reinstated under Girija Prasad Koirala.

After ten years of war and stagnation, the pace of political change was now astonishing. In June, the mysterious Comrade Prachanda arrived in Kathmandu for talks with the SPA. His public arrival caused a sensation: most Nepalis had never even seen a photograph of the guerrilla leader, who had spent the last 25 years moving between India and secret locations in the hills. Parliament quickly moved to scrap the 1990 constitution and hold elections for a **Constituent Assembly**. The king's powers were dramatically curtailed, and Nepal was declared to be no longer a kingdom. In November 2006 the Maoists formally ended their insurgency with the **Comprehensive Peace Accord**, agreeing to put their weapons under UN supervision and send their combatants into UN-monitored cantonments. That winter, snow fell in Kathmandu for the first time in sixty years.

The Republic of Nepal

All of Nepal was determined that, this time, democracy would be made to work. But without Gyanendra's regime to unite them in opposition, the political parties were free to squabble. And without the monarchy to bind the country, the tensions that had been building between ethnic groups for years could break out. From late 2006, activists in the Terai launched the **Madheshi Andolan**, or "Movement for Madhesh", to fight for the rights of ethnically and culturally Indian people, or Madheshis, against the historic dominance (or indifference) of hill peoples and the Kathmandu elite. A host of political parties and pressure groups sprang up, aspiring to regional autonomy or a separate state – *ek pradesh, ek madhesh* ("one state, one Madhesh"), as the slogan went. In 2007 and 2008, the major Terai towns were the site of bomb blasts and violent clashes.

In April 2008, the Maoists won an astounding victory in the **Constituent Assembly elections**, taking 220 seats, over a third of the total – and twice as many as either Congress or the CPN-UML. Nepal was duly transformed into a **republic** in May 2008,

1955	1959–61	1960
Indian engineers complete the Tribhuwan Rajpath, finally linking Kathmandu to the world by road.	Following the Tibetan uprising and flight of the Dalai Lama, some 20,000 Tibetans take refuge in Nepal.	King Mahendra suspends the constitution, imprisons his opponents and begins ruling as a dictator.

and Gyanendra was given three days to quit the Narayanhiti palace. In August, Comrade Prachanda – who increasingly used his proper name, Pushpa Kamal Dahal – became the first prime minister of the secular **Federal Democratic Republic of Nepal**.

The new government quickly came up against intractable **realities**. Attempting to merge those former adversaries, the Royal National Army and the People's Army, proved predictably difficult. So too did persuading self-serving politicians to stop fighting long enough to even discuss writing the new **constitution**. Girija Prasad Koirala's Nepali Congress Party quickly established itself as an official, obstructive opposition while the Maoists began to split over issues such as the extent of federalism, and whether the new Nepal would officially be a *People's* Republic.

Across the country, highly politicized youth and ethnic identity groups proliferated, posing a serious threat to stability. As so often, a natural disaster added real injury to the insults the country was already suffering: in August 2008, floods smashed the **Koshi Barrage**, killing thousands downstream in India, and dealing a massive blow to Nepal's already faltering electricity supply. Poor maintenance, lack of new projects, "pilferage" of power, and demand growing at ten percent a year resulted in scheduled "load shedding" – ie power cuts – which blacked out the capital for up to twenty hours a day. The effect on industry – already feeling the first chill wind of global **recession** – was catastrophic; the effect on Kathmandu's morale was, if anything, even more severe.

As ever, **tourism** held out the greatest economic hope. Thousands, it seemed, had just been waiting for the conflict to end. In 2007 and 2008, more than 500,000 foreigners visited Nepal (roughly one for every Nepali working in the tourism sector), finally surpassing the record set in 1999 before the conflict really took hold and tourism halved. Once again, the trails were buzzing with trekkers.

Stasis and strain

In May 2009, Prime Minister **Dahal abruptly resigned**, supposedly because President Ram Baran Yadav had countermanded his order sacking the army's Chief of Staff. In truth, it was a tactical move. The Maoists wanted a better deal on key issues such as the integration of Maoist combatants into the new Nepal Army, and the shape of the constitution – and they were prepared to undermine the government in order to get their way.

Madhav Nepal of the left-wing CPN-UML struggled on ineffectually as the chosen prime minister of a 22-party anyone-but-the-Maoists coalition while the Maoists organized vast street protests, mobilizing up to half a million supporters in Kathmandu, and arranging endless **bandhs**, or strikes, that shut down the country day after day, and road blockades that actually cut off the capital. In May 2010, the deadline for writing a constitution and holding elections expired. The Assembly voted itself an extra year to sort out its mess. Sixteen times parliament attempted to elect a new prime minister; sixteen times it failed due to political manoeuvring.

Meanwhile, the constitution remained unwritten and the country remained barely governed. And, at the same time, the forests of the **Terai** were being plundered to the point of extinction and the wildlife reserves freely poached, while the country's social structure was under increasing strain as young people continued to flee the hills. Hundreds of thousands of **migrants** were continuing to pour into the bulging cities of Kathmandu, Pokhara and the Terai, and 200,000 young people every year were

1965	1988–93	1989
Gurkha officer and mountaineer Jimmy Roberts guides three women to Everest Base Camp: it is the first tourist "trek".	Some 100,000 "Lhotshampas" (mostly Kiranti Nepalese people), flee ethnic persecution in Bhutan, taking refuge in eastern Nepal.	The People's Movement forces King Birendra to introduce multiparty democracy.

heading overseas to take on "dirty, dangerous and demeaning" jobs in the Gulf, Korea, Malaysia or India. Their remittances of foreign currency were just about keeping Nepal afloat but, for the first time in generations, many of Nepal's hill terraces were being abandoned to weeds.

A Mustang and a Seven-Point Pact

In truth, Nepal was not going to work without the Maoists in government and, in August 2011, the perpetually squabbling parties agreed to elect Maoist co-leader **Baburam Bhattarai** as prime minister. Known as the intellectual of the party, Bhattarai is famous for coming first in Nepal's national school examinations, and for earning a PhD (for a Marxist analysis of Nepal's under-development) at an Indian university – a link which is evidence, for some, of a suspicious closeness to Nepal's neighbour. Leaving aside the issue of his role in the violent Maoist insurrection, Bhattarai is often seen as the Maoist leader with the most honesty and integrity. He was praised for choosing a basic, Nepali-made Mustang jeep as his ministerial car over the usual fancy foreign SUV, for instance. It looked less impressive when he appointed a jumbo-sized cabinet, and then got it to press the president to pardon a convicted murderer from his own party.

Bhattarai was also admired for his ability – not least his ability to cool or at least balance the revolutionary zeal of his co-leaders, including his potential rival, Dahal. In October 2011, Bhattarai pulled off a major coup by signing a **Seven-Point Pact** with the main opposition parties. Under its terms, 6500 Maoist combatants would be integrated into the Nepal Army, with generous payments for those who opted out, and the Maoists would return seized property. A Truth and Reconciliation Committee, meanwhile, would examine murders by Maoists and extra-judicial killings by the army. Predictably, the hardline faction within Bhattarai's party, led by Mohan Baidya, aka Kiran-ji, decried the deal as a sell-out, but everyone knew that few Nepalis would take up arms for the Maoists again.

However, Bhattarai soon ran into trouble. In May 2012 the Constituent Assembly missed the final deadline to agree a new constitution, and the following year the Supreme Court suspended the plans for a Truth and Reconciliation Commission over concerns that it could allow amnesties for serious crimes. No party was able to secure a majority in the November 2013 elections and Nepal was paralysed by political deadlock. Finally, in February 2014, **Sushil Koirala**, leader of the Nepali Congress, was elected as prime minister after securing parliamentary support.

India and China

One of Koirala's biggest challenges is deciding how Nepal will relate to its neighbours. **India** has long regarded Nepal as a client state, due to the onerously one-sided 1950 Treaty of Peace and Friendship, and the careful "cultivation" of individual Nepali politicians, but this may change. Many of Nepal's mainstream politicians are now looking north.

The Maoists certainly are. During the conflict, they had surprisingly little to do with the **Chinese** but, once in government, they worked to improve relations by obediently tightening up the Tibetan border and repressing Tibetan protests in Kathmandu. Nepal

1996	2001	2005	2006
The Maoists launch their People's War.	Crown Prince Dipendra shoots dead most of his family, including King Birendra, before killing himself.	King Gyanendra imposes military rule under his personal leadership.	The Seven Party Alliance brings down Gyanendra's dictatorship. The Maoists agree a ceasefire and rejoin politics.

also relaxed rules on foreign investment so that companies could be wholly owned by foreigners. The Chinese are taking advantage, with new hydro schemes in the pipeline and calls to carry the Tibet railway right through Nepal to Lumbini and the Indian frontier – engineers are already studying the feasibility of extending the line from Lhasa to Nyalam, just 35km north of the Nepali border.

The future

China has also paid for new roads to be built across the border. **Road building**, in fact, is the big story of the 2000s and 2010s: more roads were built in the five years following the end of the conflict than in the fifty years before. Right across the country, where there were once just footpaths and fields, you can now find buses (or, failing that, jeeps and tractors) bumping and crashing their way on rough roads blasted through the hills (see p.412). The economy is being transformed. **Tourism** is changing almost as rapidly. With an influx of Indian and Chinese tourists, and a rise in domestic tourism, tourist hot spots that were once geared exclusively to Westerners are adapting.

While tourism continues to prop up the economy, along with remittances from expat workers, it's never enough. The once-thriving carpet industry has been destroyed by cheap competition and other exports are still hampered by corruption, poor management, atrocious power supply and the sheer difficulty of getting goods out of the country. The budget deficit has become a yawning gulf, development issues remain intractable, and Nepal's manifold problems seem set to be exacerbated by **climate change**. Landslips, flooding and erosion are gathering pace. Meanwhile, the risk of catastrophic outburst flooding from glacial lakes is ever more serious, and the larger Himalayan glaciers have lost up to half their volume in the last fifty years.

The one feature of Nepal that has seemed a constant through centuries of astonishing transformation, its Himalayan backbone, suddenly looks as if it too is vulnerable to change. Yet for all the problems that beset it, Nepal still maintains one unbeatable resource: its **people**. It might seem strange to ascribe national characteristics to a country made up of such an extraordinary diversity of cultures, ethnicities and religions, but the fame of the Nepali for great-heartedness and resilience has not been won easily. If any people can face down the future that seems to loom ahead of them so ominously, it is the people of Nepal.

2008	February 2014	April & October 2014
The Maoists win the elections. Nepal becomes a republic.	After a period of political deadlock, Nepali Congress leader Sushil Koirala is elected as prime minister.	In April an avalanche on Everest kills 16 sherpas, the worst accident in the mountain's history. Six months later, over 40 trekkers, porters and guides are killed in freak blizzards in the Annapurna region.

The people of Nepal

The number of travellers who return from Nepal and say that, for all the breathtaking scenery, it was the people they liked the most – is astonishing. Nepali friendliness is proverbial, and hospitality is deeply embedded in the national culture. "Guest is god" is a much-used saying, and children are taught early to press their hands together in the *namaste* greeting. Alongside this refined courtesy culture exists a tough-minded, proud independence and a rare talent for laughing in the face of hardship.

But the fascination of Nepal's people is about more than charm. Despite the country's modest size, it has a continent's share of **ethnic groups**, with more than fifty languages and as many cultural traditions. Much of this diversity is owed to geography. North of the Himalayan wall live the Mongoloid peoples of central and east Asia. To the south, beyond the malarial plains, are the Indo-Aryans of the subcontinent. The people of Nepal are the descendants of daring or desperate migrants.

The Newars

The Kathmandu Valley has its own indigenous group: the **Newars** (see p.153), whose tight-knit communities are recognizable by their distinctive architecture of warm brick and carved wood. Newars are found across Nepal, however, as their enterprising merchant class founded the bazaars around which so many hill towns grew. The Newars could be said to represent a mixture of all Nepal's cultures: they are Hindus and Buddhists at the same time; they look by turns "Indian" and "Tibetan". But it would be more true to say that they created the culture that *is* Nepal – including the culture of extraordinary religious and ethnic tolerance, which persists, admirably, today.

Sherpas, Tibetans and other mountain folk

Nepal's most famous ethnic group, the **Sherpas** (see p.342), makes up less than one percent of the population. Alongside other "Bhotiya" peoples of Tibetan origin, such as the **Humlis** of Humla and the **Lo-pa** of Mustang, they live at the harshest, highest altitudes, traditionally herding yaks and growing barley, buckwheat and potatoes. All follow the Tibetan school of Buddhism (see p.401), and are in many ways indistinguishable from Tibetans – as are their communities, with their stone houses, and their chortens, prayer walls and prayer flags. Bhotiya people are noticeably less tradition-bound than Hindus, and women are better off for it. Looks aside, they're recognizable by their clothing, especially the rainbow aprons (*pangden*) and wraparound dresses (*chuba*) worn by married women.

The hilly heartlands

The Middle Hills, or *pahad* region, are occupied by an extraordinary mixture of peoples, sometimes known collectively as **pahadiyas**. Some areas, especially further west, are quite ethnically homogenous; further east it can be extraordinarily mixed: in one valley you might find a Chhetri (caste Hindu) village at low elevation, Rai and Gurung villages higher up, along with adjacent Dalit (untouchable) hamlets, and Tamangs or Sherpas occuping the high ground. Traditionally, however, the Middle Hills are the homelands of distinctive ethnic groups, known as **janajaati** or tribal peoples: the Gurungs and Magars of the west (see p.229), the Tamangs (see p.187) of the central hills, and the Rais and Limbus of the east (see p.349). The *janajaati* now make up roughly a third of Nepalis and, with Maoist encouragement (combined with a long-standing hostility towards Brahmin oppression), they are increasingly assertive about their ethnic identities.

Mongoloid features and Tibeto-Burman languages are signs of ancestral origins; short stature and muscularity say more about rugged lives. The *janajaati* follow broadly animist traditions, overlaid by shamanism and subject to varying degrees of Hindu or Tibetan Buddhist influence. Social mores are relatively relaxed: women have more independence than their caste-Hindu sisters, for instance, and meat and alcohol are consumed enthusiastically. Print skirts, heavy gold jewellery and *pote malla* (strands of glass beads) are traditional dress for women; men have mostly abandoned the elfish *daura suruwal* (shirt and jodhpur pants) of old, but a *topi* on the head and a *khukuri* (machete) in the waistband are often seen.

Caste Hindus

The majority of Nepalis descend from Hindus who fled the Muslim conquest of northern India – or their converts. In the west, especially, they're sometimes called **Parbatiyas** ("Hill-dwellers") or caste **Hindus**, since nearly all were high-caste **Baahuns** and **Chhetris** who had the most to lose from the advance of Islam. High levels of education and a sense of entitlement provided the ambition necessary to subjugate the hill tribes they encountered. In the process they provided the country with much of its cultural framework, including its lingua franca, Nepali.

Baahuns

Although **Baahuns** (Brahmans) belong to the highest, priestly caste, they're not necessarily the wealthiest members of society, nor are they all priests. However, their historic ability to read and write has long given them a significant edge in Nepali society, and they have tended to occupy the best government and professional jobs – even half the Maoists' leaders belong to the caste. Rural Baahuns have a reputation for aggressive moneylending that is sometimes deserved.

Baahuns are supposed to maintain their caste purity by eschewing foods such as onions, hens' eggs and alcohol, and they are technically prohibited from eating with lower castes – including foreigners – or even permitting them to enter the house. In practice, the stricter rules are only followed by traditional families in the remote west of Nepal. Priest-work – which usually consists of reading Sanskrit prayers and officiating over rites for fixed fees – is usually a family business. Some Baahuns make a full-time living out of it, others officiate part-time alongside other work.

Chhetris

The majority of Nepal's caste Hindus are **Chhetris**. They are ranked in the classical caste system as Kshatriyas, the caste of warriors and kings. Like Baahuns, they rank among the "twice-born" castes, because men are symbolically "reborn" at thirteen and thereafter wear a sacred thread (*janai*) over one shoulder. While Baahuns usually claim pure bloodlines and exhibit classic, aquiline "Indian" features, many Chhetris have more mixed parentage. Some descend from the Khasa people of the western hills, others are the offspring of Baahun and Khasa marriages and are known as the Khatri Chhetri, or "KC" for short. Those whose Khasa ancestors didn't convert or intermarry are called **Matwaali Chhetris** – "alcohol-drinking" Chhetris – but because they follow a form of shamanism and don't wear the sacred thread, they're sometimes thought to be a separate ethnic group. Chhetris who claim pure Kshatriya blood – notably the aristocratic **Thakuri** subcaste of the far west, who are related to the former royal family – can be as twitchy about caste regulations as Baahuns. Chhetris have long been favoured for commissions in the military and, to a lesser extent, jobs in other branches of government and industry. Significantly, the Shah dynasty was Chhetri, and their rule owed much to the old warrior-caste mentality.

Dalits – "untouchables"

A significant number of Sudras – members of the "untouchable" caste – immigrated to Nepal's hills over the centuries. The members of this caste are now known as **Dalits**, or "the oppressed", and they certainly suffer severe disadvantages in Nepali society, being typically landless and lacking access to education, health facilities or representation in government. Many villages have an attached Dalit hamlet, often a cluster of smaller, meaner dwellings. Although untouchability was officially abolished in 1963, Dalits threaten orthodox Hindus with ritual pollution, and in many parts of the country they're not allowed to enter temples, homes or even tea stalls, or they may be asked to wash up their own utensils after eating *daal bhaat*.

Another name for the Dalits is the **occupational castes**, as they fall into several occupation-based *thars*, such as the Sarki (leather-workers), Kami (blacksmiths), Damai (tailors/musicians) and Kumal (potters). While the importance of their labour traditionally helped offset their lowly status, nowadays they cannot compete with imported manufactured goods. Many are turning to tenant farming, portering and day-labouring to make ends meet.

People of the plains

Until recently, the Terai was sparsely populated by forest-dwelling groups like the Tharus (see p.240), **Danuwars** and **Majhis**. But the malaria-control programmes of the 1950s finally opened it up for several million gung-ho immigrants from the hills and India alike, and today the Terai is ethnically the most mixed area of Nepal – alongside the capital, of course.

Religion

It often surprises Western visitors to learn that Nepal is, by a huge margin, a Hindu country, not a Buddhist one. That's what the statistics say, anyway. In truth, both religions are underpinned by shared tantric traditions that are distinctively Himalayan. For long the subcontinent's last great Hindu kingdom, Nepal was also the birthplace of Buddhism. Today, you can broadly judge a Nepali's religion by altitude: Tibetan-style Buddhism prevails on the ridgetops and in the high Himalayas, where you'll find Sherpas, Tamangs and other Bhotiya or Tibetan peoples; the Madheshi peoples of the plains, and the caste Hindus of the Middle Hills, are fairly orthodox Hindu.

In the hilly heartland of the country, Nepal's ethnic groups intertwine **Hinduism** with **animist** or nature-worshipping traditions, ancestor veneration and **shamanistic** practices, often worshipping local gods under nominally Hindu names. Many Rais and Limbus, however, are partly or largely "Hinduized" in terms of religion, while Magars and Gurungs have been more strongly influenced by **Tibetan Buddhism**. In the Kathmandu Valley, the Newars practise their own extraordinary, tolerant mix of the two main religions, bound together by Nepal's vibrant **tantric** legacy.

Long supported by the monarchy and Brahmin-dominated government, many Hindu institutions are now facing a more uncertain future. Elements within the Maoist movement are aggressively **secular**, and in 2008 the government attempted to throw traditional priests out of the Pashupatinath temple and withdrew funding for key Kathmandu festivals. By contrast, **Buddhist** and **indigenous religious groups** are enjoying something of a renaissance – partly thanks to the mighty amounts of foreign funding that **Tibetan Buddhism** attracts. The ethnic groups of the hills, meanwhile, are increasingly asserting political and religious autonomy, rejecting the creeping Hinduization of past decades and turning back to local traditions.

Hinduism

Hinduism isn't so much a religion as **dharma**, meaning duty, faith – an entire way of life. Hindus seek the divine not in books or prayer meetings but in the ritual rhythms of the day and the seasons – festivals are hugely important – and in the very fabric of family and social relationships. Having no common church or institution, Hinduism's many sects and cults preach different dogmas and emphasize different scriptures, and worshippers can follow many paths to enlightenment. By absorbing other faiths and doctrines, rather than seeking to suppress them, Hinduism has flourished longer than any other major religion.

According to the philosophical **Upanishads,** the soul (*atman*) of each living thing is like a lost fragment of the universal soul – **brahman**, the ultimate reality – while everything in the physical universe is mere illusion (*maya*). To reunite with *brahman*, the individual soul must go through a **cycle of rebirths** (*samsara*), ideally moving up the scale with each reincarnation. Determining the soul's progress is its **karma**, its accumulated "just desserts" (nothing to do with **kama**, which means sexual desire), which is reckoned by the degree to which the soul conformed to **dharma** in previous lives. Thus a low-caste Hindu must accept his or her lot to atone for past sins, and follow *dharma* in the hope of achieving a higher rebirth. The theoretical goal of every Hindu is to cast off all illusion, achieve release (*moksha*) from the cycle of rebirths, and dissolve into *brahman*.

OM MANI PADME HUM

You cannot escape the sound "AUM" or "**OM**" in Nepal. Once you've learned to recognize the written form of the sacred syllable, you can see it everywhere: on temples gates and monastery walls, carved on rocks beside trails, painted on the sides of buses and hanging on pendants around people's necks. Once your ear is attuned, you'll hear it everywhere too: in Hindu prayers and the *bhajan* hymns sung at dusk, in the endlessly repeated *sotto voce* incantations of Buddhist pilgrims, and in the relentless blaring of tourist music shops playing New Age mantra recordings.

Some would say you can't escape the sound anywhere outside Nepal either, as it represents the very vital energy of the universe, of which all material things are manifestations. Among Hindus, it is known as the "four-element syllable", standing for birth, existence and dissolution, as represented by the three great gods, Brahma, Vishnu and Shiva. It also stands for the three human states of selfhood: wakefulness, dreaming and sleep. The fourth element is the eloquent silence out of which the sound arises, and into which it returns; it represents the transcendent state of "peaceful, benign pure oneness".

The syllable itself reflects the idea: the basic sound (and the core shape of the written letter) is an open "a"; this is modified by the "u" part of the vowel (represented in writing by a hook-like curl behind) before being closed off with a nasalized "m" (shown as a moon-like dash with a dot on top).

As with any good mantra, actually uttering OM is supposed to have real effects: it is said to align your body with the resonant spirit of the universe itself. For Tibetan Buddhists, OM is the first element in the most essential mantra of all: **Om mani padme hum** (pronounced "om mani peme hung" in Tibetan). It's usually translated as "Hail to the jewel in the lotus", which is a salutation to the *bodhisattva* (a kind of Buddhist saint) Avalokiteshwara, who represents compassion and is known as the jewel-lotus.

For Buddhists, the mantra's meaning is many-layered, however. Each syllable corresponds to different deities, symbolic colours and magical effects in the Tibetan tradition, and each represents one of the six *paramitas*, or "perfections". Om and Hum, for instance, do not have any meaning as words, but represent white and black respectively, and the perfections of generosity and diligence. The mantra also has political significance. Chanting it is a sign of devotion to the Dalai Lama (said to be an incarnation of Avalokiteshwara), and thus of resistance to the Chinese.

The Hindu pantheon

Hinduism's earliest known origins lie in the **Vedas**, sacred texts composed in India in the first and second millennia BC. They tell stories of a pantheon of nature gods and goddesses, some of whom are still in circulation: Indra (sky and rain) is popular in Kathmandu, while Surya (sun), Agni (fire), Vayu (wind) and Yama (death) retain bit parts in contemporary mythology. As the messenger between the gods and humanity, Agni was particularly important, and sacrifice was thus a major part of Vedic religion. Gradually, the Vedic gods were displaced by the **Brahminical "trinity"**: Brahma the creator, Vishnu the preserver and Shiva the destroyer. Every locality has its own forms, often derived from ancient nature worship. Even today, many ancestral spirits of the Nepali hill peoples are being given Hindu names, their worship adapted to fit more conventional rituals – a process known as Hinduization. When pressed, Nepalis often refer to their local deities as aspects of Mahadev (Shiva), Vishnu or one of the other mainstream gods, either out of respect for foreigners' potential bewilderment or out of a widespread notion that they all boil down to one god in the end. Shaivism, or the worship of Shiva, is the most widespread devotional cult in Nepal, as part of the tantric legacy (see box, p.401).

In art and statuary, the most important gods can easily be identified by certain trademark implements, postures and "vehicles" (animal carriers). Multiple arms and heads aren't meant to be taken literally: they symbolize the deity's "universal" (omnipotent) form. Severed heads and trampled corpses, meanwhile, signify ignorance and evil.

Vishnu

Vishnu (often known as **Narayan** in Nepal) is the face of dignity and equanimity, typically shown standing erect holding a wheel (*chakra*), mace (*gada*), lotus (*padma*) and conch (*sankha*) in his four hands, or, as at Budhanilkantha, reclining on a serpent's coil. A statue of **Garuda** (**Garud** in Nepal), Vishnu's bird-man vehicle, is always close by. Vishnu is also sometimes depicted in one or more of his ten incarnations, which follow an evolutionary progression from fish, turtle and boar to the man-lion **Narasimha**, a dwarf, an axe-wielding Brahman and the legendary heroes **Ram** and **Krishna**, as portrayed in the much-loved epics, the Mahabharata and Ramayana.

Ram is associated with **Hanuman**, his loyal monkey-king ally, while blue-skinned Krishna is commonly seen on posters and calendars as a chubby baby, flute-playing lover or charioteer. Interestingly, Vishnu's ninth *avatar* is the Buddha – this was a sixth-century attempt by Vaishnavas to bring Buddhists into their fold – and the tenth is Kalki, a messiah figure invented in the twelfth century as Muslims took the upper hand in India. Vishnu's consort is **Lakshmi**, the goddess of wealth, to whom lamps are lit during the festival of Tihaar. Like Vishnu, she assumed mortal form in two great Hindu myths, playing opposite Ram as the chaste princess Sita, and opposite Krishna as the passionate Radha.

Shiva

Shiva's incarnations are countless but to many devotees he is simply **Mahadev**, the Great God. He is the pre-eminent divinity in Nepal. The earliest and most widespread icon of Shiva is the **linga**, a phallic stone fertility symbol often housed in a boxy stone *shivalaya* ("Shiva home"), often garlanded in marigolds and dusted with red *abhir* powder, and sometimes encircled in a *yoni*, or vulva symbol. Shiva temples can be identified by the presence of a *trisul* (trident) and the bull **Nandi**, Shiva's mount.

Many sadhus worship Shiva the yogin (one who practises yoga), the Hindu ascetic supreme, who is often depicted sitting in meditative repose on a Himalayan mountaintop. In his benign form as **Pashupati** ("Lord of the Animals"), he occupies Pashupatinath as his winter home. As **Nataraja**, lord of the "dance" of life, he maintains and destroys the cosmos. As the loving husband of Parvati and father of Ganesh, he represents family life – the divine couple can be seen leaning from an upper window of a temple in Kathmandu's Durbar Square. Nearby stand two famous statues of the grotesque **Bhairab**, the tantric (see p.401) interpretation of Shiva in his role as destroyer: according to Hindu philosophy, everything – not only evil – must be destroyed in its turn to make way for new things. Bhairab alone is said to take 64 different forms.

Mahadevi – the mother goddess

The mother goddess is similarly worshipped in many forms, both peaceful and wrathful. Typically, she is the consort of Shiva, and represented as the vulva-like **yoni** symbol. In Nepal she is widely worshipped as **Bhagwati**, the embodiment of female creative power, and in the Kathmandu Valley she takes physical form as the **Kumari**, a young girl chosen to be her virginal incarnation. She is appeased by sacrifices of uncastrated male animals, a practice far more common in tantric Nepal than in more orthodox India. In art, she is most often seen as **Durga**, the many-armed demon-slayer honoured in the great Dasain festival; as angry **Kali** ("Black", but often painted as dark blue), the female counterpart of Bhairab, wearing a necklace of skulls and sticking out her tongue with bloodthirsty intent; and as the **Ashtamatrika** in the form of eight (or sometimes seven) ferocious "mothers". On a more peaceful level, she is also **Parbati** ("Hill", daughter of Himalaya), Gauri ("Golden") or just **Mahadevi** ("Great Goddess").

Ganesh, Annapurna and Saraswati

Several legends tell how **Ganesh**, Shiva and Parbati's son, came to have an elephant's head: one states that Shiva accidentally chopped the boy's head off, and was then forced to replace it with that of the first creature he saw. The god of wisdom and remover of obstacles, Ganesh must be worshipped first to ensure that offerings to other gods will be effective, which is why a Ganesh shrine or stone will invariably be found near other temples. Underscoring Hinduism's great sense of the mystical absurd, Ganesh's vehicle is a rat.

Of the other classical Hindu deities, only **Annapurna**, the goddess of grain and abundance (her name means "Full of Grain"), and **Saraswati**, the goddess of learning and culture, receive much attention in Nepal. Saraswati is normally depicted holding a *vina*, a musical instrument something like a sitar.

Prayer and ritual

In practice, Hinduism is chiefly concerned with the performance of day-to-day rituals. **Puja**, a gift to the divine that acts as worship, is particularly important. It can be done before a shrine in the home – and should in fact be performed first and last thing – at a public temple, or simply on an ad hoc basis: when encountering a sacred cow in the street, for instance, or while whizzing past a particular shrine on a motorbike. In a more formal *puja*, offerings (*prasad*) are made to the chosen god: flowers (usually marigolds), incense sticks, light (in the form of butter lamps), *abhir* (coloured powder) and "pure" foods such as rice, milk or sweets. In return for the *puja*, the worshipper often receives a mark (*tilak*, or *tika* in Nepali) on the forehead, usually made of sandalwood paste, ash or coloured powders.

If the day is regulated by *puja*, the year is measured out in seasonal festivals. The most important Nepali festivals, **Dasain** and **Tihar** (see p.36), both take place in the autumn. Life, meanwhile, is marked by key **rites of passage** (*samskaras*). Among the most important in Nepal are the ceremony for a baby's first rice and the *upanayana* or **"rebirth"** rite for higher-caste (Baahun and Chhetri) pubescent boys. The boy's head is shaved (except for a small tuft at the back) and he is given the sacred thread (*janai*) to wear sash-like over one shoulder, next to the skin, signifying his twice-born status. In some communities, especially Newari ones, girls may undergo *barha*, a purification rite around the time of first menstruation. **Weddings** are hugely important and correspondingly lengthy, involving endless processions, gifts and offerings. In Nepal, they're often loudly signalled by a live band – either the traditional Nepali ensemble of *sahanai* (shawm), *damaha* (large kettledrum), *narsinga* (C-shaped horn), *jhyaali* (cymbals) and *dholaki* (two-sided drum) or, for more urban types, a brass band in military-style uniforms. The other key rite is, of course, the **funeral**. Hindus cremate their dead, and the most sacred place to do so in Nepal is beside the river at Pashupatinath, just outside Kathmandu. Mourning sons are supposed to shave their heads and wear white.

Priests can be full-time professionals or simply the local Brahman. They officiate at the more important rites and festivals, and may also give private consultations for wealthier patrons at times of illness or important decisions. Temple priests preside over the act of **darshan** (audience with a deity), providing consecrated water for the devotee to wash him or herself and to bathe the deity, leading the *puja* and the symbolic offering of food to the deity, and bestowing the **tika** on the devotee's forehead.

HINDU BHAJAN AND TANTRIC HYMNS

The most visible form of Hindu sacred music is **bhajan** – devotional hymn-singing, usually performed in front of temples and in the half-covered loggias, or *sattals*, of rest-houses. *Bhajan* groups gather on auspicious evenings to chant praises to Ram, Krishna or other Hindu deities and to recite classical devotional poetry. Like a musical *puja*, the haunting verses are repeated over and over to the mesmeric beat of the tabla and the drone of the harmonium. The group of (male) singers usually follows one lead voice, gradually coming together as the hymn accelerates to a triumphant, energizing conclusion. During festivals, round-the-clock vigils are sometimes sponsored by wealthy patrons.

Bhajan is mostly a Hindu import, but Newars have their own style, often sung in the Newari language and sometimes even invoking Newari Buddhist deities. Some Newari Buddhist priests still also sing esoteric **tantric hymns** which, when accompanied by **mystical dances** and hand postures, are believed to have immense occult power. The secrets of these are closely guarded by initiates, but a rare public performance is held on Buddha Jayanti, when five *vajracharya* costumed as the Pancha Buddha dance at Swayambhu.

The caste system

One of Hinduism's unique features is the apartheid-like **caste system**, which theoretically divides humanity into four main *varnas*, or groups. The Rig Veda, Hinduism's oldest text, proclaimed that priestly Brahmans (Baahuns in Nepali) had issued from the head and mouth of the supreme creator, warrior Kshatriyas (Chhetris) from his chest and arms, Vaishyas from his thighs, and "untouchable" Sudras from his feet. In Nepal, the system is thought to have been instituted by the fourteenth-century king **Jayasthiti Malla**, who further subdivided his subjects into 64 hereditary occupations – a system that remained enshrined in Nepali law until 1964.

Discriminating according to **caste** is now illegal in Nepal, though most "higher" caste Hindus are still careful about ritual pollution, being careful not to accept food or water from lower castes, and avoiding physical contact with them. Marriage has been slowest to change: intercaste couplings remain shocking, often resulting in families breaking off contact – a serious punishment in a country where connections are everything.

The ethnic peoples of the hills, or **janajaati**, don't quite fit into the caste system, though internal migration has led to much intermixing, and a great deal of Hinduization. As a result, the *janajaati* have been given a place half inside Nepal's caste system: practices such as eating meat and drinking alcohol have placed them below Chhetris but above Dalits. This puts them roughly on a par with foreigners (*bideshis*), incidentally – though Westerners are technically untouchable.

The usual term for caste in Nepali is **jaat**, though it can signify ethnicity and traditional occupation, as well as caste in the proper sense. A further subdivision is **thar**, usually defined as a **clan**. Members of a *thar* have a common surname, which may or may not indicate common lineage, but may often indicate a hereditary occupation and position in the social hierarchy – and may enforce caste-like rules regarding marriage.

Buddhism

The Buddha was born Siddhartha Gautama in what is now Nepal in the fifth or sixth century BC (see p.263). His teachings sprang out of Hinduism's ascetic traditions, adapting its doctrines of reincarnation and *karma*, along with many yogic practices, but rejecting the caste system and belief in a creator God. The essence of the Buddha's teaching is encapsulated in the **four noble truths**: existence is suffering; suffering is caused by desire; the taming of desire ends suffering; and desire can be tamed by following the **eightfold path**. Wisdom and compassion are key qualities, but the ultimate Buddhist goal is **nirvana**, a state of non-being reached by defeating the "three poisons" of greed, hatred and delusion.

Buddhism quickly became a full-time monastic pursuit but it also evolved a less ascetic, populist strand known as **Mahayana** ("Great Vehicle"), which took root in Nepal from around the fifth century. Reintroducing elements of worship and prayer, Mahayana Buddhism developed its own pantheon of *bodhisattva* – enlightened intermediaries, something akin to Catholic saints, who have forgone *nirvana* until all humanity has been saved. Some were a repackaging of older Hindu deities. Nepal – and especially the Newar people of the Kathmandu Valley (see p.153) – gradually developed its own unique blend of Hindu and Buddhist traditions, with a strong **tantric** flavour (see opposite). Buddhism reached its apogee in the medieval Malla dynasty, but following the Mughal invasion of India, the arrival of orthodox Hindus from the south and west increasingly diluted the Buddhist part of the mix. When the Hindu Shah dynasty took control of Nepal, in the latter half of the eighteenth century, Buddhism went into a long decline. The fortunes of Buddhism in Nepal only recovered thanks to the arrival of another wave of refugees, this time **Tibetans** fleeing the Chinese takeover during the 1950s. They brought with them their own unique form of the religion, **Vajrayana**. As a relatively structured typeset of beliefs and practices, it is now far stronger and more visible than the indigenous Nepali strains.

TANTRISM

Nepal's highly coloured religious practices owe much to the feverish influence of **tantrism**, a ritualistic and esoteric strain of religion that courses through the religious blood of Hindus and Buddhists alike. The tantric cults originated in the Shiva worship of Nepal and the surrounding Himalayan regions in around the eighth and ninth centuries, but their influence soon spread across India, pervading both Hinduism and Buddhism. When India succumbed to first Islamic and then British overlords, Nepal became not just the last remaining Hindu kingdom, but the bastion of tantric traditions. Tibet, meanwhile, developed its own distinctively tantric version of Buddhism.

Tantra has nothing to do with the Western invention of "**tantric sex**". Or almost nothing: some extreme Hindu followers turned orthodoxy on its head by embracing the forbidden, seeking spiritual liberation by means of transgression. Ascetics from the Kapalika tantric sect took up residence in cemeteries, following "left-hand" ritual practices such as the consumption of meat and alcohol, and the use of sexual fluids in sacrifice. But these now-notorious rituals were always rare, and tantrism today is chiefly concerned with using rituals to speed up the search for enlightenment or union with the divine. Quasi-magical techniques are passed from teachers to initiates, who progress upwards through levels of understanding. Through meditation and the practice of yoga, the body's energy can be made to ascend through the seven (or sometimes six) *chakras* or psychic nodes, beginning at the perineum and ending at the crown of the head, where blissful union with the god Shiva can be achieved. **Mantras**, or sacred verbal formulas, are chanted; worship is intensified with the use of **mudras** (hand gestures). Arcane geometrical diagrams known as **yantras** or **mandalas** are drawn to symbolize and activate divine principles.

So strong did tantrism become in Nepal, that the entire Kathmandu Valley – then known as **Nepal mandala** – could be conceived as a kind of interactive map of the divine cosmos, studded with religiously supercharged sites and temples. Many sites are dedicated to the chief objects of tantric worship: the "Great God" Shiva, and his female counterpart Shakti, the mother goddess. In Nepal, they are often depicted in art as the fierce god Bhairab and his terrifying consort Kali, and sometimes seen locked in a fierce sexual embrace which symbolizes the creative unity of the male and female principles: masculinity is conceived as passive and intellectual, female as active and embodied; together, they sustain the life force of the universe.

Buddhist tantra, known as **Vajrayana** ("Thunderbolt Way"), reverses the symbolism of these two forces and makes the male principle of "skill in means" or compassion the active force, and the female principle of "wisdom" passive. In tantric rituals, these forces are symbolized by the hand-held "lightning-bolt sceptre" (*vajra*; *dorje* in Tibetan), which represents the male principle, and the bell (*ghanti*), representing the female. Expanding on Mahayana's all-male pantheon, Vajrayana introduces female counterparts to the main Buddha figures and some of the *bodhisattva*, and sometimes depicts them in sexual positions.

Vajrayana – Tibetan Buddhism

Buddhism was originally exported from Nepal to Tibet, courtesy of the Licchavi princess **Bhrikuti**, who married Tibetan emperor Songstän Gampo in the seventh century. At the time, Tibet was under the sway of a native shamanic religion known as **Bön**, and Buddhism absorbed many of Bön's symbols and rituals. (Even today vestiges of the **Bön** tradition may be encountered while trekking in Nepal: for example, a follower of Bön will circle a religious monument anticlockwise, the opposite direction to a Buddhist.)

Buddhism only really took off in Nepal and Tibet in the eighth century, however, thanks to the founding father **Padmasambhava**. Better known as **Guru Rinpoche** or "Precious Teacher" – and recognizable in paintings by his wide-eyed stare, and the thunderbolt symbol and skull-cup he holds in each hand – he introduced magical and ritualistic practices from the tantric cult (see box above) that was then sweeping across South Asia. In doing so, he apparently meditated in just about every cave in the region, frequently leaving foot or handprints in the rock as signs of his passing.

Bön and tantra proved an explosive mix, giving rise to the spectacular branch of Buddhism now known as **Vajrayana**, or "thunderbolt way" Buddhism. It takes its name from the *vajra* or thunderbolt (*dorje* in Tibetan), a diamond sceptre or dagger used in tantric rituals to signify indestructability. True to its tantric roots, Vajrayana placed great emphasis on close contact with a **lama**, or spiritual guide, who steers the initiate through the complex meditations and rituals, and progressively reveals teachings at ever higher and more esoteric levels. (It's sometimes called Lamaism for this reason.) The most important lamas are regarded as **tulkus**, reincarnations of previous teachers.

Four main sects developed in Tibet, all now represented in Nepal. The oldest, founded by Padmasambhava, is the Nyingma-pa sect – known as the "**Red Hats**" for obvious reasons. The Sakya-pa and Kagyu-pa orders emerged in the eleventh and twelfth centuries – the latter inspired by the Tibetan mystic Marpa and his enlightened disciple Milarepa, who also meditated his way around Nepal. The Gelug-pa sect, or "**Yellow Hats**", led by the Dalai Lama, is the only one that takes a significantly different theological line. Born out of a fifteenth-century reform movement to purge Lamaism of its questionable religious practices, it places greater emphasis on study and intellectual debate.

Vajrayana disciples make heavy use of quasi-magical rituals, such as the ringing of bells, the reading aloud of holy texts and the chanting of **mantras** or sacred syllables – most importantly, *Om mani padme hum* (see p.397). In part, these rituals are aids to **meditation**, the most important action of all, but they also serve to accelerate the passage of the disciple towards the ultimate goal: enlightenment.

The most visible sign of Vajrayana Buddhism is the **stupa** (chorten in Tibetan), a dome-like stone structure that serves to enshrine the relics of the saints and to act as a giant abstract representation of Buddhist beliefs. Around Kathmandu's Swayambhu stupa, for instance, stand five statues representing the transcendent or *dhyani* (meditating) Buddhas. Stupas are also surrounded by **prayer wheels and prayer flags**, Tibetan innovations that allow written mantras to be not spoken but spun or fluttered into the air.

Newari religion

Ask a Newari man whether he's Hindu or Buddhist, the saying goes, and he'll answer "yes": after fifteen centuries of continuous exposure to both faiths, the Newars of the Kathmandu Valley have concocted a unique synthesis of the two. Until the eighteenth century, most Newars held fast to the original monastic form of tantric Buddhism – as the *bahal* of Kathmandu and Patan still bear witness. Gradually, the Kathmandu Valley

---

BUDDHIST MONASTERIES

Increasing numbers of lavishly endowed **gompa**, or monasteries, have sprung up all over Nepal in the last 25 years, thanks to the growing wealth of the Tibetan community and the generous sponsorship of Western followers. Rather like medieval cathedrals, *gompa* are vehicles for esoteric religious symbolism as much as places of worship. Fierce guardian demons (*dharmapala*) flank the entrance, while the interior walls are riotously covered in paintings of deities, Buddhas and geometric mandalas, and hung all over with silken **thangka** icons. Gorgeous banners of brightly coloured silk brocade hang from the ceiling, often with elaborately carved and gilded cornices and panelling. On low trays, butter lamps burn pungently alongside heaps of rice piled onto three-tiered silver stands, rows of incense sticks and offerings of fruit, money, flowers and conical dough cakes called *torma* – sacrifices of a uniquely vegetarian kind. The eye is inevitably drawn, however, to the golden statues of **Buddhas** and **bodhisattvas** that line the altars. Often mistaken for deities, these provide a focus for meditation as well as an object of devotion. The most popular figures are **Shakyamuni**, the historical Buddha; **Avalokiteshwara** (**Chenrezig** in Tibetan), a white male figure with four arms (or, sometimes, a thousand), who represents compassion; **Tara**, a white or green female figure, also representing compassion; **Manjushri**, an orange-yellow male youth gracefully holding a sword above his head, who represents wisdom; and the founder of the monastery's sect, perhaps the Nyingma-pa's Padmasambhava, better known as **Guru Rinpoche**. Though these figures are peaceful and benign, there are also wrathful bulging-eyed figures wearing human skins and bearing skulls filled with blood; they symbolize the energy and potency of the enlightened state, and the sublimation of our crudest energies.

TIBETAN BUDDHIST RITUAL MUSIC

More astounding, even, than the polychrome decor of a **Tibetan Buddhist** monastery is the crashing, thumping, rasping ritual music that rings out during the *puja* or prayer ceremonies. (Typically, these take place at daybreak and in the late afternoon, before dusk, but timings vary.) The cacophony is supposed to shock you out of your everyday thoughts – and it works. At the core of the ritual is the recital or hymn-like **chanting of texts**, which usually begins with the master, or cantor, and spreads in rhythmic ripples down the rows of monks. Monks from the Gelug-pa order (see p.401), most dramatically, use the extraordinary overtone or "throat-singing" technique; this ultra-low, growling tone produces rich harmonics sometimes called the *gyü-ke*, or "tantric voice". Alongside the virtue regarded as inherent in the recitation of holy texts, such demanding vocal techniques create their own meditational discipline.

In the Tibetan tantric tradition chanting alternates antiphonically with **instrumental music**, whose crashes and blasts and bangs punctuate and disrupt the hypnotic vocal line – and thus serve to turbo-charge the meditation. Music can represent fierce protective Buddhas or calming, peaceful ones, and different instruments have different ritual significance or uses. The *dung-dkar* conch, for instance, embodies the clear voice of the Buddha. The *rkang-gling* trumpet, traditionally made from a human thighbone, is apparently like the whinnying of horses on their way to paradise. Cymbals can be soft and peaceful (*gsil-snyan*) or brassily fierce (*rol-mo*). The *rgna*, or double-drum with its distinctively crooked beater, typically leads the orchestra. Oboe-like *rgya-gling* shawms play intense, microtonally sliding melody lines, while the long (up to 3m long), alpenhorn-like *dung* trumpets play sustained, almost subsonic rasping notes in discordant pairs. The *dril-bu* hand bell and *damaru* rattle drum usually mark off different sections of the ritual, or guide the tempo. The *damaru* is a particularly powerful instrument: commonly used by shamans in Nepal, it may be made of two human half-skulls, and the pair of pellet beaters should ideally contain male and female pubic hairs.

became "**Hinduized**" thanks largely to the Hindu kings who ruled it. The monasteries largely disappeared, and the title of Vajracharya (Buddhist priest) became a hereditary subcaste much like that of the Baahun (Brahman) priests. When Newars refer to themselves as **Buddha margi** (Buddhist) or **Shiva margi** (Hindu), they often do so only to indicate that they employ a Vajracharya or Baahun priest. Yet many *jyapu* (farmers) will attend Hindu festivals and use Vajracharyas as well.

Animal sacrifice is an important part of Hindu – but not Buddhist – Newari religious practice. Newari priests don't perform sacrifices, but they do preside over the rituals that precede them. Similar ceremonies and feasts are held at private gatherings of patrilineal groups during the Newars' many **festivals** and during **digu puja**, the annual reunion based around the worship of the clan deity (*digu dyo*).

Many other members of Newari society function in spiritual capacities, either as full-time para-priests or in bit parts during rites of passage and festivals. Members of the Vajracharya subcaste, **Gubhajus** are tantric healers who employ *vajrayana* techniques and accoutrements to cure ailments caused by malevolent spirits. **Baidyas** play a similar role but draw from a more diverse range of Hindu, Buddhist and shamanic techniques including *jhar-phuk* ("sweeping" away bad influences and "blowing" on healing mantras), *puja*, amulets and ayurvedic medicines. **Jyotish** – astrologers – specialize in helping clients deal with planetary influences and their corresponding deities.

The Newari pantheon

All the Hindu and Buddhist deities are fair game for Newars, along with a few additional characters of local invention. Some deities specialize in curing diseases, others bring good harvests – as far as Newars are concerned, it doesn't matter whether they're Hindu or Buddhist so long as they do the job.

The widely worshipped **Ajima**, or **Mai**, the Newars' grandmother goddess, is both feared as a bringer of disease and misfortune and revered as a protectress against the same. There are innumerable Ajimas, each associated with a particular locality. Some are also worshipped as Durga, Bhagwati or Kali, including the **Ashta Matrika**, the eight mother goddesses, whose temples in and around Kathmandu are considered especially powerful. Similar are the tantric **Bajra Yoginis** (or Vajra Joginis), who command their own cults at four temples around the Kathmandu Valley. Local manifestations of Ajima are represented by clusters of round stones (*pith*) located at intersections and other strategic places. Chwasa Ajima, the Ajima of the crossroads, has the power to absorb death pollution, which is why Newars traditionally deposited possessions of deceased persons at crossroads. **Nag** (snake deities), who control the rains and are responsible for earthquakes, may be similarly indicated by modest roadside markers.

Machhendranath, the rainmaker par excellence, is known by Buddhist Newars as **Karunamaya**, and associated with Avalokiteshwara, the *bodhisattva* of compassion.

A VISIT TO THE ASTROLOGER

His name is Joshi – in Newari society, all members of the astrologer subcaste are called Joshi – and to get to his office I have to duck through a low doorway off a courtyard in the old part of Patan and feel my way up two flights of wooden steps in the dark, climbing towards a glimmer of light and the sounds of low murmuring. At the landing I take off my shoes and enter the sanctum. Joshi-ji doesn't even look up. He's sitting cross-legged on the floor behind a low desk, glasses perched on the end of his nose, scowling over a sheaf of papers and, except for his Nepali-style clothes, looking exactly the way I'd always pictured Professor Godbole in *A Passage to India*. Shelves of books and scrolls are heaped behind him, and over in one corner a small shrine is illuminated by a low-watt bulb and a smouldering stick of incense.

To Newars, the **astrologer** is a counsellor, confessor, general practitioner and guide through the maze of life. He acts as mediator between the self and the universe (which are one), and his prognostications are considered as important as a priest's blessings and as vital as a doctor's diagnosis. He knows most of his clients from birth. For new parents, the astrologer will prepare complex planetary charts based on the baby's precise time and place of **birth**, together with a lengthy interpretation detailing personality traits, health hazards, vocational aptitude, characteristics of the ideal marriage partner, and a general assessment of the newborn's prospects. When a **marriage** is contemplated, he will study the horoscopes of the prospective couple to make sure the match is suitable and to determine the most auspicious wedding date. During an **illness**, he may prescribe a protective amulet, gemstone or herbal remedy corresponding to the planets influencing the patient. He may also be consulted on the advisability of a business decision or a major purchase.

Although it's misleading to speak in terms of planetary "influences", the *karma* revealed by an astrologer's **horoscope** strongly implies the future course of one's life. The astrologer's role is to suggest the best way to play the hand one was dealt. Hindu astrology recognizes the usual twelve **signs of the zodiac**, albeit under Sanskrit names, and assigns similar attributes to the planets and houses as in the West. The basic **birth chart** indicates the **sun sign** (the sign corresponding to the sun's position at the time of birth), the ascendant (the sign rising above the eastern horizon at the time of birth) and the positions of the moon and the five planets known to the ancients, plus a couple of other non-Western points of reference. The positions of all of these are also noted in relation to the twelve **houses**, each of which governs key aspects of the subject's life (health, relationships and so on). Where Western astrologers use the **tropical zodiac**, in which Aries is always assumed to start on the spring equinox (March 21, give or take a day), Hindu astrologers go by the **sidereal zodiac**, which takes all its measurements from the *actual* positions of the constellations.

In practice, if you have a horoscope done in Nepal, you'll probably be presented with a beautifully calligraphed scroll detailing all these measurements in chart and tabular form, using both tropical and sidereal measurements. **Interpretation** of the chart is an intuitive art requiring great eloquence and finesse. The astrologer can draw on numerous texts but at the end of the day, the usefulness of the reading comes down to his own skill and experience. As I found on my visit to Joshi-ji, the specifics aren't everything. The astrologer isn't peddling facts; he's offering insight, hope, reassurance and a dash of theatre.

David Reed

Depending on his incarnation (he is said to have 108), he may be depicted as having anything up to a thousand arms and eleven heads. **Kumari**, the "Living Goddess", is another example of Newari syncretism (religious fusing): although acknowledged to be an incarnation of the Hindu goddess Durga, she is picked from a Buddhist-caste family. **Bhimsen**, a mortal hero in the Hindu Mahabharat, who is rarely worshipped in India, has somehow been elevated to be the patron deity of Newari shopkeepers, both Hindu and Buddhist. **Manjushri**, the *bodhisattva* of wisdom, plays the lead part in the Kathmandu Valley's creation myth, and is often confused with Saraswati, the Hindu goddess of knowledge. He is always depicted with a sword, with which he cuts away ignorance and attachment, and sometimes also with book, bow, bell and *vajra*. **Tara**, the embodiment of the female principle in Vajrayana Buddhism, assumes special meaning for Newars, who consider her the deification of an eighth-century Nepali princess.

Shamanism

Shamans – sometimes called medicine men, witch doctors and oracles, or **jhankri** and **dhami** in Nepali – exist to mediate between the physical and spiritual realms. Shamanistic practices are often found alongside animism, or nature-worship, and the ethnic groups of Nepal's hills, including those who would unhesitatingly describe themselves as Hindu or Buddhist, will often turn to a *jhankri*. Urbane Nepalis may publicly ridicule the shaman in favour of more "modern" beliefs such as orthodox Hinduism, but many will privately call on a shaman to exorcise a new house or deal with a case of toothache. In Kathmandu, at night, the shaman's double-headed drum is still heard beating behind closed doors.

Most ethnic groups clearly distinguish between the true shaman, whose duties, rituals and powers are concerned with the spiritual world, and other types of tribal priest, whose concerns may be with seasonal rituals, rites of passage or tribal myth, and whose roles have been more easily absorbed by mainstream religion. For all the many local variations, a *jhankri* – usually carrying a double-sided drum and often wearing a headdress of peacock feathers – is always unmistakeable. And even across ethnic and religious divides, *jhankris* may come together on high hilltops or at lakes deep in the mountains for *melas*, or religious fairs.

SUPERNATURAL FORCES

Nepal has a rich lore of **demons**, **ghosts** and **spirits** who meddle in human affairs and, like deities, must be propitiated to safeguard passage through their respective domains. Demons are sometimes thought to be the wrathful or perverted manifestations of deities, or more often as supernatural ogres, vampires and the like. Some demons, such as the *lakhe*, are regarded somewhat fondly, or, like the *betal*, can also serve as temple protectors. *Bhut pret* – restless ghosts – are thought to be the spirits of people who died an accidental or violent death and were not administered the proper funeral rites. Other evil spirits take the form of poltergeist-like dwarfs, furry balls, or temptresses with their feet pointing backwards; the design of traditional Newari windows is intended to prevent such spirits from entering the house. Since spirits are believed to attack mainly at night and are repelled by light, it is sometimes said that they are driven out when electricity arrives in a village.

Nepalis often blame their troubles on **witches** (*bokshi*), who are believed to be able to cast "black" tantric spells by giving the evil eye or reciting mantras over their victims' food. Evidence of bewitchment is often seen in bruises called "*bokshi* bites". "Witches" are usually neighbours, in-laws or other people known to their alleged victims. Although laws prohibit false accusations of witchcraft, this doesn't protect many people (particularly elderly women) from suffering unspoken fear and resentment for their alleged dark arts.

A final category of supernatural forces is negative **planetary influences** (*graha dosa*), caused by the displeasure of the deity associated with the offending planet.

The *jhankri* may be "called", or born, or both, and his (almost never her) main job is to maintain spiritual and physical balance, and to restore it when it has been upset. As a healer, he may examine the entrails of animals for signs, gather medicinal plants from the forest, perform sacrifices, exorcise demons, chant magical incantations to invoke helper deities, or conduct any number of other rituals. As an oracle, he may fall into a trance and act as a mouthpiece of the gods, advising, admonishing and consoling listeners. As the spiritual sentry of his community, he must ward off ghosts, evil spirits and angry ancestors – sometimes by superior strength, often by trickery. All this, plus his duties as funeral director, dispenser of amulets, teller of myths and consecrator of holy ground and so on, puts the *jhankri* at the very heart of religious and social life in the hills.

Few visitors to Nepal will encounter a *jhankri*, as their rituals are usually performed in homes, at night, and shamans have a tendency to guard their esoteric knowledge jealously, wrapping it up in archaic, poetic language that veers between the mystical and the mystifying. There are signs of new confidence, however, with the recent establishment of a Gurung shamanic cultural centre and training school in Pokhara.

Islam and Christianity

A significant number of **Muslims** inhabit the Western Terai, especially around Nepalgunj, where they're in the majority. **Musalmans**, as they're called in Nepal, form a distinctive cultural group. They have their own language (Urdu), clothing styles and customs – including the institution of **purdah** for women. In the hill areas, Nepali Musalmans are traditionally wandering traders. They specialize in selling bangles and in "teasing" cotton quilts, and they can often be heard in Kathmandu and other towns calling on housewives to come-buy-my-wares, or giving a prompting twang on the instrument of their cotton-teasing trade. Many are now farmers, tailors or run clothing shops.

Christianity barely registered in Nepal for centuries, due to a vigorously enforced ban on missionary conversions. The interdict was largely lifted in 1990, however, and since 2006 Nepal has been an officially secular state. The result has been a significant influx of evangelicals from all over the world, mostly targeting lower castes and other disadvantaged groups. There has been a corresponding growth of churches, especially in the Kathmandu Valley, and there may be as many as half a million Nepali Christians today.

Development dilemmas

Development – or *bikas*, in Nepali – has been the country's political mantra ever since the Ranas were booted out of office in 1950. And yet Nepal remains one of the world's poorest nations, with a per capita income of just over $1000 a year. In truth, this figure is distorted by migrant labourers' remittances, and perhaps half of Nepal's population survives on little more than a dollar a day. On the UN's 2014 Human Development Index, Nepal ranked 145th out of 187 countries – sandwiched ingloriously between Nigeria and Haiti.

Everything seems stacked against Nepal. It is landlocked, and squeezed between two economic giants. It has few natural resources. The steep terrain makes farming inefficient and communications difficult. Earthquakes and monsoons can undo dams, roads and other infrastructure as fast as they're built. A combination of Hindu fatalism, the caste system and a legacy of aristocratic paternalism has long kept the doors of opportunity tightly shut – the regime did essentially nothing for its people before 1951. Since then, governments have apparently prioritized corruption and clientism over development – despite the incredible efforts of aid workers and local activists.

THE DEVELOPMENT INDUSTRY

Everyone loves to give **aid** to Nepal. The country receives hundreds of millions of dollars annually in direct grants and concessionary loans, making it one of the world's leading aid recipients on a per capita basis. Depending on the year, foreign aid accounts for anything up to eighty percent of the money spent by Nepal's government on projects (capital expenditure), and around a quarter of total expenditure; the joke goes that the country can't *afford* to develop.

Aid comes in many forms. **Bilateral** (and multilateral) aid – money directly given or lent by foreign governments, invariably with political or commercial strings attached – has financed most of the roads, dams and airports in the country. Social programmes tend to be carried out by international **non-governmental organizations (NGOs)**, which can be anything from giants such as Oxfam, CARE and Save the Children to a couple of highly motivated people doing fieldwork and raising sponsorship money at home. Voluntary NGOs, such as Britain's Voluntary Service Overseas (VSO) and the US Peace Corps, generally slot volunteers into existing government programmes. Increasingly important are revenues from **international lending bodies** such as the World Bank and Asian Development Bank (ADB), which both provide direct grants and act as brokers to arrange loans for big projects with commercial potential – usually irrigation and hydroelectric schemes. The ADB, for instance, is now the source of over twenty percent of Nepal's foreign aid.

Many of these organizations do excellent work. But paying imported experts ten or twenty times more than Nepalis to do the same job causes resentment and distorts the local economy. Large organizations are effectively obliged to fund large-scale projects, which may not always be the most appropriate or efficient options. And many projects are crippled by short-term funding that prevents them taking a long-term view. Foreign aid can also foster a crippling **aid dependency**.

The fashionable philosophy, therefore, is to finance **local NGOs**, which supposedly have a better handle on local problems and solutions. The result has been an explosion in Nepali organizations, blurring the distinction between genuine, grass roots organizations run by the heroically dedicated, and quasi-companies tailoring themselves to fit the latest development buzz words: sustainable, small-scale, women-focused, environmental – whatever. Lack of coordination results in monumental inefficiency, and lack of scrutiny means that some aren't doing much besides writing grant proposals.

Population

Nepal's **population** was officially 27.7 million at the time of writing, but is almost certainly two or three million more. The rate of growth may be slowing down (it currently stands at some 1.2 percent per year, down from 2.25 percent ten years ago), but the population continues to increase. Each year there are some 400,000 more Nepalis to feed and employ – and, indeed, requiring health care, education, clean water, sewage disposal, electricity and roads. Population growth will continue as long as women remain comparatively ill educated and low status, and as long as children are needed to fetch water, gather fuel and tend animals – and to care for the aged parents in the absence of pensions or state support. Moreover, Nepalis tend to have large families because they can't be sure all their children will survive. Hindus, especially, may keep trying until they've produced at least one son, who alone can perform the prescribed rites (*shradha*) for his parents after their death.

It's often said that "development is the best contraceptive", and indeed, there is a close correlation between rising standards of living and declining birth rates. Unfortunately, in most countries this so-called **demographic transition** involves a period of rapid population growth until the birth rate settles down to match the lower death rate. The slowing in Nepal's growth rate is probably partly a result of improved women's education – and anxiety in the face of insecurity and inflation.

And the growth is just about balanced, for the time, by outward **migration**. The hill peoples, especially men, have long sought work in Kathmandu, the Terai and India. Nowadays, young Nepali men are as likely to emigrate to the Gulf and Southeast Asia or East Asia, or indeed the West. Some two million Nepalis currently work abroad, which is twice the number ten years ago, and for the first time in living memory, some middle hill districts are becoming depopulated. Instead of new terraces being painfully carved out by hand, old fields are lying fallow. At the same time, the country's urban population is exploding. The population of the Kathmandu Valley more than doubled between the early 1990s and late 2000s, and is set to continue rising at an unsustainable rate.

Health

The average **life expectancy** is now 67, up from 43 in 1975 – though the poor can still expect to live some fifteen years less than the average, and the average Nepali will live in poor health from his or her mid-50s onwards. The figure is heavily influenced by the distressingly high rate of child mortality: almost one out of every twenty children in Nepal dies before he or she reaches the age of five.

Still, this is a vast improvement over 1960, when the figure was almost one in three; and maternal mortality rates have virtually halved in the last twenty years alone. Cheap oral rehydration packets are largely responsible for saving these lives, as the chief cause of infant death is nothing more complicated than **diarrhoea**, itself the consequence of poor sanitation. Access to safe (or at least "improved") water has widened significantly in recent years: almost ninety percent of Nepalis now have access to a spring, well or communal tap.

Surviving infancy is only the start. Around half of Nepali children are **malnourished** and suffer from unceasing hunger and a relentless series of infections – of which the permanently snotty nose of the rural child is just one outward sign. Parasitic infections are also rife. Almost half the population is thought to carry **tuberculosis**, and some forty thousand Nepalis develop TB actively every year, leading to more than five thousand deaths. There are successes: **leprosy** is becoming more rare, though Nepal still has one of the highest per capita rates in the world, and mosquito spraying in the Terai has reduced **malaria** cases to about five thousand annually – compared with two million a year during the 1950s.

Nepal avoided the **HIV-AIDS** epidemic for many years, but sex workers, long-distance truck drivers and seasonal migrants provided a channel for transmission of the disease from India – one recent study found that two-thirds of women trafficked into India for sex work acquired HIV. The infection is common among the country's thirty thousand-odd injecting drug users and twenty to thirty thousand sex workers, and starting to spread into the general population as well: roughly seventy thousand Nepalis are currently living with HIV-AIDS.

There are no statistics on **alcoholism**, but it is certainly one of the major public health problems among men from the hill ethnic groups. Since the late 1990s, Maoist-affiliated women's community groups have aggressively tackled drinking, and in government the Maoists have introduced ever-more stringent regulation, but drinking culture is fairly embedded. Tobacco use seems if anything even more entrenched: more than half of adult Nepalis smoke.

In addition to all these problems, access to **health care** is extremely poor. Many parochial hospitals lack even a single resident doctor, since the vast majority of qualified physicians prefer to practise privately in the Kathmandu Valley. For rural Nepalis, medical assistance means a local *jhankri* (see p.405) or health post that's a day or more's walk (or piggyback ride) down the trail and where the only person on staff may effectively be the janitor, or perhaps an assistant with some ayurvedic training.

Agriculture

More than two-thirds of Nepalis still make their living from agriculture, on some of the most intensively cultivated land in the world. For some experts, this means that farming should be the focus of development – especially given the population growth. Nepal has been a net importer of rice since the 1970s, and localized **food deficits** are a serious problem, especially in the remote northwestern districts of Humla and Mugu, where famines and emergency food airlifts are a regular spring occurrence.

Clearing new land for cultivation only adds to deforestation (see below), so **productivity** has been chased instead. **High-yielding seeds** and animal breeds such as the Jersey cross – fondly known as *bikasi gai*, or "development cow" – have had some success, while **pesticides** and chemical **fertilizers** are now widely used in the Kathmandu Valley and Terai. In the hills, however, it can be impossible or uneconomic to transport these inputs. Where fertilizers are used, they're often misapplied. **Irrigation** is a promising area, but the big canal systems underwritten by the government and foreign funders are often inefficient and poorly maintained, and tend to benefit only the bigger landholdings. Tractors and other **mechanized equipment**, similarly, are only really workable on bigger farms in the plains.

Thanks to subdivision across generations, many farms have simply become too small to feed a family – which is why so many Nepalis are now undernourished. Many small farmers are locked in a hopeless cycle of debt, or have been forced to sell or hand over their land to unscrupulous moneylenders. Supplying **credit** through the official Agriculture Development Bank has grown impossibly bureaucratic, but microcredit loan programmes look more promising. Allowing farmers to grow cash crops is another possible solution, but roads are needed to export, and the development of the road network may actually make it impossible to compete with Indian imports.

In the circumstances, many younger and more educated Nepalis are abandoning the land and seeking paid employment. Areas under Maoist control during the ten-year conflict saw large areas of land seized and **redistributed**, sometimes turned over to farms working on a "cooperative" model. In government, the Maoists have come under pressure to return much of it, and whether or not their promises of country-wide, "scientific" **land reform** will bear fruit is uncertain. Even the lowering of existing ceilings on individual land ownership is in question.

Deforestation

An expanding population needs not only more land, but more **firewood** and more **fodder** for animals – which, in Nepal, is gathered by hand in the forest. The result is

deforestation, which itself causes erosion and landslides, thus reducing productivity and contributing to flooding. In practice, there are counterbalancing forces: the further people have to walk to find firewood or fodder, the more likely they are to emigrate, taking pressure off the area's resources.

No one has a clear idea of the rate of forest loss in Nepal but certainly the government got it badly wrong when it **nationalized the forests** in the 1950s. From the 1980s, however, the policy of sustainable, locally managed **community forestry** slowed or even reversed deforestation in some hill areas. The breakdown in law and order during the conflict, however, and the massively increased road network, meant that the community forests were corruptly or illegally plundered on a dramatic scale from the late 1990s onwards. The **Terai** suffered worst: trees have been clear-felled right across the south, leading to the loss of some 2640 square kilometres of forest in the five years up to 2005 alone. Overall, a quarter of Nepal's forest has vanished in the last twenty years, including almost all of the magnificent native forest outside the **national parks** and wildlife or forest reserves. Perhaps a quarter of Nepal's total land cover is woodland today, and less than half of that is true, "primary" forest.

Efforts to reduce deforestation produced one apparently brilliant solution: the "**smokeless**" **chulo** (stove), which burns wood more efficiently. The positive side effect, however – reducing levels of health-destroying kitchen smoke – turned out to be problematic: insects were no longer smoked out of traditional thatched roofs, leading to infestations and increased use of corrugated metal. The miracle stoves also emit less light, causing increased dependency on kerosene for lamps or electricity – both of which require hard cash to purchase.

Waste and pollution

An astounding number of foreign news stories relating to Nepal focus on **pollution** – usually of the "Everest is a rubbish dump" sort. There's a bit of truth to these reports. The most popular "yak route" up Everest is indeed bestrewn with the remnants of old expeditions, and expeditions regularly find funding by offering "clean-up Everest" missions – one removed 8000kg of rubbish from Everest Base Camp. There's a lot of Himalaya beyond Everest, however. Even the environmental pressure on trekking routes is restricted to a few ribbons of the country – admittedly, in relatively fragile mountain areas.

Waste disposal is a major national problem, of course. Consumption of manufactured goods has boomed, yet there are few organized methods of waste disposal outside the major cities (and precious few within them). The less visible pollution issues are arguably more serious, however. **Air pollution** in the cities is life-threatening, due to a lethal combination of brick manufacture in kilns, burning of fuel woods and rubbish (including plastics), and ever-swelling volumes of traffic. **Vehicular pollution** is exacerbated by the routine adulteration of fuels (low-taxed, subsidized kerosene is illegally added to petrol and diesel), and the dust clouds caused by unsealed road surfaces. After an hour on Kathmandu's Ring Road, you can feel the grit between your teeth and the black snot in your nose.

LITTER

Western visitors are frequently horrifed by the amount of visible **rubbish** in Nepal, but often forget to ask themselves how they would manage their own waste if no one ever came to take away their bins. Tourists also consume items that are particularly hard to get rid of (bottles, toilet paper, batteries and plastic, for instance), and with a much greater intensity than locals. The traditional, local methods of waste disposal – composting in the fields and burning – just can't keep up. Next time you're horrified by the sight of a child dropping a sweet wrapper, consider that the average carbon emission of a Nepalese person is 1 tonne per capita: about a tenth of most Europeans, and a twentieth of the average North American. Next time you buy a bottle of mineral water, consider that, at best, it's going to be burned in someone's courtyard.

Human waste also presents a major challenge. Defecation in the open pollutes water sources and assists in the transmission of many diseases, as flies may alight on human waste and then food. Many development programmes have focused on the building of toilets in recent years, from the "one family one toilet" scheme, to Eco Himal's "public toilets for Everest" campaign and Kaski District's proud declaration of itself as "Nepal's first open-defecation-free zone". Yet sewer systems are still poor where they exist at all (and they certainly struggle to cope with the toilet paper used by tourists – paper should be put in separate bins for burning later). Composting toilets and pit latrines are becoming ever more sophisticated, however, and more common.

Water pollution is easy to see, but a relatively little-known environmental threat is the extraction of sand, gravel and stone from rivers, fuelled by the construction boom. Drive along any riverside road in Nepal, and you'll see the trucks and the diggers. As many as one hundred lorry-loads of sand can be legally removed per day from a river site, but real volumes may be three times higher, and there are scores of illegal sites. The result is disturbance or destruction of wildlife habitat, the exacerbation of landslides and the acceleration of erosion. In the Churia Hills of the Terai, meanwhile, hundreds of illegal crusher industries operate, quarrying rock and exporting it as sand and stone to India.

Electricity

Nepal's steep, mountain-fed rivers have enormous **hydroelectric** potential – enough to power the British Isles, by some estimates. Unfortunately, getting materials and technical experts into the rugged backcountry, not to mention handling the Himalayan-scale seismic problems, has made this potential difficult to harness. Currently, only five percent of rural Nepalis have access to **electricity** – at night the hills still remain largely swathed in darkness. And access is no miracle solution: electricity itself costs rupees, and electric appliances cost dollars. Electrification can actually add to the pressure on forests, too, because good lighting encourages people to stay up late, burning more wood to keep warm.

Small-scale successes have been achieved with **microhydro** projects, which supply electricity for a few hundred households each. Locally manufactured **solar water-heaters** are also promising, as are **biogas** plants, tank-like super-composters of manure and agricultural waste which collect the gas given off for burning. But to satisfy demand growing at ten percent a year, and currently estimated at 850MW (megawatts) at peak, Nepal has to persuade international donors and lending bodies to finance **hydroelectric** projects.

The idea of building huge-scale storage dams fell out of favour in 1995, after the World Bank finally withdrew from the monstrous (404MW) **Arun III** project, citing environmental and social concerns. The emphasis now is on licensing of private sector companies to build mostly small- to medium-sized "**run-of-river**" diversions. Many such projects were mothballed during the Maoist conflict, but political stability and an

LOAD-SHEDDING

Despite its goal of exporting clean hydropower to India, Nepal cannot begin to keep up with domestic demand and is forced to import dirty power from its southern neighbour – a fact which became painfully clear after the Koshi flood of 2008, which washed out a crucial transmission line. Domestic electricity supply is also threatened by seasonal fluctuations: only one of Nepal's hydro projects, the 92MW Kulekhani, has a reservoir, and the power output of the other schemes drops along with river levels over the course of the winter. From as early as October onwards, the country now operates policies of **load-shedding** (scheduled power cuts), which means all power is lost for anything up to eighteen hours a day. During the blackouts, industry and government is crippled and foreign investment and tourism stifled; only criminals profit – plus, of course, amateur stargazers who want to *really* see the night sky.

improved climate for foreign investment may lead to an explosion: plans exist for two dozen hydropower projects, capable of producing over 1000MW, and construction is starting on some of them.

In recent years, two 70MW projects on the **Marsyangdi**, on the east side of the Annapurna range, and the 144MW **Kali Gandaki "A"** project, on the west, have started production. Work has started on others – notably on the **Upper Trisuli** – and it is still possible that some huge dams may go ahead. In August 2011, plans for the huge (and hugely controversial) 750MW **West Seti** dam project, in Nepal's Far West region, were shelved after the Asian Development Bank finally admitted that the scheme met none of its own criteria for information disclosure, public participation, environmental assessment or proper acknowledgement of the rights of local people. Then, in November, the Chinese agreed to provide a $1.6 billion loan for the project – and it looked as if it was back on. At the time of writing, the project had a prospective completion date of 2019.

Roads and paths

Until the 1950s, the only way to get to Nepal was to **walk**. In fact, the only way to get anywhere within Nepal was to walk. VIPs might be carried in palanquins, the royal elite could drive up and down a few kilometres of road in cars dismantled and imported piecemeal from India, and valuable freight was swung over from the plains on a 42km ropeway (which operated from the 1920s to the early 1990s) – but otherwise, you had to walk.

Nepal began to open in the 1950s. Cows in a field outside Kathmandu were surprised when the first plane landed, in 1953. Three years later, the tortuous **Tribhuwan Rajpath** was completed, connecting Nepal's capital to India. In the 1960s, the Chinese managed to blast the **Arniko Highway** down from the Tibetan border (the bridges, it was said, were exactly strong enough to carry a Chinese tank), and they funded the **Prithvi Highway**, which joined Kathmandu with Pokhara. India chipped in with a link from Pokhara to its own border, at Sonauli, and by the end of the 1960s, a faster route from Kathmandu to India was opened, via Narayangadh.

In the hills, meanwhile, scores of rivers and gorges were being spanned by spidery **suspension footbridges**, which saved villagers hours or even days of walking. Airstrips were being hammered out in remote areas, while in the south, the plains and forests were being pierced by the **Mahendra Highway** which, by the early 1980s, sped east–west though the Terai in one unbroken (if not smooth) ribbon.

The pace of change seemed to slow in the 1990s, but picked up in the 2000s, as the army pushed "feeder roads" into the Maoist heartlands while government "green roads" crept towards the district capitals. In the last five years, more roads have been built in Nepal than in the last fifty, and only a handful of the country's 75 districts now remains roadless. Even the extravagantly beautiful **Kali Gandaki gorge**, on the Annapurna Circuit, has been penetrated, and it now links up with the Chinese border at Mustang. The **Trisuli road** now creeps beyond the Langtang trailhead at Syabrubesi, and before long it will be possible to bump through to the Tibetan town of Kerung. New roads snake due south from the Kathmandu Valley, making for the Terai – and work has begun on a "fast track" link, which will reduce the journey time to India by around half. (It is supposed to hit the East–West Highway at Nijgadh, where there is a proposal to build a new international airport.) Kathmandu is also supposed to get an Outer Ring Road – one day – and there's even talk of a grand Mid Hill East–West Highway.

The perennial problem is **maintenance**. Foreign donors rarely fund upkeep, and with every monsoon, many roads are washed away or buried in landslides. Even Kathmandu suffers: during the monsoon in 2010, the main highway to India was blocked, causing a two-day traffic jam; that same season, the road to Tibet was shut for a week. The other, greater problem is that roads are not universal panaceas. With every new road, barefoot porters will no longer people the trails, while only those Nepalis who can afford a bus ticket will be able to get to hospitals and universities. Cheap imports of goods and foodstuffs will arrive in ever greater quantity. And what was once a country whose every step – political, developmental, cultural – was measured at walking pace, whose people met and talked with each other (and with foreign visitors) on the hill trails, will become more like the rest of the world.

Education

Education is one of Nepal's relative success stories: the result, perhaps, of how well respected it is in Nepali culture: "book is god", as the saying goes. The system has certainly come a long way in a short time: before 1951 schools only existed for the children of the ruling elite, and two percent of the population was literate. There are now government primary schools within walking distance of most villages, and secondary schools in most areas of denser population, and **literacy** has soared to 66 percent.

Of course, that's still an appalling figure by international standards. **Government schools** are chronically underfunded, especially in rural areas, and the current policy of handing over school management to communities is unlikely to address the problem. Teachers may be unqualified, poorly trained, underpaid or simply absent. Classes regularly number eighty or more, and are held in rooms with mud floors and no glazing. Toilet facilities, if they exist at all, are execrable – a major factor in putting children off school. There are rarely enough benches, let alone desks – even though many children will be off school on any given day due to illness, the need for their labour in the fields, or lack of funds to buy a book or pen, or to find the modest subscription fee.

In these conditions it's no surprise that while three-quarters of young Nepalis now attend primary school, around half fail to finish. Girls and disadvantaged castes make up the bulk of the dropouts. Secondary attendance is under a third, and many rural secondaries fail to get even one of their final-year students through their School Leaving Certificate (SLC). As a result, any family that can afford it sends its children away to one of the legion of private "**English medium**" boarding schools which have sprung up in the cities and towns, teaching in the English language. Those who make it to one of Nepal's **colleges** or **universities** often find that there's no work for them when they graduate. Frustrated by a lack of opportunities or just plain bored, the educated youth of the cities make up a growing class of angry young men.

Women

Women have particularly **low status** in much of Nepal, making them exceptionally vulnerable to exploitation. Their status is generally slightly higher among the ethnic groups of the hills, and considerably so among Buddhists and in wealthy urban families, but even these women rarely enjoy true power-sharing. Rural women may still be considered their husband's or father's chattel. They work far harder than men, by and large: rising before dawn to clean the house, doing the hardest fieldwork and all of the cooking. Women wait for men to finish eating before they begin.

Typically married off in their teens, women are often subject to institutionalized **domestic violence**. In orthodox Baahun families, low status is underpinned by religious sanction. The touch of a menstruating woman, for example, is traditionally considered as polluting as that of an untouchable. During their menstrual period, or in the wake of childbirth, women in the far west may still be sent into ritual seclusion.

It's estimated that each year, some 10–15,000 Nepali girls and women – twenty percent of them under the age of sixteen – are **trafficked** into sexual slavery. Kathmandu's sex industry is burgeoning, but most are bound for India, where Nepali girls are reputed for beauty (partly on account of their relative pallor), purity and supposed lack of inhibition. To poor families in Nepal, a daughter is a financial burden; when a broker comes offering

> ### DALITS
>
> Nepal's "**untouchables**" (see p.395) – are still held back by poverty, lack of education and flagrant discrimination. Thanks in part to Maoist pressure, the Constitutional Assembly has taken significant steps to improve political representation, and the old barriers are breaking down in the cities, but it is unlikely that attitudes will change quickly at village level. The pre-Maoist democratic government did act dramatically in 2000 to free the **kamaiyas** (bonded labourers), victims of a system of indentured servitude prevalent in the mid- and far west. Unfortunately, it failed to accompany the liberation with any policy on land redistribution or job training, with the result that most *kamaiyas* found themselves suddenly homeless and jobless.

thousands of rupees for a pubescent girl, many agree. This trade is most pronounced in the Central Hills north of Kathmandu, where it has historical roots: Tamang girls were forced to serve as court concubines for generations, and some men are still complicit in the enslavement of their own female relatives. A sex worker may eventually buy her freedom, but few escape without acquiring HIV or are able to return to their home communities.

One solution to women's low status is to boost education and earning power. The Bangladesh-based Grameen Bank and the Nepali government's Production Credit for Rural Women programme, make **microcredit loans** to small, self-organizing groups of women, and support the borrowers with literacy, family-planning and other training. Another route is political. Legally, the position of women has vastly improved in recent years, with the **Maoists** being particularly vociferous about improving the status of women; female involvement in the insurgency has presented Nepal with a new image of women's empowerment.

Children

However much their parents love them, children in poor families are counted as an economic resource from an early age. **Child labour** has always been essential in agriculture, and despite laws barring employment of anyone of fourteen or under, more than half of all Nepali children between six and fourteen work. They are often porters, domestic servants and labourers in the brick and construction industries – menial or hazardous jobs, by and large – and some are forced into the sex trade. Children working in domestic service are also at risk of **sexual abuse**, and there are cases of foreign paedophiles preying on Kathmandu's numerous – and exceptionally vulnerable – **street children**.

Some children are effectively sold by their families into "**adoption**" rackets – though little of the money received by the foreign agency ever gets back to the family. Many Western countries have now frozen adoption of Nepali children. Other children find their way into "**orphanages**" in Nepal or India, where income from charitable donations may be milked by the management, and toys brought by well-meaning volunteers may be sold on when the volunteer leaves his or her placement. Among Kathmandu's four hundred-odd orphanages there are some excellent ones, but many poor or corrupt ones too – the worst may be fronts for organized abuse. There is a registration scheme, but it's not backed up by government vetting.

Trade and industry

Agriculture simply cannot absorb the country's growing workforce, and unemployment and underemployment are rife. Nepal also desperately needs to earn foreign exchange to pay for the imported technology and materials it needs for development. All of this means boosting **industry**, which in Nepal's case accounts for an unusually low proportion of gross domestic product – import values are roughly six times those of exports.

Other countries in the region have used their low wages and high unemployment to attract the sweatshops of Western brand-name companies. Without a seaport, Nepal can't even do that. It achieved surprising success in the 1990s, with **carpet manufacture**, though the industry has collapsed since due to quality-control problems, bad PR over child labour, saturation of the market and undercutting by more mechanized competitors. Where once one million Nepalis worked in the industry, the number is now less than a tenth of that. **Pashmina** (cashmere) items have seen less dramatic rises and falls, while ready-made **clothes** and **shoes** seem to be on the up. Beer and cigarettes, curiously enough, are two other success stories, alongside the more prosaic bricks and cement, and agricultural products like sugar and timber (most of the latter being illegally exported). There is also a brisk trade in Himalayan **medicinal herbs**, along with the fabled *yarsagumba* caterpillar, which is used as a stimulant and aphrodisiac, and various essential oils. In herbs and medicines, there is a thriving illegal market.

Recent liberalization of rules on foreign ownership and investment may stimulate entrepreneurship but in many of its industries, Nepal finds itself in a classic Third World bind. Even if it could fairly access external markets, it can't compete with high-volume market leaders in manufacture. But importing even modest amounts of high-value items quickly runs up a nasty trade deficit. The government therefore subsidizes the production of run-of-the-mill goods for domestic consumption, according to the economic theory of **import substitution**: for a country short on foreign exchange, a penny saved is a penny earned.

Nepal's main trading partner, India, is as much a part of the problem as it is the solution. It levies high import duties to protect its own industries, thus benefiting Nepali border traders (who can sell imported goods for less than their Indian competitors), but crippling Nepali exporters (whose goods become uncompetitive with duty added on). The balance of power is so disproportionate that India can always present Nepal with take-it-or-leave-it **terms of trade**. Thus, when India imposed a "luxury tax" on Nepali tea leaves, it instantly pulled the rug from under the Nepali growers' market.

Tourism

Nepal has three religions, or so the saying goes: Hinduism, Buddhism and **tourism**. The last is Nepal's top foreign-exchange earner (not counting the massive remittances from **migrant workers**). Around 800,000 tourists a year bring in some $700 million, and give work to roughly half a million people. With the return of relative political stability, and the growth of tourism from India and China, visitor arrivals to Nepal are once again growing, but the infrastructure to cope with them is still lacking – and all tourism jobs tend to be both seasonal and intensely vulnerable to economic and political downturns. The fruits of tourism, so arbitrarily awarded, have turned legions of Nepalis into panhandlers, in much the same way that aid has done to politicians and institutions. And while tourism can claim some credit for shaping Nepal's environmental record, it has imposed its own ecological and cultural costs. Independent trekking may encourage tourists to spend money at the local level in rural areas, but it has placed an environmental strain on the fragile "honeypot" areas in the mountains.

Kathmandu Valley problems

Solutions often create their own problems. For five decades, people have been trying to get Nepal to develop – now that it has, in the **Kathmandu Valley**, many are nervously fumbling for the "off" switch. Overpopulation and conflict has driven a growing **rural exodus**; new roads and bus services pull the landless poor away from their villages, while jobs in the tourism and manufacturing industries push them towards the Kathmandu Valley. Many immigrants land jobs in the big city, but there's no safety net for those who don't. They may end up squatting in unhealthy shacks on waste ground, in empty buildings, in the streets – and scrounging a living from the rubbish heaps or prostitution.

FATALISM

Most of Nepal's institutional problems – bureaucracy, corruption – are common to most poor countries, but some may be unique to Nepal. One of Nepal's foremost anthropologists, Dor Bahadur Bista, controversially argued that along with Nepalis' beguilingly relaxed *ke garne* ("what to do?") attitude comes a crippling **fatalism**. Responsibility is supposedly passed on to higher-ups (whether a boss, an astrologer or a deity), and the relationship between present work and future goals glossed over, resulting in haphazard planning. Nepali society also values **connections** very highly. The cult of the *aafno maanche* (one's "own man") makes it hard for minorities to advance, while the tradition of patronage ensures that loyalty is rewarded rather than skill or innovation.

While poverty is a perennial problem in the valley, it is prosperity that's creating the brand-new headaches, starting with **traffic** and **pollution** caused by a fleet of vehicles that is doubling every six to eight years. Smoke from brick kilns has long contributed to air pollution in the valley, as has its geographical shape as a bowl into which cool air sinks, trapping pollutants – but new vehicle emissions are blamed for the alarming increase in respiratory problems (asthma, allergies, lead-related developmental disorders in children), which now occur at twelve times the national average in Kathmandu. Those who can afford to are moving out to the suburbs – but then they have to commute by vehicle. On the positive side, the success of electric-powered Safaa ("clean") tempos is providing a highly visible reminder that there are cleaner alternatives. Assuming there is power, that is: centralized "load-shedding" threatens the viability of all electric vehicles, as there simply may not be enough time to recharge their batteries.

In Kathmandu, demand for **drinking water** vastly exceeds the supply, with the result that residents pump what water they can get up to rooftop storage tanks, and supplement it with deliveries by tanker. Leaks account for most of the shortfall, but development money, chasing the mega-project as ever, is all going to the $700 million **Melamchi project**, which plans to pipe water from the Helambu area northeast of the valley through a 27km tunnel. Almost twenty years late at the time of writing, millions over budget, and mired in corruption and environmental controversy (it will desiccate irrigated farmland downstream of the tunnel mouth in the dry season), the big donors have withdrawn one by one. The Asian Development Bank is one of the few to stay the course, but has insisted on the part-privatization of Kathmandu's water supply as a condition for its loan. Demand is likely to have overtaken supply by the time Melamchi comes on tap.

Water is not only scarce in the valley, it's also contaminated by **sewage** permeating the soil and infiltrating old, leaky pipes. Less than a third of the valley's sewage is properly treated, as municipal treatment plants don't operate properly and raw waste and toxic effluents drain directly into rivers. **Rubbish** is another problem, and the valley's municipalities still haven't agreed on a permanent dump: the Gokarna landfill in the valley is full, and the "temporary" site established at Sisdol, 25km north of Kathmandu, is frequently closed off by protesting locals. Rubbish is often dumped in horrific landfills right beside the Bagmati River, or burned, adding to air pollution.

The damage that has been done to the valley's **culture** in the name of progress is less easy to quantify, but is arguably more profound. Traditional architecture is only valued by a few. Members of the younger generation are drifting away from the religion of their parents. *Guthi* (charitable organizations) are in decline and have been forced to leave the upkeep of many temples to foreign preservationists. Tourism has robbed crafts of their ritual purpose and performance arts of their meaning. Work and schooling outside the home has loosened once-tight family ties, and the influx of strangers – especially refugees from the Maoist conflict, including thousands of families whose homes were destroyed or requisitioned – has introduced social tensions and crime.

To an encouraging extent, valley residents are prepared to accept these problems as the price of **progress**: a little pollution or crime may seem a fair trade for improvements that keep children from dying and give people greater control over their lives. But, increasingly, Kathmanduites are worrying that they might have a "Silent Spring" in the making. What will be the effects on their children of growing up breathing air, drinking water and eating food that is not only contaminated with germs but also laced with chemicals and heavy metals?

The future

Many development workers succumb to periodic despair. Every solution seems to create more problems. Better health and sanitation increases population growth, for example – and will do until poverty and the status of women is addressed. In the meantime, agriculture has to be improved to feed all those new mouths, deforestation must be reversed to solve the fuel wood and fodder crisis, and industry developed. So **irrigation projects**, **roads** and **hydroelectric schemes** are needed – all requiring **foreign support**. If development is left entirely to Nepalis, **better education** is required, which means addressing the poverty that prevents children attending classes and teachers from working in rural areas.

Encouragingly, it's the newcomers to the field that tend to be the gloomiest. Older hands can see the slow successes behind the seemingly intractable problems. Literacy, life expectancy and access to health care have all improved. **Community forests** are re-greening the hills. Microhydro and micro-loan schemes are bringing power – real and metaphorical – into remote areas. And, most excitingly, Nepalis themselves are demanding change. **Women's groups** are combating domestic violence, alcoholism and gambling. **Environmentalists** are pioneering a renewed concern for woodland and wildlife. Activists are doing anything from building community trekking lodges and leading birdwatching walks for children to picking up litter in Kathmandu's Ratna Park – small steps, maybe, but signifying a refreshing culture of home-grown activism. For all the many problems besieging this terrifyingly young, post-monarchical republic, a smell of spring is undoubtedly in the air.

Wildlife

Nowhere in the world is there a transition of flora and fauna so abrupt as the one between the Terai and the Himalayan crest. In a distance of as little as 60km, the terrain passes from steaming jungle through monsoon rainforest and rhododendron highlands to glacial valleys and the high-altitude desert of the Himalayan rain shadow. As a result, Nepal can boast an astounding diversity of life, from rhinos to snow leopards.

Flora

Nepal's **vegetation** is largely determined by altitude and can be grouped into three main divisions. The **lowlands** include the Terai, Churia Hills and valleys up to about 1000m; the **midlands** extend roughly from 1000m to 3000m; and the **Himalayas** from 3000m to the upper limit of vegetation (typically about 5000m). Conditions vary tremendously within these zones, however: south-facing slopes usually receive more moisture, but also more sun in their lower reaches, while certain areas that are less protected from the summer monsoon – notably around Pokhara – are especially wet. In general, rainfall is higher in the east, and a greater diversity of plants can be found there.

The Terai

Most of what little **lowland forest** remains in the Terai consists of **sal**, a tall, straight tree much valued for its wood – a factor which has caused its catastrophic decline outside protected areas. *Sal* prefers well-drained soils and the purest stands were once found along the Bhabar, the sloping alluvial plain at the base of the foothills; in the lower foothills, stunted specimens are frequently lopped for fodder. In spring, its cream-coloured flowers give off a heady jasmine scent. Other species sometimes associated with *sal* include **saj**, a large tree with crocodile-skin bark; **haldu**, used for making dugout canoes; and **bauhinia**, a strangling vine that corkscrews around its victims.

The wetter **riverine forest** supports a larger number of species, but life here is more precarious, as rivers regularly flood and change course during the monsoon. **Sisu**, related to rosewood, and **khair**, an acacia, are the first trees to colonize newly formed sandbanks. **Simal**, towering above mangrove-like buttresses, follows close behind; also known as the silk-cotton tree, it produces bulbous red flowers in February, and in May its seed pods explode with a cottony material that is used for stuffing mattresses. **Palash** – the "flame of the forest" tree – puts on an even more brilliant show of red flowers in February. All of these trees are deciduous, shedding their leaves during the dry spring. Many other species are evergreen, including **bilar**, **jamun** and **curry**, an understorey tree with thin, pointed leaves that smell just like their name.

Grasses dominate less stable wetlands. Of the fifty-plus species native to the Terai, several routinely grow to a height of 8m. Even experts tend to pass off any tall, dense stand as "elephant grass", because the only way to get through it is on an elephant (the most common genera are *Phragmites*, *Saccharum*, *Arundo* and *Themeda*). Most grasses reach their greatest height just after the monsoon and flower during the dry autumn months. Locals cut **khar**, a medium-sized variety, for thatch in winter and early spring; the official thatch-gathering season in the Terai parks (two weeks in January) is a colourful occasion, although the activity tends to drive wildlife into hiding. Fires are set in March and April to burn off the old growth and encourage tender new shoots, which provide food for game as well as livestock.

The Middle Hills

The decline in precipitation from east to west is more marked in the **Middle Hills** – so much so that the dry west shares few species in common with the moist eastern hills. Central Nepal is an overlap zone where western species tend to be found on south-facing slopes and eastern ones on the cooler northern aspects.

A common tree in dry western and central areas is **chir pine** (needles in bunches of three), which typically grows in park-like stands up to about 2000m. Various **oak** species often take over above 1500m, especially on dry ridges, and here you'll also find **ainsilo**, a cousin of the raspberry, which produces a sweet, if rather dry, golden fruit in May.

Although much of the primary forest in the wet midlands has been lost to cultivation, you can see fine remnants of it above Godavari in the Kathmandu Valley and around the lakes in the Pokhara Valley. Lower elevations are dominated by a zone of **katus** (*Castanopsis indica* or Nepal chestnut) and **chilaune** (*Schima wallichii*), the latter being a member of the tea family with oblong concave leaves and, in May, small white flowers. In eastern parts, several species of **laurel** form a third major component to this forest, while alder, cardamom and tree ferns grow in shady gullies.

The magical, mossy oak-rhododendron forest is still mostly intact above about 2000m, thanks to the prevalent fog that makes farming unviable at this level. **Khasru**, the predominant oak found here, has prickly leaves and is often laden with lichen, **orchids** and other epiphytes, which grow on other plants and get their nutrients directly from the air. It's estimated that more than three hundred orchid varieties grow in Nepal, and although not all are showy or scented, the odds are you'll be able to find one flowering at almost any time of year. **Tree rhododendron** (*Lali guraas*), Nepal's national flower, grows to more than 20m high and blooms with gorgeous red or pink flowers in March and April. Nearly thirty other species occur in Nepal, mainly in the east – the Milke Danda, a long ridge east of the Arun River, is the best place to view rhododendron, although impressive stands can also be seen between Ghodapani and Ghandrung in the Annapurna region. Most of Nepal's three hundred species of **fern** are found in this forest type, as are many medicinal plants whose curative properties are known to ayurvedic practitioners but have yet to be studied in the West. Also occurring here are **lokta**, a small bush with fragrant white flowers in spring, whose bark is pulped to make paper, and **nettles**, whose stems are used by eastern hill-dwellers to make a hard-wearing fabric.

Holly, magnolia and **maple** may replace oak and rhododendron in some sites. **Dwarf bamboo**, the red panda's favourite food, grows in particularly damp places, such as northern Helambu and along the trail to the Annapurna Sanctuary. **Cannabis** thrives in disturbed sites throughout the midlands – including beside roads and paths, handily enough.

The Himalayas

Conifers form the dominant tree cover in the **Himalayas**. Particularly striking are the forests around Rara Lake in western Nepal, where **Himalayan spruce** and **blue pine** (needles grouped in fives) are interspersed with meadows. Elsewhere in the west you'll find magnificent **Himalayan cedar** (*deodar*) trees, which are protected by villagers, and a species of **cypress**. Two types of **juniper** are present in Nepal: the more common tree-sized variety grows south of the main Himalayan crest (notably around Tengboche in the Everest region), while a dwarf scrub juniper is confined to northern rain-shadow areas. Both provide incense for Buddhist rites. In wetter areas, **hemlock fir** (distinguished from spruce by its upward-pointing cones) and even the deciduous **larch** may be encountered.

One of the most common (and graceful) broadleafed species is **white birch**, usually found in thickets near the tree line, especially on shaded slopes where the snow lies late. Shivery **poplars** stick close to watercourses high up into the inner valleys – Muktinath is full of them – while **berberis**, a shrub whose leaves turn scarlet in autumn, grows widely on exposed sites. Trekking up the Langtang or Marsyangdi valleys you pass through many of these forest types in rapid succession, but the most dramatic transition of all is found in the valley of the Thak Khola (Upper Kali Gandaki): the monsoon jungle below Ghasa gives way to blue pine, hemlock, rhododendron and horse chestnut; then to birch, fir and cypress around Tukche; then the **apricot** orchards of Marpha; and finally the blasted steppes of Jomosom.

Alpine vegetation predominates on the forest floor and in moist meadows above the tree line, and – apart from the dwarf rhododendron (some species of which give off a strong cinnamon scent and are locally used as incense) – many **flowers** found here will be familiar to European and North American walkers. There are too many to do justice to them here, but primula, buttercup, poppy, iris, larkspur, gentian, edelweiss, buddleia, columbine and sage are all common. Most bloom during the monsoon, but rhododendrons and primulas can be seen flowering in the spring and gentians and larkspurs in the autumn.

Mammals

Most of Nepal's rich **animal life** inhabits the Terai and, despite dense vegetation, is most easily observed there. Along the trekking trails of the hills, wildlife is much harder to spot due to population pressure, while very few mammals live above the tree line. The following overview progresses generally from Terai to Himalayan species, and focuses on the more charismatic or visible animals – anyone interested in identifying some of Nepal's 55 species of bats or eight kinds of flying squirrel will need a specialist guide.

The **Asian one-horned rhino** (*gaida*) is one of five species found in Asia and Africa, all endangered, and all at risk from poaching. In Nepal, about five hundred rhinos, or a quarter of the species total, live in Chitwan – something of a success story. Forty-eight were introduced to Bardia, but only half have survived the period of instability. Rhinos graze singly or in small groups in the marshy elephant grass, where they can remain surprisingly well hidden.

Although trained **elephants** (*hatti*) remain important to Nepali culture, their wild relatives are seen only rarely in Nepal by tourists – though they kill literally dozens of Nepalis every year, especially near the eastern border, where hundreds of wild elephants roam between Nepal and India. Since elephants require vast territory for their seasonal migrations, the settling of the Terai is putting them in increasing conflict with humankind. More than half of Nepal's resident wild elephants, some eighty animals or so, are found in Bardia National Park; Chitwan has another thirty or so.

Koshi Tappu is the only remaining habitat in Nepal for another species better known as a domestic breed, **wild buffalo** (*arnaa*), some two hundred of which graze the wet grasslands there in small herds. Majestic and powerful, the **gaur** (*gauri gaai*), or Indian bison, spends most of its time in the dry lower foothills, but descends to the Terai in spring for water.

Perhaps the Terai's most unlikely mammals, **gangetic dolphins** – one of four freshwater species in the world – are present in increasingly small numbers in the Karnali and Sapt Koshi rivers (see box, p.292). Curious and gregarious, they tend to congregate in deep channels where they feed on fish and crustaceans, and betray their presence with a blow-hole puff when surfacing.

The most abundant mammals of the Terai, *chital*, or **spotted deer**, are often seen in herds around the boundary between riverine forest and grassland. **Hog deer** – so called because of their porky little bodies and head-down trot – take shelter in wet grassland, while the aptly named **barking deer**, measuring around half a metre high at the shoulder, are found throughout lowland and midland forests. **Swamp deer** gather in vast herds in Sukla Phanta, and males of the species carry impressive sets of antlers (their Nepali name, *barhasingha*, means "twelve points"). **Sambar**, heavy-set animals standing 1.5m at the shoulder, are more widely distributed, but elusive. Two species of antelope, the graceful, corkscrew-horned **blackbuck** and the ungainly **nilgai** (blue bull), may be seen at Bardia and Koshi Tappu respectively; the latter was once assumed to be a form of cattle, and thus spared by Hindu hunters, but no longer.

Areas of greatest deer and antelope concentrations are usually prime territory for the endangered Bengal **tiger** (*bagh*). However, your chances of spotting one of Nepal's hundred-odd tigers on the average visit to a National Park are exceedingly slim, and not just because they're rare: they're mainly nocturnal, and incredibly stealthy. In the deep shade and mottled sunlight of dense riverine forest, a tiger's orange- and black-striped coat provides almost total camouflage. A male may weigh 250kg and measure 3m from nose to tail. Tigers are solitary hunters; some have been known to consume up to twenty percent of their body weight after a kill, but they may go several days between feeds. Males and females maintain separate but overlapping territories, regularly patrolling them, marking the boundaries with scent and driving off interlopers. Some Nepalis believe tigers to be the unquiet souls of the deceased.

Leopards (*chituwa*) are equally elusive, but much more widely distributed: they may be found in any deep forest from the Terai to the timber line. As a consequence, they account for many more maulings in Nepal than tigers, and are more feared. A smaller animal (males weigh about 45kg), they prey on monkeys, dogs and livestock. **Other cats** – such as the fishing cat, leopard cat and the splendid clouded leopard – are known to exist in the more remote lowlands and midlands, but are very rarely sighted. **Hyenas** and **wild dogs** are scavengers of the Terai, and **jackals**, though seldom seen (they're nocturnal), produce an eerie howling that is one of the most common night sounds in the Terai and hills.

While it isn't carnivorous, the dangerously unpredictable **sloth bear**, a Terai species, is liable to turn on you and should be approached with extreme caution. Its powerful front claws are designed for unearthing termite nests, and its long snout for extracting the insects. The **Himalayan black bear** roams midland forests up to the tree line and is, if anything, more dangerous; some believe the bear is the origin of the Yeti myth (see p.346). **Wild boars** can be seen rooting and scurrying through forest anywhere in Nepal.

Monkeys, a common sight in the Terai and hills, come in two main varieties in Nepal. The delightful **grey langurs** have silver fur, black faces and hands, and long, ropelike tails; in forested trekking areas, it's quite common to see and hear them crashing about in the trees, or sitting around in placid family groups. Nepalis know them as "Hanuman" monkeys, after the monkey god: one story has it that they have been blackened since the fire that singed the monkey god when he tried to rescue Sita from the demon Ravana. Russet-brown **rhesus macaques** (red monkeys or *raato bandar*) are more shy in the wild, but around temples are tame to the point of being nuisances. There is a third species, the Assamese macaque, but it's found only in small populations in remoter areas such as the Langtang region and Makalu-Barun National Park.

Many other **small mammals** may be spotted in the hills, among them porcupines, flying squirrels, foxes, civets, otters, mongooses and martens. The **red panda**, with its rust coat and bushy, ringed tail, almost resembles a tree-dwelling fox; like its Chinese relative, it's partial to bamboo, and is very occasionally glimpsed in the cloud forest of northern Helambu.

Elusive animals of the rhododendron and birch forests, **musk deer** are readily identified by their tusk-like canine teeth; males are hunted for their musk pod, just one of which can fetch well over $100 on the black market. Though by no means common, **Himalayan tahr** is the most frequently observed large mammal of the high country; a goat-like animal with long, wiry fur and short horns, it browses along steep cliffs below the tree line. **Serow**, another goat relative, inhabits remote canyons and forested areas, while **goral**, sometimes likened to chamois, occurs from middle elevations up to the tree line.

The Himalaya's highest domesticated, or at least semi-domesticated, resident is the **yak** – true wild yaks are considered extinct in Nepal. While smaller and usually gentler than cows, they look shaggier, tougher, with their long horns, and distinctly more eccentric. The female is called a **nak** (giving rise to a popular Nepali joke about what you get if you order yak cheese). The bovines more often seen on trekking paths, however, are the **dzopkio** (male) and **dzum** (female) yak-cow crossbreeds, recognizable by their more even temper, forward-curving horns and lowing – yaks can only grunt. The truly wild mammals you'll most often see above the tree line are **blue sheep**, or *bharal*, which graze the barren grasslands year-round. Normally tan, males go a slatey colour in winter, accounting for their name. Herds have been sighted around the Thorung La in the Annapurna region, but they occur in greater numbers north of Dhorpatan and in She-Phoksundo National Park. Their chief predator is the **snow leopard**, a secretive and beautiful cat whose habits are still little understood. Nepal has a critical population of 350–500 of this globally endangered species.

Amphibians and reptiles

Native to the Terai's wetlands, crocodiles are most easily seen in winter, when they sun themselves on muddy banks to warm up their cold-blooded bodies. The endangered **mugger crocodile** favours marshes and oxbow lakes, where it may lie motionless for hours on end until its prey comes within snapping distance. Muggers mainly pursue fish, but will eat just about anything they can get their jaws around – including human corpses thrown into the river by relatives unable to afford wood for a cremation. The even more endangered **gharial crocodile** lives exclusively in rivers and feeds on fish (see p.251).

Nepal has many kinds of **snakes**, but they are rarely encountered: most hibernate in winter, even in the Terai, and shy away from humans at other times of year. Common cobras – snake charmers' favourites – inhabit low elevations near villages; they aren't found in the Kathmandu Valley, despite their abundance in religious imagery there. Kraits and pit vipers, both highly poisonous, have been reported, as have pythons up to 6m long. However, the commonest species aren't poisonous and are typically less than half a metre long.

Chances are you'll run into a **gecko** or two, probably clinging to a guesthouse wall. Helpful insect-eaters, these lizard-like creatures are able to climb almost any surface with the aid of suction pads on their feet. About fifty species of **fish** have been recorded in Nepal, but only *mahseer*, a sporty relative of carp that attains its greatest size in the lower Karnali River, is of much interest; most ponds are stocked with carp and catfish.

Birds

More than eight hundred **bird species** – one-tenth of the earth's total – have been sighted in Nepal. The country plays host to a high number of birds migrating between India and central Asia in spring and autumn and, because it spans so many ecosystems, provides habitats for a wide range of year-round residents. The greatest diversity of species is found in the Terai wildlife parks, but even the Kathmandu Valley is remarkably rich in birdlife. The following is only a listing of the major categories – for the complete picture, get hold of *Birds of Nepal* (see p.426).

In the **Terai** and lower hills, raptors (birds of prey) such as ospreys, cormorants, darters, gulls and kingfishers patrol streams and rivers for food; herons and storks can also be seen fishing, while cranes, ducks and moorhens wade in or float on the water. Many of these migratory species are particularly well represented at Koshi Tappu, which is located along the important Arun Valley corridor to Tibet. Peafowl make their meowing mating call – and peacocks occasionally deign to unfurl their plumage – while many species of woodpeckers can be heard, if not seen, high up in the *sal* canopy. Cuckoos and "brain fever" birds repeat their idiotic two- or four-note songs in an almost demented fashion. Parakeets swoop in formation; bee-eaters, swifts, drongos, swallows and rollers flit and dive for insects, while jungle fowl look like chickens as Monet might have painted them. Other oddities of the Terai include the paradise flycatcher, with its lavish white tail feathers and dragonfly-like flight; the lanky great adjutant stork, resembling a prehistoric reptile in flight; and the giant hornbill, whose beak supports an appendage that looks like an upturned welder's mask.

Many of the above birds are found in **the midlands** as well as the Terai – as are mynas, egrets, crows and magpies, which tend to scavenge near areas of human habitation. Birds of prey – falcons, kestrels, harriers, eagles, kites, hawks and vultures – may also be seen at almost any elevation. Owls are common, but not much liked by Nepalis. Babblers and laughing thrushes populate the oak-rhododendron forest and are as noisy as their names suggest. More than twenty species of flycatchers are present in the Kathmandu Valley alone.

Nepal's national bird, the iridescent, multicoloured *danphe* (impeyan pheasant), can often be spotted scuttling through the undergrowth in the Everest region. *Kalij* and *monal*, two other native pheasants, also inhabit the higher hills and lower **Himalayas**. Migrating waterfowl often stop over at high-altitude lakes – ruddy shelducks are a trekking-season attraction at Gokyo – and snow pigeons, grebes, finches and choughs may all be seen at or above the tree line. Mountaineers have reported seeing choughs at up to 8200m on Everest, and migrating bar-headed geese are known to fly *over* Everest.

Invertebrates and insects

Perhaps no other creature in Nepal arouses such squeamishness as the **leech** (*jukha*). Fortunately, these segmented, caterpillar-sized annelids remain dormant underground during the trekking seasons; during the monsoon, however, they come out in force everywhere in the Terai and hills, making any hike a bloody business. Leeches are attracted to body heat, and will inch up legs or drop from branches to reach their victims. The bite is completely painless – the bloodsucker injects a local anaesthetic and anticoagulant – and often goes unnoticed until the leech drops off of its own accord. Removing them, however, can be tricky (see p.40).

More than six hundred species of **butterflies** have been recorded in Nepal, with more being discovered all the time. The monsoon is the best time to view butterflies – in fact, they provide a reason in themselves for a visit in that season – but many varieties can be seen before and especially just after the rains: look beside moist, sandy banks or atop ridges; Phulchoki is an excellent place to start in the Kathmandu Valley. Notable hill varieties include the intriguing orange oakleaf, whose markings enable it to vanish into forest litter, and the golden birdwing, a large, angular species with a loping wingbeat. **Moths** are even more numerous – around five thousand species are believed to exist in Nepal, including the world's largest, the giant atlas, which has a wingspan of almost 30cm.

Termites are Nepal's most conspicuous social insects, constructing towering, fluted mounds up to 2.5m tall in the western Terai. Organized in colonies much the same as ants and bees, legions of termite workers and "reproductives" serve a single king and queen. The mounds function as cooling towers for the busy nest below; monuments to insect industry, they're made from tailings excavated from the colony's galleries and bonded with saliva for a wood-hard finish. **Honey bees** create huge, drooping nests in the Terai and especially in the lush cliff country north of Pokhara. **Spiders** aren't very numerous in Nepal, although one notable species grows to be 15cm across and nets birds (it's not poisonous to humans). **Fireflies**, with orange and black bodies, give off a greenish glow at dusk in the Terai. For many travellers, however, the extent of their involvement with the insect kingdom will be in swatting **mosquitoes**: two genera are prevalent in the lowlands, one of them, *Anopheles*, the infamous vector of malaria.

Books

In the reviews that follow, publishers are only listed for books published outside the UK and US. Most titles – including those that are out of print (o/p) – are a lot easier to come by in Nepal, and some will only be available there. Books marked with the ★ symbol are particularly recommended.

TRAVELOGUE

Barbara Crossette *So Close to Heaven*. A survey of the "vanishing Buddhist kingdoms of the Himalayas", including a chapter focusing on Nepal's Tibetans, Bhotiyas and Newars.

★ **Harka Gurung** *Vignettes of Nepal* (Sajha Prakashan, Nepal). This vivid travelogue, illuminated by a native's insights, is one of the best books written by a Nepali in English about his country.

★ **Toni Hagen and Deepak Thapa** *Nepal: The Kingdom of the Himalaya*. No person alive has seen as much of Nepal as Hagen, who literally surveyed the entire country in the 1950s. His groundbreaking book was first published in 1961, and revised in 1999.

★ **Peter Matthiessen** *The Snow Leopard*. Matthiessen joins biologist George Schaller in a pilgrimage to Dolpo to track one of the world's most elusive cats, and comes up with characteristically Zen insights and magnificent writing on landscape.

Dervla Murphy *The Waiting Land* (o/p). A personal account of working with Pokhara's Tibetan refugees in 1965, written in the author's usual entertaining and politically on-the-ball style.

★ **Charlie Pye-Smith** *Travels in Nepal* (o/p). A curious and surprisingly successful cross between a travelogue and a progress report on aid projects. Mixes impressionistic writing with hard facts.

Barbara J. Scot *The Violet Shyness of Their Eyes: Notes from Nepal*. An American woman crash-lands in the Nepali hills; the writing strikes a nice balance between observation and introspection.

Eric Valli and Diane Summers *Caravans of the Himalaya* (o/p). A journey along the old Nepal–Tibet trade route, packaged for maximum armchair impact. The authors' *Hunting for Honey* (o/p) also made a splash.

CULTURE AND ANTHROPOLOGY

John Burbank *Culture Shock! Nepal* (o/p). Sensitivity training for tourists, with valuable insights into social mores, religion, caste and cross-cultural relations.

Broughton Coburn *Nepali Aama: Life Lessons of a Himalayan Woman* (Adarsh Enterprises). Delightful study of an old Gurung woman in a village south of Pokhara. Told in her own words, and includes photos.

Monica Connell *Against a Peacock Sky* (o/p). Beautiful, impressionistic rendering of life among the *matawaali* (alcohol-drinking) Chhetris of Jumla District, capturing the subtleties of village life in Nepal.

★ **Hugh R. Downs** *Rhythms of a Himalayan Village* (o/p). An extraordinarily sensitive synthesis of black-and-white photos, text and quotes, describing rituals and religion in a Solu village.

William P. Forbes *The Glory of Nepal: A Mythological Guidebook to the Kathmandu Valley* (Vedic Books, India). A lively retelling of myths from the Nepal Mahatmya and other medieval texts, linking them to modern-day locations.

Jim Goodman *Guide to Enjoying Nepalese Festivals* (o/p). All the arcane whys and wherefores of the Kathmandu Valley's festivals: authoritative, though not very user-friendly.

Eva Kipp *Bending Bamboo, Changing Winds: Nepali Women Tell Their Life Stories* (Pilgrims, Nepal). Powerful oral histories and photographs of women from all over Nepal, revealing not only the country's amazing cultural diversity but also the universal trials of being a Nepali woman.

Robert I. Levy and Kedar Raj Rajopadhyaya *Mesocosm: Hinduism and the Organization of a Traditional Newar City in Nepal*. A heavy anthropological study of Bhaktapur, but its thesis – that the city's inhabitants collectively operate a sort of well-oiled cultural and spiritual machine – is fascinating.

Kathryn S. March *If Each Comes Halfway: Meeting Tamang Women in Nepal*. Compelling oral history collected from highland, rural Tamang women, with accompanying photographs.

Rashmila Shakya and Scott Berry *From Goddess to Mortal* (Vajra, Nepal). Gripping window into the life of a Kumari, as told by the ex-goddess herself.

★ **Mary Slusser** *Nepal Mandala: A Cultural Study of the Kathmandu Valley* (o/p). A gorgeous but exorbitant two-volume set, this is the definitive study of Newar culture and religion.

David L. Snellgrove *Himalayan Pilgrimage* (o/p). A classic travelogue/anthropological account of a trip through northwestern Nepal in the 1950s.

HISTORY AND POLITICS

Dor Bahadur Bista *Fatalism and Development* (o/p). Controversial analysis of the cultural factors that stand in the way of Nepal's development, by the country's best-known anthropologist.

Jonathan Gregson *Blood Against the Snows*. Occasionally lurid account of the royal massacre, prefaced by rather dustier diggings into the history of Nepal's monarchy.

Michael Hutt *Himalayan People's War: Nepal's Maoist Rebellion*. Has dated fast since publication in 2004, but remains one of the most detailed academic analyses of the insurrection's origins and early years.

Percival Landon *Nepal* (o/p). The most comprehensive study of the country when it was written (1928), and still a classic – but having been commissioned by the Maharaja, it has a distinct political bias.

John Parker *The Gurkhas*. One of many books lionizing Nepal's famous Gurkha soldiers.

Michel Peissel *Tiger for Breakfast* (Time Books International, India). This biography of Boris Lissanevitch, the Russian émigré who ran Kathmandu's first tourist hotel, opens a fascinating window on 1950s Nepal.

Anirban Roy *Prachanda, The Unknown Revolutionary* (Mandala Book Point, Nepal). Journalistic and anecdotal account of the Maoist leader.

★ **Manjushree Thapa** *Forget Kathmandu: An Elegy for Democracy*. Published just before the royal coup in 2005, this trenchant account of the early years of the Maoist insurrection weaves it into the context of Nepal's deeper history. Thapa is a novelist, and uses personal memoir and travelogue – she visits the Maoist heartland – to bring the politics alive.

Ludmilla Tüting and Kunda Dixit *Bikas-Binas, Development-Destruction* (o/p). Dated but classic collection of articles covering the whole gamut of dilemmas arising out of development, environmental degradation and tourism.

★ **John Whelpton** *A History of Nepal*. The best and most up-to-date general history of Nepal, published in 2005.

RELIGION

★ **Kevin Bubriski and Keith Dowman** *Power Places of Kathmandu*. A collaboration by two eminent authorities on Hindu and Buddhist holy sites. Rich colour photographs are accompanied by well-researched text.

★ **Claudia Müller-Ebeling, Christian Rätsch and Surendra Shahi** *Shamanism and Tantra in the Himalayas*. Impressive on-the-ground research and superb photographs make this a magnificent production – though marred somewhat by its credulous stance.

★ **Georg Feuerstein** *Tantra: The Art of Ecstasy*. Clear-sighted and readable introduction to tantra, dispelling the usual "tantric sex" myths and offering a vision of an alternative thread in subcontinental spirituality.

James McConnachie *The Book of Love: In Search of the Kamasutra*. Investigates the role of sex in Hinduism, touching on tantra, and traces how those ideas became known in the West.

Axel Michaels *Hinduism Past and Present*. Heavyweight, and still one of the most insightful books on Hinduism. Written by a Nepal specialist, it focuses on living practices rather than texts and mythology.

Barbara Stoler Miller (trans.) *The Bhagavad-Gita*. A poetic English rendering of Krishna's teaching.

Stan Royal Mumford *Himalayan Dialogue: Tibetan Lamas and Gurung Shamans in Nepal*. An account of myths and rituals practised in a village along the Annapurna Circuit – fascinating, once you get past the anthropological jargon.

R.K. Narayan (trans.) *The Ramayana of Valmiki*. One of the most engaging retellings of this magnificent tale. The Clay Sanskrit Library's seven-volume version offers an elegant, high-minded (and full-length) alternative.

John Powers *Introduction to Tibetan Buddhism*. A thorough introduction for beginners.

Robert A.F. Thurman *Essential Tibetan Buddhism*. Weaves together classic texts with modern commentary; not for beginners.

ART AND ARCHITECTURE

Lydia Aran *The Art of Nepal* (Sahayogi, Nepal). Good overview of Nepalese religion as well as stone, metal and wood sculpture and *thangka* paintings.

Hannelore Gabriel *Jewelry of Nepal* (o/p). A thorough cataloguing of traditional highland jewellery (less coverage is given to hill and Terai styles), with lavish illustrations.

Michael Hutt *Nepal: A Guide to the Art and Architecture of the Kathmandu Valley* (o/p). An in-depth discussion of iconography, design and construction, from one of the leading scholars of Nepal.

Eva Rudy Jansen *The Book of Buddhas: Ritual Symbolism Used in Buddhist Statuary and Ritual Objects* (Binkey Kok, Netherlands; Motilal Banarsidass, India) and *The Book of Hindu Imagery: The Gods and Their Symbols* (New Age, India, plus Weiser, UK). Good introductory guides to the iconography of religious statuary.

Jnan Bahadur Sakya *A Short Description of Gods, Goddesses and Ritual Objects of Buddhism and Hinduism in Nepal* (Handicraft Association of Nepal). This extremely handy, inexpensive pamphlet is fairly widely available in Nepal.

Madanjeet Singh *Himalayan Art* (South Asia Foundation). Dated – this is a reprint of the 1968 original – but still scholarly and fascinating. Focuses on wall paintings and sculptures.

FICTION AND POETRY

Laxmi Prasad Devkota *Muna Madan* (Nirala, Nepal). The most famous work by one of Nepal's best-loved poets recounts the tragic, almost Shakespearean tale of a young Newari trader who leaves his young wife to travel to Lhasa.

Michael Hutt (ed.) *Himalayan Voices: An Introduction to Modern Nepali Literature* (Indian Book Company, India, plus University of California Press). An excellent survey of Nepali poetry and fiction, with some commentary.

★ **Manjushree Thapa** *The Tutor of History* (Penguin, India). Tensions build before an election in a small roadside town between Kathmandu and Pokhara. Hugely vivid evocation of politics, social mores, alcoholism and a quintessentially Nepali struggle against what appears to be fate. *Seasons of Flight*, her most recent novel, follows a navel-gazing young Nepali woman on her journeys through the post-globalization Nepali diaspora.

★ **Samrat Upadhyay** *Arresting God in Kathmandu*. This acclaimed collection of stories, written by a Nepali living in the US, takes on typically introspective Nepali themes – jealousy, self-doubt, desire, family tension. Upadhyay's debut novel, *The Guru of Love*, tells a story of disturbed domesticity against the charged atmosphere of late-1990s Kathmandu.

★ **Narayan Wagle** *Palpasa Café* (Nepa-laya, Nepal). Perhaps the definitive novel of the Maoist conflict era, written by a leading journalist. Conveyed in a direct, youthful, Murakami-like style, it puts a blighted romance between a drifting artist and a Nepali-American girl in the highly charged context of the troubles.

NATURAL HISTORY

Richard Grimmett, Carol Inskipp and Tim Inskipp *Birds of Nepal*. The authoritative guide. The authors have published numerous shorter guides as well.

K.K. Gurung *Heart of the Jungle* (o/p). The essential guide to Chitwan's flora and fauna, written by the former manager of *Tiger Tops Jungle Lodge*.

George Schaller *Stones of Silence: Journeys in the Himalaya* (o/p). Written by the wildlife biologist who accompanied Peter Matthiessen on his quest for the snow leopard, this book provides a detailed view of ecosystems of the high Himalayas.

Rishikesh Shaha and Richard M. Mitchell *Wildlife in Nepal* (Nirala, India). Brief but handily illustrated guide, with a fascinating section on the history of hunting in Nepal.

Colin Smith *A Photographic Pocket Guide to Butterflies of Nepal* (Rohit Kumar, Nepal). Beautiful colour plates show butterflies in typical settings. Smith is the authority on butterflies, and has published a series of books of varying degrees of comprehensiveness.

★ **Adrian and Jimmie Storrs** *Enjoy Trees* (Book Faith India). Great beginner's guide to the more common flora of Nepal, covering flowers as well as trees, and with sections on medicinal and religious plants.

MOUNTAINEERING

W.E. Bowman *The Ascent of Rum Doodle*. This much-loved parody of a mountaineering expedition is the *Spinal Tap* of the Himalayan climbing scene. It even has a bar in Kathmandu named after it.

Chris Bonington and Charles Clarke *Everest: The Unclimbed Ridge*. The classic story of the bold but ill-fated first attempt of Everest's fearsome Northeast Ridge in 1982.

★ **Maurice Herzog** *Annapurna*. One of the greatest true adventure stories ever written, describing the search for, and first successful ascent of, an 8000m peak. Herzog's dreamlike description of his summit stupor and the tale of the desperate descent are riveting.

Maurice Isserman and Stewart Weaver *Fallen Giants: A History of Himalayan Mountaineering*. This authoritative overview has great insights into the culture of mountaineering in different ages, but it has to cover too many climbs to be a truly gripping read.

★ **Jon Krakauer** *Into Thin Air*. The best-selling first-person account of the 1996 Everest tragedy reads like a whodunnit and has all the elements of high tragedy: hubris, heroism, angry mountain gods, rivalry, vanity, triumph and agony.

Sherry Ortner *Life and Death on Mt Everest: Sherpas and Himalayan Mountaineering*. The great anthropologist of the Sherpas brings all her knowledge to bear on this controversial topic, weaving some amazing stories as she does so.

H.W. Tilman *Nepal Himalaya* (Pilgrims, Nepal). A chatty account of the first mountaineering reconnaissance of Nepal in 1949–51. Tilman was one of the century's great adventurers, and his writing remains fresh and witty.

TREKKING GUIDES

Stephen Bezruchka and Alonzo Lyons *Trekking Nepal: A Traveler's Guide* (Mountaineers). Covers only the "teahouse" treks, not those in restricted areas, but is perhaps the most culturally sensitive book, containing background pieces on Nepali language, culture and natural history.

Robin Boustead *Nepal Trekking and the Great Himalaya Trail*. A solid general trekking guide from Trailblazer, though it doesn't offer all that much more detail in terms of the standard routes than is covered by this *Rough Guide*. That said, it's good on more remote areas, and of course covers the monumentally ambitious, country-length, high-altitude Great Himalaya Trail, as pioneered by Boustead himself.

Bob Gibbons and Sian Pritchard-Jones *Mustang: A Trekking Guide* (Pilgrims, Nepal). A great guide to Mustang, despite the 1997 publishing date, which means it is hugely out of date on matters like roads and lodges. The authors also wrote the definitive guide to the Mount Kailash trek, heading out from Simikot into Tibet.

Margaret Jefferies *Highest Heritage: The Mount Everest Region and Sagarmatha National Park* (Pilgrims, Nepal). Superbly detailed guide to the Everest region, covering Sherpa culture, landscape, history and wildlife, as well as giving brief trekking itineraries.

Bradley Mayhew and Joe Bindloss *Trekking in the Nepal Himalaya*. This Lonely Planet guide divides treks into fixed days, which can be limiting, but is hugely detailed and written in an enjoyably breezy style, and the maps are decent. Unless you're doing lots of treks, however, it makes more sense to buy a dedicated, single-region guidebook.

Jamie McGuinness *Trekking in the Everest Region; Trekking in Langtang, Helambu and Gosainkund*. The Trailblazer series has a friendly, useable feel, with hand-drawn maps and a chatty tone. The guides to all these routes are written by a vastly experienced leader of treks and climbs.

Steve Razzetti *Nepal: Trekking and Climbing – 25 Classic Treks and 12 Climbing Peaks* (New Holland). Currently the only book in print – published in the US by Interlink – that describes trekking peaks in any detail.

Kev Reynolds *Annapurna; Everest; Manaslu; Kangchenjunga; Langtang; Gosainkund & Helambu*. British publisher Cicerone produces well-written guides to all these areas, all by the indefatigable Reynolds, with plentiful colour photos, simple but easily readable maps, detailed route guides and lots of cultural background.

Bryn Thomas *Trekking in the Annapurna Region*. A good, workmanlike guide to this popular region from Trailblazer, though the 100 pages of trek descriptions are rather overshadowed by general information on Nepal, Kathmandu, Pokhara and so on. Reviews of trekking lodges are unusually detailed.

MOUNTAIN BIKING AND WHITEWATER RAFTING GUIDES

James Giambrone *Kathmandu Bikes & Hikes* (o/p). Now over twenty years old, this book still gives a decent account of cycling routes in and around Kathmandu, especially when paired with an up-to-date map.

Peter Knowles and Darren Clarkson-King *White Water Nepal*. Updated in 2011, this is the definitive guide.

MISCELLANEOUS

Jim Duff and Peter Gormly *The Himalayan First Aid Manual* (World Expeditions, Nepal). Handy pocket-sized booklet.

★**Jyothi Pathak** *Taste of Nepal*. Authoritative, comprehensive and mouthwatering cookbook.

Andrew J. Pollard, David R. Murdoch and James S. Milledge *The High Altitude Medicine Handbook* (Book Faith India). Everything you need to know for a trek.

Language

Basic Nepali is surprisingly easy to learn, and surprisingly useful: nearly all Nepalis who deal with tourists speak English, but almost all enjoy attempts to reciprocate. Off the beaten track, a few phrases are essential, as good English is rare.

Nepali is closely related to Hindi, so Nepalis and North Indians can usually get by – and many Nepalis in the Terai speak languages that are even closer to Hindi, such as Bhojpuri and Maithili. The ethnic groups of the hills and mountains speak utterly unrelated Tibeto-Burman languages – some Rai languages are only spoken by a few thousand people within a single valley – but almost all have adopted Nepali as a lingua franca. Fortunately for foreigners, many hill people use a relatively simple form of Nepali that's easy to learn and understand. Nepali is written in the **Devanaagari** script but signs, bus destinations and so on are usually written in English (see box, p.23).

There are lots of useful **phrasebooks** available in Kathmandu; internationally the choice is limited to Lonely Planet's useful *Nepal Phrasebook & Dictionary*. For a full-blown **teach-yourself book**, by far the best is *Complete Nepali: Teach Yourself*, by Michael Hutt and Abhi Subedi (Teach Yourself, UK), which comes with a CD; David Matthews' *A Course in Nepali* (SOAS, UK) offers a more literary perspective.

Pronunciation

Nepali has to be transliterated from the Devanaagari script into the Roman alphabet; the resulting spellings may vary, and aren't always exactly phonetic.

a as in "alone"	**e** as in "bet"	**r** lightly rolled; can sound	**u** as in boot
aa as in "father"	**i** as in "police"	like a cross between "r"	**w** sounds like a cross
b sounds like a cross	**j** as in "just"	and "d"	between "w" and "v"
between "b" and "v"	**o** as in "note"	**s** can sound almost like "sh"	**z** sounds like "dj" or "dz"

Nepali has lighter accents than English, but the accent almost always goes on any syllable with "aa" in it. If there's no "aa", it usually falls on the first syllable.

Vowels

The distinction between "a" and "aa" is important. *Maa* (in) is pronounced as it looks, with the vowel stretched out and open. *Ma* (I), by contrast, sounds shorter and more closed: something like "muh" or perhaps the "mo" in "mob"; *mandir* (temple) comes out like "mundeer".

Some Nepali vowels are nasalized – to get the right effect, you have to honk nasally, rather like a French "en". Nasalized vowels aren't indicated in this book, but they're something to be aware of: listen to a Nepali say *tapaai* (you) or *yahaa* (here) – it's like saying "tapaaing" or "yahaang", but stopping just before the end.

Aspirated consonants

The combinations "ch" and "sh" are pronounced as in English, but in all other cases where an "h" follows a consonant the sound is meant to be aspirated – in other words, give it an extra puff of air. Thus *bholi* (tomorrow) sounds like *b'holi* and Thamel sounds like *T'hamel*.

chh sounds like a very breathy "ch", as in "pitch here"; almost like "tsha"

ph sometimes sounds like an "f" (as in phone) but may also be pronounced like a breathy "p" (as in haphazard)

th is pronounced as in "put here" (as in Kathmandu, not as in think)

Retroflex consonants

The sounds "d", "r" and "t" occur in two bewildering forms, dental and retroflex; to Nepali ears, English "t" falls somewhere between the two. The retroflex sound is made by rolling the tip of the tongue back towards the roof of the mouth – a classic "Indian" sound. The dental form is like saying a "d" with the tip of the tongue right up against the teeth. An obvious example of a retroflex (and aspirated) "t" is Kathmandu, which sounds a little like a breathy "Kartmandu". Rarely, retroflexion changes meaning: *saathi* means friend, but with a retroflex "th" it means sixty.

GREETINGS AND BASIC PHRASES

For advice on the nuances of some of these basic phrases, check "Cultural and etiquette" (see p.40). Separate words for "please" and "thank you" are rarely used, though **dhanyebaad** is increasingly common in tourist areas. Politeness is indicated by manner and the grammatical form of the verb.

Hello, Goodbye (formal)	Namaste	I don't know	Malaai thaahaa chhaina
Hello (very formal)	Namaskar	I didn't understand that	Maile tyo bujhina
Thank you (very formal)	Dhanyebaad	Please speak more slowly	Bistaarai bolnus
Yes/No (It is/isn't)	Ho/Hoina	Please say that again	Pheri bolnus
Yes/No (There is/isn't)	Chha/Chhaina	I speak a little Nepali	Ali ali Nepali aunchha
How are things?	Kasto chha?	Pardon?	Hajur?
	or Sanchai chha?	No thanks	Pardaina (I don't want it)
It's/I'm OK, fine	Thik chha or Sanchai chha	I'm sorry, excuse me	Maph garnus
OK!/Sure thing! (informal)	La!	Let's go	Jaun (often sounds like
OK!/Sure thing! (formal)	Hos!		djam)
What's your name?		It was an honour	Hajur lai bhetera dherai
(to an adult)	Tapaaiko naam ke ho?	to meet you	khushi laagyo
(to a child)	Timro naam ke ho?	Thank you [very much]	Sabai kurako laagi [dherai]
My name is...	Mero naam...ho	for everything	dhanyabaad
My country is...	Mero desh...ho	See you again	Pheri betaaula

FORMS OF ADDRESS

Excuse me...	O...	Father	Buwa (a man old enough
(more polite)	Hajur...		to be your father)
Elder brother	Daai; Daajyu (said to men	Mother	Aama (woman old enough
	your age or older; more		to be your mother)
	respectful)	Grandfather	Baje (old men)
Elder sister	Didi (women your age or	Grandmother	Bajei (old women)
	older)	Shopkeeper, Innkeeper	
Younger brother	Bhaai (men or boys	(male)	Saahuji
	younger than you)	(female)	Saahuni
Younger sister	Bahini (women or girls		
	younger than you)		

BASIC QUESTIONS AND REQUESTS

Whether you're making a statement or asking a question, the word order is the same in Nepali. To indicate that you're asking, not telling, raise your voice at the end.

Do you speak English?	Tapaailaai Angreji	Please help me	Malaai madhat garnus
	aunchha?	Please give me...	...dinus
Does anyone speak English?	Kasailaai Angreji aunchha?	I'm [hungry]	Malaai [bhok] laagyo
I don't speak Nepali	Ma Nepali boldina	I'm not [hungry]	Malaai [bhok] laageko
Is/Isn't there [a room]?	[Kothaa] chha/chhaina?		chhaina
Is [a meal/tea] available?	[Khaanaa/chiya] painchha?	I like...[very much]	Malaai...[dherai]
Is [smoking] okay?	[Curot khaane] hunchha?		manparchha

I want/don't want	Malaai...chaahi nchha/ chaaidaina	How?	Kasari?
What's [this] for?	[Yo] ke ko laagi?	What?	Ke?
What's the matter?	Ke bhayo?	When?	Kahile?
What's [this] called in Nepali?	[yas] laai Nepali maa ke bhanchha?	Where?	Kahaa?
		Who?	Ko?
What does [chiya] mean?	[chiya] ke bhanchha?	Why?	Kina?
Really?	Hora?	Which?	Kun?

NEGOTIATIONS

How much does this cost?	Esko kati parchha?	Is there a cheaper one?	Kunai sasto chha?
How much for a [room]?	[Room] ko kati parchha?	I don't need/want it	Malaai chaaidaina
Is there somewhere I can stay here?	Mero laagi basne thau chha holaa?	I don't have any change	Masanga khudra chhaina
		Please use the meter	Meter-maa jaanus
How many people?	Kati jana?	Just a moment	Ek chin (literally, "one blink")
For [two] people	[Dui] jana ko laagi		
Only one person	Ek jana maatrai	I'll come back	Ma pharkinchhu
Can I see it?	Herna sakchhu?	Good job, Well done	Kyaraamro
Go away! (to a child)	Jaau!	Don't worry	Chinta nagarnus
It's very/too expensive	Dherai mahango bhayo		

TRAVEL/DIRECTIONS

Where is the...?	...kahaa chha?	Here	Yahaa
Where is this [bus] going?	Yo [bas] kahaa jaanchha?	There/Yonder	Tyahaa/Utyahaa (the "u" is drawn out on a high note to indicate a long distance)
Which is the way/ trail/ road to...?	...jaane baato kun ho?		
Which is the best way?	Kun baato raamro chha?		
How far is it?	Kati taadhaa chha?	[To the] right	Daayaa [tira]
Where are you going?	Tapaai kahaa jaanuhunchha?	[To the] left	Baayaa [tira]
		Straight	Sidhaa
I'm going to...	Ma...jaanchhu	Near/Far	Najik/Taadhaa
Where have you come from?	Tapaai kahaabaata aaunubhaeko? – (also means "where are you from?")	Rough/tarmac road	Kachi baato/pitch road
		Car/wheeled vehicle	Gaadi

TIME

What time is it?	Kati bajyo?	Day	Din
What time does the bus leave?	Yo bas kati baje jaanchha?	Week	Haptaa
		Month	Mahina
When does this bus arrive [in Kathmandu]?	Yo bas kati baje [Kathmandu-maa] pugchha?	Year	Barsaa
		Today	Aaja
		Tomorrow	Bholi
How many hours does it take?	Kati ghanta laagchha?	Yesterday	Hijo
		Now	Ahile
[Two] o'clock	[Dui] bajyo	Later	Pachhi
[Nine]-thirty	Saadhe [nau] bajyo	Ago, Before	Pahile
[Five] past [six]	[Chha] bajera [paanch] minet gayo (formal); chha paanch (informal)	Next week	Aarko haptaa
		Last month	Gayeko maina
		[Two] years ago	[Dui] barsa aghi
[Ten] to [eight]	[Aath] bajna [das] minet bakichha	Morning	Bihaana
		Afternoon	Diuso
Minute	Minet	Evening	Belukaa
Hour	Ghanta	Night	Raati

NOUNS

Bag, Baggage	Jholaa	Mistake	Galti
Bed	Khat	Money	Paisaa
Blanket, Quilt	Sirak	Mouth	Mukh
Bus	Bas	Nose	Naak
Candle	Mainbatti	Pain	Dukhyo
Clothes	Lugaa	Problem	Samasya
Ear	Kan	Restaurant	Resturent, bhojanalaya
Eye	Akha	Road	Baato, rod
Food	Khaanaa	Room	Rum, kothaa
Foot	Khutta	Shoe	Jutta
Friend	Saathi	Shop	Pasal
Hand	Haat	Son	Chori
Head	Taauko	Stomach	Pet
Hotel/Lodge	Hotel/Laj	Teahouse	Chiya pasal, chiya dokan
House	Ghar	Ticket	Tikot
Job, Work	Kaam	Toilet	Chaarpi (rural), toilet
Lamp	Batti	Town, Village	Gaaun
Mattress	Dasna, ochhan	Trail/Main trail	Baato/mul baato
Medicine	Ausadhi		

ADJECTIVES AND ADVERBS

One tricky thing about Nepali adjectives: the ones that describe feelings behave like nouns. Thus to express the notion "I'm thirsty", you have to say *Malaai thirkaa laagyo* (literally, "To me thirst has been felt").

A little	Alikati, thorai	Heavy	Garungo
A lot	Dherai	Hot (person or weather)	Garam
After	Pachhi	Hot (liquid, food)	Taato
Again	Pheri	Hungry	Bhok (laagyo)
All	Sabai	Hurt	Dhukyo
Alone	Eklai	Late	Dhilo
Always	Sadai	Less	Kam
Another	Aarko	Lost	Haraayo
Bad	Kharaab, naraamro	Loud	Charko
Beautiful	Sundari	Many	Dherai
Best	Sabbhandaa raamro	More (quantity)	Aru
Better	Ajai raamro	More (degree)	Ekdum, ajai
Big	Thulo	Near(er)	Najik(ai)
Cheap	Sasto	Never	Kahile paani
Clean	Safaa	New	Nayaa
Closed	Banda	Noisy	Halla
Cold (person or weather)	Jaado	Often, usually	Dheraijaso
Cold (liquid, food)	Chiso	Old (thing)	Purano
Difficult	Gaaro	Old (man)	Budho
Dirty	Phohor	Old (woman)	Budhi
Downhill	Oraallo	Only	Maatrai
Early	Chaadai	Open	Khulaa
Empty	Khali	Quick	Chitto
Enough	Prasasta	Pretty, good	Ramaailo
Expensive	Mahango	Right (correct)	Thik
Far	Taadhaa	Similar	Jastai
Few	Thorai	Slowly	Bistaarai
Full (thing)	Bhari	Small	Saano
Good	Raamro	Soon	Chaadai, chittai

Stolen	Choreko	Thirsty	Tirkha
Strong	Baliyo	Tired	Thakai
Tasty	Mitho	Too much	Atti
Terrible	Jhur	Uphill	Ukaalo

VERBS

The following verbs are in the infinitive form. To turn a verb into a polite command (eg, "Please sit"), just add -s (Basnus); for a request, replace the -nu ending with just -u, said through the nose, almost like "Basun?". For an all-purpose tense, drop the -u ending and replace it with -e (eg *jaane* can mean go, going or will go, depending on the context). The easiest way to negate any verb is to put na- in front of it (*nabasnus, najaane*).

Arrive	Aaipugnu	Need	Chaahinu
Ask	Sodhnu	Open	Kholnu
Buy	Kinnu	Receive	Paunu
Carry	Boknu	Rent	Bhadama linu
Close	Banda garnu	Rest	Aaram garnu
Come	Aunu	Run	Daudinu
Cook	Pakaaunu	Say, Tell	Bhannu
Do	Garnu	Sleep	Sutnu
Eat	Khaanu	Speak	Bolnu
Feel	Laagnu	Steal	Chornu
Forget	Birsinu	Stop	Roknu
Get	Paunu, linu	Think	Bichaar garnu, sochnu
Give	Dinu	Try	Kosis garnu
Go	Jaanu	Understand	Bujnu
Hear, Listen	Sunnu	Wait	Parkhanu
Help	Madhat garnu	Walk	Hidnu
Hurry	Hatar garnu	Want	Chahanu
Leave	Chodnu	Wash (face, clothes)	Dhunu
Lie (speak untruthfully)	Jhutho bolnu	Wash (body)	Nuhaaunu
Look, See	Hernu		

OTHER HANDY WORDS

Most of the following words are what we would call prepositions. However, those marked with an asterisk (*) are actually postpositions in Nepali, meaning they come after the thing they're describing (eg, "with me" comes out *masanga*).

Above, Over, Up	Maathi*	Near	Najik*
Behind	Pachhadi*	Out, Outside	Bahira*
Below, Under, Down	Talla*	That	Tyo
Each	Pratyek	This	Yo
From	Baata*	To, Towards	Tira*
In, Inside	Bhitra*	With	Sanga*
In front of	Agaadi*	Without	Chhaina*

NUMBERS

Unlike the English counting system, which uses compound numbers above twenty (twenty-one, twenty-two, etc), Nepali numbers are irregular all the way up to one hundred – the following are the ones you're most likely to use. A further complication is the use of quantifying words: you have to add *wotaa* when you're counting things, *jana* when counting people. Thus "five books" is *paanch wotaa kitaab*, "three girls" is *tin jana keti*. But note these irregular quantifiers: *ek wotaa* (once) = *euta*; *dui wotaa* (twice) = *duita*; *tin wotaa* (three times) = *tintaa*.

half	aada	3	tin
1	ek	4	chaar
2	dui	5	paanch

6	chha	20	bis
7	saat	25	pachhis
8	aath	30	tis
9	nau	40	chaalis
10	das	50	pachaas
11	eghaara	60	saathi
12	baara	70	sattari
13	tera	80	asi
14	chaudha	90	nabbe
15	pandra	100	ek say
16	sora	1000	ek hajaar
17	satra	first [time]	pahilo [palta]
18	athaara	second	dosro
19	unnais	third	tesro

DAYS

Sunday	Aitabar	Thursday	Bihibar
Monday	Sombar	Friday	Sukrabar
Tuesday	Mangalbar	Saturday	Sanibar
Wednesday	Budhabar		

FOOD AND DRINK

KEY FOOD PHRASES

Alikati	A little
Dherai	A lot
Aarko	Another
Bil dinus!	Bill, please!
Mitho	Delicious
Pugchha!	Enough!
Malaai pugyo!	I'm full!
Aru	More
...dinus	Please give me ...
Sahakaari	Vegetarian
Ma maasu khaanna	I don't eat meat

BASICS

Umaaleko [paani]	Boiled [water]
Roti	Bread
Makhan	Butter
Achhaar	Chutney, Pickle
Chiso	Cold
Paakeko	Cooked
Taareko	Deep-fried
Phul	Egg
Khaanaa	Food
Kaata	Fork
Gilaas	Glass
Taato	Hot
Chakku	Knife
Dudh	Milk
Tel	Oil
Marich	Pepper (ground)
Plet	Plate
Sahuji	Proprietor (male)

Sahuni	(female)
Bhaat	Rice (cooked)
Chaamal	Rice (uncooked)
Chiura	Rice (beaten)
Nun	Salt
Piro	Spicy
Chamchaa	Spoon
Chini	Sugar
Bhuteko	Stir-fried
Guliyo	Sweet
Mithaai	Sweets, Candy
Paani	Water
Dahi	Yogurt, Curd

COMMON NEPALI DISHES

Daal bhaat tarkaari	Lentil soup, white rice and curried vegetables
Dahi chiura	Curd with beaten rice
Momo	Steamed dumplings filled with meat and/or vegetables
Pakora	Vegetables dipped in chickpea-flour batter, deep fried
Samosa	Curried vegetables in fried pastry triangles
Sekuwa	Spicy, marinated meat kebab
Taareko maachhaa	Fried fish

COMMON NEWARI DISHES

Chataamari	Rice-flour pizza, usually topped with minced buffalo
Choyila	Buffalo cubes fried with spices and greens

NEPALI NUMBERS

?	?	?	?	?	?	?	?	?	?°
1	2	3	4	5	6	7	8	9	10

Kachila	Paté of minced raw buff meat mixed with ginger and oil
Kwati	Soup made with sprouted beans
Momocha	Small meat-filled steamed dumplings
Pancha kol	Curry made with five vegetables
Woh	Fried lentil-flour patties served plain (**mai woh**) or topped with minced buff (**la woh**) or egg (**khen woh**)

COMMON TIBETAN DISHES

Kothe	Fried meat or veg dumplings (**momo**)
Thukpa	Soup containing pasta, meat and vegetables
Tsampa	Toasted barley flour

VEGETABLES (TARKAARI OR SAABJI)

Bhanta	Aubergine (eggplant)
Simi	Beans
Gaajar	Carrot
Kaauli	Cauliflower
Chaana	Chickpeas
Dhaniyaa	Coriander (Cilantro)
Makai	Corn
Lasun	Garlic

Daal	Lentils
Chyaau	Mushroom
Pyaaj	Onion
Kerau, Matar	Peas
Alu	Potato
Pharsi	Pumpkin
Mulaa	Radish (daikon)
Palungo, Saag	Spinach, Chard, Greens
Golbheda	Tomato

MEAT (MAASU)

Raangaako maasu	Buffalo ("buff")
Kukhuraako maasu	Chicken
Khasiko maasu	Goat
Bungurko maasu	Pork

FRUIT (PHALPHUL) AND NUTS

Syaau	Apple
Keraa	Banana
Nariwal	Coconut
Nibuwaa	Lemon
Kagati	Lime
Aaph	Mango
Suntalaa	Orange, Mandarin
Badaam (Mampale, near India)	Peanut
Kismis	Raisin
Ukhu	Sugar cane

A glossary of Nepali, Newari and Tibetan terms

Avalokiteshwara The *bodhisattva* of compassion (also known as Chenrezig)

Avatar Bodily Incarnation of a deity

Baahun Nepali term for the Brahman (priestly) caste

Baba Holy man

Bagh Tiger

Bahal (or **Baha**) Buildings and quadrangle of a former Buddhist Newar monastery (a few are still active)

Bahil (or **Bahi**) Newari term for Buddhist monastery

Bajra see vajra

Bajra Yogini (or **Vajra Jogini**) Female tantric counterpart to Bhairab

Bakshish Not a bribe, but a tip in advance; alms

Ban Forest

Bar Banyan (fig) tree

Barahi (or **Varahi**) Vishnu incarnated as a boar

Bazaar Commercial area or street – not necessarily a covered market

Beni Confluence of rivers

Betel see paan

Bhaat Cooked rice; food

Bhairab Terrifying tantric form of Shiva

Bhajan Hymn, hymn-singing

Bhanjyang A pass (Nepali)

Bharat India

Bhatti Simple tavern, usually selling food as well as alcohol

Bhojanalaya Nepali restaurant

Bhot Tibet

Bhotiya Highland peoples of Tibetan ancestry (pejorative)

Bideshi Foreigner (or **gora** – "whitey")

Bidi Cheap rolled-leaf cigarette

Bihar (or **Mahabihar**) Buddhist monastery (Sanskrit)

Bodhisattva In Mahayana Buddhism, one who forgoes *nirvana* until all other beings have attained enlightenment

Brahma The Hindu creator god, one of the Hindu "trinity"

Brahman Member of the Hindu priestly caste (Baahun in Nepali); metaphysical term meaning the universal soul

Chaitya Small Buddhist monument, often with images of the Buddha at the four cardinal points

Charash Hashish

Chautaara Resting platform beside a trail with trees (bar and/or pipal figs) for shade

Chhang (or **Chhyang**) Home-made beer brewed from rice or other grains

Chhetri Member of the Hindu ruling or warrior caste

Chilam Vertical clay pipe for smoking tobacco or ganja

Cholo Traditional half-length woman's blouse

Chorten Another name for a *chaitya* in high mountain areas

Chowk Intersection/crossroads, square or courtyard (pronounced "choke")

Chulo Clay stove

Daada (or **Danda**) Ridge, often used to signify a range of connected hilltops

Damaru Two-sided drum

Danphe Nepal's national bird, a pheasant with brilliant plumage

Daura Suruwal Traditional dress of hill men: wrap-around shirt and jodhpur-like trousers

Devi see Mahadevi

Dewal (also **Deval**, **Degu**) Stepped temple platform; temple with prominent steps

Dhaara Communal water tap or tank

Dhaba Indian-style fast-food restaurant

Dhaka Colourful hand-loomed material made in the hills

Dhami Shaman; the word is often used interchangeably with *jhankri*, or even as *dhami jhankri*

Dharma Religion (especially Buddhist); correct behaviour

Dharmsala Rest-house for pilgrims

Dhoka Gate

Dhoti Indian-style loincloth

Dhyani Buddhas meditating figures representing the five aspects of Buddha nature

Doko Conical cane basket carried by means of a headstrap

Dorje Tibetan word for *vajra*

Dun Low-lying valleys just north of the Terai (sometimes called inner Terai, or *bhitri madesh* – "inner plains")

Durbar Palace; royal court

Durga Demon-slaying goddess

Dyochhen Private "home" of a Newari deity

Dzopkio Sturdy yak-cattle crossbreed; the female is called a dzum

Gaalne Wandering minstrel of the western hills (**ghandarba** is now the preferred term)

Gaida (or **gainda**) Rhinoceros

Gajur Brass or gold finial at the peak of a temple

Ganesh Elephant-headed god of beginnings and remover of obstacles

Ganja Cannabis, marijuana

Garud Vishnu's man-bird carrier

Gaun Village

Ghandarva Traditional musician

Ghanta A bell, usually rung at temples as a sort of "amen"

Ghat Riverside platform for worship and cremations; any waterside locality

Ghazal Crooning, poetic, sentimental form of Indian music

Gidda Vulture

Gompa Buddhist monastery (Tibetan)

Goonda Hooligan, thug

Gupha Cave

Gurkhas Nepali soldiers who serve in special regiments in the British and Indian armies

Guthi Newari benevolent association that handles funeral arrangements, temple maintenance, festivals, etc

Hanuman Valiant monkey king in the Ramayana

Hatti Elephant

Himal Massif or mountain range with permanent snow

HMG His Majesty's Government (as was)

Jaand (or **Jaar**) Nepali word for *chhang*

Jaatra Festival

Janai Sacred thread worn over left shoulder by high-caste (Baahun and Chhetri) Hindu men

Jhankri Shaman, or medicine man, of the hills

Jyapu Member of the Newari farming caste

Kali The mother goddess in her most terrifying form

Karma The soul's accumulated merit, determining its next rebirth

Kata White scarf given to lamas by visitors

Khat A litter or platform on which a deity is carried during a festival

Khola Stream or river

Khukuri Curved knife carried by most Nepali hill men

Kora Circumambulation or pilgrimage around a Buddhist monument

Kot Fort (pronounced "coat")

Krishna One of Vishnu's avatars, a hero of the Mahabharat

Kumari A girl worshipped as the living incarnation of Durga

Kund Pond, water tank

La Pass (Tibetan)

Lakshmi Consort of Vishnu, goddess of wealth

Lali Guraas Rhododendron

Lama Tibetan Buddhist priest or high-ranking monk

Lek Mountain range without permanent snow

Linga (or **lingam**) The phallic symbol of Shiva, commonly the centrepiece of temples and sometimes occurring in groups in the open

Lokeshwar see Avalokiteshwara

Lokta Traditional Nepali paper made from the bark of an indigenous shrub

Lungi Brightly coloured wrap skirt worn by hill women

Machaan Watchtower used by Terai farmers to ward off wild animals

Machhendranath Rain-bringing deity of the Kathmandu Valley; also known as Karunamaya or Bunga Dyo

Mahabharat (or **Mahabharata**) Hindu epic featuring Krishna and containing the Bhagavad Gita

Mahabharat Lek Highest range of the Himalayan foothills

Mahadev "Great God", an epithet for Shiva

Mahadevi The mother goddess

Mahayana Form of Buddhism followed in Nepal, Tibet and East Asia; follows deities, saints and teachers

Mahout Elephant handler

Mai Common name for any local protector goddess

Mandala Mystical diagram, meditation tool

Mandap Pavilion

Mandir Temple

Mani Stone stone inscribed with the mantra *Om Mani Padme Hum*

Mantra Religious incantation

Maobaadi Maoist

Masaala Spice; any mixture (thus masaala films, with their mixture of drama, singing, comedy, etc)

Math Hindu priest's home

Mela Religious fair or gathering

Nadi River

Nag Snake deity or spirit, believed to have rain-bringing powers

Nagar City

Nak Female yak

Namaste Polite word of greeting

Nandi Shiva's mount, a bull

Narayan Common name for Vishnu

Nath "Lord"

Nepali The adjective Nepalis use when referring to themselves and their language

Nirvana In Buddhism, enlightenment and release from the cycle of rebirth

Om Mani Padme Hum The mantra of Avalokiteshwara, roughly translating as "Hail to the jewel in the lotus"

Paan Mildly addictive mixture of areca nut and lime paste, wrapped in a leaf and chewed, producing blood-red spit

Padma Sambhava alias Guru Rinpoche, the eighth-century saint who brought Buddhism to Tibet

Pahad Hill, or the area of Nepal also known as the Middle Hills; hence *pahadiya*, hill person

Panchayat Council or assembly, the basis for Nepal's pre-democratic government

Pandit Hindu priest

Parbat Mountain

Parbati (or **Parvati**) Shiva's consort

Pashmina Nepali equivalent of cashmere

Pati Open shelter erected as a public resting place

Phanit Elephant driver

Phedi Foot (of a hill, pass, etc)

Pipal Holy fig (*ficus religiosa*); also known as *bodhi*, the tree under which Buddha attained enlightenment

Pokhari Pond, usually man-made

Poubha Newari-style scroll painting

Prasad Food consecrated after being offered to a deity

Puja An act of worship

Pujari Hindu priest or caretaker of a particular temple

Pul Bridge

Raksi Distilled spirit

Ram (or **Rama**) Mortal avatar of Vishnu, hero of the Ramayana

Ramayana Popular Hindu epic in which Sita, princess of Janakpur, is rescued by Ram and Hanuman

Rath Chariot used in religious processions

Rinpoche "Precious jewel": title given to revered lamas

Rudraksha Furrowed brown seeds, prized by Shaivas

Sadhu Hindu ascetic or holy man

Sahib Honorific term given to male foreigners, pronounced "sahb"; women are called memsahib

Sajha Cooperative

Sal Tall tree of the Terai and lower hills, valued for its timber

Sanyasin (or **Sunyasan**) Hindu who has renounced the world, usually in old age

Sarangi Nepali four-stringed violin

Saraswati Hindu goddess of learning and the arts

Sati (or **Suttee**) Practice of Hindu widows throwing themselves on their husbands' funeral pyres

Sattal Public rest-house

Shaiva Member of the cult of Shiva (pronounced "Shaib")

Shakti In Hindu tantra, the female principle that empowers the male; the mother goddess in this capacity

Shaligram Fossil-bearing stones found in the Kali Gandaki River, revered by Vaishnavas

Sherpa Man from one of Nepal's highland ethnic groups, originally; sometimes (incorrectly) used by foreigners to mean any Nepali guide or climber. A woman is a **Sherpani**

Shikra (or **Shikhara**) Indian-style temple, shaped like a square bullet

Shiva "The destroyer", one of the Hindu "trinity" – a god of many guises

Shivalaya One-storey Shiva shrine containing a *linga*

Shradha Prescribed rites performed after a death

Shri An honorific prefix

Sindur Red mark on the parting of married women

Sirdar Nepali trek leader

Sita Ram's wife, princess of Janakpur, heroine of the Ramayana

STOL "Short Takeoff And Landing" (read "hair-raising") landing strip

Stupa large dome-shaped Buddhist monument, usually said to contain holy relics

Tal (or **Taal**) Lake

Tantra Esoteric path to enlightenment, a major influence on Nepali Hinduism and Buddhism

Tara Buddhist goddess; female aspect of Buddha nature

Tashi Delek Tibetan for welcome, *namaste*

Tempo Three-wheeled scooter; also called *autoriksha*, tuk-tuk

Thangka Buddhist scroll painting

Tika Auspicious mark made of rice, *abhir* powder and curd, placed on the forehead during *puja* or festivals or before making a journey

Tol Neighbourhood

Tola Traditional unit of weight (115g); precious metals are sold by the tola, as is hashish

Topi Traditional Nepali brimless hat, either black (called *bhadgaonle*) or multicoloured (*dhaka*)

Torana Elaborate wooden carving, or metal shield, above a temple door

Torma Dough offerings made by Buddhist monks

Trisul The trident, a symbol of Shiva

Tudikhel Parade ground

Tulku Reincarnation of a late great teacher in the Tibetan Buddhist tradition

Vaishnava Follower of the cult of Vishnu (pronounced "Baishnab")

Vajra Sceptre-like symbol of tantric power (pronounced "bajra")

Vajracharya Buddhist Newari priest

Vajrayana "Thunderbolt Way": tantric Buddhism

Vedas The oldest Hindu scriptures (pronounced "Bed" by Nepalis); hence Vedic gods

Vipassana Ancient and austere Buddhist meditation practice

Vishnu "The preserver", member of the Hindu "trinity", worshipped in ten main incarnations (pronounced "Bishnu")

Yangsi Reincarnated successor of a Tibetan lama

Yoni Symbol of the female genitalia, usually carved into the base of a *linga*

Small print and index

A ROUGH GUIDE TO ROUGH GUIDES

Published in 1982, the first Rough Guide – to Greece – was a student scheme that became a publishing phenomenon. Mark Ellingham, a recent graduate in English from Bristol University, had been travelling in Greece the previous summer and couldn't find the right guidebook. With a small group of friends he wrote his own guide, combining a highly contemporary, journalistic style with a thoroughly practical approach to travellers' needs.

The immediate success of the book spawned a series that rapidly covered dozens of destinations. And, in addition to impecunious backpackers, Rough Guides soon acquired a much broader readership that relished the guides' wit and inquisitiveness as much as their enthusiastic, critical approach and value-for-money ethos.

These days, Rough Guides include recommendations from budget to luxury and cover more than 120 destinations around the globe, as well as producing an ever-growing range of ebooks.

Visit **roughguides.com** to find all our latest books, read articles, get inspired and share travel tips with the Rough Guides community.

Rough Guide credits

Editor: Claire Saunders
Layout: Jessica Subramanian
Cartography: James MacDonald
Picture editor: Lisa Jacobs
Proofreader: Susanne Hillen
Managing editor: Keith Drew
Assistant editor: Payal Sharotri
Production: Nicole Landau

Cover design: Nicole Newman, Daniel May, Jessica Subramanian
Editorial assistant: Freya Godfrey
Senior pre-press designer: Dan May
Programme manager: Helen Blount
Publisher: Joanna Kirby
Publishing director: Georgina Dee

Publishing information

This eighth edition published July 2015 by
Rough Guides Ltd,
80 Strand, London WC2R 0RL
11, Community Centre, Panchsheel Park,
New Delhi 110017, India
Distributed by Penguin Random House
Penguin Books Ltd,
80 Strand, London WC2R 0RL
Penguin Group (USA)
345 Hudson Street, NY 10014, USA
Penguin Group (Australia)
250 Camberwell Road, Camberwell,
Victoria 3124, Australia
Penguin Group (NZ)
67 Apollo Drive, Mairangi Bay, Auckland 1310,
New Zealand
Penguin Group (South Africa)
Block D, Rosebank Office Park, 181 Jan Smuts Avenue,
Parktown North, Gauteng, South Africa 2193
Rough Guides is represented in Canada by Tourmaline
Editions Inc. 662 King Street West, Suite 304, Toronto,
Ontario M5V 1M7
Printed in Singapore

© Rough Guides, 2015
Maps © Rough Guides
No part of this book may be reproduced in any form
without permission from the publisher except for the
quotation of brief passages in reviews.
448pp includes index
A catalogue record for this book is available from the
British Library
ISBN: 978-0-24118-472-1
The publishers and authors have done their best to
ensure the accuracy and currency of all the information
in **The Rough Guide to Nepal**, however, they can accept
no responsibility for any loss, injury, or inconvenience
sustained by any traveller as a result of information or
advice contained in the guide.
1 3 5 7 9 8 6 4 2

MIX
Paper from
responsible sources
FSC™ C018179
www.fsc.org

Help us update

We've gone to a lot of effort to ensure that the eighth edition of **The Rough Guide to Nepal** is accurate and up-to-date. However, things change – places get "discovered", opening hours are notoriously fickle, restaurants and rooms raise prices or lower standards. If you feel we've got it wrong or left something out, we'd like to know, and if you can remember the address, the price, the hours, the phone number, so much the better.

Please send your comments with the subject line "**Rough Guide Nepal Update**" to ✉ mail@uk.roughguides .com. We'll credit all contributions and send a copy of the next edition (or any other Rough Guide if you prefer) for the very best emails.

Find more travel information, connect with fellow travellers and plan your trip on 🌐 roughguides.com.

ABOUT THE AUTHORS

Charles Young has been travelling since university and, as well as working on over a dozen Rough Guides titles, has taught English in Catalunya, run a coffee shop in Hong Kong, been a publican in South Korea and worked in the spice trade in India. He currently lives in deepest, darkest China and should, perhaps, be older than he is.

Shafik Meghji A travel writer, journalist, editor and photographer based in south London, Shafik Meghji has travelled throughout Nepal for both work and pleasure. He has co-authored/updated more than 25 Rough Guides, and he writes regularly for newspapers, magazines and websites around the world. Shafik is a fellow of the Royal Geographical Society, a member of the British Guild of Travel Writers and a trustee of the Latin America Bureau. His website is shafikmeghji.com, his blog is unmappedroutes.com and his Twitter handle is @ShafikMeghji.

Acknowledgements

Charles Young I'd like to thank Mark, Siobhan and all their friends in Kathmandu for their kind hospitality (but not the man who sold me a second-hand Chinese copy of an Indian motorbike that they don't make any more), Yogesh for taking me round the buffer zone in Chitwan, all the guys I met at the Bardia Wildlife Resort (especially for helping me out when my bike conked out in the middle of the river) and at the Bardia Guides Association, the people of the village where I crashed for helping patch both myself and my bike up so I could drive five hours to the nearest decent hospital at Kolhalpur, and the doctors there for stitching up my eye and setting my broken hand (for free). I'd also like to thank Purna and his family at the Narawanga in Dhulikhel for being old school, as well as the hundreds of Nepalis I met on the road who stopped to help me when the bike broke down, gave me shelter when

it rained, and generally made this trip an unforgettable experience with their kind hospitality. I'd also like to thank at Rough Guides, Claire for her excellent editing, Shafik for his advice and Keith for organizing it all.

Shafik Meghji Thanks to the many travellers and locals who helped out along the way. A special *dhanyabaad* must go to: David Reed and James McConnachie, whose work remains at the centre of this book; Claire Saunders for her sterling editing; Ellie Aldridge at Rough Guides HQ; Niraj Shrestha of Himalayan Encounters for his invaluable help with my travel itinerary; Ramesh Chaudhary for his insight into the trekking scene; Pat O'Keefe for his help with the Rafting and kayaking chapter; Sam Voolstra; Jean, Nizar and Nina Meghji; and Sioned Jones, for her love and support.

Readers' updates

Thanks to all the readers who have taken the time to write in with comments and suggestions (and apologies if we've inadvertently omitted or misspelt anyone's name):

Jill Allegretti; Sylvia Bailey; Darren Van Blois; Freya Chapman Amey; Noémie Christen; Tilman Evers; Jos Groenendijk; Paul und Erika Hakenesch; Max Helber; Laurence Hupays; Katja Jezersek; Philipp Keel; Klaas Kelchtermans; Oliver Leask; Martina Manders; Bram Oers; Uschi Overhage; Nadia Persaud; Phillipa; Sara Ricardo; Pascale Strugalla; Tom Stuart; Cesar Vallejo; Michel Vandeweghe; Alistair Weir; Stijn De Winter; Gabriela Wyland; Gawain Young.

Photo credits

All photos © Rough Guides except the following:
(Key: t-top; c-centre; b-bottom; l-left; r-right)

Index

Maps are marked in grey

Map symbols

The symbols below are used on maps throughout the book

	Road	✈	Major airport		Zoo
	Dirt road/4-wheel drive road	✈	Minor airport/airstrip	E	Embassy/consulate
→	One-way street	H	Helipad		Airline office
	Steps	✉	Post office		Travel & tour operator/outdoor equipment stockist
	Tunnel	@	Internet access		Hindu temple
	Bridge/mountain pass	☾	Telephone office		Hindu shrine/site
	Railway	✚	Hospital/clinic		Buddhist monastery
- - -	Footpath/trail	♦	Place of interest		Buddhist temple/chorten/stupa
......	Minor footpath/trail	⊠	Gate/entrance		Ghat
	Mountains		Fountain/gardens		Mosque
▲	Mountain peak		Museum		Notable tree
	Mountain ridge		Tower		Building
	Hill slope		Viewpoint		Stadium
	Waterfall	☉	Statue		Parkland or National park/reserve
★	Bus park/transport stop		Golf course		

Listings key

■	Accommodation
●	Eating
■	Bar & live music
●	Shopping

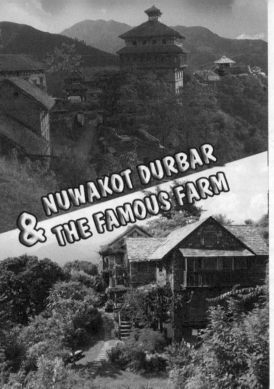